# Religion and the Early Modern State

## Views from China, Russia, and the West

How did state power impinge on the religion of the common people? This perennial issue has been sharpened as historians uncover the process of confessionalization or acculturation, by which state and church officials collaborated in ambitious programs of Protestant or Catholic reform, intended to change the religious consciousness and the behavior of ordinary men and women. For England, in particular, the debate continues as to whether a reformation in this broad sense, up and down the social ladder, was in the end able to prevail over the stubborn resilience of ancient habits and beliefs. In the belief that specialists in one area of the globe can learn from the questions posed by colleagues working in the same period in other regions, this volume sets the topic in a wider framework. Thirteen essays, grouped in themes affording parallel views of England and Europe, Tsarist Russia, and Ming China, show a spectrum of possibilities for what early modern governments tried to achieve by regulating religious life and for how religious communities evolved in new directions, either in keeping with or in spite of official injunctions.

James D. Tracy teaches in the history department of the University of Minnesota. He is the author of *Emperor Charles V, Impresario of War* (Cambridge, 2002) and *Europe's Reformations, 1450–1650*. He is the editor of *City Walls: The Urban Enceinte in Global Perspective* (Cambridge, 2000), *The Political Economy of Merchant Empires: State Power and Global Trade, 1350–1750* (Cambridge, 1991), and of the *Journal of Early Modern History*.

Marguerite Ragnow is the associate director of the Center for Early Modern History at the University of Minnesota.

Studies in
Comparative Early Modern
History

Center for Early Modern
History
University of Minnesota

Cambridge University Press

Previously published in series:

# RELIGION
## and the
# EARLY MODERN STATE

VIEWS FROM CHINA, RUSSIA, AND THE WEST

*Edited by*

JAMES D. TRACY

*University of Minnesota*

MARGUERITE RAGNOW

*Center for Early Modern History,*
*University of Minnesota*

CAMBRIDGE
UNIVERSITY PRESS

PUBLISHED BY THE PRESS SYNDICATE OF THE UNIVERSITY OF CAMBRIDGE
The Pitt Building, Trumpington Street, Cambridge, United Kingdom

CAMBRIDGE UNIVERSITY PRESS
The Edinburgh Building, Cambridge CB2 2RU, UK
40 West 20th Street, New York, NY 10011-4211, USA
477 Williamstown Road, Port Melbourne, VIC 3207, Australia
Ruiz de Alarcón 13, 28014 Madrid, Spain
Dock House, The Waterfront, Cape Town 8001, South Africa

http://www.cambridge.org

© Cambridge University Press 2004

First published 2004

Printed in the United States of America

*Typeface* Palatino 10/12 pt.    *System* LATEX 2$_\varepsilon$  [TB]

*A catalog record for this book is available from the British Library.*

*Library of Congress Cataloging in Publication Data*

Religion and the early modern state : views from China, Russia, and the West / edited
by James D. Tracy, Marguerite Ragnow.
p.   cm. – (Studies in comparative early modern history)
Includes bibliographical references and index.
ISBN 0-521-82825-2
1. Religion and state – History.   I. Tracy, James D.   II. Ragnow, Marguerite, 1955–
III. Series.
BL65.S8R445   2004
322′.1′09–dc22

2003068731

ISBN 0 521 82825 2 hardback

In honor of
STANFORD E. LEHMBERG
on the occasion of his retirement
from the University of Minnesota

# Contents

### PART III: THE SOCIAL ARTICULATION OF BELIEF

### AN EPILOGUE AT THE PARISH LEVEL

# Contributors

**Robert O. Crummey**
University of California at Davis

**Eamon Duffy**
Magdalene College, Cambridge University

**Willem Frijhoff**
Vrije Universiteit Amsterdam

**Susan C. Karant-Nunn**
University of Arizona

**Stanford E. Lehmberg**, emeritus
University of Minnesota

**Eve Levin**
University of Kansas

**Caroline J. Litzenberger**
Portland State University

**Thomas Mayer**
Augustana College

**Raymond A. Mentzer**
University of Iowa

**Sara T. Nalle**
William Paterson College

**Nicholas Orme**
University of Exeter

**Paul S. Seaver**
Stanford University

**Richard Shek**
California State University at Sacramento

**Frank E. Sysyn**
University of Alberta

**Romeyn Taylor**, emeritus
University of Minnesota

**James D. Tracy**
University of Minnesota

# Acknowledgments

This volume represents the work of many hands and voices. The conference on which it is based had financial support from the University of Minnesota's Department of History, the College of Liberal Arts, the University's McKnight Special Events Fund, and the Center for Early Modern History. This made it possible to include colleagues from England in our discussions: Eamon Duffy, Nicholas Orme, and Pamela Tudor-Craig, Lady Wedgewood. To assist the presenters in revising their papers, several of our graduate students kept a précis raisonné of the discussion: Jodi Campbell, Noel Delgado, Jonathan Good, Don Harreld, Diana Laulainen-Schein, Dorothea Sartain, Anne Thompson, and Jennifer Turnham. The conference ran smoothly thanks to Debra Salata, then the assistant director of the Center for Early Modern History. Editorial assistance was ably provided by Noel Delgado. Finally, the volume presented here is a small but heartfelt thanks to a friend and colleague of many years whose hard work, natural graciousness, and keen wit have sustained us in times good and bad: Stanford Lehmberg.

Stanford Lehmberg, at the lych-gate of St. Clement's Episcopal Church, St. Paul, MN, where he was organist and choir director for many years. Photo by Mike Long.

# *Preface*

## STANFORD E. LEHMBERG, HISTORIAN

ALTHOUGH officially a student of Christopher Morris at Cambridge, Stan Lehmberg was really the first Ph.D. of the dean of Tudor historians in the second half of the twentieth century, Sir Geoffrey Elton, if indeed it is not closer to the mark to speak of the two as fellow laborers at that early stage in both their careers. Like Elton, Lehmberg made his mark on Tudor history by importing the methods pioneered by medievalists in the study of English history, replacing the heavy reliance on printed sources characteristic of earlier generations of historians of the sixteenth century, including Elton's teacher Sir John Neale, with the gospel of original documents and their careful exploitation. In part, Lehmberg's and Elton's careers ran parallel in their emphasis on political and administrative history, but in an equally large part they diverged in two significant ways: the importance of ideas and of religion. While Elton was never entirely comfortable in – or persuaded of the centrality of – either domain, not even in the case of his hero Thomas Cromwell, Lehmberg made them both very much his own.

This process began with Lehmberg's first book on Sir Thomas Elyot, best known for his *Book named the governor*, which Lehmberg edited at the same time for Everyman. In the early sixties, it was daring to work on Elyot, in part because Pearl Hogrefe had already laid claim to him, in part because intellectual history was fading fast. And it has always been dangerous for historians to venture into biography. None of this deterred Lehmberg, no more than it did when he later added a major study of the Elizabethan minister Sir Walter Mildmay. In tandem with these works, Lehmberg published a series of articles on early Tudor humanism, especially its relation to nascent Henrician state religion. A similar concern with the exercise of authority, especially over religion, came through in a pair of ground-breaking articles, one on the use of parliamentary attainder in Henry VIII's reign and another on the exercise of the royal supremacy through the king's vicegerent, his chief minister Cromwell.

Lehmberg's most important work, like these early biographies and articles, comes in pairs. First, at Elton's urging, were two volumes on the Henrician parliaments from 1529 to Henry's death, excluding the earliest ones for which insufficient evidence survives. (One of Lehmberg's Ph.D. students would nonetheless complete a thesis on this topic, especially Cardinal Wolsey's role.) *The Reformation Parliament, 1529–1536* (1970) adopted a novel approach to this well-known turning point in English history by treating all of the parliament's work, not just the cataclysmic legislation ushering in the break with Rome, and all of the parliament, that is, including the House of Lords, which in the past usually had been ignored completely, as well as the southern convocation of the clergy, which met in conjunction with parliament. Eschewing the statistical analysis of parliamentary behavior then in vogue, Lehmberg chose a basically narrative approach, supplemented with analysis of the membership. A second volume, *The Later Parliaments of Henry VIII, 1536–1547* (1977), completed the legislative history of this turbulent reign. Both books adhered fairly closely to the now under pressure Eltonian line that the 1530s saw a revolution in English history, engineered by Cromwell. Perhaps more important, if almost subconsciously, the volumes on parliament demonstrated how a medieval occasion for taking counsel, the literal meaning of parliament, gradually became an institution with a self-conscious identity founded in procedure, helping to explain Elizabeth I's epic struggles with her parliaments as well as the English Civil War.

These books have a permanent place in the study of Tudor history as they have already helped to reorient the study of parliament as demonstrated in the work of Jennifer Loach, Michael Graves or Norman Jones, and David Dean. Perhaps nearer to Stan's heart and likely to be even more enduring, is his second duo, two studies of the English cathedrals in the sixteenth and seventeenth centuries: *The Reformation of Cathedrals: Cathedrals in English Society, 1485–1603* (1988) and *Cathedrals under Siege: Cathedrals in English Society, 1600–1700* (1996). Here again, Lehmberg extended the medievalists' work into a period about which very little had been known, linking the well-studied medieval cathedrals to the magisterial work of Norman Sykes and other works on the eighteenth-century English church. Following much the same approach as in the books on parliament, Lehmberg tried to get at how these great churches worked. He assembled a massive prosopography of all cathedral clergy, ransacking the archives of every cathedral in England in the process. Focusing once more on institutional change, including a fascinating investigation of cathedral finance, Lehmberg yet made room for a good deal of attention to perhaps his first love, cathedral music and musicians, as well as writing by the clergy. His abiding passion for his adopted church comes through in both, perhaps especially in the lavish illustrations, many of which he provided. Finally, in both volumes, Lehmberg pioneered for professional historians the now very important study of funeral monuments. The conclusion of the second volume is tinged with melancholy in the judgment that the cathedrals had lost a great deal of ground by the year 1700.

His is an imposing if somewhat elegiac corpus of work. It may yet be that Stan had his most important impact as a teacher of both undergraduate and graduate students. A gripping lecturer who always had time for questions and made himself easily approachable, he achieved great renown on the first score. His lunches with particularly favored students are legendary. He fostered many an incipient interest in Tudor England into nearly his own intense involvement with it. The collapse of the job market for Ph.D.s, which coincided almost exactly with Lehmberg's move to Minnesota, limited his success in maintaining the university's proud tradition of international leadership in his field, stretching back to Wallace Notestein at the beginning of the twentieth century. Nevertheless, Stan managed to attract good students and make them better. He treated them all with the same affection he showed for his undergrads and, perhaps most important, allowed them sufficient latitude to make their own mistakes on the way to finishing their degrees (and after!). This is a rare quality among teachers of graduate students and another mark of Stan's stature as a historian, secure in his own work and the knowledge that he has contributed a great deal to the study of state and religion in early modern England.

Thomas Mayer
Augustana College, 2002

# Religion and the Early Modern State

Views from China, Russia, and the West

# Introduction

## STANFORD E. LEHMBERG AND JAMES D. TRACY

This book owes its origins to a desire to bring together two divergent approaches to the English Reformation. Early writers, most notably John Strype, viewed the Reformation primarily as an event in political history; they collected and analyzed the documents which established the independent Church of England.[1] Writing in 1936, Sir Maurice Powicke went so far as to say that "the one definite thing which can be said about the Reformation in England is that it was an act of State."[2] The classic modern account of Reformation politics is that by A.G. Dickens, first published in 1964.[3] This approach remained dominant through the 1970s. Several of Sir Geoffrey Elton's magisterial works described the religious policies of Henry VIII's chief minister Thomas Cromwell,[4] while the statutes passed by Henry VIII's parliaments to regulate religion were studied by Stanford Lehmberg in his books *The Reformation Parliament* and *The Later Parliaments of Henry VIII*.[5] Biographies of Thomas Cranmer naturally emphasized the primary role of the archbishop of Canterbury in enforcing reforms.[6]

Works of this sort see the Reformation as coming rapidly and being imposed from the top down. But another sort of historiography, gaining popularity in the 1980s, viewed Reformation as a slow process working its way up from the bottom as Lutheran, Zwinglian, and Calvinistic

---

[1] John Strype, *Ecclesiastical Memorials* (London, 1721); *Annals of the Reformation*, 4 vols. (London, 1709–31).

[2] Sir Maurice Powicke, *The Reformation in England* (Oxford, 1941), 1.

[3] A.G. Dickens, *The English Reformation* (London, 1964; 2nd ed., University Park, PA, 1989).

[4] G.R. Elton, *Policy and Police* (Cambridge, 1972); *Reform and Renewal* (Cambridge, 1973).

[5] Stanford E. Lehmberg, *The Reformation Parliament, 1529–1536* (Cambridge, 1970) and *The Later Parliaments of Henry VIII, 1536–1547* (Cambridge, 1977).

[6] Jasper Ridley, *Thomas Cranmer* (Oxford, 1962); Diarmaid MacCulloch, *Thomas Cranmer* (New Haven, CT, and London, 1996).

1

views gradually gained acceptance by common people.[7] Another perspective on popular belief emphasized the reluctance of many men and women to abandon their traditional Catholic beliefs. J.J. Scarisbrick and Robert Whiting were among the early exponents of this argument; Scarisbrick providing a general account and Whiting a more specialized examination of the southwest of England.[8] The finest study of "Traditional Religion in England 1400–1500" – that is its subtitle – is *The Stripping of the Altars* by Eamon Duffy.[9]

Despite some attempts to draw these different approaches together,[10] they have tended to remain separate. Historians of official religion do indeed talk with their colleagues examining popular belief and culture,[11] but they have not yet attempted a synthesis of their work. It may be that the time has come for such a comprehensive new interpretation to gain acceptance. In any case, it was our hope that pulling together a series of essays by leaders of both camps might be an appropriate step in that direction.

Each section of this volume includes a study of a part of England. Interestingly enough, these are pieces of local or regional history, a fact suggesting the growing importance of local studies upon which more general future accounts can be based. Eamon Duffy considers the changes in a single church, Salle in Norfolk; Caroline Litzenberger deals primarily with the diocese of Gloucester and its bishop, John Hooper; and Nicholas Orme examines popular religion and the Reformation in Cornwall. Paul Seaver's study of state religion and Puritan resistance in the early seventeenth century, while it has a broader context, is based on events in London. All of these suggest fascinating comparisons and contrasts, some of them purely English but some with theoretical implications stretching far beyond the British Isles.

Memories of England's Reformation traveled around the globe, carried by the agents of Tudor–Stuart England's commercial outreach. During the period when Iran's Shah 'Abbâs I (ruled 1587–1629) was extending the trading network of his Shi'ite kingdom – while fighting wars with the Sunni sultans of the Ottoman Empire – Anthony Sherley arrived in

---

[7] The distinction between these two approaches was first set out in "The Recent Historiography of the English Reformation" by Christopher Haig, in *The English Reformation Revised*, ed. Haig (Cambridge, 1987), 19–33.

[8] J.J. Scarisbrick, *The Reformation and the English People* (Oxford, 1984); Robert Whiting, *The Blind Devotion of the People* (Cambridge, 1989).

[9] Eamon Duffy, *The Stripping of the Altars* (New Haven, CT, and London, 1992).

[10] The most important is Christopher Haig, *English Reformations: Religion, Politics, and Society under the Tudors* (Oxford, 1993).

[11] Lehmberg and Scarisbrick were both students of Elton and for a time corresponded occasionally.

Iran as a merchant adventurer (1598). With an implicit bow to Elizabeth I's success in repressing Catholic worship in Protestant England, Sherley regarded with approval the shah's policy of enforced religious uniformity in Iran, dictated, he assumed, by reasons of state: "On the one hand, the shah thus eliminated internal division within his realm; on the other, he strengthens himself against the Turk."[12] Nearly sixty years later, Paul Rycaut began a long period of service as English consul in Smyrna. During England's Civil War, members of Rycaut's family lost their offices because of their adhesion to the royalist cause; Rycaut was reminded of these events by a zealous *mufti* who had persuaded the grand vizier (1662) to raze all Christian churches that had been rebuilt in Istanbul after the fire of 1660: "Thus we may see how troublesome Hypocrisie and Puritanism are in all places where they gain a superiority."[13]

As these comments suggest, observers of politics in the early modern era took it for granted that a state conscious of its own interests would or at least ought to guide the religious behavior of its subjects. Until fairly recently, similar assumptions about the primacy of state policy in religious affairs have informed historical writing about Europe's Protestant and Catholic Reformations. For example, Karl Brandi's *German History in the Age of the Reformation and Counter-Reformation* covers much of the same ground as his monumental *Emperor Charles V*, stressing conflicts between Charles V (ruled 1519–1555) and Germany's Protestant princes.[14]

But scholarship of the last four decades or so has made it abundantly clear that one cannot imagine the religious life of the people as simply decided for them by their rulers. The term "popular religion" seemed useful for differentiating the beliefs of ordinary men and women from those of the governing elite, until it was pointed out that the common folk and their betters often shared the same religion, even if each locality preserved usages frowned on by church authorities.[15] "Folk belief" is perhaps a better way of describing the whole complex of traditional thinking and ritual against which reformers of all persuasions directed their fire.

---

[12] Antony Sherley, *Opmerckelijke Reistochten na Persien* (Leiden, 1706), 14; copy in the James Ford Bell Library, University of Minnesota.

[13] Paul Rycaut, *A History of the Turkish Empire, from the Year 1623 to the Year 1673* (London, 1680), 104–5; copy in the James Ford Bell Library, University of Minnesota. Cf. sig. B-Bv, where Rycaut mentions having served for eighteen years as consul in Smyrna, "prior to which my loyal family was banned from office."

[14] Kárl Brandi, *Deutsche Geschichte im Zeitalter der Reformation und Gegenreformation* (Munich, 1928/1942/1960); *Kaiser Karl V* (Munich, 1938).

[15] William A. Christian, Jr., *Local Religion in Sixteenth-Century Spain* (Princeton, 1981).

But if the "lived" religion of the people was somehow different from the "official" religion promoted from on high, what was the relation between the two? As Willem Frijhoff notes in this volume, scholars pursuing "a narrative that tries to get hold of neglected dimensions" in religious history have conceptualized this relationship in several different ways. "Protestantization" is a good description of the aims of the reformers in Calvinist areas like the Dutch Republic, where the aim was to expunge altogether the idea that prayer and worship could ever be instruments for inducing the Lord God to intervene directly in human affairs. "Acculturation" points to the fact that religious reform was often a program of social elites, aiming to raise the uneducated and unwashed to their own higher level.[16] "Confessionalization" defines a paradigm especially appropriate for small and medium-sized princely territories in Germany – whether Lutheran, Calvinist, or Catholic – where civil and ecclesiastical authorities worked hand-in-glove to instruct the people in the doctrine of the chosen confession and to make them conform to its way of life.[17] But though each of these categories has merit, none of them recognizes the common folk who were the object of various meliorative ministrations as having an active will of their own. Hence three of the authors represented here – Willem Frijhoff, Caroline Litzenberger, and Susan Karant-Nunn – prefer to characterize the relationship between "lived" and "official" religion as a process of "accommodation," in which people took what they wanted from the message of reform, and reshaped it according to their own needs. But a clarification of concepts only permits the real questions to emerge more sharply. If (as seems to be the case) programs of religious change were pushed through most thoroughly where state and church authorities worked closely together, what was the basis of their collaboration? In particular, what was the state's perceived interest in religious reform? And if the objectives of state officials and zealous pastors differed – as surely they must have – how did they differ? As for the commoners, one would like to know which parts of the message of reform they found appealing, and why. But since most inhabitants of most European countries in the sixteenth and seventeenth centuries were illiterate peasants, how does one determine what they thought one way or the other? Perhaps the first step toward an answer is to accept the idea that the religious individualism

---

[16] Robert Muchembled, *Popular Culture and Elite Culture in France, 1400–1750*, trans. Lydia Cochrane (Baton Rouge, 1985).

[17] Wolfgang Reinhard, Heinz Schilling, *Die Katholische Konfessionalisierung* (Münster, 1995); Heinz Schilling, "Confessional Europe," in *Handbook of European History, 1400–1600*, Thomas A. Brady, Jr., Heiko A. Oberman, and James D. Tracy eds., 2 vols. (Leiden, 1994), II: 641–82.

of these early modern centuries seems now to have been overrated by earlier scholars – on this point see Eamon Duffy's essay. This means that questions about the beliefs and behavior of ordinary men and women have to focus on the communities in which they lived.[18] But here further questions arise: are we to believe that villages and small towns of four or five hundred years ago were communities in a moral sense, as well as a physical or legal sense? Or were they merely collections of warring factions and competing material interests, each seeking to cloak its private purposes under the mantle of the common good?

Paradoxical as it may seem, one can sometimes see complex issues more clearly by raising the complexity to a higher level. When Antony Sherley and Paul Rycaut compared their home country to one or another Islamic realm, they applied familiar categories to a new and unfamiliar situation, as travelers invariably do. But is it not also possible that each gained a sharper view of England's experience by observing what seemed to be analogous phenomena in a strange land? The premise of this volume is that students of religious history in a given area can indeed gain perspective from the findings of colleagues working on what seem to be analogous problems in different parts of the globe. The point is perhaps easiest to grasp in reference to the Christian tradition. Just as much has been gained by moving beyond the denominationally oriented historiography of an earlier era, as proponents of the "confessionalization" thesis do by discerning common patterns in Catholic and Protestant efforts at reform, there is much to be gained also by looking for common patterns at a deeper historical depth, between Eastern and Western Christianity. There are elements of religious life that transcend the limits of any particular tradition. China's imperial government shared with European states an interest in promoting orthodoxy, even if the respective definitions of orthodoxy were quite different; and its subjects shared with Europeans a remarkable facility for interpreting religious teachings in their own way.

The essays are grouped under three major headings. In keeping with the volume's focus, each section concludes with an essay on England. Part I, "Lived Religion and Official Religion," frames the basic contrast between the two. Richard Shek's "The Alternative Moral Universe of Religious Dissenters in Ming-Qing China" defines orthodoxy in China as having a "social-ethical" content that all of the officially approved

---

[18] Bernd Moeller, *Imperial Cities and the Reformation*, ed. and tr. H.C. Erik Middlefort, Mark U. Edwards (Durham, N.C. 1982). Prof. Moeller's essay, originally published in German in 1961, launched a whole subfield of scholarship on the urban Reformation, especially in Germany.

religious traditions promoted; accordingly, adherents of the "Eternal Mother" tradition were persecuted for refusing to conform to these behavioral norms. Robert Crummey's "Ecclesiastical Elites and Popular Belief and Practice in Seventeenth-Century Russia" examines the complex reasons for resistance to the imposition of uniform service books by Tsar Aleksei and his reform-minded churchmen; the "Old Belief" movement rested on popular attachment to specifically Russian ritual gestures, the courage of martyrs, and apologetic writings circulated by dissident monastic communities. Willem Frijhoff's "The State, the Churches, Sociability, and Folk Belief in the Seventeenth-Century Dutch Republic" distinguishes the aims of the Dutch Reformed Church from those of the magistrates; while the former struggled to root out the "instrumental religion" that was a legacy of the Catholic era, the latter supported the "official church" for reasons of social control, while seeking also to build "civic values" that transcended sectarian differences. Caroline Litzenberger's "Communal Ritual, Concealed Belief: Layers of Response to the Regulation of Ritual in Reformation England" centers on what the reformers sought to change, as exemplified by two episcopal visitations of the diocese of Gloucester; so as to school the people to trust in God's Word alone, no traditional gesture or cult object that suggested the old idea of the efficacious power of ritual was to be allowed to continue. In fact, since compliance depended on the cooperation of local parish leaders, worship spaces were changed a good deal less than ardent reformers desired.

Part II, "Forms of Religious Identity," gets at the collective aspect of religious behavior by looking at some of the ways in which shared belief and worship can form a sense of group identity. Romeyn Taylor's "Spirits of the Penumbra: Deities Worshiped in more than one Chinese Pantheon" starts from a distinction between popular religion broadly understood and no less than four forms of worship officially promoted by imperial officials (Confucianism, Daoism, Buddhism, and an officially sanctioned form of popular belief). The "spirits" of the title are witness to the flexibility of religious practice, as supernatural beings keep their names (but not much else) when cultivated in nonofficial places of worship. Frank Sysyn's "Orthodoxy and Revolt: The Role of Religion in the Seventeenth-Century Ukrainian Uprising Against the Polish-Lithuanian Commonwealth" traces the emergence of a sense of distinctiveness among Ruthenians or Orthodox Ukrainians to their disadvantaged position in the Commonwealth of Poland-Lithuania; when the accommodation with the state sought by church leaders was frustrated by the rising zeal of the Counter-Reformation, the hierarchy turned to the cossacks, defenders now not just of their own interest but of the Ruthenian people and their faith. Raymond Mentzer's "The Huguenot Minority in Early Modern France" explores what it meant for France's Protestants to live under an increasingly hostile Catholic state: Huguenots lacked the state support that promoted implementation of moral reform in Calvinist lands, and their numbers were depleted through intermarriage. Yet official measures directed against them seem to have combined with their own internal discipline to create a community strong enough to withstand persecution, including Louis XIV's Revocation of the Edict of Nantes (1685). Paul Seaver's "State Religion and Puritan Resistance in Early Seventeenth-Century England" examines a case in which state pressure was even less effective in discouraging beliefs deemed undesirable; efforts by England's bishops to discipline wayward Puritan preachers had the full backing of the crown, especially under Charles I (1625–1642), but failed utterly to suppress a movement that had strong social roots, especially among lay leaders at the parish level.

Part III, "The Social Articulation of Belief," gives examples of how religious belief is itself shaped and reconfigured by being implanted in a given social framework. Eve Levin's "False Miracles and Unattested Dead Bodies: Investigations into Popular Cults in Early Modern Russia" deals with eighteenth-century efforts to impose limits on the popular credulity that allowed saints to sprout up in great profusion; though supported in their efforts by Tsar Peter the Great, the churchmen who tried to channel popular belief within canonical rules of scrutiny were not always consistent among themselves, partly because of sharp divisions between men who quite consciously drew their ideas of reform from Protestant or Catholic sources. Susan Karant-Nunn's "Liturgical Rites: The Medium, the Message, the Messenger, and the Misunderstanding" broaches the question of how reforms of worship were received by ordinary men and women. If Lutheran pastors in Germany had the firm intention of counteracting all vestiges of the Catholic belief that ritual might influence God, their success was only partial, for worshipers clung stubbornly to their belief in the warding-off of evil through ritual, especially the ritual of baptism. Sara Nalle's "Self-Correction and Social Change in the Spanish Counter-Reformation" takes a more optimistic view of what the reformers could accomplish, at least in the sphere of behavior. In keeping with the new idea that sexual relations between engaged couples were sinful, one finds a decline in the rate for first children born sooner than nine months after marriage; and in keeping with an emphasis on the Catholic doctrine of Purgatory, the faithful spent more on soul-masses for their dear departed and less on the elaborate funeral processions dating back to pre-Christian times. Eamon Duffy's "The

Disenchantment of Space: Salle Church and the Reformation" shows in detail what the Protestant program of worship meant at the parish level. Instead of a worship space marked by "multiple corrals" for gild and family chapels, there was but the one space, for the hearing of God's Word; instead of a congregation compartmentalized as the village itself was, with groups like plough-boys and village maidens each having a role, there was but the one parish community, in which no one but the traditional lay leaders had a specific function.

Finally, by way of an Epilogue, Nicholas Orme's "Popular Religion and the Reformation in England: A View from Cornwall" takes a long-term view of religious life in a part of England where many people still spoke the Celtic language of their ancestors. The Reformation had real popular support in Cornwall, and it changed the landscape of worship forever: as opposed to multiple chapels scattered throughout the parish, devoted to multiple saints, there was now only the parish church itself, in keeping with the reformers' aim of "emphasizing the community of the people of God, rather than allowing it to divide into coteries" centered on the cults of different saints. But people did not so readily abandon their social habits; well into the eighteenth century, each parish still had its annual church-ale, and the festival of the patron saint was still observed, albeit now in private houses, not in public.

Quite apart from the division of the volume into three parts, there are many points at which essays on different parts of the world link up with one another, of which three might be mentioned by way of illustration. The first is the tendency of ordinary worshipers to attach more importance than their religious superiors do to the "instrumental" or apotropaic properties of ritual action. To undermine this common belief was a major aim of Protestant reformers, regardless of their theological differences (Litzenberger, Karant-Nunn); Dutch Calvinists took the same view, while their Catholic rivals saw this aspect of folk belief as "recoverable, within an ecclesiastical strategy" of emphasizing Catholicism's distinctive features (Frijhoff). In Russia, where Christianity was "a religion of the sign, not the word," the fact that one was now commanded to make the sign of the cross with three fingers instead of two became a matter of utmost seriousness for seventeenth-century believers from all levels of society (Crummey). In the next century, the question of how vigorously to pursue the offensive against popular superstition was one that divided reformers of "Catholic" and "Protestant" sympathies (Levin). In China, officially approved teachers of religion, though often (at least in the Confucian tradition) deeply skeptical of popular superstition, were venerated among the people not as men of learning, but as men "endowed with numinous powers to command the spirits" (Taylor).

Second, it seems that state attitudes toward religion may have something in common in different parts of the world. Russian historians have found it useful to adopt the paradigm of "confessionalization" (Crummey), developed by historians of the Protestant and Catholic Reformations in Germany as a way to describe the interest of the state in correct religious observance. The Chinese officials for whom orthodoxy had a "social-ethical content" (Shek) would perhaps not have found it so difficult to understand the magistrates in the Dutch Republic, whose commitment to the official church was more a matter of "social control" than of doctrine (Frijhoff).

Third, it is apparent that differing ways of worship express differing understandings of community, and vice versa. In China, where the pluralistic official religion "constituted the social order," it nonetheless "provided no socially inclusive space" where men and women and young and old of high and low social standing could all worship together (Taylor). This was surely one of the attractions of the cult of the Eternal Mother, for the bonds that socially heterogenous devotees formed among one another were "much stronger" than those formed among worshipers at the same temple or shrine, always segregated according to age or station (Shek). In Europe during roughly the same period, the long Catholic–Protestant struggle for the allegiance of the faithful turned in part on two competing visions of community, one in which the whole parish came together to form a single body of believers, the other in which the worshiping community was a coming-together of smaller communities defined by affinities of various kinds (Duffy, Litzenberger, Orme, Seaver).

Readers will no doubt find their own connections among the essays, perhaps even more intriguing than those just listed. Despite such parallels, however, this volume is not conceived as a step toward a generalized science of past belief; rather, it is a shared conviction among the authors represented here that our knowledge of the past advances by differentiation, not by homogenization. Our hope is thus that the consideration of phenomena that are properly analogous – that is, somewhat alike, but simply different – will help to bring out for each area those features that stand out more sharply by virtue of comparison.

PART I

# Lived religion and official religion

CHAPTER I

# The alternative moral universe of religious dissenters in Ming-Qing China

RICHARD SHEK

ELSEWHERE in this volume, Professor Romeyn Taylor offers a nuanced portrayal of Chinese religions.[1] He identifies four traditions, with overlapping deities and shared common assumptions, but with different rituals and varying degrees of "officialness." There is, however, a fifth tradition in the Chinese religious world, one that is qualitatively different from the other four. One can argue that the other four traditions are expressions of one orthodox camp, while this fifth tradition is indisputably heterodox by contrast. It is the late imperial version of this fifth tradition, making its appearance at the beginning of the sixteenth century in China, that is the focus of this essay.

Couched in the framework of orthodoxy versus heterodoxy, this chapter attempts to establish the following points: (1) an orthodoxy existed in China since the middle of the second century before the common era and lasted until the turn of the present century; (2) this orthodoxy was not articulated by a religious authority, but rather by a political authority; (3) the content of this orthodoxy, sociopolitical and ethical in emphasis, was defined not by narrow sectarian doctrines but by a compromise consensus among all the major religious traditions in China; (4) challenge to this orthodoxy, long-lasting and variegated in nature, crystalized at the turn of the sixteenth century into a potent tradition revolving around a central matriarchal deity and a strong millenarian and eschatological vision; (5) this heterodox tradition, though similarly socioethical in content, was by definition

---

[1] See Chapter 5: "Spirits of the Penumbra: Deities Worshiped in More Than One Chinese Pantheon."

13

also politically subversive and occasionally erupted into antidynastic
rebellions.

### MORAL ORTHODOXY AND RELIGIOUS PLURALISM

In his seminal study of the religion of China, the early twentieth-century
sociologist Max Weber offered an instructive, though ultimately misin-
formed, framework of analysis. He proposed that China could be understood most usefully when Confucianism was regarded as the orthodox
tradition, while Daoism was deemed its heterodox counterpart. In this
analysis, Confucian doctrines, buttressed by political authority, served
as the official ideology of the land. Daoism, on the other hand, played a
subversive role throughout Chinese history, offering an alternative view
of the world that engaged in a protracted struggle with Confucian orthodoxy. In this struggle, Weber further observed, the Chinese emperor,
unopposed by an independent church, was the *pontifex maximus* who
stood at the head of this Confucian orthodoxy.[2] This analytical scheme
is attractive because of its simplicity, as well as its apparent validity.
After all, Confucianism and Daoism often have been seen as the *yang*
and the *yin*, respectively, of Chinese religion, and as such they meet the
dualistic expectations of those familiar with the monotheistic traditions.
Since Confucianism had been closely related to the power of the state
from the Han dynasty on (205 B.C.E.–220 C.E.), its orthodox status was
assumed. By contrast, Daoism had been associated with antisocial and
countercultural ideas and behavior as well, thus its heterodox nature
also seemed to be beyond question.

What this Weberian thesis seems to have failed to take note of, however, is that numerous rulers in imperial China have been ardent supporters of Daoism and have used Daoist doctrines as the guiding principles of the state. Moreover, this framework also ignores the prominent
role played by Buddhism and other faiths in traditional China, which
on numerous occasions also served as the dominant ideology. Overall,
Weber's analysis suffers from a simplistic approach that sees only the dichotomy between Confucianism and Daoism as relevant, thereby being
unable to account for Buddhism's place in Chinese society, while at the
same time treating both of China's indigenous traditions as monolithic
entities devoid of internal tensions and variations.

A recent study of the same subject is far more nuanced and complex. In his symposium volume on *Orthodoxy in Late Imperial China*,

---

[2]  Max Weber, *The Religion of China: Confucianism and Taoism*, trans. Hans Gerth (New York,
1951), esp. 152–67.

Kwang-ching Liu offers a richly textured and far more suggestive discussion of Chinese orthodoxy.[3] Liu argues from the outset that, just as
Max Weber had observed, the espousing of "right and correct teaching"
(*zheng*)[4] in China was undertaken and enforced by the state, namely
the imperial ruler, precisely because of the absence of a distinction between political and religious authorities. The Chinese monarch during
the entire imperial period performed dual roles as both caesar and pope.
As such, he viewed as his prerogative the imposition of a normative
teaching on his subjects, one that supposedly would induce them toward proper understanding and ideal behavior. This normative teaching, however, should not be seen merely as an official ideology because
it was deeply rooted in the religious beliefs and values of China since
the classical period.

Liu calls this teaching *lijiao* – "doctrine of propriety-and-ritual."[5] It is
grounded in familial and political assumptions and expressed in inter-
personal conduct. It is encapsulated by the cardinal prescriptive behavior demanded by the Three Bonds (*sangang*), that is, obligations of subject
to ruler, child to parents, and wife to husband. These obligations, along
with the relationships between juniors and seniors and among peers,
are enacted through a set of behavioral patterns generally referred to
as *li* – rituals. These rituals are in turn governed by the principles of
propriety, decorum, deference, and harmony. This orthodox tradition
maintained that it is through performance of such situational rituals
that one's authentic humanity can be established.

It is precisely at this juncture that the religious nature of such ritual
behavior can be discerned. Herbert Fingarette has contended elsewhere
that these rituals contain elements of the numinous.[6] For behind these
rituals, Fingarette maintains, lies the ultimate entity known as *Tian* –
Heaven. *Tian* is the Will that presides over both the natural and the social cosmos, ordaining the functions of nature as well as human society.
It is, moreover, a Will that controls not only the fate of the universe but
also the destiny of humanity, and it demands goodness and harmony for
all to survive and prosper. Proper and ritualistic human behavior, therefore, is mandatory to attain a good and harmonious cosmos, as well as
community. In this connection, such ritual and ethical conduct in social
intercourse is fraught with religious implications, as human behavior

---

[3] Kwang-ching Liu, ed., *Orthodoxy in Late Imperial China* (Berkeley, 1990), esp. the introduction and 2.
[4] This term, interestingly, has a cognate word and homophone which means "politics"
and "the affairs of the people."
[5] Liu, *Orthodoxy*, 53.
[6] Herbert Fingarette, *Confucius – The Secular as Sacred* (New York, 1972).

is now linked inextricably to the ultimate concern of *Tian*. Ritual, seen in this light, is holy rite;[7] the secular is indeed sacred. *Tian* is the this-worldly transcendental being that makes every human act a religious act. Thus loyalty to the monarch, filial piety to the parents, and wifely submission are religiously sanctioned behavior and are themselves holy and numinous in nature. It is by according oneself to these providential social conventions that one aspires to accord with the Will of *Tian*.

While Confucianism was principally responsible for the articulation of such a view, it was by no means alone in its effort. Despite intrinsic doctrinal differences and even fundamental incompatibilities, Daoism and even Buddhism have, over the course of the imperial period, come to embrace just such a view and have contributed to upholding its validity and immutability. Both the Daoist and the Buddhist establishment have produced learned texts as well as moral exhortations of behavior to lend support to the sanctity of the Three Bonds.[8] Whether they came to this position out of expediency or through strong conviction remains to be debated. What is noteworthy is the apparent accommodation agreed upon by the three major religious traditions. Diversity in doctrine and belief might be tolerated, but there was a convergence and unanimity among the three on matters relating to social morality and ethical behavior. Different deities, or none at all, could be worshiped; the world could be understood alternatively as ultimately illusory or concrete and real. Yet with respect to social and ethical conduct, a rigid and axiomatic insistence on loyalty, filial piety, and wifely submission was shared by the three mainstream religions. Liu calls this phenomenon "religious pluralism and moral orthodoxy,"[9] a unique Chinese feature that the aforementioned Weberian thesis has failed to capture.

Having thus defined China's moral orthodoxy, which, as indicated, was formulated during the Han dynasty (third century B.C.E. to third century C.E.), persisted through the invasion of Central Asian tribes and the importation of Buddhism in the subsequent centuries, and finally was consolidated and provided with an elaborate metaphysical underpinning by the Neo-Confucians of the Song-Ming era (tenth through sixteenth centuries), it becomes easy to see how heterodoxy can be identified. It is the defying of the ritual propriety and social morality ordained

---

[7] Fingarette, *Confucius*, Chapter 1.

[8] For Daoism's subscription to this ethical convention, see Akizuki Kan'ei, *Chugoku kinsei Dokyo no kenkyu – Jomyodo no kisoteki kenkyu* [A Study of Early Modern Daoism – Basic Research on the Pure and Brilliant Sect] (Tokyo, 1978). For Buddhism's similar conversion, see Michibata Ryoshu, *Bukkyo to Jukyo rinri* [Buddhist and Confucian Ethics] (Kyoto, 1968) and Kenneth Ch'en, *The Chinese Transformation of Buddhism* (Princeton, 1973).

[9] Liu, *Orthodoxy*, 2.

by *Tian* to be universally valid and perennially immutable that makes one deviate from orthodoxy and verge on heterodoxy. In other words, it is the espousal of an alternative moral universe in which the Three Bonds have no relevance that makes one a true heterodox dissenter.

This heterodox tradition came into being as soon as orthodoxy took shape, paralleling the experience of Christian Europe. In some sense, the need to define orthodoxy was prompted by the awareness of the existence of heterodoxy. Thus from the Han dynasty onward, numerous individuals, groups, movements, and traditions had rejected the essentialness of one, or another, or all of the Three Bonds. Some Buddhists had waged a protracted battle with imperial authority on the issue of clerical autonomy and their refusal to pay obeisance to the monarch. Some Daoists had steadfastly shown their aversion toward social obligations as a result of their firm belief in spontaneity and ethical relativity. Others, such as the Maitreyans, Manichaeans, and numerous chiliastic groups, had subscribed to a radical eschatological doctrine that envisioned the impending demise of the existing order, thereby depriving it of any claim of immutability and permanence. Yet the vast majority of these individuals and groups were scattered and sporadic in their opposition to orthodoxy. By their very nature, there was no sense among them of belonging to or drawing from a common heterodox tradition.[10]

### THE ETERNAL MOTHER TRADITION

By the sixteenth century, however, both orthodoxy and heterodoxy in China had solidified into distinct camps with clear lines of demarcation between them. By then the phenomenon of "religious pluralism and moral orthodoxy" had become fully entrenched. The imperial ruler as arbiter and articulator of moral orthodoxy was unrivaled; likewise, the heterodox tradition had coagulated around a definable set of doctrines that espoused an alternative moral universe. In what follows I will discuss the nature and development of this tradition.

The most characteristic feature of this tradition is the worship of a central supreme female deity named *Wusheng laomu* (Eternal Venerable Mother). Her appearance, most noticeably around the turn of the sixteenth century, signaled a new and more mature version of unorthodox beliefs. She herself symbolized all of the ideas and practices that could be considered "heterodox." Superseding, but by no means totally displacing, the Maitreya Buddha as the ultimate source of eschatological

---

[10] Kwang-ching Liu and Richard Shek are co-editing a volume entitled *Heterodoxy in Late Imperial China* (Honolulu, 2004) in which several of these groups are studied.

salvation, the Eternal Mother inspired numerous rebellious movements throughout the Ming-Qing period. For this, the government chose to call her believers White Lotus sectarians, as the White Lotus was the most feared and notorious of all sectarian organizations since the Yuan dynasty.[11] In actuality, however, few if any of her followers used the name White Lotus. Instead, they adopted a plethora of names and showed much diversity in their practices.[12] For a more accurate description, therefore, I have decided to refer to them here as Eternal Mother sects and the religion they subscribed to as the Eternal Mother religion.

The central vision of these sects was salvation through the Eternal Mother and her emissaries. But how did the figure of the Eternal Mother originate? In what manner did the myth surrounding this deity evolve? What messages did she have for her believers and what implications did these messages have for orthodoxy?

## THE ORIGIN OF THE ETERNAL MOTHER

While most historians of Chinese sectarianism speculate that the Eternal Mother myth may be traced to Luo Qing, a Shandong man who lived between 1443 and 1527 in the Ming dynasty, there are arguments advanced that point to a much earlier appearance of the deity, perhaps going back to the beginning of the thirteenth century.[13] The Chinese scholar Ma Xisha has located a sacred scroll in the Shanxi Museum that he determines to have first appeared in 1212, to be reprinted in 1290.[14] Entitled *Foshuo Yangshi gui xiu hongluo Huaxiange baozhuan* [Precious scroll on the Buddha telling the story of the ghost of Lady Yang embroidering red brocades and her son Huaxiange], this text contains interesting

---

[11] Susan Naquin has followed this designation and refers to all the Eternal Mother cults since 1500 as White Lotus religion. See her article, "The Transmission of White Lotus Sectarianism in Late Imperial China," in *Popular Culture in Late Imperial China*, David Johnson, Andrew J. Nathan, and Evelyn Rawski eds. (Berkeley, 1985), 255–91. However, as B.J. Ter Haar has recently argued in his monograph, *The White Lotus Teachings in Chinese Religious History* (Leiden, 1992), this designation is extremely problematic. I concur with Ter Haar's concerns.

[12] The *Longhua jing* (Dragon Flower Sutra), one of the most important sectarian texts belonging to the Eternal Mother tradition, lists eighteen sects in the mid-nineteenth century, none of which used the name White Lotus. A printed copy of the text is in the possession of Richard Shek. See also, Sawada Mizuho, *Kochu haja shoben* [annotated edition of the *Poxie xiangbian*] (Tokyo, 1972), hereafter referred to as *Kochu*. Susan Naquin distinguishes between two major types of Eternal Mother sects, which she calls, respectively, "sutra-recitation sects" and "meditational sects." See her "Transmission of White Lotus Sectarianism," 260–88.

[13] See the article by Ma Xisha, "*Zuizao ibu baozhuan de yanjiu*" [A study of one of the earliest precious scrolls], *Shijie zongjiao yanjiu* [Study of World Religions] (January 1986): 56–72.

[14] Ma Xisha, "*Zuizao ibu baozhuan de yanjiu*," 59.

references to the *Wusheng laomu* and the need for all believers to return to the native place (*jiaxiang*).[15] Yet these references have no organic relationship to the rest of the text, and even Ma, himself, now suspects that they may be later interpolations.[16] In the absence of further and irrefutable evidence that puts the appearance of the *Wusheng laomu* belief at a time before Luo Qing, therefore, we are compelled to regard Luo as the precursor in articulating the notion of the Eternal Mother.

A soldier turned religious teacher, Luo was the grand patriarch who gave both direction and content to much of Chinese folk sectarianism from the sixteenth century on.[17] His complete writings, known as *Wubu liuce* (Five books in six volumes), were published as a set for the first time in 1509. They served as model for many later sectarian texts and inspired a whole new brand of beliefs, namely, the Eternal Mother religion. To be sure, he never mentioned the Eternal Mother as a saving deity, nor did his writings provide any concrete details of her personality. Yet an examination of his *Wubu liuce* will reveal that most of the basic ideas of the Eternal Mother myth were adumbrated by him. It took only a little imagination on the part of his followers to translate them into full-scale, vivid images. In what follows I will show how these ideas were originally presented and later transformed.

Luo Qing's writings include the following titles: (1) *Kugong wudao zhuan* [The text of attaining enlightenment through rigorous discipline];

---

[15] Ma Xisha, "*Zuizao ibu baozhuan de yanjiu*," 70–1.

[16] Mr. Ma raised this suspicion in a March 14, 1993, conversation with me in Davis, California.

[17] For a rather complete bibliography of studies on Luo Qing in Japanese, see Sawada Mizuho, *Zoho hokan no kenkyu* [An Expanded and Annotated Study of Precious Scrolls] (Tokyo, 1975), 458–9, hereafter referred to as *Zoho*. For more recent works in Japanese, see Asai Motoi, *Min-Shin jidai minkan shukyo kessha no kenkyu* [Study of Folk Religious Associations in the Ming-Qing Period] (Tokyo, 1990), esp. 23–113. For works on Luo in English, see Daniel Overmyer, *Folk Buddhist Religion* (Cambridge, MA, 1976), 113–29; also his "Boatmen and Buddhas: The Lo Chiao in Ming Dynasty China," *History of Religions* 17.3–4 (February–May 1978): 284–302. Also see Richard Shek, "Elite and Popular Reformism in Late Ming: The Traditions of Wang Yang-ming and Lo Ch'ing," in *Rekishi no okeru minshu to bunka* [The Common Masses and Culture in History, Festschrift Commemorating the Seventieth Birthday of Prof. Sakai Tadao] (Tokyo, 1982), 1–21; and David E. Kelley, "Temples and Tribute Fleets: The Luo Sect and Boatmen's Associations in the Eighteenth Century," *Modern China* 8.3 (1982): 361–91. The most detailed study of Luo Qing in Chinese is Zheng Zhiming's *Wusheng laomu xinyang suoyuan* [Exploring the Origins of the Eternal Mother Belief] (Taipei, 1985). See also Song Guangyu's earlier article, "*Shi lun 'Wusheng laomu' zongjiao xinyang de I'xie tezhi*" [On Some Characteristics of the Religious Belief in the Eternal Venerable Mother], *Bulletin of the Institute of History and Philology*, Academia Sinica 52.3 (September 1981): 559–90. See also Yu Songqing, *Ming-Qing bailianjiao yanjiu* [Study of White Lotus Sects in Ming and Qing] (Chengdu, 1987), and the most recent compendium by Ma Xisha and Han Bingfang, *Zhongguo minjian zongjiao shi* [History of Chinese Folk Religion] (Shanghai, 1992), esp. 165–339.

(2) *Tanshi wuwei zhuan* [The text of lamentation for the world and un-contrived action]; (3) *Poxie xianzheng yaoshi zhuan* [The text on the key to refuting heresy and revealing the truth], in two volumes; (4) *Zhengxin chu'i wuxiuzheng zizai baozhuan* [The self-evident precious scroll, needing no cultivation, that rectifies belief and dispels doubts]; and (5) *Weiwei budong Taishan shen'gen jieguo baozhuan* [The precious scroll, imposing and unperturbed as Mt. T'ai, which has deep roots and bears fruits]. The *Kugong wudao zhuan* was the first completed and is thematically the most coherent, with the remaining four providing sometimes rambling expositions of the ideas mentioned in it. Moreover, the *Kugong zhuan* documents the religious odyssey of Luo Qing, describing in graphic de-tail the arduous path by which he arrived at his spiritual awakening. The following analysis of Luo's religious search relies chiefly on the *Kugong* text, with the discussion of key concepts supplemented by quotations from Luo Qing's other books.

* * * * *

The driving forces behind Luo Qing's spiritual quest were his realiza-tion of the impermanence of life and his feeling of anxiety caused by the awareness of his own ephemeral self. Subscribing to the conventional Buddhist notion of *samsara*, Luo was troubled by the gnawing thought of endless and meaningless existences of births and deaths, rebirths and redeaths: "Where can this soul of mine attach itself? Since eons ago it has gone through innumerable births and deaths, in various shapes and forms. Though assuming human form this time, its life-span of at most a hundred years is nothing more than a dream, while its next incarna-tion as another suffering creature is yet to be decided.... This incessant samsaric transmigration is truly frightening!"[18] From this disturbing observation, he concluded that all beings are cut adrift and have gone astray from their native place ( *jiaxiang*).[19]

This conclusion prompted Luo to embark on a religious journey to find a solution to this perennial problem and to put an end to this wandering of his soul. His first teacher was apparently a Pure Land monk[20] who, after putting him through a half-year apprenticeship, taught him the technique of reciting the Amitabha Buddha's name. His

---

[18] *Kugong zhuan*, 1:12b. (The edition used in this study is the 1596 reprint, with commentaries.)

[19] *Kugong zhuan*, 1:14b, 16a; see also *Taishan zhuan*, Section 23.

[20] Pure Land is a mature form of the Mahayana (Great Vehicle) tradition of Bud-dhism, which emphasizes the Buddha's compassion and the believers' dependence on it.

master explained that by incessantly and earnestly invoking the name of Amitabha Buddha, one could stop the *samsaric* migration and attain rebirth in the Western paradise. What was unusual about this Pure Land master's teaching was, however, his identification of Amitabha Buddha as the Eternal Venerable Parent (*Wusheng fumu*) and the believer as infant (*ying'er*).[21]

This represents the earliest recorded usage of the term *Wusheng fumu*, a term that would come to assume great significance in sectarian belief, and one that later would be changed to *Wusheng laomu* by Luo's followers. From the context in which it occurs, however, it is obvious that Luo Qing did not invent this term, but merely repeated what must have been a common or popular reference to the Amitabha Buddha among certain Pure Land groups in the second half of the fifteenth century. These Pure Land believers must have employed this parent-child motif to characterize the intimate relationship between the Amitabha Buddha and the human race. In any event, Luo Qing followed the instruction of his master faithfully and devoted himself wholeheartedly to the chanting of the Amitabha Buddha's name with vigor. Thus the text reads:

> With utmost effort, I utter the single cry of *Wusheng fumu*, lest the Amitabha Buddha will not hear me!
> I single-mindedly recite the name of the Amitabha Buddha, thinking that if I say it too slowly, my *Wusheng fumu* in heaven will not hear me![22]

For Luo, and perhaps for some Pure Land practitioners of his time as well, Amitabha Buddha was the Eternal Parent who would deliver the children from endless suffering.

Luo Qing's experimentation with *nianfo* (chanting the Buddha's name) lasted eight years. Yet he confessed that his devotion did not bring him the peace of mind and liberation from anxiety he sought. He was still filled with doubt and restlessness. How could one be sure that one's earnest chanting actually would be heard? When one was old and near death, would one not slacken in vigor while chanting, thereby missing the opportunity for deliverance? In what manner would this final encounter with the Eternal Parent take place? These concerns were causing him doubts about *nianfo* devotionalism altogether. In the end, the dependence on the saving grace of a deity, however compassionate, was for Luo too uncertain and risky.

Luo Qing's next religious search was triggered by a death in a neighbor's family, when a group of Buddhist monks came to recite sutras

---

[21] *Kugong zhuan*, 1:18a.
[22] *Kugong zhuan*, 1:19a, 20b.

for the deceased. The sutra used on that occasion happened to be the *Jingang ke'i*, a simplified version of the Diamond Sutra that had been popular among the lay and less educated Buddhists since its compilation in the Song dynasty. When Luo heard the recitation of it from the street late one night, he was deeply moved and resolved to study this sutra intensively to probe its meaning. This account of Luo's introduction to the Diamond Sutra is certainly reminiscent of a similar experience of Huineng (638–713), the Sixth Patriarch of the Chan School.[23] It may be indicative of Luo's conscious, or at least subconscious, attempt to imitate Huineng and to enhance his own stature among fellow religious teachers. The episode is, moreover, a clear indication of Luo's transition from Pure Land to Chan in his search for salvation and enlightenment.

Luo's intensive study of the Diamond Sutra continued for three years, during which time he read the text with devotion by day and practiced quiet-sitting by night. Yet complete understanding of the text still eluded him. This distressed him tremendously, as he believed that only through genuine comprehension of this text would he achieve enlightenment. With no prospect for any quick comprehension and therefore illumination, he became almost neurotic, forgetful of food and drink. Meditation, *gong'an* puzzles, and other religious practices he found too restrictive and confining. His anxiety reached the breaking point.

It was at this particular juncture that Luo redirected his inquiry. Instead of preoccupying himself with his own salvation, he now focused his attention on the question: What was it like before Heaven and Earth were created?[24] His answer was a surprising discovery and a real breakthrough for him: Before the creation of Heaven and Earth, there existed only the unchanging Vacuous Emptiness (*xukong*), or True Emptiness (*zhenkong*).[25] This Emptiness antedated the universe and would last longer than it. Limitless and inexhaustible, it was the source of all beings. In a flash of insight, Luo found in this True Emptiness a new focus of his religious quest. At the same time, it gave him a new challenge: How could one attach oneself to this Emptiness? How could one enter or return to it?

His rumination and musing on such questions led him to the startling but pleasant realization that True Emptiness is ultimately omnipresent and pervasive. It already exists in all things, therefore there is no need

---

[23] In contrast to Pure Land, Chan Buddhism stresses the completeness of each individual believer's buddhahood. It calls for self-reflection and quiet meditation to rediscover one's original perfection.

[24] *Kugong zhuan*, 1:33a, 34b.

[25] *Kugong zhuan*, 1:34a–36a.

to seek attachment or entry to it. It is, moreover, all things – from the time of their very creation! This realization resulted in Luo's euphoric proclamation:

All of a sudden, during my meditation, I experience great joy in my heart. Not belonging to Being, and not belonging to Non-Being, I am True Emptiness. The Mother (*niang*) is me, and I am her – there is originally no distinction. With Emptiness within and without, I am True Emptiness![26]

The reference to the Mother here is most intriguing. In Luo's usage, the Mother is another name for True Emptiness, which, as the source of all things, has a mother-like quality. For Luo Qing at this time, however, this Mother has no personality and is certainly no deity. She is the generative and transformative force in the universe, very much like the Daoist usage of the term in the *Daodejing*, the Daoist classic reportedly authored by Laozi. It can thus be seen that Luo's religious quest was not confined to Buddhist motifs but was instead quite eclectic, involving native Daoist notions as well. Once this highly emotive image was used, however, its personification was only one step away, as we shall see.

As a matter of fact, Luo himself was the one who initiated this process of personification, although the term he personified was "True Emptiness" rather than "Mother." This occurred in his recounting of his final and thorough awakening, which came two years after his insight into True Emptiness and thirteen years after he first began his spiritual search. As he described it, the "Venerable True Emptiness" (*Lao zhenkong*), showing pity on his sincerity and devotion, enlightened him on the ultimate reality of things by shining on him a stream of white light while he was absorbed in meditation, facing the southwest.[27] This brought about an immediate opening of his mind and the complete illumination of all things. He experienced a total sense of unity with all the myriad phenomena around him, which he described as the sensation of "absolute freedom and ease" (*zongheng zizai*).

This awakening brought Luo Qing's spiritual odyssey to an end. From then on he felt so sure and confident of his religious understanding that he became a teacher himself and propagated his new found faith among the people. His teaching, which he called the *wuwei fa* (teaching of

---

[26] *Kugong zhuan*, 2:44b.
[27] This episode is given much significance by most scholars studying Luo Qing's thought. See, in particular, Kaji Toshiyuki, "Raso no shinko no seisei katei to 'hikari' ni tsuite" [On the 'Light' and the Process of Formulation of the Cult of Luo Qing] in *Chutetsu bungaku kaiho* no. 10 (1985); also his "*Sen yonhyaku hachijyuni nen no 'hikari' – futatabi goburokusatsu o yomu*" [The 'Light' of 1482 – Again on Reading the Five Books in Six Volumes], in *Yamane Yukio kyojyu taikyu kinen Mindaishi ronso* [Essays on Ming History in Honor of Professor Yamane Yukio's Retirement] (Tokyo, 1990), II: 1151–70.

actionless action), dispensed with all outward forms of religious piety and theoretical discourse, but insisted only on self-reflection and intuitive understanding.[28] The most interesting part of his teaching, for our purposes at least, remains his discussion of the ontological source and the creative progenitor of the myriad things and how human salvation could be effected with knowledge of it. In my view, Luo Qing's elaboration on this subject in the *Wubu liuce* provided all the groundwork for the later evolution of the Eternal Mother belief.

In addition to the terms "Vacuous Emptiness" and "True Emptiness," Luo Qing used a variety of labels to refer to the ontological entity which is the source and origin of all creation: "Original Face" (*benlai mianmu*),[29] "Authentic Self" (*zhenshen*),[30] "Light" (*guang*) or "Sentient Light" (*lingguang*),[31] "Native Place" (*jiaxiang*),[32] "Mother" (*niang* or *mu*),[33] "Nonbeing" (*wu*),[34] "Eternal Unbegotten" (*wusheng*),[35] and "Ultimate of Nonbeing" (*wuji*).[36] All of them were used as interchangeable terms to denote the "First Cause" or "Unmoved Mover" from which all beings are created and to which all existences shall return. The last named, however, was also portrayed by Luo as a personified deity, the Sagely Patriarch (or Matriarch?) of Ultimate of Nonbeing (*Wuji shengzu*).[37] As the unbegotten origin of the universe, the deity was the creator of all the buddhas, the myriad worlds, the heavenly bodies and the earthly mountains and oceans, the grains and all vegetation, the human race, and the teachings of the Three Religions.[38] But more significantly, this *Wuji shengzu* was a conscious supreme deity, who showed boundless compassion for the virtuous and administered stern punishment to the wicked. Furthermore, the *Wuji shengzu* had undergone numerous transformations and manifestations as a shining embodiment of morality to enlighten the human race.

In Luo Qing's mind, this understanding of the ontological basis of all existences carried with it a simple solution to his quest for the cessation

---

[28] For a discussion of Luo's religious iconoclasm and his Chan affinity, see Shek, "Elite and Popular Reformism in Late Ming," esp. 7–11. See also Zheng Zhiming, *Wusheng laomu xinyang suoyuan*, esp. Chapters 3–5.

[29] *Taishan zhuan*, Sections 4, 6, 7. *Poxie zhuan*, Section 4. *Tanshi zhuan*, Section 1.

[30] *Kugong zhuan*, 2:59b–60a. *Tanshi zhuan*, 44–5.

[31] *Kugong zhuan*, 2:73a, 74a–75b. *Poxie zhuan*, 2:17, 22. *Zhengxin zhuan*, 42.

[32] *Poxie zhuan*, Sections 4, 7. *Zhengxin zhuan*, Section 13. *Kugong zhuan*, 2:59b–60a, 73a.

[33] *Kugong zhuan*, 2:44b, 63b. *Taishan zhuan*, Section 4.

[34] *Kugong zhuan*, 2:55a. *Poxie zhuan*, 21.

[35] *Poxie zhuan*, Section 4.

[36] *Zhenxin zhuan*, Prologue, Sections 1, 5. *Taishan zhuan*, 1.

[37] *Zhengxin zhuan*, Prologue, 1, 16, Section 5.

[38] *Taishan zhuan*, Section 17.

of suffering and for salvation. Since all things are the manifestations and transformations of *Wuji*, they are equal to and unified with one another. At the same time, they are all as exalted and complete as *Wuji* itself. This led Luo to declare with perfect conviction that "Before creation I already existed; before Heaven and Earth came into being I was already there!"[39] Thus salvation involves nothing more than the removal of all previous ignorance and the recognition of one's identity with this ontological source before creation – one's equality with the buddhas, and one's unity with all things.

Having thus thought through the nature of the human predicament and its resolution, Luo was able to draw the conclusion that all the teachings and practices of the other schools were superfluous, if not inimical, to salvation. He felt particularly compelled to reject the earlier instruction he had received, which compared the Amitabha Buddha to the Eternal Venerable Parent. In his *Zhengxin zhuan*, he derided the "ignorant simpletons who say that our nature is the Infant and the Amitabha Buddha is the Eternal Parent." Reasoning that the Amitabha Buddha was a man and not a woman, he asked rhetorically, "How could he have given birth to you?"[40] On the other hand, the *Wuji shengzu* was more appropriate as the progenitor, not only of the human race, but also of all the buddhas as well. In fact, this generative and procreative ability of *Wuji* was very much mother-like. "The names of all the buddhas, the scriptures, the human race, and the myriad things originate from a single word. This word is 'Mother'. The Mother is the Patriarch (Matriarch?), and the Patriarch (Matriarch?) is the Mother (*mu ji shi zu, zu ji shi mu*)."[41]

Luo Qing's religious views can thus be summarized as follows: All creatures and beings originate from, and partake of, the same source. This source has various names, including *zhenkong* and *jiaxiang*. Moreover, it is understood to be Eternal and Unbegotten (*wusheng*) and is the Parent or Mother (*fumu* or *mu*) of the universe and the myriad things. Separation from and ignorance of this origin constitute human suffering, while a return to and unity with it signal salvation. It is thus apparent that Luo's religious writings supplied all the key terms for the later sectarian chant of *zhenkong jiaxiang, wusheng fumu* (Native Land of True Emptiness, Eternal Venerable Parent). To this chant the Ming-Qing sectarians added a whole new mythology of the Eternal Mother and her salvational message for her prodigal children. Yet in an amazing way,

---

[39] *Poxie zhuan*, Sections 2, 7.
[40] *Zhengxin zhuan*, Section 16.
[41] *Taishan zhuan*, Section 4.

Luo Qing had already drawn the broad outline of this mythology in his
*Poxie zhuan*:

*Wuji* gives birth to Heaven and Earth, regulates them, and provides for the
human race.
The people of the Earth are the poor children: you have been admonished to
return home; yet you lack faith.
*Wuji* is our original forebear, *Wuji* the elder is thinking of her/his descendants.
The people of the Earth are the poor children; they have experienced numerous
kalpas and are lost, failing to recognize their parents.
With faith, the poor children can return home and occupy an exalted position
in this vast universe.
There will be boundless joy; yet you are not returning. Instead you go through
endless *samsara* in the sea of suffering.
With faith, the poor children can return home and fulfill the vow of the elder.
The people of the Earth are the poor children, while the elder is the Buddha.
The Buddha on Mt. Ling is originally me; when I realize this *wusheng*, I can
avoid hell.
*Wusheng* is True Thusness (*zhenru*), I myself am originally the Amitabha
Buddha.[42]

This depiction of the human predicament and the nature of salvation
anticipates much of the Eternal Mother myth that came to be developed
later. The human race is alienated from its creator, ignorant of its divine
origin, and mired in *samsaric* suffering. On the other hand, the creator
cares for the well-being of her/his children and is distressed to see them
suffer. She/he seeks to enlighten them and beckons them to return.
Their reunion with this unceasing, unbegotten, and eternal ground of
being marks a genuine salvation. It can be seen that while the later
sectarian myth has a much stronger eschatological theme and contains
more pronounced personality traits for the Eternal Mother, Luo Qing
has essentially formulated the main story line.

THE ETERNAL MOTHER

Indeed, the emotive image of a divine mother who tearfully awaits the
return of her estranged and suffering children is so appealing that it
did not take long for some sectarians, inspired by Luo Qing, to propose
it.[43] This took place even before Luo's death in 1527, as evidenced by

---

[42] *Poxie zhuan*, Section 24.
[43] The motif of the reunion between mother and child may have received inspiration from
the Manichaean cosmogonic story. See my article on "Maitreyanism, Manichaeanism,
and Early White Lotus," in *Heterodoxy in Late Imperial China*.

a sectarian text "reprinted" in 1523.[44] The text is *Huangji jindan jiulian zhengxin guizhen huanxiang baozhuan* [Precious scroll of the golden elixir and nine lotuses of the imperial ultimate, which leads to the rectification of beliefs, the taking of refuge in truth, and the return to the native place], hereafter, the *Jiulian baozhuan*.[45]

A text composed during the lifetime of Luo Qing, the *Jiulian baozhuan* represents both a continuation of his main themes and the addition of new ones. Written probably by a follower of Luo Qing's daughter, it makes frequent references to his teaching. The progenitor of all things, for example, is referred to at one point as "Venerable True Emptiness," even though she is more commonly addressed as the Eternal Mother. Moreover, the method of cultivation to prepare oneself for the return to the Native Place is described as *wuwei fa*, a direct echo of Luo's teaching. In deference to him, the principal expositor of the Eternal Mother's salvational message is referred to in this text as the Patriarch of Wuwei, who is in turn the incarnation of the Amitabha Buddha. This clearly indicates that Luo Qing was regarded with high esteem by the author of the text. The identification of Luo Qing with the Amitabha Buddha is interesting, as Luo himself repeatedly insisted that when one is truly enlightened, one is the equal of all the buddhas, especially Amitabha, because one embodies the same buddha nature.[46]

Yet the *Jiulian baozhuan* is more than a text that simply repeats or parrots Luo Qing's teaching. It takes Luo's characterization of the ontological ground of being for all things as "Parent or Mother" as a point of departure and ingeniously creates a vivid, emotive, and homey picture of a mother who tearfully awaits reunion with her estranged children. In a remarkably well-developed form, the Eternal Mother myth, which was later the shared belief of so many Ming-Qing sectarian groups, unfolds enthrallingly before the reader and the listener. She is portrayed as the matriarch of all the gods, buddhas, and immortals; the progenitor

[44] It is more likely that it was the first printing of the text, which had previously existed in manuscript form, as Susan Naquin suspects.

[45] Apparently the text has another name, *Wudangshan xuantian shangdi jing* [Sutra of the august lord of mysterious heaven from Mt. Wudang]. Mt. Wudang has been a major Taoist center since the early Ming. It was associated with the Taoist adept Zhang Sanfeng and the Ming court's fascination with him. See Anna Seidel, "A Taoist Immortal of the Ming Dynasty: Chang San-feng," in *Self and Society in Ming Thought*, ed. Wm. Theodore de Bary (New York, 1970), 483–516. See also Mano Senryu, "*Mincho to Taiwazan ni tsuite*" [The Ming Dynasty and Mt. T'aihe (Wudang)], *Otani gakuho* 38.3 (1959): 59–73; also his "*Mindai no Butozan to kangan no shinshutsu*" [Mt. Wudang in the Ming and the Ascendancy of the Eunuchs], *Toho shukyo* 22 (1963): 28–44. For access to the sutra I would like to thank Susan Naquin, who kindly allowed me to photocopy her copy of it, which she had acquired from Mr. Wu Xiaoling, Peking, 1981.

[46] See *Poxie Zhuan*, Section 6, and *Zhengxin zhuan*, Section 12.

of the cosmos and the myriad things; and the compassionate savior of the faithful. In addition, the text introduces a distinct eschatological scheme not present in Luo Qing's writings. Finally, the text reveals a much more complex sectarian organizational structure, as well as a far more pronounced sectarian mentality. All these will be discussed in the following pages.

The *Jiulian baozhuan* opens with the assembly of all the buddhas and immortals called by the Eternal Mother.[47] The gathering notices a distinct fragrance, which is called the Trefoil Nine Lotus Fragrance of the Three Phases (*Sanyuan ru'i jiulian xiang*). The presence of this fragrance signals an impending change in the *kalpa*, as it did on two previous occasions, when *Wuji* and *Taiji* (Supreme Ultimate) took their turn to be in charge of the world. Whereupon, the Amitabha Buddha is summoned before the Eternal Mother, who explains to him that he shall descend to earth to save the divine beings created originally by the Eternal Mother to populate the world. Ninety-six myriads in number, they are mired in worldly passions and are totally forgetful of their sacred origin. Four myriads of them have reunited with the Mother when two previous *kalpic* changes occurred. Now it is Amitabha's turn to locate the rest of the lost souls and to bring them back to her. When they do return, they will escape the Three Disasters of flood, fire, and wind, which will scourge the world.

Unable to disobey this command given by the Mother, the Amitabha Buddha reluctantly leaves this blissful heaven and prepares for his descent. To better enable him to identify the divine beings and facilitate their return, the Eternal Mother entrusts the Amitabha Buddha with numerous "tools," including: *hunyuan ce* (Roster of undifferentiated origin), *guijia biaowen* (Document for returning home), *jiulian tu* (Nine lotus diagram), *sanji xianghuo* (Incense of the Three Ultimates), *shibu xiuxing* (Ten-step method of cultivation), *touci shizhuang* (Oaths of allegiance

---

[47] *Jiulian baozhuan*, Section 1. The possible Manichaean influence on the Eternal Mother myth should not be overlooked. As I have shown in my essay on the Maitreyan and Manichaean challenge, Mani's original teaching contains the story of the "Mother of Life" who, having given birth to the Primeval Man, sent him into battle against the forces of Darkness. Primeval Man was defeated, his armor of light stripped away, and he lay in a stupor. Later, he was rescued by the Living Spirit and was reunited with his Mother in a moving scene. The rest of the Manichaean story involves complicated efforts undertaken to retrieve all the light particles left behind by Primeval Man, leading up to the climatic conclusion of the second Epoch in cosmic history. Although the main thrusts of the two myths differ, the Manichaean motif of the rescue of Primeval Man, the union with the Mother, and the retrieval of the rest of the light particles lost in Darkness bears a striking resemblance to the later Eternal Mother story of the return of the primordial beings, their union with the Mother, and the deliverance of other primordial beings still mired in ignorance and suffering.

and submission), and *mingan chahao* (Overt and covert checking of signs).[48]

The rest of the text describes how the incarnated Amitabha Buddha, now appearing as the Patriarch of *Wuji*, explains and elaborates on the Eternal Mother's message of salvation to the faithful. With much verbiage and repetition, this message is delivered. The following is typical:

From the beginningless Beginning until now, the Eternal Mother has undergone numerous transformations. She secures *qian* and *kun* (male and female), administers the cosmos, and creates humanity. The divine beings are *qian* and *kun*. They come to inhabit the world. Entrapped by passions, they obscure their original nature and no longer think of returning. . . . The Eternal Mother on Mt. Ling longs for her children, with tears welling up in her eyes whenever she thinks of them. She is waiting for the day when, after I have descended to this Eastern Land and delivered this message for her, you will return home to your origin and to your matriarch.[49]

The Amitabha Buddha ends his explanation with the admonition for everyone to "head for Mt. Ling, return home, meet with the Mother, have a reunion between mother and child, and smile broadly."[50]

In the course of acting as the Eternal Mother's messenger, the Amitabha Buddha gives expression to several noteworthy themes. First and foremost is the three-stage salvational scheme. Historical time, according to this scheme, is marked by three great *kalpas*, each with its respective buddhas in charge. The past age, the age of *Wuji*, is ruled by the Dipamkara Buddha (Lamp-lighting Buddha), who sits on a three-petaled lotus flower and hosts the Yellow Sun Assembly (*huangyang hui*). The present age, the age of *Taiji*, is under the control of the Sakyamuni Buddha, who sits on a five-petaled lotus flower and convenes the Azure Sun Assembly (*qingyang hui*). The future age, the age of Imperial Ultimate (*huangji*), will be dominated by the Maitreya Buddha, who is seated on a nine-petaled lotus flower and summons the Red Sun Assembly (*hongyang hui*).[51] This scheme establishes the basic eschatology of Eternal Mother sectarianism and promises that the salvation of the believers will take place in the near future.

---

[48] *Jiulian baozhuan*, Section 2.
[49] *Jiulian boazhuan*, Section 4.
[50] *Jiulian boazhuan*, Section 12.
[51] *Jiulian boazhuan*, Sections 4, 10, 12. It should be pointed out that earlier in the text, the Amitabha Buddha is referred to as the Future Buddha (Sections 1, 2, 3). It is only later that the more standard version treating the Maitreya Buddha as the future buddha is presented. It is equally interesting that the Amitabha Buddha is at one point called the *Sanyang jiaozhu* [Patriarch of the Three Suns]; see Section 2.

Second, Amitabha's teaching reveals a highly "sectarian" character, warning that only the predestined faithful will be saved, while the unbelieving are doomed. Repeatedly such terms as "fated ones" (*youyuan ren*), "primordial beings" (*yuanren*), "remnant sentient beings" (*canling*), "worthies" (*xianliang*), and "offspring of the imperial womb" (*huangtai*) are used to refer to the religious elect who alone will heed the message of the Mother and return to her. The rest of humanity are expected to perish at the time of *kalpic* change.[52]

Third, the later sectarian organizational pattern and initiation practices are already mentioned in this text. The terms "*sanzong wupai*" (Three schools and five factions), as well as "*jiugan shibazhi*" (Nine poles and eighteen branches), characteristic of the organizational structure of later sectarian groups such as the *Yuandun* (Complete and Instantaneous Enlightenment) Sect in the seventeenth century,[53] occur numerous times in this text.[54] Moreover, the practices of "registering one's name" (*guahao*) and "verifying the contracts" (*dui hetong*),[55] both performed at the time of initiation by numerous sectarian groups in the Qing dynasty to ritualize and guarantee the salvation of their members, are also mentioned frequently throughout the text.

The *Jiulian baozhuan* thus reveals unmistakably that as the Eternal Mother myth was formulated, the attendant cosmology and eschatology so characteristic of this belief were also developed. At the same time, the sectarian nature of this religion, together with much of its organizational framework and many of its initiation practices, also made their appearance.

### FURTHER DEVELOPMENT OF THE ETERNAL MOTHER MYTH

The *Jiulian baozhuan* was followed by a long tradition of sectarian writing that repeated and expanded on the Eternal Mother motif, although in both doctrine and style there was much diversity. A datable text after the *Jiulian baozhuan* is the *Yaoshi benyuan gongde baozhuan* (Precious scroll on meritorious deeds based on the original vow of the Buddha of Medicine, or Baisajya-guru), published in 1543. It echoes much of

---

[52] *Jiulian baozhuan*, Prologue, Sections 6, 15.

[53] See Richard Shek, "Religion and Society in Late Ming: Sectarianism and Popular Thought in 16th and 17th Century China," Ph.D. dissertation (University of California–Berkeley, 1980), 287–301.

[54] *Jiulian baozhuan*, Sections 9, 20.

[55] Both practices are designed to give the impression of official and bureaucratic recognition of the believers' confirmed status as the saved elect.

the language found in the *Jiulian* text, with the same promise of returning home and salvation by the Eternal Mother. Much emphasized is
the joy of reunion with the Mother.[56] In 1558, the *Puming rulai wuwei
liaoyi baozhuan* (Tathagata Puming's precious scroll of complete revelation through nonaction) was completed by the founder of a Yellow
Heaven Sect (*huangtian dao*), whose background and religious awakening bore a strong resemblance to those of Luo Qing.[57] The text also
preaches the now familiar theme of salvation by and reunion with the
Eternal Mother. It contains vivid descriptions of the encounter between
Mother and child, and the following passage is representative:

When I finally come before the Eternal Mother, I rush into her embrace. Together
we weep for joy at our reunion. Ever since our separation on Mt. Ling, I have
been left adrift in samsara because of my attachment to the mundane world.
Now that I have received the family letter from my Venerable Mother, I have
in my possession a priceless treasure. Mother, listen to me! Please deliver the
multitudes from the sea of suffering![58]

In 1562, a text entitled *Erlang baozhuan* [Precious scroll on Erlang] appeared, providing further information on the emerging Eternal Mother
myth. Based on the story of Erlang's valiant fight with the Monkey
King, a famous and entertaining episode from the classic novel *Journey to
the West* (which, incidentally, was given the finishing touches around the
same time), the *Erlang baozhuan* describes the final subjugation of the
Monkey King by the semidivine Erlang, thanks in large measure to
the assistance provided by the Eternal Mother.[59] This text also seems to
presage the legend surrounding the building of the Baoming Si, Temple
Protecting the Ming dynasty, as described later. In it the story of the
Bodhisattva Guanyin incarnating as a nun by the name of Lu is first
being told. According to this text, the nun had tried unsuccessfully

---

[56] See Shek, "Religion and Society in Late Ming," 226. See also Zheng Zhenduo, *Zhongguo
suwenxue shi* [History of Chinese Folk Literature] (Peking, 1954), 2: 312–17.

[57] For a detailed study of the Yellow Heaven Sect, see Richard Shek, "Millenarianism
without Rebellion: The Huangtian Dao in North China," *Modern China* 8.3 (July 1982):
305–36. See also Sawada Mizuho, "*Shoki no Kotendo*" [The Early Yellow Heaven Sect],
in his *Zoho*, 343–65. For a reproduced and annotated version of the *Puming baozhuan*,
see E.S. Stulova, *Baotszuian o Pu-mine* [The Precious Scroll of Puming] (Moscow, 1979).
The most recent study of this sect is done by Ma Xisha; see his chapter in Ma Xisha
and Han Bingfang, *Zhongguo minjian zongjiao shi* [History of Chinese Popular Religion]
(Shanghai, 1992), 406–88.

[58] See Stulova, *Baotszuian o Pu-mine*, 80.

[59] The content of this precious scroll is given brief description by Wu Zhicheng in his
"*Bailianjiao de chongbaishen 'Wushengmu'*" [The Eternal Mother – A Deity worshiped
by the White Lotus], *Beijing shiyuan xuebao* [Journal of the Peking Normal College] 2
(1986): 46.

to dissuade Emperor Yingzong from fighting the Oirat Mongols prior to his debacle at Fort Tumu in 1449. When Yingzong was restored to the throne in 1457 after his long captivity, he rewarded the nun for her loyalty and courage and built a temple for her, naming it the Baoming Si.[60] The temple had been reportedly in existence since 1462. By the late Jiajing reign (1522–67), however, it came under the sway of believers in the Eternal Mother religion.

In the 1570s, a sectarian group composed primarily of nuns and affiliated with the Baoming Si in the western suburb of Beijing created a sizable corpus of texts to dramatize its intimate relationship with the Eternal Mother. One of the nuns was a young girl by the name of Guiyuan [Returning to perfection], who produced a set of texts circa 1571–3, when she was only twelve years old. Modeling after Luo Qing's collected works, she also named them "Five books in six volumes." The following passage from the *Xiaoshi dacheng baozhuan* (Explanatory precious scroll on the Mahayana teaching), one of her five books, is revealing:

To illuminate the mind and look into our nature, let us discuss a wondrous teaching.
When we return home, there will no longer be any worry.
We will be free and totally unimpeded, for we have probed the most mysterious teaching.
Let us deliver all the infants and children and return them home.
When we return home, the way will be fully understood and immortality will be secured. We sit upon the lotus flower, enwrapped in a golden light.
We are ushered to our former posts; and the children, upon seeing the Mother, smile broadly.
The Venerable Mother is heartened to see you, for today is the time of reunion.
We walk the path of enlightenment to attend the Dragon Flower Assembly.
The children will rush into the Mother's embrace.
They will sit on the nine lotus seat, being free and joyful, with bright illumination all around them.
This trip leads us to extreme bliss; the children, upon seeing Mother, burst out laughing![61]

Other texts written by this group of Eternal Mother believers at the Baoming Temple include the *Pudu xinsheng jiuku baozhuan* [Precious

---

[60] For a history of the Baoming Temple, see Thomas Shi-yu Li and Susan Naquin, "The Pao-ming Temple: Religion and the Throne in Ming and Qing China," *Harvard Journal of Asiatic Studies* 48.1 (1988): 131–88.

[61] Quoted in Sawada, *Zoho*, 47–8.

scroll of the new messages of universal salvation from suffering] and the *Qingyuan miaodao xiansheng zhenjun Erlang baozhuan* [Precious scroll of the perfect lord Erlang, who is of pure origin, teaches the wondrous way, and manifests sageliness].[62] Both of them link the nun Lu, founding abbess of the Baoming Temple and now respectfully referred to as Bodhisattva Lu, with the Eternal Mother. In fact, she is asserted to be the incarnation of the Eternal Mother. This group continued to produce texts well into the seventeenth century,[63] when it was known as the West Mahayana Sect (*Xi dacheng jiao*).

Yet another sectarian group active in propagating the Eternal Mother faith was the Red Sun Sect (*Hongyang jiao*) founded by Han Piaogao, probably in the 1580s.[64] Central to this group's teaching is the doctrine of *linfan shouyuan* [descending to earth to retrieve the primordial beings]. Elaborating on the basic Eternal Mother motif, this group asserted that its founder was the youngest son of the Eternal Mother, who had been sent into the world to help with the salvation of the original beings before the world was to be devastated by *kalpic* disasters. It contributed to the Eternal Mother tradition by standardizing the three-stage scheme, making it a progression from Azure Sun (*qingyang*) to Red Sun (*hongyang*) and finally to White Sun (*baiyang*).[65] This was the scheme accepted and shared by all Eternal Mother sectarians in the Qing dynasty.[66]

Perhaps by far the most successful and influential sectarian group around the turn of the seventeenth century was the East Mahayana Sect (*Dong dacheng jiao*) founded by Wang Sen of Northern Zhili. Also known as the Incense-smelling Sect (*Wenxiang jiao*), Wang Sen's organization at one point boasted a following of more than two million. It was the most systematically organized sect at the time, with a clear division of labor and specific titles for different levels of sect leadership.[67] It is interesting

---

[62] Whether this latter text is identical to the one bearing a similar title but appearing earlier is uncertain. See note 46 in this chapter.

[63] Sawada, *Zoho*, 278–9.

[64] See Shek, "Religion and Society in Late Ming," 276–87. See also Sawada Mizuho, "*Koyokyo shitan*" [A preliminary study of the Red Sun Sect], in his *Zoho*, 366–408. Ma Xisha has also written extensively on this group. See his *Zhongguo minjian zongjiao shi*, 489–548.

[65] See the quote from *Hunyuan jiao hongyang zhonghua baojing* in Sawada's *Zoho*, 397.

[66] Actually, as early as 1579, a certain Wang Duo was known to have organized an Assembly of Three Suns between Heaven and Earth [*Tiandi sanyan hui*] and had a following of six thousand. He was later captured and executed. See *Ming shilu* [Veritable Records of the Ming Dynasty], 83:5a, Wanli 7/1/23.

[67] The most thorough study of Wang Sen's sect has been undertaken by Asai Motoi. His recent work, which is the culmination of over a decade of research and writing, is *Min-Shin jidai minkan shukyo kessha no kenkyu* [Folk Religious Associations in the Ming-Qing Period] (Tokyo, 1990), esp. 133–310. Yu Songqing is also an ardent student of this

to note that this sect subscribed to the *Jiulian baozhuan*,[68] as its leaders were found to have in their possession numerous copies of the text each time the sect was investigated. Wang Sen himself was arrested in 1595, released through the payment of bribes, and arrested again in 1614. He died in prison in 1619; his preachings, however, lived on. The apocalyptic message he taught generated a full-scale rebellion in 1622, headed by his follower Xu Hongru and Wang's own son Haoxian.[69] The rebellion lasted three months but was ruthlessly suppressed by the Ming government after heavy fighting. Even then Wang Sen's teaching survived this setback, for his descendants continued to be sectarian practitioners and leaders for the next two hundred years.[70]

It was through one of the off-shoots of Wang Sen's organization that the Eternal Mother cult was brought to a fully mature form. This was the *Yuandun* Sect mentioned earlier. Founded by one Gongchang (split-character version of the word *Zhang*) in the aftermath of the 1622 rebellion, this sect was responsible for the compilation of the *Gufo tianzhen kaozheng longhua baojing* [The heavenly perfect venerable Buddha's authenticated dragon flower precious sutra], the most doctrinally developed text on the Eternal Mother religion in Ming-Qing China.[71] Published in the 1650s, this text contains the most mature form of the Eternal Mother myth. It describes the familiar three-stage salvational scheme, the Dragon Flower Assembly, the procreation of humanity by the Eternal Mother, the trapping of her children in the samsaric world, and the joyful return she prepares for them. It also mentions the organizational structure of *sanzong wupai* (Three schools and five factions) and *jiugan shibazhi* (Nine poles and eighteen branches), which made their first appearance in the *Jiulian baozhuan*, as observed earlier. It stresses

---

tradition; see her *Ming-Qing bailianjiao yanjiu*. Ma Xisha also has substantial chapters on this group and its off-shoots in his *Zhongguo minjian zongjiao shi*, 549–652, 859–907. Finally, Susan Naquin also studies the later transmission of the Wang Sen tradition in her "The Transmission of White Lotus Sectarianism," as well as her "Connections between Rebellions: Sect Family Networks in Qing China," *Modern China* 8.3 (July 1982): 337–60.

[68] See Naquin, "Connections between Rebellions," 340.

[69] For a detailed description of this rebellion, see Shek, "Religion and Society in Late Ming," 352–67. See also Xu Hongru's biography by Richard Chu in *Dictionary of Ming Biography* (New York, 1976), I:587–89. Noguchi Tetsuro also has a substantial chapter on this rebellion in his *Mindai byakurenkyoshi no kenkyu*, 255–68.

[70] See Yu Songqing, *Ming-Qing bailianjiao yanjiu*, 37–56, 131–62; Ma Xisha, *Qingdai bagua jiao* [The Eight Trigrams Sect of the Qing dynasty] (Beijing, 1989), esp. 36–44.

[71] For an analysis of the Dragon Flower Sutra, see Shek, "Religion and Society in Late Ming," 176–92. A more recent brief treatment is given by Daniel Overmyer in his "Values in Chinese Sectarian Literature: Ming and Ch'ing Pao-chuan," in *Popular Culture in Late Imperial China*, 238–43. See also Sawada Mizuho, "*Ryugekyo no kenkyu*" [A study of the Dragon Flower Sutra], in his *Kochu*, 165–220.

the importance of the rituals of "registration" (*guahao*) and "verifying the contracts" (*dui hetong*), as does the *Jiulian baozhuan*. But what is most characteristic about the *Longhua jing* is its preoccupation with *kalpic* disasters, which are asserted to be imminent. Three disasters will take the form of famines and floods, avalanches and earthquakes, pests and epidemics. There is a palpable sense of urgency in preparing oneself for this cataclysmic devastation not present in other texts.

The Eternal Mother cult thus reached its mature form by early Qing. Thereafter, partly because of governmental vigilance and partly because of the loss of creative momentum, few new sectarian texts were composed. Sometime in the eighteenth century, however, the Eternal Mother belief came to be encapsulated in the eight-character chant of *zhenkong jiaxiang, wusheng laomu* [Native land of true emptiness, the Eternal Venerable Mother]. Thus the vague and hazy ideas that began with Luo Qing finally reached their culminated form as a creed-like chant, binding all the believers of the Eternal Mother into one nebulous but potentially powerful community.

When sectarian writing was resumed in fits and starts in the late nineteenth century, particularly through the *bailuan* (worshiping the phoenix) techniques, it seldom surpassed the grandeur and sophistication of the earlier texts. The scriptures of the *Iguan dao* (Unity Sect) and the *Longhua zhaihui* (Dragon Flower Vegetarian Assembly) invariably portray a teary-eyed Eternal Mother, wringing her hands and anxiously waiting for her estranged children to come home. The following passage from the *Jiaxiang shuxin* [Letters from home] of the *Iguan dao* is representative:

In her heavenly abode the Venerable Mother lets out a cry of sadness, with tears running continuously from her eyes and drenching her clothes. This is all because the children of buddhas are attached to the samsaric world. The ninety-six myriads of the imperial womb's offspring know not how to return home.... The people of the world are all my children. When they meet with disaster, the Mother is distressed. She dispatches immortals and buddhas to the human world below to set up the great way in order to convert people from all corners. The Venerable Mother cries in a heart-wrenching way. Is there any way to call her children back?[72]

In the preceding pages, the genesis and development of the Eternal Mother myth have been traced in some detail. What impact did this myth have upon state and society? What kind of challenge, however potential and theoretical, to orthodoxy did it pose? What were the

---

[72] See Song Guangyu, "*Shi lun 'Wusheng laomu' zongjiao xinyang de I'xie tezhi*," 575.

implications of the Eternal Mother belief in ethics and in rituals?[73] These are the questions to be explored in the remainder of this chapter. Three aspects of the Eternal Mother religion will be examined: its challenge to state authority, its eschatological salvationism, and its challenge to patriarchal-familial authority.

## CHALLENGE TO STATE AND POLITICAL AUTHORITY

By its very nature, folk sectarianism presented a "competing hierarchy of authority" to the government.[74] On this point Max Weber's observation is instructive: "The Confucian subject was expected to practise virtue privately in the five classical social relations. He did not require a sect for this and the very existence of a sect violated the patriarchal principle on which the state rested."[75] Sectarian membership was regarded as dangerous and subversive precisely because "the value and worth of the 'personality' were guaranteed and legitimated not by blood ties, status group, or publicly authorized degree, but by being a member of and by proving oneself in a circle of specifically qualified associates."[76] In other words, the sect had usurped the prerogatives of the state and family to provide meaning and value for the life of the sect member, a decidedly intolerable situation for the authorities. Even more worrisome was the crowd-gathering propensity of the sects. As shall be explained more fully later, folk religious sects performed numerous social functions for their members, including mutual aid and mutual protection. This was particularly popular among the dispossessed and deprived segments of society, which needed these services the most to counter exploitation and other economic hardship. As such, these sectarian groups offered themselves as "alternatives" to the state and local communities.[77]

Furthermore, the sectarian nature of the organization of these groups created a far stronger sense of identity and solidarity among

---

[73] It should be pointed out that there is no consensus among students of the Eternal Mother tradition over the issue of the political and ethical nature of its doctrine. Daniel Overmyer, for example, prefers to focus on the "orthodox" and accommodating nature of sectarian thought. He also downplays the "subversive" potential of the sects. See his "Attitudes Toward the Ruler and State in Chinese Popular Religious Literature: Sixteenth and Seventeenth Century *Pao-chuan*," *Harvard Journal of Asiatic Studies* 44.2 (1984): 347–79. What I am offering here is an alternative assessment of the same tradition.

[74] Borrowing David Kelly's characterization in his "Temples and Tribute Fleets," 370.

[75] Weber, *Religion of China*, 215, 216.

[76] Weber, *Religion of China*, 218.

[77] On this point even Overmyer agrees. See his "Alternatives: Popular Religious Sects in Chinese Society," *Modern China* 7.2 (April 1981): 153–90.

the members than existed among ordinary temple- and shrine-goers. This "congregational" power of the sects was potentially troublesome for the government. The statement made by Huang Yubian, the Qing magistrate who zealously hunted down sectarian groups and confiscated their scriptures in the nineteenth century, bears eloquent witness to this official concern. In his celebrated *Poxie xiangbian* [Detailed refutation of heterodoxy], Huang unequivocally declared: "The texts of the heterodox sects make no overt references to sedition and rebellion, yet why is it that members of these sects invariably end up becoming rebels? The cause of rebellion lies in the assembly of large numbers of people."[78] Seen from this standpoint, any sect was potentially threatening to the stability that orthodoxy strove to maintain, regardless of its belief.

The subversive nature of the sects should not, however, be determined by their inherent power to attract crowds. Their challenge to the state was evidenced by some outright cases of disregard for the government's penal sanctions.[79] It was, of course, the monarch's prerogative to inflict punishment on transgressors of the law. Usually his threat of punishment was enough to deter most people from breaching the law, given the severity of the penal code. But when applied to some Eternal Mother believers, this threat became empty and ineffectual. In the late Wanli period of the Ming dynasty (1573–1620), officials of the Ministry of Rites complained in one of their memorials: "The sects avoid using the name White Lotus, yet in practice they espouse White Lotus teaching. For every sect there is a different patriarch, and ignorant men and women delude themselves and spread the sects' doctrines.... They would rather be executed [by the government] than dare to disobey the order of the sect master."[80] This is a strong indication that some sectarians had turned to another locus of authority – their sect master – and that the emperor had lost his sway over them. Huang Yubian also made the following observation:

The sectarians blatantly claim that all men who become believers are incarnated buddhas and that all women who become believers are incarnated buddha mothers.... Ignorant men and women, who have swallowed the charm water [of the sects], become convinced that they are indeed buddha incarnates. They are

[78] Sawada, *Kochu*, 67, 113.
[79] It should be noted that most of the records of the activities, behavior, and beliefs of the sectarians come from hostile sources written by government officials and unsympathetic literati. There is a decided bias there. Nevertheless, whether real or perceived, these descriptions do point to the subversive or heterodox nature of such allegations.
[80] *Ming shilu*, Wanli 43/5/gengzi.

therefore eager to return to heaven. Thus they earnestly practise their religion. Even after they have been apprehended by the authorities and sentenced to decapitation and slow-slicing, they show no regret.[81]

In other words, some of the sectarians did not fear death because they were convinced that they could benefit from it. For them, death would hasten the recovery of their original divinity. Indeed, it would enable them to return to their paradise once lost. There was also a sectarian claim that the heavier the punishment one receives at death, the more glorious one's ascent to heaven will become. "Non-capital punishment will enable one to avoid hell, but not enough to reach heaven. Death by strangulation will enable one to ascend to heaven; there will be, however, no red capes [to wear in celebration]. Death by decapitation will enable one to ascend heaven wearing a red cape. Death by slow-slicing will enable one to enter heaven wearing a red gown."[82] Huang Yubian thus acknowledged in despair: "Ignorant men and women are not fearful of violating the law or committing seditious acts. As they are eager to return to heaven, they are happy to face capital punishment. Thus penal sanction is useless in deterring them."[83] This sectarian denial of government authority in enforcing the law, admittedly commented upon with some exaggeration by Huang, was nevertheless a principal factor in earning for the sects the label of heterodoxy. Their supposed zealous commitment to their religious beliefs had made them unaccommodating to the rules and regulations of the state. Yet their unregulated congregation and their disregard for state authority, serious as they were, paled in comparison to their central beliefs and practices in terms of the potential challenge they posed to orthodoxy.

## CHALLENGE TO PATRIARCHAL AND FAMILIAL AUTHORITY

It has been observed earlier that the sects, by virtue of their organization, conferred upon their members a new identity and a sense of separateness from the rest of society. This new identity as one of the religious elect, moreover, set the sect member apart even from parents, spouse, children, other relatives, and friends unless, of course, they became members of the sect. The sect member's loyalty was now transferred to the family of the religious elect, together with whom he or she awaited the arrival of the millennium. This disruption to familial and lineage

---

[81] Sawada, *Kochu*, 130.
[82] Sawada, *Kochu*, 113, 152.
[83] Sawada, *Kochu*, 152.

cohesion and the transferring of obligation to a surrogate kinship group was cited, for example, in a memorial to the throne in 1584:

Nowadays heterodox sects are proliferating. Their assembly places and chanting halls increase in number rapidly. These sectarians would rather be remiss in paying taxes to the government, but dare not be parsimonious in making financial contributions to their sects. They would rather be negligent in keeping appointments with the officials, but dare not be absent from sect meetings. Through incurring debts and selling their valued belongings, they try to meet the demands of their sects.[84]

An official investigating sectarian activities in 1615 charged that the sectarians regarded their fellow believers as more important than their kin: "Though unwilling to contribute to the public coffer, the sectarians support their own organizations with enthusiasm. They treat their own kin with indifference, but embrace their fellow believers with devotion."[85]

What these reports indicate was a new ethics that belittled obligations to the state and kin, but instead stressed solidarity with the community of fellow religionists. The bond forged by one's religious affiliation now took precedence over the ties to lineage as well as loyalty to the state. The charge that such severance of traditional ties had resulted in tax resistance is most intriguing, as it certainly brought home to the government how potentially destabilizing and subversive such sectarians could become.

Yet even more serious was the charge of unfiliality leveled against the sectarian followers. The late Ming scholar Fan Hen reported in his *Yunjian jumu chao* [Eyewitness accounts from Yunjian] that followers of the Wuwei Sect refused to perform the prescribed funeral rites for their deceased parents and ancestors.[86] A local gazetteer of Wuxi (in present-day Jiangsu), compiled in 1574, contains the following description of another Wuwei Sect:

The people of Kaiyuan and Yangming are fairly affluent. Since the Jiajing period (1522–1566), they have come to embrace the Wuwei belief . . . and refuse to worship their ancestors. Men and women mingle together to burn incense and take vegetarian meals.[87]

[84] *Ming shilu*, Wanli 12/12/xinyu.
[85] *Ming shilu*, Wanli 43/6/gengzi.
[86] Swada, *Zoho*, 61.
[87] Quoted in Kawakatsu Mamoru, *"Minmatsu Nankyo heishi no hanran"* [The Nanking army mutiny in late Ming] in *Hoshi hakase taikan kinen chugokushi ronshu* [Essays on Chinese History in Commemoration of the Retirement of Dr. Hoshi Ayao] (Yamagata, 1978), 198.

Zhu Guozhen, an observant late Ming essayist, noted in his *Yongchuang xiaopin* [Short essays from the Yongchuang studio] that Wuwei sectarians in the Wenzhou area in Zhejiang did not worship their ancestors or any other deity.[88]

Though admittedly fragmentary, these accounts appear to be compatible with the basic belief of the Ming-Qing sectarians regarding the relative importance of the Eternal Mother as compared with their own ancestors. Their basic eight-character chant of *zhenkong jiaxiang, wusheng laomu* is indicative of this ethical heterodoxy. One's ultimate native place is not the village or county where one was born and reared, but is the realm of True Emptiness where one originated and eventually will return. Thus the attachment to the locality and submission to the village power structure is weakened. Moreover, one's ultimate parents are not the biological father and mother, but instead the Eternal Mother who makes life possible in the first place. One's obligation to the earthly family and ancestry is therefore undermined and made relative.

This subversive attitude toward family and lineage is further illustrated by the precious scrolls of some sects. One *Xiaoshi zhenkong saoxin baozhuan* [Precious scroll on True Emptiness and the sweeping of the mind], possessed by a late Ming Wuwei Sect, relates that its patriarch attained enlightenment despite his total ignorance of and disregard for human relations (*renlun*) and ethical proprieties (*liyi*).[89] Another, the *Hongyang tanshi jing* [Red Sun text of lamentation for the world], contains a picture of Piaogao the patriarch receiving kowtow from his eighty-one-year-old grandfather. This led Huang Yubian to complain vehemently that Piaogao was totally devoid of human feelings, that he knew of no hierarchical distinctions in the family, and therefore in the state as well, and that he deserved the severest punishment in hell.[90]

Such an iconoclastic attitude toward patriarchal authority and the traditional practice of ancestor worship had serious religious and political implications. In religious terms, it was heterodox to deny the validity of the most exalted and lasting aspect of Chinese religious behavior. Politically, it was seditious to dissent from the patriarchal form of authority on which Chinese polity was based. As Weber has so pointedly observed:

To reject the ancestor cult meant to threaten the cardinal virtue of politics, i.e., piety, and on this depended discipline in the hierarchy of offices and obedience of subjects. A religiosity which emancipated [the subjects] from believing in the

---

[88] Zho Guozhen, *Yongchuang xiaopin* (Shanghai, repr., 1959), 777.
[89] Swada, *Kochu*, 161.
[90] Swada, *Kochu*, 133–4.

all-decisive power of imperial charisma and the eternal order of pious relations was unbearable in principle.[91]

This countercultural iconoclasm was reflected in another feature of Ming-Qing sectarianism: the disproportionally heavy participation of women and the relative equality they enjoyed with their male counterparts.[92] Though most of the sects had male leaders, it remains true that they were the only voluntary organization in traditional China that had a sizable female membership. Indeed, some sects such as the Red Sun Sect (*Hongyang jiao*) were comprised predominantly of women believers.[93] This substantial female participation in sectarianism is also evidenced by the often-cited official charge against the sects: "gathering at night and dispersing at dawn, with men and women mingling together" (*yeju xiaosan, nannu hunza*). The fact that women could intermingle freely with men in sectarian worship was decidedly objectionable to the guardians of orthodoxy. In their opinion, such unsegregated assembly at night was an open invitation to all kinds of immoral and illicit sexual contacts. Indeed, government sources do contain allegations of lustful behavior and even sex orgies performed by the sectarians.[94]

While some of the allegations may not have been groundless for some groups, for the majority of the female followers of the Eternal Mother faith, deeper and more fundamental reasons for joining the sects can be identified. The female, motherly character of the supreme deity of the believers was a factor that must be reckoned with. In her mature form, the Eternal Mother was no mere goddess who answered people's dire calls for help, as in the case of the Bodhisattva Guanyin or the folk goddess Mazu. Instead, she was matriarch of the pantheon of buddhas, gods, and immortals, as well as supreme savior of the human race. In the mature Eternal Mother cult, her position was even more exalted than that of the Jade Emperor, an assertion against which Huang Yubian railed with particular harshness.[95] At her command, awe-inspiring deities such as the Maitreya Buddha would descend to earth to scourge it of all evil elements. Yet her power was tempered by her matronly compassion.

---

[91]  Weber, *Religion of China*, 216.

[92]  For a discussion of this interesting subject, see Kobayashi Kazumi, "*Kozoteki fusei no hanran*" [The rebellion of the structurally antithetical elements]; *Rekishigaku no saiken ni mukete* [Towards a review of historiography] 4 (1979), and his "*Chugoku byakurenkyo hanran ni okeru teio to seibo*" [Sacred mothers and imperial monarchs in White Lotus rebellions in China], *Rekishigaku no saiken ni mukete* 5 (1980). See also Yu Songqing, *Ming-Qing bailianjiao yanjiu*, 295–311.

[93]  Swada, *Zoho*, 402–3. Suzuki Chusei, *Chugokushi ni okeru kakumei to shukyo* [Rebellion and religion in Chinese history] (Tokyo, 1974), 212.

[94]  Suzuki, *Chugokushi ni okeru kakumei to shukyo*, 193; Sawada, *Kochu*, 30, 57, 64.

[95]  Swada, *Kochu*, 38.

In sectarian literature, she was portrayed as the concerned mother who tearfully awaited the return of her wayward offspring. Her superiority over all deities, combined with her motherly character, must have formed an extremely appealing image to women who were by and large dissatisfied with their lot in life or unfulfilled in their aspirations. More importantly, the Eternal Mother motif must have provided a sense of equality, worth, and liberation for the female followers, a feeling that was denied them by society at large.

Numerous precious scrolls make reference to this equality between women and men. The *Longhua jing*, for example, declared: "Let it be announced to all men and women in the assembly: 'there should be no distinction between you.'"[96] Similarly, the *Jiuku zhongxiao yaowang baozhuan* [Precious scroll on the god of medicine who is loyal, filially pious, and who delivers people from suffering] proclaims emphatically that "Men and women are originally not different. Both receive the pure breath of Prior Heaven (*xiantian i'qi*) from the Venerable Mother."[97] Finally, the *Pujing rulai yaoshi tongtian baozhuan* [Precious scroll by the Pujing Buddha on the key to reaching heaven] voices a similar theme: "In the realm of Prior Heaven, there are five spirits of *yin* and five pneuma of *yang*. When men gather the five spirits of *yin*, they become bodhisattvas. When women collect the five pneuma of *yang*, they become buddhas."[98]

To each of these passages, in particular to the last one, Huang Yubian reacted with moral outrage. He vehemently accused the sectarians of making a mockery of the proper separation between the sexes. He further charged that these statements were an open invitation to lustful behavior and sexual promiscuity among the sect members.[99] Whether or not these statements encouraged licentiousness is beside the point. What is noteworthy is their insistence that men and women are no different and are equally worthy of salvation. To be sure, such equality may be only theoretical and may exist only in the future world. Yet this admission alone is a stark contrast to the orthodox maxim of "distinctions must exist among the sexes" (*nannu youbie*).

In actuality, some sects did implement, up to a point, this egalitarian notion. The *Huangtian* Sect in the seventeenth century referred to its female members as the "alternative way" (*erdao*).[100] In view of the orthodox claim of "under heaven there is no alternative way (*tianxia wu erdao*),

---

[96] Swada, *Kochu*, 30.
[97] Swada, *Kochu*, 97.
[98] Swada, *Kochu*, 57.
[99] Swada, *Kochu*, 30, 57.
[100] Yan Yuan, *Sicun pian* [Four Preservations] (Hong Kong, repr., 1978), 152–3.

this play on words was clearly not accidental, but was meant to tease the orthodox authority. Yan Yuan was adamant in his criticism of this blurring of sexual distinctions. He accused the sectarians of "destroying the way of humanity and disrupting established customs." This, he declared, "was utterly shameless."[101] Prosper Leboucq, a French Catholic missionary who traveled extensively in North China in the 1860s and reported on the activities of the sects in his letters, noted that women were very active in most of the sects. His explanation was that women were given a status equal to men. He further observed that if a wife joined a sect earlier than her husband, then in sectarian matters she would have superiority over him, as seniority within the sects was determined by length of membership.[102]

### SECTARIAN APOCALYPTIC ESCHATOLOGY AND SALVATIONISM

The one truly distinguishing feature of the belief in the Eternal Mother is its apocalyptic eschatology. By that I mean an acute, burning vision of the imminent and complete dissolution of the corrupt, existing world and its replacement by a utopian, alternative order. Furthermore, this esoteric knowledge is shared only by a religious elect whose faith and action will guarantee their exclusive survival of this cosmic event.[103] Basic to the Eternal Mother belief is the idea of the *kalpa* (*jie*), a drastic and cataclysmic turning-point in human history. Originally a Buddhist notion that marks the cyclical passage of time on a cosmic scale, *kalpa* for the Eternal Mother believers assumed an immediacy and urgency that it originally did not possess.[104] The belief in an eventual occurrence of *kalpic* crisis was commonly shared by the Ming and Qing Eternal Mother followers. Virtually all the sectarian texts from the sixteenth century on subscribed to a three-stage salvational scheme in which heavenly emissaries would descend to earth at predestined times and at the command of the Eternal Mother to deliver the faithful. While the first two stages, representing past and present, excited little interest, it was the third stage, the stage to come, that created apprehension and fired the imagination of the believers. After all, it was their anticipation that the arrival

---

[101]  Yan Yuan, *Sicun pian*, 152–3.

[102]  Prosper Leboucq, *Association de la Chine* (Paris, 1880), 11–12, 19.

[103]  For a comparative framework, consult Christopher Rowland, *The Open Heaven: A Study of Apocalyptic in Judaism and Early Christianity* (London, 1982) and D.S. Russell, *The Divine Disclosure: An Introduction to Jewish Apocalyptic* (Minneapolis, 1992).

[104]  For the early history of eschatological notions among Buddho-Taoist groups, see Chapters 1 and 2 in Liu and Shek, eds., *Heterodoxy*.

of this third stage would signal their return to and reunion with the Mother. The third stage, it was widely believed, would be ushered in by a messianic figure (usually the Maitreya Buddha, but in some cases the founding patriarchs of the various sects) whose coming would be accompanied by an unprecedented wave of natural and social upheavals so catastrophic that the heavenly bodies as well as human society would be literally torn asunder and then reconstituted. The following description of the honors and devastation of the *kalpic* turmoil, related with apparent relish by the compilers of the *Longhua jing*, is illustrative:

In the *xinsi* year [1641?] there will be floods and famines in North China, with people in Shantung being the hardest hit. They will practise cannibalism upon one another, while millions will starve to death. Husbands and wives will be forced to leave one another, and parents and children will be separated. Even those who manage to flee to northern Zhili will be afflicted by another famine and will perish by the roadside. In the *renwu* year [1642?] disasters will strike again with redoubled force. There will be avalanches and earthquakes. The Yellow River will overflow its banks and multitudes will be drowned. Then the locusts will come and blanket the earth, devouring what little crop that remains. Rain will come down incessantly and houses will crumble. . . . In the *guiwei* year [1643?] widespread epidemics will occur.[105]

Keeping in mind that the *Longhua jing* was compiled during the Ming-Qing transition, and assuming that the specific years mentioned in the text refer to that critical period as the Ming dynasty was about to fall, the devastation and misery described here may indeed be offering an uncannily authentic picture of the real situation itself. Thus the *kalpic* change, for some of the sectarians at least, was not an event that might happen in some distant future eons from the present but was in fact taking place right before their very eyes and being confirmed by their own experience! Their overriding concern was to "respond" to this *kalpic* disaster (*yingjie*) and to survive it. The urgency for action was understandable.

Equally noteworthy in this apocalyptic vision of the sectarians is the notion of their own "election." Not only was the apocalyptic conflagration impending, it would at the same time separate the elect from the doomed. The Eternal Mother believers were convinced that they belonged to a minority of "saints" destined to survive the cataclysm that would terminate the existing order. Indeed, they and they alone would

---

[105] *Longhua jing* 3:21. I would like to thank Prof. Overmyer for supplying me with a photocopy of an early twentieth-century edition of this text. For the apocalyptic beliefs of some later sects, see Susan Naquin, *Millenarian Rebellion in China: The Eight Trigrams Uprising of 1813* (New Haven, 1976), 12.

inherit the new age that was soon to dawn, when they would enjoy the fruits of reunion with the Eternal Mother. All their religious practices were designed to confirm their election, to ensure their survival in the final moments of this doomed order, and to prepare themselves for the eventual admission into the new one. A corollary of this view was the expected annihilation of the nonbelievers (the wicked and evil ones) prior to the arrival of the millennium. Since the onset of the new age would confirm the salvation of the elect, it was not surprising that some sectarians would look forward to its early arrival when the saved and the doomed would be separated and the latter would be destroyed and cast away without mercy.

The notion of election figures prominently in sectarian texts. The elect are variously referred to as *youyuan ren* (predestined ones), *huangtai zi* (offspring of the imperial womb), and a host of other names.[106] The *Longhua jing*, in particular, contains a pronounced theme of election for the *Yuandun* Sect members. Describing the Dragon Flower Assembly after the *kalpa*, the text mentions "city in the clouds" (*yuncheng*) where it will be held. The survivors of the apocalypse will proceed to enter the city gate, where their identity will be individually checked before admission. Those who fail to produce a valid registration or contract will be turned away and cast into oblivion.[107]

While this portrayal reveals glimpses of the bureaucratic tendency in Chinese folk mentality – salvation is seen here as "certified" by registration slips and "confirmed" by admission through the city gate – it nevertheless highlights the sense of solemnity and pride felt by the elect. For this reason, the initiation rituals of *guahao* (registration), *biaoming* (submitting names), and *dui hetong* (verifying contracts),[108] performed by the novices at the time of their admission into the sect, assumed great significance. These rites not only ritualistically conferred upon the members a new identity but also dramatized their election as the destined remnant of humanity after the *kalpa*. Assured of their salvation, many Eternal Mother followers thus concerned themselves with "the life to come" (*laishi*), which meant both "the life one might expect after death and the millennium one might experience in this world."[109] When captured and interrogated, these people repeatedly insisted that the principal motivation for their conversion to sectarianism was to "pray for

---

[106] See *Longhua jing* 2:29; 3:21a–b, 22a–b, 23a–b, 24a–b. See also the *Puming baozhuan* in Stulova, *Baotszuian o Pu-mine*, 10, 62, 130, 207.

[107] *Longhua jing*, 2:15; 3:16b; 4:5b, 8b.

[108] *Longhua jing*, 1:24b; 2:6, 12b, 13b, 14b, 18b; 4:21, 25. See also Sawada, *Kochu*, 63.

[109] Naquin, "Transmission of White Lotus Sectarianism," 279.

protection in the life to come." They were confident that they would get it too.

This sense of election was evident in many Eternal Mother sects. An untitled precious scroll in Huang Yubian's *Poxie xiangbian* declared that "All non-believers are destined for hell. Only devout sect members will have direct access to the Celestial Palace, not be condemned to descend into hell."[110] At the time of the Eight Trigrams uprising in 1813, one of the faithful claimed, "In the future, those who are not in our assembly will meet with disasters accompanying the arrival of the kalpa." Another put it more bluntly, "If you join the sect, you live; if you don't, you die."[111] Members of a *Yuan Chiao* Sect [Perfect completion] in the early part of the nineteenth century held the belief that "when the Maitreya comes to rule the world, there will be chaos for forty-nine days. The sun and moon will alter their course, the weather will change and only those who adhere to the Yuan Chiao will be saved from the cataclysm."[112] It was precisely this exclusionist view of election that made the sectarians stand apart from their local communities and even kins; their commitment to the existing order came under doubt.

When, and if, they did survive the catastrophic disasters of the *kalpa*, some sectarians expected to find a radically changed cosmos with a totally different time scale and alternative calendar. The *Puming baozhuan* of the Yellow Heaven Sect, the first edition of which probably appeared in 1558, has a vivid description of this new world:

The land is rearranged; the stars and constellations re-established. Heaven and earth are put in order again. Oceans and mountains are relocated. After nine cycles, the elixir [of life] is refined. Together humans reach the other shore. The compass stops and the two unbroken lines [of a trigram] meet. The eighteen kalpic disasters have run their full course, and the form of all things is about to change. Eighteen months will make one year, and thirty-six-hours constitute a day. There will be forty-five days in a month. One day will have one hundred and forty-four quarter-hours, and eight hundred and ten days form one year.[113]

This vision of a reconstituted cosmos with an altered time scale appears to have been shared by other sectarians as well. During the early Daoguang reign in the Qing dynasty (1821–51), a White Sun Sect espoused a similar belief in a thirty-six hour day for the new age. Moreover, its members claimed that "The *hongyang* [red sun] age is about to have run its full course. It is time to prepare for the arrival of *baiyang*

---

[110] Swada, *Kochu*, 116, 152.
[111] Quoted in Naquin, *Millenarian Rebellion in China*, 113.
[112] Adopted with emendation from Overmyer, *Folk Buddhist Religion*, 160.
[113] See Stulova, *Baotszuian o Pu-mine*, 223–5.

[white sun]. In the present age, the moon remains full until the eighteenth day of each month. When it stays full until the twenty-third day, the kalpa is upon us."[114] It is thus obvious that some sectarians were not content with the thought of a new cosmos, but were actively observing phenomena in the night sky, ever ready to detect the first signs of the arrival of the new age.

Another sect displayed keen interest in astronomical matters: the Imperial Heaven Sect (*Huangtian dao*) of the seventeenth century.[115] The famous neo-Confucian scholar Yan Yuan (1635–1704) has left a brief account of this group:

In my native province of Zhili, the people's mores were uncontaminated prior to the Longqing (1567–1572) and Wanli (1573–1620) periods [of the Ming dynasty]. Since the last years of Wanli, however, there appeared a Huangtian Sect which has become very popular. From the capital to the neighboring prefectures and counties, and even down to the distant villages and mountain retreats, members of this sect can be found. . . . They rename the stars *Can* and *Shu* "Cold Mother" and the two constellations *Fang* and *Xin* "Warm Mother."[116]

The entire eschatology of the Eternal Mother sectarians, represented by the concepts of *kalpa*, election, and cosmic reconstitution, was most threatening to orthodox thinking. The notion of *kalpa*, to begin with, was predicated on the assumption that the existing order, with its ethical norms and sociopolitical institutions, was finite, mutable, and destined to be replaced. Moreover, the new age promised to be a far better substitute. This kind of thinking might create a frame of mind that expected, even welcomed, the demise of the present age. It would at least render untenable the orthodox claim that "Heaven is immutable, so also is the Way" (*tian bubian, dao yi bubian*). The notion of *kalpic* upheaval ran directly counter to this claim of immutability, for it called for total, cosmic, cataclysmic change. The validity of the present age, including the existing moral authority, was at least theoretically undermined, since moral norms must rest on certain assumptions of stability and continuity.

The threat of the *kalpa* was further aggravated by its urgency. It was expected to take place at least in the foreseeable future, if not here and now. It was to be accompanied by a series of disasters so severe that the entire realm would become one big chaos (*tianxia daluan*). To survive it one could no longer rely on one's own efforts alone, but must

---

[114] Swada, *Kochu*, 67. See also his "Doko Byakuyokyo shimatsu" [The Full Story of the White Sun Sect of the Daoguang Period], in his *Zoho*, 434–5.

[115] It is highly probable that it is merely another name for the Yellow Heaven Sect, as "imperial" and "yellow" are homophones in Chinese.

[116] Yan Yuan, *Sicun pian*, 152–3.

entrust oneself to a savior or deliverer, follow his injunctions, and completely suspend all personal values and judgment. This abandonment and surrender ran counter to the orthodox teaching that prevailed at the time, made popular by morality books and religious instructions, that one could shape one's own destiny and receive karmic rewards through moral behavior. For some sectarians, this salvational path of conformity to the moral norm was no longer acceptable. They believed instead in redemption through a messianic figure whose deliverance they eagerly awaited. For the guardians of orthodoxy, this sectarian view of messianic salvation meant total contempt for their teaching and authority.

The idea of election was equally unacceptable to orthodox belief, which subscribed to a universalist approach to salvation. The infinite compassion of the Amitabha Buddha or of the Bodhisattva Guanyin was believed to be available to all. Similarly, the saving power of Laozi and the other Daoist deities was all-embracing. The sectarian view that sect membership alone could guarantee salvation was thus assailed with vehemence by the orthodox-minded. Huang Yubian thus asked teasingly in his *Poxie xiangbian*: "If those who are practising heterodox religion are the children of the Eternal Mother, then whose children are those who do not follow such deviant ways?"[117] A few paragraphs later, Huang again attacked this sectarian view: "If indeed there is a compassionate Eternal Mother up in Heaven, she should certainly not be discriminating in extending her saving grace, and should treat everyone equally. Why should she be so partial toward the heterodox sectarians?"[118]

The sectarian attention to astronomical matters was found most troubling by the state. The changes in time scale, the alteration in calendrical calculations, the predicted deviation in the movement of the heavenly bodies, and the renaming of the stars all infringed upon the prerogatives of the emperor as the supreme astronomer and diviner. In a culture in which the Son of Heaven claimed a monopoly of interpretation of all astronomical phenomena and of all calendrical calculations, and in an agrarian economy in which such powers conferred enormous control over the timing of planting and harvesting, such sectarian concerns carried serious ethical and political implications. Chinese monarchs had traditionally warned that "those who recklessly talk about astronomical phenomena are to be executed" (*wang tan tianxiang zhe zhan*). It is small wonder that orthodoxy would find this sectarian interest in celestial matters most disturbing.

[117] Sawada, *Kochu*, 61.
[118] Sawada, *Kochu*, 63.

All in all, the sectarian espousal of an eschatology and the attendant millenarianism posed a direct, frontal challenge to orthodoxy. With little to lose and all the fruits of the coming millennium to gain, some sectarians might be psychologically disposed to take drastic, even violent, action to usher in the new era. Seen in this light, Huang Yubian's bitter attack on the sectarian millennial yearning becomes understandable:

For those who do not practise heterodox religion, men till the land and women weave their cloth. Food will be plentiful and clothing will be abundant. Is it not delightful? . . . The joy of this world is concrete and tangible, while the bliss of heaven is illusory and unreal. The heterodox sects focus their attention on heavenly bliss, but in the end they lose even the joy of the human world. . . . When they say that they are going to enjoy their blissful paradise, who can prove it? Their claim is not to be believed.[119]

### CONCLUDING REMARKS

The first part of this chapter attempts to establish the fact that an orthodox tradition existed in China. Socioethical in content, this orthodoxy can be characterized as "religious pluralism and moral orthodoxy." Next I try to define heterodoxy in light of this Chinese orthodoxy. I identify the Eternal Mother belief as the mature and coherent version of heterodoxy in late imperial or early modern China. I then examine the genesis and development of the Eternal Mother belief. It has been demonstrated how certain originally abstract and disparate ideas were transformed into vivid imagery and even concrete objects of worship. The argument is advanced that Luo Qing played an important role in the final emergence of the Eternal Mother motif, although he was by no means the first person to have used the term or its variant. Furthermore, it is asserted that once formed, this Eternal Mother cult began to inform the religious content of most Ming-Qing sectarian groups. The last part of this essay is concerned with the implications and the heterodox nature of this myth. A number of the sects at different times implicitly or explicitly challenged the power of the monarch through casual discussion of astronomical matter, deliberate defiance of law and punishment, evasion of taxes, and arrogating the power to bestow titles and princely honors on the faithful. Some sectarians also undermined patriarchal and kinship authority with their creation of a new sense of community based not on blood relationship but on religious commitment, as well as their advocacy of the theoretical equality of the sexes. Their otherworldly

119 Sawada, *Kochu*, 37.

salvational goals, in the last analysis, were not compatible with the existing social and cultural order. Through their religious affiliations, they subverted the control of society through familial and monarchical authority, replacing the orthodox moral norm with their alternative socioethics.

The most heinous crime in the Chinese tradition was "disloyalty and unfiliality, having no regard for monarch and father" (*buzhong buxiao, wufu wujun*). The sectarians discussed in this study fit this description of heterodoxy rather well, even though the vast majority of them never raised the banner of rebellion. When describing the Wuwei Sect in the Wenzhou area in Zhejiang, Zhu Guozhen noted that "some of the curses these sectarians heaped upon monarch and father are unbearable when heard by loyal subjects and filial sons."[120] Commenting on the *Huangtian* and several other sects, the philosopher Yan Yuan remarked, "When their houses are temples or nunneries which observe no monastic rules, when they themselves are untonsured monks and nuns, it is rare that they do not worship evil spirits who show contempt for ruler and father; it is also rare that they do not chant heterodox slogans which show contempt for ruler and father."[121] Likewise, Huang Yubian noted repeatedly that sectarian beliefs would result in disloyalty and unfiliality.[122] Seen from the perspective of orthodoxy, these sects would have to be regarded as heterodox. If one may borrow the title of Christopher Hill's famous work on the English sectarians, one can indeed say that many of the Ming-Qing Eternal Mother followers had conceptualized a world "turned upside down." Commenting on the precious scroll, Huang Yubian made the following observation:

The sectarians consider those who lead a tranquil, stable life as "having gone astray from home." ... They make other people abandon their parents, spouse, and children to join them, and call this "return home." They regard prosperous, law abiding, and peaceful life as "suffering in samsara," but refer to punishments received after their arrest, including decapitation, slow-slicing, and slaughter of family and lineage members, as "returning to Pure Land and Mt. Ling." What is heterodox they maintain as orthodox, evil as moral, transgression as merit, misfortune as blessing, harm as benefit, and disaster as fortune.[123]

Although the sectarians only infrequently took up arms to overthrow the existing government, the reversal of values inherent in their belief was what made the sects so threatening to the guardians of orthodoxy.

---

[120] Zhu Guozhen, *Yongchuang xiaopin*, 77.
[121] Yan Yuan, *Sicun pian*, 152–3.
[122] Sawada, *Kochu*, 33, 65.
[123] Sawada, *Kochu*, 160.

The current value system simply lost its validity and immutability when these sectarians subscribed to an alternative system. Their antinomian values, combined with an intense eschatological vision, had made them suspect in the eyes of orthodoxy.

To be sure, most of the sects did not translate this alternative value and practice system into radical political action. In fact, it would be safe to say that the vast majority of the sects remained docile and pacific throughout their history, while their organization remained quite hierarchical and authoritarian. Nevertheless, the existence of this potentially subversive tradition in direct opposition to the orthodox mode of thinking must be recognized, and some sectarians did use this radical tradition to realize their political goals. The resilience and tenacity of this tradition must not be underestimated. Indeed, in studying the historical origins of revolutionary movements such as the Taipings in the nineteenth century and perhaps even the Chinese communists in the twentieth, the Eternal Mother tradition needs to be carefully examined for comparison.

# CHAPTER II

# Ecclesiastical elites and popular belief and practice in seventeenth-century Russia

### ROBERT O. CRUMMEY

THE Russian church schism of the seventeenth century is the focal point of this brief examination of popular belief and practice and the struggles of ecclesiastical elites to shape, control, and change them. The chapter will review and reflect on the most important phases of the interaction between the leaders of Russian Orthodoxy and ordinary parishioners between the late 1630s and the beginning of the eighteenth century in light of recent studies of Christian communities elsewhere in early modern Europe. It contains no new archival discoveries: Most of the documents and monographs on which it draws have long been familiar to historians of Russia. These sources, moreover, reflect the perceptions of government officials or ecclesiastical polemicists. Thus, as Eve Levin cautions, when describing popular religious beliefs and practices, they are likely to focus on "the most heterodox elements" that diverge most dramatically from established norms.[1]

In spite of the country's enormous territory, the discussion will consider Russia as a single unit for two reasons. First, even a glance at scholarship on Western and Central Europe shows how limited and scattered are the surviving sources on Russian parish life and popular religious practice.[2] For one thing, historians of Russia must live without systematic parish records. Second, in spite of the Muscovite monarchy's vast size, movements of popular religious protest spread quickly, in large measure through the efforts of itinerant agitators and exiles.

---

[1] Eve Levin, "Supplicatory Prayers as a Source for Popular Religious Culture in Muscovite Russia," in *Religion and Culture in Early Modern Russia and Ukraine*, Samuel H. Baron and Nancy Shields Kollmann eds. (DeKalb, IL, 1997), 96–114, here p. 96.

[2] As compared, for example, with England. See Eamon Duffy, *The Stripping of the Altars. Traditional Religion in England, c. 1400–c. 1580* (New Haven, CT, and London, 1992).

What then is the purpose of this reexamination of familiar territory? First, in recent years, scholars – Vera Rumiantseva[3] and Georg Michels,[4] in particular – have uncovered new sources, primarily reports of governmental investigations, on religious movements in the seventeenth century. Their publications have added significantly to our knowledge of popular movements of religious dissent and the enforcement of the Nikonian liturgical reforms and resistance to them. Second, recent writing on the development of religious communities elsewhere in Europe provides a stimulating conceptual vehicle on which to revisit the Russian scene. As we shall see, in Russia, as elsewhere on the continent in the early modern period, the government and the ecclesiastical leadership collaborated in maintaining confessional uniformity and enforcing "decency and good order" in worship and public morals.[5] Indeed, the concept "confessionalization" and its implications have long been axiomatic to historians of Russian religion and society.

In undertaking comparative analysis, we must of course keep in mind that Russian Orthodoxy is, above all, a religion of the sign, not of the word. Believers communicate with God primarily through their

[3] V.S. Rumiantseva, *Narodnoe antitserkovnoe dvizhenie v Rossii v XVII veke* (Moscow, 1986) and two collections of archival documents she has edited, *Narodnoe antitserkovnoe dvizhenie v Rossii XVII veka. Dokumenty Prikaza Tainykh Del. 1665–1667 gg.* (Moscow, 1986) and *Dokumenty Razriadnogo, Posol'skogo, Novgorodskogo i Tainogo Prikazov o raskol'nikakh v gorodakh Rossii. 1654–1684 gg.* (Moscow, 1990).

[4] Georg Michels's publications include "The Place of Nikita Konstantinovich Dobrynin in the History of Early Old Belief," *Revue des Études slaves* 49 (1997): 21–31; "Muscovite Elite Women and Old Belief," in *Rhetoric of the Medieval Slavic World: Essays Presented to Edward L. Keenan on his Sixtieth Birthday by his Colleagues and Students (Harvard Ukrainian Studies* 19), 428–50; "The Violent Old Belief: An Examination of Religious Dissent on the Karelian Frontier," *Russian History* 19 (1992): 203–29; "The First Old Believers in Ukraine: Observations about their Social Profile and Behavior," *Harvard Ukrainian Studies* 16 (1992): 289–313; "The Solovki Uprising – Religion and Revolt in Northern Russia," *Russian Review* 51 (1992): 1–15; "Myths and Realities of the Russian Schism: The Church and its Dissenters in Seventeenth-Century Muscovy," unpublished Ph.D. dissertation (Harvard University, 1991); and his book, *At War with the Church: Religious Dissent in Seventeenth-Century Russia* (Stanford, CA, 1999).

[5] For treatments of "confessionalization" that are helpful from a Russian perspective see Duffy, *Stripping the Altars*; R. Po-chia Hsia, *Social Discipline in the Reformation: Central Europe, 1550–1750* (London and New York, 1989); R.W. Scribner, *For the Sake of the Simple Folk. Popular Propaganda for the German Reformation* (Cambridge, 1981); Heinz Schilling, "Between the Territorial State and Urban Liberty: Lutheranism and Calvinism in the County of Lippe," in *The German People and the Reformation*, ed. R. Po-chia Hsia (Ithaca, NY, 1988), 263–83 and "Die Konfessionalisierung im Reich. Religiöser und Gesellschaftlicher Wandel in Deutschland zwischen 1555 und 1620," *Historische Zeitschrift* 246 (1988): 1–45; Wolfgang Reinhard, "Zwang zur Konfessionalisierung? Prolegomena zu einer Theorie des konfessionellen Zeitalters," *Zeitschrift für Historische Forschung* 10 (1983): 257–77; and Jean Delumeau, "Déchristianisation ou nouveau modèle de Christianisme," *Archives de sciences sociales des religions* 40 (1975): 3–20.

participation in the church's rites. In Orthodoxy, liturgy, belief, and practice are ultimately inseparable. Thus, in spite of minor differences in theology, major divergences in church organization and discipline, and a long history of animosity, Orthodoxy has far more in common with Roman Catholicism – and to some degree Anglicanism – than with any branch of Protestantism.[6] Moreover, in seventeenth-century Russia, religious struggles took place in a large, long-established, comparatively centralized monarchy which, in spite of many obvious differences, bore much closer resemblance to England, France, or Spain than to the small city-states and principalities of Central Europe.[7]

The title of this chapter contains two terms that require further explanation. "Ecclesiastical elites" refers to two groups of people. First are the patriarch, bishops, and parish priests of the Eastern Orthodox Church. Second, during and after the church schism of the mid-seventeenth century, the conservative opposition to the Nikonian reforms, later known as the Old Belief, began to bring forth its own leaders and create its own unofficial organizational structures. Over the latter half of the seventeenth century and into the eighteenth, its leaders formed a second "ecclesiastical elite" – to be sure, canonically self-appointed, internally divided, and often fugitive from the power of official church and state.[8] "Popular religion" refers to the beliefs and practices of ordinary

---

[6] Some historians have suggested parallels between Old Belief and Protestantism for two reasons (for example, James Billington, *The Icon and the Axe. An Interpretative Study of Russian Culture* [New York, 1966], 193). First, the priestless Old Believers rejected the priesthood and created self-generating communities led by laypeople. In spite of these superficially "Protestant" arrangements, the priestless regard themselves as the faithful remnant of Eastern Orthodoxy and regret the loss of the full sacramental ministry of the church. Time and again, individuals among them have, for this reason, rejoined the priestly Old Belief or uniate affiliates of the "synodal" Orthodox church when they can overcome their canonical scruples. In the last two decades, all of the major Old Believer communities in North America have relived this recurring story.

Second, the Old Believers' ascetic way of life and success in business seems to parallel Calvinism. As I have argued elsewhere, the "Weber" thesis seems inappropriate to Old Belief for theological reasons (Robert O. Crummey, *The Old Believers and the World of Antichrist. The Vyg Community and the Russian State, 1694–1855* [Madison, 1970], Chapter 7, esp. pp. 135–7). I accept Manfred Hildermeier's counterargument that Weber's more general concept of "this-worldly asceticism" fits the Old Believers and, for that matter, many other religious or cultural minorities. His essay on this subject is in press. See also his "Alter Glaube und neue Welt: Zur Sozialgeschichte des Raskol im 18. und 19. Jahrhundert," *Jahrbücher für Geschichte Osteuropas* [hereafter *JfGO*] 38 (1990): 372–98, 504–25 and "Alter Glaube und Mobilität. Bemerkungen zur Verbreitung und sozialen Struktur des Raskol im frühindustriallen Russland (1760–1860)," *JfGO* 39 (1991): 321–38.

[7] Much of the recent literature on the Reformation concentrates on the latter. See, for example, the essays in Hsia, *German People*.

[8] Robert O. Crummey, "The Origins of the Old Believers' Cultural Systems: The Works of Avraamii," *Forschungen zur osteuropäischen Geschichte* [hereafter *FzOG*] 50 (1995): 121–38.

parishioners or those of comparatively uneducated or marginal individuals and groups in defiance of established authority.[9]

The following discussion will focus on six important points of contact between ecclesiastical leaders and ordinary parishioners. These are: the reform movement of the so-called Zealots of Piety and the popular beliefs and practices they attempted to change; the Nikonian liturgical reforms and their initial enforcement; the popular movements of religious renewal or protest uncovered by governmental and ecclesiastical investigators in the middle decades of the seventeenth century; the campaign of the royal government and the hierarchy to root out opposition to Nikon's reforms; the explosion of violent resistance to changes in church and state, particularly self-immolation; and the initial efforts of the leaders of the conservative movement of resistance, the Old Believers, to channel and discipline the beliefs and practices of their followers.

\* \* \* \* \*

Ecclesiastical reform became a burning issue in seventeenth-century Russia on the accession of Tsar Aleksei Mikhailovich (1645–76).[10] A small, informal group of would-be reformers, known to later generations as the Zealots of Piety, gathered around the young monarch who was already establishing a reputation for sincere piety and intense interest in ecclesiastical matters.[11] Among its prominent members were the tsar himself; his friend, F.M. Rtishchev; his confessor, Stefan Vonifat'ev; the prominent parish priest, Ivan Neronov; his younger protegee, the priest Avvakum; and the rising star of the ecclesiastical firmament, Metropolitan Nikon of Novgorod. As they looked at life in the parish,

---

[9] The literature on popular religion in Europe is enormous. General overviews include Natalie Zemon Davis, "From 'Popular Religion' to Religious Cultures," in *Reformation Europe: A Guide to Research*, ed. Steven Ozment (St. Louis, 1982), 321–42; R.W. Scribner, "Interpreting Religion in Early Modern Europe," *European Studies Review* 13 (1983): 89–105; Richard van Dulman, "Volksfrömmigkeit und konfessionelles Christentum im 16. und 17. Jahrhundert," *Volksreligiosität in der modernen Sozialgeschichte*, ed. Wolfgang Schieder (Göttingen, 1986), 14–30 and the works cited in footnote 4. For a recent discussion of the literature on popular religion as applied to Russia, see Robert O. Crummey, "Old Belief as Popular Religion: New Approaches," *Slavic Review* 52 (1993): 700–12.

[10] For a narrative of the events discussed in this paper, see the two best general works on ecclesiastical reform and the church schism, Pierre Pascal, *Avvakum et les débuts du raskol* (Paris, 1936; repr., Paris and The Hague, 1963) and Serge Zenkovsky, *Russkoe staroobriadchestvo* (Munich, 1970).

[11] On the Zealots of Piety, see Wolfgang Heller, *Die Moskauer "Eiferer für die Frömmigkeit" zwischen Staat und Kirche (1642–52)* (Wiesbaden, 1988). Since the Zealots were an informal group of friends and acquaintances, any interpretation of their aims and activities depends, in part, on assumptions about who can be considered a member.

the Zealots, some of them experienced parish priests, saw two fundamental problems: confusion and disorder in worship and the survivals
of pre-Christian rites that still captivated and entertained many villagers. In attacking these problems, the Zealots implicitly confronted an
even deeper problem. In comparison with much of Western Europe, the
parish was loosely organized and, in practice, only tenuously connected
to the higher ecclesiastical authorities. As individual reformers were already discovering, a parish priest, usually a descendant of priests, could
minister to his people most easily by abiding by village tradition and
not pressing them too hard to fulfill their ritual and moral obligations
as Orthodox Christians.[12] In a crisis, he might well find that his bishop
was far away indeed. Paradoxically, as we shall see, the government
and ecclesiastical hierarchy acted as though they could exercise effective control over parish life and the behavior of ordinary believers.

The Zealots' aspirations closely resembled those of ecclesiastical reformers in Western and Central Europe, especially Roman Catholics.
They envisioned a vibrant Christian community in which, under the
supervision of the hierarchy, priests celebrated the Eucharist and other
offices with dignity and order and maintained high moral standards
among their flocks. Popular devotional life was to be purified by removing extraneous elements and dubious forms of devotion.[13] A revival of
preaching was one step toward their lofty goals. In Russia, achieving
liturgical uniformity and good order was a daunting challenge. Full
Orthodox worship requires a variety of service books; over centuries
of hand copying, significant inconsistencies had crept into these texts.
From about 1500, the more enlightened Russian hierarchs had realized
the importance of establishing standard, authoritative texts. In the early
seventeenth century, the problem remained unsolved and, with the aid

---

[12] Parishioners' enthusiasm was undoubtedly dampened by the custom of paying priests
for their services, including confession and administering the Eucharist. See S. Smirnov,
"Drevnerusskii dukhovnik," in *Chteniia v Imperatorskom Obshchestve Istorii i Drevnostei Rossiiskikh pri Moskovskom Universitete* [hereafter *ChOIDR*] 249 (1914, book ii): 1–
283, here p. 73. See also A. Amfiteatrov, *Russkii pop XVII veka* (Belgrade, 1930), esp.
pp. 109–14.
   To distract the authorities from their real activities and goals, peasant radicals in Pudozh in 1693 made a formal complaint that they had been deprived of the sacraments
because their village priests charged very high fees for their services. Whatever the truth
of the charges, the people who made them evidently believed that they were plausible
enough to be taken seriously (*Akty istoricheskie, sobrannye i izdannye Arkheograficheskoiu
komissieiu*, 5 vols. [St. Petersburg, 1841–3] [hereafter *AI*], 5: 383–5 [no. 223]).

[13] Duffy, *Stripping the Altars*, Chapter 16, characterizes the Counter-Reformation in much
these terms. See also Wolfgang Reinhard, "Gegenreformation als Modernisierung?
Prolegomena zu einer Theorie des konfessionellen Zeitalters," *Archiv für Reformationsgeschichte* 68 (1977): 226–52, and A.G. Dickens, *The Counter Reformation* (New York,
1969).

of that dangerous foreign innovation, the printing press, the leaders of the Russian church began once again to address the problem. The Zealots fully supported the effort.

Initially, however, the Zealots gave special attention to two issues, neither of which was new. Ivan Neronov and his fellow parish priests in Nizhnii-Novgorod sent a petition to Patriarch Ioasaf in 1636, asking for his support in restoring order and dignity to services of worship. The petitioners recited a litany of apparently long-standing abuses – *mnogoglasie* (the practice of chanting up to "five or six" different parts of the service simultaneously); other liturgical short-cuts (for example, omitting the hours before the Divine Liturgy); and singing vespers in the morning. They also complained at length about rowdy behavior during services. Priests' children played noisily in the altar area while, in the congregation, men and women came and went, talked loudly, and acted the fool. False monks, fake fools-in-Christ, and other panhandlers harassed worshipers. In a particularly ingenious scam, beggars, giving false names and addresses, asked the faithful for money to redeem them from bond-slavery.[14]

From the patriarch's point of view, many of these complaints were clearly justified and the remedies obvious. In 1646, Ioasaf issued a general decree that all priests, deacons, and "all Orthodox Christians fast, live in purity with all discipline (*vozderzhanie*)[15] and distance themselves from drunkenness, injustice and all kinds of sin." The clergy should see to it that their parishioners "should stand in God's church with fear and trembling and love, silently without any whispering," and focus their minds on God and pray "over their sins with tears, humble sighs and contrite hearts without malice or anger." A tall order indeed! The patriarch ordered parish clergy to put a stop to precisely the forms of irreverent behavior about which the Nizhnii-Novgorodians had complained.[16]

Attacking *mnogoglasie* was more controversial. Liturgical short-cuts had crept into Russian Orthodoxy for good reason.[17] In Orthodoxy, there is no such thing as a *missa brevis*. Over the centuries, monastic services had become the norm in parishes. The Divine Liturgy and the other services put severe demands on the patience and stamina of even the

---

[14] N.V. Rozhdestvenskii, "K istorii bor'by s tserkovnymi bezporiadkami, otgoloskami iazychestva i porokami v russkom bytu XVII v.," *ChOIDR* 201 (1902, book ii): 1–31, here pp. 19–23.

[15] I have used the Library of Congress system of transliteration from Cyrillic.

[16] *Akty, sobrannye v bibliotekakh i arkhivakh Rossiiskoi imperii Arkheograficheskoiu ekspeditsieiu Imperatorskoi Akademii nauk*, 4 vols. (St. Petersburg, 1836–58) [hereafter *AAE*] 4: 481–2 (no. 321).

[17] For an extensive list of examples, see *AAE* 4: 487–9 (no. 327).

most devout laypeople. Thus the willingness of many priests and parishioners to do almost anything to shorten services is, if not admirable, at least quite understandable. When the first attempts to end these traditional practices encountered vigorous opposition, Patriarch Ioasaf retreated and, in 1649, an ecclesiastical council supported a return to the status quo.[18] The reformers, however, would not give up their demand for an orderly liturgy with no overlapping or short-cuts (*edinoglasie*).

The second of the reformers' agendas – the survival of pre-Christian rites and impious entertainments – had troubled the leaders of the church for centuries. The Nizhnii-Novgorod petition of 1636 took up and expanded on the complaints of the church fathers in the Stoglav council of 1551 and, once Tsar Aleksei ascended the throne, royal decrees echoed the cry.[19] The list of sinful behavior is lengthy and remarkably – indeed suspiciously – consistent throughout the documents. In midwinter and late spring, instead of coming to church, ordinary people went out to drink, gamble, tell fortunes, and enjoy the performances of the traditional folk entertainers (*skomorokhi*) with their irreverent and obscene patter and songs, their musical instruments, their trained bears, and their dancing dogs. Women and girls swung on swings. For their health, villagers bathed in the nearest river or lake at the new moon or the sound of thunder or washed themselves with silver coins. They also allowed folk healers into their houses to practice their arts.

The documents describe the observance of the annual rituals of Rusalii and Koliada.[20] Between the feasts of the Ascension and John the Baptist, villagers in the Nizhnii-Novgorod area gathered four times in different villages: women and girls brought food offerings and danced around a birch tree. Beginning on Christmas Eve, revelers celebrated Koliada, the winter solstice, with drinking, musical instruments, pagan songs, and all kinds of fortune telling. Masked mummers entertained them, including several young men representing a mare (*kobylka*).

Even in Lent, the devilish entertainments went on. The *skomorokhi* went the rounds of houses and streets and swings appeared in the central square. Entertainers even parodied the Resurrection.[21]

---

[18] S.A. Belokurov, "Deianie Moskovskago tserkovnogo sobora 1649 goda," *ChOIDR* 171 (1894, book iv), 1–52.

[19] D.E. Kozhanchikov, ed., *Stoglav* (St. Petersburg, 1863), 135–41.

[20] On these festivals, see V. Ia. Propp, *Russkie agrarnye prazdniki* (St. Petersburg, 1995), esp. 45–7, 70–5, 122–4, 136–43; Linda J. Ivanits, *Russian Folk Belief* (Armonk, NY, and London, 1989), 9–10; and Russell Zguta, *Russian Minstrels. A History of the Skomorokhi* (Philadelphia, 1978), 9–12.

[21] Rozhdestvenskii, "K istorii bor'by," *AI*, 4: 124–26 (no. 35); N. Kharuzin, "K voprosu o bor'be Moskovskago pravitel'stva s narodnymi iazycheskimi obriadami i sueveriiami v

As we would expect, these graphic descriptions come exclusively from prominent Orthodox priests and the government. How literally can we take the details of these accounts? In general, the picture they present harmonizes with earlier written sources and later ethnographic observation. Moreover, it seems improbable that conscientious parish priests would not know roughly what their parishioners were up to, no matter how much they disapproved of their conduct. At the same time, a pinch of skepticism seems justified. For one thing, the government's decrees describe "pagan" practices in remarkably consistent, stereotypical phrases. In addition, the documents assume that folk practices were essentially the same all across Russia, from Nizhnii-Novgorod to Dmitrov, near Moscow, Belgorod in the south, and Verkhotur'e in western Siberia.

What did these rituals and entertainments mean to the participants? On this we can only speculate. They were certainly carnivalesque with a vengeance.[22] They allowed the participants to shed their inhibitions (on occasion, their clothes), drink, sing and dance, and, in the process, mock the respectable world and its powers. But what did participants think they were doing? Were they practicing a pre-Christian nature religion or just having a riotous good time?[23] While any answer must be hypothetical, the most likely explanation lies somewhere in between. In the lives of seventeenth-century peasants, these survivals of ancient systems of belief were part of a complex syncretism of Christian and pre-Christian elements, of faith and magic expressed in annual cycles of rituals governed by two complementary calendars.

The ecclesiastical reformers' view of these popular practices was unequivocal. They were determined to abolish them for reasons that would make good sense to confessional leaders elsewhere in Europe.[24] In origin, they were clearly pagan and the *skoromokhi* who led the revels had once functioned as priests or shamans; they distracted parishioners from their Christian duties during some of the great festivals of the

---

polovine XVII v.," *Etnograficheskoe Obozrenie*, no. 1 (1879): 143–51; and Pascal, *Avvakum*, 161–4.

[22] Peter Burke, *Popular Culture in Early Modern Europe* (New York, 1978), 213–15, rightly includes these Russian practices in this category. Relying primarily on ethnographic materials of the nineteenth and twentieth centuries, Propp, *Agrarnye prazdniki*, Chapter 7, also classified many of the practices that shocked the Zealots as "games and amusements."

[23] Historians of popular religion in England on the eve of the Reformation have a clear answer to this question. In Ronald Hutton's words, "there is absolutely no evidence that the people who kept these customs were anything but Christian or had any notion that by carrying on these activities they were commemorating other deities." Ronald Hutton, *The Rise and Fall of Merry England* (Oxford, 1994), 72.

[24] For the dynamics of the parallel process in England, see Hutton, *Rise and Fall*.

church year; the disorderly and licentious behavior they encouraged undercut Christian morality and decency; and they had bad practical consequences, not least deaths and injuries in the ritual brawls and the usual consequences of illicit sexual encounters.

In Russia, as elsewhere, Lent appeared to defeat Carnival. At the prodding of the reformers, Tsar Aleksei, already known for his personal antipathy toward folk entertainment, issued a series of decrees, beginning in December 1648, ordering local governors to ban *skomorokhi* and suppress the rituals associated with them. The tsar ordered governors to proclaim his decree in every village and hamlet in their jurisdiction and authorized them to flog or, for repeated offenses, exile those who persisted in the old ways.[25]

Issuing decrees was much easier than changing deep-rooted patterns of behavior. Scattered evidence suggests that the *skomorokhi*, driven underground or into the remote countryside, continued to practice their ancient trade into the eighteenth century.[26] Many of the agrarian rites and folk entertainments survived long enough for modern ethnographers to record them. And, in subtler ways, ordinary Russians continued – indeed continue – to incorporate ancient folkways such as charms, incantations, and folk healing into a Christian or post-Christian way of life.

Not surprisingly, the implementation of the Zealots' program of reform aroused violent opposition among the laity. The prominent Zealot Avvakum's hagiographic autobiography, written roughly twenty years after the events, describes his clashes with a prominent aristocrat, V.P. Sheremetev, local notables, and ordinary parishioners while he was parish priest of Lopatitsy. To be sure, Avvakum's methods of enforcing order and decency were hardly subtle. He describes his encounter with folk entertainers:

… and again the devil raised up a storm against me. There came to my village dancing bears with tambourines and domras, and I, sinner that I am, being zealous in Christ I drove them out; one against many I smashed their masks and tambourines in a field and took away two great bears. One of them I clubbed, and he came to life again; the other I set loose in the fields.[27]

[25] Kharuzin, "K voprosu"; P.I. Ivanov, *Opisanie gosudarstvennogo arkhiva starykh del* (Moscow, 1850), 296–99 (unavailable to me); *AI*, 4: 124–6.

[26] Zguta, *Minstrels*, 63–5.

[27] N.K. Gudzii, ed., *Zhitie Protopopa Avvakuma im samim napisannoe i drugie ego sochineniia* (Moscow, 1960), 62; *Archpriest Avvakum, The Life Written by Himself*, trans. Kenneth N. Bystrom (*Michigan Slavic Translations*, no. 4) (Ann Arbor, MI, 1979), 46. The translation is Bystrom's.

In return, Avvakum survived berating, beatings, a severely bitten hand (by a parishioner), and an assassination attempt in which the weapon misfired.[28] Twice, in 1648 and 1652, in fear for his life, he fled his parish for the safety of Moscow. The second time, he received a major promotion to become dean of the cathedral in Iurevets on the Volga. The assignment lasted only eight weeks until:

> The devil instructed the priests and peasants and their women; they came to the patriarchal chancellery where I was busy with church business, and in a crowd they dragged me out of the chancellery (there were maybe fifteen hundred of them). And in the middle of the street they beat me with clubs and stomped me, and the women had at me with stove hooks. Because of my sins, they almost beat me to death and they cast me down near the corner of a house. The Commandant rushed up with his artillerymen, and seizing me they raced away on their horses to my poor yard. But people came up to the yard and the town was in tumult.[29]

Unfortunately, in only a few instances does Avvakum's "Life" give the specific reasons for these clashes. In Sheremetev's case, he refused to bless the boyar's son because, contrary to time-honored custom, the young man was clean-shaven. One of the clashes with local officials occurred when he intervened to rescue a young woman toward whom the grandee had dishonorable intentions. Similarly, he explained the riot in Iurevets on the fact that he had rebuked the priests and their women for "fornication" (*bludnia*). It is, of course, entirely possible that the disorders had causes other than Avvakum's rigor. Between 1648 and 1652, many urban centers in Russia exploded in uprisings against rising taxes and a depersonalized and more intrusive bureaucratic administration.[30]

Other reformist priests suffered through similar tribulations. As foot soldiers in a campaign to reform parish worship and morals from above, they took the brunt of parishioners' anger at the demand that they abruptly and radically change their traditional way of life. One after another, they found parish ministry untenable, trapped as they were between the aspirations of the reformers in Moscow and the recalcitrance of their flocks. The reform campaign took a sharp turn when Nikon succeeded Ioasaf as patriarch in 1652. As metropolitan of Novgorod, Nikon had proved to be an energetic reformer, a capable and courageous

---

[28] *Zhitie*, 61–4; Bystrom, *Life*, 45–50.

[29] *Zhitie*, 63–4; Bystrom, *Life*, 48–50. I have slightly altered Bystrom's translation.

[30] For a survey of the vast literature on this subject, see Robert O. Crummey, "Russia and the 'General Crisis of the Seventeenth Century'," *Journal of Early Modern History* 2 (1998): 156–80. Valerie A. Kivelson, "The Devil Stole His Mind," *American Historical Review* 98 (1993): 733–56, is an imaginative analysis of the symbolic significance of the Moscow uprising of 1648.

administrator, and an ardent advocate of the church's leadership in society. In the stormy seven years of his active tenure as patriarch, however, the reforming coalition and ultimately the Russian Orthodox Church as a whole were fatally divided.

What took place must be examined in its international context. Religious reform from above – "confessionalization" if you like – began in Russia roughly a century later than in Catholic and Protestant Europe.[31] And, although cautious, Russian political and ecclesiastical leaders were, by the mid-seventeenth century, becoming aware of some of the implications of developments elsewhere. Some of the Zealots – the tsar, Rtishchev, and Nikon, among others – responded enthusiastically to international currents in ecclesiastical learning and culture, especially when transmitted through other Orthodox churches with which they desired closer contact.

The messages they received were often ambivalent. From the Orthodox in Ukraine, battleground against revitalized and aggressive Catholicism, the Muscovite church received a body of apocalyptic literature summarizing biblical and later Eastern Christian teachings on the End Time. These works achieved considerable influence not only among the defenders of Orthodoxy in Ukraine, but also in Muscovy.[32] At the same time, Ukraine provided Russia with new styles of Orthodox scholarship, education, and art, all taken from Counter-Reformation Catholicism and recruited for the defense of the Eastern church. The more analytical, rationalistic approaches of the Ukrainian scholars who began to enter Russian service made all but the most sophisticated and tolerant Muscovites uneasy.[33] Frank Sysyn's essay in this volume makes clear why these learned clergymen, whose erudition suited the needs of their homeland so well, had such a divisive impact on the Muscovite church and Russian cultural life.

Nikon's elevation to the patriarchal throne brought another source of inspiration to the fore. The tsar, the new patriarch, and some of their collaborators turned toward ecumenical Eastern Orthodoxy as represented by the Greek church in order to revitalize Russian Orthodoxy. For his part, Nikon also hoped that closer ties with the rest of the Orthodox world would help him recapture for the church the legal autonomy

---

[31] Indeed, this was precisely the time when, according to Schilling, the process of confessionalization ended in the German lands ("Konfessionalisierung," 28–30).

[32] H.P. Niess, *Kirche in Russland zwischen Tradition und Glaube? Eine Untersuchung der Kirillova kniga und der Kniga o vere aus der 1 hälfte des 17 Jahrhunderts* (Göttingen, 1977).

[33] K.V. Kharlampovich, *Malorossiiskoe vliianie na velikorusskuiu tserkovnuiu zhizn'* (Kazan', 1914); Paul Bushkovitch, *Religion and Society in Russia. The Sixteenth and Seventeenth Centuries* (Oxford and New York, 1992), Chapters 6 and 7.

and moral hegemony that, in his view, it had lost in a series of defeats and compromises culminating in the Law Code of 1649. Although the Russian church had never lost touch with its Greek sister and had, in recent decades, received a steady stream of needy Greek prelates, to say nothing of charlatans, the admiration of tsar and patriarch for the practices of Greek Orthodoxy and their increasing dependence on Greek émigré advisers shocked their contemporaries. After all, it was the Greeks' apostasy at the Council of Florence that had thrust Orthodox Russia into the center of world history. Here, too, ironies abound. For the center of Greek Orthodox scholarship and publishing was Roman Catholic Venice. Moreover, in his defense of the dignity of the church and its personification, Patriarch Nikon began to adopt the arguments and language of the popes of the High Middle Ages.[34]

The link between these developments and life in the parish lay in the continued republication of service books. For, as all of the reformers had long understood, consistent and dignified worship was impossible without consistent liturgical texts. Nikon quickly gave this campaign a new twist. His Greek advisers had convinced him that, in cases where the two Orthodox traditions diverged, the Greek church had preserved the authentic practices of the early church while Russians, in their ignorance, had introduced local eccentricities into the liturgy. Accordingly, the new Psalter of 1653 omitted the customary instructions on the sign of the cross. Nikon soon issued new ones instructing the faithful to cross themselves with three fingers extended in the Greek manner rather than two as Russian tradition decreed.[35] Thereafter, new editions and changes in liturgical practice followed one another in rapid succession.[36]

The Nikonian editions of liturgical texts deliberately attacked customary Russian practice. In addition to the sign of the cross, the more

[34] Valerie Tumins and George Vernadsky, eds., *Patriarch Nikon on Church and State. Nikon's "Refutation"* (Berlin, New York, and Amsterdam, 1982). English translation in William Palmer, *The Patriarch and The Tsar*, 6 vols. (London, 1871–6), vol. 1.

[35] The classic study of Nikon's reforms is still N.F. Kapterev, *Patriarkh Nikon i Tsar' Aleksei Mikhailovich*, 2 vols. (Sergiev Posad, 1909–12). The current state of the literature on many topics discussed in this paper reflects the fact that, during the Soviet period, scholars were, in effect, forbidden to publish serious work on explicitly religious subjects. Russian colleagues relate that, even in the late 1980s, censors required them to remove theological language from their studies of popular ideology or religious practices as a precondition for publication.

[36] For a systematic analysis of the changes in the liturgy, see Paul Meyendorff, *Russia, Ritual and Reform. The Liturgical Reforms of Nikon in the 17th Century* (Crestwood, NY, 1991). On the theological implications of the liturgical reform, see Karl Christian Felmy, *Die Deutung des Göttlichen Liturgie im Rahmen der russischen Theologie* (Berlin and New York, 1984), 80–111; and Bushkovitch, *Religion and Society*, 61.

dramatic changes included the four-pointed instead of eight-pointed cross on the sacred wafer and on church buildings; the triple rather than double Alleluia after the Psalms and the Cherubic hymn; the number of prostrations and bows in Lent; a new transliteration of "Jesus" into Slavonic ("Iisus" instead of "Isus"); and small but significant alterations in the wording of the Nicene Creed.[37] For ordinary parishioners, these changes would probably have seemed less jarring than the enforcement of *edinoglasie* or the suppression of agrarian festivals and carnivalesque entertainment. They were significant enough, however, involving as they did some of the most frequently repeated words, gestures, and visible symbols in the liturgy. Nikon did not help matters by insisting, against the advice of the patriarch of Constantinople and his royal protector, that only reformed usage was acceptable. In 1656, Nikon repeatedly branded the two-finger sign of the cross and other traditional Russian practices as heretical.[38]

The reforms and the patriarch's intransigence in enforcing them split the reform coalition in two. In a series of increasingly agitated letters written in late 1653 and early 1654 to the tsar and to Vonifat'ev, Ivan Neronov severely criticized Nikon's abandonment of Russia's heritage and the arrogance with which he was treating his former friends. The three-finger sign of the cross and the altered number of deep bows (*poklony*) in services were specific examples of these destructive policies.[39] In one letter to Vonifat'ev, he told of hearing a voice from an icon urging him to resist Nikon's reforms.[40] In his later autobiography, Avvakum told the same story and claimed that both he and Neronov had immediately realized that Nikon had destroyed Russian Orthodoxy, the last bastion of true Christian faith.[41] The two priests quickly fell afoul of the ecclesiastical superiors. The authorities imprisoned Neronov in a remote northern monastery; Avvakum was exiled to Siberia. According to tradition, the one bishop who in 1654 openly questioned the reforms, Paul of Kolomna, lost his see and perhaps his life for his stand.[42]

Prominent clergymen were not the only vocal opponents of the reforms. In 1657, the ecclesiastical and governmental authorities arrested the Rostov weaver, Sila Bogdanov, and two companions for

---

[37] These were the changes on which later Old Believers concentrated their sharpest criticisms (Crummey, "Origins," 132).

[38] Kapterev *Patriarkh Nikon* 1: 192–8; Meyendorff, *Russia*, 61–2.

[39] N. Subbotin, ed., *Materialy dlia istorii raskola za pervoe vremia ego sushchestvovaniia*, 9 vols. (Moscow, 1874–90) [hereafter *Materialy*] 1: 51–78.

[40] *Materialy*, 1: 99–100.

[41] *Zhitie*, 65; Bystrom, *Life*, 52.

[42] *Materialy*, 1: 100–2; Pascal, *Avvakum*, 248.

publicly condemning the new service books. Under intense interrogation, Bogdanov flaunted his convictions and, for his pains, was imprisoned in the same monastery to which Neronov had earlier been sent.[43]

Thus, even though the first protests against the Nikonian reforms were isolated and easily suppressed, they began the process of division within Russia's ecclesiastical elite. From these small beginnings, there emerged two competing elites with two competing visions of reform from above, one consistent with contemporary international standards in the Orthodox world and beyond, however poorly understood, the other faithful to local Russian tradition.

The first version of reform triumphed. Supported by the Tsar Aleksei's government, the Orthodox hierarchy under Nikon's authoritarian leadership rigorously enforced the new canons and, even after the patriarch withdrew from office in 1659 and was deposed for dereliction of duty in 1666, the process of confessionalization continued unabated. Using the records of the patriarchal Printing Office, Georg Michels has shown that the new books sold well in Moscow and that, over time, their use spread downward from the ecclesiastical hierarchy throughout the church.[44]

What does the hierarchy's apparent success in enforcing the new canons suggest? That most Russians, clergy and laypeople alike, had little interest in the minutiae of liturgical change, as Michels argues? The willingness of a priest to accept the new service books does not, of course, tell us whether his parishioners followed their instructions in practice or continued to cross themselves in the old way. Or, as Duffy argues in the case of England, did the coercive power of the royal administration and the church overpower potential opposition before it had a chance to form? The speed and vigor with which the authorities pursued individuals as diverse as Neronov and Bogdanov surely set an intimidating example for their contemporaries. One example illustrates the interpretative dilemma. In his study of the first Old Believers in Ukraine, Michels points out that the priest Koz'ma, traditionally viewed as the first missionary of the old faith in Starodub, had perforce used the reformed liturgy in his parish in Moscow before leaving the capital. Therefore, the author argues, Koz'ma must have left Moscow for reasons unconnected with the Nikonian reforms and come out in opposition to

---

[43] Rumiantseva, *Dokumenty*, 29–58; "Sudnye protsessy XVII–XVIII vv. po delam tserkvi," ed. E.V. Barsov, *ChOIDR*, 122 (1882, book iii): 1–42, here 3–13. Bogdanov illustrates the difficulties of drawing neat divisions between "elite" and "popular" religious culture. On one hand, he consistently told his interrogators that he was illiterate; on the other, he carried around a notebook hidden in his hat.

[44] Michels, *War*, Chapter 1.

them in Ukraine only because, given local political conditions, it was expedient for him to do so.[45] But may his move to a more congenial setting not have allowed him to give public expression to deep-seated doubts and convictions that, if openly revealed in Moscow, would have brought extremely unpleasant consequences? Either explanation is, in the end, a matter of speculation.

Faced with such pressure, opposition to the Nikonian reforms coalesced very slowly. From within the ecclesiastical elite, individual opponents of Nikon's reforms wrote treatises attacking both the general philosophy and specific details of the changes in the liturgy. Spiridon Potemkin, the learned archimandrite of the Pokrovskii monastery, composed the first tract of this type, probably in 1658. Between 1665 and the late 1670s, his successors produced a "canon" of anti-Nikonian polemical and devotional texts – Nikita Dobrynin "Pustosviat's" lengthy petition; the "scrolls" of the priest Lazar'; Deacon Fedor's "Response of the Faithful" and letters; Avraamii's "Secure Shield of Faith" and petition; and the autobiographies of Avvakum and his cellmate, Epifanii.[46] To this list, Michels rightly adds Bishop Alexander of Viatka who, although he did not write a major anti-Nikonian tract, collected a library of raw materials for such a task.[47] This remarkable body of literature, whose authors wrote at great risk or from prison, met several pressing needs. It responded to the official publications defending the reforms, the *Skrizhal'* (1656)[48] and the *Zhezl pravlenie* (1668) of Simeon Polotskii, the most prominent representative of Ukrainian scholarship at the tsar's court. In a broader sense, these writings expressed the growing frustration of Nikon's opponents within the clergy: These men may well have hoped that the obvious truth of their position would convince the tsar and the hierarchy to abolish the new liturgical usages or, at the very least, allow the continued practice of the old. In this, they were profoundly disappointed.

The ecclesiastical council of 1667 destroyed all hope of restoring Russian ecclesiastical tradition. Led by visiting Greek prelates, the fathers of the church required the exclusive use of the Nikonian practices, declared heretical such traditional Russian practices as the two-finger

---

[45] Michels, "Old Believers in Ukraine," 292–3.
[46] Crummey, "Origins," esp. 125–6; N. Iu. Bubnov, *Staroobriadcheskaia kniga v Rossii vo vtoroi polovine XVII vv.* (St. Petersburg, 1995), an indispensable guide to Old Believer polemical literature.
[47] Michels, *War*, Chapter 2.
[48] This work of the Greek hieromonk, John Nathaniel, had been published in Venice in 1574. Members of Nikon's inner circle translated and edited it to support their patron's program (Meyendorff, *Russia*, 61).

sign of the cross and the double Alleluia, and anathematized all those who refused to give up their opposition to the new order.[49] The categorical nature of the council's protocols destroyed any hope of future reconciliation. The anathemas were to remain in force until the 1970s.

The council's intransigence put the defenders of tradition in an impossible position. Their ranks divided. Through threats and appeals to preserve the unity of the Body of Christ, the leaders of the church convinced some prominent opponents – Neronov, Bishop Alexander and Nikita Dobrynin – to recant.[50] Avvakum, Fedor, Lazar', and Epifanii chose the path of resistance and martyrdom.

Thus, in the late 1660s and early 1670s, a conservative intelligentsia emerged within the ecclesiastical elite and constructed the intellectual and polemical foundations of Old Belief. Prominent parish priests for the most part, they wrote their most ambitious works for men like themselves who knew the Bible and the Orthodox liturgical and devotional texts that circulated in Muscovy before the mid-seventeenth century. Over the following decades, later sympathizers copied many of these works – some of them remarkably abstruse – and circulated them among their followers.[51] The core messages of the canon of Old Believer sacred texts were clear and dramatic. First, the Nikonian reforms were wrong for clear canonical and historical reasons. Second, they violated the Orthodox traditions of Russia. As conservative polemicists repeatedly pointed out, if only the Nikonian usages were correct and all others heretical, all earlier Russian saints, princes, and laypeople must literally be damned. Third, the Nikonian reforms marked the beginning of the End Time. This conclusion came naturally to those who accepted the symbolic statements of earlier Muscovite ecclesiastical writings that the Russian church was the last – and last possible – refuge of true Christian faith and took seriously the apocalyptic prophesies imported from Ukraine.

It is not difficult to imagine the appeal of these general messages to ordinary laypeople, men and women who could not possibly have read the great petitions of Nikita Dobrynin or Avraamii. How these

---

[49] *Deianiia Moskovskikh soborov 1666 i 1667 godov* (Moscow, 1893), 2: 3v–8, 30v–33v; *Materialy*, 2: 210–18, 264–79.

[50] Dobrynin later broke once again with the reformed church and, in 1682, was the most prominent Old Believer leader in Moscow.

[51] Some of the important early Old Believer writings were copied much more frequently than others. The works of men who made their peace with the official church in 1667 survive in comparatively few copies. Far more copies of the works of the intransigents of 1667 have survived.

convictions spread downward from the elite to significant numbers of ordinary people is a complex and open question.

*\* \* \* \* \**

Some clues can be found in the official investigations of the so-called Kapiton movement of reform and protest in the middle decades of the century.[52] Most of what we know about Elder Kapiton himself comes from later official Orthodox and Old Believer sources. Probably a self-appointed prophet of humble origins, Kapiton led a succession of small informal monastic communities in various corners of Northern and Central Russia between the 1620s and about 1660. Insofar as it can be reconstructed, his teaching had several central features. He advocated an asceticism far more extreme than the most rigorous teachings of Eastern Orthodoxy. One manifestation was continuous, severe fasting even in the church's feasting seasons. He and his followers also rejected the authority of the Orthodox clergy on grounds of moral corruption. Although the sources are less clear on this point, his moral and ascetic rigor seems to have sprung from the conviction that the Apocalypse was at hand.

Much more precise evidence about some of Kapiton's followers in Viazniki survives in records of their interrogation in 1665. These itinerant or self-proclaimed monks and ordinary laypeople lived in informal monastic settlements. By their own admission, they fasted rigorously throughout the year. One of their accusers, Bishop Ilarion of Riazan', charged them with going even farther and preaching ritual suicide through starvation in anticipation of the Apocalypse.[53] When investigators arrested the monks Vavila and Leonid and some of their followers, others burned themselves to death rather than surrender.[54] Under torture, the leading suspects remained defiant. They admitted that they would, on principle, have nothing to do with official Orthodoxy and its clergy. Several, moreover, specifically referred to the Nikonian reforms – a "schism of the books (*knizhnoi raskol)"* – as one of the reasons

---

[52] The following discussion summarizes Robert O. Crummey, "Religious Radicalism in Seventeenth-Century Russia: Reexamining the Kapiton Movement," *FzOG* 46 (1992): 171–86 and relies heavily on Rumiantseva, *Antitserkovnoe dvizhenie* and *Antitserkovnoe dvizhenie. Dokumenty*.

[53] Illarion also accused them of forcing unwilling followers to starve themselves to death in "graves" or pits. Ia. I. Barsukov, *Pamiatniki pervykh let russkago staroobriadchestva. Letopis' zaniatii Arkheograficheskoi Komissii* 24 (1912): 1–424, here pp. 330–1.

[54] Rumiantseva, *Antitserkovnoe dvizhenie. Dokumenty*, 57–9.

why they rejected the church's authority.[55] In 1666, the investigation uncovered more of Kapiton's followers in the Vologda and Nizhnii-Novgorod areas. One of those arrested, Stepanida L'vova, defiantly described her austere way of life and her angry rejection of the clergy. "She said that she has hands of her own that can make the sign of the cross without a priest. And she does not go to church because now they celebrate by the new service books."[56]

Thus, at this early date, the disciples of Kapiton displayed several of the defining characteristics of later Old Belief: the creation of self-generating monastic communities, radical opposition to the authority of the royal administration and the clergy, a belief in the imminence of the Apocalypse, and, in extremis, the practice of group suicide. The available evidence suggests that, in the 1660s, such groups were small, scattered, and eccentric. Moreover, the radicals' statements under interrogation suggest that Nikon's reforms were not the primary reason for their hostility to church and state.

The world of the radicals in Viazniki and Vologda could not have been farther removed from the patriarch's court or the Moscow mansion in which Boiarynia Morozova, leading patroness of the anti-Nikonians, hid Avraamii and a number of women devoted to the old ways. The radicals surely were a "popular" religious movement, however we define that elusive term. Nevertheless, the two groups shared a deep antipathy to the reformed church and an increasing willingness to defy its leaders and their royal protector whatever the cost.

Miracle cults were a far more widespread form of popular devotion in mid-seventeenth century Russia than the "*Kapitonovshchina.*" Devotion to wonder-working icons and saints – well-known, obscure, or, in some cases, imaginary – appears to have proliferated among the clergy and all classes of the laity in the sixteenth and early seventeenth centuries to the increasing consternation of the hierarchy.[57] Suppressing even the most dubious of popular cults raised the specter of serious opposition to church and state. Allowing miracle cults to flourish without the scrutiny and sanction of the hierarchy also presented dangers, however, not least the very real possibility that the Old Believers would use them to support their attack on the Nikonian reforms.[58]

---

[55] Rumiantseva, *Antitserkovnoe dvizhenie. Dokumenty*, 94, 98–9, 111.

[56] Rumiantseva, *Antitserkovnoe dvizhenie. Dokumenty*, 189.

[57] Bushkovitch, *Religion and Society*, 89–127.

[58] For example, Old Believer polemicists often used the Life of St. Evfrosin of Pskov to defend the two-finger sign of the cross.

Thus, in spite of the risks, beginning with Patriarch Nikon himself, the ecclesiastical hierarchy strove with the government's backing to regulate the cults and, in the latter half of the seventeenth century, suppressed public manifestations of a number of the more dubious or threatening of them.[59] In the best-known example, Patriarch Ioakim convened church councils in 1677 and 1679 to reexamine the case of Anna of Kashin, a fourteenth-century princess whose popular cult had led, by about 1650, to officially sanctioned local veneration and preparations for her formal canonization. After a review of the evidence, including a detailed analysis of the historical inaccuracies in Anna's "life" and the miracles attributed to her remains, the councils concluded that, while a lady of undoubted piety, Anna did not merit recognition as a saint.[60] Eve Levin's essay in this collection analyzes popular miracle cults and their regulation in the eighteenth century.

$$* * * * *$$

From the very beginning of the Nikonian reforms and the opposition to them, the royal government and the Orthodox hierarchy worked together to suppress any overt manifestations of religious dissent or "schism" (*raskol*). The urgency of this task largely distracted them from the struggle against pagan rites and entertainments.

Two of the cases we have described illustrate this collaborative campaign. Metropolitan Iona of Rostov first brought Sila Bogdanov and his disciples to Patriarch Nikon's attention. After the metropolitan had questioned the suspects, Tsar Aleksei ordered the boyar, Prince A.N. Trubetskoi, and the powerful chancery official, Almaz Ivanov, to take over the investigation. These two prominent statesmen carried the investigation to its conclusion. Meanwhile, the metropolitan interrogated the two priests who were the suspects' confessors and sent them on to Moscow for further questioning. Moreover, the tsar's government asked the metropolitan to report in greater detail on the "subversive words" (*neistovye slova*)[61] that Bogdanov had uttered in his presence. The accused, it turned out, had said that "he did not fear the tsar or his courts

---

[59] Michels, "Place," 25–9, draws attention to a complex dispute in 1659 and 1660, one element of which appears to have been an attempt by the autocratic Bishop Stefan to suppress a local Marian devotion. Significantly, Nikita Dobrynin was his most vociferous opponent.

[60] Bushkovitch, *Religion and Society*, 92–4; E.E. Golubinskii, "Istoriia kanonizatsii sviatykh v Russkoi tserkvi," *ChOIDR* 204 (1903, book iv), here pp. 159–69; "Moskovskii sobor o zhitii blagoverynia kniagini Anny Kashinskoi," *ChOIDR* 79 (1871, book iv): 45–62.

[61] Literally, "crazy words."

and that the reign of the Antichrist had begun." He called Nikon the "precursor of the Antichrist."[62] Similarly, in 1665, the parish priest Vasilii Fedorov and, some months later, Bishop Ilarion of Riazan' informed the ecclesiastical authorities and the tsar, respectively, of the existence of the Viazniki radicals. In response, the government dispatched a detachment of musketeers (*strel'tsy*) to round them up and an investigative commission, led by the boyar, Prince I.S. Prozorovskii, to conduct the interrogations. At the end of the process, some of the lesser defendants who escaped execution were imprisoned in several monasteries, where, predictably, they proved difficult to control.[63]

Thus from the time of the Nikonian reforms, the royal government and Orthodox hierarchy collaborated in suppressing opposition, which, as they understood, was directed indiscriminately against both.[64] The decrees of the council of 1667 made effective collaboration an even more urgent necessity. Responsibility for enforcing the Nikonian rites and suppressing dissent and schism (*raskol*)[65] fell to the clergy. Parish priests bore the primary responsibility for enforcing the reformed canons. As a check on the loyalty of their flocks, they were to make sure that their parishioners fulfilled their minimal obligations as Orthodox Christians – annual confession and communion – and to report those who failed to do so. They were also to inform higher authorities of any individuals who openly held to the old rites or engaged in other forms of suspicious conduct.[66]

Clearly, then, this design for the imposition of the new order was part of the larger process of giving the Orthodox hierarchy more effective control over the beliefs and practices of ordinary parishioners. As Michels carefully demonstrates, the leaders of the church gradually succeeded in disseminating the new liturgical order downward through the provincial dioceses and large monasteries to the parish level. The process of dissemination was not complete in the remotest corners of the realm until the 1680s or 1690s. Moreover, as this process went on, some of the reform's most vociferous opponents were the itinerant monks and nuns whose entire way of life made them opponents of tighter discipline in the church.[67]

---

[62] Rumiantseva, *Dokumenty*, 29–58. The quotes are on p. 54.
[63] Rumiantseva, *Antitserkovnoe dvizhenie. Dokumenty*, 50–137.
[64] Schilling describes essentially the same phenomenon in "Konfessionalisierung," 43–4.
[65] In official documents, "*raskol*" and "*raskolniki*" (schismatics) are extremely broad, heterogeneous categories and include all real or imagined dissent against the official church and its teachings and practices.
[66] Smirnov, *Dukhovnik*, 224–41.
[67] Michels, *War*, Chapters 4 and 5.

The responses of the angry and dispossessed of Russian society mirrored the policies of state and church. Increasingly, in the last decades of the seventeenth century, opposition to the Nikonian liturgical reforms became inextricably entangled with defense of corporate rights, local autonomy, or traditional practices against the incursions of the increasingly intrusive central bureaucratic structures of state and church. In 1668, the Solovetskii monastery revolted and, for eight years, held off besieging government forces. A variety of motives drove the rebels. Successive abbots and their monks defended the monastery's traditional freedom from the control of the hierarchy and the secular authorities. Rejection of the Nikonian reforms, however, was their chief rallying cry.[68] As the siege continued, the monks and their allies became ever more militant and the government more frightened and desperate. When the great fortress finally fell, government forces killed all of its surviving defenders.[69] In similar fashion, defense of the traditional rites became entangled with the struggle to preserve Cossack freedoms in both northern Ukraine and the lower Don valley.[70] Most frightening of all, in 1682, the rebellious garrison of Moscow in alliance with Old Believers led by Nikita Dobrynin took control of the capital and brought the government to its knees.[71]

In response to this dramatic demonstration of its vulnerability, the regency government of Princess Sophia made a more determined effort than ever to suppress religious dissent and subversion in the name of faith. Calling the government's police agencies and parish priests to arms, the decree of December 1684 ordered them to hunt down and interrogate any parishioners who had been lax in their religious duties. Those who rejected the new rites had a radical choice: submission to the reformed church or death. The death penalty was automatic for any missionaries of the Old Belief or anyone who, after submission, reverted to the old ways. Even impeccably loyal

---

[68] The monastery's leaders sent Tsar Aleksei a series of petitions protesting the Nikonian reforms. The fifth of these is one of the most thorough early attacks on the changes in the liturgy: *Materialy*, 3: 45–6, 160–71, 209–12, 213–75.

[69] Historians continue to debate the relative importance of these causes in inciting and sustaining the revolt. In addition to the monastery's traditional freedom from the control of the hierarchy, Michels, "Solovki Uprising," stresses the importance of exiles and other inveterate troublemakers among its leaders. Earlier studies include N.A. Barsukov, *Solovetskoe vosstanie 1668–1676 gg.* (Petrozavodsk, 1954); A.A. Savich, *Solovetskaia votchina v XV–XVII v.* (Perm', 1927); I. Ia. Syrtsov, *Vozmushchenie Solovetskikh monakhov-staroobriadtsev v XVII v.* (Kostroma, 1888).

[70] Michels, "Old Believers in Ukraine"; V.G. Druzhinin, *Raskol na Donu v kontse XVII veka* (St. Petersburg, 1889).

[71] See V.I. Buganov, *Moskovskie vosstaniia kontsa XVII v.* (Moscow, 1969).

church members who gave shelter to Old Believers were to be severely punished.[72]

\* \* \* \* \*

Savage persecution begot desperate opposition. In the late 1680s and early 1690s, the government confronted an epidemic of mass suicide by fire. The most spectacular episodes took place in Karelia. Twice, in 1687 and 1688, a sizable number of rebels captured the Paleostrovskii monastery and, when surrounded by government troops, burned themselves to death rather than submit to interrogation and execution or, perhaps even worse, apostasy. Similar cases of self-immolation occurred in an informal monastic community at Berezov "na Voloku" in 1687 and around the village of Pudozh in 1684 and 1693.[73]

Contemporaries knew that the leading figures in these shocking episodes were a motley lot. Some were itinerant monks; others were local peasants. Their motives and actions were equally mixed. In the best tradition of "social banditry," many had weapons and did not hesitate to use them. Emel'ian Ivanov Vtorogo, a prominent local peasant, chose to escape from the first siege with the monastery treasure instead of dying for the old faith, and lived to raid Paleostrov again. Moreover, as the contemporary Old Believer, Evfrosin, charged, some of the rebels forced others to die by fire unwillingly.[74]

For all that, self-immolation was an extreme and shocking expression of religious convictions. When they lived in informal monastic communities or conducted armed assaults on villages and monasteries, the rebels claimed that they acted in defense of the old rites. In the Pudozh case of 1693, for example, the rebels turned the churches "upside down." They took out all of the liturgical books, icons, crosses, altar cloths, and liturgical vessels and washed them down, leaving only "local" icons and crosses. With these they blessed the waters of the local lake, bathed themselves, and rebaptized all of the onlookers.[75] In a word, they reconsecrated these churches and their people into the Old Belief.

---

[72] *Polnoe sobranie zakonov Rossiiskoi Imperii*, sobranie pervoe, 45 vols. (St. Petersburg, 1830–43) [hereafter *PSZ*] 2: 647–50 (no. 1102), summarized in Crummey, *Old Believers*, 41–2.

[73] For contrasting interpretations of the events, see Michels, "Violent Old Belief" and Crummey, *Old Believers*, Chapter 3. For a broad chronological survey of self-immolation, see D.I. Sapozhnikov, "Samosozhzhenie v russkom raskole," *ChOIDR* 158 (1891, book iii), 1–170.

[74] Evfrosin, *Otrazitel'noe pisanie o novoizobretennom puti samoubistvennykh smertei. Pamiatniki drevnei pis'mennosti* 108: 37, 56–7.

[75] *AI* 5: 378–94 (no. 223), here 389, 392. Michels summarizes this evidence in "Violent Old Belief," 211. It is unclear whether the rebels' plunge into the lake represented a form of

Mass suicide was a direct extension of their campaign. To be sure, all branches of Christianity regard suicide as a grave sin. Nevertheless, the leaders of frightened and emotionally overwrought communities of men, women, and children saw it as the best response to an unbearable dilemma. Several strands fed into this response. First, the leaders of the Kapiton movement allegedly regarded suicide as the ultimate expression of Christian asceticism. Second, the first Old Believers were extremely angry men and women, even by the standards of an angry and violent age, for they were convinced that the rulers of church and state had destroyed true Orthodoxy, damned millions of their fellows, and put their own souls in mortal peril. Future martyrs like Avvakum and the Boiaryna Morozova[76] took every opportunity to express their rage and contempt at the new order in church and state. In their minds, the End Time had come. The government's increasingly relentless pursuit of religious dissenters strengthened the conviction that, in some sense, the Antichrist reigned.

All of these convictions and emotions fed into the wave of self-immolations in the 1680s and 1690s. In 1684, for example, the monks Andronnik and Iosif "preached that the world had come to an end and that the only way ... to be saved was by committing suicide."[77] Moreover, if the Antichrist's power was reaching even the remotest corners of the northern forest, the faithful remnant of true Christians had to make a stand. Impatience for a confrontation with the forces of evil may well have reinforced less edifying motives for capturing nearby monasteries, churches, and administrative centers. Once government troops came in pursuit, the preachers of self-immolation followed a scenario that, in their eyes, transformed suicide into martyrdom. Imprisonment was to be avoided at all costs, for with it came torture and the risk of apostasy and damnation. Instead, when government troops approached, the Old Believers barricaded themselves into their stockades, often prepared in advance to be ignited quickly,[78] and fought back as long as possible. Once capture was imminent, they set the buildings alight and died.

To such incidents, the government and Orthodox hierarchy reacted with shock, outrage, and disbelief. The regency government, for example, ordered both Metropolitan Kornilii of Novgorod and the governor of Olonets to take energetic action to preserve order and uniformity

---

baptism or harkened back to pre-Christian ritual bathing denounced by the Zealots of Piety earlier in the century.

[76] On Morozova, see A.I. Mazunin, ed., *Povest' o boiaryne Morozovoi* (Leningrad, 1979).

[77] Michels, "Violent Old Belief," 220, citing documents in fund 163 of the Russian State Archive of Ancient Acts, Moscow. He stresses that some of those rescued from the conflagration claimed that they had been forced to participate in the ritual suicide.

[78] For example, *AI* 5: 389.

within their jurisdictions. In the wake of the first occupation of Paleostrov, the metropolitan received orders to clean up the ravaged monastery and resettle it with reliably Orthodox monks, while the *voevoda* and his troops were to capture the surviving rebels and dissenters.[79] Self-immolation presented the authorities with a particularly painful dilemma. The government gave its local representatives guidelines that, in practice, were impossible to implement: to round up all opponents of the regime as quickly as possible without, at the same time, doing anything that would set off mass suicide.[80]

Prominent Old Believers were equally ambivalent. From his Arctic dungeon, Avvakum expressed his admiration of the early martyrs by suicide and gave the appearance of encouraging the practice.[81] Other Old Believers strongly opposed self-immolation. Writing in 1691, Evfrosin attacked the practice as contrary to traditional Christian teaching and charged that its advocates were fanatics who resorted to deceit, drugs, and violence to control their gullible and frightened followers.[82] In the end, Evfrosin won the argument. In later generations, the leaders of the main Old Believer communities revered the earlier victims as saints and martyrs but did everything they could to avoid further incidents in their own day.[83] It was an ongoing struggle, for the memory of the earlier martyrs continued to tempt the most militant Old Believers when they faced persecution.

\* \* \* \* \*

In the 1690s, a new generation of Old Believer leaders emerged from the movement's burgeoning network of informal monastic communities. In the best-known example, Daniil Vikulich and the Denisov brothers, Andrei and Semen, founded the Vyg community in 1694 in a remote corner of Karelia. At about the same time, other centers appeared at Vetka along the Polish frontier, Starodub in northern Ukraine, Kerzhenets east of Nizhnii-Novgorod, and in the Pskov area.

At the beginning of the eighteenth century, the leaders of these communities made up the Old Believer "ecclesiastical elite." Like the founders of their movement, they aspired to direct their followers into

---

[79] *AI* 5: 252–62 (no. 151).
[80] For example, AI 5: 380.
[81] *Zhitie*, 126; P. S. Smirnov, *Vnutrennie voprosy v raskole v XVII v.* (St. Petersburg, 1898), 61–6.
[82] Evfrosin, *Otrazitel'noe pisanie*.
[83] See, for example, the treatment in I. Filippov, *Istoriia Vygovskoi pustyni* (St. Petersburg, 1862). A leader of the Vyg community, Ivan Filippov, wrote his history in the years just before his death in 1744.

an austere and disciplined Christian life, centered on pre-Nikonian liturgical practices and cultural forms. They faced a formidable task. As the years passed, priests consecrated before Nikon died out. And without validly consecrated priests, there could be no sacraments except for those such as baptism, which laypeople themselves could celebrate in extreme circumstances. Thus, early Old Believer communities faced a difficult choice. Some attempted to maintain a full sacramental life by receiving and anointing renegade priests from the official church. Others, like Vyg, became priestless out of necessity and canonical principle, not by choice. Adapting traditional Orthodox worship to fit these new circumstances was an undertaking of the most pressing urgency. Moreover, the new generation of Old Believer leaders had to maintain its authority over the ordinary believers who followed them without the support of the state or a hierarchical ecclesiastical structure. Indeed, the state was the enemy; all of the new communities played cat-and-mouse with the imperial government and, in the end, several were devoured.

In these challenging circumstances, the new leaders of the Old Belief adapted several techniques to establish and maintain their authority. Like Avvakum and other early leaders – and, indeed, like their Orthodox counterparts – they could be spiritual directors to their followers.[84] Following the giants of the 1660s and 1670s and, later, Evfrosin, they wrote polemics defending their position and refuting their enemies. Within a generation or two, they had created a history and martyrology of their movement. Works like Filippov's *History* and Semen Denisov's *Vinograd rossiiskii*[85] both sanctified and sanitized the Old Believer tradition: They glorified the memory of past martyrs and, at the same time, told their followers how to live in the present. How these long and elaborate works reached and influenced ordinary believers, especially those outside the main monastic communities, is a complex issue. The later history of the Old Belief provides several partial answers. First, since Old Belief is a "textual community," its leaders valued literacy and saw that boys learned to read in the best medieval Orthodox manner. Second, the men and especially the women of the Old Believer communities made innumerable copies of manuscript books of pre-Nikonian texts and the classics of their own movement. To this day, such books turn up regularly in peasant houses in the remotest corners of Russia, where, if not avidly read, they are at least deeply revered as holy objects. Finally, Old Belief developed its own elaborate oral culture which, through

---

[84] Smirnov, *Dukhovnik*, 205–24.
[85] Semen Denisov, *Vinograd rossiiskii ili opisanie postradavshikh v Rossii za drevletserkovnoe blagochestie* (Moscow, 1906).

stories and spiritual verses (*dukhovnye stikhi*), spread the principal messages of the old faith even among the illiterate.[86]

Ultimately, the key to the survival of Old Belief and its leaders was the structure of the monastic communities themselves. In order to provide stable refuges and centers of inspiration and learning in a threatening world, the Denisovs and their contemporaries required the residents of their settlements to live by a strict rule, which, over the years, became more and more elaborate. Vyg and the companion Leksa convent adopted clear hierarchical structures of authority; their leaders enjoyed a measure of power that would have made a traditional abbot jealous. The first rule, adopted in 1702, makes the priorities of the leaders clear: austerity and rigor in worship and in daily life. Frivolousness, wavering, or any hint of sexual impropriety were the enemy.[87] Oddly enough, although leading peasant followers in a remote area, the Denisovs showed no concern at all about the pagan survivals that had irritated their precursors among the Zealots of Piety. Had the church succeeded in suppressing the more flamboyant of these practices in the intervening years? Or did avoiding these temptations simply have lower priority for the Denisovs than the task of creating a godly community? Both suggestions may have some merit.

* * * * *

At the beginning of the eighteenth century, the official Orthodox Church stood on the brink of radical reorganization. The decision of Peter I to leave the office of patriarch vacant and then, in 1721, to create the Holy Synod to govern the church had momentous consequences for the ruler, the members of the hierarchy, and the laity.[88] If anything, the change served only to increase the responsibility of bishops and priests for the political loyalty and orderly behavior of their flocks. To mention the most extreme case, the notorious decree of 1722 required confessors to report any conspiracies or evil thoughts against the emperor to his security organs. Refusal to violate the sanctity of confession brought savage

---

[86] See the essays of S.E. Nikitina and M.B. Chernysheva in *Russkie pis'mennye i ustnye traditsii i dukhovnaia kul'tura* (Moscow, 1982).

[87] Crummey, *Old Believers*, 101–34; L.K. Kuandykov, "Razvitie obshchezhitel'nogo ustava v Vygovskoi staroobriadcheskoi obshchine v pervoi treti XVIII v.," *Issledovaniia po istorii obshchestvennogo soznaniia epokhi feodalizma v Rossii* (Novosibirsk, 1984), 51–63. The limited evidence on the organization of the other communities suggests that their structures were more flexible and their leaders had less control over the other members than in Vyg.

[88] See James Cracraft, *The Church Reform of Peter the Great* (Stanford, CA, 1971).

penalties.[89] At the same time, as the works of Gregory Freeze show, the synodal church continued to struggle through the eighteenth and much of the nineteenth century to create effective parishes by nurturing an educated clergy and making ordinary parishioners fulfill their liturgical duties with real understanding and conform to the moral teachings of the church.[90]

For most Old Believers, Peter's reign was equally disastrous, for it meant paying double taxes, wearing discriminatory markers, and, for those overheard calling Peter the Antichrist, serving a life sentence at hard labor. There were, however, some encouraging signs. Although we have no statistics, the Old Believers probably gathered many new adherents among the millions of ordinary Russians battered by Peter's skyrocketing taxes, military conscription, and forced labor and repelled by the forced Europeanization of the ruling elite.[91] Moreover, when it suited him, Peter adopted a policy of de facto toleration: In the best-known case, the emperor agreed to leave the Vyg community alone in return for services rendered.[92]

Like their counterparts among the Orthodox clergy, the leaders of the growing Old Believer denominations or, as they prefer, "accords," continued to struggle to keep discipline and order among their followers. In addition to insisting on dignity and austerity in worship and a strictly moral life, the leaders of Vyg and the other main communities also worked hard to rein in the extremists among them who advocated confrontation with the rulers of the world of Antichrist or preached self-immolation. The absence of clearly defined hierarchical structures of authority within the Old Belief made the task extremely difficult.

Finally, two features of Russian popular religious life remained essentially unchanged. Throughout the eighteenth and nineteenth centuries, prophets and prophetesses appeared in Russian villages and, no matter how eccentric or extreme their teaching in Orthodox eyes, attracted a following to the consternation of the state, the official church, and the leaders of Old Belief. And, even though Lent seems to have triumphed

---

[89] Cracraft, *Church Reform*, 238–44; *PSZ* 6: 685–9 (no. 4012).

[90] Gregory L. Freeze, *The Russian Levites: The Parish Clergy in the Eighteenth Century* (Cambridge, MA, 1977); *The Parish Clergy in Nineteenth-Century Russia: Crisis, Reform and Counter-Reform* (Princeton, 1983); his introduction to I.S. Belliustin, *Description of the Clergy in Rural Russia: The Memoir of a Nineteenth-Century Parish Priest* (Ithaca, NY, 1985); as well as his many articles on this subject, including "The Rechristianization of Russia: The Church and Popular Religion, 1750–1850," *Studia Slavica Finlandensia* 7 (1990): 101–36.

[91] On popular responses to Peter's policies, see Michael Chernavsky's classic article, "The Old Believers and the New Religion," *Slavic Review* 25 (1966): 1–39.

[92] Crummey, *Old Believers*, 66–91.

and the more dramatic forms of carnival disappeared, the change took place very slowly, and magic charms and incantations remained an integral part of the lives of peasants whatever their formal confessional affiliation.[93] In that sense, as Hsia puts it, "For the vast majority of the populace, confessionalism represented a veneer that preserved traditional practices and beliefs."[94]

[93] The literature on this subject is very large. See for example, Ivanits, *Folk Belief*, passim. For a few examples from our own day, E.B. Smilianskaia, "'Iskra istinnago blagochestiia.' Religioznye vozzreniia staroobriadtsev Verkhokam'ia," *Rodina* no. 2 (1995): 101–3; F.F. Bolonev, *Mesiatseslov semeiskikh Zabaikal'ia* (Novosibirsk, 1990), and his "Archaic Elements in the Charms of the Russian Population of Siberia," in *Russian Traditional Culture. Religion, Gender and Customary Law*, ed. Marjorie Mandelstam Balzer (Armonk, NY, and London, 1992), 71–84. These works are all based on the culture of rural Old Believers.

[94] Hsia, *Social Discipline*, 154.

# CHAPTER III

# The state, the churches, sociability, and folk belief in the seventeenth-century Dutch republic

WILLEM FRIJHOFF

From the outset, any reflection on religion and the state in the early modern Netherlands is confronted with some major conceptual problems. In the perception of many seventeenth-century Netherlanders, the state was multiform, and at times vanishing. Similarly, the historical concept of state religion is inappropriate for that country and period. Besides, more perhaps than in most other European countries, there is reason to distinguish for the United Provinces, at least analytically, between religion, church, and belief.

## DEFINITIONS

It might be useful to propose some working definitions. *Religion* is meant here as the whole field of more or less intuitive forms of symbolic agency and interpretation of natural and human reality, prior to intellectual reflection and to "rational" organization (whatever rationality that may be), but from the intimate conviction that there is something beyond visible reality. Forms of magic may pertain to religion, just like the recourse to healing saints, and other elements of what currently is called "popular religion." *Belief* is the intellectual legitimation and/or the emotional motivation of religion, centered around a personal or a joint encounter with God, as the ultimate reason of being. The social organization of religion refers to *church* (or its equivalents): The church is the sociocultural framework that enables belief to be organized in socially meaningful ways of thinking, ritual expressions, and norms and values for group behavior. Whereas religion stands for symbolics and ritual acting, church stands for its streamlining and legitimation into liturgy. Whereas belief refers to thinking about religion, church refers to dogmatics and intellectual authority. The focus of religion is the symbolic interpretation of reality, belief stresses the personal involvement, and church stands for social organization.[1]

Although historically, in many cases and in many countries, religion, belief, and church overlap, the three terms are not really equivalent. The ambition of church organization being to encompass and control in one single movement these three dimensions of religious life, its outlook depends very much on the actual relations between social life, political power, cultural values, and church organization. A symbiosis between political power and church organization (theocracy) will bring about a form of religious life that differs notably from a harmony between the church and the broad cultural values of society, but without any involvement of the state (as may be the case in secular societies).

### A PUBLIC CHURCH

Early modern Dutch society presents in this respect a particular configuration. Formally, there was no state religion in the early modern United Provinces, but only a "public church." This church, the Reformed Church of Dutch expression,[2] was acknowledged by the secular authorities of the individual Dutch provinces and towns as the only church allowed to perform religious functions publicly and to intervene publicly in moral affairs. No other public religious services were allowed except those organized by the Reformed Church. As the public church, the Reformed Church was endowed with all the privileges of a public body, whether pertaining to the position of its ministers and other officials or with respect to its right to proclaim and defend norms and values. As a successor to the medieval public church, it inherited part of

---

[1] For these definitions, see the Epilogue in Willem Frijhoff, *Embodied Belief: Ten Essays on Religious Culture in Dutch History* (Hilversum, 2002), 275–89. For an attempt to operate on the biographical level, see my *Wegen van Evert Willemsz. Een Hollands weeskind op zoek naar zichzelf 1607–1647* (Nijmegen, 1995), 28–35 and my "Popular Pietism and the Language of Sickness: Evert Willemsz's Conversion, 1622–23", in *Illness and Healing Alternatives in Western Europe*, Marijke Gijswijt-Hofstra, Hilary Marland, and Hans de Waardt eds. (London and New York, 1997), 98–119.

[2] As from 1578, there exists in the Dutch Republic also a Reformed Church of French expression (the so-called Walloon Church) with its own synodal organization, but in close relation with the Dutch Reformed Church. Formally, it had the same privileges as the Dutch Reformed Church. During the eighteenth century, it developed into the church of the Frenchified élites. See Willem Frijhoff, "Uncertain Brotherhood: The Huguenots in the Dutch Republic," in *Memory and Identity. The Huguenots in France and the Atlantic Diaspora*, eds. Bertrand van Ruymbeke and Randy J. Sparks (Columbia, SC, 2003), 128–71.

the income from former church property, as well as some of the public church buildings.

The rituals of the Reformed Church were adopted by the civil authorities for the religious design of civic life, and the Reformed Church had to supervise the norms of public morality. Civil meetings and conferences were opened and closed by prayers, days of public prayer and fasting were prescribed on important occasions (catastrophes, victories, plagues, etc.), baptisms and marriages performed in the Reformed Church received a civil recognition. However, the Reformed Church never had exclusive authority; from the very beginning, dissenters, Catholics, and all those who for whatever reason wanted to avoid Reformed ceremonials had the benefit of a secular marriage administration in the town halls, in front of the aldermen or the village authorities. In Amsterdam, the town authorities enforced almost from the beginning a compulsory civil registration of marriage intentions for everybody, regardless of the customs of the public church. On the other hand, Peter van Rooden has recently shown how the Reformed practice of the public day of prayer was, in fact, considered by the provincial Estates and the States-General as a supraconfessional ritual involving, by and large, all the individual confessions in a unique, great "fatherland."[3]

In the past, this double track has brought about much confusion among historians familiar with less ambiguous relations between church and state, as was the case in the nineteenth century. It means, in fact, that a "church" ritual performed within the Reformed Church has not forcibly a "Reformed" meaning (i.e., pertaining to the order of "belief"), neither is an apparently civil function necessarily destitute of a "Reformed" background; the main problem for present-day historians is that "public," "civil" (or secular), and "Reformed" meanings are not immanent to the religious acts themselves but can be traced only by contextual evidence. Thus, at least for some decades after the Dutch Revolt against the authority of the Spanish king, and the change of public religion (1579), newborn children of all confessions were in many villages and towns baptized by a Reformed minister, in the building of the local Reformed Church, without their baptism being a sign of adhesion to the Reformed Church itself.

Earlier historians started, anachronistically, from the assumption of an equivalence between confessional rituals and church adhesion. They translated attendance at religious functions into numbers of church members or into a degree of penetration of the Reformed Church into

---

[3] Peter van Rooden, *Religieuze regimes. Over godsdienst en maatschappij in Nederland, 1570–1990* (Amsterdam, 1996), 78–120.

the global society. The very quick penetration of the Reformed Church into Dutch society at large that resulted from this assumption was, however, obviously in contradiction to the persistence of very large religious groups outside the new public church. These included Catholics, still estimated at – according to the sources and their interpretation – about 30 to 50 percent of the population at the time of the Peace of Westphalia (1648), eighty years after the introduction of Protestantism in public life; the Mennonites, whose numbers (difficult to retrieve due to the absence of infant baptism) could locally run to 10 or 20 percent of the population (as at Haarlem or in the province of Friesland); as well as the Lutherans of either Netherlandish or German origin, and a wide range of more or less dissenting groups organized on a congregational basis.

## NONCONFESSIONAL CHRISTIANS

Some time ago, Juliaan Woltjer introduced the concept of the "middle groups" (i.e., the undecided who postponed for many years, sometimes for decades or a lifetime, their decision for adhesion to one church or another). The best known example is the recently studied case of the Utrecht lawyer Arnoldus Buchelius, whose diaries reveal a very gradual shift from traditional Catholicism (with a strong accent on popular ritual) through a period of indecision to orthodox and militant Calvinism, the decisive role for this latter shift having been played by a phase of despair and an attempt at suicide.[4] Interestingly, Buchelius's choices, however decidedly he finally may have made them, do not reveal a strong commitment to "belief." For example, though he was an elder of the Utrecht consistory, he does not really seem to have understood what predestination is about. His commitment as a Christian and a Calvinist went much more to social control, cultural conformity, and individual piety. Those were precisely the aims of the public church as viewed by the civil authorities: the moral control of the whole civic community, a useful form of civic religion meant to safeguard society's unity, and a pervasive nonconfessional piety as exemplified by the works of Erasmus and Thomas à Kempis, always bestsellers in the United Provinces. Ongoing research in several parts of the Netherlands, especially in Friesland by Wiebe Bergsma, clearly shows the numerical importance of the provisionally or permanently undecided people in the maritime and central provinces for several decades, at least until the

---

[4] Judith Pollmann, *Religious Choice in the Dutch Republic: The Reformation of Arnoldus Buchelius, 1565–1641* (Manchester, 1999).

Twelve Years' Truce (1609–21) and the Synod of Dordrecht (1618–19). Though considering themselves to be Christians (but not always even that), they rejected the need of a quick choice, and for some of them, indeed, the need of any choice at all, in favor of one of the existing confessions; the public church – as a public church, not as the Reformed community of the elect – provided religious shelter enough for their demands, for the time being.

Therefore, I presume that it was mainly owing to the very concept of a public church that large groups of Netherlanders postponed adhering to one church or another. An indication for this argument is the public status of the church building. Administered by publicly appointed churchwardens, who normally were of the Reformed confession but whose elite status determined their nomination, the church building was indeed a public building: it served as a public burial place regardless of confession; the town council often kept its archives there and maintained other goods, including some form of public library. The organ was also the property the town council, which appointed the organist and set musical programs, though not for religious services. The town council could also place the church at the disposal of whatever corporation needed it, like the grammar school or a guild. In a town with complex confessional cleavages like Woerden (Holland), where the Catholics had been succeeded by the Lutherans, then by the liberal Calvinists (the later Remonstrants), and finally by a Pietist and Puritan Orthodoxy, the church in the center of the town embodied the continuity of religious praxis notwithstanding the changes of confession. It was consequently and uninterruptedly called the *stadskerk* (the town church). This public character determined the church building's religious meaning. At least for the transition to Lutheranism and thence to liberal Calvinism, there is reason to argue that "belief" played only a minor role in Woerden. Rather, the public character of the religious service must have been the main focus of loyalty for the majority of the population. After all, several ministers changed their own confession, just as the confessional affiliation of church building itself was changed.

The acknowledgment of this evolution has far-reaching implications for the relation between state and belief in the early modern Netherlands. It means not only that the Calvinists took a very long time to impose their theological and ecclesiological positions on the majority of the population, but also that, contrary to the old claims of Catholic historians of a previous generation, the decline of the Catholic population was precipitate, not slow and gradual, as a result of an ongoing process of more or less forced Protestantization. Having lost its status as public church, the Catholic Church was quickly reduced to the two other dimensions of religious life: as a provider of instrumental rituals of the sacred sphere and as a community of believers. In the latter sense, during the first half of the seventeenth century, the Catholic Church obviously was reduced to a minority. Local estimates that point to very small groups of practicing Catholics (for example at Rotterdam), which were formerly looked at with some skepticism, may well reflect the actual size of the true community of Catholic believers after the breakdown of the old church structures and before the reconstruction of a new, socially meaningful church organization.

## RELIGIOUS RITUALS

On the other hand, popular religious rituals could continue on an autonomous track, far from Catholic ecclesiastical control, and there are many indications that they did so. The apologetic, confessional historiography of the nineteenth and the early twentieth centuries, together with allies such as the historian W.P.C. Knuttel and the folklorist P.J. Meertens, have drawn abundantly on the complaints of Reformed consistories and synods against "papistic superstitions," and on the repeated resolutions and decrees of the civil authorities, to demonstrate the long survival of religious practices considered Catholic: the use of rosaries, images of the saints, the holy cross, and the *agnus dei*, as well as sacred wells, pilgrimages, and the like, not to mention exorcisms, healing practices, and other rituals for the persuasion of the sacred. Whether as tokens of piety or of the instrumentalization of religion, it is obvious that such practices were slow to die out; indeed, they really did not die out at all, for they were picked up again by a revitalized Catholic Church during the latter part of the early modern period, or revived in a new, "pillarized" context during the nineteenth century. The recently published analytical and historical dictionary of pilgrimages in the Netherlands gives a marvelous example of the complex process of the survival, reinterpretation, and revitalization of traditional rituals.[5]

However, we should be very careful in ascribing such practices solely to one confession. On the one hand, each confession maintained or developed rituals that could be used somehow in an instrumentalized way. Some were quite close to former "Catholic" popular rituals, such as the use of the Bible as a sacred book among the Calvinists, the propensity to popular prophecy among the Mennonites, or the expressive funeral

---

[5] Peter Jan Margry and Charles Caspers, eds., *Bedevaartplaatsen in Nederland*, 4 vols. (Hilversum and Amsterdam, 1997–2004), in particular *Deel 1: Noord- en Midden-Nederland* (Amsterdam, 1997).

services among the Lutherans. Eighteenth-century Dutch Pietism even developed new rituals for sanctifying the gestures of everyday life, such as the important new ritual of drinking coffee or tea together, celebrated in 1740 with a hymn by the popular Calvinist minister Willem Schortinghuis.[6] In a general situation of confessional noncommitment, it may be assumed that such similarities favored the blurring of the confessional boundaries.

On the other hand, instrumental religion went its own way, and the recourse to the sacred did not bother very much about confessional identity. As late as 1713–14, a cattle plague in northern Holland drove the peasants of the region, Catholics and Protestants alike, to the sacred well of the Holy Virgin at Heiloo near Alkmaar, one of the oldest shrines in the Netherlands.[7] Yet it would be erroneous to postulate in this case an unbroken continuity since the Middle Ages. Of course, there was a formal continuity of the ritual, but its functions and meanings may have changed considerably in the meantime, as some engraved images of the holy place suggest. Whereas after the Reformation, the shrine became essentially a nonpublic place of gathering for Catholic believers, who could not exercise their religion publicly in town, it later recovered its former, semipublic function as a sacred instrument of healing, and the two functions continued henceforth on autonomous tracks. In fact, instrumental religion, including successful exorcisms, eventually was incorporated into the new pastoral strategy of the Catholic Church; thus the efficacy of the sacred became an apologetic argument for the Catholic faith, thereby giving it a new meaning for outsiders, while subjecting the faith of the insiders to various forms of ecclesiastical control.[8]

## CATEGORIES OF BELIEVERS

At least three categories of "believers" must be distinguished among the early modern consumers of Reformed Church services in the United Provinces: (1) the church members, who were admitted to the community of the Church by a public ceremony and entitled to partake in Holy

---

[6] Willem Schortinghuis, *Geestelike gesangen* (Groningen, 1740), 133.

[7] For this and other examples, and their interpretation, see Frijhoff, *Embodied Belief*, 111–36.

[8] See Willem Frijhoff, "Vraagtekens bij het vroegmoderne kersteningsoffensief," in *Religieuze volkscultuur. De spanning tussen de voorgeschreven orde en de geleefde praktijk*, Gerard Rooijakkers and Theo van der Zee eds. (Nijmegen, 1986), 71–98. And more generally for the evolution of pilgrimages, Marc Wingens, *Over de grens. De bedevaart van katholieke Nederlanders in de zeventiende en achttiende eeuw* (Nijmegen, 1994).

Communion; (2) the so-called *liefhebbers* or "devotees" of the Reformed Church, first identified by A. Th. van Deursen but visible everywhere as soon as one adopts the proper angle of view (i.e., men or women who called themselves "Reformed" and normally attended public church services, but without committing themselves to ecclesiastical discipline or theological orthodoxy); and (3) the occasional users, interested in consuming some religious commodity for momentary needs: a pious word, moral advice, bread from the poor relief authorities, a love of reading or singing together, some form of conflict mediation, or simply basic sociability. By now, these categories have been clearly singled out for the Reformed Church, but there is reason to believe that they are equally valid for the other churches and congregations, beginning with the Catholic Church and the Lutherans. But we should not forget to include in this pattern the more important Mennonite congregations, whose sharp numerical decline in a rather short time suggests both a variegated membership, comparable to that of the established churches, and more of a dependence on the practice of the "public church" than Mennonite orthodoxy has pretended in later times.

Among the Catholics, such a categorization would distinguish between active church members, simple communicants, and occasional consumers of "Catholic" ritual (i.e., instrumental forms of religion rooted in pre-Reformation practice, assimilated to more recent, Counter-Reformation forms of Catholic devotion, or ascribed to Catholicity owing to their symbolic or ritual character). This distinction should be coupled with an analysis of the various strategies of the Church authorities for the recuperation of their original flock. One might proclaim the "Dutchness" of the Catholic faith by stressing the continuity of the local Church organization and by purifying folk belief and ritual; this was roughly what the secular clergy did. One also might emphasize the new, "missionary" situation of the country, which required a Counter-Reformation strategy of international outlook, and renewed attention to the meaning of religious symbolism and the importance of ritual acting; this was the strategy of the regular clergy dominated by the Jesuits.

A two-sided analysis of this kind would account much better for the apparent fluctuations in Church membership, and for the penetration of Catholicism into different layers of the local populations, particularly as the "clandestine," nonpublic character of the Catholic Church organization in the Netherlands favored the involvement of lay elites in Church affairs and the growth of a particular lay piety. The best example is provided by the thousands of so-called *klopjes* (i.e., female laypersons), who acted as auxiliaries to the clergy, as quasi-nuns, or as small-scale entrepreneurs on the religion market (teaching, singing, nursing, making or selling religious objects, etc.).[9]

Still other, broader categorizations cut across such intraconfessional stratifications. In his seminal study on the Reformation in Utrecht, Benjamin Kaplan has argued that, contrary to the historical evolution in most of Europe, the real opposition in the early modern Netherlands was not between Catholics and Protestants but between Calvinists and Libertines, the Libertines being Calvinists who rejected essential aspects of Calvinism, including ecclesiastical discipline.[10] Although the Utrecht case is rather peculiar, the opposition between Calvinists and Libertines really is one of the major issues of early modern Dutch history, and one with tremendous consequences for later centuries, as structural oppositions of the same kind recur among new groups and creeds.

As Kaplan points out, three basic interpretations of the Calvinist– Libertine conflict have prevailed in Dutch historiography, but they are not mutually exclusive.[11] This first makes it essentially a political struggle between church and state, the Libertines being prominent among the urban magistrates. In this interpretation, the concept of a "public church" underpins the opposition, since the Libertine regents viewed the Calvinists as defenders of theocracy and therefore a potential threat to their authority. Hence, "the Libertines championed toleration for essentially political reasons." The second interpretation draws on the meaning of "belief" discussed earlier, since it stresses the intellectual oppositions between Catholics on the "right" (conservative) wing of the spectrum of beliefs and Calvinists on the "left" (progressive) wing, the Libertines being the Erastian, often irreligious humanists in the middle. The third interpretation, political and ecclesiological at the same time, sees the concept of the "public church" at the heart of the matter: While the Calvinists wanted the church to be an exclusive company of committed believers, the Libertines sought a comprehensive, open body that welcomed all persons to communion and full membership.

## CHURCH AND STATE

Kaplan argues that none of these three interpretations suffices, even in combination. In his view, the phenomenon has been too long considered

---

[9] See Marrit Monteiro, *Geestelijke maagden. Leven tussen klooster en wereld in Noord-Nederland gedurende de zeventiende eeuw* (Hilversum, 1996).

[10] Benjamin J. Kaplan, *Calvinists and Libertines. Confession and Community in Utrecht, 1578–1620* (Oxford, 1995).

[11] Kaplan, *Calvinists and Libertines*, 3–4.

in terms of a uniquely Dutch situation, whereas it was in fact "a local manifestation of a much broader struggle between the champions and opponents of confessionalism." Be that as it may, the important point for our purposes is that Kaplan's stress on the question of confessionalization helps to account for the religious evolution of the Netherlands in the long run.

In fact, given the religious situation of the United Provinces, the further development of confessionalism was permanently blocked for two reasons. First, the Reformed Church could not make an unequivocal and unanimous choice in favor of the public church model, which would have meant giving the "ruling church" (as the Reformed Church was currently called) the major prerogatives enjoyed by state churches elsewhere. Instead, Reformed opinion was divided between the idea of a church of the elect (*Ecclesia purior*), with a restricted social scope, and a full theocracy that would have subjected all citizens to the moral control of the Church. This latter option was unacceptable to the civil authorities because of the second reason: the coexistence of a flourishing variety of confessions, churches, and/or religious congregations, resulting from the very conditions in which the Dutch Republic had been created, and also to the culture of sociability and mediation that permeated the conviviality of everyday life, including the way power was exercised. The articles of the Union of Utrecht (29 January 1579), the treaty of union between the rebellious provinces, considered ever since to be the charter of the Dutch Republic, recognized freedom of conscience but let the individual provinces determine their own religious policy (article 13). In fact, all the provinces opted for the Reformed Church as the unique public church, but none of them went so far as to call into question the freedom of conscience that remained the foundation of the state's religious policy, notwithstanding the profound distrust toward the Catholics as potential allies of the Spanish enemy. The Great Assembly of the States-General (*Grote Vergadering*), convened in 1651 after the Peace of Westphalia to regularize the matters of the now formally independent Union, left religious affairs as they were, adding only the canons of the Synod of Dordrecht to the founding principles of the State: among Reformed believers, Calvinist orthodoxy had to be the only community authorized in public life.

One of the main problems of the Dutch Republic was, in fact, the ambiguous relationship between church and state at the very origin of the nation. Though, in retrospect, the Revolt of the Netherlands against Spain has often been interpreted as a rebellion for the sake of Calvinism, this historiographical option, which pervades much of the nineteenth- and twentieth-century literature on the Netherlands, suffers from a double bias. First, other Protestant communities did exist; some of them were older, and locally stronger, than the Calvinist community. Second, the Dutch Revolt had started as a fight for freedom, in an inextricable mix of political liberty and freedom of conscience. Humanists, Mennonites, some Lutherans, several smaller religious communities, but also an important group of moderate Catholics had fought for a concept of freedom that did not admit any encroachment on the very principle of a rather loose relation between the church and the state itself.

## CENTRIFUGALITY

Hence, dissenting opinions were structurally numerous, the more so as the horizontal, consensus-oriented forms of decision making encouraged free association of congenial spirits, if only for a free discussion on matters of political or religious interest.[12] This discussion culture pervaded all levels of early modern life in the Netherlands. Over and over again, pamphlet writers defended freedom of discussion (and of the forms of association that such a free discussion presumed) as the hallmark of political freedom. In fact, for a state that, destitute of a really hierarchical power structure, consisted of an assemblage of freely united groups, towns, and provinces, which intended to keep their autonomy of decision, despite the obvious balance of power in favor of the most wealthy, full discussion entailed the risk of dissolution. As Joke Spaans has shown for the city of Haarlem, the need to fight political centrifugality led the Haarlem town council to the active promotion of secular civic values going back before the religious divisions; for example, the council patronized the works of art extolling the civic courage of the undivided community of Haarlem burghers at the siege of Damietta during the Crusade of 1218–19.[13] On a national level, the need for *concordia* was inscribed in the emblem of the state itself, as it was on the façades of the town halls and on all of the public buildings.

In the past, historians have had very different views on the acceptance of the state, by inhabitants of the Dutch Republic, as an umbrella organization embodying their common interests. Roughly, some scholars have emphasized factors conducive to the unity of the state as a national

---

[12] The cultural characteristics of early modern Dutch society are discussed in: Willem Frijhoff and Marijke Spies, *1650: Hard-won Unity*, trans. Myra Heerspink Scholz (Assen and Basingstoke, 2004), originally *1650: Bevochten eendracht* (The Hague, 1999, 2nd ed. 2000).

[13] Joke Spaans, *Haarlem na de Reformatie. Stedelijke cultuur en kerkelijk leven, 1577–1620* (The Hague, 1989), 127–30; Willem Frijhoff, "Ritual Acting and City History: Haarlem, Amsterdam and Hasselt," in *Urban Rituals in Italy and the Netherlands. Historical Contrasts in the Use of Public Space, Architecture and the Urban Environment*, Heidi de Mare and Anna Vos eds. (Assen, 1993), 93–106.

community, while others have stressed the factors that thoroughly divided this would-be national community, making the Dutch Republic so peculiar on the European continent. Among the unifying elements we may count the centralizing role of international commerce, the colonial ventures, the demands of culture and education, the national science network, the great national myths (the Batavian myth, the Calvinist myth of the Dutch Israel, the reputation of the Nassau-Orange family as the founders of the state), and international policy and warfare. The image of division, on the contrary, stems mainly from the exercise of provincial and local autonomy, the discussion culture, and religious pluriformity, that is, precisely those elements that are at stake for our theme.[14]

During the two centuries of the rise of Dutch nationalism, dating from the end of the eighteenth century, the historical narrative has essentially emphasized the unity of the Dutch confederation: It has been seen as a single state unified from the beginning by virtue of the Union of Utrecht. The seven individual provinces composing this union were considered, as it were, potentially disturbing factors. In fact, they disturbed the union very often indeed by promoting local interests – the more so given the great weight of the province of Holland (and within it the great city of Amsterdam), by far the richest and the most populous of the seven.

Formally, the confederate republic of the seven United Provinces had a dual structure: Internally, the individual provinces were vested with sovereignty; externally, foreign policy was decided by the States-General as the common political body of the confederation. Although the States-General embodied Dutch sovereignty for the outside world, it exercised only the sovereignty delegated to them by the provincial states, the real bearers of sovereignty. To make things even more complicated, the provincial states shared sovereignty with the lower bodies whose deputies they were: the nobility, the numerous towns with voting rights, even a few representatives of ecclesiastical corporations. Of course, foreign policy needed money, an army, and some general measures to maintain, morally and politically, the unity of the state.

Initially, national feeling did not uniformly focus on the Dutch Republic as a whole: Lesser corporations such as the town or the province

---

[14] Another discussion point is the relationship between northern and southern Netherlands, separated from each other after the Unions of Utrecht and Arras, but striving for reunion until the Peace of Westphalia. How different were the southern Netherlands from their northern counterpart? Actually, one of the main discussion themes of Dutch history is the economic, cultural, and religious influence exerted by the huge migration of southerners to the north from the 1580s onward. As H. A. Oberman and H. Schilling have argued, the religious narrative of the migration has certainly benefited a posteriori from a form of theology of exile (*Exulantentheologie*) due to the numerous exiled intellectuals.

could be seen as the nation, while the federal state could at best claim the reputation to be the "fatherland," as it was considered overseas. Hence, in a series of articles – and now in a book on 's-Hertogenbosch[15] – the social historian Maarten Prak has brought forward the essentially corporative nature of the Dutch national community during the early modern period. On all the levels of community-building, corporative forms of association, of symbolic representation, and of social protection prevailed. They formed the real tissue of the Dutch state. Even the founding myths of the nation were written, or rewritten, in a provincial form or in a corporative spirit. The Batavian myth, for instance, carried the foundation of the Dutch Republic as a political body, endowed with democratic virtues and a congenial spirit of liberty, back to the German tribe of the Batavians, celebrated by Tacitus in classical times. But the myth was appropriated both by the province of Holland, as a legitimation of its central position in the Republic and its traditional leading qualities, and by the province of Gelderland, which, as a duchy, ranked first in the confederation. In fact, Gelderland had the better claim, since the *Insula Batavorum* [Betuwe] and the *oppidum Batavorum* [Nijmegen] of Roman times were situated within its boundaries. The Nijmegen Reformed minister Smetius spent a fair portion of his time attempting to prove the justice of Gelderland's claims.

The unstable equilibrium between political and religious motivations of national unity found a practical resolution in the power structure as it developed during the Dutch Revolt. Contrary to those who in the past have contended that the civil authorities of genuine Calvinist conviction would have accepted some form of theocracy, it must be emphasized that in the eyes of all the civil authorities, orthodox and liberal alike, the Reformed Church was, in the end, at the service of the state. Not a single Dutch alderman or burgomaster would have agreed to receive from the church authorities any orders for town policy, notwithstanding the fact that magistrates and ministers may have shared intellectual commitments, especially when the very foundations of religiously legitimated authority seemed to be at stake (as in the case of Spinozism and other alleged forms of a virtual atheism that seemed to undermine the foundations of society itself).

Even during the strongly Calvinist periods of town government in cities with an orthodox tradition – like Leiden, Middelburg, Utrecht, or (in the 1620s) Amsterdam, or the main towns in the inner provinces, with their strong grip on the countryside – the town hall always made its own

---

[15] Maarten Prak, *Republikeinse veelheid, democratisch enkelvoud: Sociale verandering in het Revolutietijdvak, 's-Hertogenbosch 1770–1820* (Nijmegen, 1999).

decisions. The church was considered to be a public part of the political domain that had to be controlled by the state; hence the presence of "political commissioners" in the meetings of the consistories and other congregations, in whatever sense they may have worked. This structural difference between the two levels of authority, and indeed the distrust of the church by the civil authorities, was expressed in social status. As Groenhuis and F.A. van Lieburg have convincingly shown, ministers did not form part of the ruling elites, at least not during the seventeenth century, and not really afterward either.[16] At most they could pretend to marriages within the sub-elite, but though the function of a minister could be a step up on the social ladder, theology remained the lowest of academic positions, unfashionable for a young man born of a regent family, just as it was for an aristocrat or a nobleman.

Virtually all of the conflicts between church and state ended with a victory of the civil authorities, though sometimes, as in the case of the Synod of Dordrecht (1618–19), church authorities succeeded in having the political authorities impose their view of orthodoxy. But in important conflicts concerning the orthodoxy of individual ministers, civil authorities never submitted to the will of the church. This is strikingly shown in the case of Balthasar Bekker (1634–98), the famous critic of demonology, who certainly was one of the most frequently criticized intellectuals of his time. In spite of his dismissal by the Reformed Synod in 1692, Amsterdam's town regents maintained him in his position and salary. The Bekker case shows that the civil authorities considered the church mainly as a public service organization, not as a body of knowledge. They were interested in "church," not really in "belief," and still less in "religion"; conversely, the Reformed Church identified itself as a "church" with authority on "belief," and tried again and again to eradicate those aspects of "religion" that were considered harmful to "church" and "belief" taken together.

### A RESEARCH PERSPECTIVE: THE CONCEPT OF "APPROPRIATION"

One of the key notions of the essays presented in this volume is "folk" belief, an idea closely related to the older concept of popular religion. This concept has gone through a long evolution since its appearance in

---

[16] G. Groenhuis, *Depredikanten: de sociale positie van gereformeerde predikanten in de Republiek der Verenigde Nederlanden voor ± 1700* (Groningen, 1977) and, for example, F.A. van Lieburg, *Profeten en hun vaderland: de geografische herkomst van de gereformeerde predikanten in Nederland van 1572 tot 1816* (Zoetermeer, 1996) and van Lieburg et al., eds., *Vier eeuwen domineesland* (Utrecht, 1997).

historical discourse during the 1960s and 1970s, first in France and later in the other countries of Europe. At first, sociologists (Serge Bonnet) and historians (Bernard Plongeron and his team) used it as a descriptive tool to account for other and older layers of religious belief and practice.[17] But, it was soon adapted to new historical views on the evolution of Christianity. As an historical notion going back to the early modern period itself (abbé Thiers[18]), it has been recognized as a strategic concept of the Counter-Reformation era, subsequently used by historians like Jean Delumeau and Robert Muchembled to identify a sociocultural process of differentiation between desirable and unlawful forms of religious belief and practice: the so-called Christianizing offensive that, within the framework of the "church," aimed at excluding from Christian "belief" all forms of popular "religion."[19] In the context of this discussion I have argued for the Netherlands that popular religion was, at least in Catholicism, not simply an undesirable form of religious expression but that it could be recovered as useful within an ecclesiastic strategy intended to stress the peculiar features of the Church, against the Calvinist discourse that tried to reduce any form of ritual to its narrowest expression.[20] But there is more. Given the only moderately hierarchized social structures of the Dutch Republic, the notions of "popular" and "folk" refer much more to cultural differences within specific social layers, groups, and indeed the individuals themselves than to differences between social groups. In fact, the concept of "popular" is first and foremost a narrative that tries to get hold of perceived differences in religious culture that escape the customary definitions of religion.

As such, this concept competes with other major narratives on religious differentiation during the early modern period. The first of these narratives was, of course, that of gradual *Protestantization* as a process

---

[17] For example, Serge Bonnet, *Sociologie politique et religieuse de la Lorraine* (Paris, 1972) and Bernard Plongeron, *Religion et sociétés en occident, XVIe–XXe siècles: recherches françaises et tendances internationales, 1973–1981* (Paris, 1982).

[18] Jean-Baptiste Thiers, *Traité des superstitions selon l'Écriture Sainte, les décrets des conciles et less entimens des saints pères, et des theologiens* (Paris, 1679).

[19] Jean Delumeau, Catholicism between Luther and Voltaire: A new view of the Counter-Reformation, trans. Jeremy Mosier (London, 1977), originally *Le catholicisme entre Luther et Voltaire* (Paris, 1971; 6ᵗʰ ed. 1996); and Robert Muchembled, *Popular Culture and Elite Culture in France, 1450–1750*, trans. Lydia G. Cochrane (Baton Rouge, 1985); originally *Culture populaire et culture des élites dans la France moderne (XVe–XVIIIe siècles)* (Paris, 1978).

[20] Willem Frijhoff, "Official and Popular Religion in Christianity: The Late Middle Ages and Early Modern Times (13th–18th Centuries)," in *Official and Popular Religion. Analysis of a Theme for Religious Studies*, eds. P.H. Vrijhof and J. Waardenburg (The Hague, 1979); idem, "Problèmes spécifiques d'une approche de la 'religion populaire' dans un pays de confession mixte: le cas des Provinces-Unies," in *La Religion Populaire; Paris, 17–19 octobre 1977* [Colloques internationaux du CNRS, 576] (Paris, 1979), 35–43.

of the internalization of belief, which was violently opposed to all forms of instrumentalization and eager to ban as quickly as possible all physical forms of ritual expression. This concept has been given, as it were, a second life in the acculturation thesis, brought forward by Robert Muchembled in his earlier works and almost immediately rejected by other historians.[21] *Confessionalization* may be considered as the most recent metamorphosis of this old concept. Olav Mörke has convincingly shown how delicate the application of this notion to the situation of the early modern Netherlands would be, although it might be able to illumine particular features of the Dutch situation.[22] In the strongest sense of the word, as applicable to Germany, confessionalization never could have been introduced into the Netherlands: There was no real uniformity of religion in society, not even within the churches themselves; moreover, in spite of its formal commitment to a public church, the state could not really be identified with any single religion, not even in the inland provinces where Calvinism had a much stronger grip on social life than in the province of Holland.

A second narrative explaining religious differentiation is that of religious *toleration*. Toleration is conceived essentially as a top-down movement involving either political permissiveness or an enlightened and intellectually legitimated form of religious relativism.[23] Traditionally, as early as the later seventeenth century, the narrative of toleration has been used to justify the diverging path of the Dutch. This narrative is particularly popular outside the Netherlands, especially in those countries where clericalism and laïcité oppose each other, such as France and still more Italy, where it has sometimes a distinctly political flavor; those who seek the roots of secular thought and indeed of laïcité often find them in the seventeenth-century Netherlands. In the final analysis, the stress on toleration is meant to justify the evacuation of religion from community life.

Recently, the Italian scholar Antonio Rotondó has rightly warned against an uncontrolled, overly extensive use of the notion of toleration. For Rotondó, that tolerance in the seventeenth-century sense encompasses three elements, but in changing combinations: philosophical

---

[21] Muchembled, *Popular Culture*; Jean Wirth, "Against the Acculturation Thesis," in *Religion and Society in Early Modern Europe, 1500–1800*, ed. Kaspar von Greyerz (London, 1984), 66–78; Stuart Clark, "French Historians and Early Modern Popular Culture," *Past & Present* 100 (1983): 62–99.

[22] Olav Mörke, "'Konfessionalisierung' als politisch–soziales Prinzip? Das Verhältnis von Religion und Staatsbildung in der Republik der Vereinigten Niederlande im 16. und 17. Jahrhundert," *Tijdschrift voor sociale geschiedenis* 16.1 (1990): 31–60.

[23] C. Berkvens-Stevelinck, J. Israel, and G.H.M. Posthumus Meyjes, eds., *The Emergence of Tolerance in the Dutch Republic* (Leiden, 1997); *Calvinism and Religious Toleration in the Dutch Golden Age*, eds. R. Po-chia Hsia and H. F. K. van Nierop (Cambridge, 2002).

irenicism, civil and ecclesiastical toleration, and freedom of conscience.[24] Since intellectual debate about toleration has dominated historiography until now, the flourishing of dissenting groups in the seventeenth-century Netherlands has traditionally been considered a proof of toleration in civil society.

A third narrative proposes a more horizontal view of religious differentiation: that of peaceful *coexistence*.[25] Against the reputation of the early modern Netherlands as a national community where peaceful coexistence prevailed from the very beginning, Jonathan Israel has argued that the provincial and town governments of the new Republic supported from the very beginning, with full conviction, the concept of a new public church, giving it every possible assistance, in hopes that the public church would dominate society, confessionalize the population, and overcome all rival confessional blocs.[26] Public criticism of the Reformed Church was not tolerated, at least not in the first decades of the Republic's existence. Yet from the beginning, the national community of the Netherlands was perceived by foreigners as a community where people of various confessions could coexist without being bothered for their faith. Even within the public church, various Reformed convictions coexisted, and the Church's inner identity was far from clear. The celebrated Dutch toleration was mostly little more than a precarious form of confessional coexistence.

Given the imperfection of all these narratives, I would propose here a fourth, supplementary narrative applicable to the Dutch social structures: the narrative of *group-bound appropriation* of the sacred and the *group satisfaction* of religious demands. Because of the growing accent on human agency in history, "appropriation" has become a key concept in cultural history.[27] The narrative of appropriation is inscribed in the very structures of Dutch society itself: Its basic sociability and its culture of mediation make appropriation the best way to account for how the Dutch shaped the actual forms of their religious group culture, from the bottom up, and in permanent dialogue with the supply of religious forms, contents, and meanings provided by the public church and by

---

[24] Antonio Rotondó, *Europe et les Pays-Bas. Évolution, réélaboration et diffusion de la tolérance aux XVIIe et XVIIe siècles. Lignes d'un programme de recherches* (Firenze, 1992).

[25] Willem Frijhoff, "Dimensions de la coexistence confessionnelle," in *The Emergence of Tolerance*, 213–37, and Frijhoff, *Embodied Beliefs*, 39–65.

[26] Jonathan Israel, "The Intellectual Debate about Toleration in the Dutch Republic," in *The Emergence of Tolerance*, 3–36.

[27] On the fate of this concept in historiography, see Willem Frijhoff, "Toeëigening: van bezitsdrang naar betekenisgeving," *Trajecta. Tijdschrift voor de geschiedenis van het katholiek leven in de Nederlanden* 6.2 (1997): 99–118.

the other religious mainstreams. Instead of giving a supply-side account of religion, through the factor "church," appropriation accounts for the transformation of religion into a religious structure adapted to the current values and norms of the civil society: It gives religious history back to the believers, since it stresses the active, dynamic dimension of any religious involvement.

The concept of appropriation gives a better insight into the famous propensity of the Dutch to separate from existing groups and to form new religious communities, such as the so-called conventicles of the seventeenth century. Instead of interpreting this as a form of sectarianism, we may see it as a peculiar way – adapted to Dutch social values and cultural models – of appropriating through group discussion and in a corporative spirit the religious message and its meanings and to secure its effects in social life. Similarly, the concept of appropriation, stressing the factor of demand, explains much better the apparent fluctuations in Dutch religious life. Whereas the demand for church provisions was low at the end of the sixteenth century, it rose considerably in the second half of the seventeenth and in the eighteenth century until reaching its zenith in the nineteenth and early twentieth centuries, when, in the context of the so-called process of pillarization, church affiliation became the dominant mode of Dutchness and the stereotypical view of Dutch Calvinism was born, together with a renaissance of Dutch Catholicism.

# CHAPTER IV

# Communal ritual, concealed belief: Layers of response to the regulation of ritual in Reformation England

CAROLINE J. LITZENBERGER

In 1551, John Hooper, fresh from his battle with Archbishop Cranmer over vestments and his consecration as bishop of Gloucester, prepared for the initial visitation of his new diocese. Twenty-five years later, in one of a number of nearly concurrent moves to define English Protestantism more fully, Archbishop Edmund Grindal prepared for a similar visitation of that same diocese as part of a general visitation of the province of Canterbury. In each case, the emphasis was on the reformation of ritual, and the concerns expressed were prompted by the condition of worship across the realm.

A year before his elevation to the bishopric, John Hooper had written to his friend and mentor, Heinrich Bullinger in Zurich, expressing his frustration with the pace of religious reform in England. "Partly through ignorance, and partly fascinated by the inveiglements of the bishops, and the malice and impiety of the mass-priests," the people were not turning to the new religion nearly fast enough.[1] Now Hooper was in a position to hasten the pace of reform and to promote and enforce policies associated with English Protestantism in at least one corner of the kingdom. As bishop, he would carry out his duties with impressive vigor and attention to detail.[2] He clearly believed, as did most of the other English reformers, that the reformation of ritual was

---

[1] John Hooper to Heinrich Bullinger, from London, 5 February 1550, in *Original Letters Relative to the Reformation*, trans. and ed. H. Robinson, vol. I, Parker Society (Cambridge, 1846), 76.

[2] Even before he became bishop, Hooper's wife, Anne, worried that his preaching schedule would exhaust him. Anne Hooper to Heinrich Bullinger, from London, 3 April 1551, in *Original Letters*, 107–8.

a key to establishing "true religion" among the clergy and people of England and thereby creating a kingdom with which God would be pleased. As Hooper and other reformers saw it, both the people and the realm needed to be freed from the tyranny of superstition before they could profess their faith in the "true religion of Christ." The way to that freedom was through the elimination of all ritual practices that might evoke beliefs associated with "papistry," and their replacement by reformed rituals. For the most part, the rituals used to define Reformed religion were those associated with public worship. However, some attention was also given to those that marked significant points in the lives of individuals, and those ritual acts of piety that individuals employed in the privacy of their homes. Once John Hooper was bishop of Gloucester, he would prepare for a thorough visitation of his diocese to replace the last vestiges of the traditional faith with the new religion. Having only recently returned from Zurich, he had a clear vision of that new faith, especially its ceremonies. The situation would be different in 1576. It would be the archbishop, rather than the diocesan bishop, who would initiate the visitation, and the purpose of the visitation would be to assess the progress of reform rather than to initiate it. However, in each case, the visit was prompted by the need to ensure that the latest religious policies were being faithfully implemented in the localities.

The process of gaining acceptance for those policies, however, was fraught with difficulties, as they were transmitted through the multiple layers of enforcement from the Crown and Privy Council to the individual layperson. Each layer served as a filtering prism, sifting and modifying provisions of religious change being transmitted to the next lower level. In addition, some layers became barriers, insulating and isolating those below from those above. In the process, otherwise public entities, such as parish communities and worship spaces, were sometimes redefined as private, when those within or below were shielded from both the policies and the penalties associated with the enforcement of religious conformity by such actions as parish leaders' refusals to respond to inquiries. Both Bishop Hooper's and Archbishop Grindal's visitations provide examples of the multiple layers of enforcement. Looking above these strata of episcopal and archiepiscopal authority, it becomes apparent that the vision of the "true church" presented in each set of visitation articles was in fact a variant of that promoted as the official religion of the realm: Each was more radically Protestant than the state religion. Looking toward the lower layers, we first encounter local parishes – the clergy and parish leaders, as well as the corporate entity itself – and finally individuals, both clergy and laypeople. At these lower levels, the nature of compliance was as varied as the shapes and colors created by a kaleidoscope.

Two theories concerning ritual have influenced this work significantly. Hooper's mentor, Heinrich Bullinger (along with his predecessors, Ullrych Zwingli in Zurich and Andreas Karlstadt in Germany, and the leaders of the English Reformation), believed that ritual practice shaped or at least greatly influenced belief. Of course, their first goal was the elimination of anything that would distract worshipers from focusing on the Word of God, including decorations of various kinds, but especially images.[3] However, there was more to Reformed worship than the absence of pernicious distractions. Edward Muir has suggested that what distinguished the Protestants' approaches to ceremonies in the sixteenth century was their emphasis on the meaning of ritual, and further that in the absence of images, "Protestant ritual . . . provided clarity of meaning through the declaration of seemingly unambiguous words [albeit] at the cost of visual impoverishment."[4] Reformers, such as John Hooper, thus revised ritual space and reformed rites so that, by entering into the discipline of participating regularly in particular rituals, people would come to understand and accept beliefs consistent with those rituals.[5]

However, Catherine Bell's comments on enforcement of ritual also pertain. When those in authority impose rituals on the people as did the sixteenth-century Protestant reformers, then those ceremonies do not necessarily reveal the actual beliefs of the subjected portion of society. Rather, through "complicity, struggle [and] negotiation" the powerless agree to accept a form of the official policy, a form that they then appropriate and modify.[6] I would suggest that this process is inherent in the internalization essential for any substantive change in religious beliefs. Furthermore, Bell's theory suggests that it is in the liminal areas between official public policy and unofficial public and private ritual actions where one can discern the effects of those policies and the actual beliefs of the people most clearly. New or modified rituals not only changed people's pious practices but were in turn changed by those same practices. In addition, as noted earlier, the actual rituals in use were sometimes concealed when parish clergy and lay leaders in concert resisted all pressure to respond fully to visitation inquiries. Such action

---

[3] Heinrich Bullinger, "The Ceremonial Laws of God," in *The Decades of Henry Bullinger*, ed. T. Harding (Cambridge, 1850), 3:127–30; Carlos Eire, *War against the Idols: The Reformation of Worship from Erasmus to Calvin* (1986; repr., Cambridge, 1990), 60–88, passim.

[4] Edward Muir, *Ritual in Early Modern Europe* (Cambridge, 1997), 155–98.

[5] This also describes Thomas Cranmer's understanding of the efficacy of liturgy. Diarmaid MacCulloch, *Thomas Cranmer: A Life* (New Haven, CT, and London, 1996), 224.

[6] Catherine Bell, *Ritual Theory, Ritual Practice* (Oxford and New York, 1992), 189–91.

would require a coordinated, unified stance by all leaders of a parish, but there is evidence that such a strategy was occasionally adopted. In this way, parish leaders could create a wall of secrecy between the official visitors and their parishioners, thus effectively redefining otherwise public spheres, such as their parish communities, as private. Hence, the degree to which religious rituals imposed by the Crown and Council were modified in the course of their implementation, and the nature of those modifications, ultimately defined English Protestantism more accurately than either official proclamations and statutes or theological treatises.

Two discreet periods – Hooper's episcopate in the early 1550s and the period of the 1570s – offer an opportunity to examine the layers of enforcement and response at times when official religious policy was clearer and differences between policy and practice were greater than at any other times during the English Reformation. In each period, the authorities conducted a thorough visitation of the diocese of Gloucester, offering a window into the realities of the enforcement of religious conformity, revealing the complexity of responses at two crucial times in the history of Reformation England. Established English religion became more radically Protestant in the early 1550s under Edward VI (1547–1553) than it would ever be again, and Bishop Hooper, in his visitation of the diocese of Gloucester in 1551, defined and at least attempted to enforce what was arguably the most radically Protestant set of rituals in Edwardian England. Less effective and significantly less radical bishops followed Hooper, but then a fervent reformer and leader of the Vestiarian Controversy, Laurence Humphrey, became dean of Gloucester Cathedral in 1571. He and one of his most zealous prebendaries, Arthur Saule, represented Archbishop Grindal in the metropolitical visitation of the diocese in 1576.[7] The early 1570s had been a time of definition for the embryonic Church of England, and the need to communicate and enforce the resulting policies prompted the later visitation.

＊ ＊ ＊ ＊ ＊

In Gloucestershire, as elsewhere, the series of contrasting and at times conflicting religious policies during the last years of Henry VIII's reign and the early years under Edward appear to have been honored as often in their breach as in their observance. Perhaps the shifts in acceptable belief and practice confused people as some historians have

---

[7] Caroline Litzenberger, *The English Reformation and the Laity: Gloucestershire, 1540–1580* (Cambridge, 1997), 130–1.

speculated. However, the laity in particular may have welcomed the lack of consistency, hoping to be allowed to continue their familiar and traditional rituals in the absence of clear, consistent directives to the contrary. Thus, while some parishes probably purchased the English Bible "of the largest volume" when ordered to do so in the late 1530s, the expense was too great for most, and they still did not have the requisite tome some ten years later. In 1548, they may have purchased the Order of Communion (in English), and a year later they probably obtained the Book of Common Prayer as required by statute, but new problems emerged.[8] How did the clergy use these books? Could worshipers distinguish the new Reformed liturgies from the familiar traditional rites? The Royal Injunctions of 1547, the Order of Communion of 1548, and the Prayer Book of 1549 were all intended as steps in the process of establishing Protestantism in the hearts, minds, and institutions of Edwardian England, but how could those responsible for official religious policy ensure the faithful implementation of what they had declared to be the "true religion of Christ"? This was the problem that faced everyone in the English ecclesiastical hierarchy, and typically, visitations (whether episcopal, archiepiscopal or royal) were the chosen means of inquiry and enforcement.

Through the 1540s in the diocese of Gloucester, religious practices were allowed to drift, albeit in a generally Protestant direction. Newly formed in 1541, the diocese lacked the infrastructure and the resources for efficient implementation of the state religion. In addition, it lacked effective leadership. The first bishop, John Wakeman, had been the last abbot of Tewkesbury Abbey and may not have welcomed religious change, in which case the condition of the diocesan administration would have provided a convenient excuse for less-than-vigorous enforcement of reform under Edward. The see was then vacant from his death in December 1549 to the time of John Hooper's consecration in March 1551.

Indeed, few people in Gloucestershire had even begun to embrace the new religion when Hooper became their bishop, but he was not daunted. In typically vigorous fashion, he set out to conquer every obstacle and bring his people and his diocese to a fully reformed state, similar to that which he had witnessed in Zwinglian Zurich in the 1540s.[9] He

---

[8] For a more detailed discussion of the acquisition of the required Protestant service books by parishes in Edwardian England, see Ronald Hutton, "The Local Impact of the Tudor Reformations," in *The English Reformation Revised*, ed. C. Haigh (Cambridge, 1987), 114–38.

[9] John Hooper to Heinrich Bullinger, from Strasbourg, 27 January [1546], *Original Letters*, 33–5; Charles Nevinson, "Biographical Notices," in John Hooper, *Later Writings of Bishop Hooper*, ed. C. Nevinson (Cambridge, 1852), vii–xii.

thought he knew what to do and how to do it. He would be vigilant; he would preach regularly; he would examine every detail of public and private ritual to which he could gain access. He would root out superstition and ignorance in all its manifestations and replace them with "true religion." By the summer following his consecration, he had made arrangements for the first episcopal visitation of his diocese and had issued arguably the most detailed set of articles, injunctions, and inquiries seen in sixteenth-century England. His interests ranged from institutional concerns such as clerical qualifications and behavior, and matters relating to parish worship, to the pious practices of the laity, especially during important points in their lives such as childbirth and death. Predictably, he inquired as to whether the Mass was still being said in any parish, but he also wanted to know about less obvious, less public actions, such as the conduct of midwives and the provisions in wills.

Hooper's vision of Reformed ritual included the actions of the clergy, the characteristics of the space where worship took place, and the behavior of the laity. With regard to the clergy, he seems to have been particularly concerned that they not incorporate any actions into the liturgy that would evoke memories of the Latin Mass. Thus, he admonished his priests not to wash their hands or fingers after the Gospel, not to shift "the booke from one place unto another," not to show "the Sacrament openly before the distribution," and not to "kiss their vestments, booke, chalice, corporas, or any thing about the Table as they did in their Mass."[10] Rather, "the minister in the use of the Communion and prayers... [was to] turne his face towards the people" and "reade and use the Common Prayers, lessons, Homilies, and other such service... plainly, distinctly, openly,... solemnly, honourably and devoutly." With a typical eye for detail and anticipating one specific potential problem, he went further. He directed that

if the Psalmes spoaken by the minister cannot be heard in the lowest part of the church, or els if the curate or minister have so small and soft a brest or voice that he cannot be heard... then every [one] of them [should] come into the body of the church, and there reverendly, plainly as is afore spoaken, see that all things be read in such sorte that all the people may understande.

This latter provision reflects yet another aspect of Hooper's concern: his insistence that the words spoken by the clergy always be audible to the worshipers. He addressed this in several different ways, but his

<hr>

[10] "A True Copy of Bishop Hooper's Visitation Booke, made by Him. AD 1551, 1552," Dr. Williams's Library, Morice MS 31L, Item 3 [hereafter "Visitation Booke,"], 5, 14.

real concern was to ensure that the clergy were in fact following the rites prescribed in the Book of Common Prayer. There was to be no possibility that the congregation might be able to imagine that they were attending a Mass, but further, they were to be edified by the Word of God and the words of the liturgy as established by the Crown.[11]

If the clergy's liturgical actions were important to Bishop Hooper, the nature of the space within which worship occurred was no less crucial. He wanted to be sure that all objects, images, and pieces of liturgical furniture that might distract the worshipers from the Word of God or remind them of the old religion – of old "superstition" practices – were removed. Images on walls were to be obliterated or at least concealed beneath layers of whitewash, because they were "contrary and injurious to the honour of Christ." Meanwhile, images in stained glass were apparently viewed as less pernicious. When glass windows were repaired the new glass was not to have any image of a saint painted on it, but Hooper did not insist on the removal of existing glass in good repair.[12] Meanwhile, all "tabernacles, . . . [Easter] sepulchres, . . . rood-lofts, and such other monuments, signs, tokens, reliques, leavings, and remembrances . . . [of] superstition" were to be taken down and removed. Altars were to be replaced with tables that were in turn to be covered with a single, simple cloth. In addition, however, to ensure that no one could mistake a communion table for an altar, the area where the altar had stood was to be lowered to the level of the nave where the people assembled for worship, or alternatively, the communion table was to be placed in the nave. Finally, all side chapels (and side altars), "partitions and separations" within churches were to be removed to create a worship space without any closures or separations between the ministers and the people, and to eliminate areas that had previously been dedicated to particular saints or set aside specifically for masses for the dead.[13]

However, Bishop Hooper did not give all his attention to clerical actions and liturgical space; he also was concerned about the laity. Thus, for instance, they were to worship regularly, both on Sundays and on specified weekdays, and were to behave with decorum during services. More specifically, they were not to "talke, walke, molest, unquiet or grieve the minister . . . [while he was presiding over] the Divine Service . . . with any noise, brute cryes, clamours, playes, games, sports, dancing or such like." They were not to use "any primers, or bookes of Prayers

[11] "Visitation Booke," 6, 7.
[12] M. Aston, *England's Iconoclasts: 1. Laws against Images* (Oxford, 1988), 260 n, 404.
[13] "Visitation Booke," 2, 6, 9, 11.

in Laten, . . . or any beades, knotts, [or] reliques," and in addition, no man was to "pray in the church his private and own prayer while the Common Prayer is a saying."[14] However, Hooper's concerns with lay piety were not confined to parish churches or regular worship services. He also wanted to know if any "man or woman maintaine openly or privately . . . the defence of transubstantiation," and if anyone kept any "monuments of superstition" in their churches or in private houses.[15]

Moving into the interstices between the public and the private, he also addressed those rituals that were associated with illness, preparation for death, and dying. He admonished the clergy that when they brought the Sacrament to the sick, they were not to give any sign to the people that would cause the latter to honor it in any way. The ministers were not to cover their heads with their surplices, accompany the Sacrament with any light, or "suffer the people to kneele" when they came into the house. In addition, if the sick person wanted to be anointed before death, the minister was to discourage the person from putting any trust in the oil. Furthermore, a bell could be tolled to let people know that someone was deathly ill and in need of their prayers, but once death had come, the bell was to be rung only once. To ring it more than once might prompt the hearers to pray for the dead, which would be an acknowledgment of the existence of Purgatory. Furthermore, the minister was not to allow anyone to place a cross or any other object secretly with the body for burial, and no offices for the dead were to be said after the corpse was buried.[16]

Turning to rituals associated with birth, he inquired into the words and actions of midwives. He wanted to know whether they "use any prayers or invocations, unto any saint, saving to God in Christ, for the deliverance of the woman, and whether they do use any salt, herbs, water, wax, clothes, girdles, reliques, or any such other like thing, or superstitious meanes." Here he was anxious to ensure that even in childbirth no one was invoking the saints, especially those feminine images of the divine that had previously been a source of comfort and courage to women giving birth. However, he was also determined to ensure that midwives were not baptizing infants, even in an emergency, as they had before the advent of Protestantism.[17]

In all his inquiries and directives Hooper had a common goal: to reform the public rituals of the English church, and by that means to bring the people to "true religion." His energy and his penchant for detail led

---

[14] "Visitation Booke," 9, 11, 12, 13.
[15] "Visitation Booke," 9, 13.
[16] "Visitation Booke," 10, 15, 16.
[17] "Visitation Booke," 12.

him to include aspects of the material culture of worship and nuances of gesture and presentation that other bishops seem to have ignored. While few sets of episcopal visitation articles survive from Edward's reign, among those that do, only Bishop Nicholas Ridley of London came close to Hooper in the degree of reform advocated. Ridley did require that every parish remove its altars and install a communion table. However, not even he ordered the level of the floor beneath the table lowered to the level of the nave, as did Hooper. In addition, his visitation did not traverse nearly as many layers of ritual as did Hooper's.[18] Among those for whom records survive, Hooper was the only bishop to address the conduct of midwives or the precise language used in wills. From the extant evidence, then, Hooper appears to have been both the most radical and the most vigorous episcopal agent of religious change in Edwardian England.

Several historians have asserted that the sluggish acceptance of Protestantism in England was owing to a prevalent policy of removing the old religion without replacing it with the new. It was after all much easier to define what was forbidden than to educate people in the complexities of Protestantism. However, such an analysis overlooks the strategy of introducing new rituals as a vehicle for inculcating the new beliefs into the populace. Hooper was unstinting in his efforts both to eradicate traditional faith and practice and to implement reform. To what degree was he effective?

Within the layers of liturgical practice associated with parishes, reformed worship spaces and rituals only became the standard in a few parishes, even after Hooper's visitation. While only fragmentary evidence survives, it appears that Tewkesbury and Minchinhampton were probably typical. Despite the presence of Robert Erean, a learned and reform-minded curate, the Tewkesbury parish leadership seems to have done little to implement reforms. Erean may indeed have presided over worship services that were in accordance with Hooper's directives in terms of priestly words and actions. However, the lay leaders of the parish do not seem to have made any significant changes in the worship space, and extant evidence indicates that they retained the accoutrements of traditional worship prohibited by Hooper. Minchinhampton similarly seems to have held onto its vestiges of the old religion, and with Gilbert Bourne, the future Marian bishop of Bath and Wells as rector, that parish probably wrapped itself in a layer of silence, creating a barrier of privacy between Bishop Hooper and the actual ritual life of

---

[18] "Ridley's Injunctions for London Diocese, 1550," in *Visitation Articles and Injunctions of the Period of the Reformation*, W.H. Frere and W.M. Kennedy eds., Alcuin Club Collections, vol. 15 (London and New York, 1910), 243–4.

the parish.[19] Meanwhile, the parish of St. Michael's, Gloucester, chose a very different response to Hooper's promotion of Protestantism. There the parish leaders complied fully and promptly with every aspect of the bishop's articles of visitation. They dismantled their rood-loft and side chapels; they sold the wood from those structures of superstition, along with prohibited books, vestments, and other remains of the discredited past. They removed their altar and replaced it with a communion table, but they did not stop there. They even paid two men 4s. to remove the dirt from the area where the altar had stood, to lower that area to the level of the nave in compliance with Hooper's order.[20] However, such compliance was the exception, not the rule.

If parishes were reluctant participants in Hooper's program of reform, then it is probably not surprising that Gloucestershire testators were as well, despite their bishop's best efforts. Hooper may have hoped, and even believed, that by insisting on the reformation of ritual at all levels, in all layers of the ecclesiastical and social structure from the most public to the most private, he would actually be able to convert the people to Protestantism. His visitation injunctions even included a prohibition against the use of the most traditional form of soul bequest in wills. However, despite his most vigorous efforts, he does not appear to have been successful. In addition to the resistant behavior of some parish leaders, testators from all levels of society also revealed a reluctance to embrace the new beliefs. They might have gone through at least some of the motions of public Protestant ritual, but such actions should not necessarily be read as evidence of their beliefs. While traditional soul bequests nearly vanished from wills between the time of Hooper's visitation and the end of Edward's reign, they were not replaced by Protestant declarations. Instead, those leaving wills opted for ambiguity, apparently choosing to "duck for cover" in the face of Hooper's vigorous promotion of Protestantism, concealing their true beliefs behind one last screen of privacy. Not even his thoroughgoing efforts in the name of Protestantism could force the people to convert.[21]

\* \* \* \* \*

The years between the visitations in 1551 and 1576 were a time of dramatic changes in religious policies and in the ritual manifestations of

---

[19] Litzenberger, *The English Reformation and the Laity*, 100.

[20] Gloucestershire Record Office [hereafter GRO], P154/14 CW 1/5.

[21] For a more complete analysis of the religious content of early modern English wills, see Caroline J. Litzenberger, "Local Responses to Religious Changes: Evidence from Gloucerstershire Wills," in *Religion and the English People, 1500–1640: New Perspectives/ New Voices*, ed. E.J. Carlson (Kirksville, MO, 1998), 245–70.

those policies in England, and this may be best exemplified by looking further at the actions of St. Michael's, Gloucester. Prominently placed at the geographical and political center of the city, this parish appears at least at first blush to have been the model of conformity, working diligently to adhere to the latest official pronouncements, no matter how much they differed from the previous policies. The dramatic changes they made immediately following Bishop Hooper's visitation in 1551 exemplify this strategy, as do their actions two years later. Then they spent 6s. 8d. for dirt and labor to raise the altar area to support a proper Catholic altar, following the accession of Mary (1496–1558) to the throne and the concomitant restoration of Catholicism. At that time they also purchased vestments and Mass books, paid for the creation of a new altar, rebuilt the rood-loft and had a carver begin work on the crucifix and the statues of the Virgin Mary and John, which would adorn it. In 1558, just months before Mary's death, the statues were put in place, only to be removed within the year following Elizabeth's accession to the throne, probably in response to the royal visitation that accompanied the official reestablishment of Protestantism.[22]

By the time Elizabeth (1533–1603) became queen, Gloucestershire actually was without any active leadership at the diocesan level. The Marian bishop, James Brookes, had died a few months earlier. Unfortunately, no replacement would be named for nearly three years, and then the choice was anything but auspicious. Richard Cheyney was chosen to fill the last remaining seat on the early Elizabethan episcopal bench.

Historians have characterized Bishop Cheyney variously as "a round man [placed] in a square hole," "pathetically weak [and] irresolute," and "dreamy."[23] However, his contemporaries were even harsher in their condemnations. A priest in his charge labeled Cheyney "an infidill of his religion" in 1570.[24] A few years later, his one-time protégé Edmund Campion, the Jesuit missionary to England and future martyr, was at least as critical, telling the bishop he was "the hatred of heretics, the pity of Catholics, the talk of the people, the sorrow of your friends,

---

[22] GRO, P154/14 CW 1/6–1/11, passim. Cf. Eamon Duffy, *The Stripping of the Altars: Traditional Religion in England, c. 1400–c. 1580* (New Haven, CT, and London, 1992), 563–4, for further discussion of the centrality of the crucifix in the lay piety of Marian Catholicism.

[23] Frederick O. White, *Lives of the Elizabethan Bishops* (London, 1898), 174; F. Douglas Price, "Bishop Bullingham and Chancellor Blackleech: A Diocese Divided," *Transactions of the Bristol and Gloucestershire Archaeological Society* 91 (1973): 175; Patrick Collinson, *The Religion of Protestants: The Church in English Society, 1559–1625* (Oxford, 1982), 63.

[24] GRO, GDR, vol. 9, 9.

the joke of your enemies."[25] In sharp contrast to John Hooper, Richard Cheyney was typically a rather passive presence in his diocese. He allowed a very corrupt chancellor to preside over the diocesan consistory court through most of his episcopate. He responded to most instances of nonconformity by ignoring them or at most by asking the Privy Council for guidance and thus postponing any action. He only occasionally asserted his episcopal authority with any vigor or energy, and then the beliefs he was promoting were usually significantly more traditional than those espoused in official religious policies, while those he rose up to punish were typically more reformed. His general policy seems to have been one of occasional, selective enforcement of the precepts of established Protestantism. In most such instances, he carefully chose to enforce those portions of religious policy that were consistent with his own beliefs, or which at least did not impinge on those beliefs, and to discipline most vehemently those whose actions were so radically Protestant as to be outside the bounds of acceptability.[26]

Bishop Cheyney's episcopal administration affected the ways in which parishes, as well as individuals and less formal groups of co-religionists, received and conformed to official policy regarding public ritual. The pattern of Cheyney's responses to official policy on the one hand, and to nonconformity on the other, reveal a complex strategy of benign neglect, combined with occasional assertions of his authority, which effectively created a screening protective layer of enforcement between the Crown and the diocese. Those so inclined could have taken advantage of this apparent opportunity for concealment offered by their bishop. However, that same layer interposed between the Crown and the diocese also hid official changes in religion from the parishes and people in Bishop Cheyney's charge. Through his administrative style, he thus created a screen of privacy, which not only protected him from his superiors, but also served to protect those within from the prying eyes of higher authority. In addition, by hindering the flow of information between the Crown and those worshiping within this artificially created "private" region, Bishop Cheyney may have weakened local popular pressure for reform.

In addition, during the early years of Elizabeth's reign, the absence of vigorous episcopal leadership in the diocese of Gloucester was matched

---

[25] "Campion the Martyr to Cheney, Anglican Bishop of Gloucester," *The Rambler: A Catholic Journal and Review*, n.s., 8 (1857): 61–2.

[26] For further discussion of Richard Cheyney's episcopate, see Caroline J. Litzenberger, "Richard Cheyney, Bishop of Gloucester, an Infidel in Religion?" *Sixteenth Century Journal* 25 (1994): 567–84.

by a lack of clarity in the Crown's religious policies. In some cases, specific policies were even in conflict with each other. For instance, one aspect of Reformed ritual that was the subject of much confusion and contention concerned the nature of communion bread. Unfortunately, two official publications issued in the first months of the reign contained conflicting directives on this eucharistic element: The Royal Injunctions of 1559 called for wafer-bread, while the Book of Common Prayer declared that bread that "is usual eaten at table" was to be used.[27] This caused so much debate in the diocese of Norwich that Bishop John Parkhurst wrote to Archbishop Parker to express his concern and ask for advice. The archbishop's response was similar to that given to the bishop of Chester by the Privy Council some years later. In each case, the bishop was urged to allow both practices to continue unhindered, as Parker said, "for peace and quitenes heare and theare."[28] Bishop Cheyney similarly discovered a lack of conformity in communion bread, and based on his behavior in numerous other instances one might have expected him to dither and ask Archbishop Parker or the Privy Council for help and guidance, as had Parkhurst. However, in this instance he did not; rather, he forced his priests to use traditional wafers, bringing them before his court to enforce his order.[29] The lack of definition, which was a hallmark of early Elizabethan Protestantism, thus provided Cheyney with the latitude to enforce his own interpretation of official policy.

As a result of Bishop Cheyney's administrative style, the diocese of Gloucester lagged behind most of the rest of the realm when official policy began to change in the late 1560s. At that time, the Church of England began to define itself further through semiofficial pronouncements, parliamentary statutes, and archiepiscopal visitations. The metropolitical visitation in 1576 was one of the later acts undertaken to enforce the emerging religious policy.

The visitation of 1576 would, however, not be as detailed as that conducted by Hooper in 1551. Hooper's interest in private as well as public aspects of ritual, in fact, stands in sharp contrast to much of what

---

[27] P.L. Hughes and J.F. Larkin, eds., *Tudor Royal Proclamations*, vol. 2 (New Haven, CT, and London, 1964), 131; W.K. Clay, ed., *Liturgical Services: Liturgies and Occasional Forms of Prayer* (Cambridge, 1847), 198.

[28] John Parkhurst to Matthew Parker, 6 June 1574, from Ludham; Matthew Parker to John Parkhurst, 14 June 1574, from Lambeth, in *The Letter Book of John Parkhurst, Compiled during the Years, 1571–5*, ed. R.A. Houlbrooke, Norfolk Record Society Series, vol. 43 (Norwich, 1974/5), 243, 247; K.R. Wark, *Elizabethan Recusancy in Cheshire*, Chetham Society, 3rd ser., vol. 19 (Manchester, 1971), n.18.

[29] GRO, GDR, vol. 24, 709, 722; vol. 40, fols. 160v, 167.

happened in the cause of establishing Protestantism during Elizabeth's reign. With a monarch who eschewed "windows into men's souls," the enforcement of Elizabethan religious policy was tightly focused on public ritual. When the Crown and the Church moved to clarify the limits of acceptability in English religion in the late 1560s and 1570s, they focused on ritual and related public behavior. Thus, they vigorously prosecuted those who were recusant, while people who attended services regularly but did not receive Easter communion were frequently ignored or reported but not punished, unless other more public behavior brought them to the attention of the authorities.[30] Meanwhile, the authorities were much less likely to concern themselves with private or semiprivate religious rituals, such as those surrounding childbirth or those associated with death and dying, than had Bishop Hooper.

Nonetheless, the archiepiscopal visitation in 1576 made the boundaries of approved liturgy more evident in the diocese of Gloucester than had been the case earlier in Elizabeth's reign. As with Hooper's visitation articles, so too Grindal's articles addressed clerical and lay actions, as well as the accoutrements of worship and other characteristics of the worship space. Similarly, they included prohibitions against some actions that had not been forbidden previously. For instance, priests were not to wear copes. Rather, they were to wear surplices (but only when presiding over rituals within the church itself). On the other hand, for the perambulation of the boundary of the parish, typically conducted during Rogationtide, ministers were not to wear surplices or any other special garment or vestment, and additionally there were to be no banners or handbells, and no "staying at crosses."[31] Furthermore, they were to obtain a communion cup with cover, and the cover was to be used for the distribution of the bread. Priests and people alike also were to refrain from any action or rite not specifically mentioned in the Book of Common Prayer. These included "crossing or breathing over the sacramental bread and wine, or shewing the same to the people to be worshipped and adored," using "any oil and chrism, tapers, spattle [spittle], or any other popish ceremony in the ministration of the sacrament of Baptism."[32] Additionally, they were not to promote, "maintain or defend any heresies,

---

30 1 Elizabeth, c. 1, passim. Cf. John LaRocca, "Time, Death and the Next Generation: The Early Elizabethan Recusancy Policy, 1558–1574," *Albion* 14 (1982): 103–17, passim.

31 "Articles to be enquired of within the Province of Canterbury" [hereafter "Grindal's Visitation Articles"], in *The Remains of Edmund Grindal*, ed. W. Nicholson (Cambridge, 1843), 168. Not all were happy with the official prohibition, however. Alice Huddleston, wife of John, gent., called the curate a "hunter" because he did not wear a surplice in perambulation. GRO, GDR, vol. 40, fol. 51.

32 "Grindal's Visitation Articles," 159–60.

false opinions, or popish errors," or say mass, either "openly or privately." However, in contrast to Hooper, not all prohibitions were against Catholic or traditional practices. Priests and laypeople, alike, also were to refrain from keeping "any secret conventicles, preachings, lectures, or readings contrary to law," an obvious attempt to curtail some of the more radical Protestant actions.[33]

In addition to the previously mentioned activities, which involved both the clergy and the laity, other regulated actions pertained exclusively to the laity. The people were to refrain from walking, talking, "or otherwise unreverently behav[ing] themselves in the church," or using "any gaming or pastime abroad or in any house, or sit[ting] in the streets or churchyard, or in any tavern or ale-house, upon the Sunday or other holy day, in the time of Common Prayer."[34] Similarly, they were not to sell goods during services, and there were to be no "wanton gestures," dancing or other antics during services. Popish practices, on the other hand, were prohibited at all times, not just during services. Hence, praying in English or Latin "upon beads ... or upon any superstitious popish Primer" and bequeathing "any jewels, plate, ornaments, cattle or grain ... for the erections or finding [funding] of any obits, ... torches, lights, tapers, lamps, or any such like use, [were] now by law forbidden."[35] (Of course, these prohibitions were not new, but apparently they were not being observed consistently.) On the other hand, the people were to receive communion at least three times a year, including once during the Easter season, and all householders were "faithfully and diligently [to] endeavour themselves to resort with their children and servants to their parish church ... on holy days, and chiefly upon the Sundays, to Morning and Evening Prayer." Once there, they were to "abide orderly and soberly, ... reverently and devoutly giving themselves thereof, and occupying themselves at times convenient in private prayer."[36]

Predictably, the worship space was to reflect the priorities of the reformed liturgy, especially the emphasis on the Word. Thus, it was to be devoid of all images and other hints of superstition. Gone were the statues, wall paintings, images in glass, altars, and rood-lofts so recently refurbished during the Marian Restoration of Catholicism. In their place were excerpts from scripture painted on the walls, especially the Lord's Prayer, the Apostle's Creed, and verses from the Psalms. A table of the

---

[33] "Grindal's Visitation Articles," 160, 164–5.
[34] "Grindal's Visitation Articles," 170, 175.
[35] "Grindal's Visitation Articles," 169, 173.
[36] "Grindal's Visitation Articles," 169–70, 172.

Ten Commandments was typically hung above the communion table, and the Queen's arms were often suspended from the top of the rood screen where the crucifix and the images of the Virgin Mary and John had been. And yes, there was to be "a comely and decent table, standing on a frame, for the Holy Communion, with a fair linen cloth to lay upon the same, and some covering of silk, buckram, or other such like, for the clean keeping thereof," and also "a convenient pulpit well placed." Furthermore, each parish was to have a Prayer Book and psalter, an English Bible "of the largest volume," two volumes of the Homilies, and the *Paraphrases* of Erasmus in English.[37]

Some parishes acted in anticipation of the visitation, whitewashing their walls to conceal forbidden images, and in some cases (both in Gloucestershire and elsewhere) also whitewashing at least the faces of the images in their stained glass to the same end, before the arrival of the archiepiscopal visitors.[38] In fact, a significant majority of the laypeople and clergy in the diocese either had similarly anticipated the approved standards for Reformed ritual or at least were not detected by the archbishop's visitors, given the evidence contained in the visitation records. However, there were people and parishes who still openly resisted the pressure to conform to established Protestantism. Many parishes were required to replace their chalices with communion cups following the archiepiscopal visitation, and a surprising number also had to obtain one or more of the requisite books.[39] Other parishes were even less responsive to the visitors and appear to have continued as before, after only token compliance. Thus, while Tewkesbury's lay leaders replaced their chalice with a communion cup and sold some vestments and portions of the rood, as required, they kept several items that had been prohibited. An inventory of church goods made in 1577 shows that they still had "one riche coape, ... vij albes" and "a pece of imagery," as well as a tall candlestick. A short distance to the south, the parish of Bishop's Cleve listed even more prohibited items in their inventory from the same year: bells, candlesticks, a censor and cross, a pyx, and "certen vestmentes and copes."[40]

---

37 "Grindal's Visitation Articles," 157.
38 Litzenberger, *The English Reformation and the Laity*, 130–5; Christopher Haigh, *English Reformations: Religion, Politics and Society under the Tudors* (Oxford, 1993), 245.
39 Of course, the absence of required books may have been due to the combined pressures of previous, ruinous hard use and inadequate funds, rather than to resistance to official policy. Litzenberger, *The English Reformation and the Laity*, 137–9.
40 GRO, P329, CW 2/1, 55, 62, printed in *Tewkesbury Churchwardens' Accounts, 1563–1624*, ed. C. Litzenberger, Gloucestershire Record Series, vol. 7 (Gloucester, 1994), 35–6, 40; GRO, GDR, vol. 40, fol. 50v.

Additionally, numerous individuals were reported for selling food and such like during the time of divine services, while others were accused of gaming, eating, and drinking during that sacred time. More generally and perhaps more significantly, by 1576, a substantial proportion of all the parishes in the dioceses named at least one individual who either abstained from communion or refused to attend services at all. This was a marked change from earlier visitations in Elizabeth's reign, when statistics indicated that although numerous people were either recusants or noncommunicating attendees, those so named were associated with only a small number of parishes. The new statistics indicate that, rather than objecting to particular manifestations of the new religion in particular parishes, as Elizabethan Protestantism came to be more clearly defined, individuals in many parishes who had previously been ambivalent now chose to turn their backs on the new religion in general. Resistance to the state religion was becoming more broadly based.[41]

However, even in Elizabeth's reign, not all reformation of ritual was initiated from above. While most parishes did not typically make changes immediately after Elizabeth's accession and the reestablishment of Protestantism, many modified their worship space in the 1560s without waiting to be prodded by those in authority. They whitewashed their walls several times during that decade, repeatedly choosing to conceal their images rather than obliterate them more permanently. Many then painted over those images with excerpts from scripture.[42] In Minchinhampton, following the arrival of their new reforming rector, arrangements were made for the "pullynge downe dystroyenge and throwynge out of the church sundrye superstycyous thinges tendinge to the maintenance of Idolatry."[43] Anticipating directives that would be included in Grindal's visitation articles, several parishes also purchased tables of the Ten Commandments and the Queen's arms, and mounted them in the appropriate places. In addition, many parishes built communion pews in the chancel around the communion table so that people could receive communion seated, rather than having to kneel as they had in the Mass. Others opted to continue to kneel to receive communion and purchased kneeling boards for that purpose.[44]

---

[41] GRO, GDR, vol. 40, fols. 20, 109v, 143v, 188, 208, 249–49v, 253v; Litzenberger, *The English Reformation and the Laity*, 143.

[42] GRO, P154/14 CW 1/17–1/25, passim; P124 CW 2/4, fol. 6; P197 CW 2/1, fols. 3–3v.

[43] GRO, P216, CW 2/1, 54.

[44] Both sitting and kneeling to receive communion were permitted, and parishes both in Gloucestershire and elsewhere made changes to support local custom. Among the many changes made, the Gloucestershire parishes of Dursley, Lechlade, Minchinhampton,

Again, as in Edward's reign under Bishop Hooper, ritual practices in the diocese of Gloucester had been scrutinized to determine the level of conformance to official policy. However, the situation in 1576 was different than it had been twenty-five years earlier. Hence, the effects of the visitation were also different, not only because of the level of ecclesiastical authority represented and because of the particular layers of ritual examined but also because of differences in the religious and political landscape. England now had an adult monarch, albeit a woman who had not yet married, whose reign had now lasted for seventeen years, significantly longer than either Edward's or Mary's. This lent a sense of stability to her reign, in general, and to state religion, in particular. However, a stable religious policy was not all that was required. A series of challenges to her authority had also led to the clarification of the boundaries of acceptable religious practices, and to the more vigorous prosecution of those whose actions were outside the newly defined limits.[45]

By the same token, however, by defining the established religion more exactly, Elizabeth and her advisers had also given those who opposed the new religion a more substantive entity to reject. Additionally, Mary's reign had given those who preferred Catholicism a vivid reminder of what they had lost. The religious changes under Henry, and even to some extent under Edward, may have been, as some historians have asserted, so subtle and gradual that their effects were obscured. People may indeed not have realized what they had lost until it was restored under Mary. Then, experiencing the Mass anew with all its sensory riches, some would have been reminded of the old and may not have wanted to lose it again. Those people may have held out hope for a return to Catholicism during the early years of Elizabeth's reign, and in the diocese of Gloucester that period of hopefulness would have lasted until the middle of the 1570s, as a result of Bishop Cheyney's episcopate.

---

and St. Michael's, Gloucester, erected communion pews; Ashburton in Devon purchased a board "to knele on at the recevynge of the communyon," as did Ludlow in Shropshire; St. Nicholas, Strood, in Kent had the Queen's arms painted on the top of the rood screen. GRO, P124 CW 2/4, fols. 5–6, 10v; P197 CW 2/1, 4, 5; P217 CW 2/1, 54; P154/14, CW 1/11–11/25, passim; *Churchwardens' Accounts of Ashburton, 1479–1580,* ed. A. Hanham (Torquay, 1970), 171; *Churchwardens' Accounts of the Town of Ludlow, in Shropshire,* ed. T. Wright, Camden Society (London and New York, 1869), 93–103, passim; *The Churchwardens' Accounts of St. Nicholas, Strood,* ed. H.R. Plomer, Kent Archeological Society (1927), 13, 15, 20.

[45] For further discussion of the clarification of Elizabethan religious policy, see Caroline J. Litzenberger, "Defining the Church of England: Religious Change in the 1570s," in *Belief and Practice in Sixteenth Century England: A Tribute to Patrick Collinson from His Students,* C. Litzenberger and S. Wabuda eds. (Aldershot, 1998), 137–53.

The archiepiscopal visitation in 1576, then, effectively stripped away the layer of religious authority represented by Cheyney, and with it, the protective or concealing barrier between the state, on the one hand, and the parishes and people, on the other. Of course, that barrier had not been totally effective. As noted earlier, some parishes had undertaken changes that anticipated the archiepiscopal visitation. Similarly, some individuals had proclaimed beliefs that were far more radically Protestant than the established religion.[46] However, even in the cases of greatest conformity and even with Bishop Cheyney's barrier in place, we can see evidence of the shaping and molding of official versions of Protestant ritual to accommodate local customs and preferences. The parish of Minsterworth, for instance, complained in 1563 that their curate refused to wear a cope and preached "over longe" without the benefit of either a university degree or a preaching license. Parishioners at Fairford and Tewkesbury continued to worship in a space adorned with a magnificent array of images in stained glass. The parishes of Woodchester and Minchinhampton complained that their reform-minded rector refused to proclaim the required commination or to teach the catechism, believing he could achieve greater reform through his own preaching.[47]

However, St. Michael's, Gloucester, had a different problem, one most likely shared by others. There, the successive demands of the series of liturgical changes, faithfully implemented, had taken a financial toll. The parish had gained substantial revenues from the sale of forbidden church goods, but the proceeds were consumed in changing the worship space and purchasing the requisite books for Protestant services during Hooper's episcopate. Any money that remained was quickly spent as a result of the Marian Restoration. By the end of 1558, all the requisite liturgical changes had been made to support the full and complete restoration of Catholic worship at St. Michael's, but those changes had depleted the parish coffers. Even a special parish rate had not generated sufficient funds to cover the cost of both liturgical change and urgently needed maintenance, previously deferred in the face of pressure to conform to changes in ritual. Hence, even this model parish found it difficult to respond promptly to the official policies associated with the reestablishment of Protestantism following Elizabeth's accession. They did have the rood-loft with its recently completed statues removed

---

[46] GRO, GDR, vol. 26, 31, 135–7; vol. 28, 168–70; vol. 29, 71, 88; vol. 31, 81–7; vol. 35, passim; printed in *The Commission for Ecclesiastical Causes within the Dioceses of Bristol and Gloucester, 1574*, ed. F.D. Price, Bristol and Gloucestershire Archaeological Society, Record Section, vol. 10 (Gateshead, 1972), 49–108, passim.

[47] GRO, GDR, vol. 20, 32; vol. 40, fol. 189.

almost immediately, as noted earlier, and like most other parishes, they did obtain the new Prayer Book promptly. However, it would take two years before they would once again remove both the altar and the extra dirt under it and install a communion table. In the interim all the available resources that might have gone to support liturgical changes were required to repair the tower and keep it from collapsing.[48]

Once again, as in the time of John Hooper's episcopate, conformity to the established religion varied widely in the parishes. They may all have used the words of the Book of Common Prayer, but the actual worship experience included much more: It was comprised of numerous visual cues, including parish decorations and furnishings, priestly attire and movements, and the actions of the laity, as well. Once again, as in the early 1550s, the wide variation in liturgical practice is also evident in the beliefs espoused in wills. Predictably, given Elizabeth's aversion to "windows on men's souls," the visitation of 1576 did not include any reference to wills, as had Hooper's. However, such documents still included statements of faith and provided evidence of the nature of belief at the lowest, most private layer involved in the creation of a Protestant England. In the 1570s, these statements revealed a populace still reluctant to embrace Protestantism, although the tide was beginning to shift. Following Edward's death and the return to Catholicism under Mary, testators too returned to the old religion in their wills, but then, the reintroduction of Protestantism following Elizabeth's accession ushered in another overwhelming swing toward ambiguous statements. In the 1560s, over 85 percent of the Gloucestershire wills included such statements, while only approximately 2 percent made Protestant declarations of faith. Protestant statements only began to appear in statistically significant numbers in the late 1570s, following the clarification of official religious policy and the metropolitical visitation of the diocese. Nonetheless, the numbers were still small, and Protestant will preambles would not become the norm until the last decade of Elizabeth's reign. Thus, testators often used their wills as one final way to either conceal or disclose their religious beliefs, as one final layer of response to official policy and religious change.[49]

---

[48] Minchinhampton devoted parish funds to a similar project at about the same time. Meanwhile at Tewkesbury, they did not act soon enough, and the steeple came crashing down on Easter Day 1559. GRO, P154/14 CW 1/12; P217 CW 2/1, 13–15, 20–1; P329 CW 2/1, fol. v. For further discussion of the cost of liturgical change, see Caroline J. Litzenberger, "St. Michael's, Gloucester," 1540–80: The Cost of Conformity in Sixteenth-Century England," in *The Parish in English Life 1400–1600* (Manchester and New York, 1997), 230–49.

[49] See Litzenberger, "Local Responses to Religious Changes," 259–70, passim.

The enforcement of religious change was a multilayered, multidimensional process involving people at all levels in church, state, and society. Within each layer of implementation, regional, local, and individual pious practices and beliefs created prisms that modified the policies promulgated by the Crown and Privy Council. Practical considerations, such as the cost of liturgical change and the conflicting demands on parish funds for repairs and ongoing maintenance, also hindered this process. In addition, where the dichotomy between official expectations and traditional practices was too great for accommodation, people and institutions developed strategies of concealment to protect themselves from having to change too quickly, if at all.

Layers of response to religious change thus included disclosure and concealment, as well as nuanced responses, all of which reflected the previous traditions and experiences of parishes and individuals. Thus, changes in ritual, and through ritual in religion, may have been initiated from above by those in authority. However, the shape of official religion and its ritual manifestations in the localities, and in the hearts and minds of the people, were determined by a reflexive, recursive process, which involved both the powerful and the powerless as reluctant participants in a collaborative struggle. The result was not the "true religion" envisioned by John Hooper or Edmund Grindal; rather it was a religion of the people as richly diverse as the English landscape.

## PART II

# Forms of religious identity

CHAPTER V

# Spirits of the penumbra:
# Deities worshiped in more
# than one Chinese pantheon

ROMEYN TAYLOR

## INTRODUCTION: CHINESE ORTHODOXY

In his contribution to this volume, Professor Richard Shek has illuminated the "alternative moral universe" of the Eternal Mother sects, a universe made by dissenters from a "Chinese orthodoxy" that he defines as the "doctrine of propriety-and-ritual" (*lijiao*). Under their religious aspect, the rites of the *lijiao* were understood to have been an expression of the will of Heaven and its correct performance was necessary for the maintenance of social and cosmic harmony. The sociopolitical content of the *lijiao* is reduced to its core, the "three bonds" (*sangang*), which were the paradigmatic relationships between subject and ruler, child and parents, and wife and husband.[1]

In what follows, I turn from Professor Shek's "alternative moral universe" to look at the other term of his polarity – "Chinese orthodoxy."[2] I start from the assumption of a Chinese social whole, and I understand the social whole under its religious aspect as a hierarchically ordered system comprising four distinct religions (each with its *own* evolving orthodoxy). These were, first, the legally prescribed official religion of

---

[1] Other formulations of the Chinese sociopolitical order as constituted by the practice of *li-jiao* (by whatever name) may be found in Gary Hamilton, "Heaven is High and the Emperor Is Far Away," *Revue europeenne des sciences sociales* 27.84 (1989); 141–67 Liu Kuang-ching, "Introduction," and "Socioethics as Orthodoxy: A Perspective," in *Orthodoxy in Late Imperial China*, Liu ed. (Berkeley, 1990), 4–8, 53–100, respectively; and Romeyn Taylor, "Chinese Hierarchy in Comparative Perspective," *Journal of Asian Studies* 48:3 (1989): 490–511.

[2] I avoid the term "*li-jiao*" as descriptive of Chinese orthodoxy because it suggests the rites of the official religion and their foundation in the Confucian canon. "Chinese orthodoxy," as I understand it, refers to the domain of fundamental religious orientations that was shared by the four religions. Professor Shek's "three bonds" would be an important instance of this.

the empire,[3] followed in rank order by Buddhism and Daoism (both of which were quasi-legal, i.e., accommodated and regulated, but not mandated by the law), and, finally, the diffuse popular religion that was embedded in the "natural" communities of village, neighborhood, and household.[4]

I understand Chinese orthodoxy as the continuous *process* of mutual accommodation among these four religions. It is further argued here that this process of mutual accommodation mobilized practice across religious boundaries and across a broad social spectrum in support of the imperial social order, a social order that was ultimately reducible in principle to Professor Shek's "three bonds."

Mutual accommodation among the religions was achieved in the face of persistent underlying tensions. The official religion represented, in principle, the whole religious obligation of humankind, but *in practice* it was primarily the religion of the imperial government and, more specifically, of the ruling class of civil administrators. The inadequacy of the official religion in practice to satisfy all spiritual needs of the ruling and subject classes was evident from the continued flourishing of the other religions.

The official and popular religions, as religions of this–worldly salvation, were both relativized by the world-transcendent visions of

---

[3] The main legal texts are the sections of the *Collected Statutes* of the Ming and Qing dynasties under the heads of "Ministry of Rites" and "Directorate of Sacrifices." The *canonical* foundations of the official religion were primarily the conventional genres of "classics and history," where "classics" denotes the ancient texts associated with Confucius and his school with their commentaries, and where "history" denotes the archives of successive imperial dynasties and their authoritative summation in official historiography. One ought not on this account to label the official religion as "Confucian." The historical roots of the official religion were pre-Confucian; the development of Confucian thought was not always closely tied to the development of the official religion; and the official religion, shaped as it was to the exigencies of rulership, routinely accommodated certain non-Confucian practices.

[4] I owe the concept of "diffuse" religion in contradistinction to "institutionalized" to C.K. Yang's *Religion in Chinese Society: A Study of Contemporary Social Functions of Religion and Some of Their Historical Factors* (Berkeley, 1967), esp. 20–21. I have not followed his inclusion of the official religion under the heads of "diffuse religion" and "ethicopolitical cults," however. (See 127 and especially 297, where he speaks of "the diffusion of religion into the central and local political order.") Rather, I have taken the presence of canon, ordained clergy, and sacred places as indicative of institutional religion, and the official religion satisfies all three conditions. For treating the government officials as clergy in their roles as ritualists, see Henri Maspero, "Mythologie de la Chine moderne," in Maspero, *Le Daoisme* (Paris, 1971), 90. By "natural communities" I mean settlements that were formed as an effect of economic and societal forces and not by administrative action. See also Martin Heijdra, "The Socio-Economic Development of Rural China during the Ming," in *The Cambridge History of China*, eds. Denis Twitchett and Frederick W. Mote: vol. 8, pt. 2. *The Ming Dynasty, 1368–1644* (Cambridge, 1998), 468–72.

Buddhism and Daoism.[5] But Buddhism, however well adapted it was to its Chinese home, was still seen as a religion of alien origin from the perspective of Daoism and the official religion, both of which were essentially indigenous.

Popular religion enlisted the aid of Buddhist or Daoist clergy and religious specialists in the performance of its rites and ignored the hierarchical structure of the official liturgy in pursuit of numinous power. It allowed the humblest worshipers to address their offerings and their prayers to the highest deities without benefit of official mediation. In doing so, it bypassed the liturgical foundation of the ruling-class dominion over the common people. At the same time, however, this violation of social and political hierarchy was generally tolerated by the officials as evidence of the ignorance of the common people and their necessary subordination to the tutelage of the scholar–official class.

Chinese orthodoxy, when understood as a process of mutual accommodation, thus constituted and reconstituted the ideology of the social whole. But that whole was not a harmonious, frictionless, and static universe; rather it was complex and subject to contradictions and tensions. These contradictions and tensions were not the enemy of the social whole, however; they kept the entire religious ensemble alive as long as the process of mutual accommodation kept its several parts together.

### Official religion

The structure of the official religion as prescribed by law was identical with that of the empire under its liturgical aspect (i.e., the empire-as-church with the emperor as high priest, the civil officials as ordinary priests, sub-bureaucratic functionaries as community officiants, and finally, the household heads as domestic ritualists). It was built upon a tripartite cosmogony modeled on the nuclear family. In Chinese thought, cosmogony was understood as a continuous process that was both spontaneous and orderly. Heaven as cosmic "father" engendered and ruled all phenomena, while Earth as cosmic "mother" nurtured and brought them forth. Heaven and Earth were completed as "parents" by Humankind as their "offspring." The distinguishing attributes of Heaven were activity, intelligence, and order, while those of Earth were quiescence, submissiveness, and affection.

Humankind, however, was complex and unstable, and therefore dangerous. On the one hand, humans shared with lesser creatures a

---

[5] Official religion could be thus transcended because transcendent concepts of late imperial Confucian *thought* do not seem to have been encoded in the liturgy.

powerful appetitive nature tending toward disorder and strife, and on the other hand they were uniquely endowed by Heaven with intelligence and a capacity for creating order.[6] Actions associated with these two aspects of human nature were partial (*si*) and impartial (*gong*), respectively. This fundamental duality was mediated by a free will (*zhi*).[7] The obligation to choose the right and to act accordingly was therefore inescapable. Observance of the prescribed rites, when it was done with understanding and reverence, instructed the mind and steadied the will. The musical performances that often accompanied the rites were intended to evoke the appropriate emotional response.

The abstract elements of the cosmic order found ample and aesthetically satisfying expression in the official liturgy. In late preimperial times, the archaic polytheism and its mythology had been systematized and translated into several abstract cosmogonic systems. By the end of the Han, these had been sufficiently, if imperfectly, reconciled to form an enduring framework for the official religion. The mythology and the deities of the archaic religion were not obliterated by their translation into the new cosmology, however. They and their cults were integrated with the new cosmology, and they mediated between Humankind and the abstract cosmic forces. Thus, for example, the cosmic abstraction of Heaven was worshiped during most of the Han period as an astral court comprising the five sovereigns of the four cardinal directions and the center. These, in turn, were identified as the apotheoses of the five "emperors" of the old mythology. Earth, as Heaven's complement, was usually worshiped in Han by the more modest cult of Empress Earth (Houtu).

In late imperial times, Heaven was worshiped at the winter solstice on the great three-tiered, marble, and blue-tiled round altar south of Beijing as Exalted Emperor of August Heaven (*Haotian shangdi*). Earth was worshiped at the summer solstice on the two-tiered, yellow-tiled square altar north of the city as August Earth Spirit (*Huang diqi*). This association of anthropomorphic deity with cosmic abstraction accommodated the use of hymns, dance-dramas, prayers, and sacrificial offerings in the worship of the cosmic powers. In the words of the *Official History of the Ming Dynasty*: "The distinction that is being made here [i.e., between

---

[6] For this formulation of the duality of human nature, see Feng Yu-lan, *A History of Chinese Philosophy*, 2 vols. (Princeton, 1952–3), I:119–27; *The Works of Mencius*, trans. James Legge (1895; repr., New York, 1970), VI, A, 15, 16, pp. 416–19.

[7] See, inter alia, Confucius, *Confucian Analects*, in *The Great Learning & the Doctrine of the Mean*, trans. James Legge (1893; repr., New York, 1971), *Analects* IX, 15, p. 224; *Mencius*, trans. Legge, V, B, 7, pp. 389, 390; II, A, 9, p. 188; *Reflections on Things at Hand*, comps. Zhu Hsi and Lü Tsu-ch'ien, trans. Wing-tsit Chan (New York, 1967), 149, 161.

Heaven (*Tian*) and the Exalted Emperor (*shangdi*)] is that between the body (*xingti*) of Heaven and its directing intelligence (*zhuzai*)."[8]

The deities and spirits of the official pantheon were registered in the *Sacrificial Statutes* (*Sidian*) and divided into three domains corresponding to Heaven, Earth, and Humankind in that order of dignity. There were celestial deities (manifested in stars, planets, and constellations), terrestrial deities (of mountains, lakes, and rivers), and the spirits of human history or legend (sages, heroes, and paragons of male and female virtue). It needs to be added here that the same human spirits who were properly worshiped locally or throughout the empire were also worshiped as ancestors by their own descendants. The deities of Heaven and Earth and the spirits of deceased humans were clearly distinguished in the liturgy. The celestial and terrestrial spirits were coeval with the universe and formless. They received their offerings on open-air altars, while the latter received theirs in the mansion-like temples in which their spirit tablets were kept. Moreover, the pantheon and its cults were fitted to the sociopolitical hierarchy. The emperor alone (or his qualified deputy) presided over the great rites on the metropolitan altars and in the imperial ancestral temple, and the prefectural and county magistrates presided over the worship of deities and spirits proper to their own jurisdictions.

Beyond the spheres of the imperial court and the administrative hierarchy, the prescribed liturgy and ritual reached down to the offering rites of village, neighborhood, and family. Included under this head were the communal tutelary deities of soil and grain, the five spirits of the household (gate, door, impluvium, stove, and well), and the ancestors. This point, which is often missed, informs us that in principle the official religion was meant to provide fully for the religious life of all the empire's subjects. In reality, however, the rules at the communal and domestic levels were largely not enforced, and practice was subject to local variation and to "corruption" by Buddhist and Daoist doctrine and practice.

### Buddhism, Daoism, and the popular religion

From the end of the Han, the official religion had to share the Chinese world with the institutionalized religions of Buddhism and Daoism. By the early eighth century, a *modus vivendi* had been worked out in relation to Buddhism that preserved the this-worldly supremacy of the Chinese

---

[8] Quoted in Romeyn Taylor, "Official Religion," in *Cambridge History*, 8 2:891.

orthodoxy by distinguishing the Buddhist clergy from the laity. The laity, living as they did in the bosom of their families, were still the emperor's subjects and owed him full obedience in all things, while the clergy in their monasteries and convents were exempted from this obligation in their religious practice and from their obligation to pay taxes. They were obliged as a condition, however, to submit to their own monastic discipline. The imperial government retained the right to investigate and punish such monastic offenses as ordaining unqualified novices, harboring criminals, or accepting false donations of land by tax-evading lay patrons. The government also undertook periodically to limit or even to reduce the numbers of Buddhist temples and to impose quotas on the ordination of monks. These regulations were administered by a hierarchy of monk-officials that descended from an office in the Ministry of Rites downward to the prefectural and county registries. Such controls appear to have been more or less effective at different times in the large public monastery-temples. The far more numerous small "hereditary" temples that were owned by master-disciple "lineages" largely escaped routine government control.

In emulation of Buddhism, the Daoists evolved an ordained, celibate, and monastic clergy,[9] few in number however, who existed apart from the much larger numbers of married, home-dwelling priests and the more humble ranks of exorcists, and from the village and neighborhood temple attendants who attached themselves to the clergy as their subordinates. Their few large public monasteries, like their Buddhist counterparts, were subject to governmental regulation from the early eighth century.[10] In late imperial times, government control was exercised by a hierarchy of Daoist registries that paralleled the Buddhist offices.

The three institutionalized religions were deeply interconnected with a diffuse popular religion. The term "popular religion" is intended to imply something more than a residual category of whatever religious activity was left after the institutionalized religions are subtracted. It is best understood as a religion first by recognizing its role in constituting hierarchies of small communities.[11] Leaving aside for the moment the

---

[9] For a description of early twentieth-century Daoist monasticism, see Yoshitoyo Yoshioka, "Taoist Monastic Life," in *Facets of Taoism*, Holmes Welch and Anna Seidel eds. (New Haven, CT, 1979), 229–52, based mainly on the Quanzhen Daoism of the White Cloud Monastery Temple (Baiyün Guan) in Bejing and its branches.

[10] Judith A. Berling, "Taoism in Ming Culture," in *Cambridge History*, 8 2:959–62.

[11] G. William Skinner's work on Chinese urban and commercial networks highlights the tension, varying in degree over time between "natural" and politically directed urbanization. This bears significantly on the issue of the partially autonomous formation of settlement hierarchies within the Chinese empire. See, for example, his introduction to *The City in Late Imperial China*, ed. Skinner (Stanford, CA, 1977), 3–31.

question of the nominal identification of many of the local deities and their cults as "official," "Buddhist," or "Daoist," communal life was organized around the temple. Construction and repair of the temples, several annual festivals, including those celebrating the god's birthday, and occasional communal rites of supplication, exorcism, or renewal in times of peril all required the assignment of roles such as leadership, fundraising, skilled crafts, and performance arts. The numinous core of each temple was located precisely in its incense brazier, and it was through the braziers that the temples were linked into hierarchies. When a new temple was founded, it was given its place in the local hierarchy when ashes were taken from its superior temple and placed in its own brazier.

In terms of doctrine and practice, the popular religion and the official religion shared a fundamentally similar orthodox cosmology. A hierarchy of realms furnished a core or armature for the "orthodoxy" in question: the celestial, the terrestrial, and the human (including the chthonic realm in the popular religion). The popular pantheon in its organization roughly mirrored the imperial administrative hierarchy and its official religion.[12] Deities of the popular pantheon descended from the Jade Emperor and his court around the north celestial pole, to his terrestrial viceroy, the spirit of the Eastern Peak, Dongyue or Taishan, to the county-level city gods (*chenghuang zhishen*), to the local tutelaries (*tudi*), and finally to the domestic stove gods. Also, as in the imperial administrative hierarchy, the popular spirit-officials were appointed and removed at the pleasure of the Jade Emperor. Thus a Daoist priest managing a city god temple, for example, might announce that a new deity had been appointed to that office.

The underworld of the popular religion was ruled by Yanluo (Skt. Yama) and the other nine kings of Hell. In one account, the kings were assisted in their rule by the city gods, who had custody of the newly dead for forty-nine days, after which they delivered them to the infernal courts.[13] The chthonic court system meted out justice in a purgatory that was furnished with horrific instruments of torture. These were graphically depicted on the walls of the Eastern Peak and city god temples.

---

[12] For the interconnection of official and popular religion within a "popular orthodoxy," see Myron Cohen, "Souls and Salvation," in *Death Ritual in Late Imperial and Modern China*, James L. Watson and Evelyn Rawski eds. (Berkeley, 1988), esp. 195–7. Also see Maurice Freedman, "On the Sociological Study of Chinese Religion," in *Religion and Ritual in Chinese Society*, ed. Arthur P. Wolf (Stanford, CA, 1974), 19–41.

[13] Henri Maspero, "La religion chinoise dans son développement historique" and "Mythologie de la Chine moderne," in Maspero, *Le taoïsme et les religions chinoises* (Paris, 1971), 62 and 205–8, respectively. Also see Yang, *Religion in Chinese Society*, 156–8.

Under Buddhist influence, the popular orthodoxy had linked the ideas of reincarnation and retributive justice. Survivors of the deceased might appeal to their local tutelary spirits, the gods of their communal temples, or their city gods to intervene with the underworld authorities so as to facilitate their progress toward release from the underworld and a longed for reincarnation. The performance of powerful rites by Buddhist monks or Daoist specialists offered the best prospects of successful intervention.[14]

Other deities were gathered around this core of popular belief and practice. Some, such as Guandi, God of War, and Guanyin, Goddess of Mercy, were immensely popular, and temples dedicated to them were found in every part of the empire. Others were regional, such as The Empress of Heaven, Tianhou (heavily concentrated on the southeast and south coasts), and the daughter of the God of the Eastern Peak, Princess of the Azure Clouds, Bixia Yuanjun, whose temples were found mainly in northeast and northwest China. Still others were members of a uniform class, such as the city gods and the local tutelaries, which were at once ubiquitous and local.

Because the popular religion had no discrete clergy or sacred canon of its own, the performance of important communal rites required the participation of religious specialists living in the community who might be rustic Daoist or Buddhist clergy.[15] The imperial government also had a hand, albeit a modest one, in shaping the popular religion. The county magistrates' responsibility for education extended beyond the elite county schools to the rudimentary village or neighborhood schools (*shexue*) and charity schools (*yixue*), which were often neglected. They were also responsible for overseeing certain communal rites, such as the township banquet (*xiangyin*), which brought minor functionaries and commoners together in a formal setting for the purpose of reinforcing adherence to the rules of the *lijiao*.[16]

---

[14] Major examples included the Buddhist plenary mass *shuilu fahui* (for which see Holmes Welch, *The Practice of Chinese Buddhism, 1900–1950* [Cambridge, 1967], 190–7); the Ghost Festival *guijie* performed in the middle of the seventh moon (for which see Stephen F. Teiser, "Introduction," in Teiser, *The Ghost Festival in Medieval China* [Princeton, 1988]; also see Laurence G. Thompson, *Chinese Religion: An Introduction*, 4th ed. [Belmont, 1989], 133–4), and the Daoist communal rites of cosmic renewal *jiao* and retreat *zhai* (for which see Berling, "Taoism in Ming Culture," 968–9; Cohen, "Souls and Salvation," 193–4; Kristofer Schipper, *The Taoist Body*, trans. Karen C. Duval [Berkeley, 1993], 72–82; Kristofer Schipper, "The Written Memorial in Taoist Ceremonies," in *Religion and Ritual*, 309–24).

[15] Berling, "Taoism in Ming Culture," 968–9.

[16] Ch'ü T'ung-tsu, *Local Government in China under the Ch'ing* (Cambridge, 1962), 161–4; Hsiao Kung-chuan, *Rural China: Imperial Control in the Nineteenth Century* (Seattle, 1960), Chapter 6.

## Limits of mutual influence among the religions

Chinese empire and society do not seem to have been compromised by their engagement with four distinct major religions. Professor Shek has suggested an explanation of this point with his formula, "moral orthodoxy and religious pluralism." That is, the sociopolitical order was not threatened as long as the religions shared a consensus on a "moral orthodoxy." It may also be to the point that all four religions were polytheistic and that their pantheons overlapped. Most of the population was devoted to communal cults, which could be nominally associated with Daoism or Buddhism, and they were not thereby prevented from approaching other deities for personal aid and comfort.

It was also the case that the official religion, Buddhism, Daoism, and the popular religion all survived their long immersion in the Chinese Empire and society. Each of the institutionalized religions had its own fundamental religious orientation, canon, ordained clergy, pantheon, iconography, liturgy, and sacred places, while the popular religion had a secure place in the life of the small communities that it sanctified.[17]

The offering rites of the official religion were, in principle, collective acts of submission to the gods and spirits and, most importantly, of submission to the cosmic and human order for which they stood. They were to be conducted with reverence and in a disinterested spirit unsullied by self-seeking. It was in part by their ritual manifestation of this quality of mind and character that the officiants claimed membership in the ruling class. The supreme exemplary rite of the official religion was the Son of Heaven's own three kneelings and nine prostrations before the tablet of the Exalted Emperor of August Heaven in the presence of a large retinue of officials.[18]

---

[17] On the evidence of certain emperors' patronage of Daoist clergy and the rites, Lagerwey asserts that "for the larger part of the last two millennia, Taoism was, like Christianity in Europe, the official religion of the state." John Lagerwey, *Taoist Ritual in Chinese Society and History* (New York, 1987), 253 ff. This, it seems to me, is to make rather too much of Daoist participation in the official religion. See Schipper, *The Taoist Body*, 8–9, for a more temperate assessment by a scholar of Daoism. Also see my chapter, "Official Religion," in *Cambridge History*, 877–9, 883–4.

[18] It is often supposed that in the official religion the emperor and his officials commanded the spirits. See inter alia, Benjamin I. Schwartz, *The World of Thought in Ancient China* (Cambridge, 1985), 411, and Patricia B. Ebrey and Peter N. Gregory, eds., *Religion and Society in T'ang and Sung China*, (Honolulu, 1993), 8. The emperors' conferral of ranks and titles on spirits, and a rite in which a county magistrate responds to a drought by exposing the city god image to the sun, or even thrashes it are adduced as evidence. In the first case, the emperor is in principle correcting the liturgy or adjusting it to changes that were thought to have occurred within the pantheon. In the second case, the rite is not only not found in the *Sacrificial Statutes* but violates the legally defined relationship between the magistrate and the city god. Performance of this rite satisfies popular

Daoist doctrine and liturgy sprang from the same indigenous roots as those of the official religion, but the Daoist priests stole a march on the emperor and his officials by transcending their universe. They claimed to acquire from certain secret rites the power to identify themselves with the ineffable Way, the ultimate source from which Heaven and Earth and all else were ultimately differentiated.[19] They also claimed to have achieved mastery over the gods and spirits, including some that were found in the official pantheon.[20] Their exclusion of "bloody sacrifice" from the orthodox Daoist rites must have further reinforced their sense of spiritual superiority vis-à-vis the officiants of the official religion.[21] The ordained Daoist clergy as learned in the canon and as masters of esoteric rites constituted a religious elite and, at least in the context of their worldview, shared pride of place with the literati.

The ordained Buddhist clergy similarly aspired, after their fashion, to world-transcendence, and for the laity they offered hope of progress toward a happier state through successive rebirths. This was to be accomplished in part by the seeker's own righteous efforts in this world, and in part with the helpful intercession of a pantheon of deities, mostly of Indian origin but enlarged by the inclusion of some Chinese deities. Again, the same line of social demarcation passed between the learned monks on one side and the laity and rustic clergy on the other.

The fundamental and enduring social fact that constituted the Chinese Empire and society was its division between a ruling class qualified by learning, and a subject class of commoners who were under the tutelage of their social betters. This fact also may have obstructed the merging of the learned clergy of Buddhism and Daoism into the laity and the popular religion, and favored the survival of their canons and liturgies.

### SPIRITS OF THE PENUMBRA

Pantheons and their worship were central to the practice of all four of the religions we have considered: the official, Buddhist, Daoist, and popular. It is easy enough, if laborious, to compile lists of deities from readily available sources such as the *Collected Statutes*, official histories, local gazetteers, encyclopaedias, canonical texts of the institutionalized

---

expectations of the magistrate and is consistent with popular notions of the magistrate as having the shamanic powers of a Daoist priest or specialist.

[19] This is my reading of John Lagerwey's understanding of the *jiao* or, commonly, the "rite of cosmic renewal." See his *Taoist Ritual*, 269.

[20] Schipper, *The Taoist Body*, 53.

[21] Schipper, *The Taoist Body*, 61; Lagerwey, *Taoist Ritual*, 249; Welch and Seidel, eds., *Facets of Taoism*, 6, 7.

religions, and collections of "folk" iconography. On the other hand, the deities cannot be sorted by religion because the same deity may appear in the contexts of several religions.

By "spirits of the penumbra" I mean those spirits that are found in more than one pantheon; the penumbra is the resulting overlap. The clergy of the institutionalized religions were well aware of these overlaps and were careful to limit their effects.

The institutionalized religions were selective in their embrace of new cults. They required either that a cult satisfied their liturgical rules, or that it must first be purged of its heterodox elements. The popular religion was more accommodating, requiring only that a deity display numinous power, whether for good or for ill. Both the official and the popular religions were prolific generators of new cults. On the official side, this would be mainly accounted for by the installation of thousands of tablets in the school shrines for offerings to the spirits of good officials, local worthies, chaste widows, and so forth. On the popular side were other such exemplary spirits that might have escaped the attention of the officials. An account of the Temple of the Old Salt Lady, Yanmu miao, illustrates the way in which new cults were generated within the popular religion.

The Temple of the Old Salt Lady, also called Temple of the Holy Lady (Shenmu miao), was situated at the Lutai salt works in Baochi County, near Tianjin. In the period of the Five Dynasties (907–60), because of a division of the kingdom of Yan, more and more people were cut off from their supply of salt. Suddenly, an old woman said to the people, "In this place, we can boil the earth to make salt cakes." Her method for doing this was eventually lost, and people came to think of her as a goddess (*shen*), and they built a temple for her called the Temple of the Old Salt Lady. At some later time, someone restored her image in the temple. The next day, over an area of a thousand *mu*, the ground was covered with a pure white substance like snow. When people hastened there to see for themselves, they found that it was salt. The people of that place then vied with one another to gather it. There is a song about this called the "Song of the Blessed Salt."[22]

The fact that this temple stood at the site of a salt works suggests that it may have served a tutelary cult of the local salt workers. Most cults such as this one, which grew out of a small community's immediate experience, ran their course and eventually disappeared without ever having been formally inducted into the official pantheon by the Ministry

---

[22] *Tianjinfu zhi* 天津府志, 1895, 25.14a–b.

of Rites and on the authority of the emperor. However, if a benign popular cult found favor with the local government, it might enjoy official
protection and even sponsorship, and an extralegal status that might be
called "official by magistrate's option."

Other cults, including some of those we will shortly consider in detail,
entered the penumbra when they were legally inducted into the official
religion by imperial edict and provided with a suitable liturgy. When
this occurred, as in the case of Guangong, the popular martial paragon,
the cult would assume a double aspect. While it would now be practiced in one form under official auspices, it would still be practiced as
a popular cult among the laity. Still more complex patterns of doctrine
and practice resulted from the popular appropriation of certain sites of
the official religion. The official liturgy was itself subverted to the point
of becoming internally inconsistent and subject to recurrent controversy
among members of the imperial court and civil administration.

### God of the Eastern Peak (Dongyue)

Deities that inhabited the mountains and rivers were conspicuous in
the pantheons of the three indigenous religions. The God of the Eastern
Peak was a case in point. People living near the mountains must have
felt a numinous presence in them. Mountain spirits were worshiped as
early as the Shang, and the cult of the Five Sacred Mountains was well
established by the end of the Zhou. The most august of these five was
the Eastern Peak, or Taishan, in modern Shandong Province. In the official orthodoxy, the mountain's summit was the *axis mundi*, the point of
contact between Heaven and Earth. In the former Han, the emperors not
only worshiped the in-dwelling god of the Eastern Peak, but Emperor
Xiao Wu ascended the mountain and deposited at the summit a written message addressed to the Exalted Sovereign of August Heaven. The
same emperor had another reason for visiting Taishan and the offshore
islands. He believed that they were home to the Daoist immortals (*xian*),
and he sought, in vain as it proved, to find them and to learn their secrets
of physical immortality. By the end of Han, moreover, in the domain of
popular religion, it was widely believed that the mountain, or a hill at
the foot of it, was the gateway to the underworld, through which all
mortals must pass upon their death.

The basic pattern set in Han, when the God of the Eastern Peak was
served by an official cult, a Daoist cult of the immortals, and a popular
cult of the underworld, continued and flourished through late imperial times. There were now two distinct forms of the late imperial official cult: the one classical and the other evidently of popular or Daoist

inspiration. In the austere classical liturgy, the God of the Eastern Peak was represented by a simple tablet placed (with those of other terrestrial spirits) on the open-air altar of the August Earth Spirit north of the imperial capital. All the earth spirits were worshiped there at the summer solstice. In the popular or Daoist form of the official rites, the god was represented by an image in the human likeness of an emperor. He was worshiped on his "birthday," the twenty-eighth day of the third month, and on the emperor's own birthday in either of two temples: a splendid one on the eastern side of Beijing and a still more splendid one at the foot of Taishan.

The popular cult of the Eastern Peak had undergone a baroque elaboration since the early empire. The gateway to Hell was still found at the foot of the mountain, now on Haoli Hill, but the underworld itself had been transformed under Buddhist influence into the vast spirit bureaucracy described earlier. The God of Taishan had meanwhile acquired a "sacred mother" (*shenmu*) and a daughter, the Princess of the Azure Clouds, Bixia Yuanjun. During late Ming and Qing, the Princess far eclipsed her father, and pilgrims came to visit her temple, not her father's. The Daoist clergy residing in the temples situated along the granite pathway to the summit assisted the pilgrims with their worship and sold Eastern Peak talismans to assist them in the quest for immortality if they were so inclined. Even as the popular cult had become richly elaborated, it had also become universal throughout the empire by the fifteenth century and was reinforced across north China by the popularity of his daughter, the Princess, in late Ming and Qing.

The main distinction to be drawn among the different personae of the mountain god with his family was that between the classical worship of the Taishan god as a cosmological phenomenon, and the other forms, all of which were anthropomorphic. The Ming founder offered an official explanation of the origin and nature of the terrestrial deities of the cosmos. In 1370, he said that they were spontaneously and mysteriously formed out of the "brilliant, numinous pneuma *qi*" of the great mountains and waters. By their numinous power, they activated all terrestrial and atmospheric phenomena. The mountain spirits produced the rain-bearing clouds that shrouded their summits and caused, or prevented, earthquakes and landslides. It was consistent with this theology cult that the emperor worshiped the spirits of the Five Sacred Peaks, which were represented by their spirit tablets, on the altar of the August Earth Spirit at the summer solstice.

*God of the Eastern Peak in the local histories.* According to the law, the god of the Eastern Peak could legally be worshiped only in three places. These were the imperial altar of the August Earth Spirit and the Eastern Peak temples in Beijing and Taishan. Nevertheless, the extra-legal Dongyue temples were important centers for the practice of the popular cult; their high importance is indicated by the fact that more than eighty percent of them were *Miao* (i.e., major temples). Their wide geographical distribution is also apparent. By late Qing, the gazetteers for 53 randomly selected counties recorded 114 unsanctioned temples distributed among 40 of the counties and all the provinces but Guangdong, which testifies to the robust state of the popular religion during that time.

The late imperial history of the cult presents a picture of extraordinary stability. Already well established in the Song, especially in the eastern provinces and Sichuan, its temples gradually spread west and south until the late sixteenth century, when they were recorded in our sample in every province except Yunnan, Guizhou, and Guangdong, all of which are in the extreme south. This may be taken as an indication that the popular religion was well established in the Song and that it spread throughout the empire during Yuan, Ming, and Qing.[23]

The genesis and spread of the Dongyue cult was closely associated with the strong secular trend toward commercialization throughout the Song through the Qing. Most of the temples were built in urban settings. Of eighty-seven temples whose exact location can be determined, thirty-seven were in county seats. Of these, sixteen were within the city walls, fifteen at the gates, two by the city wall, and four were nearby at the cities' customs posts. Of fifty others that were elsewhere in the county, eighteen were in important towns, which makes a total of fifty-five urban temples or sixty-three percent of those known.

There was little agreement among the gazetteer editors, however, on the question of how to classify the temples. As a rule, they were noncommittal on the question, but thirty-five were assigned to the "Buddhist and Daoist" *siguan* category, four were classified as official, and it was even reported of one of these that the local officials conducted the god's annual birthday offering there.[24] Four others were described as having been customary among the common people (*minsu*). The difficulty of classifying the cult is illustrated by the fact that the clergy residing in the Dongyue temples could be either Buddhist or Daoist. The county-level Daoist registry was housed in one; a Daoist residence (*daoyuan*) was attached to another, and still another was classified as Buddhist because monks resided in it.

---

[23] This finding tends to confirm Maspero's assertion that what he called "the mythology of modern China" was fully formed in the Song period.
[24] 1816D069, 3.22b.

Another indication of the temples' local status is the recorded participation of local people in their construction and repair. Evidence of this kind lends stronger support to the assumption that local officials often actively supported the cult in their counties. Of thirty-two recorded construction or repair projects where sponsorship was indicated, eighteen were sponsored by officials, three by Buddhist monks, and only one by a Daoist priest. The remaining sponsors were "local persons" (six), "common persons" (three), and a scholar (one). The active roles played by Buddhist and Daoist clergy may have been far larger than these numbers suggest, but they may have solicited nominal sponsorship from the local officials in order more easily to mobilize the needed resources.[25] It was also the case, however, that difficult questions remained for the defenders of orthodoxy.

Several gazetteer compilers explicitly acknowledged that their counties' Eastern Peak temples were "contrary to the Rites" (*feili*), which is to say that they were in violation of the *Sidian*.[26] The issue raised by these admissions was that it was "contrary to *li*" for the emperor's subjects to make offerings to any spirit whose place of residence lay within another local jurisdiction. This rule and the cosmological reason for it were clearly set forth in a fourteenth-century text quoted in an 1880 gazetteer for Kunshan and Xinyang counties in Suzhou prefecture.

The universal ruler sacrifices to the spirits of the mountains and rivers everywhere He stands as it were at the center of Heaven and Earth, where the *qi* (pneumas) of all three [Heaven, Earth and Humankind] interpenetrate. The feudal lords,[27] on the other hand, may not sacrifice to those spirits that do not reside within the boundaries of their domains. When spirits do not reside within their frontiers they dare not transgress against the rites because their own pneumas cannot interpenetrate with theirs.

The author of the text, however, sought and found another authority that offered a way around this limitation:

According to the *Gongyang Commentary* (on the *Spring and Autumn Annals*), if, when you hurl a rock it bounces up a handbreadth, there will be rain before dawn, and the clouds everywhere in the world are produced by Taishan. Such is Taishan's ability to produce clouds. And when it makes rain the rain falls

---

[25] Timothy Brook, *Praying for Power: Buddhism and the Formation of Gentry Society in Late-Ming China* (Cambridge, 1993), 283.

[26] 1882C010, 2.19a.; 1906I003, 11.7b.; 1599M000, 10.2b.

[27] This is an archaic term denoting prefectures and counties, which replaced the states with which the Zhou dynasty nobility were invested.

everywhere. Why is it appropriate for people everywhere to worship Dongyue? It is because the other sacred peaks have nothing to do with this.[28]

This justification for the spread of the Dongyue cult throughout the empire was applicable only to Dongyue's classical, cosmological persona however, and it did not address the popular cult, which was pointedly overlooked. The popular cult is attested in various ways. Worshipers in one temple made offerings to the "ten kings of hell."[29] Other temples organized an annual festival to celebrate the god's birthday on the twenty-eighth day of the third month, or at the time of the Qingming festival of "sweeping the graves." Festivals were held at other temples at the beginning of the year.[30]

*Implications.* In late imperial times, Dongyue was worshiped as an important deity of the official and popular religions, and civil officials and Buddhist and Daoist clergy presided over its rites in different locations. Local officials commonly violated the letter, if not the spirit, of the law by giving their sanction to the popular practice. In view of the strength of the cult in the context of the popular religion, one may ask why the cult in its classical altar form was preserved at all if it was so shallowly rooted in the society at large. The answer would seem to have been that reenactment of the archaic rites of the sage kings was still the indispensable foundation of the imperial order and the means by which the emperor as high priest, and the civil officials as his fellow officiants, established their authority in the world.

### The eight spirits of agriculture (Bbazha)

The Bazha rites presented the case of a cult that was deeply anchored in popular religious practice in north China and that repeatedly entered, left, and reentered the domain of the official religion. In the time of the Zhou dynasty, there was a joyous bacchanalian harvest celebration, the *dazha*, in the last month of the Zhou calendar year (roughly equivalent to our November). One of Confucius' disciples complained to him that the revelers seemed to have gone mad. Confucius suggested that this was the common people's well-earned day of celebration after a hundred days of toil: "The bow cannot always be drawn, it must sometime be loosened." His reply might have served as a text for those civil officials

---

[28] *Kunxin liangxian xuxiu zhi* 昆新兩縣志 10.24b–25b.
[29] 1894F056, 3.23b–24a.
[30] And in the third month. See *Gujin tushu jicheng, Shuntianfu fengsukao*, ce 64, p. 40; *Gujin tushu jicheng, Baodingfu fengsu*, ce 69, p. 19; 18821038, 17.7a; and at new years, *Gujin tushu jicheng*, ce 64, p. 40.

of later times who were disposed to be indulgent toward occasional excesses among the common folk.[31]

One of the rites associated with the ancient festival was the king's plenary sacrifice (*dazha*; also eight sacrifices, *bazha*) that was offered to eight kinds of spirits associated with agriculture. The *locus classicus* is the *Record of Rites* where the eight are listed as (1) First Husband-man, *Xianse* (a.k.a. First Farmer, *Xiannong*); (2) the (ancient) ministers of agriculture, *sise*; (3) the tutelary spirits of inspectors of the fields, *nong*; (4) of the laborers' huts and the field boundaries, *you biaozho*; (5) of wild animals, *qinshou* (glossed as cats and tigers, *maohu*, valued as natural enemies of rodents and wild boars); (6) of the dikes, *fang*; (7) of the ir-rigation channels, *shuiyong*; and (8) of the swarming insects, *kunchong*. In conjunction with the popular festival, the sovereign, and at least in the later Zhou reigns the lesser rulers as well, performed a plenary rite of offering to the spirits. The First Husbandman was the most honored, and he was the subject of his own official agricultural cult throughout imperial history.[32]

The festival in the Han dynasty appears to have been perpetuated in the year-end La festival, with which it was subsequently confused by some commentators.[33] The La and its offering rites survived during the VI Dynasties period and the Sui and Tang, but the imperial Bazha rites only reappeared under that name as an "archaistic revival" in the official religion of the Northern Zhou dynasty. Revived and abolished in Sui, it was revived yet again in the Tang in 638.[34] Derk Bodde sees nothing to celebrate in this retention of the La and the revival of the Zha, however. "In this embalming of two once vital festivals within the compartmentalized framework of official ritual, we see the end result of that process of festival impoverishment."[35] In 962, two years after he had reunified the empire, the Song founder accepted a suggestion that he resume the rites as they had been performed in Tang.[36]

---

[31] For this story, see *Li Ki*, trans. Seraphin Couvreur, S.J., 2 vols., 2nd ed. (Hejianfu, 1913), 1:190–1. As to the time of year, the last month of the Zhou calendar corresponded to the twelfth month of the Han calendar and the eleventh month of our own. See Derk Bodde, *Festivals in Classical China: New Year and other Annual Observances during the Han Dynasty 206 B.C.–A.D. 220* (Princeton, 1975), 71.

[32] *Li Ki*, trans. Couvreur, 1:594–5, and *dazha* entry in *Cihai*, 752.

[33] "Zha," in Cihai 2 vols. (Shangai, 1937; repr. Taipei, 1965) 2570, cites a *Liji* commentary to the effect that this rite was called Qingsi in Xia, Jiaping in Shang/Yin, Zha in Zhou, and La in Han. For the relation of preimperial Zha rites to the early imperial La, see Bodde, *Festivals*, 73, 74.

[34] *Li Ki*, trans. Couvreur, 1:594–8. See also Bodde, *Festivals*, Chapter 3. As the first of the Bazha, Xiannong is named Xianse, who was also the demiurge Yandi (Fire Emperor), a.k.a. Shennong (Divine Farmer).

[35] Bodde, *Festivals*, 74.

[36] *Shitong* 十 通, comp. Yang Jialuo 楊家 駱 (rprt., Taipei, 1975), 70.5a.

But once again, during Liao, Jin, Yuan, and Ming, a period of more than five hundred years, the Zha rites disappeared from the official religion,[37] only to be revived once again in the Qing.

The Manchu rulers had adopted the rites "outside the passes" (i.e., before their occupation of the Ming capital in 1643). The liturgy is sketched in the official Qing history.[38] The Bazha temple was built inside the south gate of the city. In spring and autumn, an altar was prepared for the "offering-from-a-distance" (*wangji*). The rites were performed in spring and autumn, which corresponded to the ritual calendar for the offerings to First Farmer, Xiannong. This suggests that the Manchu Bazha rites had been subsumed under the Xiannong cult.[39] By this early use of a south-facing offering-from-a-distance, the Manchu rulers may have been consciously appropriating a Chinese imperial prerogative in anticipation of their own later conquests.

The Qing regime continued to perform the imperial Bazha rite after they had made Beijing their capital in 1644. In an extraordinary display of favor, the Yongzheng emperor (r. 1723–35) ordered the rites performed in all the counties of the empire. This measure was evidently adopted in response to good omens reported on the agricultural front.[40] Before this decree had been universally implemented, however, the Qianlong emperor "for the first time ignored the liturgical statutes" and terminated the official rites in 1745 over the protests of his court officials. The emperor justified his decision with a barrage of objections to continued practice of the cult. The Dazha rite, he said, originated with Yiqi[41] and was continued by the Xia, Shang, and Zhou, but that was long ago, and disagreements among the classical commentators had made it impossible to restore the liturgy in its original form. The last of the eight *zha* was Kunchong (Insect Spirit), and to present offerings to him could only be harmful to agriculture. The emperor cited a commentary on the "Ordinances of the Months" (*Yueling*) to the effect that prayers for a good harvest should be offered to sun, moon and stars, and not to

---

[37] *Shitong*, 70.8b.

[38] *Qingshi* (Taibei, 1961), 1073.7.

[39] For assimilation of different rites of the Zha festival to other contexts, see Bodde, *Festivals*, 72–3.

[40] 1733H040; 1816D069; 1915G051; *Suzhoufu zhi*, comp. 1878, 36.2b. The edict concerning the Bazha was merely one of several endorsing agricultural rites at this time. They were inspired by reports in 1724 and 1726 of auspicious omens in the form of four- and even nine-headed stalks of grain. See *Qingshi* juan 84, p. 1061.0.

[41] According to different commentators, Yiqi was either Shennong or the emperor Yao. See *Cihai* entry, 194. A history of the Bazha cult, including the Qianlong emperor's long discussion is found in *Qingshi*, 1073.7–.9.

the Bazha.[42] Whether or not Zha and La rites were the same remained unclear, and the Han had performed the La but not the Zha. After the Han, the Wei and Jin dynasties had inconsistently abolished or restored the rite. At times, the rites had been taken over by alchemical quacks, and the numbers of spirits of all sorts that shared in the offerings had grown to one hundred and ninety-two, including celestial and human emperors, dragons, unicorns, and red birds. This, according to expert opinion, constituted a ritual fault.

The emperor then cited the eminent Song scholar Su Shi, who had said with reference to the fifth *zha*, the cat and tiger spirits:

"When you welcome the cat [spirit to the ceremony,] it is but a cat-personator; when you welcome the tiger [spirit], it is but a tiger personator. It is [like] taking an actor to be the person he represents.[43]

This [said the emperor] explains why [the cat and tiger ritual] has long been treated as theatre [by the learned], and why the Yuan and Ming put a stop to it. How much more should this be the case with the *zha* offerings to the several spirits? As for the First Husbandman, the Ministers of Agriculture, Sun, Moon, Stars, Chronograms, Mountains, Forests, Rivers and Marshes, they all have their own altars on which to receive their offerings."[44]

The legal status of the cult in the provinces was less clear. Several gazetteers reported that the Yongzheng emperor ordered the counties to make annual offerings to the Bazha in the twelfth month.[45] Detailed liturgical instructions were also provided at this time.[46] When the imperial rites were abolished twelve years later, the Qianlong emperor left it to the local officials and the commoners to determine whether to continue the rites on their own account. "If the common people wish to retain the *zha* offerings in their thanksgiving observances and unify their villages in happiness, they may follow their own customs."[47] Thus, from 1745, the Bazha rites were no longer official at any level, but they were tolerated if not actively encouraged as a popular cult by the imperial

---

[42] The "Ordinances of the Months" here probably refers to the section of that name in the *Liji*. See *Li Ki*, trans. Couvreur, 1:330–410. I have not found the passage to which he referred.

[43] The "personators" were evidently theatrical performers who were supposed to have been possessed by the spirits they represented. The cat and tiger spirits were invoked for their protection of the crops from rodents and wild boars.

[44] *Qingshi*, 1073.9.

[45] The decree, if there was only one, was variously dated to 1728 in 1889K019, 8.8a, 1730 in 1915G051.

[46] *Suzhou fuzhi* 蘇州府志 1878. 36.2b. 1816D069 3.20b. 1915G051, 9.2b. According to the Suzhou gazetteer, the rites were to be performed on the first *wu* day of the twelfth month, and the spirit tablets of the eight spirits were placed on Xiannong's altar.

[47] *Qingshi*, 1073.9.

government, and in some counties, they were accepted by the local officials. The Qianlong emperor's abandonment of the official rites without proscribing the local and popular may have had two objects: While smiling upon the harvest-time happiness of his lesser subjects, he disconnected the superstitious absurdities of the festival from the official religion.

*Bazha in the local histories.* In the fifty-three sampled counties, the legal status of the county-level Bazha rites during most of their late imperial history is best described as "magistrates' option." During the Ming, the cult had no formal standing, but the rites were offered in three sampled counties between 1425 and 1566 and in seven between 1567 and 1619. The Bazha temples were built and maintained by the local officials on their own authority. In no case was there more than one temple reported in any county, and the temples were either within the walls of the county seat or just outside the east gate. Where the information is provided, three temples were constructed and one repaired between 1425 and 1619, and in every case the work was done under local official auspices. In early Qing, although the Bazha rites in the capital were legally sanctioned, those in the provinces were not. During late Ming and early Qing (1620–1722), there were ten temples in ten counties and the one reported construction was officially sponsored.

The Yongzheng edict was soon reflected in increased temple construction and repair. During the period 1723–45, five projects were recorded in the sampled counties (three constructions, all officially sponsored, and two repairs, of which one was officially sponsored). This was as many as were recorded for the three hundred years before, and for the first time Bazha temples appeared in the middle Yangtze provinces of Huguang and Jiangxi. During the period 1723–95, seventeen were reported in as many sampled counties. In late Qing, long after the Qianlong emperor had ended the official status of the Bazha, thirteen of the temples were still reported between 1796 and 1874, and the one rebuilding project reported was sponsored by the local government.[48]

*Bazha and popular religion.* If official support for the Bazha rites was weak and sporadic, what prevented their complete extinction? In spite of the strictures of the Qianlong emperor, passages describing the offering

---

[48] For popular Bazha temples elsewhere, also see Yang, *Religion in Chinese Society*, 446, and W.A. Grootaers, "The Sanctuaries in a North-China City: A Complete Survey of the Cultic Buildings in the City of Hsuan-hua (Chahar)," in *Melanges Chinois et Bouddhiques*, no. 26 (Bruxelles, 1995), 112–14.

in the canonical texts were always available to those who would re-vive them or, at least, to tolerate the popular practice. Moreover, an episode recounted in the *Liji* has Confucius officiating at the Bazha rites in the state of Lu.[49] The story may be apocryphal, but the source was impeccable.

May there also have been support for the Bazha in popular belief and practice? There is some reason to believe that this was the case. The vitality of popular cults depends on their proven efficacy. A Jiangnan gazetteer entry for the Bazha temple includes the story of a disastrous infestation of locusts in 1814 that was cut short by the sudden appear-ance of locust-eating worms and immense flocks of hungry birds. This extraordinary event was reported to the throne, and the emperor re-sponded by inscribing an honorific signboard for the temple.[50]

There is also evidence of popular support from the annual cycle of festivals in north China. A casual search of the "Manners and Customs" chapters in gazetteers for the sampled counties in north China turned up many references to popular La observances on the eighth day of the twelfth month, but no Zha. Here one finds the custom of making *labazhou* (gruel), sometimes with lists of the meatless ingredients, and a *lajiu* (wine). In some accounts, the gruel is shared with friends, and in some it is claimed that eating the gruel will ward off the plague (*wen*). In one instance, monks of the neighboring monasteries participated in the rite as well.[51] Given the generally assumed association of La and Zha, it is reasonable to count these remote echoes of the ancient La festival as having supported the late imperial *zha* offerings.

*Implications.* The Bazha offerings to the agricultural deities evolved both official and popular forms. The popular forms were the more robust be-cause they developed freely outside the law and because of their place at the heart of a communal harvest festival. The official rites, on the con-trary, were restrained in their development by the relative weakness of their basis in the canonical texts and by the fact, noted by the Qianlong emperor, that they were rendered superfluous by the more august rites for Xiannong and the Spirits of Soil and Grain. The toleration, or active support, of the local rites on the part of the imperial government and the local officials reflected their recognition of the complementarity of

---

[49] *Li Ki*, trans. Couvreur, 1:496–7.
[50] 1915G051, 9.2b.
[51] For these observances, also see also Li-ch'ên Tun and Derek Bodde, *Annual Customs and Festivals in Peking as Recorded in tl e Yen-ching Sui-shih-chi*, 2nd rev. ed. (Hong Kong, 1965), Chapter 12.

the "dionysian" temper of the popular rites and the "appollonian" manner of the official.

## Guanyin

In Chinese Buddhism, the Bodhisattva Guanyin [Skt. Avalokitesvara] presided over the Pure Land, or Western Paradise, together with the Amitabha Buddha and the Bodhisattva Dashi [Skt. Mahasthamaprapta]. In the popular religion, Guanyin was refashioned as a goddess of infinite compassion and perhaps the most widely worshiped female deity in the pantheon. She may even have outshone her male popular counterpart, the ubiquitous Guan Yü (the divinized paladin and god of wealth). Her help was accessible to all in need and to those who aspired to rebirth in her paradise. Women especially turned to her in her role as Guanyin Bringer of Children (Songzi Guanyin).[52]

Guanyin and her cult of the Pure Land shared in the legitimacy extended to Buddhism under the Ministry of Rites. However, perhaps because of her Buddhist and alien origin, she was excluded from the pantheon of the official religion in the Ming and Qing.[53] From the Buddhist side, a partial accommodation was reached with the official religion, or at least with its cosmological foundation. The official pantheon's four sacred peaks of the cardinal directions were mirrored in the establishment of the main Buddhist monastery temples of four great bodhisattvas at the four corners of the Chinese world. As Guanyin resided in the east in her Putuo Shan grotto,[54] so Manjusri (Wenzhu) resided in the north on Wutai Shan in Shanxi; Samantabhadra (Puxian) in the west on Emeishan in Sichuan; and Ksitigarbha (Dizang) in the south on Jiuhuashan in Anhui.[55.]

*Guanyin and popular orthodoxy.* Guanyin was accompanied in the popular pantheon by such other powerful goddesses as the Princess of the Azure Clouds, Bixia Yuanjun (daughter of the god of the Eastern Peak and wife

---

[52] Maspero, "Mythologie," 190.

[53] Her temples in Hangzhou and Yongcheng were recorded in the official *History of the Qing*, but this may have reflected patronage by the local magistrates. *Qingshi*, juan 85, p. 1072.7, .8. However, Guanyin had been adopted by Emperor Taizong of the Khitan Liao as a tutelary spirit of his ruling house. *Liaoshi*, 遼史, comp. Toghto (Beijing, Zhonghua Shuju edn.) juan 49, p. 835.

[54] Putuo Shan is a small island off the Zhejiang coast, in the Zhusan archipelago, approximately seventy miles east of Ningbo. See Chün-fang Yü, "P'u-tuo Shan," in *Pilgrims and Sacred Sites in China*, Susan Naquin and Chün-fang Yü, eds. (Berkeley, 1992), 202, 203.

[55] Maspero, "Mythologie," 142–3.

of the God of the Eastern Ocean, a.k.a. Divine Mother or Shenmu, a.k.a. Lady of Taishan or Taishan Niangniang); and the Empress of Heaven or Tianhou (a.k.a. Mazu). Temples dedicated to Bixia Yuanjun were common across north China, while those dedicated to Tianhou were found mainly along the east coast and in Lingnan, but Guanyin was conspicuously present in every region of China from the fifteenth century through the nineteenth.

She appeared in the ubiquitous popular shrines and temples dedicated to her and in Buddhist temples where she was installed in a shrine of her own behind the principal image and facing north. She faced north, it was said, because she was awaiting repentant sinners from the darker regions to come and seek her help.[56] Her shrine was often made to resemble a rocky grotto, which was a reference to her dwelling place on Putuo Shan Island. She also was a familiar presence in the popular pantheon temples (*zongshen miao*).[57] As an object of domestic worship, her image was found on household altar tables throughout the empire.[58]

Guanyin was integrated into the hierarchy of the popular pantheon where she mediated between Yanluo's underworld and the bereaved survivors. Although the Bodhisattva Dizang was specifically responsible for offering hope of release to souls in Hell, Guanyin also had a role in the infernal justice system. In one account, when prayers were offered to Guanyin on behalf of the souls of the blameless, she would come for them on her raft of lotus blossoms before they could be escorted below to Yama, and bring them to the Western paradise.[59]

The popular cult of Guanyin bore the marks of Daoist as well as Buddhist influence. According to a legend of her mortal life, she suffered martyrdom at the hands of her royal father, whom she had enraged by her refusal to marry. She was subsequently rescued from the underworld and restored to life by the Jade Emperor. The Buddha then appeared to her, gave her a "peach of immortality," and bore her to Putuo Shan. There she subsequently was enthroned as the Most Merciful and

---

[56] Grootaers, "Sanctuaries." Also see Karl Ludvig Reichelt, *Truth and Tradition in Chinese Buddhism* (Shanghai, 1934), 246–8, and Welch, *Practice*, 92.

[57] I.e., *Qisheng miao* or *zongshen miao*. 1808B010, 12.2b. (In these temples, of which there were "more than ten," Guanyin was given the highest place, followed by Guandi.) 1911D037, 12.14b.

[58] Maspero, "Mythologie," 140–1. Also see Clarence Burton Day, *Chinese Peasant Cults: Being a Study of Chinese Paper Gods* (Shanghai, 1940; repr., Taipei, 1969), especially, "Triads and Pantheons," 154–9. Also, Le P. H[enri] Dore, *Manuel des superstitions chinoises ou petit indicateur des superstitions les plus communes en Chine* (Shanghai, 1936), 93, 122.

[59] Cohen, "Souls and Salvation," 181.

Benevolent Bodhisattva.[60] It is also significant that her Putuo Shan Island
had already been sanctified as a haunt of the Daoist immortals.[61]

*Guanyin in the local histories.* Unlike the worship of Bazha or Dongyue,
the worship of Guanyin was historically of foreign origin, although her
Chinese "home" on Putuo Shan Island (approximately one hundred
miles east of Hangzhou) was identified by the faithful with Potolaka (the
Indian home of Avalokitesvara/Guanyin).[62] For those who accepted this
identification, it may have "naturalized" her in China. In any event, her
many appearances to worshipers and her benefactions left no doubt as
to her living presence.[63] Putuo Shan Island's situation astride the sea
lanes to Hangzhou and Ningbo made it a lively maritime entrepôt. It
also exposed it to pirate raids, and its temples were often destroyed.[64]

Just half of the temples reported in the sampled counties throughout
the empire were built in urban centers and, therefore, under the eyes
of the local officials. Of the 178 temples, 64 were located in the county
seats (35 within the walls, 16 at the gates, and 13 at the customs posts).
Another 25 were in smaller towns.

Guanyin's cult flourished under the protection afforded by the quasi-
official status of the registered Buddhist temples and clergy. This may
have contributed to the fact that some eighty-five percent of the recorded
shrines and temples that were dedicated to her (155 of 178 in the sampled
counties) were listed in the gazetteers under the head of the registered
Buddhist and Daoist temples (*siguan*). Official acceptance of her cult is
also attested by the fact that of thirty-one construction or repair projects
where sponsorship was recorded, the sponsors of thirteen were officials,
and one was sponsored by a literatus (*ru*). In eight cases, the sponsor
was a Buddhist monk, and in one, a Daoist priest. The sponsors of the
remaining eight were "local people," not further identified. At least
one of the Guanyin temples served as the county's Buddhist Registry.
At times during the Ming, Guanyin also had patrons in the imperial
court. The Yongle emperor's empress, Xü, and the Wanli emperor and
his mother were among her devotees.[65]

---

[60] Maspero, "Mythologie," 99, 191–2.

[61] Yü, "P'u-tuo Shan," 204–5.

[62] Yü, "P'u-tuo Shan," 191, 192, and Richard Robinson, *Buddhist Religion*, 3rd ed. (Belmont,
   1982), 169–70. The Potala Palace of Tibetan Buddhism is yet another Potalaka. See R.A.
   Stein, *Tibetan Civilization*, trans. J.E. Stapleton Driver (Stanford, CA, 1972), 84–5. The
   canonical source for the sacred history of Potolaka is the *Avatamsaka* (*Huayan*) Sutra.

[63] The island sometimes lent its name to Guanyin's temples (e.g., the "Putuo an" 1928F017,
   7B.11b, located in Sichuan).

[64] Yü, "P'u-tuo Shan," 202–4, 210–13.

[65] Yü, "P'u-tuo Shan," 210–11.

The formal status of Guanyin's own temples and shrines was not in any way problematic for the authorities except insofar as they may have had personal objections to Buddhism. The pantheon temples, and Guanyin's presence in them, were something else again, however. On this matter, one compiler expressed his anxiety about this breakdown of order in religion:

The main spirits in the pantheon temples (*zongshen miao*) are: the *Sanqing* (i.e. the Three Pure Ones of Daoist cosmology) followed by *Yudi* (the Jade Emperor), the *Sidi* (the Four Emperors of the four directions), *Shouuxing* (the Longevity Star), *Sanguan* (the cosmogonic Three Agents of Daoism), and the Princess of the Many-Hued Clouds *Bixiayuanjun*. They [also] indiscriminately select Guanyin along with earth spirits and warrior spirits. Thus they combine Buddhist and Daoist [deities] in one [pantheon]. And among these [spirits] there are some that are verified and [others] that are unverified and are all treated alike. The categories of spirits are thus mixed up.[66]

Implicit in the complaint is the compiler's assumption that the mixture of spirits of different kinds in the temple resulted from the ignorance of those responsible; no consideration is given to the possibility that this may have been the valid expression of a "popular orthodoxy." It was for modern scholars to define and name this fourth Chinese religion.

The popular cult of Guanyin was largely observed by women.[67] Women devotees observed vegetarian fast days in her honor two or, in some cases, nine days each month. They also made offerings three times each year, on the nineteenth days of the second, sixth, and ninth months. The first of these days was conventionally counted as the goddess' birthday.[68] Her flourishing cult was sustained by the wonders she wrought. Although these often were answers to prayers for offspring, according to one of her legends she had refused marriage and died a martyr.[69] She therefore also aided women who chose not to marry. In her life as a young woman, and before her deification, the Empress of Heaven Tianhou or Mazu had taken a vow of chastity and devoted

---

[66] 1808B10 B1A123.

[67] A similar observation regarding Tian Hou may be found in James Watson, "Standardizing the Gods: The Promotion of T'ien Hou ('Empress of Heaven') along the South China Coast 960–1960," in *Popular Culture in Late Imperial China*, David Johnson et al. eds. (Berkeley, 1983), 320.

[68] J.J.M. DeGroot, *Les fêtes anuellement celebrées à Emoui (Amoy): étude concernant la religion populaire des chinois* (1886; repr. San Francisco, 1977), 199–200. Also see Dore, *Manuel*, 132, and *Gujin tushu jicheng, Damingfu fengsu* 大明府風俗 ce 74, p. 21.

[69] Maspero, "Mythologie," 191–2.

herself to Guanyin.[70] At the nether end of the social scale, Guanyin's boundless compassion also extended to the courtesans of Amoy.[71]

In a Jiangnan county, the commoner, Ting Fu, was unhappy because he had no heirs. He dreamed of Guanyin, who spoke to him. [Ting] Fu subsequently donated land and raised money to build [a convent]. After the convent was finished, he did in fact have two sons.[72]

Her powers extended to the control of natural forces as well. This story comes from a Sichuan county:

A sculpted figure of Guanyin stood on the embankment of Whitefish Shop. In the Chunxi reign (1174–89) the town suffered persistent flooding. The assembled townspeople prayed to the goddess. When the floods had subsided they built her a temple in that place.

Guanyin's other benefactions included answering prayers for good fortune in general (*Zhuli*)[73] and fostering a candidate's success in the civil examinations. In this case, the young man took up residence in a Guanyin temple while he prepared himself for his ordeal. After passing the examinations, he expressed his gratitude by a handsome donation of endowment fields.[74]

*Implications.* Guanyin's cult was a vehicle for the salvific power of compassion in Mahayana Buddhism and for the practical power of compassion, accessible especially to women, in the popular religion. Her presence in both religions complemented the relatively severe and male-dominated world of the official religion, from which she was firmly excluded.

### Lü Dongbin: The immortal Lüzu

Lü Dongbin, or *Lü Zu* (Master Lü), was the most illustrious of the *Baxian* (Eight Immortals) of Daoism. He owed his greater fame to the fact that he was taken up as a deity in the popular pantheon. According to his legend, he was an unsuccessful examination candidate in the Tang dynasty. The futility of life in the world of men was then revealed to him in a dream; he became the disciple of a Daoist master and attained immortality.[75] In Daoism, the immortals are liberated spirits who have no mission in the

---

[70] Maspero, "Mythologie," 164–5.
[71] Maspero, "Mythologie," 169.
[72] *Gujin tushu jicheng*, ce 114, 24.
[73] 1911D037, 12.10a; Maspero, "La religion chinoise," 53.
[74] *Gujin tushu jicheng*, ce 174, 48a.
[75] According to Dore, *Manuel*, 128, he was born in 798 in Yonglezhen, Shanxi. For his examination story, see Maspero, "Mythologie," 183–4.

world, heed no prayers, and are the objects of no cult. It is the stories about them that instruct the world in the ways to liberation.[76] In the Yuan dynasty, however, Lü was invested with an exalted Daoist title of *Chunyang yanzheng jinghua zunyou dijun* (Purely Yang, Expansively Governing, Reverently Transforming, Venerated and Beneficent Lord).[77]

In the popular religion, several occupations, including the jewelers, the barbers, and the merchants of Guangdong, adopted him as their tutelary deity. A legend among the jewelers had it that Maitreya fled the palace of the Buddha Sakyamuni with ingots of gold and silver. He descended to Earth where he hid himself among the living and set up shop as a jeweler. The Buddha then dispatched Lü Dongbin to find him. The immortal then arrested and subdued him with a magic cord and brought him back to the palace. According to a legend (from the early Qing dynasty, when Chinese were required to shave their heads in Manchu fashion) Lü was summoned to shave the emperor's head because his sensitive skin required special care.[78] As a failed examination candidate who had found happiness, the immortal also became a tutelary of scholars, although in this role he was overshadowed by the more powerful Wenchang (Literary Glory). In his most important role in the popular religion of the late Qing, Lü Zu was adopted by the merchants of Guangdong and installed in their guildhalls. He also was a patron of druggists and ink-stick makers.[79] The breadth of his presence in Chinese society is reflected in his domestic cult. Dore found him especially in the homes of scholars;[80] and Day found his likeness in popular pantheon prints of Zhejiang.[81]

Lü Zu's membership in the official pantheon had to wait for the reign of the emperor Renzong (1796–1820). The following terse entry appears under that reign in the Qing standard history's Rites Monograph: The capital region and the provinces made offerings to the "Purely Yang Expansively Governing Reverently Transforming Venerated and Beneficent Lord, LüYan."[82] It is not clear whether the performance of rites for Lü Zu was mandated at this time or, which is more likely, it meant only that a petition or petitions for official authorization of the cult had been approved. Some of the sampled gazetteers clarify this point.

---

[76] Schipper, *The Taoist Body*, 160–6.
[77] See entries in Cihai, 564, and *Gwoyeu tysrdean*, 4 vols. (Shangai, 1937; rept. Taipei, 1965), 625. *Dijun* was a title with which Daoist divinities were invested, and not a title used in the official religion.
[78] Maspero, "Mythologie," 167–8.
[79] Day, *Peasant Cults*, 111; Dore, *Manuel*, 126.
[80] Dore, *Manuel*, 93; Day, *Peasant Cults*, 158.
[81] Day, *Peasant Cults*, 158, where he appears in his persona as Zhun Zang, patron of druggists.
[82] *Qingshi*, 1072.4.

There was a flurry of activity regarding the official status of the cult around 1800. According to one source, the emperor acknowledged the completion of a Lü Zu temple in 1800 by bestowing an honorific signboard and prescribed regular offerings in spring and autumn. The liturgy was the same as that for the more illustrious Zhenwu (Immortal Warrior, a.k.a. Xuanwu, the Dark Warrior).[83] In 1805, when the Jiangnan director-general of the Grand Canal and the Ministry of Rites had discussed and reported on the offerings for Lü Zu, they were ordered to enter the rites into the *Sacrificial Statutes*. Subsequently, upon petition by the Grand Secretariat, four characters were added to Lü Zu's original title: "Assists Transformation in Harmony with the Origin." Moreover, the director-general (whose headquarters were at Huai'an) built shrines and urged performance of the rites for Lü Zu throughout the Huai region.[84]

*Lü Zu in the local histories.* Although a single Lü Zu temple appeared in Zhejiang in the Song, others did not begin to appear elsewhere in the sampled counties until the seventeenth century, and they were not numerous or widespread until the nineteenth century. The seventeen reported during that time were found in eight provinces and every region except the northwest and the southeast coast. Throughout the late imperial period, the cult was disproportionately represented in the Yangtze valley from Sichuan to the east coast.

The cult's association with the Guangdong merchants (thirteen of the thirty-five temples or shrines were in the guildhalls) may account for the concentration of temples in a relatively small number of counties, thirty-five temples in fourteen counties. This was an average of two and one-half per county (as many as seven in one county), and none at all were reported from the other thirty-nine.

The temples were sixty percent urban (twenty-seven percent were within the city, fourteen percent outside the gates, and eighteen percent in other towns). Two of the shrines were built within Buddhist temples, and one in a Wenchang temple. Of fifteen construction or repair projects with known sponsorship, nine, or sixty percent, had official sponsors, one was sponsored by a scholar (*ru*), four by "local persons," and one by a commoner. In another temple, the county government offered material

---

[83] 1882I015, 17.7b; 1932F040, 5.77a–7b. This entry is more specific: The annual offerings were presented on the fourth day of the first decade of the second and eighth months. Essentially the same information appears in 1889K019, 8.9b.

[84] 1889K019, 8.9b. For a different version of Lu Zu's official title, see Grootaers, "Sanctuaries," 9.

support when it defrayed the cost of the rites.[85] The high level of official sponsorship points to cooperation between the magistrates and the local merchants.

We learn from accounts in the gazetteers that worshipers consulted Lü Zu with divining sticks and that he "wrought many wonders."[86] A county magistrate built another temple in 1849 upon a gate tower, a place that was usually reserved for the Dark Warrior, and here he displayed his numinous power to protect the city.[87]

*Implications.* Lü Dongbin made his first historical appearance in the Tang and his first appearance as one of the Daoist Eight Immortals (*Baxian*) in the Song. In Yuan he was elevated to the rank of Imperial Lord (*Dijun*), appropriate to a major Daoist deity, and he was finally given a place in the official pantheon in 1805. His career went from unsuccessful civil service candidate to Daoist free spirit, immortal, and popular deity to member of the official pantheon. The vigor of his cult owed much to his role in the popular religion as the patron deity of the Guangdong merchants and other occupational groups.

### SUMMARY AND CONCLUSIONS

In contradistinction to the "alternative universe" of the Eternal Mother sects, I have presented Chinese orthodoxy as a continuous process of mutual accommodation among four functionally distinct religions: the official religion of the Chinese Empire, Buddhism, Daoism, and the popular religion. An aspect of their mutual accommodation was the overlapping of their respective pantheons, which has been explored here through a few illustrative cases. This overlap neither obliterated the distinctions among the four religions, nor did it give rise to irreconcilable conflicts among them. The stability of this religious system depended in part upon the functional complementarity of the religions and in part upon the multivalence of the Chinese deities – their assumption of different roles and personae in the different social contexts in which they were worshiped.

Each of the religions was necessary for the stability of the whole. Their ordained clergy and minor religious specialists, and the common laity were sufficiently invested in the stability of the existing order to accept it or, at least, not to challenge it directly. Thus, despite the secession of the

---

[85] 1882I038, 4.43a.
[86] 1932F040, 5.77b–78a.
[87] 1882K036, 2.27a.

sectarians, the "orthodox" center held. It has sometimes been supposed that it was power exercised from the center, rather than the acquiescence of the governed that held the empire together, and it is true that military and police power were resorted to. But given the relatively thin layer of imperial administration,[88] the chaotic and antiquated imperial fiscal administration,[89] and the limited availability of coercive force to mobilize resources and secure compliance with the laws,[90] the sociopolitical order must have depended during most of the late imperial period upon the widespread acquiescence, or at least the passivity, of its members for its survival. It is argued here that the formation of the "Chinese orthodoxy" contributed to this acquiescence.

There was a complementary relationship between the three institutionalized religions and the popular religion. The three were institutionalized in the sense of having their own canonical texts, ordained clergies, and sacred places. The popular religion had its sacred places as well as a social base in the villages and neighborhoods, but it depended upon the validating patronage of local officials and the participation of Buddhist and Daoist religious specialists in its major rites.

In conformity with the nested spatial hierarchy of the imperial administration, the official religion strictly limited the territorial jurisdictions of the deities of the official pantheon. The popular religion, on the contrary, constructed local and regional versions of the pantheon without regard for jurisdictional boundaries. This provided for *lateral* integration, which complemented the *vertical* provided by the official cults. Lateral integration was also provided by the Buddhist monastery temples, which maintained pilgrimage sites and which accommodated visiting laity and wandering monks.

Another kind of complementarity appeared in the fact that Buddhism and Daoism were world-transcendent in their highest aspirations whereas the official and popular religions were bounded by the phenomenal world under its spiritual aspects. This was evidently not to the disadvantage of the latter two religions, however. Because the resolution of transcendental issues was left to the Confucian philosophers

---

[88] Charles Oscar Hucker, "Ming Government," in *Cambridge History*, 29–30.

[89] R. Huang, "The Ming Fiscal Administration," in *Cambridge History*, 168–71. Note especially Huang's observations for late Ming that "Tax regulations became inseparable from social custom, the one perverting the other," and his local reference to "local attempts to change the system."

[90] See Martin Heijdra's observation that the late Ming efforts at governmental reform at the local level could not be adopted at the imperial level because it was not until early Qing and the "Manchu reliance on violence, fear, and intimidation created conditions under which the implementation of the late Ming reforms could be enforced on a wider scale than before. In "Socio-Economic Development," 578. Also see Hucker, "Ming Government," 62–70.

and to the learned monks and priests of Buddhism and Daoism, the official and popular religions were spared the tensions that might have resulted from their having been torn between aspirations to world-transcendence above, and engagement with the quotidian affairs of the empire and its subjects below.

The predominantly masculine, civil, and exclusive world of the official religion was complemented especially by the popular religion's openness and its greater hospitality to female deities and to the women who worshiped them. It was complemented in its civil aspect by the popular religion's deified warrior heroes such as Guan Yü, who was worshiped as a paragon of loyalty, pillar of justice, and god of wealth. Finally, the popular religion was constantly being replenished locally by new cults, some of which flourished and were selectively added to the lower ranks of the other pantheons.

Buddhism and Daoism were necessarily less open to women's participation than the popular religion was, but they complemented the official religion to some degree. Although there were ordained Buddhist nuns who shared in ministering to the needs of laywomen, their convents were subordinate to the monasteries to which they were attached and they were forbidden to travel about.[91] The case of Daoism is less clear, but the *vocation* of Daoist priest, *daoshi*, has always been open to women; however, it is not clear that a woman could hold that *title* in late imperial times.[92] With regard to the balance between the civil and martial aspects of rulership as these were expressed in religion, the official religion in Ming times lacked a conspicuous martial presence. The Manchus, who constituted a ruling military elite in the empire, soon altered the balance by enshrining the immensely popular warrior god Guan Yü in the official pantheon and building him a temple in every prefecture and county. Both Buddhism and Daoism also found room for martial deities. The entrance halls of Buddhist temples present a martial aspect to the outside world with the terrifying forms of the Four Heavenly Kings in the entrance hall. Similarly, one of the most popular figures in the Daoist pantheon is the Dark Warrior, Xuanwu.

This mutual accommodation of the four religions is reflected in the selected cases of particular deities and their cults. The God of the Eastern

---

[91] Reichelt, *Truth and Tradition*, 255.

[92] Information on Buddhist convents and their management is relatively hard to come by, but see Reichelt, *Truth and Tradition*, 255. Convents were associated with the monasteries and subject to their control. The question of Daoist nuns and convents is obscure. Berling, "Taoism in Ming Culture," 961, says that she "has been unable to locate any information on the organized religious life of Taoist women." Schipper, *The Taoist Body*, 58, says only that women may now "become masters only by vocation."

Peak makes a good starting point because of its ancient origins, its prominence throughout the empire, and the relatively abundant literature surrounding it. The classical, open-altar worship continued through the imperial period and was joined under official auspices by the anthropomorphic temple form no later than the Song. The Daoist and popular forms were almost equally ancient, and flourished in late imperial times. In his official roles, the god kept faith on the open altar with the ancient cosmology, and in his temples he forged links with the Daoist and popular religiosity of the imperial subjects. When his compassionate daughter joined him at the summit of Taishan, her cult greatly enhanced the feminine aspect of the popular religion. In the face of all this, the objections that have been noted to the "promiscuity" of worship offered to the God of the Eastern Peak and his daughter without regard for administrative geography were of little avail. Local officials grudgingly tolerated their cult when they did not actively patronize it.

The sovereign's offerings to the Eight Spirits of Agriculture enjoyed canonical status in the preimperial texts, and, at the same time, they were loosely connected with a plebeian folk festival. Subsequently throughout imperial history, the imperial offering rites appeared and disappeared from the *Sacrificial Statutes*, but the rites survived independently in popular practice in north China. The imperial offerings were resumed in Song and then abandoned again until the Manchus reintroduced them to the Chinese Empire from their preconquest capital in Mukden around 1644. The Yongzheng emperor (ca.1730) took the additional step of mandating them for the prefectural and county governments. The Qianlong emperor promptly overruled him and abolished the official rites in 1745. At the same time, the latter expressly gave his blessing to the performance of the popular rites "in accordance with local custom." Despite his having been appalled at some of the absurdities he saw in the popular rites, he also saw redeeming value in their contribution to communal solidarity, agricultural output, and popular morale.

As one of the triumvirate presiding over the Western Paradise – Amitabha, Avalokitesvara (Guanyin), and Mahasthamaprapta – Guanyin was assured of an eminent place in Mahayana Buddhism. In this role, she enjoyed the protection extended by the imperial government to orthodox Buddhism. Her greatest flourishing came in the popular religion as the most eminent of a small group of compassionate and powerful goddesses where she was without formal standing in the law but still enjoyed the support of local officials and local gentry as well as the Buddhist and Daoist clergy.

In the popular religion, she and the other goddesses complemented the masculine character of the official religion, but their worship still fell within the Chinese orthodoxy of the four religions. Although Guanyin's compassion was infinite and always accessible, her salient image is that of the bringer and protector of children and, therefore, that of a guardian of the family and a pillar of the very social order that had been rejected by the devotees of the Eternal Mother.

In orthodox Daoism, Lü Dongbin was an immortal *xian* and not a god (*shenming*). As the beloved favorite of the illustrious Eight Immortals, however, he came to be worshiped as a god in the popular religion. In late imperial times, Lü Dongbin was a versatile tutelary deity of jewelers, barbers, merchant guilds, druggists, and ink-stick makers. He also extended his protection to certain cities. Emperor Renzong recognized his immense popularity when he invested him with an additional title and enacted the liturgy to be used in his worship. Lü Dongbin now had a foot in three pantheons: as an immortal in Daoism and as a god in the official and popular religions.

In conclusion, by their mutual accommodations, and their selective adoptions and exclusions, the four religions constituted the imperial social order of late imperial China under its religious aspect. Thus reinforced, the orthodox order withstood the defections of the sectarians and their radical transvaluation of the orthodox values.

GAZETTEERS CITED

1599M000 *Guangxi tongzhi* 廣西通志
17250000 *Gujin tushu jicheng* 古今圖書集成
1733H040 *Leanxian zhi* 樂安縣志
1808B010 *Yuchengxian zhi* 禹城縣志
1816D069 *Mengjianxian zhi* 孟津縣志
1882C010 *Shouyangxian zhi* 壽陽縣志
1882I015 *Guian xian zhi* 歸安縣志
1882I038 *Ninghaixian zhi* 寧海縣志
1882K036 *Yingchengxian zhi* 應城縣志
1889K019 *Dangyangxian zhi* 當陽縣志
1894F056 *Yongchuanxian zhi* 永川縣志
1906I003 *Fuyangxian zhi* 富陽縣志
1911D037 *Ninglingxian zhi* 寧陵縣志
1915G051 *Huainingxian zhi* 懷寧縣志
1932F040 *Quxian zhi* 渠縣志

# Orthodoxy and revolt: The role of religion in the seventeenth-century Ukrainian uprising against the Polish-Lithuanian Commonwealth

FRANK E. SYSYN

THE sixteenth and seventeenth centuries were an age of wars of religion. From the Catholic-Huguenot struggle in France to the Defenestration of Prague (1618), religious differences both caused and justified numerous civil and foreign wars. In one case – the English Civil War – political and social radicalism grew out of religious disputes.[1] Although modern historians have come to question religious motives and justifications as the principal catalysts in struggles such as the Dutch war of independence, they have not questioned the importance of religious divisions within societies and monarchs' attempts to impose religious uniformity as major issues in early modern struggles. The European phenomenon stretched from the Urals to the Atlantic. In Russia, religious disputes and millenarianism played a major role in all revolts after the Old Believer schism of the late seventeenth century.

Few events in early modern Ukrainian history drew such widespread contemporary attention as the Khmel'nyts'kyi uprising against the Polish-Lithuanian Commonwealth. Rumors of the slaughter of landlords, Jews, and Catholics in 1648 reverberated in the grain ports on the Baltic, in the Jesuit houses in central Europe, and in Jewish communities on the Mediterranean. The destruction of the armies of the

---

[1] On the role of religion in early modern revolts, see Perez Zagorin, *Rebels and Rulers, 1500–1660*, vol. 1 (Cambridge, 1982), Chapter 6.

154

Polish-Lithuanian Commonwealth led Sweden, the Habsburgs, France, and many other powers to reevaluate their view of the balance of power. The Cossack leader Bohdan Khmel'nyts'kyi had upset this balance by his alliance with the Crimean khan in early 1648. Within a year after he had started his revolt, Muscovite, Transylvanian, Moldavian, Polish, and Turkish emissaries came to the Ukraine to treat with this Zaporozhian Cossack hetman. A decade after the revolt began, all of eastern and northern Europe was involved in wars that had their origin in the Cossack stronghold on the lower Dnieper. By the late 1650s, Hetman Khmel'nyts'kyi and his successor, Hetman Ivan Vyhovs'kyi, planned (with Sweden, Brandenburg-Prussia, and Transylvania) to partition the Polish-Lithuanian Commonwealth, and then, when this plan did not work, Hetman Vyhovs'kyi arranged an agreement with the Commonwealth to create a Duchy of Rus' in Ukraine and to abolish the Union of Brest, the agreement of 1596 through which Rome had gained control over some of the Commonwealth's Orthodox believers. Small wonder that the revolt and new political power in Ukraine attracted widespread attention.

The aspects of the Ukrainian revolt that received international attention in the 1640s and 1650s also draw today's specialist in early modern revolts to its study. It is one of the few popular uprisings in seventeenth-century Europe that defeated the upper classes and resulted in an improvement in the legal and economic position of the peasants, the urban populace, and other disadvantaged groups. Whether the Ukrainian revolt constituted a "social revolution" may be questioned, but it did serve as a rallying point for opposition to economic, social, and political repression well into the eighteenth century.[2]

The Ukrainian revolt shifted the balance of power in Eastern Europe. Although the Polish-Lithuanian Commonwealth survived the onslaught, it never regained the position it held before 1648. Muscovy suffered setbacks and defeats after Tsar Aleksei Mikhailovich accepted the allegiance of Hetman Bohdan Khmel'nyts'kyi in 1654; however, that allegiance laid the foundation for the growth of the Russian Empire in the decades to follow. The Ottomans ultimately failed in their last effort to conquer the north, but the conspiracies and plots that began with the revolt so shook the political order in Eastern Europe that they challenged the Ottomans to attempt to assert control. By the early eighteenth century, a new balance of power had emerged in the eastern half of the

---

[2] See Frank E. Sysyn, "War der Chmel'nyc'kyj-Aufstand eine Revolution? Eine Charakteristik der 'grossen ukrainischen Revolte' und der Bildung des kosakischen Het'manstaates," *Jahrbücher für Geschichte Osteuropas* 43.1 (1995): 1–18.

continent, with a dominant Russian Empire under Peter I. Try as he would, Khmel'nyts'kyi's successor, Ivan Mazepa, could not shake that dominion.

The revolt in the Ukraine also produced a new political entity, the Cossack hetmanate. Although its period of full independence was relatively brief, the political order that endured until 1783 constitutes one of the few examples of "state-building" through a revolt that established the borders of a new polity. The Ukrainian revolt is comparable to the Dutch war of independence in this respect. Both conflicts encouraged the development of a national culture and consciousness that was associated with the new political order. In the Ukrainian case, both the political entity and the culture disintegrated in the eighteenth century and were submerged into the Russian Empire and Russian imperial culture, only to reemerge in the modern Ukrainian national awakening. But the more than one hundred twenty-five years of Ukrainian autonomy after 1648 nonetheless constitutes one of the most important instances of an early modern revolt creating a new political entity and reshaping a cultural pattern.[3]

Since the late seventeenth-century Ukrainian Eyewitness Chronicler, who asserted that the reason for the "war" was the "Poles' persecution of Orthodoxy," many commentators have believed that religious conflict caused the Khmel'nyts'kyi uprising of 1648.[4] Historians have also described the religious strife during the conflict and the function of religion in motivating both sides. Certainly the long-term outcomes of the war, the decline of religious pluralism in Ukraine with the establishment of the Orthodox Cossack hetmanate, and the triumph of Catholicism in the right-bank Ukraine and Poland speak for the importance of religion in the conflict. The tsarist government and Russian Orthodox Church in the nineteenth century viewed the religious issue as cardinal in their retrospective justification of revolt, war, and tsarist claims to Ukraine after 1654. Even Soviet historians admitted the importance of the religious issue, though they usually saw religious disputes as reflecting national and social tensions.[5]

The Polish-Lithuanian Commonwealth and Ukraine seem to fit a general European pattern of strife caused by religious divisions and differences. Yet they differ in one way. In the Polish and Lithuanian

---

[3] See Frank E. Sysyn, "The Khmel'nyts'kyi Uprising and Ukrainian Nation-Building," *Journal of Ukrainian Studies* 17.1–2 (Summer–Winter 1992): 141–70.

[4] *Litopys samovydtsia*, ed. Ia. Dzyra (Kyiv, 1971), 45.

[5] See V. Nikonov, "Rol' pravoslavnoi tserkvi v osvoboditel'noi voine ukrainskogo naroda," *Zhurnal Moskovskoi patriarkhii* 12 (1953): 31–43, and John Basarab, *Pereiaslav 1654: A Historiographical Study* (Edmonton, 1982).

states, contending Christian faiths – Catholic, Orthodox, and Armenian Apostolic – had long been permitted. No European states had developed societies with religious pluralism in the medieval period except for Poland and Lithuania.[6] The Utraquist-Catholic split in Bohemia may be seen as an exception, but this situation was never stable. Some states also occasionally gave toleration to non-Christians, Jews or Muslims, but none permitted the existence of "error" among their Christian inhabitants. Christian diversity could only flourish in states such as the Ottoman Empire, where the rulers cared little about their subjects' views about the Trinity or church governance.[7] Only in the sixteenth century did the monolith of Western Christendom break down, occasionally leading to experiments in toleration such as in Transylvania after the 1560s and in the Holy Roman Empire after 1648 (at least on a territorial basis). Poland and Lithuania, states on the divide between Western and Eastern Christianity, had to accept religious pluralism from the fourteenth century because both states had numerous and well-established Ruthenian (Ukrainian-Belarusian) populations (a minority in Poland, a majority in Lithuania).[8]

From the late sixteenth century, the relations of the Polish-Lithuanian state with its Orthodox inhabitants became confrontational. As the Orthodox Church stood in opposition to the state's religious policies and Orthodox believers opposed attempts at accommodation by their hierarchs, the Orthodox faith in the early seventeenth century came to symbolize revolt and challenge to authority. Therefore, when the great uprising in Ukraine against the Polish-Lithuanian Commonwealth broke out in 1648, religious grievances intermixed with economic, social, and national issues. This chapter outlines how the Polish-Lithuanian state estranged its Orthodox inhabitants despite periods of attempted accommodation. It also analyzes to what degree Orthodoxy and the Orthodox Church caused and took part in the revolt. It is the story of

---

[6] See Wiktor Weintraub, "Tolerance and Intolerance in Old Poland," *Canadian Slavonic Papers* 13 (1971): 21–44.

[7] On Ottoman religious policies, see Steven Runciman, *The Great Church in Captivity* (Cambridge, 1968).

[8] In this chapter, "Ruthenian" is used to render the noun *Rusyn* and the adjective *rus'kyi*, both of which are derived from the word *Rus'*, the name of the medieval East Slavic polity. In the seventeenth-century Polish-Lithuanian Commonwealth, the terms were most often used to describe the Ukrainians and Belarusians, who shared a common literary language. Forms of these terms were also used by the Muscovites to refer to themselves, but were more seldom used to describe Muscovy and Russians in the Commonwealth, where Ruthenians (*Rusyny*) and Muscovites (*Moskva*) were often described as two peoples alongside other peoples of the region. The varying fates of Ukraine and Belarus in the seventeenth century greatly furthered the distinction between these otherwise closely related peoples and cultures.

how a conservative faith became revolutionary and how churchmen who sought to maintain the established political and social order found their Church and their faith increasingly drawn into and associated with the uprising.

The Polish-Lithuanian Commonwealth, like the medieval kingdom of Poland, offered only limited toleration to Orthodox subjects.[9] The Orthodox faced discrimination from statutes such as the Union of Horodlo of 1413 in Lithuania, only fully rescinded in 1563, and the Magdeburg law regulations in both states. Catholic theologians argued for rebaptism of Orthodox converts in the fifteenth century. After 1439, attempts were made to entice or pressure the Orthodox into accepting the Union of Florence (1439). Nevertheless, for three hundred years, Ukraine and Belarus were lands of overlapping Christian religious jurisdictions.[10] The Orthodox-Catholic conflict did not, therefore, have the poignant newness that the religious divisions in France or England had in the sixteenth century. Indeed the initial climate of tolerance in Polish-Lithuanian society toward Western Christian schisms in the mid-sixteenth century may have stemmed, in part, from the long-term experience of Eastern and Western Christians coexisting.

Political developments shaped the evolution of the church of the Ruthenians, which had originated in the conversion of Kyivan (Kievan) Rus' in the tenth century.[11] The Tatar-Mongol conquest of the thirteenth century that decimated the land and destroyed that state had profound consequences for the Church. After a relatively short time under the Tatars, the Orthodox of Ukraine and Belarus came under Catholic rule. The political divisions of the territories of the vast metropolitanate of Kyiv (Kiev) that had arisen in medieval Rus' and the migration of the metropolitans to the Russian northeast of their see in the early fourteenth century led to numerous attempts in the fourteenth and fifteenth centuries to recover the metropolitanate or to create a separate metropolitanate in the Ukrainian and Belarusian lands. The Orthodox Galician-Volhynian, pagan Lithuanian, and Catholic Lithuanian and Polish rulers all pursued this policy at times. A lasting separation occurred in the mid-fifteenth century in the wake of the unsuccessful Union of the Eastern and Western Churches at Florence (1439), the fall

---

[9] See Kazimierz Chodynicki, *Kościół prawosławny a Rzeczpospolita Polska: Zarys historiczny 1370–1632* (Warsaw, 1934) on the situation of the Orthodox Church.

[10] See Eduard Winter, *Byzanz und Rom im Kampf um die Ukraine, 955–1939* (Leipzig, 1942).

[11] On the Christianization and the culture of Rus', see Mykhailo Hrushevsky, *History of Ukraine-Rus'*: vol. 1. *From Prehistory to the Eleventh Century* (Edmonton and Toronto, 1997); A.P. Vlasto, *The Entry of the Slavs into Christendom* (Cambridge, 1970); and Simon Franklin and Jonathan Shepard, *The Emergence of Rus': 750–1200* (London, 1996).

of Constantinople (1453), and the establishment of a self-proclaimed autocephalous metropolitanate of Moscow. The erection of a Kyiv metropolitanate limited to the Lithuanian and Polish states ensured ever greater influence of the Catholic rulers of Poland and Lithuania in the appointment of Orthodox metropolitans and bishops, albeit with the metropolitans turning to Constantinople for consecration. The Kyiv metropolitanate became a church on the defensive against state-supported Catholicism, which sought to undermine its authority.[12]

The Protestant Reformation and the Catholic Reform or Counter-Reformation radically changed the relation of rulers and ecclesiastical institutions in the Kingdom of Poland and the Grand Duchy of Lithuania, united as the Polish-Lithuanian Commonwealth after the Union of Lublin of 1569.[13] The Catholic Church split as reform groups such as the Lutherans, Calvinists, Antitrinitarians, Anabaptists, and Czech Brethren founded their own religious establishments and began successful missions among the Orthodox. While toleration for the Orthodox in the fourteenth century could be explained largely by the extent and populousness of the Ukrainian-Belarusian territories amassed by the Polish and Lithuanian rulers, the acceptance of religious multiplicity in the sixteenth century, legalized in 1573, derived chiefly from the decay of royal power and the sweeping rights of the nobility.[14] Still, the decision of the last Jagiellonian kings not to adhere to any of the Reformed groups, and the increasing Catholic dedication of the elected kings of the late sixteenth century and early seventeenth century, above all of Sigismund Vasa, greatly benefited the Catholic Church. The ability of the king to favor Catholics in royal appointments and the presence of Catholic bishops in the Diet of the Commonwealth strengthened the Church's position. As the Counter-Reformation won over large numbers of the nobility, including Orthodox, in the early seventeenth century, the position of non-Catholics began to decline, as did the relative spirit of tolerance of the late sixteenth century.

---

[12] On the early church, see Andrzej Poppe, *The Rise of Christian Russia* (London, 1982) and his *Państwo i kościół na Rusi w XI wieku* (Warsaw, 1968); Sophia Senyk, *A History of the Church in Ukraine*, vol. 1 (= *Orientalia Christiana Analecta* 243) (Rome, 1993); John Lister Fennell, *A History of the Russian Church to 1448* (London and New York, 1995); and John Meyendorff, *Byzantium and the Rise of Russia* (Cambridge, 1981).

[13] See Ambroise Jobert, *De Luther à Mohila: La Pologne dans la crise de la chrétienté 1517–1648* (= *Collection Historique de l'Institut d'Etudes Slaves* 21) (Paris, 1974).

[14] See Janusz Tazbir, *A State without Stakes: Polish Religious Toleration in the Sixteenth and Seventeenth Centuries*, trans. A.T. Jordan (New York, 1973); Miroslaw Korolko, *Klejnot swobodnego sumienia: Polemika wokół Konfederacji warszawskiej w latach 1573–1658* (Warsaw, 1974); and Henryk Wisner, *Rozróżnieni w wierze: Szkice z dziejów Rzeczypospolitej schyłku XVI i połowy XVII wieku* (Warsaw, 1974).

In crossing the line between the Western Christian Polish, Lithuanian, and German populations to the Eastern Christian Ruthenian population, the Protestants and Catholics challenged both the national and religious identity of the Ukrainians and Belarusians. The metropolitanate of Kyiv was usually referred to as the Rus' or Ruthenian Church, and the Ruthenians were seen as an ethno-religious community in which adherence to the Church was a necessary characteristic of Ruthenian identity. Indeed on this religious borderline, the Ruthenian faith was often placed in opposition to the Polish faith (the Liakhs' faith), with Western Christianity being defined by the major local ethno-cultural group that professed it.[15] Hence conversion was generally perceived as a change of ethno-cultural allegiance.[16]

In addition to losses to Protestantism and Catholicism, the Orthodox Church suffered a schism in the late sixteenth century. Initially, reform movements within the Church, responding to Protestant and Catholic challenges, had produced divergent factions but no schisms.[17] When some hierarchs negotiated an agreement recognizing papal jurisdiction over the metropolitan see of Kyiv (Union of Brest, 1596), however, a permanent schism resulted between Orthodox and Uniates. Unlike the Union of Florence, which was an attempt at a universal union, the Union of Brest was a local submission to a papacy that was now more centralized and less favorable to acceptance of other traditions and churches.[18] In addition, the Latin-rite Church never gave equal status to Uniate Catholics, that is, the Christians of the Ruthenian rite who now accepted papal authority. Many Roman clergy would have preferred full

---

[15] The identification of ethnicity with faith in Ukrainian territories was strengthened by the existence of the Armenian Church, a clearly defined ethno-national religious institution.

[16] See Frank E. Sysyn, "Ukrainian-Polish Relations in the Seventeenth Century: The Role of National Consciousness and the National Conflict in the Khmel'nyts'kyi Movement," in *Poland and Ukraine: Past and Present*, ed. P. Potichnyj (Edmonton and Toronto, 1980), 58–82. On the evolution of Ukrainian national identity in the early modern period, see the essays by T. Chynczewska-Hennel, Frank E. Sysyn, and Z. Kohut in *Concepts of Nationhood in Early Modern Europe*, Ivo Banac and Frank E. Sysyn eds. (= *Harvard Ukrainian Studies* 10.3–4) (Cambridge, MA, 1986), 377–92, 393–423, and 559–76, respectively; and Ihor Ševčenko, "The Rise of National Identity to 1700," in his *Ukraine between East and West: Essays on Cultural History to the Early Eighteenth Century* (Edmonton and Toronto, 1996), 187–96.

[17] On the religious revival of the late sixteenth century in Ukraine, see Ihor Ševčenko, "The Rebirth of the Rus' Faith," in *Ukraine between East and West*, 130–48, and William K. Medlin and Christos G. Patrinelis, *Renaissance Influences and Religious Reforms in Russia* (Geneva, 1971).

[18] On the question of union, see Joseph Franz Macha, *Ecclesiastical Unification: A Theoretical Framework together with Case Studies from the History of Latin-Byzantine Relations* (= *Orientalia Christiana Periodica* 198) (Rome, 1974).

conversion to the Latin rite. Also, the Uniate bishops were never given equality with the Latin-rite bishops by gaining seats in the Diet of the Commonwealth.[19]

Resistance to the Union of Brest among the clergy and the faithful undermined any chance of strengthening the Ruthenian Church through union with Rome. Acceptance or rejection of the Union dominated religious and political discussions from 1596 to the Khmel'nyts'kyi uprising. The Orthodox revulsion for the Uniate minority, especially in the Ruthenian palatinate (western Ukraine) and the Dnieper Basin (central Ukraine), split the Ruthenian community. The support of the king and the Diet for the Union and the Uniate hierarchy, stiffened by Rome whenever it wavered, made the "Rus' Church of the Greek religion from the East" illegal from 1596 to 1632.[20] This was an anomalous situation in a state that permitted toleration for Protestant and Armenian Churches, as well as communal autonomy for the Jews and rights of worship for the Muslims.

The Commonwealth could not act decisively against the widespread resistance to the Union because to do so would attack the liberties of Orthodox nobles, who could turn to Protestant nobles as allies, and because the adherents of Orthodoxy included armed supporters in Ukraine. Foreseeing collapse of their Church with the dying out of the hierarchy if the king refused to authorize new elections of bishops (a situation that the Old Believers in Muscovy later faced for their clergymen), the Orthodox had to resort to defiance of the state and to a show of arms in order to obtain a new hierarchy in 1620 from a visiting patriarch of Jerusalem (who was empowered by the patriarch of Constantinople). The "legal" Uniate and "illegal" Disuniate (the government's term for the Orthodox) Churches struggled for the loyalty of believers, each claiming to be the only legitimate Ruthenian Church and negating the right of the other to exist. Orthodox persistence forced royal recognition of Orthodox legality by the newly elected King Władysław IV in 1632, because the king needed Orthodox nobles' support for this election and had to ensure Ukraine's and Belarus's loyalty in an impending war with Muscovy. The government's attempts to divide the eparchies, churches,

---

[19] On the Union of Brest, see Oskar Halecki, *From Florence to Brest, 1439–1596*, 2d ed. (New York, 1968); Borys Gudziak, *Crisis and Reform: The Kyivan Metropolitanate, the Patriarchate of Constantinople, and the Genesis of the Union of Brest* (Cambridge, MA, 1998); and M. Dmitriev, "The Religious Programme of the Union of Brest in the Context of the Counter-Reformation in Eastern Europe," *Journal of Ukrainian Studies* 17.1–2 (Summer–Winter 1992): 29–44.

[20] On papal policy, see Sergei Nikolaevich Plokhy (Plokhii), *Papstvo i Ukraina. Polititka Rimskoi kurii na ukrainskikh zemliakh v XVI–XVII vekakh* (Kyiv, 1987).

and benefices of the Kyiv metropolitanate between the Orthodox and Uniates only unleashed new conflicts.[21]

Pressure from Catholic nobles and occasional defections of Orthodox dignitaries to the Uniates (Meletii Smotryts'kyi and Kasiian Sakovych) increased anxiety among the Orthodox. Suspicion reigned that betrayal would occur, particularly since the Church hierarchs could be attracted to enter into discussions with the Catholic Church by promises of legalization (before 1632), or later of elevation of their own social and economic status.[22] Within the Orthodox community, each attempt to introduce new educational, publishing, and liturgical practices, a process that had been going on since the 1560s, made the innovators vulnerable to charges that they were betraying the true Orthodox tradition.[23] Attempts to define the place of the Orthodox in the matrix of contending Christian confessions appeared dangerous, especially when such discussions revealed how much was shared with the Latin-rite Catholics as opposed to with the more radical Protestants.[24]

Fatigue owing to the constant efforts to defend properties, which required frequent mobilization of the embattled faithful, appeared among the Orthodox bishops and nobles. These efforts could backfire, such as when the burghers of Vitsebsk killed the Uniate archbishop of Polatsk, Iosafat Kuntsevych, thereby giving their opponents a martyr and calling forth persecution from the government. In addition, the endangered situation of the Church had spawned a whole series of institutions (e.g., brotherhoods[25]) and practices (e.g., cooperation with Cossacks[26] and

---

[21] On the religious policies of Władysław IV, see Jan Dzięgielewski, *O tolerancje dla zdominowanych: Polityka wyznaniowa Rzeczypospolitiej w latach panowania Władysława IV* (Warsaw, 1986).

[22] In the Western Ukrainian Kholm eparchy in the 1630s and 1640s, the activist Uniate bishop Metodii Terlets'kyi spread the Union by force against the wishes of local burghers. In the Peremyshl' eparchy, the Orthodox nobles conducted armed struggles with the Uniate bishop Atanazii Krupets'kyi, but the courts passed strict sentences against them.

[23] See William K. Medlin, "The Cultural Crisis in Orthodox Rus' in the Late 16th and Early 17th Centuries as a Problem of Socio-Economic Change," in *The Religious World of Russian Culture*, ed. Andrew Blane (The Hague, 1973), 173–88, and the essay and appended bibliography to Ihor Ševčenko, "Religious Polemical Literature in the Ukrainian and Belarus' Lands in the Sixteenth and Seventeenth Centuries" in *Ukraine between East and West*, 149–63.

[24] See Frank E. Sysyn, "The Formation of Ukrainian Religious Culture: The Sixteenth and Seventeenth Centuries," in *Church, Nation and State in Russia and Ukraine*, ed. Geoffrey A. Hosking (Edmonton, 1991), 1–22.

[25] On the brotherhoods, see Iaroslav Dmytrovych Isaevych, *Bratstva ta ïkh rol' v rozvytku ukraïns'koï kul'tury XVI–XVII st.* (Kyiv, 1966).

[26] The Cossacks were an armed frontier population of the borderlands between the states of the Great Principality of Muscovy, the Grand Duchy of Lithuania, and the Kingdom of Poland (after 1569, the former composed the Polish-Lithuanian Commonwealth)

noble participation in synods) that were not always to the liking of the hierarchs. Frequent intervention by Eastern patriarchs (based in the Ottoman Empire) opened the Kyiv metropolitan see to accusations that the Orthodox hierarchs were spies for the Ottomans, of whom the patriarchs were subjects. Indeed, Patriarch Cyril Lucaris of Constantinople included Kyiv in his plans for an anti-Catholic Orthodox-Protestant league. Search for support from Muscovy also lay the Church in the Commonwealth open to charges of disloyalty.[27]

The position of the Orthodox Church entered a new phase under Metropolitan Peter Mohyla (1633–1646), a member of a once ruling family of Moldavia,[28] who tried to reinforce episcopal authority and the power of the metropolitan, define the faith, unify liturgical practices, and adapt the leading Catholic educational model to Orthodox education.[29] Selected as part of the compromise by which the new king, Władysław, and the Diet recognized the legality of the Orthodox Church, Mohyla sought to break with the rebellious Cossacks and demonstrate full loyalty to the Warsaw government. The opposition of Orthodox diehards and the growing Catholic intolerance in the Commonwealth hindered his efforts. Internally, the Orthodox Church remained free of full schism, despite considerable dissatisfaction, but no matter what Mohyla did, he could not stop the decline of the Orthodox Church's position in a Commonwealth ever more influenced by the Counter-Reformation. At the same time, he could not obtain permanent security for the Church since the policies of a new king, a diminishing number of Orthodox representatives in the Diet, or successful papal political pressure could undermine the Orthodox position and strengthen the Uniates. In the 1640s, Mohyla responded favorably to initiatives from Rome and other quarters to enter into negotiations that might heal the breach in the

---

and the Muslim Turkic steppe societies. Groups of Cossacks were enlisted in a register and paid to defend the frontier by the Commonwealth's government, but far larger numbers of the population considered themselves Cossacks and organized themselves to carry on campaigns in the Black Sea region and to resist the encroachment of the Commonwealth's social order.

[27] On the Orthodox Church in international affairs, see Gunnar Hering, *Ökumenisches Patriarchat und europäische Politik (1620–1638)* (Wiesbaden, 1968).

[28] Moldavia had a predominantly Romanian-speaking population but shared the Church Slavonic liturgical language with the Orthodox Slavs. Its culture had been greatly influenced by the West Ukrainian Galicia, and the Mohyla family had close contacts with Lviv. Therefore, in some sense, Mohyla could be seen as a Ruthenian, in a way that a Greek or South Slav would not have been.

[29] See the essay and bibliography of Ihor Ševčenko, "The Many Worlds of Peter Mohyla," in *Ukraine between East and West*, 164–86, and the classic study of Stefan Timofeevich Golubev, *Kievskii mitropolit Petr Mogila i ego spodvizhniki (opyt tser'kovno-istoricheskogo issledovaniia)*, 2 vols. (Kyiv, 1883–98).

Ruthenian Church, but he may have merely been mollifying the king and the Catholics; he also had to take into account continued widespread popular opposition to the Union.[30] At any rate, the increasing Catholic confessional consciousness among the Uniates and the Orthodox confessional consciousness among those who rejected the Union were undermining the common attachment to a Ruthenian Church.

What role did the Orthodox issue play in inspiring the revolt of 1648? Religious controversy greatly undermined the legitimacy of the Polish administration in the eyes of many of the Orthodox. To have had to maintain an "illegal" Church for thirty-five years inevitably inspired disaffection with the existing regime even among the otherwise loyalist nobility. The settlement of 1632 did not satisfy Orthodox complaints of discrimination.[31] The Orthodox found that royal commissions were slow in assigning buildings and properties to them and that Catholic potentates could obstruct decisions and the law. In a land in which each noble aspired to be a law unto himself and each magnate virtually became one, the Orthodox could hold little hope for lasting amelioration of their situation. With the defection of more and more magnates to Catholicism, the Orthodox had to fear the consequences of the existing political arrangements.[32] In a society in which violence was endemic, they learned that force and arms were better than any privilege. Seize the Kyiv Caves monastery or the St. Sophia cathedral and it was likely to remain yours.[33] The Orthodox understood that they could best wrest concessions during times of danger for the Commonwealth – such as the Turkish conflict of 1620 and the threat of Muscovite war in 1632. They also had learned to turn to foreign centers for support: spiritual from the Middle East and material and political from Moldavia, Wallachia, and Muscovy. Most importantly, they had come to realize

---

[30] See Atanasii Welykyj (Velykyi), "Anonymnyi proiekt Petra Mohyly po z'iedynenniu ukraïns'koï tserkvy 1645r," in *Svitla i tini ukraïns'koï istoriï: pry chynky do istoriï ukraïns'koï tserkovnoï dumky* (Rome, 1969).

[31] On the atmosphere surrounding the compromise of 1632, see Paulina Lewin and Frank E. Sysyn, "The *Antimaxia* of 1632 and the Polemic over Uniate-Orthodox Relations," *Harvard Ukrainian Studies* 9 (1985): 145–65.

[32] On conversion, see H. Litwin, "Stosunki wyznaniowe na Kijowszczyźnie i Bracławszczyźnie," *Przegląd Powszechny* 10 (1985): 58–70.

[33] Occasionally such techniques might backfire, as when the bishop of Peremyshl, Sylvestr Hulevych, and the local nobility were sentenced harshly for their seizure of properties that the Uniate bishop illegally retained. Still, the long discussions of the Peremyshl affair eventually ended with Hulevych retaining the properties for his own lifetime. See Frank E. Sysyn, "The Buyer and Seller of the Greek Faith: A Pasquinade in the Ruthenian Language against Adam Kysil," *Harvard Ukrainian Studies* 19 (1995): 655–70.

that the Zaporozhian Cossacks served as an important guarantor of their position.

From the 1590s, the Orthodox cause and Zaporozhian Cossack rebellions were linked in the popular mind as "Nalyvaiko," the name of a Cossack leader of the 1590s, which became an epithet hurled by the Catholics at the Orthodox.[34] By the same token, the Commonwealth's need for Zaporozhian military support in time of war ensured Orthodox successes in 1620 and 1632. Against the common view that the original Cossacks were warriors for the faith, a counterpart to the Muslim *ghazis* whom they encountered in the steppe borderlands, it has been argued that they might have used the issue of Orthodoxy to further their revolt in the 1590s. In time, however, the Cossacks increasingly identified with the Orthodox cause. Cossacks assisted in seizing the Caves monastery in 1607, they enrolled in the Kyiv brotherhood in the 1610s,[35] and they prevented concessions to the Uniates at the Synod of Kyiv in 1629.

During the Smolensk War (1632–4), Metropolitan Mohyla had blessed the Cossack artillery to be used against the Orthodox Muscovites, but he soon tried to break with the Cossacks and dispense with their support for the Church. This break by the Mohylan Church seemed at first to work to the detriment of the Cossacks, as the failed revolts of 1635 and 1637–8 demonstrated. Ultimately, however, the Mohylan policy was a fragile one, for if the Commonwealth found a final resolution for the Cossack problem, the Catholic circles in the Commonwealth would have less reason to tolerate Orthodoxy.

The defense of Orthodoxy had mobilized the Ruthenian population of the Commonwealth for over seventy years before the great uprising of 1648. Nobles had threatened to break up Diets and dietines, they included Orthodox demands in the programs of confederations such as the Zebrzydowski revolt (1606–9), and they took part in the defense and seizures of church properties.[36] Burghers had formed brotherhoods,

---

[34] On the Cossacks and the religious issue, see Mykhailo Hrushevsky, *History of Ukraine-Rus'*: vol. 7. *The Cossack Era (to 1625)* (Edmonton and Toronto, 1999), which contains updates on the literature by the editor, Serhii Plokhy. While the designation may have referred originally to the Orthodox cleric Demiian Nalyvaiko, it was interpreted as referring to his more famous brother, the Cossack leader Severyn Nalyvaiko. Of course, the very fact that a Cossack and an Orthodox leader were brothers showed how closely Church and Cossacks were connected. For a recent examination of the role of religion in the revolt, see Serhii Plokhy, *The Cossacks and Religion in the Early Modern Ukraine* (Oxford, 2001).

[35] See Iaroslav Dmytrovych Isaievych, "Zv"iazky bratstv iz zaporiz'kym kozatstvom u XVII st.," in his *Ukraïna davnia i nova: Narod, relihiia, kul'tura* (Lviv, 1996), 105–13.

[36] On the religious issue in noble political culture, see Frank E. Sysyn, "Regionalism and Political Thought in Seventeenth-Century Ukraine: The Nobility's Grievances at the Diet of 1641," *Harvard Ukrainian Studies* 6.2 (June 1982): 167–90.

financed delegations to the Diet, and occasionally participated in Cossack revolts. Peasants had been drawn into conflicts as early as the 1590s, but little is known about their views on religion or any other topic.[37] Although it is questionable to accept uncritically that the peasants were "conservative" in religion, it is more certain that they hated Catholicism and Protestantism as landlords' faiths and viewed the attempt to impose the Union as but another interference of the lords in the peasants' world.[38]

The clergy were most closely identified with the Church and its policies. By the sixteenth century, the Orthodox clergymen of the Polish-Lithuanian Commonwealth differed greatly from their predecessors. The metropolitans and bishops of the Kyivan Rus' period had frequently been Greeks, and as late as the fifteenth century South Slavs were prominent. But by the late sixteenth century, Ruthenian nobles, appointed by the king and frequently tonsured and ordained to receive their office, dominated the higher clergy. Inferior hierarchs had been one of the causes of the Church's decline and the rise of a reform movement among the laity. But the bishops were inferior not only because they often came to their posts with no clerical education but also because they lacked the power and status of Roman Catholic prelates since they did not have seats in the Diet. Hence the Union of Brest was partially an attempt by the bishops to regain control of the Church and to achieve equality with the Latins. In their plans, they would have improved the positions of all of the clergy by reducing control over monastic and ecclesiastical offices by lay patrons, many of whom were not Orthodox, and by abolishing the humiliating, virtually subject status of the village clergy. The bishops sought a reform and elevation of their Church through union with Rome, but their plans miscarried because they underestimated the need to gain a consensus among their own faithful before proceeding, and they themselves broke ranks. Opposition to the Union ranged from powerful Orthodox magnates to enserfed peasants.

---

[37] On popular views on the basis of Russian sources, see B. Floria, "Natsional'no-konfesiina svidomist' naselennia Skhidnoï Ukraïny v pershii polovyni XVII stolittia," in *Beresteis'ka uniia ta vnutrishne zhyttia Tserkvy v XVII stolitti*, ed. Borys Gudziak (Lviv, 1997), 125–47.

[38] On social groups, see Frank E. Sysyn, "The Social Causes of the Khmel'nyts'kyi Uprising," in *Religion and Culture in Early Modern Russia and Ukraine*, Samuel Baron and Nancy Shields Kollmann eds. (Dekalb, IL, 1997), 52–70. There were also Orthodox landlords, but in relations with them religion was not a factor of demarcation and Orthodoxy was a faith that included various social strata. In rural areas in much of Ukraine, however, almost all Protestants and Catholics were nobles, whether landowners or their servitors, or clergy.

The Orthodox Church after 1596 presents a mixed picture of decline and of growth.[39] On the one hand, most bishops left the Church, large numbers of benefices were lost, and the conversion of the upper social strata to Catholicism continued. On the other hand, new monasteries were founded, schools were established, and the educational level of the clergy was improved. The Mohylan solution provided stability for this growth by a compromise with the government. Hence in contrast to the virtual opposition to the government by the hierarchy of 1620, which actively sought help from the enemies of the Commonwealth, the post-1632 hierarchy was solidly loyalist. In addition, while bishops before 1632 had given tacit approval to Cossack and peasant rebels who struggled for the Church's interests, the Mohylan hierarchy withdrew this support. It did not abandon violence as a solution, as the Peremyshl bishopric affair and the forceful assertion of Orthodox rights by Mohyla demonstrated, but these ventures were undertaken by nobles and Church retainers.

At the highest level, the Church had begun to reach an accommodation with the Commonwealth. But the bishops could not undo the consequences of the long years of struggle: suspicion from Catholics, indictment from the Uniates, and popular Orthodox distrust of the Catholic state and the hierarchs' accommodation. Closely allied to the bishops were the archimandrites of the great monasteries, many of which had revived activities in the early seventeenth century. Institutions such as the Caves monastery had been crucial to saving the Orthodox position, and the monasteries had reemerged as centers of education and book production. In the 1630s, the monasteries of the Trans-Dnieper region had resisted Mohyla's religious and political policies, but they had been brought in line with dissidents fleeing to Muscovite territory. By the 1640s, many monastic leaders (*hegumen*) favored cooperation with the Commonwealth's authorities, partially because many of them came from the nobility. In contrast, the lower ranks were less committed to such a course. In one case, Heguman Afanasii Filipovich had rejected Mohyla's line of conciliation and had even disrupted a Polish Diet in an attempt to have the Union abolished.[40] Other monks may have been closer to the tradition of withdrawal from the corrupt world preached by Ivan Vyshens'kyi, a monk trained at Mount Athos.[41] This was not a

---

[39] On the state of the Orthodox Church in this period, see Ivan Wlasowsky (Vlasovs'kyi), *Outline History of the Ukrainian Orthodox Church*, 2d ed., vol. 2 (New York, 1979).

[40] See A.F. Korshunov, *Afanasii Filippovich: Zhizn' i tvorchestvo* (Minsk, 1965) and my discussion of this work in *Kritika* 8.2 (Spring, 1972): 1–12.

[41] See Harvey Goldblatt, "Ivan Vyšens'kyj's Concept of St. John Chrysostom and his Idea of Reform for the Ruthenian Lands," *Harvard Ukrainian Studies* 16 (1992): 37–66.

course available to educators and chaplains, men who had to confront the Catholic challenge and to respond. Some, like Kasiian Sakovych, capitulated, probably reinforcing discontent at lower levels.[42] In the struggle for control of churches in the towns, the urban clergy played a major role. At the base, the village clergy, frequently treated as virtual serfs by the largely non-Orthodox lords, had little reason to support the accommodations. In sum, the troubled clergymen were not a united group, but they did provide considerable numbers of detractors of the Polish administration.

The policies of the Commonwealth and the tactics of the Orthodox Ruthenians had led to a climate of confrontation between the state and the Orthodox that Metropolitan Mohyla and King Władysław IV had been unable to defuse. Did Church circles, clergy and laity, actively conspire in the planning and execution of the great revolt? How important were Orthodox demands for the rebels? What did the revolt mean for the Church as an institution?

In some ways, it made little difference whether the clergy supported the revolt or the rebels made religious demands. From the very first, Counter-Reformation opponents of Orthodoxy focused on the religious issue, seeing the "schismatic" clergy and nobles as masterminds of the revolt, in part because they refused to believe that the lower orders could be so ingenious. They argued that the very toleration of the Orthodox had brought divine retribution on the Commonwealth.[43] Certainly Polish retribution against the clergy as planners and supporters of the revolt both radicalized the Church and enhanced its position in rebel ranks. The execution of Afanasii Filipovich in Brest in 1648 on charges of supporting the Cossacks gave the Church and the revolt a martyr.

As in so many early modern revolts, the attempt of the government to bring about change provoked a revolt. The Polish-Lithuanian Commonwealth of the seventeenth century was a republic, in which power was shared among the king, the Diet, and local dietines. Hence, the attempt of the king to embark on a foreign war against the will of the Diet and most of the nobility destabilized Ukraine. Before the revolt, the king hoped to incite a war to humble the Ottoman foe of Christendom, to be paid for by Venice, which was then involved in the War of Candia. A foreign war also could have strengthened his own power in his realm.

---

[42] On Sakovych, see David A. Frick, "'Foolish Rus': On Polish Civilization, Ruthenian Self-Hatred and Kasijan Sakovyc," *Harvard Ukrainian Studies* 18.3–4 (December 1994): 210–48.

[43] For treatment of religious issues in contemporary literature, see Frank E. Sysyn, "Seventeenth-Century Views on the Causes of the Khmel'nyts'kyi Uprising," *Harvard Ukrainian Studies* 5.4 (December 1980): 430–66.

Therefore he had negotiated a defensive alliance with Muscovy against the sultan's vassals, the Tatars, in 1647, though given the Diet's suspicions, all the terms had to be left vague. In this strategy, the Cossacks were essential, particularly because the king might need them to incite a Tatar attack, thus setting his plans in motion, and certainly would need them in any war. His secret negotiations with the Cossacks from 1646 raised their expectations that they could undo the harsh terms imposed after the revolt of 1638.

At the same time, the king sought to assure the support of the Orthodox Church. In what seems to the modern eye a flight of fantasy, he hoped to heal the split in the Ruthenian Church in order to create a united front and also to be able to hold out to Rome, an important partner in the anti-Turkish plan, the chance of bringing the entire Kyiv metropolitanate into union. Mohyla's death had not halted discussions for a new religious compromise. Religious affairs may have been the issue that led Crown Chancellor Jerzy Ossoliński to confer with the new Orthodox metropolitan, Sylvester Kosiv, and the leading Orthodox layman and senator, Adam Kysil, in the summer of 1647. At any rate, it seems certain that the metropolitan must have been apprised of the plans afoot. Certainly Ossoliński's and Kysil's later actions seemed to indicate that they thought Kosiv their man. Well into 1648 the papal nuncio saw the matter of an accommodation coming to fruition with the call for meetings in Vilnius. But the king's plans aroused great suspicion in the Commonwealth that he was conspiring with the Cossacks and the Orthodox against the interests of the Polish nobility. For the Orthodox hierarchy, the war plan could strengthen their position, though it would also involve them in an intricate game. At the same time, the plans put zealous Orthodox on guard that some new sell-out might occur. Then King Władysław IV, who inspired considerable trust in Orthodox circles for his attempts to moderate the Counter-Reformation, died unexpectedly in May 1648, thus removing the linchpin for all arrangements with the Cossacks and the Church.[44]

While the higher clergymen may have known of the Ottoman war plans, which involved the Zaporozhians, did they conspire with Khmel'nyts'kyi in late 1647 and early 1648 in his great change of plans and alliance with the Tatars to launch the revolt? In the late fall of 1647, Bohdan Khmel'nyts'kyi, persecuted by borderland officials, fled to the Cossack stronghold and from there made an alliance with the Crimean Tatars. There is no evidence, but circumstances seem to show that the

---

[44] On this period, see Frank E. Sysyn, *Between Poland and Ukraine: The Dilemma of Adam Kysil, 1600–1653* (Cambridge, MA, 1985), 117–28.

Cossack campaigning of the spring of 1648 came as a shock to the Church leadership. It has been argued that Khmel'nyts'kyi was an outsider in the Orthodox milieu, little known or trusted by the clerical establishment, which only came to terms with him after his great victories.[45] In contrast to Karpo Skydan, leader of the Cossack revolt in 1637–8, who immediately focused on the religious issue in calling for support, Khmel'nyts'kyi was muted in discussing the religious issue, perhaps indicating that he expected little active support from the Church. Although we know little of the particulars of Khmel'nyts'kyi's first negotiations with the Tatars and Turks, there seems to have been no active participation by the Eastern patriarchs.

Thus the Church did not plan with the Cossacks to initiate the revolt. Still, the event of 1648 was much more than a Cossack revolt; it was also a popular uprising. Here it seems we can give credence to the Polish charges that the clergy incited and led the masses. There is no Motryns'kyi monastery as a center of the revolt and no Archimandrite Melkhizedyk Znachno-Iavors'kyi as in the eighteenth-century Kolii uprising, but there are too many accounts of priests with swords in hand to disregard. What this phenomenon revealed was the limited nature of the success of the government's and Mohyla's policies. Despite the policy of accommodation, the Church was drawn into a Cossack revolt both because the Poles were sure that it was implicated and because the lower clergy, in fact, joined it. However tactful the Mohylas and Kosivs might be, the lower clergy seethed with hatred against the haughty Latins. They had also suffered the socioeconomic humiliation visited on their peasant flocks. Hence the Church was tied to the Cossacks as protectors; however, its hierarchs might have wished otherwise: The Cossacks, as fellow Orthodox, felt they had full rights to intervene in Church affairs. By the same token, however little interest Khmel'nyts'kyi initially may have had in Church affairs, he put the alleviation of the grievances of the Church forward as a way of gaining popular support and legitimacy.[46] The Church and the Cossacks may have been on the outs from 1638 to 1648, but their links were too strong to be sundered by a mere falling out.

For the hierarchs, the revolt called for rapid decisions. First, they had to choose sides quickly, if for no other reason than to decide whether

---

[45] See Mykhailo Hrushevs'kyi, *Istoriia Ukraïny-Rusy*, vol. 8, pt. 3 (Kyiv, 1995), 122–9.

[46] See S. Plokhy, "Sviashchenne pravo povstannia: Beresteis'ka uniia i relihiina legitymatsiia Khmel'nychchyny," in *Derzhava, suspil'stvo i tserkva v Ukraïni XVII stolitti*, ed. Borys Gudziak (Lviv, 1996), 1–13.

to remain in Ukraine or to flee with the landowning nobility. In general, bishops and archimandrites remained at their posts. While we may never know whether the bishop of Luts'k, the brotherhood of Lviv, or the archimandrite of Brest sent gunpowder and information to the approaching rebels, as the Polish side alleged, we may be sure that they would have seen the need to appear to be on the side of the victorious armies. By late 1648, the Church could see that the Cossack victories had ended the necessity of keeping up the intricate and dangerous discussions with the Latins and presented great opportunities for abolishing the Union and limiting Latin Catholic influence in Ukraine.[47] The patriarchs and clergy reinforced this positive evaluation of the revolt, since they could see the revolt as rooting out Latin influence. In addition, traveling so frequently to Moscow for alms, they could envisage a new Orthodox alliance, comprising a Muscovy recently awakened to the outer world, particularly in religious affairs, a Cossack Ukraine, and the Romanian principalities. They could also support Khmel'nyts'kyi's negotiations with the Ottomans, since even a Ukraine as an Ottoman vassal would revive Orthodox fortunes.[48]

While foreign Orthodox prelates could see the revolt as offering a chance for better times for the Orthodox oecumene, the Orthodox metropolitan saw the delegation sent by the Commonwealth in early 1649, led by the Orthodox Adam Kysil, as constituting recognition that the Orthodox issue had come to the fore as one on which the government might make concessions. Polish members of the delegation had charged that secret negotiations had taken place between the rebels and the Orthodox members of the delegation; the demands subsequently made by the rebels, that three Senate places should be reserved for Orthodox nobles, and that the metropolitan, Sylvester Kosiv, should enter the Diet, as well, seem to confirm this allegation. The negotiations came to naught and soon Kosiv could see the negative as well as positive consequences of the revolt. He had to fear reprisals against his Church in the lands where the Cossacks did not triumph. After the Zboriv Agreement between the Cossacks and the Commonwealth

---

[47] On the Church in this period, see Metropolitan Ilarion (Ivan Ohiienko), *Ukraïns'ka tserkva za Bohdana Khmel'nyts'koho 1647–1657* (Winnipeg, 1955).

[48] On the Eastern patriarchs, see P. Nikolaevskii, "K istorii snoshenii Rossii s vostokom v polovine XVII stoletiia," *Khristianskoe chtenie*, pt. 1 (1882): 242–67, 732–75; D. Olianchyn, "Do stosunkiv het'mana Bohdana Khmel'nyts'koho z Ierusalyms'kym patriiarkhom Paisiiem u 1648–1649," *Bohoslovs'kyi vistnyk* 2 (1948), 51–3; and Maria Kowalska, *Ukraina w połowie XVII w. w relacji arabskiego podróżnika Pawła, syna Makarego z Aleppo. Wstęp, przekład, komentarz* (Warsaw, 1986).

(August 1649), he became increasingly dependent on Cossack power, which, despite the agreement, did not secure his place in the Diet in 1650 and did not protect his titular city of Kyiv from the Commonwealth's armies when war resumed in 1651. Kosiv's noble background and his fear of social turmoil caused him to backslide toward a pro-Commonwealth position in 1651. Just as importantly, Metropolitan Kosiv had to fear for the unity of his see if indeed Khmel'nyts'kyi broke away from Poland.[49]

When, in 1653, Khmel'nyts'kyi turned decisively toward Moscow, the metropolitan and higher clergy saw another danger for their Church: a forcible break with the distant and lightly enforced jurisdiction of Constantinople and incorporation into the Muscovite Church. With its traditions of clerical privileges and self-government, and its higher clergy's noble political culture, the Ukrainian Church could only look with apprehension at the Muscovite Church, dominated by the tsar. In addition, these two Churches, which had emerged from the final division of the metropolitanate of Kyiv in the fifteenth century, had taken on very different cultural and ecclesiastical practices. In the 1620s, the Muscovites had burned Ruthenian books and rebaptized Ukrainians. Hence there arose the opposition of Metropolitan Kosiv and the higher clergy to the 1654 Pereiaslav Agreement, which sought Orthodox reconciliation between the Ukraine and Muscovy, and the willingness of some of his successors to side with the Commonwealth and the Ottomans.

The establishment of the Cossack hetmanate did, however, improve the Church's position, granting the Church rights to peasant labor services on its lands, even if these privileges were hard to enforce.[50] The homogenous Orthodox Cossack Ukraine that emerged from the revolt underwent a religious revival, and the wealth of the new elite poured into monasteries and church building. It was clear by the 1650s that Orthodoxy would be secure as far west as the border of the Cossack polity extended.

To what degree did religion serve to justify and legitimize the revolt? Did Orthodoxy serve as an "ideology" of the rebels? While there was no theological decision in support of revolt, statements and actions of the Orthodox Church from within and from outside Ukraine allow us to address this question.

[49] On the relationship of Kosiv and Khmel'nyts'kyi, see O. Ohloblyn, "Problema derzhavnoï vlady na Ukraïni za Khmel'nychchyny i Pereiaslavs'ka uhoda 1654 roku," *Ukraïns'kyi istoryk* 2.1–2 (1965): 2–13; 2.3–4 (1965): 11–16.
[50] See M. Chubatyi, "Pro pravne stanovyshche tserkvy v kozats'kii derzhavi," *Bohosloviia* 3.1–2 (1925): 19–53, 181–203.

Many of the Orthodox statements on the political order came in religious polemical works.[51] The Church had to answer the challenges of the Catholic and Protestant Churches, which had been so successful in winning away the Orthodox upper classes, and which represented clearly superior "modern" civilizations. After 1596, the formation of the Union of Brest made this challenge an assault on the very existence of the Orthodox Church. Before the revolt of 1648, the Orthodox thus had to cope with the triumph of wrong-believing states, the loss of social elites, and the desertion of the bishops and leaders entrusted to preserve Orthodoxy. In dealing with these difficult questions, they did realize that they were not alone, as the Council of Florence and the fall of Constantinople showed, but the common humiliation of defeat they shared with the Eastern patriarchates could hardly give them comfort. In this situation, they differed from the Muscovites, who remained safe in their isolated Orthodoxy, but who were for that reason to suffer a more traumatic and permanent shock less than a century later during the reign of Peter the Great.

That Orthodoxy did not split into various sects and groups in Ukraine and Belarus as it did in Muscovy was partially owing to the gradual nature of the challenge to the Ruthenian Orthodox worldview and partially owing to the need to maintain unity in the face of Catholics, Protestants, and later the Uniates. The Western Christian challenge, the debates of the various Protestant groups, and the redefinition of Catholicism at the Council of Trent forced the Kyiv metropolitanate and the Ruthenians to formulate more clearly their confessional allegiance. Indeed in the Ukrainian and Belarusian territories, new precision in defining the structure of an "Orthodox Church" and its dogmas arose in response to the new confessionalism of the Western Christians. As the Kyiv metropolitanate and the Rus' Church made more explicit their relationship with other Eastern Churches, the conception of Orthodoxy became clearer, and wider circles of adherents of the Ruthenian community came to think in confessional terms.

As to their existence in a heretic state, there was little the Orthodox could say: They had endured in such a way for a very long time. The Eastern Orthodox Church had taken shape in a transformed Christian Roman Empire and conceived of the emperor as essential to its wellbeing.[52] In converting a number of Slavic and East European peoples

---

[51] In addition to Ševčenko, "Religious Polemical Literature," see David A. Frick, *Meletij Smotryc'kyj* (Cambridge, MA, 1995) and A. Martel, *La langue polonaise dans les pays ruthène: Ukraine et Russie Blanche 1569–1667* (Lille, 1938).

[52] See Joan Mervyn Hussey, *The Orthodox Church in the Byzantine Empire* (Oxford, 1986).

through the Slavonic tongue, Orthodoxy became associated with specific state traditions and cultures, albeit as part of the Byzantine Commonwealth centered on the imperial city.[53] Yet by the late sixteenth century, many Orthodox had existed for hundreds of years in non-Orthodox states, deprived of the support of a right-believing empire. For most Orthodox peoples, this meant existence in the Ottoman state. Despite Ottoman pressure on the Church, the institution gained a certain authority as the representative of its faithful and bearer of the Byzantine-Hellenic legacy. The Russians were to undergo a similar, if shorter, experience under the Mongol-Tatars, who in many ways improved the situation of the Church, preparing the way for its reemergence as an ideological force in sixteenth- and seventeenth-century Muscovy.

For the Orthodox of the Polish-Lithuanian Commonwealth, God had seen fit to send the Mongols against Kyiv in the thirteenth century, to bring an end to the Orthodox rulers of Galicia-Volhynia, to convert the grand dukes of Lithuania to Catholicism in the fourteenth century, and to destroy the Christian empire in the fifteenth century. The grand princes of Orthodox Muscovy might theoretically lay claim to all the Rus' lands, but in the late sixteenth century no one foresaw the extension of their rule to Kyiv and Vilnius. Their newly proclaimed patriarchate (1589) also counted for little except as a source of alms. The Orthodox Church in Ukraine and Belarus conceived no new worldview to square its present status with the vision inherited from Byzantium. Only at the end of the sixteenth century did increasing Western influences and pressures force the Church to express new views on church, state, and people. On the one hand, the Church asserted that the faith it professed was the ancient and correct one, even if in recent times the Church of Rome had enjoyed more success than that of Constantinople. The metropolitanate constantly asserted its identity as the Greek faith adopted six hundred years earlier in Kyiv. With this assertion came the contention that the Church enjoyed the privileges granted by the Rus' princes, Lithuanian grand dukes, and Polish kings, though Catholics pointed out that the major privileges had been issued at times when it could be argued the Union of Florence was in force. In political terms, the Orthodox simply had to stand by their ancient privileges and, after 1596, to point out that the Ottomans were less repressive of the Greeks than were the Catholic Poles of the Ruthenians.

---

[53] For a treatment of the relationship of the East Slavs, in general, and the Ukrainians, in particular, with Byzantium and the Byzantine Church, see Ihor Ševčenko, *Ukraine between East and West*, essays 2–4, 6–7; and Dimitri Obolensky, *The Byzantine Commonwealth* (New York and Washington, DC, 1971).

In practice, the political culture of the Orthodox Church had been deeply penetrated by the political culture of Poland. While the Church might lack a right-believing ruler, it did claim the allegiance of many members of the political nation, that is, the nobility. Since this political nation had secured the right of freedom of conscience by the late sixteenth century, the Church could depend on its great men. Because the most powerful of these men were princes who descended from former ruling families, the Church could even locate them in the political ideology it had inherited from Kyivan Rus'. This amalgam of old and new authority within a noble political nation was reflected in the very structure of the Church in matters such as the role of Orthodox nobles at synods. Consequently, when the princes and other nobles continued to desert the Church after the Union of Brest, Orthodoxy faced a new crisis. In tracts like Smotryts'kyi's *Trenos* (1610) or Kopyns'kyi's call to Iarema Vyshnevets'kyi (Jeremi Wiśniowiecki, the scourge of the rebels in 1648) in 1631 not to convert to Roman Catholicism and to return to the faith of his fathers,[54] the Church expressed its alarm over these defections. Ascetics and monks such as Ivan Vyshens'kyi cited biblical passages on the relative chances of rich and poor men to enter Heaven, and other polemicists argued that, freed of worldly power, the Orthodox Church increased in sanctity. Still, the leaders of the earthly Church knew that without nobles their Church could not survive. Hence Kopyns'kyi had reminded Vyshnevets'kyi that one could hardly call the faith of the Greek emperors a peasant faith. But the image of past glories could not overshadow the cultural and social realities of the present, which meant that noble converts went directly over to the dominant Latin-rite Church, bypassing the Uniate Church. Before the Union of Brest, the Orthodox Church had taken some extraordinary measures to ensure its continuity. Monasteries and brotherhoods were placed under the Eastern patriarchs, whose role in the Church was augmented. It was almost as if the Church knew it could not depend on its hierarchy.

The Union of Brest might appear to the modern eye as a moderate plan to solve the Church's predicament. Yet its initial failure cannot be explained solely by the powerful opposition of Prince Kostiantyn Ostroz'kyi, the palatine of Kyiv and one of the richest men in Europe.[55] Nor can it be attributed merely to some deep-seated conservative Orthodox faith of the masses. Rather, the fact that obedience to Rome

---

[54] The text is published in *Z dziejów Ukrainy*, ed. Viacheslav Lypyns'kyi (Wacław Lipiński) (Kyiv and Cracow, 1912), 121–2.
[55] See Tomasz Kempa, *Konstanty Wasyl Ostrogski* (Torun, 1997).

was so roundly rejected, even with the seemingly acceptable retention of all the externals of the Ruthenian Church, must also be explained by the long seige mentality of the Orthodox Ruthenian population, which viewed the Union as a symbol of unacceptable social, cultural, and political innovations. The rejection of the Union also demonstrated how limited the power of the bishops was in an already fragmented Church, and how far the Orthodox had already advanced in answering the Latin challenge.

The Union had introduced a new dimension to the religious struggle in Ukraine and Belarus. Latin Catholicism might be abhorred, but it was the proper faith of the native "Liakhs" and had long existed in the Ukrainian land. Protestant groups were a "heresy" from the Latin schism.[56] But no loathing could compare to that which the Orthodox held for the Uniate "turncoats." The Uniates, after all, had gained recognition for the privileges and institutions that the Orthodox claimed and almost had succeeded in interrupting the apostolic continuity of the Orthodox Church. But in essence, neither Uniate nor Orthodox could accept the other as legitimate. There was room for only one Ruthenian Church and the compromise of 1632 never gained sincere acceptance from either side. The increasing Catholic confessionalism of the Uniate Ruthenians inevitably stimulated the Orthodox to think in more confessional terms. In 1648, the Uniates were still a long way from challenging the Orthodox claim to be the Ruthenian Church, particularly in Ukraine, but they had shown disturbing signs of becoming more than an artificial implant.[57] Indeed, Archbishop Smotryts'kyi, even before accepting the Union, had issued a challenge to one of the major premises of the Orthodox defense by insisting that it was blood and descent, not faith,

---

[56] The Protestants had occasionally demonstrated good will toward the Orthodox, assisting them intellectually and politically. In the end, the Orthodox masses showed a greater antagonism toward the Protestant innovations than toward their old Latin opponents. This partially may be due to the continuing dynamism of the Protestant group in Ukraine in the 1630s and 1640s, long after they had peaked in Poland. The Protestants also represented a landlords' faith in Ukraine and Belarus, while Catholicism had a more socially varied constituency. Most telling, the Protestants, in particular the Antitrinitarians, held "abominable" heresies. On Protestants in Ukraine, see George H. Williams, "Protestants in the Ukraine during the Period of the Polish-Lithuanian Commonwealth," *Harvard Ukrainian Studies* 2.1–2 (1978): 41–72, 184–210.

[57] By the 1640s, the Uniates had succeeded in taking root among a mass following in some areas (the Belarusian towns after the suppressions following Iosafat Kuntsevych's martyrdom and the Kholm area, under Bishop Metodii Terlets'kyi's energetic rule). Even more importantly, Metropolitans Potii, Ruts'kyi, and Seliava had trained a group of clergy dedicated to the Union. See Sophia Senyk, "Methodius Terlec'kyj – Bishop of Xolm," *Analecta OSBM* 12 (1985): 342–73, and "Dva mytropolyty – Potii i Ruts'kyi," in *Istorychni kontekst, ukladennia Beresteis'koï uniï i pershe pouniine pokolinnia*, ed. Borys Gudziak (Lviv, 1995), 137–48.

that defined a Ruthenian.[58] For the Orthodox, one issue was clear – any way the Union could be destroyed was legitimate.

The Orthodox had not evolved a justification for rebellion, but in the decades after Brest, they had tacitly come to accept that the state had to be challenged if the Church was to survive, and that lower orders had to be depended upon if the upper classes proved unreliable. Their most concentrated effort went into giving the Zaporozhian Cossacks historical and political legitimacy in the 1620s. In that decade, the legitimacy of the Church depended on a defiance of royal authority that would not have been possible without the Cossack army. In declaring the Cossacks Christian knights and the descendants of the followers of the tenth-century Rus' Prince Oleh, the clergymen had decided to draw the Cossacks into the defense of the Rus' inheritance.[59] They could not easily expel them from this role later. Mohyla tried to build his image of a hierarchically ruled Church in accordance with the political and social structure of the Commonwealth, but he built his edifice on Ukrainian quicksand. The Church could not depend long on a government in which men such as the zealous Catholic Stanisław Albrycht Radziwiłł, Lithuanian vice-chancellor, were becoming more and more numerous.[60] It also could not expel from its laity the Cossacks and burghers whom it had formerly courted.

Did the Church give legitimacy to the revolt? In the popular imagination, it did so immediately. In the face of the Cossack armies, Uniates, Catholics, Protestants, and Jews fled, converted, or were destroyed. The Cossack realm would be an Orthodox one, even though in the first agreements expulsion of Catholics (as distinct from expulsion of the Jesuits) was not a demand. It is not until Christmas of 1648 that echoes of an active program by the Church to legitimize the revolt appear. The students and professors of the Kyiv Academy, who had so enthusiastically greeted a Polish-appointed Orthodox castellan of Kyiv in 1646, now greeted a Zaporozhian hetman as "Moses, well-called Bohdan (God-Given)" liberator of his people from the Polish servitude.[61] Also important was the role of the Ottomans, who, in trying to maintain "Byzance aprés Byzance," had a custom of extending their sphere of influence with the cooperation of leading Christians at the Ottoman court and the great families of Moldavia and Wallachia; in this case, the patriarch

---

[58] For Smotryts'kyi's view on nationality, see Frick, *Meletij Smotryc'kyj*, 227–45.

[59] This text is the epigraph of volume seven of Hrushevsky's *History of Ukraine-Rus'*.

[60] The diaries of Radziwiłł constitute one of the most graphic testimonies of the new Counter-Reformation thought. See *Memoriale Rerum Gestarum in Polonia 1632–1656*, 5 vols. (Wrocław, 1968–75).

[61] See Sysyn, *Between Poland and Ukraine*, 164–5.

of Jerusalem sent greetings to the hetman as *Illustrissime Princeps*, and the metropolitan of Corinth presented him with a sword from the Holy Sepulchre. Impressed by a hetman who had scored so many victories over the Polish state, seeming to ensure God's deliverance of his true believers and chastising the evil Latins, the Eastern clergy could dream of a new Orthodox order.[62] But the new Orthodox order proved ephemeral in 1649. Instead of seizing the mantle of authority, Khmel'nyts'kyi continued to negotiate with the Poles. Worse, the Crimean khan's politics and the Zboriv agreement deprived Khmel'nyts'kyi and Orthodoxy of final victory. The Ottomans were too cautious to envision Ukraine as an Orthodox vassal. By 1650, the metropolitan of Kyiv could see the negative side of a Cossack yoke, that is, intervention in Church affairs, and the possible dangers a separate Cossack Ukraine would hold for the patriarchate. Thus when the metropolitan of Corinth perished at the Battle of Berestechko, with the holy sword blessed in Jerusalem beside him, the metropolitan of Kyiv preferred to intervene personally with the Lithuanian authorities to gain clemency for his city of Kyiv. Cossack hetman and metropolitan often clashed after this time, including at the Pereiaslav oath of 1654, by which the Cossacks submitted to the tsar of Muscovy. Hence the Ukrainian Church was not present to bless this new relationship with Moscow. The Greek and Arab clergy remained more enthusiastic about Khmel'nyts'kyi, perhaps seeing him as a more vigorous Vasile Lupu, the contemporary Moldavian *hospodar* who served as a protector of the Orthodox. At any rate, Paul of Aleppo praised to the skies the hetman and his pious Orthodox subjects. For the Arab prelate, at least, the Orthodox triumph over non-Orthodox believers (Catholics, Protestants, Armenians, and Jews) remained the major reason and justification for the war.[63] It was not just any Orthodox ruler and people that Paul praised. He made clear that he preferred the Church and political culture of Ukraine to that of Muscovy, even though the Pereiaslav Agreement had already been negotiated at the time of his journeys.

In contacts with Muscovy, Orthodox justifications of the revolt emerged most clearly. The Muscovite state feared social unrest and remembered the damage done to Muscovy when the Cossacks intervened during the Time of Troubles and sided with the Commonwealth during

---

[62] On contacts with the Eastern patriarchs, see Olianchyn, "Do stosunkiv."

[63] The relish with which Paul of Aleppo described attacks on the Armenians reflected antagonisms in the Middle East. Kowalska's edition has information on the original and English, French, and Russian translations. Volodymyr Sichynsky, *Ukraine in Foreign Comments and Descriptions from the VIth to the XXth Century* (New York, 1953), contains excerpts, including on Khmel'nyts'kyi.

the Smolensk War. The Muscovite Church had until recently condemned the innovations of the Ruthenians' Orthodoxy. Therefore, it was the Ukrainian side that had to play the pan-Orthodox card first. If Muscovy was to be convinced to renege on its defensive alliance agreement of 1647 with the Commonwealth against the Tatars, or to break its Eternal Peace of 1634 and come to the rebels' assistance, only arguments of religious persecution and Orthodox solidarity could be used as a justification. Fortunately for the Ukrainians, the new Muscovite patriarch, Nikon, sought to make his see a center of the Orthodox world, so he was receptive to the entreaties carried back and forth by the Greek clergy.[64] By 1650, Muscovy had introduced religious issues into its negotiations with the Commonwealth; by 1653, it had decided to break with the Commonwealth and take a Ukraine in dire need of foreign support under the "high hand of the tsar."[65]

It is at Pereiaslav that we see the most clear-cut use of Orthodoxy as an ideology. The Ukrainians put forth common Orthodoxy as the major theme of the negotiations, and this argument resonated with the Muscovites. For them, persecution of the Orthodox legitimized the Ukrainians' breaking their oath to the Polish king and the Muscovite tsar's breaking his eternal peace with Poland. Desire to live under an Orthodox ruler explained the decision at Pereiaslav. In the later Muscovite interpretation, only heretics opposed this Orthodox reconciliation – particularly in 1658 the "Jew" or "Lutheran" (i.e., Antitrinitarian) Iurii Nemyrych. A number of Ukrainian petitions to Muscovy and the accounts by the Muscovites of Khmel'nyts'kyi's conducting of the Pereiaslav council also reflect this ideology. But these Ukrainian accounts are difficult to evaluate. The Ukrainian texts of 1654 are extant only in a Russian translation prepared for the Muscovite court. Also, the Ukrainians and Khmel'nyts'kyi knew well how to frame their petitions and letters to fit with the differing political cultures of Muscovy, the Commonwealth, the Crimean khanate, and the Ottoman Empire. But whatever the true feeling of the Cossack administration and the Church in 1654, they were soon to show that they could conceive of other possibilities for an Orthodox people than life under an Orthodox tsar. At the negotiations for the Hadiach Union (1658–9), the convert to Orthodoxy, Nemyrych, and Khmel'nyts'kyi's successor, Hetman

---

[64] On the consequences of the Russian Church reform, see Hedwig Fleischhacker, "Der politische Antrieb der moskauischen Kirchenreform," *Jahrbücher für Geschichte Osteuropas* 2 (1937): 224–33.

[65] See Robert Stupperich, "Der Anteil der Kirche beim Anschluss der Ukraine an Moskau (1654)," *Kirche im Osten* 14 (1971): 68–81.

Ivan Vyhovs'kyi, supported by Metropolitan Dionisii Balaban, gained a position for the Orthodox Church in the Commonwealth that would not have been dreamed of by Mohyla.[66] But here was the rub. Once again the Orthodox masses would not trust the "Liakhs," and the revolts against the agreement took on a religious coloration. Considering the trouble that the Commonwealth had in accepting the Hadiach Union and the papal nuncio's protests, the masses were quite correct. The Counter-Reformation was gaining the upper hand in the Commonwealth, as the expulsion of the Antitrinitarians in 1658 demonstrated, and there could be no real accommodation with the Orthodox Cossack hetmanate.

In the long run, while Moscow's theme of common Orthodoxy may not explain the Pereiaslav oath, it did come to serve as a binding ideology, particularly after the annexation of the Kyiv metropolitan see to the Moscow patriarchate in 1685–6.[67] The guarantees to maintain the autonomy and traditions of the Kyiv metropolitanate were soon broken, just as Moscow undermined the political autonomy of the hetmanate. Once the Orthodox clergy found themselves in a political arrangement with a universally recognized Orthodox sovereign, they could reorient themselves to return to more traditional Orthodox relations with the state. In addition, the Muscovite ruler laid hereditary claim to the core lands of Kyivan Rus', and the Ukrainian clergy, who had spent so much of their energy defending the rights of the Church on the basis of the conversion of Kyivan Rus', could now turn their knowledge to the service of the Muscovite tsar. In the same way, they could shift their focus from the Ruthenians to an East Slavic unity, characterized by the Greek derived name for Rus', *Rossiia*, of which Muscovy was "Great"; Ukraine, "Little"; and Belarus, "White." During the 1620s, they had developed some of the basis for this view in the appeals for assistance, above all in emphasizing the use of Little and Great *Rossiia*. Hence the Ukrainian clergy came to play a major role in reconceiving identities from the old divide between Ruthenians and Muscovites to a new concept of Little and Great Russians as part of an Orthodox East Slavic people, though for them the distinction between Ukrainians and Russians remained quite sharp. Midcentury, Muscovy offered tremendous opportunities to the Ukrainian clergy, above all in carrying on the Nikonian reform in the Russian Church. Even those clergy who remained in Ukraine would

---

[66] See Janusz Tazbir, "The Political Reversals of Jurij Nemyryč," *Harvard Ukrainian Studies* 5 (1981): 306–19.

[67] See Natala Carynnyk-Sinclair, *Die Unterstellung der Kiever Metropolie unter das Moskauer Patriarchat* (Munich, 1970).

come to find the tsar and the Russian Empire more stable and appropriate as civil authorities than the Cossack hetman and the hetmanate, though this issue was not fully resolved until the defeat of Hetman Ivan Mazepa at the Battle of Poltava (1709). Tsar Peter the Great used the Church to anathematize this great patron of Orthodox culture, thereby showing how the Church could be mobilized against political dissidence and revolts in Ukraine.

\* \* \* \* \*

This discussion of the role of Orthodoxy in the revolt against the Polish-Lithuanian state has concentrated almost entirely on inter-Christian relations. In doing so, it has reflected the major religious trend within the conflict and the discourse of the age. Two important issues have not been explored here: Muslim-Orthodox relations and Orthodox-Jewish relations. Despite the long-term conflict between the Cossacks and the Muslim world, the leaders of the revolt were able to ally with a Muslim power and ignore the Commonwealth's appeals to Christian solidarity. The degree to which they succeeded remains to be fully explored.

The cultural and national convergence of Orthodox Ukraine and Muscovy was based, to a considerable degree, on a joint struggle against the Tatars and Islam. Yet prior to the last third of the seventeenth century, the Ukrainian struggle with the Tatars and the Ottoman Empire was not sharply reflected as a religious issue. Ukrainian writings on Islam date only from Ioanikii Galiatovs'kyi's works of the 1670s and 1680s. Perhaps the focus on the struggle with the Catholics had hitherto muted the Muslim issue earlier. The original plan of an assault against the Tatars came from the Polish court in the 1640s and was framed as a general Christian alliance including Muscovy. Khmel'nyts'kyi had begun his revolt by allying with the Muslim Tatars, and in the Polish tradition this break in Christian solidarity was widely condemned, though this did not stop the Poles from wooing the Tatars away from Khmel'nyts'kyi and allying with them. The Orthodox clergy, who had so long pointed out that the Greeks fared better under the Ottomans than they did under the Poles, had in some sense laid the groundwork for Khmel'nyts'kyi's alliance. Earlier countervailing plans for an Orthodox or Orthodox-Protestant alliance against Islam came largely from the Greek and Arab clergy. With the formation of a Ukrainian-Russian bloc, however, the intervention of the Ottomans in Ukraine could be condemned in religious terms, though Hetman Petro Doroshenko still succeeded in the 1670s in winning the support of the Orthodox metropolitan in his plans to bring Ukraine under Ottoman protection. The popular historical songs (*dumas*) may reflect an anti-Muslim spirit of the masses, but it is difficult to establish their time of composition.[68]

More essential to the origins of the revolt and its course was the relationship of the Orthodox Church and population to Jews and Judaism. Despite the considerable literature on the massacres of Jews during the revolt, their religious context has not been fully examined. The revolt of 1648 resulted in the killing of many of Ukraine's approximately 100,000 Jews. Resentment of Jews – especially of Jewish estate managers – intertwined with the new economy of enserfment, manorial estates, and leaseholds that was being introduced in Ukraine. The social and religious aspects of anti-Semitism in Ukraine are very difficult to distinguish. The revolt of 1648 also resulted in widespread massacres of landlords and Catholic clergy. Yet prior to the revolt, relatively little anti-Jewish literature emanated from Orthodox sources (in comparison to Catholic circles). The most common refrain was that the Jews were given more freedom in the Commonwealth than were the Orthodox (also said of the Armenians). During the revolt, the major Orthodox expressions of antagonism toward the Jews came from Paul of Aleppo in correspondence with Muscovy. Indeed, Shmuel Ettinger saw Muscovite influence as decisive in the formation of anti-Jewish sentiments. In these sources, and in later justifications and discussions of the revolt, anti-Jewish themes (e.g., purported Jewish leaseholds for use of churches and performance of sacraments) came to play a greater role. The only source during the revolt making the same allegations was authored by a Dominican.[69] Popular sentiments are harder to gauge, but it seems certain that the fact that daily contacts with the new manorial enserfment and taxation systems were frequently with Jews rather than with the Orthodox or other Christians must have further alienated the masses from the existing order. The *dumas* are the major popular source on attitudes.[70]

---

[68] For the *dumas*, see George Tarnawsky and Patricia Nell Warren, *Ukrainian Dumy* (Toronto and Cambridge, MA, 1979).

[69] See Frank E. Sysyn, "A Curse on Both Their Houses: Catholic Attitudes towards Jews in Father Ruszel's *Fawor Niebieski*," in *Israel and the Nations: Essays Presented in Honor of Shmuel Ettinger* (Jerusalem, 1987), ix–xxiv.

[70] For bibliography on the topic, see Majer Bałaban, comp., *Bibliografia historii Żydów w Polsce i w krajach ościennych za lata 1900–1930* (Warsaw, 1939); Gershon Hundert and Gershon Bacon, *The Jews in Poland and Russia: Bibliographic Essays* (Bloomington, IN, 1984); *Sistematicheskii ukazatel' literatury o evreiakh (1708–1889)* (St. Petersburg, 1892); Joel Raba, *Between Remembrance and Denial: The Fate of the Jews in the Wars of the Polish Commonwealth During the Mid-Seventeenth Century as Shown in Contemporary Writings and Historical Research* (Boulder, CO, 1995); and my review, "The Jewish Massacres in the Historiography of the Khmel'nyts'kyi Uprising: A Review Article," *Journal of Ukrainian Studies* 23.1 (Summer 1998): 83–9. For additional literature, see the notes in

Contrary to the statement of the Eyewitness Chronicler, the primary and immediate cause of the revolt was not the religious issue. The Byzantine-Latin Christian divide was, however, a faultline in the Polish-Lithuanian state. The religious ferment of the sixteenth century that had increased missionary activity and improved the institutions of Western Christians upset the balance between Western and Eastern Christianity in Ukraine and Belarus. The intervention of the state in the failed attempt to respond to this challenge that the Ruthenian bishops attempted at Brest and the increasing religious consciousness among all nobles made the maintenance of the older coexistence untenable. Almost against its will, the Orthodox Church had come to destabilize the state and legitimize revolt and resistance in the early seventeenth century. Once the Cossacks began the great revolt, both sides in the conflict almost

the articles by J. Pelenski, "The Cossack Insurrections in Jewish Ukrainian Relations" and Frank E. Sysyn, "The Jewish Factor in the Khmelnytsky Uprising," in *Ukrainian-Jewish Relations in Historical Perspective*, Howard Aster and Peter J. Potichnyi eds., 2d ed. (Edmonton, 1990), 31–42, 43–54; the introduction to Jacob Schatzky et al., *Gzeires takh* (Vilnius, 1938), and S. Borovoi, "Natsional'no-osvoboditel'naia voina ukrainskogo naroda protiv pol'skogo vlaychestva i evreiskoe naselenie Ukrainy," *Istoricheskie zapiski* 9 (1940): 81–2, 102.

For general literature, see the notes in Salo Wittmayer Baron, *A Social and Religious History of the Jews*: vol. 16. *Poland-Lithuania 1500–1650*, 2d ed. (New London, 1976); Bernard D. Weinryb, *The Jews of Poland: A Social and Economic History of the Jewish Community of Poland from 1100 to 1800* (Philadelphia, 1972); and Simon Dubnov, *History of the Jews in Russia and Poland*, vol. 1 (Philadelphia, 1916).

On the works of Ukrainian historiography, see Mykhailo Hrushevs'kyi, *Istoriia Ukrainy-Rusy*, vol. 8, pt. 2 (repr., New York, 1956), 199–224, and O. Efymenko (Aleksandra Iakovlevna Stravrovskaia Efimenko), "Bedstviia evreev v Iuzhnoi Rusi XVII veka," in her *Iuzhnaia Rus': Ocherki, issledovaniia i zametki*, vol. 2 (St. Petersburg, 1905), 1–11. The forthcoming volume from the conference held at Bar-Ilan University on May 18–20, 1998, "Gezeroit Tah-Tat/Eastern European Jewry in 1648–49: Context and Consequences," will contain many contributions on this topic.

A number of sources and secondary works hitherto only in Hebrew have appeared in translation recently. See Saul Iakovlevich Borovoi's translation of three of the Hebrew chronicles in *Evreiskie khroniki XVII stoletiia. (Epokha "Khmel'nichiny")* (Jerusalem and Moscow, 1997); the Russian translation of Samuel Ettinger's work *Rossiia i evrei* (Jerusalem, 1993); and the English translation, "The Legal and Social Status of the Jews of Ukraine from the Fifteenth Century to the Cossack Uprising of 1648," *Journal of Ukrainian Studies* 17.1–2 (1992): 107–40. On demography and the number of victims, see Frank E. Sysyn, "Ievrei ta povstannia Bohdana Khmel'nyts'koho," in *Mappa mundi: Zbirnyk naukovykh prats' na poshanu Iaroslava Dashkevycha z nahody ioho 70-richchia* (Lviv, Kyiv, and New York, 1996), 479–88; Bernard Weinryb, "The Hebrew Chronicles on Bohdan Khmel'nyts'kyi and the Cossack-Polish War," *Harvard Ukrainian Studies* 1 (1977): 153–77; Maurycy Horn, *Żydzi na Rusi Czerwonej w XVI i pierwszej połowie XVII wieku: Działalność gospodarcza na tle rozwoju demograficznego* (Warsaw, 1975), 310; and Samuel Ettinger, "The Participation of the Jews in the Settlement of Ukraine" (in Hebrew), *Zion* 24.3–4 (1956): 107–42 (in Russian translation: *Rossiia i evrei*, 87–154) and "Jewish Participation in the settlement of Ukraine in the Sixteenth and Seventeenth Centuries," in Aster and Potichnyi, *Ukrainian-Jewish Relations*, 23–30.

automatically saw it as a war of religion. What the masses of the population thought is more difficult to ascertain. Clearly the religious issue, associated with Ruthenian identity and xenophobia against alien faiths and communities, had great resonance. Ultimately, the religious issue played a major role in the negotiations with Muscovy and the swearing of allegiance to the tsar. With the formation of the hetmanate and the new link with Muscovy, Orthodoxy no longer found itself allied with the forces of social and political discontent.

# CHAPTER VII

# The Huguenot minority
# in early modern France

RAYMOND A. MENTZER

Despite substantial, sustained effort and encouraging initial success, the Protestant movement in France never advanced beyond the status of a permanent if vigorous religious and political minority. The Reformation clearly attracted a sizable following among the elite, drawing in particular from the nobility and urban bourgeoisie. Protestantism also appealed to many artisans and even persons from the rural agricultural world. Yet the protracted strife over the second half of the sixteenth century took its toll. Overall numerical strength among the Huguenots probably peaked in 1572 on the eve of the St. Bartholomew's Day massacre, or perhaps already a decade earlier at the beginning of the Wars of Religion. Scholars have suggested a total of some two million Protestants in 1560, roughly ten percent of the French population. More importantly, among the politically influential nobles, Huguenot strength may have been close to fifty percent. Fortunes declined steadily thereafter, and by the end of the sixteenth century, Protestants were no more than six to seven percent of the French population. The best estimates appear to be in the range of 1.2 million persons, perhaps slightly more.[1]

At the same time, the Huguenots were heavily concentrated in the western and southern portions of the kingdom. They lived on the Atlantic coast at La Rochelle and were spread across the provinces of Normandy and Poitou. To the south, Reformed communities at towns such as Castres and Montauban, Montpellier, and Nîmes have become legendary in the history of French Protestantism. In addition, a dense network of Protestant villages permeated the Cévennes mountains. Roughly four-fifths of all Huguenots lived in these areas – the west and the south. Here they established the churches and consistories that,

---

[1] Menna Prestwich, "Calvinism in France, 1555–1629," in *International Calvinism, 1541–1715*, ed. Menna Prestwich (Oxford, 1985), 73; Émile G. Léonard, *Histoire générale du protestantisme*, 3 vols. (Paris, 1961–4), 2: 313.

in turn, formed the basis for an extensive and uniform national ecclesiastical system.[2]

The Huguenots never enjoyed sustained support from the French monarchy or its governing officials. At best, they aspired to harmonious alliances with local secular authorities in the towns and regions that they dominated. In this respect, the situation differed from the generally cooperative affiliations that existed between the Reformed churches and the German princely states or the municipal councils that ruled the Swiss city-states. Accordingly, the circumstances in France placed an enormous burden on the minority Calvinist community. The Protestant faithful, their churches, and the associated ecclesiastical institutions had a strained and ambivalent relationship with the political powers. From a Catholic and royalist perspective, the Huguenots were a troublesome and dangerous group. They were, at best, grudgingly tolerated and, more often than not, actively oppressed. All too frequently, they found themselves fiercely persecuted. The religious situation was extremely difficult and tense throughout the ancien régime. The continual strain and strife inevitably shaped, restricted, and blunted the ambitious Reformed effort to revive the pristine splendor of the primitive Church.

Protestants in France were fundamentally a religious minority. Although their situation had political and legal repercussions, the Huguenots possessed none of the reinforcing distinctions – race, ethnicity, language, or unique cultural traditions – that we typically associate with religious minorities in our contemporary world. Reformed congregations thought of themselves as a moral community distinguished by a biblically sanctioned understanding of Christianity. They were, in the ideal, the community of saints, who sought to differentiate their religious beliefs and ritual forms from the "superstitious" views and "idolatrous" practices of a scandalous medieval Church. On a practical level, the absence of a cooperative relationship with royal political officials severely restrained the Protestant attempt to realize the reform of society that, in Calvinist tradition, complemented the theological and liturgical changes customarily associated with the Reformation.

* * * * *

The centerpiece in the reform of lifestyle was a moral and social disciplining of the community. Calvinists created elaborate mechanisms for the

---

[2] Elisabeth Labrousse, "Calvinism in France, 1598–1685," in *International Calvinism*, 285–6; Samuel Mours, *Les églises réformées en France* (Paris, 1958), 157–67. For Huguenot demographic history after the Edict of Nantes: Philip Benedict, *The Huguenot Population of France, 1600–1685: The Demographic Fate and Customs of a Religious Minority* (Philadelphia, 1991).

maintenance of moral order and supervision of the faithful. The pastors and elders, who met regularly in an administrative body known as the consistory, energetically sought to encourage virtue and suppress vice. They offered guidance and religious edification with frequent sermon services and catechism lessons. At the same time, these church authorities worked arduously to identify sin and impose penitential discipline through a graduated system of shaming techniques that included censure and admonition, private and public repentance ceremonies, and excommunication. In short, the Church and its officials sought to mold behavior and cement confessional identity. Not surprisingly, the meaning of this endeavor toward a more general social and communal reform has elicited enormous discussion and is a major focus of recent historical interest.

A number of German scholars, drawing on their understanding of Calvinism in the Empire, argue that the attempt at social discipline reached well beyond the ecclesiastical sphere. Given the close association of religion and politics in early modern Europe, the drive to modify human conduct and sentiment had broad reverberations. In what has come to be known as the confessionalization model, the Church restored, nurtured, and corrected a morally weak human community. The state, for its part, recognized that the advance of social discipline and confessional solidarity served its interests too. Confessionalization, according to its proponents, contributed significantly to state formation for it allowed governing elites to utilize ecclesiastical discipline as an effective instrument for general social control. The powerful process benefited both spiritual and temporal governors. There was a vigorous, mutually reinforcing affiliation of confessional consolidation, social discipline, and state-building.[3]

Yet the symbiotic relationship between state-building and the construction of a unified Protestant identity did not exist for France, at least not in the same manner as it did for a number of other Western European countries. The French absolutist state and Counter-Reformation Catholic Church unquestionably cooperated for mutual benefit. But the extent to which the development furthered discipline or fits within the confessionalization paradigm remains largely unanswered.[4] The

---

[3] Gerhard Oestreich, *Geist und Gestalt des frühmodernen Staates. Ausgewahlte Aufsatze* (Berlin, 1969); Heinz Schilling, *Die reformierte Konfessionalisierung in Deutschland* (Gütersloh, 1986) and "Confessionalization in the Empire," in Heinz Schilling, *Religion, Political Culture and the Emergence of Early Modern Society* (Leiden, 1992), 205–46.

[4] For a preliminary discussion of confessionalization in a French Catholic context, see Marie-Antoinette Gross, "Die frühneuzeitliche Konfessionalisierung und ihre Konsequenzen für das Verhältnis von Staat und Kirche in Deutschland und Frankreich – eine Zwischenbilanz," in *Gesellschaften im Vergleich. Forschungen aus Sozial- und Geschichtswissenschaften*, Hartmut Kaelble and Jürgen Schriewer eds. (Bern, 1998), 53–83.

Huguenot presence led to confrontation and opposition. Their status as a minority meant that social discipline and Reformed religious culture acquired a character different from that which unfolded in the German world. A distinctive Gallican flavor developed within the unique context of Huguenot history.

In investigating these issues, let us first examine religious developments internal to the Reformed Church of France. Afterward, we can turn to Huguenot political relationships with the crown and the wider Catholic community. With respect to the former, attention focuses on questions of ecclesiastical and social control as well as the ways in which they evolved among the Protestants of early modern France. How did their status as a religious and political minority affect the Huguenots' effort at instructing and chastising the faithful? What were the results? What were the limitations? Did the monumental attempt at regulating human moral frailty and fostering righteous comportment change significantly over time, especially during the difficult decades after the mid-seventeenth century when a strident Catholic crown applied ever greater pressure?

The logical starting point is the local Reformed church and its consistory. The activities of individual pastors and elders, resolutely engaged in transforming Protestant religious ideas into a set of everyday ethical habits and devotional observances, suggest the dynamics of reform at the level of the village or municipal parish church and can reveal the often tense situation of local Protestant congregations, hard pressed as they were by Catholic religious and political authorities. They also disclose the tight limits and unique traits of social discipline among the Huguenots as the result of their status as a minority.

The French Reformed Church pursued ecclesiastical discipline through a broad range of key activities, including the implementation of new liturgical practices and prayer in the vernacular, catechism instruction for both children and adults, the organization of social welfare programs, and, most conspicuously, morals control. Close attention to proper ethical conduct is perhaps the most striking element of the Reformed attempt to supervise and regulate the faithful. Wrongdoers summoned by the French consistories embodied a wide spectrum of misbehavior; the offenses divide into two major groupings. Many of the infractions were of an ecclesiastical nature: failing to attend the communion service, the Sunday sermon, or catechism lessons; pursuing contaminating contacts with Catholicism; participating in "idolatrous and superstitious" celebrations such as Carnival or Catholic votive festivals; relapsing into "popery"; practicing irregularities of marriage; breaching the sabbath; blaspheming; and using magic. The other general category of offenses belongs to the realm of moral delinquency: verbal disputes and violent quarrels, sexual misconduct (mostly fornication but also adultery), dancing, immodest dress, playing various games of chance, and drunkenness. Some faults were obviously more serious than others, some were more common than others, and finally there was, over time, an evolution in the consistory's interest in and attention to these shortcomings.

French Protestants always lived in close proximity to Catholic society and culture. Even in those cities and regions where the Huguenots constituted a majority, Catholic neighbors within the towns or in nearby villages were an ever-present reality. In light of the necessity of practical coexistence with Catholicism, the Huguenots found that harmful, indeed contaminating contacts with Catholicism were a permanent and persistent problem. The offenses eventually settled into a regular pattern. The principal difficulties were participation in various Catholic festivals and marriage in a Catholic ceremony.

Throughout the early years of the Reformation, especially during moments of intense fighting, Protestants were sometimes forced to attend Mass or to have a child baptized by a Catholic priest. It was understandable, although the Reformed churches thought it unacceptable and polluting.[5] The alternatives could be destruction of a person's property, physical injury, or even death. Curiously, the problem did not diminish in the decades that followed. Among later generations, Protestants occasionally stole away to hear Mass from a sense of inquisitiveness. They wanted a closer look at the abomination of the Antichrist, which their pastors denounced vehemently and frequently.[6] Other contacts with Catholicism were more closely related to what the Reformers labeled its superstitious nature. A Protestant man from Gascony had masses said at a local Catholic chapel in expectation of curing an ailing leg.[7] A peasant from the Cévennes stopped at the Catholic church in a distant village to collect some holy water, perhaps out of respect for its alleged healing properties.[8]

In addition, Protestant men and women could always sneak away to an adjacent Catholic village and join in a votive festival honoring Mary Magdalene, Saint Blaise, or some other revered local patron. It could mean attending Mass, marching in a procession, or perhaps more to the

---

[5] Raymond A. Mentzer, "The Persistence of 'Superstition and Idolatry' among Rural French Calvinists," *Church History* 65 (1996): 221.

[6] Bibliothèque Nationale (hereafter BN), MS fr. 8667, fols. 287, 293–4, 297, 300v, 313.

[7] Archives Départementales [hereafter AD], Gers, 23067, 17 et 31 août 1607, 2 septembre 1607.

[8] AD, Hérault, E Dépôt, Ganges GG 24, fols. 102, 124–124v.

point, attending a market, dancing, and participating in the games and other collective endeavors that made up the larger celebration of a saint's feast. Some of the Huguenot faithful embraced with similar abandon the revelry surrounding Carnival on the eve of Lent. The Reformed rejection of Lenten penitential practices during the six weeks prior to Easter did not entirely overcome people's passion for the delights of Mardi Gras and the accompanying raucous distractions and merriment. Invariably, there was a neighboring Catholic hamlet where they could play violins and other musical instruments, don costumes and masks, dance, feast, and generally carouse.[9]

The greatest difficulty relating to infectious contacts with Catholicism concerned marriage. Religiously mixed unions were a grave and intractable problem, one which only worsened over time. Given the strong patriarchal notions of the age, Protestant women, when betrothed to Catholic men, often deferred to their future husbands' religion. They married in Catholic ceremonies or, as the consistory would have phrased it, "*à la messe*" and "*à la papauté*." Reformed pastors and elders throughout France summoned numerous fathers during the sixteenth and seventeenth centuries and severely scolded them for permitting their daughters to marry Catholics.[10] Not only were Protestant women placed in religiously threatening circumstances, but the children born of these unions risked being raised Catholic. Indeed, Gregory Hanlon has suggested that mixed marriages became, in the seventeenth century, the principal vehicle for incorporation of the Huguenot minority into the dominant Catholic religious culture.

Hanlon's study of several Huguenot towns in Gascony poses an especially compelling question that links confessionally mixed unions to the gradual absorption of the Huguenots. Why was the Protestant minority increasingly assimilated during the seventeenth century, despite the absence of overt oppression, at least in the region of France that he examined? The issue is complex. Hanlon begins with the observation that no significant cultural gap existed between Protestant and Catholic. While the Counter-Reformation, embodied above all in various lay confraternities, was vigorous in Gascony, it was not strident. Conversion to Catholicism frequently occurred in conjunction with a confessionally

---

[9] Marianne Carbonnier-Burkard, "Jours de fêtes dans les Églises Réformées de France au XVIIe siècle," *Etudes théologiques et religieuses* 68 (1993): 347–58; Philippe Chareyre, "'The Great Difficulties One Must Bear to Follow Jesus Christ': Morality at Sixteenth-Century Nîmes," in *Sin and the Calvinists: Morals Control and the Consistory in the Reformed Tradition*, ed. Raymond A. Mentzer (Kirksville, MO, 1994), 93–5; Mentzer, "Superstition and Idolatry," *Church History* 65 (1996): 222–4.

[10] AD, Gers, 23067, 29 décembre 1607, 26 mars 1608.

mixed marriage. Here, Hanlon underscores the importance of family alliances and solidarities that went beyond personal religious identity. Kinship requirements, the search for economic stability, even social and political aspirations could push in directions that contradicted religious commitment. Individual believers were, in any event, subject to intense, competing demands. Group dynamics slowly but inexorably eroded Huguenot society.[11]

Along similar lines, Philippe Joutard's highly regarded interpretation of the revocation of the Edict of Nantes in 1685 and the persecution of French Protestants in the decades that ensued focuses on the events as a spur to renewal of Reformed society. The revocation was not, in Joutard's view, an utter calamity. Rather, a Protestant religious community that was being slowly absorbed by the majority Catholic culture through intermarriage, conversion, and other pressures was, after 1685, fired with the will to resist.[12] Huguenot confessional identity and their position as a persecuted minority pushed them to endure.

In general, the Reformed effort to regulate marriage proved from the beginning to be an extremely frustrating affair. It figured prominently in the Reformed churches' endeavors to promote discipline. Yet the developments surrounding the Huguenot reform of marriage are evidence of the limitations born of their status as a religious minority living in a state of substantial antagonism with the Catholic monarchy. While the Reformed system for marrying generally followed the canon law model developed during the Middle Ages, John Calvin, Theodore Beza, and others made several critical changes, notably in the nature of the betrothal promises and in the dissolubility of a legally contracted marriage.

Marriage within the Reformed tradition occurred in two stages. The first step was the betrothal, which involved much more than the modern engagement. It was a formal ritual in which the couple exchanged reciprocal, binding promises to wed. They are often referred to as the "words of the future tense." For persons possessing economic resources, these promises were usually fixed in a notarial contract specifying the financial arrangements between bride, groom, and their families. The exchange had to be public and, toward this end, required at least two witnesses to be valid. Calvinist reformers were determined to avoid clandestine marriage, which had, in their opinion, seriously undermined

---

[11] Gregory Hanlon, *Confession and Community in Seventeenth-Century France: Catholic and Protestant Coexistence in Aquitaine* (Philadelphia, 1993), 102–11.

[12] Philippe Joutard, "The Revocation of the Édict of Nantes: End or Renewal of French Protestantism?" in *International Calvinism*, 339–68.

matrimony, family, and parental authority during the late medieval period.[13] The second stage, the wedding vows or the "words of the present tense" and solemnization of the marriage before the pastor, occurred in the temple several weeks later. The interval permitted further requisite publicity through the announcement of banns on three successive Sundays. The process would presumably disclose any impediments or obstacles to the union. Finally, written parental permission was necessary for women to the age of twenty-five and for men to thirty. French royal legislation enacted under Henry II in 1556 established the specifics of this latter requirement. The Reformed Church with its strong sense of patriarchal dominion readily agreed with the king's reinforcement of parental power over marriage.[14]

Many persons, accustomed to the somewhat less strict requirements of the medieval Church and communal custom, found this two-step system with *binding* promises at each stage complicated and confusing. A seemingly irresolvable tangle of problems centered on the reciprocal promises of the betrothal ceremony. Already in 1559, the first edition of the national *Discipline of the Reformed Churches of France* stipulated that "promises of marriage legitimately made cannot be dissolved, not even by the mutual consent of those who made them."[15] Yet the initial exchange of vows was no more than a solemn engagement. Couples were not yet allowed to set up a common household nor could they consummate their relationship sexually. Sexual intercourse following the betrothal but before the celebration of the marriage was fornication. Consistories everywhere in France severely censured couples who behaved otherwise. The church of Bédarieux in the Cévennes mountains amply illustrated the point when it excommunicated a couple who began living together "as if their marriage had been solemnized." According to ecclesiastical officials at Pont-de-Camarès, people were to "live virtuously during the betrothal period."[16] Another major category of persons, mostly men, declined to wed after having committed

---

[13] Beatrice Gottlieb, "The Meaning of Clandestine Marriage," in *Family and Sexuality in French History*, Robert Wheaton and Tamara K. Hareven eds. (Philadelphia, 1980), 52–3.

[14] Pierre Bels, *Le mariage des protestants français jusqu'en 1685* (Paris, 1968); Jean-Baptiste Molin and Protais Mutembe, *Le rituel du mariage en France du XIIe au XVIe siècle* (Paris, 1974); John Witte, Jr., *From Sacrament to Contract: Marriage, Religion, and the Law in the Western Tradition* (Louisville, 1997), 74–129.

[15] François Méjan, *Discipline de l'Église Réformée de France annotée et précédée d'une introduction historique* (Paris, 1947), 285–6.

[16] Frank Delteil, "Institutions et vie de l'Église réformée de Pont de Camarès," in *Les Églises et leurs institutions au XVIe siècle. Actes du Vème Colloque du Centre d'Histoire de la Réforme et du Protestantisme*, ed. Michel Péronnet (Montpellier, 1978), 98.

themselves in the betrothal ceremony. The reasons for their hesitation varied widely. Some may have found a more attractive marriage prospect. Others delayed finalization of the marriage until payment of the dowry. Women occasionally balked at their fathers' choice of a husband for them.[17] Local churches, predictably enough, endeavored tirelessly to rectify these matters.

Still, after struggling for more than a half century to institute and enforce a change of attitude toward the betrothal vows, the French Reformed Church yielded and abandoned the rigid and cumbersome system in the early seventeenth century. Members of the congregation did not always understand the Church's position. Nor were long-standing folk observances always in accord with the innovations. Finally, Catholic practice, which the crown sanctioned, did not regard the betrothal vows as irrevocable. The differences between the Reformed and Catholic views simply exacerbated an already difficult situation, especially since the Catholic view was the legal requirement. In the end, the Reformed Church adopted the Catholic and royal system whereby the engagement did not entail an irrevocable promise to marry.

The National Synod of the Reformed Church, meeting at Privas in 1612, revised the nature of the betrothal promises. They no longer represented binding consent to marry, but only a promise to give consent to wed.[18] The shift placed Reformed theory and practice in conformity with French law as expressed in the Ordinance of Blois of 1579. The royal legislation, of course, had created great pressure for the French Protestants to revise their concepts. It also embraced many of the decisions made by Catholic bishops at the Council of Trent.[19] Accordingly, the change enacted by the Huguenots in 1612 marked a break with the system of marriage laid out in the late 1550s and 1560s. It was a tacit admission of failure in the attempt to impart an indissoluble character to the initial espousal promises. The marriage bond among Protestants would henceforth be formulated according to rules nearly identical to those of the Catholic Church.[20] The decision taken at Privas in 1612 was

---

[17] AD, Tarn-et-Garonne, I, 1, fols. 79–79v, 226v. Archives Nationales [hereafter AN], TT 234, dossier 6, fols. 814, 816, 817; TT 269, dossier 25, fol. 960; BN, MS fr. 8666, fols. 57, 86v–89, 113, 122–122v, 167, 168; MS fr. 8667, fols. 15v–16, 80v, 91, 134v, 135, 141, 142v, 144v, 149, 157, 161v, 166, 168v, 174v, 178, 191v, 194v, 238, 241–241v, 248v, 249v, 308, 314, 333, 363v, 371–371v, 372v.

[18] [Jean] Aymon, *Tous les synodes des Églises réformées de France*, 2 vols. (The Hague, 1710), I: 402–3.

[19] Paul Ourliac and J. de Malafosse, *Histoire du droit privé*, 3 vols. (Paris, 1957–68), III: 205–9.

[20] Bels, *Le mariage des protestants*, 126–7, 132–5, 159–63; Méjan, *Discipline*, 280.

a stunning acknowledgment of Huguenot inability to impose ecclesiastical discipline fully and to resist successfully the relentless pressure of the Catholic Church and Bourbon monarchy.

The other aspect of marriage with which reformers attempted innovation was in the realm of divorce with the right to remarry. French Protestants joined leading theologians such as Luther and Bucer, Calvin and Beza in rejecting a long medieval tradition that had progressively limited divorce.[21] The changes, however, had little practical effect in France. Again, they were thwarted by lack of support or even cooperation from the state. Canon law allowed, under certain limited circumstances, divorce in the sense of judicial separation without the possibility of remarriage. The Catholic crown, however, forbade divorce with permission to remarry, and Protestants generally found the royal prohibition difficult to circumvent. Part of the disincentive to dissolve marriage was internal to Protestantism in France. With their insistence on the sacred character of the family and the fundamental importance of familial responsibilities,[22] Protestant officials frowned upon legal separation. They preferred that husband and wife patch up their differences, resume their marital life, and thereby restore the household. While divorce was theoretically possible, the Reformed churches laid great emphasis on preserving and fortifying the ties of marriage. When couples quarreled and marital breakdown threatened, pastors and elders went to substantial lengths to counsel and reconcile the disputing parties.

Nevertheless, French Protestants admitted two grounds for divorce in the sense of dissolution of the marriage bond and hence permission to remarry: adultery and desertion. Both had to be established before the secular magistrate.[23] In theory, when the court convicted an adulterous spouse, the consistory could declare the innocent party free to remarry. The offending party might eventually remarry as well, but only after deliberate, often lengthy inquiry. Early on, a number of Protestants, mostly men, tested the new system. The Nîmes consistory reluctantly agreed to a carder's divorce and remarriage after he established his wife's adultery. Apparently he had also proven his accusation before the secular magistrate. Other men made similar claims. In each instance, the

---

[21] Theodore Beza, *Tractatio de repudiis et divortiis* (Geneva, 1569); Robert Kingdon, *Adultery and Divorce in Calvin's Geneva* (Cambridge, MA, 1995); H.J. Selderhuis, *Marriage and Divorce in the Thought of Martin Bucer* (Kirksville, MO, 1999).

[22] Calvin, for instance, described the family as a small individual church. Janine Garrisson, *Les Protestants au XVIe siècle* (Paris, 1988), 37–9, 88–91.

[23] Lay judges traditionally had jurisdiction over adultery and recognized it as legitimate reason for legal separation of a couple. Ourliac and Malafosse, *Histoire du droit privé*, III: 198–207.

consistory counseled them to prove their wives' adultery in the royal courts before proceeding to discussion of dissolution of marriage.[24] Individuals petitioning for divorce on the basis of abandonment, though far fewer, received similar advice from consistorial officials. Before receiving permission to remarry, they had to establish the fact of their desertion before the secular magistrate. In reality, the civil authorities dramatically restricted the ability of Protestant Church authorities to grant divorces, whether for reason of adultery or abandonment. By the end of the sixteenth century, the consistories acknowledged that royal legislation effectively forbade remarriage even if a spouse had been found guilty of adultery or desertion. The civil law obstructed (admittedly unenthusiastic) Protestant willingness to permit divorce. One of the few options for Huguenots seeking divorce and remarriage was to obtain the legal conviction of an adulterous spouse. While the judgment allowed no more than legal separation in France, the innocent party could sometimes remarry outside the kingdom. Several couples followed this tack and the French Reformed churches recognized these second marriages.[25] In the main, however, the French state set strict limits on Reformed attempts to reconceptualize and modify the sacred vows, cultural practices, and legal structures surrounding marriage.

These restraints also shaped the punishments that the consistory imposed upon sinners and the ways in which they were utilized. Officials censured or admonished most offenders – individuals whose sins were relatively minor. More serious faults merited repentance ceremonies, both private and public. The French consistories never had the power to imprison, banish, or inflict corporal punishment. Initially, some churches prescribed monetary fines (as did their counterparts in Scotland, for example), but without support from the state, the penalty was probably difficult to enforce, infringed on the prerogatives of the civil magistrate, and quickly fell into disuse.[26] The gravest of all punishments was excommunication, which excluded a person from participation in the celebration of the Lord's Supper. It also curtailed normal social and economic dealings with other members of the congregation. Here

---

[24] AD, Gard, 42 J 29, fol. 90. BN, MS fr. 8666, fols. 29, 30, 45v; MS fr. 8667, fols. 20, 33v; Aymon, *Tous les synodes*, I: 10, 25, 35, 39, 68, 74, 76, 79, 107, 125, 141, 158; Bels, *Le mariage des protestants*, 239–47; Delteil, "Pont-de-Camarès," 98–9; Méjan, *Discipline*, 286–7.

[25] AD, Gard, 42 J 28, fol. 155; 42 J 29, fols. 589–90, 596; Bels, *Le mariage des protestants*, 248–9.

[26] Raymond A. Mentzer, "*Disciplina nervus ecclesiae*: The Calvinist Reform of Morals at Nîmes," *Sixteenth Century Journal* 18 (1987): 112; Michael Graham, "Social Discipline in Scotland, 1560–1610," in *Sin and the Calvinists*, 142–3, 152; Geoffrey Parker, "The 'Kirk By Law Established' and the Origins of 'The Taming of Scotland': St. Andrews, 1559–1600," in *Sin and the Calvinists*, 180–1.

the absence of a close rapport between church and state gave French ecclesiastical officials a freer hand than they would have had in many imperial and Swiss city-states where the secular magistrate generally exercised strict control over excommunication. Still, there were complications. Without backing from the state, the consistory was incapable of restricting the legal rights of excommunicates. It could not, for instance, prevent them from pursuing civil or criminal legal actions as had been the case under earlier medieval arrangements.[27]

As a practical matter, the elders composed detailed lists of excommunicates. There could be no ambiguity about who had been barred from the sacred communal meal. At the same time, they maintained rolls of the members of the congregation eligible to participate in the Lord's Supper. The Communion celebration, which occurred quarterly, was very well regulated. In order to avoid desecration of the sacrament, the elders screened the faithful during the several weeks prior to the service. They gave special admission tokens (*méreaux*) to those judged worthy in terms of belief and behavior. Each communicant presented the token at the time of the service and, accordingly, was allowed to receive the bread and wine.[28] In truth, Huguenot ecclesiastical officials were tireless enumerators. They pioneered in the preparation and maintenance of baptismal, marriage, and burial registers. These record keeping activities also extended to lists of persons received into the Church, the destitute who needed social assistance, individuals who attended catechism, and so forth. Collectively, the endeavors defined the Church's membership with astonishing thoroughness for the early modern period. The techniques identified Huguenot believers with reasonable accuracy and differentiated them from Catholic neighbors.

There was, in this broad consistorial attempt to discipline the congregation and inculcate a sense of religious and moral obligation, a progression or evolution over time. Take, for example, the church of Nîmes. During the first years of its existence – in the early 1560s – ecclesiastical matters loomed large. Getting people to participate in the Lord's Supper, attend sermon services, recite catechism lessons, and learn their prayers consumed a great deal of the elders' time and energy. Later, by the 1580s,

---

[27] Raymond A. Mentzer, "Marking the Taboo: Excommunication in French Reformed Churches," in *Sin and the Calvinists*, 97–128.

[28] E. Delorme, "Le méreau dans les Églises réformées de France," *Bulletin de la Société de l'Histoire du Protestantisme Français* 37 (1888): 204–13, 316–25, 371–81, 483–92; Ch.-L. Frossard, "Description de quarante et un méreaux de la communion réformée," *Bulletin de la Société de l'Histoire du Protestantisme Français* 21 (1872): 236–42, 286–96; Henri Gelin, *Le méreau dans les Églises Réformées de France et plus particulièrement dans celles du Poitou* (Saint-Maixent, 1891).

attendance at worship, catechism, and the like seem to have improved markedly and the elders turned their attention to other, perhaps less pressing shortcomings: dancing, playing games, frequenting taverns, and immodest dress. The pattern of consistorial activity at Nîmes during the early 1560s may well be typical of a newly established Reformed church. It concentrated on the reform of people's religious conduct and piety. These were difficulties that demanded quick resolution. The later behavioral concerns, those of the 1580s at Nîmes, probably reflect the interests of a church more confident and assured of its survival, despite a continuing hostile environment.[29]

In his study of the church of Saint-Jean-du-Gard, a small town in the heart of the Cévennes mountains, Didier Poton demonstrates that in the seventeenth century there was a far more ominous evolution in consistorial affairs. Besides examination of the consistory's handling of religious faults and moral failings among the faithful, Poton traces the consistory's attention to ecclesiastical administration. He methodically examines the time and effort that the pastor and elders of Saint-Jean-du-Gard devoted to planning the worship, managing the church's financial affairs, and, above all, guiding its relationship with the larger universe beyond their mountain community. The latter included contacts with Reformed ecclesiastical institutions such as the colloquies and synods on the one hand, and with the administrative and political officials of the monarchical Catholic state on the other.

Predictably, consistorial attention to the political and administrative goings-on of the outside world increasingly occupied the pastor and elders over the course of the seventeenth century. The great shift occurred with the so-called "strict application" of the Edict of Nantes, which began with the personal rule of Louis XIV in the early 1660s. Issues of religious and moral behavior dominated the consistory's deliberations until the late 1620s. Beginning in 1628, however, and extending to 1660, the consistory of Saint-Jean-du-Gard found itself discussing matters of ecclesiastical administration as often as those regarding religious behavior and moral control. Then, in the two and a half decades starting in 1661 and leading up to 1685 and the revocation of the Edict of Nantes, the elders and pastors became wholly preoccupied with the furious government offensive against their church. The nightmare of dealing with a Catholic state determined to suppress and eliminate Reformed society dominated the discussions among the members of the consistory. Social discipline and the close supervision of the

---

[29] Mentzer, "Reform at Nîmes," 108–9.

faithful became far less urgent. Simple survival was the central critical concern.[30]

* * * * *

An analogous progression of Huguenot interests along with a corresponding deterioration of their position is evident in the political sphere. Protestant demands for security along with the full exercise of their civil liberties and political rights figured prominently in the many negotiated peace arrangements and royal edicts that sought, largely without success, to bring an end to the devastating religious wars, which had erupted in the early 1560s. Accordingly, the Edict of Nantes, promulgated in April 1598, contained elaborate arrangements in the massive final push to pacify the realm and promote confessional coexistence. The edict did not give Protestants equal status with Catholics in the religious sphere. It provided, nonetheless, a practical and comprehensible framework within which members of each confession might strive to live in concord. The edict contained well-known provisions recognizing the legal existence of the Reformed churches and established surety towns where Protestants could worship freely. It also promised Huguenots access to royal offices, professional occupations, and educational institutions. The edict even instituted extraordinary law courts, the so-called *chambres de l'Édit* that were attached to the sovereign high courts in Protestant regions.[31]

Protestants had voiced deep concern with religiously prejudiced Catholic judges from the beginning of the Reformation in France. Royal courts had been especially active in the arrest, trial, and punishment of "heretics." Prosecutorial – Huguenots might have said persecutory – zeal only intensified with the outbreak of organized armed conflict. Protestant litigants wished to steer clear of biased Catholic judges and, accordingly, the initial Huguenot strategy envisioned the establishment of separate tribunals, staffed entirely by Reformed magistrates. Several experiments, however, were ineffective and short-lived. Thus, by the end of the sixteenth century, the agreed solution was the creation of special

---

[30] Didier Poton, "De l'Édit à sa Révocation: Saint Jean de Gardonnenque 1598–1686," 2 vols., Thèse de doctorat d'État (Université Paul Valéry – Montpellier III, 1988).

[31] Janine Garrisson, *L'Édit de Nantes* (Biarritz, 1997) offers an annotated edition of the text of the edict. By way of context and analysis, see Bernard Cottret, *1598. L'Édit de Nantes. Pour finir avec les guerres de religion* (Paris, 1997); Janine Garrisson, *L'Édit de Nantes. Chronique d'une paix attendue* (Paris, 1998); and Mack Holt, *The French Wars of Religion, 1562–1629* (Cambridge, 1995), 152–72.

chambers for the *parlements* of Bordeaux, Grenoble, and Toulouse and, in a more limited way, for the high courts at Paris and Rouen. These chambers had jurisdiction over all suits, civil and criminal, in which at least one of the parties was Protestant. In the attempt to ensure fairness toward Protestants, the tribunals were staffed at least partially by Reformed judges. Three of the chambers, those for the *parlements* of Bordeaux, Grenoble, and Toulouse, were *mi-parties* or bipartisan, that is to say, composed of equal numbers of Protestant and Catholic judges. The chambers for Paris and Rouen, however, had but one Reformed judge.[32]

The affiliations among the Protestant judges of the *chambres de l'Édit* were at once confessional, professional, and social. The Huguenots who sat on the *chambres* during their eighty-odd years of existence came from a well-defined and limited clutch of Reformed families. They shared a religious and cultural experience, gathering in the same temples, attending school together, and passing their coveted offices on the *chambres de l'Édit* to their children or those of other judicial clans within whose families they had intermarried.[33] Members of early modern elites throughout Europe would have readily understood the need to marshal carefully and nurture these scarce economic, political, and social openings. The Huguenot magistrates had additional incentive. They had been excluded and in some cases violently removed from the royal *parlements* during the Wars of Religion. Not until the Edict of Nantes in 1598 and the subsequent establishment of *chambres de l'Édit* did positions on these as well as subordinate courts open to them.

These tightly circumscribed prospects lessened dramatically during the seventeenth century. Seats on the *chambres de l'Édit* effectively marked the limits of ambition among lesser Huguenot provincial nobles who, without extensive landholdings or independent political bases, sought to ensure their families' future through bureaucratic service to the crown. Once acquired, judicial posts could not be relinquished; they typically remained in the lineage for generations. Yet even this strategy

---

[32] Emile Brives-Cazès, *La chambre de justice de Guyenne en 1583–84* (Bordeaux, 1874); Justin Brun-Durand, *Essai historique sur la chambre de l'Édit de Grenoble* (Valence, 1873); Jules Cambon de Lavalette, *La chambre de l'Édit de Languedoc* (Paris, 1872); Stéphane Capot, *Justice et religion en Languedoc au temps de l'Édit de Nantes: La chambre de l'Édit de Castres (1579–1679)* (Paris, 1998); Diane Margolf, "The Paris Chambre de l'Édit: Protestant, Catholic and Royal Justice in Early Modern France," unpublished Ph.D. dissertation (Yale University, 1990).

[33] The history of these developments for the *chambre de l'Édit* of Languedoc can be found in Raymond A. Mentzer, *Blood and Belief: Family Survival and Confessional Identity among the Provincial Huguenot Nobility* (West Lafayette, IN, 1994). Capot, *Justice et religion en Languedoc*, 259–315.

failed Protestant officeholders toward the end of the century. The monarchy, in connection with its unrelenting attack on the Reformed churches and their followers, abolished the *chambres de l'Édit* throughout France by 1679. Though not stripped of their offices, the Protestant judges were integrated into other chambers of the various *parlements* and thereby submerged in an intensely Catholic milieu. These developments culminated with the revocation of the Edict of Nantes in 1685 when, as part of the process, Louis XIV demanded attestations of Catholicity from all royal officials.[34] Under intense royal pressure and constrained by professional and familial circumstances, the Protestant judges converted rather than lose their positions.

The *chambres de l'Édit* were, of course, law courts. Over the decades, the judges, Protestant and Catholic working together, heard thousands of cases, both civil complaints and criminal prosecutions. During the initial years of their existence, the chambers had critical responsibilities for the resolution of the innumerable disputes that had arisen between Catholics and Protestants during the Wars of Religion.[35] These tensions and their potential for renewed bloodshed had to be dissolved if the realm was to enjoy stability and peace. In the long term, these tribunals functioned as the principal institutions for the settlement of litigation among Huguenots as well as for all disputes arising between Protestants and Catholics.

Much of the success that the *chambres de l'Édit* enjoyed in curbing conflict and fostering accord derived from the bipartisan nature of the tribunals associated with the *parlements* of Bordeaux, Grenoble, and Toulouse. All three were located in areas with substantial Huguenot minorities. The chambers, in this instance, were an early experiment in what modern observers term conflict resolution. In addition, the French monarchy employed the principle of bipartisanship beyond the judicial sphere toward the overall resolution of confessional conflict. Bipartisan arrangements in broad peacemaking efforts enjoined leading figures from each confessional camp to cooperate for their common welfare. In the interests of the proper application of the Edict of Nantes, the king appointed commissioners, one Catholic and the other Protestant, to

---

[34] Madeleine Brenac, "Toulouse, centre de lutte contre le protestantisme au XVIIe siècle," *Annales du Midi* 77 (1965): 31–45; Arie Theodorus van Deursen, *Professions et métiers interdits: un aspect de l'histoire de la révocation de l'Édit de Nantes* (Groningen, 1960), 172–4.

[35] Raymond A. Mentzer, "L'Édit de Nantes et la chambre de justice du Languedoc," in *Coexister dans l'intolérance. L'Édit de Nantes (1598),* Michel Grandjean and Bernard Roussel eds. (Geneva, 1998), 321–38, and *Bulletin de la Société de l'Histoire du Protestantisme Français* 144 (1998): 321–38.

verify and execute the legislation in each province. These commissioners protected Reformed worship in towns so designated by the Edict, reintroduced the Mass to areas where Protestants had earlier proscribed its celebration, and generally made every effort to ensure the safety of Catholics and Protestants throughout the kingdom.[36]

These bipartisan endeavors proved extremely valuable in winning approval for the Edict of Nantes, advancing the pacification process, and resolving lingering points of friction between Protestant and Catholic, especially in the decade or so subsequent to the Edict's promulgation. Later, after 1629 and the conclusion of an ill-advised Huguenot rebellion, the crown invoked systems of bipartisanship in other ways and in other places, for other institutions and for other objectives. In these instances, bipartisanship would work against Protestants. By the late sixteenth century, the municipal governance of most Protestant towns was entirely under Huguenot control. A number of these cities also had municipal schools, whose teachers were exclusively Protestant. Following the Huguenot military defeats of the 1620s, the Catholic monarchy forced these municipal councils and their schools to incorporate Catholic consuls and instructors, typically in numbers equal to the Protestant members.[37] The central mechanism of the state thereby exploited the concept and practice of bipartisanship against the very religious minority that had earlier stood to gain through its employ. The emerging absolutist monarchy and allied Catholic Church were now the principal beneficiaries of the arrangement.

On the other hand, it would be misleading to insist that the effects of Huguenot minority status were entirely negative. Although their marginalized position placed a heavy burden upon them, it also served to open new possibilities, which the French Reformed Church and its followers explored in highly creative fashion. Many Protestant towns established schools or *collèges* at the same time as they adopted Reformed Christianity. Given the profound emphasis upon the Bible and the importance of literacy for appreciating God's truth contained therein, Calvinists prized education. The *collège* at Nîmes, for example, was one of the most illustrious and oldest municipal schools in France. While its origins can be traced to the pedagogical imperatives of the Renaissance,

---

[36] Francis Garrisson, *Essai sur les Commissions d'Application de l'Édit de Nantes: Règne de Henri IV* (Montpellier, 1964); Elisabeth Rabut, *Le roi, l'église et le temple. L'exécution de l'Édit de Nantes en Dauphiné* (Grenoble, 1987).

[37] Camille Rabaud, *Histoire du Protestantisme dans l'Albigeois et le Lauragais*, 2 vols. (Paris, 1873, 1898), I: 275–6; Dominique Julia and Marie-Madeleine Compère, *Les collèges français, 16e–18e siècles*: vol. 1. *France du Midi* (Paris, 1984), 206–9, 446–50, 490–6.

Protestants quickly adapted it to the requirements of their faith. Castres and Montauban, to cite additional cases, founded similar schools in the 1570s and 1580s. Calvinist civic elites created educational institutions throughout the realm for instruction in Latin, literature, grammar, and Holy Scripture.[38] Later, in the aftermath of the Edict of Nantes, Protestants engaged in a broad cultural offensive designed to demonstrate their artistic and intellectual abilities. It was a matter of determined pride, an affirmation of the strength and energy of the Reformed faith and community in the competition between Protestant and Catholic.

Members of the Protestant intellectual and professional leadership established literary salons and scholarly societies at Paris and in the provinces by mid-seventeenth century. They discussed one another's poetry as well as political, religious, historical, and scientific issues. These salons and academies often fostered ecumenical dialogue, making explicit overtures to Catholic savants, even as they sought to advance knowledge and display the depth and breadth of Reformed culture.[39]

Several historians have taken special note of Huguenot contributions in the architectural sphere.[40] Salomon de Brosse and various members of the du Cerceau family enjoyed important roles in the artistic flowering that occurred during the first half of the seventeenth century. Marie de Médicis commissioned de Brosse to design the Luxembourg palace. He also oversaw the rebuilding of an elegant Huguenot temple at Charenton outside Paris, after the first structure was ominously burned in an anti-Protestant riot of 1621. In the provincial world, local Reformed communities took great pains in the construction of temples for worship. The refined simplicity of these structures attested to the imagination, initiative, and commitment of Protestant congregations. The building projects usually meant shouldering heavy financial burdens, and the results were objects of esteem and honor. The temple was, in many ways, the principal physical reminder of the Protestant presence in France. Small wonder that the Catholic state mounted a furious offensive to pull them down in the decades preceding the revocation. In short, the

---

[38] Jules Gaufrès, "Les collèges protestants," *Bulletin de la Société de l'Histoire du Protestantisme Français* 22 (1873): 269–82, 413–23; 23 (1874): 289–304, 337–48, 385–408; 24 (1875): 4–20, 193–208; 27 (1878): 193–208; A. Poux, *Histoire du collège de Castres depuis les origines jusqu'à nos jours* (Castres, 1902).

[39] Louis Barbaza, *L'Académie de Castres et la société de Mlle de Scudéry, 1648–1670* (Castres, 1890); O. Granat, "Une académie de province au XVIIe siècle," *Revue des universités du Midi* (1898): 181–95; Léonard, *Histoire générale du protestantisme*, 2: 333–5.

[40] Anthony Blunt, *Art and Architecture in France, 1500 to 1700*, 2nd ed. (Baltimore, 1970), 80–5, 94–104; Menna Prestwich, "Patronage and the Protestants in France, 1598–1661: Architects and Painters," in *L'Age d'or du Mécénat (1598–1661)*, Roland Mousnier and Jean Mesnard eds. (Paris, 1985), 77–88.

temple was the collective creation of the entire congregation – a visible, material expression of the Reformed community. While these abundant and varied accomplishments in the intellectual and cultural realm may not have been, strictly speaking, evidence of Huguenot election in the religious sphere, they were an important manifestation of the value and virtue of Protestantism.

\* \* \* \* \*

What finally do we make of these perspectives on the French Reformation? How does the Huguenot experience help us better understand the status and nature of religious minorities in the early modern age? What were the antagonisms surrounding competing faiths? How are we to interpret the difficulties the situation posed for the construction and internalization of religious identity?

To begin, the relationship between the Huguenot minority and the dominant Catholic world was multidimensional and certainly more subtle than we sometimes recognize. It could obviously be highly destructive. The massacres of the sixteenth century, the demolition of Reformed temples beginning in the 1660s, and the imprisonment and exile of many Huguenots after 1685 were appalling in terms of the loss of life and deliberate ruin of human achievement. The commemoration of the four hundredth anniversary of the Edict of Nantes in 1998 became for many French men and women the occasion to reaffirm the fundamental importance of coexistence and toleration. Numerous modern religious and political leaders view the long and arduous Huguenot history as a painful yet instructive lesson for current discussions centering on immigration policy, racial strife, and religious prejudice.

Scholars of the early modern world, while certainly cognizant of these larger societal issues, are likely to emphasize other dimensions of the Huguenot past. Their status as a minority placed severe internal and external limitations on French Protestants. Without state support, the Reformed Church could not exercise as much control over the faithful as it would have liked. Coexistence with Catholicism, even in its most peaceful moments, meant polluting contacts with "papism" or led to a permanent hemorrhage within the community through mixed marriages. The consistory found it impossible to restrict the normal processes of sociability. Members of Reformed congregations interacted with their Catholic neighbors in ways that, from the consistory's perspective, were alarming and harmful. Protestant ecclesiastical authorities could never eradicate the unreformed habits and traditions of a debased and corrupting medieval Christianity. The Huguenots had to live side by side with people who still believed in and ordered their lives according to what their leaders regarded as vile and objectionable notions.

The Huguenot minority faced similar limitations in the civil sphere. Although the Edict of Nantes established mechanisms for providing equitable justice and guaranteed admission to bureaucratic posts and education, Protestants found that in the decades following the edict, their faith increasingly became an obstacle to professional and social advance. In addition, the crown progressively restricted and ultimately denied them access to political power and the freedom to worship.

Despite this obvious mistreatment and unacceptable persecution, there were original elements within the experience. Calvinists everywhere seem to have taken pains to define their community with greater precision than had been customary, or perhaps possible, in pre-Reformation society. They made, for example, unprecedented efforts in the area of vital statistics with the development and maintenance of uniform registers for baptisms, marriages, and burials. These records provided a detailed enumeration of those individuals who were an integral part of the community and, by extension, those who were not.

In the late seventeenth century, even as the oppressive Catholic state set about eradicating the Huguenots, it recognized in oblique, perhaps unintended fashion the value of these undertakings. After 1685, for example, royal officers examined and inventoried the voluminous archives of the (former) Reformed church of Montauban. They decided to deposit the materials relating to vital statistics – the baptismal, marriage, and burial registers – with the clerk of the local royal court because these records served, in their words, the "public interest." The enormous mass of other papers, which did no more than "preserve the memory of the false religion," were burned.[41] Though the crown and Catholic society sought to purge the very memory of Protestantism, an important exception was made for what were recognizably "public" documents.

The situation of cohabitation (to use modern French vocabulary) imbued other elements in the Huguenot attempt at classification and control with special meaning. The use of tokens to regulate admission to the Lord's Supper and the frequent application of excommunication are perhaps the most important examples. A vigorous concept of election surely reinforced the penchant for arranging and defining the community, whether through the development of vital statistics or control

---

[41] AN, TT 255, dossier 35.

devices for participation in the communion service. After all, these were the saints, active in the creation of a new godly order, nothing less than the holy commonwealth. But in France they also wished to distinguish themselves from the "papists," who had time and again proven dangerous to both body and soul.

Still other positive elements drew upon the competitive energies arising from religious rivalry. In the period immediately following the Edict of Nantes, the Huguenots embarked upon a sparkling series of intellectual and cultural enterprises. They established municipal schools and founded erudite literary associations. These Protestants also engaged in extensive building programs, erecting stylish temples in the towns that they controlled. Local congregations explicitly understood that their temples were at once a proud aesthetic accomplishment and a challenge to others. Huguenot temples came to symbolize whatever meager success the French Protestants had achieved and, above all, their defiant nature.

Was social discipline, to return to an earlier theme, a critical component in the process whereby the Huguenots resolutely survived as a minority in a decidedly hostile environment? After all, they weathered the bloody Wars of Religion, resisted the pressure of Richelieu's armies during the 1620s, adjusted to Louis XIV and his revocation of the Edict of Nantes, and persevered the general proscription of Protestantism that followed. What explains this extraordinary tenacity? At the very least, French Protestants had created a strong sense of confessional identity. Here, social discipline and minority status reinforced one another. Together, in both positive and negative fashion, they heightened and intensified a Reformed consciousness. If, moreover, we are to believe those historians who have examined Huguenot communities for the later seventeenth century, Protestants were on their way to assimilation by the Catholic majority. Was it the revocation of the Edict of Nantes that reinvigorated Huguenot society, instilling a fresh sense of determination and perseverance within an oppressed minority?

Efforts at moral discipline and social control, dynamics that we would insist upon as fundamental to the Reformation, undoubtedly worked best with the support of the state. We have numerous examples from Geneva to the Netherlands and Scotland. Developments in France proved altogether more complicated. The deep tensions between the Reformed churches and the Catholic state prompted Protestant pastors and elders to greater diligence than they might have otherwise pursued. Yet it also denied them much needed support and dramatically restricted their endeavors to establish the New Jerusalem. Theirs was not an easy task under the best of conditions, and minority status exacerbated the situation. Occasionally, the harassment and persecution redirected French Protestants in unanticipated yet productive fashion. More often than not it hindered their great struggle to reform society.

CHAPTER VIII

# State religion and Puritan resistance in early seventeenth-century England

PAUL S. SEAVER

LATE in the 1640s, an anonymous author published an account of what he termed the eleventh persecution of the Church, particularly in London, by the "Puritan Faction (so long lying like the Canaanites, as thornes in the sides of our Israel)":

And what havoc hath been made among the Sheep, since the City-Puritan Tumults cried out no Bishops, and armed fury hath forced thousands of the Clergy from their Flocks; the almost ruins of the Church and of three Kingdoms sufficiently witnesses; a just judgment of God upon a People long contending with their Priests and mocking, and misusing the Prophets and messengers of God, till like the Jews, the wrath of God fell upon them, . . . and all this vengeance executed by a generation of Vipers, styling themselves . . . the only people of God, the meek of the earth, Christ's little flock, weak Brethren.

Such a calamity was all the more remarkable in the view of the anonymous author because "all sorts of People account[ed] the Puritan faction, a simple inconsiderate party, well meaning people, tender conscienced Christians, such as deserved pity rather than punishment, little remembering our Saviour's caveat against wolves in sheep's clothing."[1]

---

[1] *Persecutio Undecima. The Churches Eleventh Persecution. Or, A Brief of the Puritan Persecution of the Protestant Clergy . . . particularly within the City of London* (1648), 1–2. On the title page of the British Library copy it is noted in a contemporary hand: "Written by Mr Chestlin," which, if true, identifies the author as the sequestered minister of St. Matthew, Friday Street, London, who was "violently assaulted in his house, imprisoned in the Compter, thence sent to Colchester Gaol in Essex, sequestered and plundered," Ibid., 17. Spelling here and throughout the paper has been modernized, and the calendar year is taken to begin on 1 January.

Whether the "Puritan faction" were wolves in sheep's clothing or a generation of vipers depended largely on one's allegiances; it could be argued that, being the meek, they had indeed inherited the earth, or at least for a moment that corner called England. However, the question explored here is whether these thorns in the side of England's Protestant Israel were an inconsiderable party, and if so, how they managed to survive the hostility of two Stuart kings and an ecclesiastical regime whose rhetoric expressed little tolerance for clerical nonconformity, however much some of the episcopal leadership may have shared an allegiance to Reformed doctrine and thus to the theological commitments of most of the Puritan clergy. It may, of course, be argued that the question is wrongly stated; that, regardless of whether the Puritans were a considerable "faction," there never was a policy of repression or suppression, and hence nothing to be explained, except perhaps why people subjected to such "mild treatment" should have wreaked such "vengeance" on their orthodox brethren, once the tables were turned in the 1640s.[2] But in this case what needs to be explained is why the early Stuart regime, both temporal and ecclesiastical, failed so signally to give any reality to their stated intentions, for their rhetoric was certainly sufficiently hostile at times to appear to give reality to Puritan fears.

From the outset of the reign of the Stuart kings, one has little difficulty in assembling statements that seem to imply a determination to eliminate the threat Puritans posed to a uniform order in the Church. In January of 1604, when King James had been on the English throne less than a year, he defied the wishes of his own bishops and convened the Hampton Court Conference, to which a small delegation of moderate Puritan divines were invited. Late on the second day of meetings, Dr. John Reynolds, the chief Puritan spokesman, launched into an explanation of what was implied by the Puritan request that "the church government might be sincerely ministered, according to God's word." Rather than the existing system of church courts, inherited from the Catholic past, Reynolds proposed a hierarchy of courts in which the parochial clergy would be much more heavily involved, at the highest level of which the bishop would preside, accompanied "with his presbytery" of ministers representative of the lower clergy. At this point, King James is reported to have interrupted Reynolds's explanation with his famous denunciation of presbyteries, which, he claimed, agreed as

---

[2] Julian Davies has recently argued precisely this point, noting that my own evidence in an earlier study scarcely substantiates charges of attempted suppression or repression. *The Caroline Captivity of the Church: Charles I and the Remoulding of Anglicanism* (Oxford, 1992), 158–61.

well with monarchy as God with the Devil: "No bishop, no king," a tirade which concluded with the threat, "If this be all . . . that they have to say, I shall make them conform themselves, or I will harry them out of this land, or else do worse."[3]

That autumn new canons were promulgated; by December the Privy Council reminded both archbishops and the bishops of their provinces that they "have regard to the execution of the said laws and constitutions in such sort as is meet and necessary for the uniformity of the Church discipline," and that such execution applied especially to those "that have heretofore under a pretended zeal of reformation, but indeed of a factious desire of innovation, refused to yield their obedience and conformity thereunto." The letter made it clear that "although it be much more agreeable to his most gracious mind and great clemency to heal and cure such distemperatures by lenity and gentleness, . . . nevertheless, his Majesty is well pleased to have it known" that the time for persuasion and sweet reason had passed and that those "guilty of disobedience to his Majesty" were to be deprived of their benefices or denied admission to any cure they "in dutifulness might hold."[4] Matthew Hutton, the archbishop of York, in a letter to Sir Robert Cecil, the principal secretary, responded that the new measures taken against the Puritans had encouraged the papists who had grown "mightily in number, courage, and insolency." As for the Puritans, "though they differ in ceremonies and accidents, yet they agree with us in substance of religion, and, I think, all, or the most of them, love his Majesty and the present State, . . . so that, if the gospel quail and popery prevail, it will be imputed principally unto you." In his reply, Cecil responded that he had always "held it for a certain rule . . . that the Papist was carried on the left hand with superstitious blindness, [but] that the Puritan . . . was transported on the right with unadvised zeal," and that while "religious men of moderate spirits

---

[3] Quoted from Bishop Barlow's account by Patrick Collinson, "The Jacobean Religious Settlement: The Hampton Court Conference," in *Before the English Civil War*, ed. Howard Tomlinson (London, 1983), 42. What actually occurred at the Hampton Court Conference is vexed by conflicting contemporary accounts, but Collinson's reconstruction seems as plausible as any we are likely to have, and while he suggests that Barlow at this point may have exaggerated James's animus, he does not deny that James made the statement Barlow reported.

[4] Public Record Office [hereafter PRO], State Papers [hereafter SP], 14/10/61. The most convincing attempt to make sense of James's apparently contradictory ecclesiastical impulses, favoring Arminian bishops despite holding orthodox Calvinist theological views, is Kenneth Fincham and Peter Lake, "The Ecclesiastical Policies of James I and Charles I," in *The Early Stuart Church, 1603–1642*, ed. Kenneth Fincham (Basingstoke and London, 1993), 23–49. As Fincham has observed elsewhere, James's rhetoric was always fiercer than his practice. See Fincham, *Prelate as Pastor: The Episcopate of James I* (Oxford, 1990), passim.

might be borne with, yet such are the turbulent humors of some that dream of nothing but of a new hierarchy (directly opposite to the state of a Monarchy)" and in so doing "to break all bonds of unity, to nourish schism in the Church, and finally to destroy both Church and Commonwealth." As a consequence, it was "his Majesty's own clear, zealous, and constant resolution for the preservation of true religion ... to have his godly and just laws duly executed."[5]

In the five years that followed, more than seventy beneficed nonconformist clergy were deprived, which, if by no means the total purge feared by the godly, nevertheless saw the expulsion of a number of the most prominent Puritans: Anthony Lapthorne, Arthur Hildersham, Thomas Stoughton, William Jackson, and Ezechial Culverwell.[6] When Richard Bancroft, the archbishop who had presided over the creation of the new canons of 1604, died in November of 1610, what little enthusiasm there was for discipline and uniformity, even at the expense of a preaching ministry, died with him. The new archbishop, George Abbot, although an orthodox Calvinist and thus prone to look on Puritan Calvinists with a certain measured toleration, was not prepared to wink at outright disobedience or nonconformity. When William Ames, shortly after having been suspended from all ecclesiastical duties for an inflammatory sermon preached at Christ's College, Cambridge, where he was a fellow, accepted the offer to become town preacher or lecturer at Colchester, already a well-known Puritan center in Essex, Abbot, at the time bishop of London, refused to give his consent and allowance.[7]

However, the enthusiasm for the enforcement of the new canons waned in the later years of Bancroft's rule; James was not committed to eliminating Puritans who did not overtly challenge his supremacy. Subscription to the three articles, now required by the canons, rather than actual uniformity of practice, was usually sufficient: "good intentions counted in the Jacobean Church."[8] As James himself wrote at the height of Bancroft's campaign to enforce the new canons, he was

wonderfully satisfied with the Council's proceedings anent the Puritans.... They have used justice upon the obstinate, shown grace to the penitent, and

[5] PRO, SP, 14/10/64; SP, 14/10/66.
[6] For a listing of those deprived, see Fincham, *Prelate as Pastor*, app. VI.
[7] Keith L. Sprunger, *The Learned Doctor William Ames: Dutch Backgrounds of English and American Puritanism* (Urbana, IL, 1972), 25. As Kenneth Fincham has shown, Abbot did not believe that those who refused subscription were to be tolerated, at least so long as King James was on the throne: Fincham, *Prelate as Pastor*, 225–6.
[8] Lori Anne Ferrell, *Government by Polemic: James I, the King's Preachers, and the Rhetorics of Conformity, 1603–1625* (Stanford, CA, 1998), 171.

enlarged them that seem to be a little schooled by the rod of affliction. In his action they have, according to the 101 Psalm, sung of mercy and of judgment both.[9]

Although the bishops were ordered in May 1611 either to bring non-conformists to an obedient frame of mind or to drive them from the Church, "throughout his reign James was to be much more interested in extracting proof of loyalty and obedience than in the small print of regular conformity."[10]

Two developments, which were to renew episcopal attention and royal hostility to the Puritans in their midst, followed in the first decade of Abbot's tenure. First, King James's appointment of a series of bishops later labeled Arminian after the leading Dutch Remonstrant theologian – Lancelot Andrewes (1605), Richard Neile (1608), Samuel Harsnett (1609), John Buckeridge (1611), John Overall (1614), George Mountaigne (1617), John Howson (1619),William Laud and Valentine Carey (1621) – created on the bench of bishops a vigorous minority who had no sympathy for old-fashioned orthodox Calvinism and who saw the evangelical thrust of English Puritanism as responsible for the ills and lack of discipline in the English Church.[11] Some years earlier, while still an undergraduate, Thomas Goodwin claimed that already "the noise of the Arminian controversy . . . began to be every man's talk."[12] As a consequence, while a Matthew Hutton or a George Abbot might be sympathetic to much of what the Puritans preached and might find Puritan ministers useful so long as they did not parade their nonconformity, there were now churchmen among the episcopal leadership for whom Puritanism in any form was anathema.[13] Where such clerics stood is illustrated in an exchange in 1615 between Archbishop Abbot and John Howson, when the latter was still an Oxford fellow. He was charged by the archbishop

---

[9] *Letters of King James VI and I*, ed. G.P.V. Akrigg (Berkeley and Los Angeles, 1984), 255.

[10] Fincham and Lake, "The Ecclesiastical Policies," 26–7.

[11] Fincham, *Prelate as Pastor*, 276–88. The use of the label "Arminian" as a term of opprobrium seems largely to date from the years after the Synod of Dort, when Calvinists of all stripes found it convenient to label their theological and ceremonial opponents with the name associated with the Remonstrants whose position at the synod King James had rejected. On the other hand, Arminius was certainly well known to the Puritan community before Dort: Witness the Paul's Cross sermon of Samuel Ward, preacher at Ipswich, on October 20, 1616, in which Ward condemned "popery and nature, and the old leaven of Pelagius, newly worse scoured by Arminius." Millar MacLure, *The Paul's Cross Sermons, 1534–1642* (Toronto, 1958), 238.

[12] As quoted in Francis J. Bremer, *Congregational Communion: Clerical Friendship in the Anglo-American Puritan Community, 1610–1692* (Boston, 1994), 20.

[13] On the other hand, the Arminian churchmen did not dominate James's episcopal appointments even in his last years: see Sheila Lambert, "Richard Montague, Arminianism and Censorship," *Past and Present* 124 (1989): 41–2.

in a lengthy interview before King James at Greenwich with factious preaching and popery. While denying in the course of his defense both of these, Dr. Howson added significantly that he "preached not so often, as some others, against the papists, because in my time here were never above 3 or 4 at once that were suspected of popery, and there were 300 preachers who opposed them by sermon and disputations; contrarywise there were over 300 suspected of Puritanism and but 3 or 4 to oppose: with both these assertions my Lord's Grace was highly offended and denied them."[14]

Where King James stood in all this controversy is suggested by a letter written by Secretary Lake several months later; Lake remarked that "his Majesty being to keep Easter by the way and desirous to make it appear to our Church that he means to preserve all the rites and solemnities thereof," wished to hear his almoner preach; when the king was reminded that his almoner, the Arminian Francis White, had been given a commission to be elsewhere, James "willed straight that Doctor [Lancelot] Andrewes should be sent in his place."[15] By this time, the king had begun the apparently endless negotiations to marry his son, Charles, to the Spanish Infanta, a dubious strategem in the eyes of most Protestant Englishmen, and one made doubly so after James's Protestant son-in-law, Frederick, the elector palatine, was elected king of Bohemia and then lost that kingdom to the Austrian Habsburgs, and subsequently lost the Palatinate itself. Even Oxford, hardly a hotbed of Puritanism, had its share of what King James termed "seditious" preaching about the Spanish match. In April 1622, the king ordered that Oxford students should dedicate themselves to "the study of divinity, . . . in the first place to the reading of the Scriptures, next the General Councils, and ancient fathers, and then the Schoolmen, excluding those heretics,

[14] PRO, SP, 14/80/113. See also the valuable introduction to "John Howson's Answers to Archbishop Abbot's Accusations at his 'Trial' before James I at Greenwich, 10 June 1615," Nicholas Cranfield and Kenneth Fincham, eds. *Camden Miscellany* 29, 4th series, 34 (London, 1987), 319–41. Howson was in trouble for his preaching as early as 1612. See Nicholas Tyacke, *Anti-Calvinists: The Rise of English Arminianism c. 1590–1640* (Oxford, 1987), 68. Nothing cowed by his interview before the king, Howson went on in 1616 to preach against the "Puritan democracy" of Presbyterianism, claiming that Puritans were "schismatics in religion who affect staticizing and cantonizing in the commonwealth." Fincham, *Prelate as Pastor*, 284.

[15] PRO, SP, 14/91/35; the letter is dated April 15,1617, from Topcliffe in Yorkshire, which explains why the almoner, Francis White, then in southern England, could not readily appear at court. As Lori Anne Ferrell points out, the "published court sermons from this period [were] overwhelmingly anti-Puritan in their orientation." Her point is not that there was not competing conformist Calvinist preaching at court, but rather that when it came to court sermons printed by royal order, the Arminian polemic was dominant; in fact "the voice of Lancelot Andrewes stands out, with eleven sermons preached before the king [and] also printed between 1603 and 1625." *Government by Polemic*, 169.

both the Jesuits and Puritans, who are known to be meddlers in matters of State and Monarchy that thereby they may be the better enabled only to preach Christ crucified."[16] In August of that year, James issued his "Directions concerning Preachers," noting that "the extravagancies of preachers in the pulpit have been in all times repressed in this realm," and that "at this present divers young students by reading of late writers and ungrounded divines do broach many times unprofitable, unsound, seditious, and dangerous doctrines, to the scandal of this church and disquieting of the State and present government."[17]

Such measures in such times were an exercise in futility. On September 1, Simonds D'Ewes, at the time a godly young law student at Middle Temple, noted in his diary that

our [London] sermons began now to grow famous, and Paul's Cross to be the theater of many passages. Last Sunday preached one that was my Lord of Holderness' chaplain, and because he talked of a Spanish sheep brought over in Edward the First his time, which infected all our sheep with murraine, and praying God no more such might come, the people cried amen, but he was clapt up and through his lord's means soon freed again. At Ipswich Mr. Ward was again in trouble and in London Dr. Everard in the Marshalsea or Fleet.[18]

The year before John Everard, the lecturer at St. Martin in the Fields, had been imprisoned in the Gatehouse for "glancing ... at the Spanish match and deciphering the craft and cruelty of the Spaniards in all places where they come."[19] The authorities did their best to stem the

---

[16] PRO, SP, 14/90/75; the letter is dated February 21, 1616/17.

[17] PRO, SP, 14/132/85. Archbishop Abbot dispatched a slightly different version of this letter to the bishops of the southern province on August 22: Bodleian Library [hereafter Bod. Lib.], Tanner MS 73, fol.169r. For the Directions themselves, see *Documentary Annals of the Reformed Church of England*, ed. Edward Cardwell, 2 vols. (Oxford, 1844), 2: 193–7.

[18] *The Diary of Sir Simonds D'Ewes (1622–1624)*, ed. Elizabeth Bourcier (Paris, 1974), 94. By noting various Puritans who managed to preach at Paul's Cross, I do not wish to suggest that these popular sermons had become a Puritan monopoly. Many sermons preached there were explicitly hostile to Puritanism. See, for example, John Donne's sermon on March 24, 1617, in which he remarked that "he was beholden to no by-religion. The Papists could not make him place any hopes upon them, nor the Puritans make him entertain any fears from them," and Robert Sibthorpe's sermon early the next year in which he said about the Puritans that "their pretended pure tender conscience is impurely polluted, and their faith worse than infidelity." MacLure, *The Paul's Cross Sermons*, 238, 239–40.

[19] The letter is dated March 10, 1620/21. On March 21, 1622/23, Chamberlain noted that "many of our churchmen are hardly held in, and their tongues itch to be talking, insomuch that Dr. Everard, the preacher at St. Martins in the Field, is committed for saying somewhat more than he should, and on Sunday last at the parish church next to us another went so far that the parson of the church caused the clerk to sing him down with a psalm before he had half done." *The Letters of John Chamberlain*, ed. Norman E. McClure, 2 vols. (Philadelphia, 1939), 2: 350, 486.

tide of anti-Spanish rhetoric. In April 1623, Bishop Mountaigne wrote to Secretary Conway that he had investigated a preacher at St. Andrew, Holborne, but found nothing in his sermon notes "of any suspicion, tending to tumult or sedition"; a second minister at Paul's Cross who had preached "in general words full of evil interpretation," such as "that papistry and treason are twins, and so inlincked, one within another, that a man cannot be a perfect Catholic unless he be ready to undertake the Pope's quarrel against his Prince"; and finally a third who preached at St. Michael, Bassishaw, "on a text concerning Solomon's marriage with an idolater," but when "he would make application of his text to these times, the . . . minister of the Church, one Dr. Gifford, a very honest man, agreeably to the Directions . . . rose up and told the congregation that he feared the preacher would speak something contrary to the Instructions and Commandment they had received from his Majesty by their diocesan and therefore willed them to sing a psalm, which they readily did."[20] As a London correspondent wrote to James Ussher, then bishop of Meath, on July 9, 1618, "the affairs of the Church here are much after one style; the better sort of preachers, some stand and are hid or winked at, and some go down the wind."[21]

That a handful of daring spirits used various London pulpits to question or condemn King James's marriage plans for his son should not be taken to suggest that James's hostility to such interference with his prerogative had no effect. In a letter of May 26, 1621, to his old tutor, Dr. Samuel Ward, master of Sidney Sussex, Dr. Robert Jenison, the Puritan preacher at Newcastle, complained that a manuscript he had sent to Richard Sibbes in London to be printed had been altered by Sibbes – "his timorousness is the cause thereof" – to eliminate mention of "Spanish cruelty" and the phrase "forbidden marriage with women popishly affected." Jenison did concede that "the times I know are dangerous, yet I might have advised [that] no such alterations should have been made."[22]

---

[20] PRO, SP, 14/142/22. Dr. John Gifford was rewarded for his "honesty" in 1628, when he was appointed a chaplain extraordinary to King Charles; his living was sequestered by Parliament in 1642 on the grounds of his Arminianism and royalism. See PRO, Lord Chamberlain's Accounts, 1628–34, 5/132/23; *Dictionary of National Biography* (London, 1885–1901), hereafter DNB.

[21] *The Whole Works of the Most Rev. James Ussher, D.D.*, Charles R. Elrington and J.H. Todd, eds. 17 vols. (Dublin, 1847–64), 16:355.

[22] Bod. Lib., Tanner MS 73/1, fol. 29r. How much such self-censorship went on in the Puritan community in those years is difficult to gauge, but Sibbes, who was divinity reader at Gray's Inn from 1617 until his death in 1635, was certainly in a more exposed position than Jenison. For the central role that Sibbes played in the London Puritan community, see Paul S. Seaver, *The Puritan Lectureships: The Politics of Religious Dissent, 1560–1662* (Stanford, CA, 1970), 235–8. For all of Jenison's complaints, he continued to

Some might wink at the activities of the Puritans, but King James never changed his tune. In the spring of 1624, commenting on a sabbatarian bill in Parliament forbidding Sunday sports, he remarked that "churches themselves have been abused, so perchance have these sports been, but let the abuses be taken away but not the churches; he could not agree to this act which is but to give the Puritans their will, who think all consists in two sermons a day."[23] The Parliament of 1624 had seen a number of complaints about Samuel Harsnett, the bishop of Norwich, charging that he had suppressed popular morning preaching while countenancing images and crucifixes in the cathedral. After the Lord Keeper had prorogued the Parliament, James is reported to have told the bishops, "as with one hand you labor to suppress papists, so with the other you be careful to sweep out the Puritans," and he went on to "praise my Lord of Norwich for thus ordering his churches, and I commend it in spite of all the Puritans," concluding that "I like none of them nor their humors, for I think that as all one to lay down my crown to the Pope as to a popular party of Puritans."[24] At the end of his reign as at the beginning, King James struck the same note of unremitting hostility to papists and Puritans alike, although not everyone was convinced of his even-handedness. In May of 1623, Chamberlain wrote that "men mutter of a toleration in religion, and a revocation, or at least suspension, of all the acts and statutes made against the Roman Catholics," and Archbishop Abbot was reported to have beseeched the king not to grant "a toleration in religion":

You labor to set up that most damnable and heretical doctrine of the Church of Rome, the whore of Babylon. How hateful will it be to God and grievous to your good subjects, the true profession of the Gospel, that your Majesty, who have disputed and learnedly written against the wicked heresies should show yourself as a patron of those doctrines, which your pen hath told the world and your conscience tells yourself are superstitious, idolatrous, detestable.[25]

---

resort to Sibbes as his London agent: Tanner MS 73/2, fol. 437r, a letter from Jenison to Ward, dated May 11, 1624. As Anthony Milton has observed percipiently, "We can only guess at the extent to which we may have gained a misleadingly moderate sense of the content of Jacobean puritan writings because of the sanitizing work of Featley, Sibbes, and others." "Licensing, Censorship, and Religious Orthodoxy in Early Stuart England," *Historical Journal* 41.3 (1998): 631.

23 PRO, SP, 14/165/61.
24 British Library, Harleian MS 159, fols. 118, 136. I owe this citation to the late Robert Ruigh.
25 John Chamberlain to Sir Dudley Carleton, from London, May 3, 1623, in *The Court and Times of James the First*, ed. Thomas Birch, 2 vols. (London, 1849), II: 393; Bod. Lib., Tanner MS 73/2, fol. 302r; another copy of this letter exists in Lambeth Palace Library, MS 9433, 79.

Whatever the ambiguities of King James's attitude toward his Catholic subjects, he remained convinced that the English Puritans, like the Scottish Presbyterians, really stood for a "democratical" church totally at variance to a monarchical state.[26]

If the hostility toward Puritans that King James publicly expressed seems at odds with the general moderation of his actions, no such ambiguity surrounds the ecclesiastical policies of his son. King Charles's convictions have to be deduced from his actions, since he was as closed-mouthed about his beliefs as his father was articulate, which may perhaps be what Julian Davies means by suggesting that "as far as can be ascertained, the king was doctrinally dyslexic rather than doctrinally illiterate"; certainly, as Kenneth Fincham and Peter Lake note, Charles "was taciturn, where his father had been positively loquacious," and his ecclesiastical policies have to be inferred by his actions rather than by his words, which were few.[27] But it was surely more than a straw in the wind when William Laud, who had never progressed further than to the bishopric of St. David's in James's reign, was now designated to preside over the king's coronation and then in rapid succession replaced the late Lancelot Andrewes as dean of the Chapel Royal and was appointed a privy counselor in 1627, where he was joined by his old patron, Richard Neile. Richard Montague, who had created a firestorm of clerical and parliamentary opposition in 1624 with his *A New Gagg for an Old Goose*, now found himself first made a royal chaplain and then a bishop. The York House conference, which was held just before the meeting of Parliament in 1626 at the behest of Calvinist peers, the earl of Warwick and Lord Saye and Sele, who apparently hoped that a clerical debate would lead to a repudiation of Arminianism in general and Richard Montague in particular, turned out to be uncomfortably inconclusive for its instigators, and Montague emerged unscathed.[28]

Charles was to demonstrate by his actions what were his religious prejudices or preferences, if not his thoughts. However, the reissuance in 1633 of the Book of Sports, which detailed those recreations lawful for Sunday pursuit, and the insistence in both Laud's metropolitical

---

[26] James's perception was not without foundation. Articles in the Court of High Commission against Samuel Ward, the Puritan preacher at Ipswich, claimed that he had "delivered that all that bear office in the Church or Commonwealth ought to be elected by the people." PRO, SP, 16/261, fols. 304–5, dated November 26, 1635.

[27] Davies, *The Caroline Captivity of the Church*, 12; Fincham and Lake, "The Ecclesiastical Policies," 36.

[28] Tyacke, *Anti-Calvinists*, 164–80; Barbara Donagan, "The York House Conference Revisited: Laymen, Calvinism and Arminianism," *Historical Research* 64 (1991): 312–30.

visitation of the archdiocese of Canterbury and Neile's visitation of York that the communion table should be placed altar-wise in the east end of churches and railed in, that communicants receive at the altar rails kneeling, and that both priest and congregation bow at the name of Jesus, all seemed to many of the king's subjects evidence of a long but determined march back to Rome. The Venetian ambassador countered this interpretation, speculating that Charles introduced Roman ceremonies in order to defeat the Puritans, but noted in 1637 that "the results are very different from his Majesty's intentions, because the more the bishops dress themselves out with the new constitutions, the more the Puritans cling to the bareness of their worship and what is worse, many of the Protestants themselves, scandalized by the new institutions, become Puritans from fear of falling into Catholicism if they follow them."[29]

However acute the Venetian ambassador was in reporting what he saw around him, he may have misread the king. It seems more likely that Charles, who favored a decorous and ceremonious court, wished a church of the same model and backed Laud and the Arminian bishops because they alone seemed to promise to deliver such a church; the Puritans were simply an unruly element in Church and State, which must be brought to order. On the other hand, the Venetian ambassador was surely correct in seeing that Charles wished to give the Puritans no quarter. As the king noted in the margin of Archbishop Neile's first annual report on the state of the archdiocese of York in 1633, it was "the neglect of punishing Puritans [that] breeds Papists," by which he appears to have meant that leaving Puritans unpunished was so alienating to right-thinking Protestants that, to escape the odium that attached to Puritanism, they perforce fled back to Rome.[30]

As for William Laud, the leading ecclesiastical figure at court from the beginning of Charles's reign (Laud was promised the archbishopric of Canterbury when Abbot died, a promise apparently conveyed by Buckingham on October 2, 1626),[31] he was, if more articulate than the king he served, equally circumspect in his utterances. As has been pointed out, Laud was "remorseless [in his] search for plausible deniability," a state of affairs partly due perhaps to personal anxieties, but surely in part learned as a consequence of the Devonshire marriage affair

---

[29] "Relazione of England by Anzolo Correr, October 24, 1637," in *The English Civil War: A Contemporary Account*: vol. 1. *1625–1639*, Edward Razzell and Peter Razzell eds. (London, 1996), 31.
[30] PRO, SP, 16/259/78.
[31] William Laud, *The History of the Troubles and Tryal of . . . William Laud* (London, 1695), 36.

early in the career of this ambitious cleric.[32] Nevertheless, he tended to associate Puritans with separatists, whom he called Brownists, and both with a determination to destroy the Church of England, personified by himself. When recounting the censure in Star Chamber of Burton, Bastwick, and Prynne in 1637 for "notorious libels printed and published by them against the hierarchy of the Church," which led them to be "sentenced to stand in the pillory and lose their ears," he noted with a clear sense of grievance that "the Brownists and the preciser part of the Kingdom were nettled at this, and their anger turned upon me." In fact, in Laud's view, the charge of treason leveled against him in the Long Parliament on December 18, 1640, could only be explained by the known malignity of the former:

The chief instruments herein were the Brownists, and they which adhered unto them, who were highly offended with rue, because I hindered and punished (as by law I might) their Conventicles and separation from the Church of England. And though I pitied them (as God knows) from my very head, yet because necessity of government forced me to some punishment, their malignity never gave me over.[33]

While Laud's propensity to act without offering an explanation for the action, or to disguise his role in a measure by obtaining the king's authorization of it, left his contemporaries in some uncertainty about his ultimate intentions, no one seems to have doubted his hostility to the Puritans. The Venetian ambassador noted in May 1637 that "the Archbishop of Canterbury, who has assumed absolute command in ecclesiastical affairs, so that they commonly call him the Pope of England,

---

[32] Fincham and Lake, "The Ecclesiastical Policies," 45. Late in 1603 Laud became chaplain to Charles Blount, the earl of Devonshire, who was living in an adulterous relationship with Penelope Devereux, the divorced wife of Lord Rich; in 1605 the earl married Penelope, Laud obligingly officiating, an act that King James thoroughly and publicly condemned and that undoubtedly delayed Laud's elevation to an episcopal post. Laud himself saw it as "serving my own ambition and the sins of others," and referred to it in his diary as "my cross about the Earl of Devon's marriage, December 26, 1605." H.R. Trevor-Roper, *Archbishop Laud*, 2d ed. (London, 1962), 35–7; Laud, *History of the Troubles*, 2.

[33] Laud, *History of the Troubles*, 144. Laud's association of Puritans with separatism can be explained by his propensity to elide opposition to Arminianism and ceremonialism with separation from the Church of England. Thus he complained that at his trial "many of the witnesses against me were Separatists. I did indeed complain of this, and I had abundant cause so to do. For there was scarce an active Separatist in England, but some way or other his influence was into this business against me. And whereas the gentleman said that the witnesses were gentlemen and aldermen, men of quality. That's nothing, for both gentlemen and aldermen, and men of all conditions (the more's the pity) as the times now go, are separatists from the doctrine and discipline of the Church of England established by law." Ibid., 434.

is pronounced by the generality to be the protector of the Catholic party, because he not only does nothing against them, but because he seems to make a very close approach to the rites of the Roman Church." However, the ambassador noted to the contrary that "the well informed know that his aims are very different, and that he lets things run with their present freedom not from inclination but from a forced connivance, because he aims at destroying the party of the Puritans, which has grown so much as to cause apprehension to the Government."[34]

But if King Charles and William Laud were both hostile to the Puritans and saw them as a "party" that should be destroyed before it undermined Church and State, why were they not more successful in doing so? It could of course be argued that they had indeed some measure of success, and to that degree the question may be badly posed. After all, in the years after 1628, some thousands followed their suspended and subsequently deprived ministers to the Netherlands and to New England's shores. Thomas Shepard had scarcely preached half a year at Earle's Colne in Essex, when Laud succeeded Mountaigne as bishop of London, "a fierce enemy to all righteousness and a man fitted of God to be a scourge to his people," and summoned Shepard before him. "After many railing speeches against me, [he] forbade me to preach, and not only so, but if I went to preach anywhere else his hand would reach me." After seeking a safe haven in various places in the archdiocese of York, Shepard tried to establish himself in the Puritan community at Newcastle, but there Bishop Morton of Durham, an old-fashioned Calvinist, "professed he durst not give me liberty because Laud had taken notice of me," and so in 1633 Shepard followed Cotton, Hooker, Stone and Weld to New England. As he noted, his reasons were "many," not the least of which was that he "saw the Lord departing from England when Mr. Hooker and Mr. Cotton were gone, and I saw the hearts of most of the godly set and bent that way."[35] The conviction that the triumph of the Arminian clergy after 1625 presaged the destruction of England by a punitive divinity was apparently widespread among the Puritan clergy. In 1631, Thomas Hooker had preached to his congregation in Chelmsford shortly before departing for the Netherlands in June that "all things are ripe to destruction": "God may leave a nation, and his elect may suffer, and why may not England (that is but in outward covenant

---

[34] Razell and Razell, *The English Civil War*, 1: 199.

[35] *God's Plot: The Paradoxes of Puritan Piety. Being the Autobiography and Journal of Thomas Shepard*, ed. Michael McGiffert (Amherst, MA, 1972), 48–9, 54–5. Thomas Morton had expressed his opposition to the doctrines of the Arminians as early as 1609, long before he became a bishop. Roger Howell, Jr., *Newcastle upon Tyne and the Puritan Revolution* (Oxford, 1967), 85.

with him)? England's sins are very great, and the greater, because the means are great, and our warnings are and have been great; . . . Yet now God may leave it, and make it the mirror of his justice."[36] While Laud may have bridled at being pictured as God's instrument to scourge England, the fact that he drove out so many prominent ministers and that so many godly laymen followed them from Kent and Essex in the south to Durham and Northumberland in the north must be seen as a measure of success.[37]

Nevertheless, the measure of failure is equally impressive. A "D.D.," writing to his cousin in Madrid from London on September 1, 1638, explained that "the Archbishop, who is most in favor, very painful and hath much subdued the puritan faction upon a sudden, though not without some oppression, which is tolerable in [the] state for public example."[38] Archbishop Laud was less sanguine, if ultimately reassuring in his report to the king in 1638. While he could report that "there is neither any increase or decrease of Papists or Puritans in the Diocese [Canterbury]," he admitted that in London "there was some heat struck by opposite preaching in the pulpit between one [John] Goodwin of St. Stephen's Coleman Street, concerning the imputation of Christ's righteousness in the justification of the sinner," a contentious theological issue on which ministers had been forbidden to speak by the king's Declaration of 1628.[39] Rather than promise to sin no more in this fashion, a group of London ministers drew up a petition to the king in which they professed to be

not a little discouraged and deterred from preaching those saving doctrines of God, free Grace in Election and Predestination, which greatly confirm our faith

---

[36] *Thomas Hooker: Writings in England and Holland, 1626–1633*, George H. Williams et al. eds. *Harvard Theological Studies*, vol. 28 (Cambridge, MA, 1975), 232.

[37] That the lay Puritans came from one end of the country to the other can be illustrated by the testimonies of the members of Thomas Shepard's congregation in Cambridge, Massachusetts: see *Thomas Shepard's Confessions*, George Selement and Bruce C. Wooley eds. Publications of the Colonial Society of Mass., Collections, vol. 58 (Boston, 1981), passim.

[38] PRO, SP, 16/401/19. The letter was found in Lincoln's Inn by a "discreet officer of the Court of Wards," and Francis Cottington on viewing it sent it to Secretary Windebank: "I guess it to be from some Scottish man, and howsoever altogether it is foolish and very contemptible, yet I am of opinion that you should show it to his Majesty."

[39] Laud, *History of the Troubles*, 553. For the Declaration, see *Documentary Annals*, 1: 43. Much to his consternation, Bishop John Davenant of Salisbury promptly got into trouble by preaching before the king on the doctrine of predestination. As he complained in a letter to Dr. Samuel Ward at Sidney Sussex, "The doctrine of predestination, which I taught, was not forbidden by the Declaration, first, because in the Declaration all the Articles are established amongst which the Article of Predestination is one. Second, because all ministers are urged to subscribe unto the truth of that Article. . . . Upon these and such like grounds I gathered it would not be esteemed amongst forbidden, curious or needless doctrines." Bod. Lib., Tanner MS 71, fol. 41v.

of eternal salvation and fervently kindle our love of God, as the XVII Article expressly mentioneth. So as we are brought into a great strait, either of incurring God's heavy displeasure if we do not faithfully discharge our embassage in declaring the whole counsel of God, or the danger of being censured for violators of your Majesty's said acts, if we preach these constant doctrines of our Church and confute the opposite Pelagian and Arminian heresies, both preached and printed boldly without fear of censure.[40]

Yet petitions were not the worst of it. In late 1637, a survey of London churches still reported irregularities – communion tables not properly railed in, some still standing in the chancel, the communion administered to the congregation in their pews, baptisms held at times other than that prescribed in the Prayer Book, boys who "put on their hats in sermon time" – and a number of the city clergy who had misbehaved. Besides John Goodwin's preaching in violation of the 1628 Declaration (he was also reported to have administered "the communion to divers strangers sitting"), Henry Burton's curate at Friday Street was charged with praying "before and after sermons loosely and factiously, as for the conversion of the Queen, [and] for a neighbor minister in persecution"; Adoniram Byfield had officiated at Allhallows Staining without his surplice; a Mr. Jenison read prayers at Allhallowes by the Wall two Sundays in his cloak; Edward Finch, vicar and lecturer at Christ Church, Newgate, created a scandal by stationing a collector by the church door who cried "pray remember the minister"; James Palmer, vicar and preacher at St. Bride's for over two decades, was found to have omitted prayers for the bishops and the rest of the clergy and to have neglected to wear the prescribed vestments when officiating; Sydrach Simpson, curate and lecturer at St. Margaret's, New Fish Street, and George Hughes, lecturer at Allhallowes, Bread Street, were noted as "scarce licensed, by which themselves avoid the practice of conformity"; John Cardell, lecturer at Allhallowes, Lombard Street, was suspended briefly; and George Walker, rector of St. John Evangelist and lecturer at St. Helen's, Bishopsgate, was imprisoned by Star Chamber for a sermon that suggested that it was a "sin to obey the greatest monarchs in things which were against the command of God" – a record that hardly suggests that the "Puritan faction" had been successfully subdued, even with the application of a little violence.[41]

---

[40] PRO, SP, 16/408/171. The petition is not signed, which is not surprising, but since it is found among the state papers, it was presumably either delivered or discovered by the government in some other way.

[41] PRO, SP, 16/371/39; Seaver, *Puritan Lectureships*, 259–61. Edward Finch was apparently of scandalous life and conversation, which may have been the source of his appeal as a preacher, but he was certainly no Puritan, and was removed by an order of Parliament on May 8, 1641. A.G. Matthews, *Walker Revised* (Oxford, 1948), 47.

The evidence for the following year was not appreciably better and suggests that a dozen years of episcopal rule by two disciplinarians, Laud and Juxon as bishops of London, had failed to produce an obedient, conformable clergy. Daniel Votier, the incumbent at St. Peter, Westcheap, was charged with "divers inconformities," but, like Joseph Symonds, formerly rector of St. Martin, Ironmonger Lane, was suspected by Laud to be preparing to avoid a censure by the High Commission by going beyond the seas.[42] Within months, Votier returned from the Netherlands and was summoned before the High Commission, as were Thomas Foxley, another Puritan who had preached in London since 1629, and Thomas Edwards, who was charged with preaching a seditious sermon at Mercers' Chapel.[43]

Elsewhere at the end of the 1630s, the taming of the "schismatical Puritans" seems to have succeeded no better. At Northampton, long a Puritan center, a letter from Samuel Clerk to Sir John Lambe, Laud's dean of the Court of Arches, reported in June of 1638 that at All Saints "some very lately have (as I am informed) cut the rail or cancel that was about the Lord's Board in pieces and have brought down the Lord's Table into the middle of the chancel"; later that summer, Dr. Robert Sibthorpe reported that "Northampton men continue still inveighing against idolatry, yet idoling their own inventions, in so much that upon Thursday, June 21, there was a preaching fast by Mr. Ball in the forenoon and Mr. Newton in the afternoon, but neither of them prayed for any archbishops or bishops nor used the Lord's Prayer at conclusion of theirs before sermon, nor did they or the people use reverend gestures of rites and ceremonies enjoined."[44]

Much more ominous in the light of the rebellion of the Scottish Covenanters was the news from the north. In January 1638/9 Alexander Davyson, the mayor of Newcastle, wrote to Secretary Windebank about the preliminary results of his inquiries into the whereabouts of John Fenwick and Thomas Bitleson, two Puritan merchants, and William Morton, a preacher there, who were suspected both to be disaffected to the present Church of England and to have been in communication

---

[42] Seaver, *Puritan Lectureships*, 261. Joseph Symonds had become co-pastor with Sydrach Simpson of one of the English churches of Rotterdam: Keith Sprunger, *Dutch Puritanism: A History of English and Scottish Churches of the Netherlands in the Sixteenth and Seventeenth Centuries* (Leiden, 1982), 168–9.

[43] Seaver, *Puritan Lectureships*, 261.

[44] PRO, SP, 16/393/15; SP, 16/393/75. For the Puritan community in Northampton and for Thomas Ball and his curate, Charles Newton, see Tom Webster, *Godly Clergy in Early Stuart England: The Caroline Puritan Movement, c. 1620–1643* (Cambridge and New York, 1997), 55, 71, passim.

with the Scots. Over the course of the next month, the mayor uncovered more of the ramifications of what he termed "the faction" of John Fenwick, including Gyles Bitleson, an even more unforthcoming witness than his brother Thomas. In the course of the investigations, Gyles Bitleson's house was searched and a letter found from Edward Hall in London, apparently like the Bitlesons in the leather trade, addressed to Gyles but also to his "good brethren and sisters," which said in part, "alas, things grow worse and worse concerning the pure worship of God; they will have now the ministers to preach in the surplice all the time by this hellish plot of Antichrist."[45]

Finally, in April 1639, Robert Jenison, who had lectured as town preacher at All Saints, Newcastle, for more than twenty years, was brought before the Court of High Commission to answer a number of charges involving a variety of nonconformist practices, apparently of many years' standing, but also more dangerously of having preached "since the late commotions in Scotland, . . . that the Scriptures mention that none should trust in horse or armor, and that Hezechiah out of the pride of his heart did shew his armor and smarted for it," which was understood to have "a seditious meaning against the King." He was also charged with having "sundry conferences with divers of the Scotch Covenanters as they passed by Newcastle." Although Jenison denied any seditious meaning to his sermon or any treasonable correspondence with the Scots, there was no hiding his long-standing nonconformity. Despite his submission to the court, he was suspended from his lectureship and in January was reported to have fled to Amsterdam.[46]

As the articles before the High Commission make explicit, Jenison's nonconformity was neither recent nor accidental. Jenison himself made clear in his correspondence that he had been crossing swords with the local Arminian clergy from his pulpit at All Saints at least since the spring of 1628. Fully conscious that he was in violation of "the canon to which I subscribed against public contradicting of fellow ministers' doctrine," he nevertheless remained on reasonable terms with Yeldred Alvey, the Arminian vicar of St. Nicholas, against whose doctrines he preached. In January 1629/30, he wrote that "I have heard a great threatening as of my silencing, especially at the Archbishop's provincial visitation the next spring," and yet what is surely significant is that this well-known

---

[45] PRO, SP, 16/410/5; SP, 16/412/10; SP, 16/412/49. For the relations between the Newcastle Puritans and the Covenanters, see Howell, *Newcastle upon Tyne*, 100–8.

[46] PRO, SP, 16/415/7; SP, 16/415/8; Bod. Lib., Tanner MS 67, fol. 123r–v; Seaver, *Puritan Lectureships*, 108–9. For Jenison's career, see Roger Howell, *Puritans and Radicals in North England* (Lanham, NY, and London, 1984), 112–27.

nonconformist was not silenced until the summer of 1639, when the threat posed by the Scots in the first Bishops' War finally led the authorities to act.[47]

In January 1640, Yeldred Alvey wrote to Archbishop Neile with a kind of desperate optimism that in view of the flight of Jenison "and Mr. Lapthorne being silenced, there is good hope that now the neck of the puritanical faction is broken." By October the Scots were once again in possession of the town, and Alvey had fled.[48] Jenison we have already met; Anthony Lapthorne, if possible, had an even lengthier record of persistent nonconformity. In 1605 he lost his royal chaplaincy and his rectory at Landrake in the diocese of Exeter for refusing subscription as required by the new canons; in 1606 he was presented for preaching without a license in Somerset, and in 1609 he was again in trouble, this time with James Montague, the bishop of Bath and Wells. When he was before the Court of High Commission in late 1631, it was on charges that since "his deprivation and displacing from the rectory of Minchinhampton in Gloucestershire [1618], from the lecture at Lewys in Sussex [1623], and from his lecture of Tamworth in Warwickshire, and namely about three years since he was promoted to the rectory of Treatire and Michaelchurch in the diocese of Hereford, . . . the said Anthony Lapthorne hath not usually read divine service, nor yet administered the sacraments according to the prescript form appointed in the Book of Common Prayer." In fact, when he read divine service and came to one of the Psalms or Lessons, he would "leave off reading and fall to expounding the Psalms or Lessons in his reading desk, and that done to go up to the pulpit and then to begin his sermon, whereby the greatest part of the divine service is commonly omitted." Perceiving some of his parishioners to bow at the name of Jesus, he "left off reading and fell to revile the parties so bowing and told them they were worse than Papists and were plain idolaters." In addition he held a fast to which "foreigners" from outside the parish were invited whom Lapthorne termed "the children of God and told them that the reason of that fast was for that the Sunday following was appointed for

---

[47] Bod. Lib., Tanner MS 72, fols. 260r–v, 150r; Tanner MS 71, fol. 30r–v. In fact, Archbishop Neile's annual report to the king for the year 1633 merely notes that Dr. Robert Jenison was lecturer at Allhallowes in Newcastle, along with Thomas Stevenson, lecturer at St. Nicholas. After noting the names of three other lecturers in the diocese, Thomas Morton, the bishop of Durham, noted that "all these lecturers are conformable to the doctrine and discipline of the Church of England, so far as I could be informed," to which Neile appended the comment: "Yet I must confess to your Majesty I have reason to suspect some of them not to be so conformable, as they ought to be." PRO, SP, 16/259/78.

[48] Seaver, *Puritan Lectureships*, 109.

making of ministers by the bishops, which he affirmed to be one of the crying sins of this kingdom." He also termed "the reverend clergy of the realm the great rabbis, the great clergy monsters, and then terming the neighboring ministers idol shepherds, dumb dogs, soul murderers, saying also that their preaching are strawberry sermons and daubing sermons." Certainly Lapthorne possessed a vivid turn of phrase, but it is hard to think of another nonconformist who managed to offend the good order of the Church in so striking a fashion. He was, needless to say, deprived and suspended from any further ministerial function.[49]

What should have been the end of Lapthorne's checkered career was but the prelude to the next stage. In February 1638/9, Thomas Morton, the bishop of Durham, confessed in a letter to Secretary Windebank that fourteen years earlier, when he was bishop of Lichfield and Coventry, he had, on the recommendation of the earl of Pembroke, placed Lapthorne, whom he had "reduced" to conformity, in "the most prophane and barbarous parish in the diocese, who took therein such pains that he brought them to be as religious and orderly as any other." In consequence, when Lapthorne turned up in the diocese of Durham in 1636 with an order that inhibited him from preaching only in or about London, Morton had placed him in "the most barbarous place in Northumberland, where there had been almost no preaching of forty years before" and had given him £40 yearly from the bishop's own funds. Although Lapthorne once again proved "laborious," Morton admitted that even before he had received notice to dispatch Lapthorne to the High Commission, he had "heard a whispering report . . . that Mr. Lapthorne was had in, as being entangled in the Scottish business."[50]

Lapthorne's career is informative. Despite a half century of notorious nonconformity, for which, as his biographer said, he "had that hard portion from the bishops to be ejected for his inconformity out of one half the dioceses of England," bishops like Morton, who sympathized with his evangelical bent, and who as Calvinists objected only to his disciplinary irregularities, repeatedly restored his preaching license and dispatched him to exercise his talents, preferably in some "dark corner" of the realm, such as Hereford or Northumberland, where his nonconformity might be less noticeable than his fervent preaching.[51] However, compared to other well-known Puritans, Lapthorne's extravagant

---

[49] Seaver, *Puritan Lectureships*, 109; Fincham, *Prelate as Pastor*, 224–5; PRO, SP, 16/261, fols. 83r–84v.

[50] PRO, SP, 16/412/58. On being examined by Morton, Lapthorne admitted having met two Scots in the course of the past year but claimed that the words exchanged involved no expression of solidarity or support.

[51] Lapthorne's biography is quoted from Fincham, *Prelate as Pastor*, 224.

misbehavior made him a relatively easy target, and what is surprising is not that he was repeatedly suspended, deprived, and silenced, but that he was continually able to find new livings and licenses to preach.

Part of the difficulty faced by episcopal disciplinarians lay in the nature of the machinery available to them. The Canons of 1604 provided a compilation of regulations on which the Church courts could act, and these were supplemented by such regulatory additions as the Book of Sports and the king's Directions to Preachers of 1622. Both archbishops and bishops were expected to carry out a primary visitation within eighteen months of their consecration, and bishops were generally expected to follow these with triennial visitations thereafter. These visitations were inquisitorial: Bishops were responsible for drawing up visitation articles, sets of questions to be put to parochial clergy and churchwardens, which were printed and sent down to each parish prior to the appearance of the bishop or his ordinary. During the visitation itself, the letters of institution of the parochial clergy and their licenses to preach (in the case of schoolmasters, teaching licenses), had to be produced, as well as written responses to the visitation articles.[52] These in turn led to so-called office cases, the bishop's court taking the initiative to summon by apparitors those clerical and lay delinquents presented at the visitation as offending one or another regulation. The accused would be put on oath ex officio to answer all questions subsequently put to them, and judgment would be given, punishing the delinquency and presumably preventing its repetition.

Certainly the articles themselves might be both searching and thorough. John Overall, bishop of Norwich, in his 1619 visitation articles, addressed twenty-one of them to "the ministers and preachers of God's holy word," beginning with the academic qualifications of the parochial incumbent, whether he was a preacher, and if so, whether he was properly licensed and by whom; going on to query how he conducted divine service at the appointed times, whether he "duly observe[d] the orders, rites, and ceremonies prescribed," whether he invariably wore the proper vestments when officiating, whether he read the prescribed homilies, and if he was not licensed to preach, whether he preached false doctrine (i.e., any teaching at variance with the Thirty-Nine Articles of 1563), and so on. Preachers or lecturers were required to read divine service at both morning and evening prayer in a surplice at least on two

---

[52] For the exceptions to this rather schematized picture of disciplinary machinery, see *Visitation Articles and Injunctions of the Stuart Church*, vol. 1, ed. Kenneth Fincham, Church of England Record Society (Woodbridge, Suffolk, 1994), xiv–xv.

Sundays during the year and twice yearly to administer the sacraments, according to Canon 56.[53]

Strict laws without strict enforcement were largely a dead letter. Lazy bishops, such as the Arminian George Mountaigne, might promulgate detailed visitation articles but fail to pursue delinquents with energy. During the years of his episcopate in London (1621–8), more than seventy Puritan lecturers preached in London, six were cited, but none appears to have been inhibited or deprived. It is hard to fault Kenneth Fincham's judgment that Mountaigne was among those bishops who left little mark on their sees.[54] But even the task of a conscientious bishop was not a happy one. First of all, churchwardens had to present their delinquent ministers and lecturers, a process that at first glance appears simple enough, but that obviously could create difficulties in a parish where loyalties were divided. On May 1, 1634, the churchwardens and sidesmen, along with ten parishioners, signed a lengthy five-folio presentment against their minister, Edward Williams, parson of Holy Trinity, Shaston, Dorset, who "hath most usually refused or neglected to read the Book of Common Prayer in such order and form as in and by the said book is prescribed, and also to observe the rites and ceremonies of the Church of England according to the ecclesiastical laws and canons established for the performance thereof." The presentment then went on to spell out Williams' lack of conformity in excruciating detail. "On the thirtieth of March and the thirteenth of April, and on divers other Sundays this year last past he did omit it, and as for Benedicte in English, he never read it," and this is the revealing phrase, "to our knowledge and remembrance, which we suppose to be about thirteen years since."[55]

The parish had suffered this blatant nonconformist all those years in part because, as the presentment states, Williams "hath always endeavored to elect such to be churchwardens and sidemen, as are factiously inclined." Those who opposed him and his Puritan followers he slighted in his sermons "as if they were not to be esteemed as good Christians, and having most times one churchwarden of his faction much at his command, he hath so often vexed his parishioners on such frivolous and unjust presentments that many of his parishioners have been fearful to find fault with or present any of his irregularities." What had precipitated the presentment appears to have been a combination of several events. First, he had refused to read the Book of Sports and instead preached that "the morality of the Sabbath in sanctifying it was

[53] *Visitation Articles*, 161–4.
[54] Seaver, *Puritan Lectureships*, 232; Fincham, *Prelate as Pastor*, 293.
[55] PRO, SP, 16/267/6, fol. 21r.

as strictly to be observed now in the time of the gospel as it was in the time of the law amongst the Jews." He then went on to question: "hath God said, thou shalt keep the sabbath holy, and shall man contradict it? How dare any then to use vain sports on that day? Shall we serve God in the morning and with vain sports go to the devil in the afternoon?" To protect himself, he apparently did read the book, or at least part of it, before morning prayer on one occasion with only the parish clerk present. He then spent much of the spring dissecting the book's iniquities in a series of inflammatory sermons. On one occasion he read part to the congregation and then read an Act of Parliament of 1625 "against certain sports or recreations forbidden by the said Act to be used upon the Sunday," and part of another act made for the better observation of the Sabbath, which he followed with relevant passages from the homilies and canons. These derelictions certainly put him in an exposed position in 1634.

However, the final precipitating event seems to have been the disputed election of the parish clerk. Although the presentment does not make clear whether Williams had succeeded in obtaining his candidate, Williams did explain to some disgruntled parishioners to whom he had refused communion that he took that action "because they or their masters whom they served opposed Mr. Williams in the election of one John Garret to be the parish clerk, who (as the common fame went) was schismatically given and maintained tenets of Anabaptism and Puritanism and a troublesome person not fit for that place." The use of the sacrament as a weapon against parishioners who opposed the minister was obviously divisive and challenging, but whether the presentment succeeded in the deprivation of Williams cannot be discovered from the imperfect remaining records of the High Commission. What is clear is that Williams was a survivor, since he had been questioned by the High Commission before, where "(we have credibly heard) he was like to have been deprived had not the suit against him been determined by a general pardon."[56]

Ideally, ministers and churchwardens cooperated in running the parish as an ecclesiastical institution. If Puritan ministers in conformist parishes were a source of contention, conformist ministers in Puritan parishes were equally so. In Brislington, Somerset, the minister, Oliver Chiver, complained in 1636 against his churchwardens that they refused to present numerous parishioners guilty of incontinence, that they slandered him in front of the whole parish, that they denied him a view of

---

[56] PRO, SP, 16/267/6, fols. 21r–25v.

the parish accounts, that they denied the necessity of "bowing the knee at the name of Jesus," insisting that Chiver "pressed more than the text did infer," and in consequence of this disagreement persuaded many of the prominent parishioners to withhold their benevolences from Chiver on the grounds that he was "a profane fellow and superstitious person." Chiver was convinced that the churchwardens and their friends were "schismatical people who often did and still to this day do go from their parish church, running up and down to hear sermons." When in the parish church at Brislington, their behavior was equally objectionable: They sat with their hats on during divine service and sermon and refused to stand at the reading of the gospel. Having rendered Chiver's life a very hell, they then had him removed from the rented house that served as a parsonage. When he petitioned Laud against his own churchwardens, Chiver was evidently at his wit's end.[57]

The Brislington case was by no means unique. Incumbents fought with their churchwardens and vestries at their peril, for while they might win a skirmish or two, they generally lost the war. When the parish clerk of St. Michael, Cornhill, died early in 1622, the parson chose his brother-in-law to be clerk, "without consent or allowance of the parishioners." The churchwardens and vestry promptly went to Sir Henry Martin, chancellor of the diocese of London, proved that they had "in themselves by ancient custom the election of their parish clerk," and with the chancellor's license, proceeded to elect their own candidate.[58] In early 1625, William Brough, an Arminian, became the new parson, and although relations remained correct in a formal sense, the vestry minutes reveal some of the mounting tension. In 1631, at a vestry that met to "mediate and end all businesses and differences" between the parson and the parish, the vestry agreed to continue his lecture "during their pleasure and good liking." In 1633 Brough and the parish were at odds over burial fees and again went to mediation; in 1638 the vestry had to order the churchwardens to reimburse Brough for newly railing-in the communion table.[59] In 1643 the parish clerk on orders from the vestry carefully copied the sequestration order ejecting Brough from his parochial living, noting that Brough had "in his public preaching and otherwise endeavored to corrupt the parishioners with the leaven of popish and superstitious doctrines of bowing to or before the altar, worshiping

---

57 PRO, SP, 16/322132. David Underdown refers to Brislington as one of the "northern Puritan parishes." *Revel, Riot and Rebellion: Popular Politics and Culture in England, 1603–1660* (Oxford, 1985), 251.
58 Guildhall Library [hereafter GL] MS 4072/1, pt. 1: Vestry Minutes of St. Michael Cornhill, 1563–1646/7, fol. 132r–v.
59 Vestry Minutes of St. Michael Cornhill, fols. 150r, 152r, 163v.

toward the East, washing away of original sin by baptism, . . . and the error of Arminianism of universal grace and free will in man fallen. . . ." In fact Brough had ceased to attend vestries after February 2, 1640/41, and presumably had left the parish long before the sequestration, realizing that with the imprisonment of the archbishop, he had little protection against a hostile parish.[60]

Given the capacity of churchwardens to hide the nonconformities of their incumbents and preachers when they shared their religious biases, it is surprising that so many found themselves brought before the Church courts. However, once there, the purpose of the court was reformative rather than purely punitive. When Abraham Grimes, who ministered at St. Catherine Creechurch, was brought before the bishop of London for preaching against bowing at the name of Jesus – "why should the name Jesus have more reverence than the name Christ, yea, why should it have so much, when as Christ is a name of office and dignity, Jesus but a bare christian name" – he was promptly suspended by episcopal order on October 22, 1629. This order was relaxed without comment the following September, presumably as a consequence of his submission and promise not to preach against the prescribed practice again.[61] Thomas Weld, the vicar of Terling, Essex, was questioned in December 1630 for preaching and administering the sacraments without having subscribed to the three articles as required by the canons of 1604, but was given time to consider his actions. After consulting William Gouge, the minister at St. Anne, Blackfriars, and by this time one of the patriarchs of the London Puritan community, Weld reappeared the following summer before the bishop and declared "that his Lordship had dealt most favorably with him and had granted him a long time to inform his judgment, but he was not yet persuaded in his conscience to subscribe nor desired any longer time of consultation." He was suspended forthwith and on September 1, 1631, excommunicated as well.[62] He departed for Massachusetts Bay shortly after.

But while Weld remained obdurate, others submitted. John Archer, who lectured at St. Antholins, also catechized, as was required both by

---

[60] Vestry Minutes of St. Michael Cornhill, fols. 169v, 166v.

[61] GL MS 9531/15: Episcopal Register of Laud and Juxon, 1628–60, fols. 21v–22r, 22v. For Abraham Gimes or Grame, see David Como and Peter Lake, "Puritans, Antinomians and Laudians in Caroline London: The Strange Case of Peter Shaw and its Contexts," *Journal of Ecclesiastical History* 50.4 (1999): 691. Grimes or Grame was later accused of saying that "if it were in his power, he would throw all the bishops of this land out of their places and put honest men in their stead," as well as retelling a story in which Laud was called to his face "the tail of the great beast." Ibid., 691.

[62] GL MS 95 31/15, fols. 23r, 23v, 24r.

the canons and by the king's recent injunctions concerning preachers; however, the catechism he used bore little resemblance to that contained in the Prayer Book. When taxed by the bishop for preaching against bowing at the name of Jesus, he is reported to have answered "in a most doubtful and ambiguous manner," which must be a prize example of clerical understatement:

although I blamed the church of Rome's superstitious bowing at the name of Jesus, yet I confidently affirm that all accustomed lowly due reverence is to be given to the Lord Jesus, for I contradict not but say according to and with the canon of the Church of England about this particular, That the Lord Jesus, when he is named in his words have all accustomed due reverence, take we this canon in the largest sense as may be according to the Scripture and the most general exposition of the Fathers.

What the bishop made of this is hard to say, but he pressed Archer to answer "whether he had read those Fathers which his Lordship had formerly quoted to him out of Dr. Andrewes, late Lord Bishop of Winchester's book." Archer is recorded as responding "that he had and found no authors that did allow thereof." He was promptly suspended, but a little over a year later, in December 1630, he submitted, and the suspension was relaxed.[63]

Some ministers obviously tried to exploit the procedural opportunities of submission, although there is little evidence that the court was taken in. In the course of his interrogation in January 1637/8 before the Court of High Commission, Giles Creech, a self-confessed former Familist, implicated a number of Londoners as participants in these heterodox congregations and mentioned at the end of his deposition that "Dr. Everet [John Everard] did use to preach such things which these people were affected to hear." Everard was ordered to submit answers to the court, and in November of 1638 the court ordered his answers to be considered by Sir John Lamb, Dr. Duck, and Dr. Eden. On October 10, 1639, the court ordered Everard to make his submission in a form they prescribed on bended knees before the commission meeting at the archbishop's palace at Lambeth, where he was to retract such views as that "God almighty was...an actual and working cause of all things, and consequently of sin...; that God is everything and all else is but accident,...and take away the accidents and you have God unclothed;...[that he] did not believe that our bodies nourished of and by beef...and the like could rise and go to heaven, affirming it to be a senseless conceit." The incorrigible Everard, rather than making the

---

[63] GL MS 95 31/15, fols. 22r, 23r.

prescribed retractions, appeared at the end of the month with his own submission, which the court realized was totally inadequate but then gave Everard additional time to negotiate his submission. At that point the record breaks off, but it does suggest to what lengths even the High Commission would go on occasion to allow ministers to abjure error and accept the tenets of the Church of England as then understood.[64]

Some sought to stave off suspension and deprivation by negotiating their submissions to authority, a move that the authorities frequently allowed, apparently because it suggested at least some movement toward conformity. Others submitted but then found that they could not live with the terms of conformity. Two years after Charles Chauncy became vicar of Ware, Hertfordshire, he was articled against in High Commission, where it was charged that he had showed his "manifest dislike of the Book of Common Prayer," parts of which in consequence he refused to read; he "purposely refused to wear the surplice"; he "omitted to use the cross in baptism"; he "seldom read" the litany on Wednesdays and Fridays; he failed to catechize and read the prescribed prayers before his afternoon sermon. In short, he displayed all the manifestations of total nonconformity, a state of affairs that he evidently did not help by telling his congregation "that those that are called Puritans are the chariots and horsemen of Israel," which, however vivid, was also perhaps needlessly provocative, as was his claim that the Sabbath began on Saturday night at sunset (a claim which, it was charged, created "much strife and heartburnings"). Chauncy answered the articles eleven days later on April 21, 1630, denying where he could and claiming that he conformed "for the most part" in answer to other charges, but offering "most willingly to submit to better judgments."[65] Chauncy next appeared as the minister of Marston St. Lawrence, in Northamptonshire, where the report of Laud's 1635 metropolitical visitation noted that "after evening prayer and catechizing [he had evidently learned to protect himself to that degree] about 4 o'clock he rings the sermon bell and so that all the country thereabouts come in and there he holds them till 6 or 7"; the visitors also noted that he administered the communion to "sitters and standers." In fact, when depositions were taken from parishioners in

---

[64] Bod. Lib., Tanner MS 67, fols. 181r–182v, 143r–145r, 149r–v. Everard, the lecturer at Kensington, had been in and out of trouble for two decades. Chamberlain records three occasions when Everard, then lecturer at St. Martin in the Fields, was imprisoned in 1621–2 for preaching against the Spanish match. *Letters of John Chamberlain*, 2: 350, 449, 486. It may have been his chaplaincy with the courtier earl of Holland that made the ecclesiastical authorities reluctant to deal with him summarily: see *DNB*.

[65] PRO, SP, 16/164/40, fols. 79r–84v; SP, 16/165/10, fols. 17r–20r. For a full account of the Chauncy affair, see Webster, *Godly Clergy in Early Stuart England*, 221–4.

January 1635/6, it became obvious that he once again was indulging in all the nonconformist practices that had got him in trouble at Ware. His parishioners and the local Puritan clergy had certified as to his conformity, but the testimony to his continued nonconformity was confirmed by two of the Arminian clergy of the diocese.[66] Chauncy then joined the stream of emigrants to Massachusetts Bay, a measure of success to be sure, but only after six years and two major efforts at ecclesiastical discipline.

The picture presented so far of individual Puritan ministers ensnared in the web of ecclesiastical discipline, which, however forgiving, could not tolerate continued dissidence, is informative, as far as it goes. It is not, however, the whole story. What sustained the Puritan clergy through several generations of attempts to force them into conformity was a combination of clerical and lay support; it is thus a story of collective, communal support rather than a story alone of heroic and defiant individualism.

When Melanchthon Jewell, "an ancient schismatic," was apprehended in London in 1604, his room was searched and the authorities found a number of papers concerning ministers in the diocese of Exeter, who were threatened or suspended and deprived for refusing subscription as required by the new canons of that year; all part of an effort mobilized in various Puritan communities in England that aimed at convincing King James that the cost of Bancroft's campaign to exact conformity from the Puritan ministers was too high. Among his papers was a diary in which Jewell had recorded his appointments for the following week, a list that reads like a roll call of prominent London Puritans and their influential allies: Edmund Snape, Stephen Egerton, Walter Travers, Arthur Hildersham, Anthony Wotton, and others. The authorities also found among his papers a list of thirty-nine "resolute Puritan ministers" in the diocese of Exeter and the petitions of "many ministers" of sundry counties, forty-three from Essex, fifty from Suffolk, twenty-three from London, and thirty from Sussex, to be presented to the king.[67]

---

[66] PRO, SP, 16/308/52; SP, 16/302/16; SP, 16/311/33. Miles Burkitt, who followed Chauncy at Marston was also a repeated offender who, it was reported in 1638, had "read his submission, yet made an apology for himself" and, when Prynne and Burton passed through the parish, preached that "though the faithful were molested, persecuted and cropped, they continued faithful still." PRO, SP, 16/406/88.

[67] PRO, SP, 14/10/81. The paper describing the search calls Jewell a mere basket-maker who had never been to university, but he was clearly a well-connected or informed emissary. For his past, which explains his connection with these prominent Puritan ministers, see Patrick Collinson, *The Elizabethan Puritan Movement* (Berkeley and Los Angeles, 1967), 409, 412–13, 441, 443.

A quarter of a century later, when the study of John Heydon, a Norwich nonconformist, was raided, the authorities found "notes of sermons taken from Mr. Taylor, Mr. Peters, Mr. Damport [Davenport], Mr. Foxley, Mr. Shaw and divers other ministers of that quality." In addition was

a certificate written and subscribed by Ignatius Jordan of Exeter [the Puritan M.P.] (but at the date thereof, being 13 June 1627, remaining in London) importing his knowledge of the great zeal and undertaking of the bearer hereof (being John Heydon) against the vices of the times, and his suffering by prosecution in the Star Chamber for the same and his deliverance from it, the weakness of his estate and several debts, with an entreaty to consider his case.

To this certificate were appended the names of those London ministers who subscribed and the amounts contributed for Heydon's relief; it reads like a directory to the Puritan clerical community assembled in London at that moment: "Thomas Taylor, William Gouge, William Chibald, Hugh Peter, John White, Gabriel Carpenter, Thomas Barnes, Ezechial Culverwell, Marmaduke Brewster, Richard Culverwell, and others."[68] Nor, as the gulf between traditional Calvinist ministers and the Arminians widened, did Puritan ministers have to rely on the support of their fellows alone. When George Walker, the parson of St. John Evangelist and the lecturer at St. Helen's, Bishopsgate, London, was imprisoned by Star Chamber in 1638 for a sermon in which he claimed that it was a "sin to obey the greatest monarchs in things which are against the command of God," fifty-six London ministers signed a certificate attesting to his being "a man of honest and peaceable life and conversation, a zealous maintainer of the doctrine and discipline established in the Church of England, and a strong opponent of all sects, schisms and heresies." Although many who signed were certainly well-known Puritans – Stephen Denison, William Gouge, Richard Holdsworth, Cornelius Burgess, John Downame, Jeremiah Leech, William Cooper, Elias Crabtree, Charles Offspring, Joseph Caryll, Henry Roborough, Lazarus Seaman and others, perhaps twenty-three in all – others clearly were not.[69] Faced with the rising numbers and power of the Arminian churchmen in the early seventeenth century, the Puritan clergy never lacked for allies among their sympathetic Calvinist brethren.

---

[68] PRO, SP, 16/119/22.
[69] PRO, SP, 16/414/23. The Petition, dated March 4, 1638/9, was needless to say a futile gesture toward a regime already panicked by the widespread and growing evidence of dissidence and disloyalty, and Walker was not released until the Long Parliament acted in 1641: see Seaver, *Puritan Lectureships*, 260–1.

After all, these men had in many cases met as students at Oxford or Cambridge, and for the young Puritan preachers, these relationships had been cemented in many cases by further studies and practical training at one or another of those clerical "household seminaries," as Tom Webster has aptly termed them: John Cotton's household at Boston, Lincolnshire, until he left for New England in 1633; Alexander Richardson's at Barking, Essex; Richard Blackerby's on the border between Essex and Suffolk; Thomas Gataker's in suburban London at Rotherhithe; and Charles Offspring's in the city itself at St. Antholin's, where the budding preachers could try their wings in the early morning weekday lectures.[70]

The correspondence of Samuel Ward, master of Sidney Sussex, testifies to another kind of network that included former tutees, such as Robert Jenison, the Puritan lecturer at Newcastle, and old colleagues such as James Ussher, first as the bishop of Meath and later as archbishop of Armagh, and John Davenant, the bishop of Salisbury. Further, these were not discreet networks of friends, known only to Ward but unknown to each other. In 1619 the already prominent Puritan John Preston wrote to James Ussher and mentioned consulting his Cambridge friends about taking on the divinity lecture, if elected; he had, he said, "communicated with my friends (to whom in such cases I resign myself, which hath been my practice formerly) as Doctor Chadderton, . . . Mr. Dodd [and] Mr. Sibbs." He concluded that he would not accept the lectureship, if Ward would take it. Three years later, Sibbes wrote to Ussher, asking among other things whether Ussher had heard that Ward had succeeded John Davenant as Lady Margaret Professor.[71] In a letter of November 27, 1627, Henry Briggs, the mathematician, wrote to Ward from Merton College that at his last being in London "Mr. Damporte [John Davenport] told me that the distressed ministers of the Palatinate had received from London . . . 600 li." In a letter dated March 20, 1627/8, addressed to his "much respected tutor," Jenison wrote that he was preaching against the views of Dr. Thomas Jackson, a neighboring minister, who "hath lately declared himself more than formerly for Arminius," and also noted that he had recently sent off a manuscript treatise called "A Word in Season" to two London Puritans, "Dr. Sibbes and Mr. Arrowsmith, because of the conveniency of printing, who will bring it to you."[72] If the king's command suppressed much of the public and printed debate over the contentious issues of predestination and

---

[70] Webster, *Godly Clergy in Early Stuart England*, 23–35.
[71] *The Whole Works of . . . James Ussher*, 16: 370, 395.
[72] Bod. Lib., Tanner MS 72, fols. 228r, 260r–v. For Jackson, see Tyacke, *Anti-Calvinists*, 66–7.

perseverance in faith in the years after 1628, Samuel Ward's correspondents, both Puritan and episcopal, continued to discuss the issue well into the 1630s.[73]

Laud and his fellow disciplinarians on the bench of bishops faced a Herculean task. The sheer size of the task of policing more than 8,500 parishes was beyond the capabilities of early modern bureaucrats, even the most efficient. Further, the clergy frequently shared their pulpits with visiting clerical friends, who would be long gone before any episcopal machinery could be mobilized. For example, Simonds D'Ewes, while a law student, heard at the Temple not only the minister and lecturer there, but also William Crashaw, the former lecturer; Thomas Salisbury, "a very good preacher"; Dr. John Everard; Dr. Richard Holdsworth (D'Ewes's former tutor); Thomas Goad; Anthony Lapthorne; Dr. Cornelius Burgess; Dr. John Downham; as well as several strangers, whom he could not identify.[74] Finally, there was little the authorities could do to the reluctant conformist. As Nathaniel Brent complained in his 1636 visitation report, "Mr. [Stephen] Marshall, Vicar of Finchingfield ... is held to be a dangerous person, but exceeding cunning. No man doubteth but that he hath an inconformable heart, but externally he observeth all." All that Brent could recommend was that "Mr. Chancellor of London should have a watchful eye over him, in regard he governeth the consciences of all the rich Puritans in those parts."[75] There was, of course, no canon against the "inconformable heart," but only the nonconforming practice.

Clerical friendships and support based on shared ideology must have done much to sustain the morale of both Puritans and Calvinist conformists alike during the years when the Church seemed dominated by an Arminian episcopate and royal supreme governor.[76] However, while it demonstrated the depth of clerical support popular preachers could amass among their fellows, it rarely stopped episcopal efforts

---

[73] See. for example, Ussher to Ward, September 15, 1635, which complains about the publication of "such rotten stuff as Shelford hath vented." Bod. Lib., Tanner MS 70, fol. 72r. For Shelford, see Tyacke, *Anti-Calvinists*, 53–7.

[74] D'Ewes, *Diary*, 88, 104, 109, 117, 125, 145, 186, 187. D'Ewes frequently heard sermons elsewhere in the City and Westminster, including one by Laud, then bishop of St. David's, about whom D'Ewes noted that he "was suspected to be somewhat popish." Ibid., 185. For clerical associations, see Webster, *Godly Clergy in Early Stuart England*, Chapter 4; Bremer, *Congregational Communion*, passim.

[75] PRO, SP, 16/351/100, fol. 261r.

[76] For a much lengthier exploration of Puritan clerical friendships before 1640, see Bremer, *Congregational Communion*, 17–122; for an exploration of the connections of a single Puritan divine, see Ann Hughes, "Thomas Dugard and his Circle in the 1630s – A Parliamentary-Puritan Connexion?" *Historical Journal* 29.4 (1986): 771–93.

to bring the wayward to book. The petition to Bishop Laud signed by forty-eight Essex ministers in 1629 on behalf of Thomas Hooker, the Puritan lecturer at Chelmsford in Essex, appears to have had little effect in changing Laud's mind, not least because it was followed within a week by a counterpetition, signed by forty Essex ministers, who complained of their "disconsolate and much discouraged estate and condition, for want of a general uniformity" in the Church.[77] Samuel Collins, the moderate Puritan minister at Braintree and one of the signatories of the petition on behalf of Hooker, wrote to Dr. Arthur Duck, urging him to persuade Laud to permit Hooker "quietly to depart out of his diocese," not because of clerical opposition to the suppression of Hooker, but because "all men's ears are now filled with the obstreperous clamors of his followers, against my Lord of London [Laud], as a man endeavoring to suppress good preaching and advance popery." Collins was worried not only because Hooker's clerical disciples, "bold and fiery spirits," would continue to stir up trouble, but because "the stop in trade hath bred such distraction and combustion in our country which for any course that hitherto hath been taken is like the rather to increase than otherwise, and whatsoever course be taken, our tumultuous vulgar will not easily again be reduced into order." A month later Collins wrote even more fearfully that "all men's heads, tongues, eyes are in London and all the counties about London taken up with plotting, talking and expecting what will be the conclusion of Mr. Hooker's business. Cambridge disputes it pro et con. It drowns the noise of the great question of tonnage and poundage."[78] Laud, of course, was not to be deterred by such counsels of prudence.

However, what followed might have given pause to a more farsighted prelate or one less determined to have his way regardless of the cost. Early in November of 1629, after Hooker's initial suspension, John Browning, the parson of Raworth, wrote to Laud a rather hyperbolic letter in which he inveighed obliquely and at length against those who "invade us and our peace," "who after all friendly and mild manner have been dealt with and convinced by argument, . . . [persist] in seditious, stubborn and disobedient courses against the public order;" surely such are "our enemy" and to be dealt with accordingly. It is only after this lengthy preamble that "one Mr. Hooker" is mentioned, when it is noted that "great heartburnings may arise against the suppressors of this man, as though thereby the Word of God should suffer in suppressing him

[77] PRO, SP, 16/151/45; SP, 16/152/4.
[78] PRO, SP, 16/142/113; SP, 16/144/36; William Hunt, *The Puritan Moment: The Coming of Revolution in an English County* (Cambridge, MA, and London, 1983), 253–6.

and his lecture." Browning went on to write that he was willing to preach the lecture "either for quieting the people, satisfying their desire, or reducing the perverted to farther obedience and accustomed discipline."[79] Tempting as such an offer must have been, for clearly Browning was a man after Laud's own heart, a combination lecture was already in train, and the list of conforming clergy who were to preach it was drawn up in mid-November.[80] However, early in the following year, Jeffrey Watt, rector of Leigh Magna, wrote to Dr. Duck that, while he and the others were willing "to uphold that lecture, upon your appointment," nevertheless to be "(as some say) thrust upon them without any desires on their parts" was bound to produce "small success of our preaching to a people nothing desiring it." In particular he anticipated trouble for the combination in trying to replace the popular Thomas Hooker, and he would in consequence (with all due respect) rather face the censure of the bishop than the anger of the people.[81] As for the unfortunate Samuel Collins, by 1636 he was writing to Bishop Juxon, Laud's successor, begging to be permitted "to remove from Braintree, for although he had attempted, as he was commanded at the bishop's visitation, "to draw my people to conformity . . . I find many of them very averse." Further, Collins claimed that he could not hope for any help from his patron, the earl of Warwick, "because I cannot symbolize with him, who rules all in that family." He added that he had heard that "the town of Harwich is almost mined with contention," but that they "much desired me," and at this point he was willing to take on even that contentious pulpit, if it could be arranged with the diocesan's approval.[82] In the increasingly polarized atmosphere of the 1630s, the position of such moderate fence-sitters had clearly become untenable.

Bishops could deal with recalcitrant Puritan clergy; silence, suspend, or deprive them of their livings or lectureships; or force them to flee to the Netherlands or New England, but their lay supporters were another matter altogether. For the clergy, there were clear canonical and doctrinal standards, which clergy violated at their peril, and well-established inquisitorial procedures for bringing the erring priest before the ecclesiastical courts. But the laity, unless guilty of refusing to attend church services in their parishes and take the required sacraments, or of holding conventicles (not always easy to distinguish from family prayers and sermon rehearsals), or of withholding tithe payments, were not

[79] PRO, SP, 16/151/12.
[80] PRO, SP, 16/152/16.
[81] PRO, SP, 16/160/66.
[82] PRO, SP, 16/339/55.

easy or obvious targets of ecclesiastical discipline. Notoriously, William Prynne and John Bastwick, although lay Puritans, were brought before Star Chamber, not the High Commission, and were tried for seditious libel, a crime against the State rather than the Church.[83]

There were exceptions. For example, in October 1636, Richard Ask, the recorder of Colchester, along with his wife and his associates were articled against in High Commission for a variety of crimes: They were charged with avoiding their parish church (St. Runwald) and with refusing to take communion thrice yearly "reverently kneeling upon their knees." Instead, Ask had indicted their rector, Thomas Newcomen, before Quarter Sessions for administering the sacrament in a "popish" and "heretical" fashion and, when this "frivolous and foolish" indictment was returned by the grand jury with an ignoramus, had encouraged another suit by an excommunicate parishioner in a second, "scandalous," indictment "merely for revenge and malice." When that parishioner was summoned by a warrant from the archbishop, Ask was accused of having the parishioner imprisoned on a fictitious action of debt, so that he could not be examined by the High Commission. Ask and his associates were also charged with waiting until divine service was finished before entering the church in time for the sermon, as a consequence of which bad example, "there are scarce 20 in the church most commonly at the hearing of divine service." Finally, when Newcomen attempted to read "an aggravation of an examination" against the excommunicate parishioner, Ask was charged with arranging to have the reading drowned out by having "two pieces shot off close by the church, which struck the congregation into great astonishment and amazement." Whether the court was successful in pursuing the egregious Ask is doubtful, since a 1638 roster of the English church at Arnhem in Gelderland lists Edward Ask as among the "worthy gentlemen" in that congregation.[84]

The Laudian regime of the 1630s clearly brought out ill-tempered displays from some angry Puritan laymen. Late in 1637, George Catesby, Esq., a Northamptonshire gentleman, was articled against in High Commission for claiming that the only way for a clergyman to advance was to appear before Laud "and rail against puritans"; that he had as soon "see the priest in his wife's smock as in the surplice"; that he "disliked the justice executed upon Mr. Prynne"; that he had read Henry Burton's book "and approved it"; that he "derided in his ridiculous

---

[83] Stephen Foster, *Notes from the Caroline Underground* (Hamden, CT, 1978), 40–57.
[84] Bod. Lib., Tanner MS 70, fols. 107r–111r; Sprunger, *Dutch Puritanism*, 226. For Thomas Newcomen, the Arminian brother of the Puritan Matthew Newcomen, see Hunt, *The Puritan Moment*, 276, 301.

gestures the ceremony of bowing towards the altar," which he regarded as "idolatry"; that he "refused to bow at the blessed name of Jesus"; that he "disparaged the High Commission court"; and that he called William Churchman, priest "fool, ass, and knave, for saying that those which loved not the church's long prayers were enemies of piety and robbed God of his honor, withal threatening to kick the said Churchman." Catesby also threatened to stone Churchman. Obviously so demonstrative an opponent of the Laudian regime exposed himself to ecclesiastical sanction (Catesby had given vent to his spleen in Ecton, Northamptonshire, to a priest from Banbury, Oxfordshire, to the parson of Alconbury, Huntingtonshire, and again in London), but had he been less vocal and public in expressing his views, or had he confined his expression of such views to a circle of Puritan friends, it is hard to see how he could have got in trouble.[85]

However, the real danger to the Laudian regime came not from such angry denunciations but from the patronage and support that, year in and year out, was given by the lay Puritan community to their godly preachers; it was this that hamstrung all attempts to force conformity on the clergy or to drive them out of the church, and it was this alliance that ultimately was to bring down the Laudian church in the 1640s. There was no mystery about it, and contemporaries were well aware of the potency of such a nexus. In 1629, in a letter to Viscount Dorchester, the principal secretary, Lionel Sharpe lamented "this difference between the king and the subjects, which do but mistake the king; discreet men cannot choose but fear the end of this difference." On the one hand, Sharpe proposed mobilizing the lord lieutenants and the "rave clergy" to "make known the excellent mind and nature of the king unto his people" and to disabuse them of their "false fears of innovation in religion and of taking from the subject their lawful liberties" – obviously no easy task in the aftermath of the Petition of Right campaign. "None," he continued, knew better "how to qualify this [Puritan] party than Queen Elizabeth":

It pleased her majesty to use this policy at such a time as this, when Martin Marprelate so violently played his part, as my Lord of Leicester and my Lord of Essex both vouchsafed to tell me for some purpose. The policy was this, that her Majesty, though she would have those Novelers to be liable to her ecclesiastical and common laws, ... yet because she then saw that her shires and corporations were so full of them, when the choice of knights and burgesses in Parliament was made, to temper and qualify that party, and either to win them wholly or in part unto herself, her Majesty was content to give way by connivance to

---

[85] PRO, SP, 16/375/82. Webster mistakenly assumes that Catesby was a priest. *Godly Clergy in Early Stuart England*, 230.

some great lord to take, as it were, the protection of the party, leaving the part of severity and injury to her bishops and judges to be extended against them, but the part of favor and lenity to the lord sometimes to obtain remission of the rigors and extremity of the law for them by his intercession, by which means her Majesty having still some in the Lower House of her counsel as Sir Francis Walsingham and Sir Walter Mildmay, who were thought to incline to them, was ever assured of a great party of that side in the House ... upon favor to be had either for themselves or their ministers that were quiet and painful men.

Sharpe went on to claim that Leicester and Essex successively played such a role as patrons of the godly and were first used to intercede on behalf of Cartwright, Fenner, and Fenn, and later Sir Richard Knightly, Travers, and others implicated in the winding up of the Marprelate and Presbyterian movements. Sharpe concluded by urging such a policy of "wise and religious moderation."[86] It was not, of course, a policy that either Charles I or William Laud were equipped by inclination or character to follow, but it does demonstrate that some realized where the ultimate support of the Puritan clergy lay.

In fact Laud realized that as well. When charged with the suppression of the Feoffees for Impropriations, that Puritan effort to buy impropriations in order to support a preaching clergy, Laud said that he "was clearly of the opinion that this was a cunning way under a glorious pretence, to overthrow the Church government by getting into their power more dependency of the clergy than the King and all the peers and all the bishops in all the kingdom had. And I did conceive the plot more dangerous for the fairness of the pretence."[87] However, while it was relatively easy to destroy the Feoffees on the grounds that they behaved like a corporation but lacked a charter, it was much more difficult to find grounds to block the fulfillment of individual bequests for similar purposes. In 1634, the vicar of St. Alkmond's parish in Shrewsbury complained that Roland Heylyn, born in that parish but late an alderman and ironmonger of London, had before his death purchased both the advowson of the parish and the impropriate tithes, which had been vested by Heylyn's London feoffees in a Shrewsbury resident, Richard Hunt, "a Puritan"; according to the aggrieved vicar, the income went to support "two Puritan preachers (nonconformists)" resident elsewhere. Now that Heylyn was dead, the Exchequer was disputing the ownership of the tithes, in consequence of which Hunt was simply retaining the income, which was intended to endow a lectureship at St. Alkmond's and not to augment the vicar's income. The vicar, who described himself as

---

[86] PRO, SP, 16/142/45.
[87] Laud, *History of the Troubles*, 372.

"always conformable," was "left to make the best he can of his poor living." It is not without significance that Heylyn had been until his death the presiding officer and treasurer of the Feoffees for Impropriations.[88] Exactly what remedy Thomas Lloyd, the vicar, expected is not clear, for, as he knew, there was nothing illegal about purchasing impropriations, the income of which then became the property of the purchaser, not the vicar.

At best the ecclesiastical authorities could block the licensing of a preacher so endowed or suspend one already installed, but such procedures, and even a royal fiat, could be subject to appeals and delays. To cite but one example, Secretary of State Windebank was informed in April of 1637 by Sir James Douglas of the "distracted estate of the church of Berwick," doubly dangerous in Douglas's estimation because of the constant intercourse of townsmen with the Scots. Berwick had been troubled by "a sect of those people we commonly call Puritans," for the better part of forty years. In addition, since 1631 the Mercers' Company of London had supplied an assistant lecturer to whom they paid a salary of £50 per annum, compared to the vicar's "scarce 20 marks," and because the bequest had been made "by a gentleman (now deceased) much addicted to these novel opinions," the mercers had appointed a Puritan preacher who pretended conformity, "as knowing he could not otherwise by law be admitted," but once admitted had shown his true colors. This lecturer, having obtained a better living elsewhere, had now been replaced by John Jemmet, who it was feared "must be a man of the same mind." Douglas suggested that either Laud himself, or the king, should deal directly with the mercers to block the appointment and to have the £50 conferred on Gilbert Dury, the conforming vicar.[89] The Crown did act, and in the following January the mercers wrote that, while they were quite willing to obey the royal wishes, they had granted Jemmet a lease of the tithes purchased to support his lectureship and, as a consequence, could only recover the tithe income by a legal process to break the lease.[90] When the king's party reached Berwick in

---

[88] PRO, SP, 16/278/117; Seaver, *Puritan Lectureships*, 91–2.

[89] PRO, SP, 16/352/13. For the Fishborne bequest, see Paul S. Seaver, "Laud and the Livery Companies," in *State, Sovereigns and Society*, ed. Charles Carlton (Stroud, 1998), 220–5. Jemmet's predecessor, Eusebius Hunt, had managed to lecture unmolested from 1631 to 1637; the Mercers had first attempted to install Jemmet in the parsonage of St. Michael Paternoster in the Royal, and it was only when that appointment was foiled that the company appointed him to the lectureship at Berwick.

[90] PRO, SP, 16/380/79. The Mercers' Company was not unique in employing such delaying tactics. When the bishop of Chester complained to the Haberdashers' Company about the nonconformist appointed to preach the Aldersey lecture at Bunbury, the company replied that they were at a loss, since the Aldersey bequest provided no

the summer of 1639, they found Jemmet still there and preaching; he was promptly removed by a command of the king, who ordered the Mercers' Company to replace him with George Sydeserffe, a safely royalist conformist. In February 1640, the company finally complied, but within the year the town petitioned the company to replace him with "a painful and profitable preacher," by which time neither Archbishop Laud nor King Charles was in a position to block such lay initiative.[91]

Lay bequests and livery company patronage were only the most conspicuous kinds of support that sustained clerical Puritanism in the early seventeenth century. Through a study of wills, Nicholas Tyacke has uncovered a rich and complex series of relationships between Puritan preachers and the London elite. For example, when a pair of London clerics set about the posthumous publication of a series of works by Paul Baynes, the Cambridge nonconformist, they dedicated the published volumes to Lady Rebecca Romney, widow of Alderman Sir William Romney; to Lady Mary Weld, widow of Alderman Sir Humphrey Weld; and to Alderman Sir Thomas Smith. Sir William Romney was the brother-in-law of William Charke, the Elizabethan nonconformist and the father of one of the editors; Lady Mary Weld left a sizable bequest, administered by the Haberdashers' Company, which, like William Fishborne's bequest to the mercers, was dedicated to the purchase of impropriations in order to endow Puritan preachers. Sir Thomas Smith was not only a neighbor of the Charkes in St. Dionis Backchurch but also apparently the patron of William Negus, an Essex nonconformist, and his son.[92] We are, as Tyacke aptly remarks, in the presence of the "London great and godly," and such examples could be multiplied. When William Priestley, merchant tailor, died in 1620, he remembered in his will Richard Stock, the Puritan parson of his parish of Allhallowes, Bread Street, and Ezechial Culverwell, a nonconformist suspended in 1609.[93] In his will of the same year, Richard Brooke, haberdasher, remembered his "friends" Stephen Egerton, Anthony Wotton, Ezechial Culverwell, Richard Stock, William Gouge, and John Vicars.[94] Much of such support was of course invisible to the authorities, if not to

---

mechanism for depriving the preacher of his income for nonconformity, and in fact the company continued to pay the lecturer's stipend until his death eleven years later. GL, MS 15, 84211, Haberdashers' Company, Court of Assistants Minutes, 1583–1652, fols. 154v, 207v, 256r, 257v.

[91] Seaver, "Laud and the Livery Companies," 225.

[92] Nicholas Tyacke, *The Fortunes of English Puritanism, 1603–1640* (London, 1989), 6–10; for Lady Mary Weld's bequest, see Seaver, "Laud and the Livery Companies," 227.

[93] *Abstract of Wills in the Prerogative Court of Canterbury . . . Register Soame, 1620*, ed. I. Henry Lea (Boston, 1904), 146–7; Seaver, *Puritan Lectureships*, 176–7.

[94] *Abstract of Wills*, 284–5.

the Puritan beneficiaries, but even had the authorities known about such wills, it is hard to imagine what they could have done about them.[95]

Much more serious from the point of view of the authorities were public displays of support, in part precisely because there was little that could be done about such demonstrations, and because they clearly encouraged others to act in defiance of the prevailing climate of repression. When Peter Smart launched a suit in common law against six of his fellow prebendaries at Durham in 1629, the case came before Judge Yelverton, not the jurist the embattled prebendaries would have chosen. When they complained in court that Smart had preached against the prescribed ceremonies, Sir Henry Yelverton remarked that he was "very sorry" to hear that the archbishop of York had publicly burned the offending sermon, for he had read it and "thought it to be a very good and honest sermon." The judge also rather gratuitously remarked that he never liked the sung service accompanied by organ music as practiced at Durham Cathedral, since the chanting, which he referred to as "whistling," prevented him from understanding the words of the service. He then added "that he had been always accounted a Puritan, and he thanked God for it, and that so he would die."[96] It was clearly not a statement that the Arminian prebendaries wanted to hear from the bench.

Yelverton, with all the arrogance of a judge, was outspoken about his ecclesiastical preferences, even though in the final analysis he conceded that such issues were matters for the ecclesiastical courts. Others by their mere presence could convey an equally vivid message. In June 1637, Samuel Clerke of Kingston informed Sir John Lambe that

Mr. [Charles] Chauncy, whom you lately corrected in the High Commission doth mend like sour ale in summer. He held a fast on Wednesday last and (as I am informed) he with another preached some 6 or 8 hours; the whole tribe of

---

[95] In 1635 both John White, parson of Holy Trinity, Dorchester, and John Stoughton, parson of St. Mary Aldermanbury, London, were investigated by the ecclesiastical authorities, who had learned that they were trustees for some monies left for pious uses, some sums of which were apparently intended to finance John Dury's ecumenical efforts, other sums for the purchase of impropriations, and further sums that were ostensibly portions due to Stoughton's stepchildren, the sons of Ralph Cudworth, the elder. Stoughton's study was sealed, and both he and White were examined before the High Commission, but in the end both were released, for although it was clear that Stoughton corresponded with both Puritans in Amsterdam and New England, neither he nor White had committed acts against the canons of the Church; see PRO, SP, 16/297/39, 16/300/2, 16/301/4, 16/302/63; PRO, *Calendar of State Papers, Domestic 1635–36*, 109, 116, 125, 470, 478, 503, 513 (Acts of the Court of High Commission, 12 November 1635 to 12 May 1636).

[96] PRO, SP, 16/147/15. Richard Sibbes position as lecturer at Gray's Inn was apparently owed to Sir Henry Yelverton. Tyacke, *The Fortunes of English Puritanism*, 11.

God did flock thither, some threescore from Northampton; the Lord Saye with his Lady did honor them with their presence.

The fast ended with a prayer that "God would deliver his servants from persecution," apparently with Burton, Bastwick, and Prynne in mind. Clerke asked Lambe to inform Laud of these events, but it is difficult to see what Laud could do that would counteract the countenancing of such a fast and such a nonconformist by Lord Saye and Sele.[97] The following winter, when Stanley Gower, the rector of Brampton Bryan, Hereford, was articled against for a whole catalogue of nonconformist practices, the bill of particulars ended with the sobering observation that "all these passages are countenanced and upholden by Sir Robert Harley, Knight of the Bath, patron to Mr. Gower, who is lord of almost all the parish and causeth every year his own servants or tenants at the least to be churchwardens." Harley also maintained a schoolmaster, Richard Symonds, "who instructs the youth with fearful doctrine," and Symonds, it was noted, was a suspended priest driven out of North Wales, then out of Shrewsbury, and finally to Brampton Bryan "where he is entertained as in a sanctuary." Gower had been presented in 1634 and had obviously escaped notice hitherto because the churchwardens refused to present him; he evidently survived being articled against in 1638, for he was still at his rectory a year later. There was little that could be done against the wishes of so powerful a patron.[98]

This was, after all, a society in which the lay elite still exercised real power and influence, a fact that no one doubted. When Dr. John Stoughton, the curate and lecturer of St. Mary, Aldermanbury (the parish of Sir Robert Harley's London residence), was arrested in 1635 and his study ransacked for incriminating evidence, it should have spelled the end of his London career. But, as John Rous, the Suffolk parson, noted laconically in his diary, within two or three days "he returned with credit in the Earl of Holland's coach."[99] No one doubted the message implied by that courtier's conveyance. However, much of the opposition to the Laudian regime came from lay Puritans of much less social stature, but it was no less disturbingly potent for all of that.[100]

---

[97] PRO, SP, 16/361/67.

[98] PRO, SP, 16/381/92. Gower had been chaplain to James Ussher, the archbishop of Armagh, and it was undoubtedly Ussher, an old friend of Harley's, who secured Gower the recommendation to the knight. Jacqueline Eales, *Puritans and Roundheads: The Harleys of Brampton Bryan and the Outbreak of the English Civil War* (Cambridge, 1990), 56–7.

[99] *The Diary of John Rous*, ed. M.A.E. Green, *Camden Society*, ser. 1, vol. 66 (London, 1856), 79; for Harley's residence in Aldermanbury, see Seaver, *Puritan Lectureships*, 50–1.

[100] Towns with a significant Puritan presence could also provide havens for Puritan ministers right through the Laudian years. See, for example, John Fielding, "Opposition to

In the late spring of 1634, John Andrewes, the parson of Beaconsfield, wrote to the chancellor of the diocese of Lincoln asking him to intervene with Laud to release Andrewes from the obligation to preach at the upcoming metropolitical visitation, for although he was "contented to shew mine obedience in the performing thereof," he knew that the sermon would not be well received. He was, he said, not in "any wise inclining to Puritanism, wherewith the greatest number (both of the priests and people) in these parts are (if not deeply infected yet) foully tainted, insomuch that he is counted the most godly, who can, and will be, most disobedient to the orders and laws of the Church." Andrewes claimed that this was not just supposition on his part, for he had preached at a visitation two years since, for which he had received "small thanks," for "because I pressed them to obedience and the sworn men to discharge their oaths conscionably and justly, all their mouths were open against me, and they exclaimed that I preached only to bring money to the (as they called it scornfully) Bawdy Court, when, God knows, mine only aim was obedience to his Majesty's ecclesiastical laws." A year later he reported to Sir John Lambe a conversation he had had with a local justice of the peace of Berkshire, who had asked whether the orders enjoined at the metropolitical visitation were truly meant to be observed. "I told him they were seriously intended. Truly, Sir (said he), then there is great abuse committed, for, I dare assure you, neither clergymen nor laymen (if they be gentlemen, or men of any wealth) do keep them, but laugh and jeer at them."[101]

By the 1630s, the regime, while winning individual battles against particular Puritan ministers, was nevertheless losing the war of public support. The kind of unthinking loyalty the Crown and Church should have commanded was seriously eroded, and, while the Puritans may have been, as Keith Lindley insists, a "zealous minority,"[102] in parts of the country the authorities could no longer count on the automatic support of the majority. There were straws in the wind. In late 1630 in London, an informant wrote that it was worth considering "the speech and opinion of the people, and they may be ranked into three sorts that I have conversed with: [Alexander] Leighton's faction, the Puritan

---

the Personal Rule of Charles I: The Diary of Robert Woodford, 1637–1641," *Historical Journal* 31.4 (1988): 774–5.

[101] PRO, SP, 16/269/36; SP, 16/286.

[102] Lindley almost always refers to Puritans as zealots, the zealous Protestant minority, the overzealous minority, or some variant: *Popular Politics and Religion in Civil War London* (Aldershot, 1997), 36–91, and elsewhere. We assume that the Puritans were a minority, zealous or otherwise, but no one has succeeded in ascertaining their numbers in London or anywhere else.

faction, and the Protestants at large (as some term them). Now for the common multitude, they rejoice at his [Leighton's] escape and are glad, saying, it was long of the bishops he had that cruel censure, because he writ a book against them to the Parliament." The informant went on to note that "not one in a thousand dislikes him for it."[103] In early 1632, Samuel Collins, the minister at Braintree in Essex, wrote an agonizing letter to Dr. Duck, complaining that a recent reprimand from Laud had renewed his "disease of the colic and stone," for he found himself caught between a bishop determined on complete obedience and conformity and a parish "that hath been disorderly these fifty years" and who remained convinced that Collins could obtain (or wink at) a toleration of their irregular practices. "If I had suddenly and hastily fallen upon the strict practice of conformity, I had undone myself and broken the town to pieces. For upon the first notice of alteration many were resolving to go to New England, others to remove elsewhere, by whose departure the burden of the poor and charges of the town had grown unsupportable to those [that] should have stayed behind." As a consequence, he "was subject to his Lordship's censure above and here beneath to the hatred and obstreperous clamors of the people."[104] Collins's position was indeed untenable, and he would shortly be pleading to be relieved of his Braintree living.

By 1637 the evidence of disaffection must have been palpable. A newsletter writer noted that following the punishment by Star Chamber of Burton, Bastwick, and Prynne, "the minister of Shoreditch, observing the humors of the people so much to compassionate these three delinquents, should deliver in his sermon that they all incurred damnation, which thought well of those three who had been justly punished for their demerits." Laud could not have put it more succinctly. However, the newsletter writer went on to say that "this doctrine made divers go out of the church, for the common people are extremely compassionate towards them."[105]

In the same year Dr. Nathaniel Nicholas wrote to his brother, Edward Nicholas, that he "performed the divine service of the Sunday at Wherwell in my hood and surplice, which were taken among certain refractory men for the marks of the beast, and my calling upon the communicants to come up into the chancel to receive drove many out of the church." He went on to say that he "did not think there had been a congregation in Hampshire so refractory to good order," but he blamed the

[103] PRO, SP, 16/175/63.
[104] PRO, SP, 16/210/41.
[105] PRO, SP, 16/363/42.

parishioners' lack of respect for the Laudian service on the vicar, "who doth not only himself connive at their unconformity, but is himself so inclined."[106] A year later it was reported by Samuel Clerk, one of Laud's adherents, that at All Saints, Northampton, some of the parishioners had taken down the altar rails and returned the communion table to the chancel. When he had suggested to the mayor and his brethren that the Thursday lecture and Sunday afternoon sermons "should be forborne in these infectious and dangerous times," his parishioners "then raised a report that I went about to starve their souls." "Schismatical Puritans" were everywhere: The churchwardens of Towcester were "questioned for not presenting some 80 or a 100 of their parish, who refused to receive the blessed sacrament" at the rail at Easter, and at Pattishal a Mrs. Clerk was in trouble "for calling the divine service porridge and the long Puritan sermons roast meat."[107]

Since all this evidence comes from the state papers, it is hard to imagine that the government was ignorant of its mounting unpopularity. Rather than a Church triumphant, the evidence from the 1630s suggests an institution coming apart at the seams. Granted that Archbishop Laud had driven a number of Puritan clergy into exile, either to the Netherlands or New England, but only at the cost of alienating their supporters and sympathizers among the laity, and the laity was largely beyond the reach of his disciplinary machinery. As for the rest, he had succeeded neither in forcing conformity nor in suppressing dissidence. Despite mounting evidence of failure, the archbishop soldiered on until his imprisonment during the opening weeks of the Long Parliament put an end to his futile labors. A conversation reported to have taken place almost two years earlier might have served as a warning that the game was about over. A party of men from Newcastle and Gateshead were drinking wine and discussing "the Scottish business." One, Ralph Fewler, said that "in his opinion... the Scottish Covenanters were no way to be accused, for they did nothing but in defense of their own right and maintenance of the Gospel, and did but defend themselves against those that would have brought in popery and idolatry amongst them, and that for his part he thought he should not fight against them in that quarrel." When asked "whether if the king should command him to fight,... he would refuse it or not," the argument being that it was "sufficient for him to obey his prince without any further examination of the cause of the quarrel," the said Fewler replied, "No, for unless his own conscience moved him to it, he would not fight for the command of

[106] PRO, SP, 16/352/29.
[107] PRO, SP, 16/393/15.

any prince in Christendom."[108] By the late 1630s, after several decades in which Crown and Church had striven to create an unaccustomed uniformity in the Church and to force the clergy to conform and the laity to obey, the regime had succeeded instead in creating, for all its unlovely narrowness, the Puritan personality, prepared to respond not to command but to conscience, a people disciplined not for conformity, but for the coming revolution.

[108] PRO, SP, 16/413/42.

## PART III

# The social articulation of belief

# CHAPTER IX

# False miracles and unattested dead bodies: Investigations into popular cults in early modern Russia[1]

## EVE LEVIN

THE *Spiritual Regulation* of 1721 embodied Peter the Great's blueprint for the perestroika of the Russian Orthodox Church. Among its many provisions outlining the public purposes of religion and establishing a new administrative structure for the Church, the *Spiritual Regulation* expressed concern for the problem of "superstitious practices": wandering holy fools, *klikushki* (hysterical women), improbable versions of saints' lives, false reports of miracles from icons, and bogus relics. The *Spiritual Regulation* charged Church authorities – parish priests, local bishops, and its new central ruling body – with investigating such inappropriate popular religious observances and stamping them out. Specifically, the new edict dictated that priests inform the appropriate ecclesiastical and secular authorities if "someone imagined in some way a false miracle, or contrived it hypocritically, and then broadcast it so that the simple and unreasoning people take it for the truth." Bishops, for their part, were to report to the Ecclesiastical College (or, as it was renamed almost immediately, the "Most Holy Governing Synod") twice annually about the state of their eparchies, including instances of "false miracles from

[1] The author acknowledges the institutional support of the International Research and Exchanges Board (IREX), the Summer Research Laboratory in Slavic Studies of the University of Illinois, and the Hilandar Research Library of Ohio State University. The author also appreciates the stimulating comments on an earlier version of this essay by the participants in the conference on "State Religion and Folk Belief" held at the University of Minnesota, May 1–3, 1998, and the members of the Early Modern Seminar at Ohio State University at their meeting on November 13, 1998. In addition, the author is particularly grateful to Febe Armanios, Nicholas Breyfogle, Carole Fink, David Hoffman, Nadieszda Kizenko, Geoffrey Parker, Tricia Starks, and Ernest Zitser for their advice and comments.

holy icons" and "unattested dead bodies" – that is, the relics of unofficial saints. After receiving such reports, the Synod then had the obligation to launch formal investigations of all such "apparitions" and "miracles." Offenders would be subject not only to ecclesiastical penalties, but also to severe civil ones.[2]

Scholars of the Petrine reforms have not previously tried to trace the methods the Russian Church hierarchy used to regulate popular religion.[3] They have largely accepted the hierarchs' derogatory opinion concerning the faith and practice of the laity, although they could not wholeheartedly endorse Peter's despotic solutions.[4] Although in the traditional historiography Peter is depicted as the great "Tsar-Transformer" who dragged a backward and obscurantist Russia into the modern world through the force of his own overbearing personality, the current generation of specialists has revised this view somewhat. They point out significant seventeenth-century precedents to Peter's reforms, and the collaboration of members of the Russian elite in the design and implementation of his program. But few scholars would dispute the alterations Peter wrought in Russian society. He recast the government in accordance with Western European models; he modernized the military in structure and technology; he harnessed the productive energies of all social groups; and he inculcated Western secular cultural styles among

---

[2] *Spiritual Regulation*, Part II, arts. 1, 3, 6–9; "On Bishops," arts. 8, 17, subsection 15; Part III, art. 4; P.V. Verkhovskoi, *Uchrezhdenie Dukhovnoi kollegii I Dukhovnyi Reglament*, 2 vols. (Rostov-na-Donu, 1916; repr., 1972), here, 2: 34–6, 40, 50–1, 73, 87. For a modern English translation, see *The Spiritual Regulation of Peter the Great*, trans. and ed. Alexander V. Muller (Seattle, 1972), 13–15, 19–20, 30, 52, 62–3. Except where indicated, all translations are mine.

[3] An exception is Gregory Freeze, "The Rechristianization of Russia: The Church and Popular Religion, 1750–1850," *Studia Slavica Findlandensia* 7 (1990): 101–36.

[4] On reform in the Russian Church in this period, the most authoritative works in English are James Cracraft, *The Church Reform of Peter the Great* (Stanford, 1971) and Gregory L. Freeze, *The Russian Levites: Parish Clergy in the Eighteenth Century* (Cambridge, MA, 1977). See also T.V. Barsov, *Sviateishii synod v. ego proshlom* (St. Petersburg, 1896); T.V. Barsov, *Sinodal'nyia uchrezhdeniia prezhniago vremeni* (St. Petersburg, 1897); Georges Bissonnette, "Pufendorf and the Church Reforms of Peter the Great," Ph.D. dissertation (Columbia University, 1962), 248, 283; Muller, *Spiritual Regulation*, xxviii–xxxviii; Alexander V. Muller, "Historical Antecedents of the Petrine Ecclesiastical Reform," Ph.D. dissertation (University of Washington, 1973), 376–82; V.M. Nichik, *Feofan Prokopovich* (Moscow, 1977), 6–8, 119–29; Hugh Y. Reyburn, *The Story of the Russian Church* (London, 1924), 184–8; S.G. Runkevich, *Istoriia russkoi tserkvi pod upravleniem sviateishago sinoda*: vol. 1. *Uchrezhdenie I pervonachal'noe ustroistvo sviateishago pravitel'stuvuiiushchego sinoda (1721–1725gg)* (St. Petersburg, 1900), 293; Iu. F. Samarin, *Stefan Iavorskii I Feofan Prokopovich*, Sochineniia Iu. F. Samarina, vol. 5 (Moscow, 1880), 391–2; N. Tal'berg, *Istoriia Russkoi Tserkvi* (Jordanville, NY, 1959), 538–55; B.V. Titlinov, *Pravitel'stvo imperatritsy Anny Ioannovny v ego otnosheniiakh k dielam pravoslavnoi tserkvi* (Vilna, 1905), 73–7, 459–66; Verkhovskoi, *Uchrezhdenie Dukhovnoi kollegii*, 1: 46–60, 108–13, 374–82, 400–1.

the elite. Utility and rationality replaced Muscovite tradition as the justification for laws, governmental procedures, and policies. In order to transform Russia into a world power, Peter used coercive measures, ruthlessly suppressing dissent and establishing a system of government investigators, called *fiskaly*, to check into the proper conduct of officials and nonofficials alike. The Russia that resulted from Peter's reforms resembled the absolutist states of Western Europe in its priorities and character.[5]

Peter's reform of the Russian Orthodox Church should be understood in the context of his other endeavors. He feared that a strong-willed patriarch at the head of the Church could stymie his policies and threaten his authority. Consequently, he allowed the office to remain vacant after Patriarch Adrian died in 1700. Doubtless the experience of his father, Tsar Aleksei, was instructive. His patriarch of the 1650s, Nikon, authored numerous reforms to improve clerical discipline and enforce conformity in rituals. Although Aleksei approved wholeheartedly of Nikon's innovations, he rejected Nikon's papal-like claims to superior authority over the tsar. The same church councils of 1666 and 1667 that deposed Nikon also mandated obedience to his reforms. Although Nikon's innovations involved no alteration in theology and relatively minor changes in observances – especially compared to the Protestant Reformation in Western Europe, or the Puritan Revolution in England – they generated strong resistance. Old Believers, as they came to be labeled, believed Nikon's reforms to signify the imminence of the Apocalypse. They spurned the changes and defied the arrogant ecclesiastical and secular authorities who sought to compel compliance.[6] Thus Peter envisioned two threats from the religious realm: from alienated believers who conceived of the tsar as the Antichrist incarnate, and from Church hierarchs who might try to claim preeminence over the autocrat.

---

[5] On the reforms of Peter the Great, see Evgenii V. Anisimov, *The Reforms of Peter the Great* (Armonk, NY, 1993); Vasili Klyuchevsky, *Peter the Great* (Boston, 1958); James Cracraft, ed., *Peter the Great Transforms Russia* (Lexington, MA, 1991); Marc Raeff, *The Well-Ordered Police State* (New Haven, CT, 1983), esp. pt. 3; John P. LeDonne, *Absolutism and the Ruling Class* (New York, 1991), esp. chs. 1, 3, 8–9.

[6] For more information on Old Believers, see Chapter 2 in this volume by Robert O. Crummey, as well as his monograph *The Old Believers and the World of Antichrist* (Madison, 1970) and his article "Old Belief as Popular Religion: New Approaches," *Slavic Review* 52 (1993): 700–12. See also, Michael Cherniavsky, "The Old Believers and the New Religion," in *The Structure of Russian History*, ed. Cherniavsky (New York, 1970), 140–88; and the articles by Georg Michels – "The Solovki Uprising: Religion and Revolt in Northern Russia," *Russian Review* 51 (1992): 1–15, and "The First Old Believers in Tradition and Historical Reality," *Jahrbücher für Geschichte Osteuropas* 41 (1993): 481–508 – and his *At War with the Church: Realities of Religious Dissent in Seventeenth-Century Russia* (Stanford, CA, 2000).

But in fact, most high-ranking churchmen of Tsar Aleksei's day and Peter's did not share Patriarch Nikon's overweening ambition. Far from challenging the tsar's power and his platform of Westernization, they reinforced them. The Petrine era witnessed the culmination in a long trend toward Westernization within the ranks of the Russian Orthodox hierarchs. From the time of Patriarch Nikon, the Russian Church imported many of its most influential churchmen from the newly annexed territories of the eastern Ukraine. Unlike their Muscovite counterparts, these Ukrainian clerics received a Western education, the better to compete with the skilled propagandists fielded by the Roman Catholic and Protestant churches of the Polish-Lithuanian Commonwealth.[7] They were trained in Biblical exegesis, patristics, canon law, and rhetoric. They knew Latin and Greek – some better than others – and they were familiar with the classics that formed the basis of Western education, although for some it was a rather sketchy familiarity.[8] Many had studied in Jesuit academies in the guise of Uniates, only to abjure their conversions to Catholicism and return to their Ukrainian homeland, from whence they were recruited into Muscovite service. By the end of the seventeenth century, virtually all the bishops and abbots of major monasteries were Ukrainian, and they also directed the new seminaries established in Russia for the training of clergy. Thus the cultural rift between the Westernized elite and the traditional-minded peasantry that plagued Russia from the mid-eighteenth century on first appeared between elite clerics and the ordinary Christian believers of the parishes.

Along with their Western educations, the ecclesiastical elite had imbibed Western attitudes about the nature of sanctity, about church organization, and about Russia itself. They could not but be aware of the drive to clarify religious doctrine – to separate true faith from superstitious practice – that so occupied the agendas of Western religious leaders. They knew, also, the importance of a disciplined organization in establishing conformity to right practice, and the necessity of gaining the backing of secular authorities for their program.[9] Unlike their native Russian predecessors, they were not inclined to see Russia as the "Third

---

[7] For more information on Eastern Orthodoxy in seventeenth-century Ukraine, see, Chapter 6 in this volume by Frank Sysyn; William K. Medin and Christos G. Patrinellis, *Renaissance Influences and Religious Reforms in Russia* (Geneva, 1971); Igor Ševčenko, "The Many Worlds of Peter Mohyla," *Harvard Ukrainian Studies* 6 (1982): 119–51.

[8] On these Ukrainians' education and a sobering assessment of their influence on Russian culture, see Max J. Okenfuss, *The Rise and Fall of Latin Humanism in Early Modern Russia* (Leiden, 1995), and a briefer but more positive assessment in Okenfuss, "The Jesuit Origins of Petrine Education," in *The Eighteenth Century in Russia*, ed. J.G. Garrard (Oxford, 1973), 106–30.

[9] For examples of the Western European experience, see Chapter 8 by Paul Seaver and Chapter 4 by Caroline Litzenberger, both in this volume.

Rome" and the "New Israel," the one true heir to pristine Christianity and its defender against Western heresy.[10] Instead, the Ukrainian hierarchs saw Russia's deficiencies: a superstitious laity ministered to by unlettered parish priests, and a church institution that was ineffectively structured and incompetently administered.

As the *Spiritual Regulation* indicates, the popular cults of icons and saints disquieted elite churchmen of Peter's day. From the perspective of Orthodox tradition, it is surprising that they regarded these cults with suspicion because for centuries the Eastern churches had not only tolerated the veneration of icons and relics, but had mandated it.[11] Both icons and relics were not only physical reminders of the saints who had departed from this world but lived still in heaven; they also were the conduits of sacred power. Icons in particular were windows into heaven, sharing with the figure depicted that saint's holy essence and miracle-working power. By the sixteenth century, if not before, icons were found not only in Russian churches but also in most Christian homes, no matter how humble their circumstances. Although all icons, by their very nature, had spiritual power, a few gained reputations for special miracle working. They likewise became the centers of cults, quite apart from the figures they depicted, and themselves became the subjects of icons.[12] Although most early miracles in the Russian setting concerned the protection of whole communities, by the late sixteenth century, most miracles performed by the saints aided individuals who turned to them "with true faith" in time of need.

The number of new saints and miracle-working icons grew rapidly in sixteenth- and seventeenth-century Russia, demonstrating Muscovy's status as the divinely protected bastion of true Orthodoxy. Muscovite tsars and churchmen alike deemed these relics to have practical value in treating epidemics and repelling invaders. While Russians readily recognized as authentic the fragments of bone and hair that constituted relics of the saints in the former Byzantine Empire and Western Europe, they preferred their own saints to manifest complete, uncorrupted bodies.[13] Patriarch Nectarius of Jerusalem voiced a similar preference in 1680,

---

[10] On this traditional view, see Daniel Rowland, "Moscow – The Third Rome or the New Israel," *Russian Review* 55 (1996): 591–614.

[11] On relics, see Otto Meinardus, "A Study of the Relics of the Saints of the Greek Orthodox Church," *Oriens Christianus* 54 (1970): 130–278; on icons, see Michel Quenot, *The Icon: Window on the Kingdom* (Crestwood, NY, 1991).

[12] Engelina Smirnov, "Iconography of Icon Worship in Medieval Russian Art: 15th–16th c.," lecture at Ohio State University, November 12, 1997.

[13] Gail Lenhoff, "The Notion of 'Uncorrupted Relics' in Early Russian Culture," in *Christianity and the Eastern Slavs*, vol. 1, Boris Gasparov and Olga Raevsky-Hughes, eds. California Slavic Studies, vol. 16 (Berkeley, 1993), 252–75; Eve Levin, "From Corpse to Cult in Early Modern Russia," forthcoming.

when he listed the uncorrupted state of the relics, or at least the emission of an ineffable aroma of sanctity from their bones, as an essential characteristic of sanctity, along with miracle working and a life of irreproachable Orthodoxy. He recognized that the standard of incorruptibility was a new one, required, he said, by the frequency of the falsification of miracles and invention of biographies.[14] As we shall see, Russian hierarchs of the eighteenth century continued to focus on these three characteristics, although they did not require all of them in every case.

The Eastern Orthodox Church did not establish the same fixed, unified standard for canonization that the Roman Catholic Church did in the later Middle Ages.[15] Instead canon law and tradition empowered every bishop to authorize veneration of local saints within his eparchy without requiring that the national church, much less all of the Eastern Orthodox oecumene, recognize them. In the absence of standardized rules for what constituted proof of sanctity, individual churches and even individual bishops could make their own decisions.

In pre-Petrine Russia, the canonization procedures were not regularized at all. The cults of many saints grew up in provincial monasteries or parish churches, outside the purview even of the local bishop. Only decades later did the devotees of the cult, who included the local clergy and a cross section of the lay community, seek recognition from central authorities, either the patriarch of Moscow or the tsar. Often the petitions for recognition came at a time when the community was planning to build a new church to house the relics, or to upgrade the old one; the petitioners hoped to secure not only approval, but also a donation. But the reason usually given in the pious tales that constitute the primary record of successful cases is spiritual: The saint's manifestation of God's glory should not be hidden "under a bushel" as written in the Gospel of Matthew 5:15, but rather should become known to all believers. The phrase "under a bushel" – in Slavonic, *pod spudom* – came to signify not only that the saint had not yet received wide publicity, but also, more concretely, that the relics were not yet unearthed and placed on public display. When the relics remained *pod spudom*, their incorruptibility could not be verified, but the saints' post mortem miracles readily served as a basis for their cults.

---

[14] E. Golubinskii, *Istoriia kanonizatsii sviatykh v russkoi tserkvi* (Moscow, 1903; repr., Westmead, UK, 1969), 28.

[15] The only comprehensive study of canonization in Russia is Golubinskii's *Istoriia kanonizatsii sviatykh v russkoi tservki*. For a summary in French based heavily on Golubinskii, see Paulus Peteers, "La Canonisation des saints dans l'eglise Russe," *Analecta Bollandiana* 33 (1914): 380–420. Paul Bushkovitch has demonstrated that Golubinskii's study is seriously flawed: See his *Religion and Society in Russia: The Sixteenth and Seventeenth Centuries* (New York, 1992), 74–99.

As part of the approval process, sponsors of the cult produced descriptions of the saints' accomplishments, in life and after death, which might or might not take the form of a formal *vita* and miracle cycle. In response to their petition, the patriarch might initiate an inquest, which would involve interviewing the recipients of miracles, but surviving records suggest that he rarely did. The exhumation of the relics and their transfer to a new site constituted, in effect, the formal canonization. But transfers of relics were sometimes accomplished without any authorization from higher ecclesiastical authorities, and some relics were never transferred from the original burial sites. Cults could gain widespread acceptance in the absence of any verification whatsoever from the higher authorities of church and state.

Two examples of canonization in the seventeenth century – both with echoes in the eighteenth century – will suffice to show the flexibility in procedure and criteria for sanctity. Both cases are atypical in that documentation of the process of canonization exists – something that is not true in the cases of most Russian saints.

Ioann and Loggin Iarenskie were unlikely candidates for official recognition because nothing whatsoever was known about their earthly life. According to legend, they had been victims of shipwreck. Their bodies, reputedly uncorrupted, lay in the village church in Iarenga already in the late sixteenth century. In addition to the local clergy and laity, the pre-eminent Solovetskii monastery patronized the cult. In 1624, the village elder of Iarenga petitioned Tsar Michael and Patriarch Filaret (son and father) to transfer the relics to a new church. They ordered an inquest, and over eighty people, both men and women, testified to the saints' thaumaturgic powers. Ultimately, in 1639, permission was granted.[16] But when Abbot Varfolomei of the Solovetskii monastery came to officiate at the transfer of the relics, he found St. Ioann's relics to be substantially whole, but St. Loggin's remains to be decayed and mixed with dust. He ordered Loggin's grave refilled, and proceeded with the translation of St. Ioann. But the devotees of the saints, including several of his own monks, begged him to reconsider. Varfolomei relented, reopened Loggin's tomb, and discovered there an ineffable aroma – probably the result of his censing of the remains the previous day! In any case, he was satisfied, and proceeded with the canonization.[17]

Like Ioann and Loggin, Sts. Vassian and Iona Unskie had no known earthly existence. Their bodies gained a reputation for working miracles,

---

[16] Russian National Library, St. Petersburg [henceforth RNB], Solovetskoe sobranie 182/182, fols. 120–41v.
[17] Hilandar Research Library, Ohio State University [henceforth HRL], Saratov State University Collection [henceforth SGU], 1344, ff. 62–3.

and the Pertominskii monastery, located on the coast of White Sea, was built over the graves containing their supposedly uncorrupted remains. The monks apparently had never sought official recognition, despite the monastery's frequent fiscal crises, until God, or fate, played into their hands. In 1694, the young Peter the Great took refuge from a storm at the Pertominskii monastery. The monks offered hospitality to the tsar and his entourage, which included Archbishop Afanasii of Kholmogory, crediting their escape from imminent shipwreck to the local miracle workers, Vassian and Iona. Then the monks decided to take advantage of the presence of the tsar to seek formal recognition of their saints. Reluctant to carry out the tsar's and monks' wish, Archbishop Afanasii insisted upon examining the relics, and the scene, as recorded in a miracle tale from the monastery, was awkward. One body was thoroughly decayed; the second tomb proved empty. Despite this disappointing outcome, Afanasii yielded to the desire of the tsar, his entourage, and the monks and pronounced the relics to be "holy." Peter himself built a wooden cross, inscribed in Dutch, to commemorate his miraculous rescue and adorn the saints' tomb.[18]

In both of these instances, two of the three essential characteristics of sanctity Patriarch Nestorius had outlined were missing. None of the four saints were known to have led godly lives, and none of their relics were totally uncorrupted. They gained recognition as saints on the strength of record of miracle working, as testified to by living persons.

From everything we know of Peter the Great, he was an unlikely candidate for the role of witness to saints' miracles. While he believed in Divine Providence and the social value of moral education, he advocated the secularization of Russian society. He also coveted the Church's property, which could be used to finance his expensive military ventures. It is hard to imagine the adult Peter, who issued the *Spiritual Regulation* and numerous decrees in the same vein, agreeing to canonize the questionable Pertominskii saints. It is likely, as James Cracraft argues, that Peter's experience with Western religious thought, still in the future in 1694, altered his perception of Russian Orthodoxy. Certainly he based his vision of the restructuring of the Russian Church on Western European Protestant models. And certainly he became apprehensive about the image the Russian Orthodox Church projected to Western Europeans.[19]

---

[18] RNB, Solovetskoe sobranie 182/182, fols. 181–200.

[19] On Peter's religious sentiments, see Cracraft, *Church Reform*, vii–x, 1–28, 130–1; and Lewitter, "Peter the Great's Attitude Towards Religion: From Traditional Piety to Rational Theology," in *Russia and the World of the Eighteenth Century*, eds. R.P. Bartlett, A.G. Cross, and Karen Rasmussen (Columbus, OH, 1988), 62–77; Verkhovskoi, *Uchrezhdenie*

Peter's heirs shared his perspective to a greater or lesser degree. His immediate successors, his widow Catherine I and his grandson Peter II, left decision making largely to favorite advisers and thus continued Peter's policies. Most like Peter in his hostility toward superstition and religious dissent and in his concern for Western opinion was his niece Anna, who ruled from 1730 to 1740.[20] Peter's daughter Elizabeth, who seized the throne from her infant cousin in 1741, backed her father's reforms in general but was deeply religious personally. She largely left government offices, including that of the Synod, to conduct their business in her name (and subject to her approval). She took an interest in saints and relics, going on pilgrimages to visit their sites. Also, she respected her churchmen's guidance on proper Christian policy, as manifested in her abolition of the death penalty.[21]

While the ruler's personal attitude toward religion was certainly influential, it was churchmen who designed and carried out ecclesiastical policies of the Petrine and post-Petrine era.[22] These included Dimitrii Tuptalo, bishop of Rostov and author of new, approved versions of saints' lives; Stefan Iavorskii, Peter's reluctant appointee to oversee the affairs of the vacant patriarchal see and later the first president of the Synod; Feodosii Ianovskii, archbishop of Novgorod and first vice president of the Synod; Gedeon Vishnevskii, an associate of Iavorskii and bishop of Smolensk; and Feofan Prokopovich the ghostwriter of his *Spiritual Regulation* and the dominant churchman in both Peter's and Anna's reigns.[23] All of these churchmen, all of them Ukrainian, shared the perception that the Russian Church needed reformation, and thus found common cause with Peter.

They did not find common cause with each other. Scholars have identified a major rift between what they called "Catholic-oriented" and "Protestant-oriented" reform-minded Russian Orthodox clergy. Stefan Iavorskii exemplified the former; Feofan Prokopovich, the latter. The

---

*Dukhovnoi kollegii,* 1: 46–60; Bissonnette, "Pufendorf and the Church Reforms of Peter the Great."

[20] Mina Curtiss, *A Forgotten Empress: Anna Ivanovna and Her Era, 1730–1740* (New York, 1974), 130–42; Philip Longworth, *The Three Empresses: Catherine I, Anne and Elizabeth of Russia* (New York, 1972), 109.

[21] On Elizabeth and her reign, see Longworth, *The Three Empresses,* 155–229; Aleksandr B. Kamenskii, *The Russian Empire in the Eighteenth Century: Searching for a Place in the World* (Armonk, NY, 1997), 165–93; Cyril Bryner, "The Issue of Capital Punishment in the Reign of Elizabeth Petrovna," *Russian Review* 49 (1990): 389–416.

[22] Gregory L. Freeze, "Handmaiden of the State? The Church in Imperial Russia Reconsidered," *Journal of Ecclesiastical History* 36 (1985): 82–102.

[23] Tal'berg, *Istoriia Russkoi Tserkvi,* 533–53; Cracraft, *Church Reform,* 49–62, 120–6, 164–73; Cracraft, "Feofan Prokopovich," in *The Eighteenth Century in Russia,* 75–105.

labels have some basis in fact, and not only because the principals involved used them to attack each other. Stefan Iavorskii indeed modeled his construction of Russian Orthodoxy on Catholicism, as his tract
*Kamen' viery* ["Rock of Faith"], a defense of Orthodoxy against Protestant
criticism, demonstrates. Feofan Prokopovich made no attempt to hide
his antipathy for Catholicism and his sympathy for German Pietism. But
the differences between the two were as much political as theological.
Although Peter valued both men, they and the other hierarchs of their
time discerned the extent to which their positions – bishops of major
sees, abbots of leading monasteries, and seats on the Synod – depended
upon the monarch's favor. Few of their number were above accusing
their fellows not only of blasphemy and apostasy but also of embezzle-
ment and treason against the crown. In the grim atmosphere of court
politics that followed Peter's death, Feofan Prokopovich found himself
under arrest, the victim of rival advisers to Empress Catherine I and
Emperor Peter II. When the throne was offered to Peter's niece Anna in
1730, Feofan Prokopovich had an opportunity to return to power. Once
again the most prominent religious adviser to the throne, Prokopovich
used his position to eliminate his enemies. Although Prokopovich died
in 1736, his influence in the Synod lingered in the churchmen whose
appointments he arranged. While they espoused views similar to his
concerning the church's institutional structure and mission, they did so
with less vituperation, having seen the effects of public denunciations.[24]

The veneration of icons and relics was one, but only one, of the issues
high-ranking churchmen used to attack their rivals. For example, Stefan
Iavorskii and Gedeon Vishnevskii opposed Feofan Prokopovich's appointment as Bishop of Pskov in 1718 on the grounds of his "Protestant"
inclinations, citing Prokopovich's scepticism about relics. Prokopovich
was forced to clarify his views in writing in order to win Iavorskii's
reluctant acquiescence. Iavorskii's own views about the veneration of
icons, as he expounded them in his *Kamen' viery*, came into question;
Peter the Great himself instructed Iavorskii to add clarification, lest
"simple folk" misunderstand.[25] Markell Rodyshevskii, Prokopovich's
former protégé and the mouthpiece of his enemies during the reign of
Catherine I, accused his patron of "iconoclasm" and the denigrating veneration of the saints, as evidenced by his calls to investigate "suspicious"
relics, whose sanctity (in Rodyshevskii's view) had been demonstrated

---

[24] Cracraft, *Church Reform*, 130–5, 162–74; I. Chistovich, *Feofan Prokopovich i ego vremia*
(St. Petersburg, 1868); Tal'berg, *Istoriia Russkoi Tserkvi*, 533–41, 551–71; Verkhovskoi,
*Uchrezhdenie Dukhovnoi kollegii*, 1: xxvii–xxxviii.
[25] Cracraft, *Church Reform*, 131–2, 133–5.

beyond question. In his own defense, Prokopovich averred his adherence to the rulings of the church councils and the positions espoused by Peter the Great, arguing that he opposed only ignorant and idolatrous worship of icons and saints prevalent among uneducated Russians. He numbered Rodyshevskii (although a Ukrainian) among them, stating, "I can say truthfully that if he ate bread as often as he read books, in three or four days he would not exist any more."[26] Rodyshevskii clearly exaggerated his accusations against Prokopovich for political gain. Although Prokopovich undeniably assailed "superstitious" veneration of icons and relics, he reaffirmed their validity for Orthodox worship, and himself authored a tract defending the miraculous preservation of the sainted monks of the Kievan Caves monastery, intended primarily for an audience with a Latin education.[27] He and the other members of the Synod reacted with great concern to reports of the theft of a sacred relic, the robe of Christ, held in the Cathedral of the Assumption in the Kremlin. They launched a full investigation, having the robe itself examined under a magnifying glass and the staff of the cathedral interrogated.[28]

Perhaps the political sensitivity of the issue explains why the Synod did not follow up immediately upon the instructions in the *Spiritual Regulation* to launch a full investigation into the cults of supposedly miracle-working icons and relics. More likely, Synod members simply did not have the time or energy to spare from the more immediate work of reorganizing the church hierarchy, implementing the seminary education of clergy, establishing the church's sphere of autonomy vis-à-vis the state, and battling among themselves. For all the bitterness of

[26] Chistovich, *Feofan Prokopovich*, 211; for a more general survey of the dispute between Rodyshevskii and Prokopovich, see pp. 154–9, 195–222, 232–9, 297–334; Tal'berg, *Istoriia Russkoi Tserkvi*, 557–8; Titlinov, *Pravitel'stvo imperatritsy Anny Ioannovny*, 86–8; Verkhovskoi, *Uchrezhdenie Dukhovnoi kollegii*, 1: xxvii–xxx. For the text of Markell Rodyshevskii's critique of Feofan Prokopovich, see Verkhovskoi, *Uchrezhdenie Dukhovnoi kollegii*, 2: 85–154, esp. arts. 32 and 33, 132–4.

[27] Verkhovskoi, *Uchrezhdenie Dukhovnoi kollegii*, 1: 116–41. Nichik, in his *Feofan Prokopovich*, depicts Prokopovich as a supreme rationalist and forerunner of Marxist materialism, 37–9, 126–9. For a text of Prokopovich's tract on the Kievan Caves saints, see Russian State Archive of Ancient Acts, Moscow [henceforth RGADA], F. 357 Rukopisnoe sobranie Sarovskkoi pustyni, op. 1, No. 274, *Razsuzhdenie o netlienii moshei ugodnikov bozhijkh v Kievskikh peshcherakh netlienno pochivaiushchikh*, manuscript of the late eighteenth century. James Cracraft identifies the Russian text as a translation of Prokopovich's Latin original; see "Feofan Prokopovich: a Bibliography of His Works," *Oxford Slavonic Papers*, n.s. 8 (1975): 27–8.

[28] No. 2710, *Polnoe sobranie vostanovlenii I rasporiazhenii po viedomstvu pravoslavnago ispoviedaniia Rossiiskoi Imperii*, 19 vols. (St. Petersburg/Petrograd, 1869–1915) [henceforth PSVR], here, ser. 1, vol. 8, 65–75; No. 2837, *PSVR*, ser. 1, vol. 8, 282–95. In 1745, the Synod issued new rules for safekeeping the relics: No. 907, *PSVR*, ser. 2, vol. 2, 410–11.

their recriminations, Russian hierarchs agreed in principle: Veneration of icons and relics was proper and orthodox, but it too often turned into idolatry among the ignorant, who included both clergy and laypeople. But distinguishing in specific cases between religion and superstition proved to be a delicate matter, especially in the atmosphere of political hostilities that marked the Russian Church of the 1720s and 1730s.[29]

One of the first cases to come to the Synod, in March 1721, turned out to be a clear-cut instance of falsification of miracles. The previous August, a scribe in the Iamskaia Novinskaia suburb of Novgorod, Vasilii Evfimov, claimed to have experienced wondrous visions connected with the copy of the famous Tikhvin icon of the Mother of God held in his church. In one vision, he saw a fiery chariot in the heavens and local notables gathered to pay homage to the icon. Knocked unconscious by the vision, he awoke to find the church alight with candles and aromatic from incense – the classic traits of an apparition from an icon.[30] He brought witnesses to see the miracle, and wrote and distributed an account of it. The church became the locus of pilgrimages and pious donations. When Feodosii Ianovskii, first vice president of the Synod and archbishop of Novgorod, got wind of the "miracle," he became suspicious, and rightly so. Under interrogation, Evfimov admitted to faking the apparition, and the investigators were able to identify where he purchased the aromatic spirits and how he obtained the key to the church. Evfimov's purpose in staging the miracle, he said, was to collect funds for the maintenance of the church. He had felt guilty about the ruse, though, and had confessed it to his priest during Lent. The priest considered the sin to be minor and imposed a mild penance. The Synod disagreed. It found Evfimov guilty of blasphemy, theft, and deceiving the public and turned him over to the civil authorities for execution "so that nobody will carry out such lies against God and his saints and icons." He was burned at the stake in front of the church containing the icon as an object lesson to the populace he had deceived. His priest, who had violated the imperial decree to report crimes heard in confession, was defrocked. Feofan Prokopovich was the first signatory on the order.[31]

---

[29] Ecclesiastical politics similarly complicated the identification of "improper" practices in early modern England and France. See, for example, B. Robert Kreiser, *Miracles, Convulsions, and Ecclesiastical Politics in Early Eighteenth-Century Paris* (Princeton, 1978).

[30] For a variety of examples of tales of apparitions, see Library of the Academy of Sciences, St. Petersburg [henceforth BAN], 38.4.40. For a contemporaneous example of this literature in a version by Karion Istomin, a prominent Ukrainian clerical scholar of the early Petrine era, see RNB, Sofiiskoe sobranoe, No. 1369.

[31] Russian State Historical Archive, St. Petersburg [henceforth RGIA], F. 796 Kantselariia Sinoda, op. 1, No. 306; No. 225, *PSVR*, ser. 1, vol. 1, 243–4.

Given this early experience with a deliberate deception, the Synod of the 1720s was not inclined to grant credence to further reports of miracles. Another case arose in 1722, involving one Ignatii, a monk in Serpukhov. He claimed to have received a vision of "some so-called saint Zakharii," and then healed people with an icon of this saint and some earth from his tomb. The Synod ruled that this was a case of "clear superstition" and a "fraudulent miracle," but Ignatii refused to recant. He was turned over to the civil authorities for punishment.[32]

The Synod also suspected falsification in the case of Agafia Miakisheva's miracle-working icon. Agafia, the wife of a printer in the Synodal office, claimed that an icon in her home, a copy of the famous Vladimir Mother of God, was shedding tears. She also claimed that she received a vision of the Mother of God surrounded by haloed maidens, who promised to heal her illness. She brought a number of people to witness the miracle, including her husband, her in-laws, and several neighbors; and, as instructed by the Mother of God, she told her parish priest. The priest, who was also a Synod "inquisitor" (the title given to ecclesiastical *fiskaly*), reported the incident, and an investigation ensued. The witnesses provided differing accounts. Agafia's mother-in-law confirmed her statement. Her husband saw moisture in the icon's eyes one day and flowing tears the next; he witnessed Agafia's collapse at the time she claimed to have had the vision. But her father-in-law denied seeing anything more than "condensation resembling tears." Three neighbors – a woman, a soldier, and an eleven-year-old boy – all said they saw a little moisture in the icon's eyes. The government clerk's wife who was interviewed last, perhaps sensing the tenor of the investigation, denied seeing anything and said that she had hurried away to the evening church service. An examination of the icon itself revealed that the linen towel protecting it was damp. The Synod took this as evidence of a fraud, perpetrated by Agafia and her mother-in-law. As further evidence of her guilt, the Synod noted that Agafia came from Ustiuzhen Zhelezopolskii, "where, it is heard, many *klikushki* and superstitious activities originate." The two women were turned over to the civil authorities for punishment.[33]

When noblewomen of the Voznesenskii convent in Moscow reported similar miraculous experiences from an icon, their statements were granted no more credence than those of their humbly born sisters. In 1721, when the investigation began, the cult surrounding a copy of the Kazan icon of the Mother of God had existed for two decades. Its chief

[32] No. 612, *PSVR* ser. 1, vol. 2, 272–3.
[33] No. 1488, *PSVR* ser. 1, vol. 5, 23–5.

promoter was the nun Princess Ioanna Boriatinskaia. She had arranged, in 1711, to have a small church built to house the icon, seeking the assistance of the tsar's sister to gain the necessary permissions (new church construction was severely regulated). She kept a notebook of miracles performed by the icon, totaling thirty-two. The icon's first miracle was its own rescue: In 1701, when the church that then housed it burned down, the icon carried itself out to safety. The icon became known for healing, and the recipients of its benefits included not only nuns of the convent but also prominent aristocratic ladies, including Princess Agrafena Khovanskaia. Perhaps it was the icon's reputation for healing *klikushki* that raised the Synod's suspicions. Or perhaps the suspicions were politically motivated; the Boriatinskii and Khovanskii clans had long been under suspicion, and by 1722, the tsar's sister was no longer alive to protect them. The records do not indicate who reported the cult, or why.[34]

When the Synod's investigators looked into the icon's supposed miracles, they heard conflicting testimony. Ioanna Boriatinskaia stood by most of what was recorded in her book of miracles, repudiating only the icon's miraculous rescue of itself. She averred that she had written that "out of ignorance"; in fact, what she had been told was that it was unknown who had rescued the icon. Of the four clergy who had been present at Princess Khovanskaia's home on the occasion of her healing, only one was willing to confirm it; the other three denied they had ever been there. One of them, the sexton Sava Fedorov, claimed that he had written an account of this and other supposed miracles on the nun Boriatinskaia's orders and only because she threatened him. One *klikushka* who had received healing, the nun Margarita, was more ambivalent in her testimony. She said that before taking vows she had suffered from fits of screaming (*klikushi*) and "great sadness" for three years, and had sought healing from the icon, but with no success. Since entering the convent, however, she did not scream any more. She did continue to pray for healing to the icon, but she admitted that she still suffered from melancholy. She stated that she had not told Princess Boriatinskaia to record a miracle. Several other women who suffered from "sorrow" and "heartache" gave unequivocal endorsements of the icon's healing powers. But the leadership of the convent – the father-confessor Paramon Grigoriev, the abbess Venedikta Pushkina, and the cellaress Olga Chirikova – refused to back up Ioanna Boriatinskaia. They denied any knowledge of healings, even secondhand, and stated

---

[34] I am grateful to Ernest Zitser for making this point to me.

that they had no need of the little church in which the icon was kept. Ultimately, the Synod ruled that Ioanna's book of miracles was written "not without fraudulence," and the little church "exceeded [the number of] churches needed by this convent and was built in an inconvenient place." It ordered that the church be razed, and the icon be removed to another church, where it be placed inside the altar, a location off limits to women.[35] Although this was done, eventually the icon was returned to the Voznesenskii convent, where it regained its reputation for working miracles.[36]

The cult of the icon of the Savior of Krasnobor was even better established when it came under scrutiny in 1723. It dated back to 1641, when women began to report apparitions of Jesus and Mary in the presence of the icon, which ordered them to carry messages to the populace: to avoid brawling, alcohol, and tobacco and to observe fasts and holidays. By the early eighteenth century, the icon was famous, with nearly 120 miracles of visions and healings to its name.[37] Thus it was not surprising that Pimin Volkov, a lay servitor of the Sestrinskii monastery, had a vision of the Savior telling him to go on pilgrimage to the Krasnobor icon. Pimin had injured his hand while hammering a stake. His son, Vasilii, had been suffering from a sore throat for six days, so he decided to go, too. Vasilii's wife, Maremiana, wished to give thanks for her recovery from a difficult delivery in childbed. At Krasnobor, the Volkov family paid the clergy to read prayers on their behalf.

It is unclear how the Solovetskii archdeacon and Synod inquisitor Aleksandr Tikhanov learned of the Volkovs, but he was dubious of Pimin's claim to a vision. Tikhanov also found the Krasnobor cult itself suspicious: The instructions from the Savior's icon sounded too much like Old Believer rhetoric, especially in its condemnation of tobacco. Tikhanov duly reported to Archbishop Varnava of Kholmogory and the Synod, who ordered Varnava to place the Volkovs and the Krasnobor priest Danilo under arrest. Varnava complied but declined to send them to St. Petersburg for interrogation as ordered, citing the winter cold and the prisoners' lack of proper clothing. Later on, he decided to release first Vasilii and Maremiana, and later Pimin, because their poverty left them without money to buy food. Come Lent, he yielded to Danilo's pleas that his parishioners needed him to administer the sacraments,

---

[35] RGIA, F. 796, op. 3, No. 839.
[36] E. Poselianin, *Bogomater': Polnoe illiustrirovannoe opisanie eia zemnoi zhizni I posvishchennykh eia imeni chudotvornykh ikon* (St. Petersburg, n.d.), 438–9.
[37] RNB, Solovetskoe sobranie No. 661/719 is a record of the icon's miracles.

and sent him back to Krasnobor. Varnava argued to the Synod that the four had erred merely because of their "simplicity," and had not violated the *Spiritual Regulation*'s prohibition on broadcasting false miracles. The Synod did not adopt as tolerant a view of the case. It ordered the Volkovs and Danilo to be rearrested, discounting both Pimin's vision and the Krasnobor icon's record of miracles. But ultimately the Synod was lenient, at least in comparison with its treatment of Vasilii Evfimov two years earlier. Pimen was ordered to recant publicly "so that nobody will have any doubt about this in the future." He complied. The clergy of Krasnobor were prohibited from perpetuating "seeming miracles out of superstitious ignorance."[38]

Archbishop Varnava was involved in another case of a questionable cult. In 1722, the Synod issued two orders to him: first, to remove "tombs revered as holy objects" and those with lifelike effigies that "common people ... in their ignorance ... confuse with holy bodies themselves"; and second, to raze unauthorized chapels in his diocese. In the case of the chapel dedicated to St. Varlaam Keretskii, Bishop Varnava had qualms. According to his *vita*, St. Varlaam had murdered his wife at the devil's instigation, and then settled in Keret as a monk after scaring away the eels. The cult had a long history in the region, and four written post mortem miracles were attributed to him. Varnava's investigators brought back conflicting reports on the status of the relics. A monastic priest of the Solovetskii monastery, which owned the village, stated that the body was dressed in monastic garb and resembled ordinary bones. The village priest, in contrast, testified that the body wore a black Russian caftan, the head and beard were entirely intact, and the relics exuded an ineffable aroma. The village priest and his deacon remarked that it was an emanation, but the monastic investigator said it was only steam. Based on this testimony, the archbishop ruled in favor of the cult, and authorized commemoration. His decision is surprising, given not only the state of the relics but Varlaam's dubious claims to a holy life. It was only some five years later that Varnava got around to sending the documentation of the cult to St. Petersburg. Perhaps he was waiting for a change in the mood of the Synod; in 1727, Feofan Prokopovich and his Protestantizing colleagues needed to demonstrate that they did, indeed, show proper devotion to relics. In any case, the Synod recognized that the evidence concerning Varlaam Keretskii was mixed, and ruled if people wanted to commemorate Varlaam, it was "not forbidden." However, Archbishop Varnava was to question under oath any persons

[38] RGIA, F. 796, op. 5, No. 375.

claiming to experience miracles and to require three witnesses to their honesty.[39]

Archbishop Varnava of Kholmogory was not the only prelate who dissented from the Synod's zeal in pursuing superstition cases. Bishop Gedeon Vishnevskii of Smolensk actually promoted a new cult of the sort Feofan Prokopovich and the reformers of the Synod despised. The cult began in November 1730, when Matfei Shukeevich, the Polish Catholic servant of Prince Drutskii-Sokolinskii, reported a vision. As he wrote in an account soon after, he fell ill while on an errand for his master at the Synod. He attributed his illness to an "evil thought": "Why is it that before now there were miracles from icons, such as we read about in books, how the blind could see, the lame walk, the sick regain health; and now such things are never heard of? I don't know if it ever was the truth." In his illness, his patron saint, Matthew, appeared to him, and instructed him to make a pilgrimage to the icon of the Mother of God in the village of Shelbitsy. He had never heard of such an icon, he averred, although previously he had venerated icons at Czestochowa and elsewhere. But St. Matthew assured him, "you may find a miracle in every icon, when God wills it." The Synod ordered medical examinations for Shukeevich; doctors confirmed that he was partially paralyzed and unable to talk but could not identify the cause of his illness. As he wrote to Feofan Prokopovich in his capacity as a member of the Synod, if he "could receive even a small part of his health," he promised to convert to Orthodoxy and serve the empress the rest of his life. He begged the Synod to pay for his transportation to Shelbitsy. The Synod did not entertain Shukeevich's request. Instead, it released him to his master, apparently regarding his delusion about a nonexistent icon to be harmless.[40]

Shukeevich's delusion, however, became reality. Two months later, Prince Drutskii-Sokolinskii had enough sympathy for his ailing servant to bring him along on a trip to the Smolensk district and arranged lodging for him in the village of Shelbitsy. Shukeevich's landlord there, Iakov Azancheev, possessed an icon of the Mother of God, as did so many Orthodox believers, and from it Shukeevich received the healing he sought. News of the miracle spread, reaching Bishop Gedeon Vishnevskii. As he reported to the Synod, he acted in accordance with the decree of February 21, 1722, which ordered the removal of miracle-working icons from private homes to cathedral churches or monasteries,

---

[39] Golubinskii, *Istoriia kanonizatsii sviatykh v russkoi tserkvi*, 451–3; No. 1968, *PSVR*, ser. 1, vol. 6, 17–21.

[40] No. 2492, *PSVR*, ser. 1, vol. 7, 362–7. The quotations are on pp. 362 and 364.

where their cults could be overseen. So Vishnevskii moved the icon from the Azancheev home and set it up for veneration in the Smolensk Cathedral of the Assumption, satisfied that its miracle was genuine.

Feofan Prokopovich was not satisfied. He had every reason not to trust Vishnevskii's judgment. The two were old rivals, dating back to their days at the Kiev Academy, and Vishnevskii had joined Stefan Iavorskii and Markell Rodyshevskii in turn in attacking him.[41] The matter, Prokopovich advised the Synod pompously, "is not so unimportant and easy as His Grace indicated at first, but, in [my] opinion, contains some not insignificant secret lawbreaking, for the confusion of the Russian Church."[42] The icon had an inscription in Polish rather than Slavonic, and in general was drawn "in the manner of the Roman superstition." That made it unsuitable for Orthodox observances. It was Prokopovich who dictated Empress Anna's decree on the matter, ordering the arrest of Shukeevich and his witnesses. The icon was to be shipped to St. Petersburg, and Vishnevskii was ordered to explain why he had authorized veneration without approval from the Synod. Still Vishnevskii resisted. Seven months later, the icon remained on display in the Smolensk cathedral; the Synod had to remind him to remove it.[43]

Although the Synod, especially under Feofan Prokopovich's ascendancy, may have wanted to suppress "superstitious" cults of icons and relics, it had to depend upon the cooperation of local bishops, not only to close them down, but even to find out about them. The *Spiritual Regulation* required bishops to report suspicious religious practices in their semiannual reports, but they did so only sporadically. In an attempt to force bishops to make a comprehensive survey of unauthorized religious observances, it issued such a decree in 1737, soon after Feofan Prokopovich's death. The ukase would have met with his approval. It ordered bishops to investigate "false miracles," "all sorts of shameful customs involving holy icons," "unattested dead bodies . . . revered as the true, holy relics of saints," "hysterical women and sham holy fools." The hierarchs were to instruct their ecclesiastical supervisors and *fiskaly* to watch carefully for any such incidents and report them assiduously to their bishops. Bishops for their part were required to respond, "that very hour . . . without any delay," arranging an interrogation of the suspects and involving secular authorities when appropriate. But apparently the

---

[41] Chistovich, *Feofan Prokopovich*, 154–9, 332; Tal'berg, *Istoriia Russkoi Tserkvi*, 538–41, 562–6; Verkhovskoi, *Uchrezhdenie Dukhovnoi kollegii*, 1: 437–9.

[42] No. 2492, *PSVR*, ser. 1, vol. 7, 366.

[43] Nos. 2492, 2568, *PSVR*, ser. 1, vol. 7, 362–7, 474.

Synod made little effort to follow up on this order, other than collecting the appropriate extracts from bishops' reports as they trickled in over the next five years and responding to them individually. Most bishops simply reported no problems.[44]

The next full-scale investigation did not occur until December 1744, after the accession of the more pious Empress Elizabeth. She had to reconstitute the Synod because nearly all the seats were vacant owing to deaths and arrests. The new appointees, wary of repeating the pattern of denunciation that had decimated their predecessors, voiced their agenda in a less hostile manner. Two new members of the Synod, Archbishop Platon of Krutitsy and Archbishop Arsenii of Pereiaslavl', drafted the 1744 decree, and it differed from its 1737 antecedent in both scope and intent. Hierarchs, including both bishops and abbots of major monasteries, were directed to investigate specifically relics on display – *"ne pod spudom,"* literally "not under a bushel" – that had not received proper attestation as to their sanctity. The hierarchs were to report back to the Synod on the following particulars: where such relics were located; when and on whose orders they were unearthed and placed on display; what the physical state of the bodies was; and what apparitions and miraculous healings were attributed to them. The reports were to be accompanied by exact copies of all supporting documentation for the cults, and they were to be sent "without any omission and as soon as possible."[45]

The change in tone is marked, compared to similar earlier decrees from the reign of Empress Anna. A decree from July 11, 1739, for example, directed Bishop Savva of Archangel to identify instances when "unattested dead bodies were revered as saints," when these cults originated, who these figures were, and what "imaginary and false miracles" were attributed to them.[46] The 1744 decree, in contrast, referred to the remains as "relics" *(moshchi)* rather than "dead bodies" *(mertvye tielesa)*, thus granting the possibility that the cults under scrutiny might be those of real saints who had not yet received proper verification, rather than mere fabrication or superstition. But if the goal was not so much to close down cults as to separate "real" saints from "fictitious" ones, the

---

[44] RGIA, F. 834, op. 2, No. 1701. The text of the decree is included on fols. 1–2v. For a brief discussion of this decree, see Golubinskii, *Istoriia kanonizatsii sviatykh v russkoi tserkvi*, 439–40.

[45] RGIA, F. 796 Kantselariia Sinoda, op. 25, No. 723, fols. 3–3v. For a published version of the text and a brief, but inexact, discussion of the investigation, see Golubinskii, *Istoriia kanonizatsii sviatykh v russkoi tserkvi*, 441–6. The text of the decree is also published in No. 788, *PSVR*, ser. 2, vol. 2, 289.

[46] No. 3436, *PSVR*, ser. 1, vol. 10, 272.

method of investigation owed its inspiration to its precedents in the previous reign.

The decree was sent to thirty-two bishops and abbots of major monasteries, as well as to the Moscow Synodal Office to be forwarded to monasteries within its domain. Unlike in previous inquests, the leaders of the 1744 investigation kept careful records of responses at the time (although some of the documentation was lost or misfiled before the archival compendium was assembled in the 1770s). Ultimately all but three hierarchs responded to the order, and the dioceses of two of the delinquents, Archbishop Amvrosii of Novgorod and Archbishop Iosif of Moscow, were covered in the reports of other prelates. But most hierarchs did not reply promptly. Eleven months after the original decree was issued, on November 18, 1745, the Synod voted to send the delinquents a stern reminder. They were warned that failure to comply with orders of the Synod carried stiff penalties: a fine of a hundred rubles for the first month's delay, twice as much for the second month, and so on to the fifth month. After that, criminal penalties would be imposed, consisting of removal from office and hard labor at the galleys.[47]

That second order generated a flurry of responses, consisting of excuses for earlier noncompliance. Archimandrite Trifillii of the Khutynskii monastery in Novgorod replied that he had already sent in his report to the Novgorod consistory to be forwarded on to the Synod.[48] Archimandrite Ioasaf of the Troitskii-Sergiev monastery blamed the diocesan staff for being slow in conveying the orders. His report stated that there were no unattested relics at the monastery, but an earlier version, still visible under the erasure, indicated otherwise.[49] Archimandrite Luka of the Troitskii monastery in Smolensk similarly blamed diocesan personnel: One senile official had failed to send the instructions, and the other members of the staff did realize that he failed to fulfill his duties.[50] Bishop Pimen of Vologda explained his failure to respond earlier as a result of the fact that the documents about relics from past years had to come from the consistory archive, and they were short-staffed there.[51] Bishop Simon of Pskov passed both the original request and the reminder on to his consistory, and did not even report personally,

[47] RGIA, F. 796, op. 25, No. 723, fols. 4–10, 81–8.
[48] RGIA, F. 796, op. 25, No. 723, fol. 97.
[49] RGIA, F. 796, op. 25, No. 723, fol. 103–4. Although I cannot be sure, I think that Ioasaf's report originally made reference to the case of Fedor Starodubskii, discussed later, which fell under the jurisdiction of the diocese of Suzdal, although the village where the body lay belonged to the monastery.
[50] RGIA, F. 796, op. 25, No. 723, fol. 107–8.
[51] RGIA, F. 796, op. 25, No. 723, fols. 110–110v.

leaving the task to his archdeacon.[52] Bishop Feofilakt of Voronezh waited until he received notice of a fine for tardiness and then wrote that his report was "in the mail"![53] The strangest cases of delinquency involved the members of the Synod themselves. Bishop Silvestr of Kostroma sent a letter from St. Petersburg dated November 23, excusing his failure to comply by stating that he had been away from his diocese and had just received the original instructions.[54] Archbishop Arsenii of Rostov's sketchy first report did no more than acknowledge receipt of the order, so he was sent a stern reprimand warning of the penalties for non-compliance. Within days he responded with a full report, listing eight cases of suspicious relics. Doubtless he had the information close to hand; his predecessor had already reported those cases to the Synod in response to the 1737 decree.[55] The last reports trickled in during June 1746.

It is not surprising that the hierarchs were loath to carry out the Synod's order; gathering the information required a great deal of work and some savvy inferences about the Synod's intentions. Eight prelates simply reported back that they did not find any unattested relics in their domains.[56] But when Bishop Simon of Suzdal, one of the first hierarchs to respond, laid claim to no unattested relics, he was lying; the disputed relics of Fedor Starodubskii lay in his diocese, as Synod officials reminded him some months later.[57]

Fedor Starodubskii was the local saint in the village of Aleksino, which belonged to the Troitskii-Sergiev monastery. The cult had been scrutinized several times previously. In 1722, in the wake of the promulgation of the *Spiritual Regulation*, a representative of the monastery had confiscated the icon of St. Fedor and the village church's list of miracles, and Bishop Varlaam of Suzdal had forbidden Father Leontii, the village priest, from commemorating him. But in 1729 Father Leontii successfully petitioned Bishop Varlaam's successor for the return of the church's icon. In 1740 a representative of the monastery returned the list of miracles to the church and put up a railing to protect the spot where St. Fedor was buried, in effect marking a shrine to him. But in 1743, the Synod ordered another investigation. Father Leontii was the primary informant

---

52  RGIA, F. 796, op. 25, No. 723, fol. 96.
53  RGIA, F. 796, op. 25, No. 723, fols. 139–139v.
54  RGIA, F. 796, op. 25, No. 723, fols. 95–95v.
55  RGIA, F. 796, op. 25, No. 723, fols. 86v–87, 112–113v; RGIA, F. 834, op. 2, No. 1701, fols. 8–10.
56  Golubinskii, *Istoriia kanonizatsii sviatykh v russkoi tserkvi*, 443, asserts mistakenly that only one hierarch admitted to having an "unattested dead body" in his domain.
57  RGIA, F. 796, op. 25, No. 723, fols. 55–55v, 117–117v.

about St. Fedor; he had learned about him from his father, a deacon, and his grandmother, whose husband had once been the village priest. According to this oral tradition, Fedor was a Russian prince martyred by the Tatar khan Uzbek. Through divine intervention, his body ended up at his estate in Aleksino, where it worked miracles, although none had occurred in Father Leontii's time.

Such testimony did not satisfy Bishop Simon of Suzdal. He found that none of the miracles could be confirmed because none of the recipients of healing was still alive. There was no convincing evidence that Prince Fedor was even buried in that church, and Bishop Simon thought it highly unlikely, because the village had never belonged to him. Bishop Simon dismissed Father Leontii's account: "[it is] from his grandmother's words, and they are hardly worthy of belief." The phrase "grandmother's words" contained a double-entendre: It also meant "old wives' tale." Bishop Simon reported to the Synod that the cult had been suppressed.[58]

The cults that Bishop Pimen of Vologda reported as suspicious were better established and better documented than that of Fedor Starodubskii. St. Martinian had been a monk at the prominent Ferapontov monastery, and the abbot could provide good documentation about him. Although in 1744 his relics were *pod spudom* and not on display, when his body originally had been uncovered in 1514 "not only was his honorable body whole and preserved healthy, but even his clothing in which he was buried was whole." The water that flowed from his tomb was credited with miracles, and a stone church had been built over his relics.[59] It is difficult to see why Bishop Pimen regarded St. Martinian as dubious, and he did not seem to intend the report to elicit from the Synod an order to terminate veneration. Technically, he did not even need to report this cult because the body was not visible. Perhaps Bishop Pimen interpreted the order as one to report any saints whose cults were in some way peculiar. Bishop Simon of Pskov seems to have read the Synod's order that way; he listed two well-established saints, Prince Vsevolod-Gavriil and Prince Dovmont, along with lesser-known ones.[60] In any case, veneration of St. Martinian continued, and he was included in an official dictionary of saints published in 1836.[61]

[58] RGIA, F. 796, op. 25, No. 723, fols. 72–3, 117–117v, 558–561v.
[59] RGIA, F. 796, op. 25, No. 723, fols. 139–44.
[60] RGIA, F. 796, op. 25, No. 723, fols. 412–13.
[61] *Slovar' istoricheskii o sviatykh proslavlennykh v Rossiiskoi tserkvi I o niekotorykh podvizhnikakh blagochestiia miestno chtimykh* (St. Petersburg, 1836), 177–8.

Bishop Pimen's second suspicious case involved St. Ignatii, founder of the Spaskaia-Lomovskaia monastery. St. Ignatii had first come under scrutiny in 1687. At that time, the cult was already well established at the monastery and in the neighboring lay parish. The saint's relics then lay *pod spudom*, but a little church dedicated to him had been built over his tomb. The cult first came to the attention of Archbishop Gavriil of Vologda when the parish priest complained to him that St. Ignatii's relics had been removed from their accustomed spot. While the priest just wanted to get St. Ignatii restored to his proper place, Archbishop Gavriil had a different agenda. His investigators found the tomb in its accustomed spot; Prior Makarii of the monastery explained that he had simply moved it temporarily in order to replace the floor of the church. But when the investigators opened the tomb, they found it empty. At that point Makarii had to confess that he had removed the relics, which consisted of a skull and bones rather than an uncorrupted body, to a safe spot behind the altar, fearing the investigation. The struggle between Archbishop Gavriil and Prior Makarii got ugly; the archbishop threatened Makarii's brothers in order to try to coerce testimony from them. Based on Gavriil's self-serving report, Patriarch Ioakim ordered the cult of St. Ignatii suppressed. His remains were to be reburied in their previous spot, and the ground there leveled. The decorative tomb cover was confiscated, "so there would be no temptation for simple people from it." The church over the tomb, which had never been properly consecrated, was sealed. Prior Makarii was shipped off to another monastery under arrest.[62]

Despite Archbishop Gavriil's efforts and Patriarch Ioakim's ruling at the end of the seventeenth century, the cult of St. Ignatii survived. Soon after, the new prior, Savvatii, petitioned Archbishop Gavriil for permission to consecrate Ignatii's church to the martyr Ignatius and to restore the founder's tomb. Although he was not successful at that time, in 1710, Savvatii tried again with the new archbishop, Iosif, claiming that the monastery desperately needed the church since the others there had burned down. Permission was granted. When Bishop Pimen investigated in 1745, the cult was in full operation. The monks then at the monastery and the priest of the local parish disavowed any knowledge of previous prohibitions on veneration of St. Ignatii; they had been there only since 1731. Only an elderly peasant man could provide any information; he recalled that a previous abbot had reestablished veneration, but he did not know on whose orders. Bishop Pimen's

---

[62] RGIA, F. 796, op. 25, No. 723, fols. 144v–147.

inspector found Ignatii's tomb empty, and nobody knew where his remains were. As Pimen reported to the Synod, he once again confiscated the items relating to the cult and sealed up the church, which was unneeded in his view because the monastery had others.[63] But still the cult of St. Ignatii survived; his relics reappeared and were transferred to another monastery after Spaskaia-Lomovskaia was closed down in 1764.[64]

When Bishop Silvestr of Kostroma finally got around to sending in his report to the Synod in April 1746, he also boasted of suppressing unauthorized cults of saints about whom nothing was known, not even their names. He ordered their graves leveled and confiscated their icons. But fearing that Old Believers would then label him an "iconoclast," he had the icons repainted with the names of authentic saints, and returned them to their places.[65] In this way, Silvestr tried to satisfy both the Synod and the local community of believers by recasting a suspect cult as a respectable one.

Concern about Old Belief also motivated Archbishop Mitrofan of Tver in his suppression of the cult of Vladimir and Agripena Rzhevskie. The princely couple had long been venerated in Assumption cathedral of the city of Rzhev. Nobody could say when or why veneration began. Archbishop Mitrofan's inspector Varlaam, who was archimandrite of a local monastery and a member of the Tver consistory, warned about the presence of schismatics in Rzhev who adhered to the cult, with the connivance of local clergy. Consequently, he arranged for the inquest to be public, summoning two other prominent churchmen, the governor, and many local officials to attend. When the graves were excavated, they revealed several levels of decayed corpses, the bottom of which were identified as Vladimir and Agripena. Archbishop Mitrofan forbade further veneration and ordered that icons of the supposed saints be collected not only from churches, but also from private homes.[66]

Other hierarchs had a different perspective on the Synod's ukase to investigate relics *pod spudom*, regarding it not as an order to suppress unofficial cults but rather as an opportunity to gain official recognition for local miracle workers. Bishop Amvrosii of Chernigov tried to make a case for approving the veneration of Feodosii Uglitskii, a prior archbishop of Chernigov who had died in 1696. He testified that upon

---

[63] RGIA, F. 796, op. 25. No. 723, fols. 139–40, 144v–52, 191–9v.

[64] *Slovar' istoricheskii o sviatykh*, 116.

[65] Golubinskii, *Istoriia kanonizatsii sviatykh v russkoi tserkvi*, 445–6.

[66] RGIA, F. 796, op. 25, No. 723, fols. 122–122v, 611–13v; Golubinskii, *Istoriia kanonizatsii sviatykh v russkoi tserkvi*, 454–9.

personal examination he found Feodosii's relics to be substantially intact: "the hair on the head and beard are a little flattened from dust, and only the nose is in the smallest part corrupted, and two toes and a small part of the left leg up to the knee are in the smallest part corrupted." Bishop Amvrosii admitted that Feodosii's miracles were not recorded in writing, although some monks of the Chernigov Cathedral of Sts. Boris and Gleb knew about them.[67] Perhaps Bishop Amvrosii did not know that even that small level of bodily decay sufficed to serve as an excuse to decanonize St. Anna Kashinskaia in 1677, when her cult was deemed dangerous because of its attraction to Old Believers.[68] St. Feodosii eventually gained official recognition in 1896.[69]

The abbot and monks of the Kozmin monastery made the best case they could for the sanctity of their founder, Kozma Iakhrinskii. As they told the investigator Savvatii, the archmandrite of another monastery in Vladimir district, they did not know for sure whether St. Kozma's relics truly lay at the spot venerated as his grave, and they did not know whether there had been any testimony to their state of preservation. Nor could they produce any listing of miracles or even a *vita* or prayer service because they had previously handed them over to the Synod's inquisitor. However, they could document that the cult had previously gained official recognition from Tsar Aleksei in 1653, when he gave permission to build a new church along with a donation of 300 rubles and a large quantity of iron. Savvatii worded his report sympathetically, referring to Kozma in terms appropriate for a saint.[70] Apparently, the Synod found no reason to suppress the cult, and St. Kozma continued to be venerated.[71]

Saints Ioann and Loggin Iarenskie similarly received sympathetic treatment. Archbishop Varsonofii of Archangel sent the archpriest Petr of his cathedral to investigate. Drawing on the written miracle stories, Petr provided a sympathetic synopsis that referred to them as saints and omitted the dispute over the sanctity of Loggin's relics. He made no reference to the extensive investigation of the testimony of miracles in the seventeenth century, but he did note Tsar Michael's approval of the

---

[67] RGIA, F. 796, op. 25, No. 732, fols. 76–76v.
[68] For a text of the decanonization records, see *Chteniia Obshchestva istorii I drevnostei rossiiskikh pri Moskovskom universitete*, 1871, no. 4, 45–62; I used the manuscript in the Russian State Library (RGB), F. 310, No. 1212. See also Golubinskii, *Istoriia kanonizatsii sviatykh v russkoi tserkvi*, 159–68, for an account of the decanonization.
[69] Nun Taisiia, *Zhitiia sviatykh; 100 let russkoi sviatosti*, 2 vols. (Jordanville, NY, 1983), 1: 103–5.
[70] RGIA, F. 796, op. 25, No. 723, fols. 624–639; Golubinskii, *Istoriia kanonizatsii sviatykh v russkoi tserkvi*, 443–5.
[71] *Slovar' istoricheskii o sviatykh*, 161.

cult. He appended eight miracles attributed to the saints. Archbishop Varsonofii's brief cover letter adopted neutral language concerning Ioann and Loggin's sanctity. Someone in the Synod office was more skeptical, especially about Loggin, entitling the document "Archangel dead bodies revered as saints."[72] But the Synod did not move to suppress the cult, and they continued to be recognized.[73]

Although the Synod's 1744 ukase did not require investigation of the cults of miracle-working icons as well as relics of saints, Archbishop Arsenii of Pereiaslavl', who was one of the authors of the decree, ordered an investigation into an icon of the Mother of God that first appeared in the city of Akhtyrka in 1739. He sent three clergy to verify the miracles recorded in a booklet, interviewing the people listed there as recipients of healing. The investigators reported that the miracles largely checked out: The verbal reports the inquest commission gathered coincided with the accounts in the written miracles, and in several cases the accounts could be corroborated by bystanders. The recipients of miracles suffered from illnesses for which "no manner of natural healing was expected," and they responded with an outpouring of devotion to the icon. The discrepancies between the published accounts of healing and testimony were the fault of an overzealous local priest, who attributed miracles to persons who did not receive them. He was removed from his office and was placed under arrest for perpetrating a fraud. In 1751 the Synod ruled that the Akhtyrka icon was a genuine miracle worker.[74]

The inquest into the veracity of the miracles of the Akhtyrka icon became the model for future investigations. Instructions for the precanonization inquest into the sanctity of Dimitrii Tuptalo (Rostovskii) directed the commission to follow the procedures established in the Akhtyrka case.[75] The investigation of Fedor Totemskii that ultimately resulted in his canonization (the report in the wake of the 1744 ukase was inconclusive and unencouraging) was modeled explicitly on that of Dimitrii Rostovskii,[76] as was that of St. Innokenti of Irkustsk.[77] In this way, the

---

[72] RGIA, F. 796, op. 25, No. 723, fols. 578–87v.

[73] *Slovar' istoricheskii o sviatykh*, 133–4.

[74] No. 774, *PSVR*, ser. 2, vol. 2, 274; No. 1229, *PSVR*, ser. 2, vol. 3, 375–6; Poselianin, *Bogomater'*, 410–14. For a comparison with investigations of icon cults in the late nineteenth and early twentieth centuries, see Vera Shevzov, "Miracle-Working Icons, Laity, and Authority in the Russian Orthodox Church, 1861–1917," *Russian Review* 58 (1999): 26–48.

[75] Golubinskii, *Istoriia kanonizatsii sviatykh v russkoi tserkvi*, 475–84; Nos. 1524, 1530, 1543, 1546, 1547, 1553, 1638, *PSVR*, ser. 2, vol. 4, 252–60, 269–71, 283–4, 285–6, 293–4, 380–1.

[76] RGIA, F. 796, op. 25, No. 723, fols. 279–313v; Nos. 145, 170, 273, 275, 471, *PSVR*, ser. 4, vol. 1, 124–5, 159–63, 274–6, 277–8, 577–8.

[77] Nos. 528, 531, *PSVR*, ser. 4, vol. 1, 649, 657–8.

procedures for the evaluation of miracle-working relics and icons developed in the mid-1740s became the norm for the Russian Orthodox Church until the Revolution of 1917.

Thus, the Synod succeeded in consolidating its control over the recognition of new miracles. The local bishops were responsible for bringing incidents to the attention of the Synod, which would in turn order an inquest. The investigatory commission, consisting of reliable churchmen, would verify documentation relating to the cult: examining prayer services and *vitae* for their orthodoxy, collecting records relating to the origin of the cult, scrutinizing lists of miracles, and comparing them with the testimony of living recipients. The commission would also examine the icons or relics themselves, filing extensive descriptions. The commission would report, the Synod would decide, and the monarch would issue the official decree authorizing the cult or suppressing it.

Although standardized and refined, this procedure was hardly novel. In fact, it resembled that used in a few seventeenth-century canonizations, such as that of Ioann and Loggin Iarengskie. Of Nectarius of Jerusalem's three proofs of sainthood – a pious life, incorruptibility of the relics, and record of post mortem miracles – none were imposed rigorously in Russia, either before the promulgation of the *Spiritual Regulation* or afterward. The criteria for evaluating the authenticity of sanctity remained malleable, if not downright murky.

The pre mortem existence of saints became more of an issue than it had been before.[78] Hierarchs of the eighteenth century were suspicious, in general, of cults surrounding secular figures or unknown bodies, but were still willing, sometimes, to grant credence to them. They were more willing to entertain the idea that individuals like themselves in past times, namely bishops and abbots, could have been saints.

The incorruptibility of the relics remained a significant piece of evidence in the determination of sanctity, and a physical examination of the relics became an essential element in the process of the inquest. But hierarchs proved very flexible in their interpretation of the physical evidence. If they wanted to promote a cult, even substantial corruption could be overlooked. However, if they wanted to suppress a cult, the corruption of the physical remains provided a cogent reason to do so. The physical state of icons was also significant, as became evident in the Shelbitsy case, when an inscription in Polish rather than Russian made the icon ineligible for official "miracle-working" status.

---

[78] The piety of saints during their lives was not even an issue in seventeenth-century canonization inquests; see Levin, "From Corpse to Cult."

It was in the evaluation of testimony to miracles that eighteenth-century hierarchs diverged most notably from seventeenth-century practice. Although they all avowed that they believed in the reality of miracles from icons and relics, they varied widely in the degree of skepticism with which they greeted manifestations of divine intervention in their own time. Protestant-influenced clerics such as Feofan Prokopovich tended to regard claims to miraculous experience as deliberate attempts to deceive the gullible populace. Other hierarchs were more willing to accept that ordinary people in their own time could experience divine grace in tangible form. However, they, too, regarded it as necessary to separate genuine miracles from honest, or dishonest, delusion. Hierarchs of both ilks agreed that ordinary laypeople and even their own parish clergy were ignorant and superstitious, and could not properly judge the authenticity of their religious experiences. They particularly discounted women's testimony, quite unlike their seventeenth-century predecessors who valued it, and quashed cults developed by women for women. Haunted by the specter of Old Belief, they suspected manifestations of popular religiosity to be covers for treasonous and schismatic activity.

But in fact, popular veneration of saints and icons conformed to traditional Orthodox specifications. The visions Agafia Miakisheva and Pimen Volkov reported replicated exactly the prototypes in accounts of miracles recorded in the previous century. The miracles evinced to justify the canonization of Dimitrii Rostovskii were identical in type to the ones that substantiated the veneration of previously recognized saints.[79] "Superstition" proved to be in the eye of the beholder; an officially sanctioned cult was not superstitious, and an unofficial one was, despite the close similarity between the actual practices in the two.

Consequently, the authentication of miracles proved tricky for the hierarchs of the eighteenth century. Instead of granting credence to laypeople's testimony and to oral tradition, the Synod privileged physical evidence and written documentation from ecclesiastical or secular authorities. But in the case of old cults, the written documentation, if it ever existed, had been lost in the intervening years, and the physical state of relics was never perfect. Thus no case was completely free from anomalies, not even those of the Akhtyrka icon and Dimitrii Rostovskii, which enjoyed enthusiastic support from powerful hierarchs.

The Synod insisted upon receiving notification of all new manifestations of popular veneration of saints and icons, and it attempted to

[79] HRL, SGU, 258, "Miracles of St. Dimitrii, Metropolitan of Rostov."

sort through the centuries' accumulation of established, but unverified, cults. But even identifying these cults, much less examining them for their validity, involved a great effort. In theory, the Synod commanded a huge network of personnel – bishops and abbots, inquisitors, seminary professors, monks, and parish clergy – but all of them had many other duties besides the investigation of cults. Even for the most fervent opponents of superstition, such as Feofan Prokopovich and the monarchs who backed him, priorities lay elsewhere. It was difficult and time-consuming enough to deal with the incidents that came to the Synod's attention, through reports from hierarchs, parish priests, informers, or laypeople, without attempting to implement the grandiose plan of review laid out in the *Spiritual Regulation*. The Synod found it much easier to issue orders directing hierarchs to gather information about unauthorized cults than it did to follow up on them.

As the bishops' reactions to the 1737 and 1744 investigation orders reveal, most of them felt no particular compunction to do more than comply with the letter of their instructions, namely to file reports. Only the most zealous used the orders to investigate as a mandate to suppress cults they found to be inappropriate. More often, they provided the required information, no sooner than they had to, and waited for further orders. The top-heavy structure of the Russian government, replicated in the Synod, discouraged bishops from taking the initiative, even in accordance with official policy. Inaction was usually the safest course.

When bishops decided to act, they could be as successful in preserving cults as they could be in suppressing them. Archbishop Arsenii of Pereiaslavl' gained official approval for the cult of the Akhtyrka icon, and Archbishop Mitrofan of Tver eradicated the cult of Vladimir and Agripena Rzhevskaia. But it would also be true to say that bishops could be as *un*successful in preserving cults as they could be in suppressing them. Bishop Gedeon of Smolensk wanted to sponsor a cult of the Shelbitsy icon, but was overruled; Bishop Pimen of Vologda wanted to suppress veneration of St. Ignatii but ultimately failed. While some bishops seem to have had ideological motivations to eliminate veneration they regarded as superstitious, schismatic, or heterodox, others seem to have been more concerned with defending the orthodoxy of traditional local observances, a goal they shared with the monastery, parish church, and community involved in the cult. The Synod succeeded in depriving local bishops of their ancient right to canonize saints and recognize miracle cults on their own authority, yet bishops retained a large measure of power over the process.

Thus the Synod did not succeed in fully implementing its program, even though it attained unchallenged authority to judge the validity of claims to sanctity. Ultimately about half of the cults that came under scrutiny in these investigations survived, including a number that fell far short of the Synod's expected standard of proof.[80]

Until the collapse of the imperial government in 1917, the Synod continued to investigate and, if deemed necessary, to attempt to suppress new cults of saints and icons. But after 1744, it did not again issue general orders to all prelates to scrutinize "false miracles" and "unattested dead bodies." That honor fell to the Bolsheviks. Communist leaders regarded the cult of the saints as a vehicle for the Russian autocracy's expression of antirevolutionary sentiment, and with good reason: The rhetoric surrounding late imperial canonizations, such as that of Serafim of Sarov, played explicitly on the theme of the Russian empire's political and religious hegemony.[81] Soon after the October Revolution of 1917, Soviet officials undertook examination of the relics of sixty-three saints as part of the Boshevik Party's antireligious campaign. Working on the assumption that both Church hierarchs and the believing populace regarded incorruptibility of the relics as a sine qua non of sainthood, party activists hoped to prove the falsehood of religion by demonstrating the corruptibility of saints' bodies. Some of the examinations of relics, including those of the most eminent Russian monastic saint, Sergei of Radonezh (founder of the Troitskii-Sergiev monastery), were recorded on film. Vladimir Ilich Lenin, himself, took a personal interest in the investigation of relics and recommended that the films be shown in all the cinemas in Moscow.[82] Party activists and medical doctors gave public lectures, sometimes illustrated with tangible examples, to refute the notion of saintly incorruptibility. In addition to showing that supposed saints' relics had, in fact, decomposed, they also presented preserved bodies of unsaintly characters, and then explained the scientific reasons that bodies might seem to remain whole. In addition, they tried to debunk miracles emanating from relics and icons.[83] Bolshevik antireligious

---

[80] The records are not complete, so it is impossible to make an exact count.

[81] Robert L. Nichols, "The Friends of God: Nicholas II and Alexandra at the Canonization of Serafim of Sarov, July 1903," in *Religious and Secular Forces in Late Tsarist Russia*, ed. Charles E. Timberlake (Seattle, 1992), 206–29.

[82] N.S. Gordienko, *Pravoslavnye sviatye: kto oni* (Leningrad, 1979), 70–3, 82–90. For a highly critical post-Soviet account published by the Russian Orthodox Church, see A. Rogozianskii, *Strasti po moshcham* (St. Petersburg, 1998). I thank Nadieszda Kizenko for providing me with a copy of this publication.

[83] Rene Fueloep-Miller, *The Mind and Face of Bolshevism: An Examination of Cultural Life in Soviet Russia* (New York, 1965), 186–7, 219–20. I am grateful to Tricia Starks for this citation.

campaigns in general met with less success than they claimed,[84] and the attempt to undermine belief in the saints did not result in the disappearance of any cults. In fact, the Bolshevik investigation generated a new cult by creating a new martyr. Archbishop Anatolii of Irkutsk was so distraught at having a Bolshevik investigatory team ransack the relics of St. Innokentii that he collapsed from a heart attack and died; he was canonized abroad.[85]

But long-standing cultural patterns are hard to break, and come 1924, a new uncorrupted dead body, Vladimir Ilich Lenin, took its place in Moscow. The Funeral Commission officially explained its decision to preserve Lenin's body on display as a response to popular demand. Although the Bolshevik Party leaders frequently created their outpourings of "popular" yearnings to order, it is quite possible that many ordinary Russians shared the sentiment of Josef Stalin that preservation of the body represented the ultimate mark of "love and veneration of the deceased." Leon Trotsky, who had little patience with Stalin's hegemonic tendencies, was appalled by his proposal:

> Apparently we, the party of revolutionary Marxism, are advised to behave in the same way [as the Russian Orthodox Church] – to preserve the body of Lenin. Earlier there were the relics of [Sergei] of Radonezh and Serafim of Sarov: now they want to replace these with the relics of Vladimir Ilich.[86]

Despite the overt parallels to Orthodox practice – or perhaps because of them – Stalin's view won out. The temptation to prove that, unlike Christian faith, Soviet science could accomplish the perfect preservation of the body, and even, someday, its resurrection, was too great to pass up.[87]

---

[84] Glennys Young, *Power and the Sacred in Revolutionary Russia* (University Park, PA, 1997).
[85] *Saint Herman Calendar, 1994* (Platina, CA 1994), 61.
[86] Quoted in Nina Tumarkin, *Lenin Lives!: The Lenin Cult in Soviet Russia* (Cambridge, MA, 1983), 174–5.
[87] Tumarkin, *Lenin Lives*, 173–89; Irene Masing-Delic, *Abolishing Death: A Salvation Myth of Russian Twentieth-Century Literature* (Stanford, CA, 1992), 14–17.

# CHAPTER X

# Liturgical rites: The medium, the message, the messenger, and the misunderstanding

SUSAN C. KARANT-NUNN

W E historians are latecomers to the study of ritual. Anthropologists have already spent a century gazing at various societies' formal rites and ritualized behavior, seeing in these a window onto, if not men's souls, at least the structures, dynamics, values, and aspirations of groups. European and North American early modernists began only in the 1960s to feel in a serious way the impact of the social sciences upon their endeavors. Part of this impact was indeed the analysis of ritual for all that it might yield. From my perspective, it has yielded much.[1] Thus, I stand on the shoulders of many predecessors, some of them giants, as I turn my attention to liturgical ritual especially before, during, and after the Reformation in German-speaking lands.[2] I wish to argue here that whether or not there was open contention over ritual content as the reformers took it on themselves to correct what they saw to have been the long-term medieval falsifications of Gospel propriety, ritual was still at the subliminal or unconscious level an ongoing bone of contention. Not only the heads of the emerging churches but their secular overlords, too, perceived the power of ritual and were determined to "get it right." One prominent level of debate was, then, between and among theologians and heads of state. But in addition, within the ranks of the hoi poloi, ritual was a commodious and potent vessel and could

---

[1] I have provided a number of examples of the resultant literature in my *The Reformation of Ritual: An Interpretation of Early Modern Germany* (London and New York, 1997), 202–3, n. 1. To these I would now have to add at least Edward Muir's recent survey, *Ritual in Early Modern Europe*, New Approaches to European History 11 (Cambridge and New York, 1997) and Peter Arnade, *Realms of Ritual: Burgundian Ceremony and Civic Life in Late-Medieval Ghent* (Ithaca, NY, 1996).

[2] Church historians have long since discussed from a theological and a liturgical standpoint the ritual changes that were made.

not be, or at any rate *was* not received in a wholly passive, detached, uninvolved manner. It might seem as though the laity would have been more inclined to focus their attention on rituals that occurred in a secular setting, even if religion occupied their core, such as Corpus Christi processions, Saint John's Day fires, and Carnival games. But in fact, many people did indicate – if we look closely and draw together even bits of evidence – a concern over what transpired inside the four walls of their parish churches.

## I. THE MEDIUM

In my recent book, concentrating most heavily on Lutheran practice, I now think that I may have put undue weight on the continuity between late medieval Catholic and the new Lutheran ritual. To be sure, Lutheran leaders believed that they were breaking dramatically with what they saw as the papist diversion away from the "pristine" practices of the early Christian church. One of the factors that attracted me to this topic in the first place was the purported wholesale revision of the liturgy that the reformers of every stripe and persuasion attempted to put in place. I would concede now that, whatever the constituent parts of the "new" rites – the order, words, language in which they were pronounced, gestures, arena of their performance – and however recognizable many of these remained, the profound departure from Catholic precedent lay in their rejection of any inherent claim to influence God.

Every Catholic ritual act and every vessel and substance with which it was carried out extended the miraculous power of the Mass into human affairs.[3] The priest's ability to convert the substance of bread and wine into the body and blood of the Most High established him, be he ever so humble and unlettered, as a performer of miracles. Moreover, this miracle was of such a magnitude that it gave mere mortals access to the physical Son of God, which is to say to God Incarnate. This magician at the heart of parish life shared his sacral power with the people by means of holy water, wax, chrism, candles, clay, and salt – to name a few of the items – and by blessing the people themselves in their various exigencies, their fields and crops, houses, loaves of bread, cheese, eggs, candles, waxen images, and animals, including hives of bees.[4] The parish priest's sacral authority radiated outward, penetrating the furthest corners of

---

[3] On the rise of the Mass to supercultic proportions, see Miri Rubin, *The Eucharist in Late Medieval Culture* (Cambridge and New York, 1991).

[4] Adolph Franz, ed., *Das Rituale des Bischofs Heinrich I. von Breslau* (Freiburg-Berlin, 1912), passim; G.H. Buijssen, *Durandus' Rationale in spätmittelhochdeutscher Übersetzung*, 3 vols. (Assen, The Netherlands, 1974–83), passim.

attics, stables, and sheds by means of everyday artifacts. The aura of the Mass, if we can imagine it as a visible force, was like a protective bubble that encapsulated the parish and extended as far as the church bell's sound. The Mass was truly a *medium* in several dictionary meanings of the term: It existed in a middle position between humans and the Deity; it was a means of transmitting divine power; it was a surrounding and enveloping presence; it was a channel of communication between the physical and spiritual realms; it promised to create an environment in which people and the world under their dominion might flourish; it gave rise to artistic expression.[5]

Every other sacrament may be seen as subordinate to the transubstantiation in the Mass, inasmuch as the priest derived his persuasive power from that signal capacity and not from his ability to baptize, confirm, forgive sin, perform marriages, or bless the dying. Of course, under Catholicism, as anthropologists would be quick to point out, ecclesiastical performances also taught doctrine, informed the people of their social location, imposed moral discipline, and inculcated elite hegemonic values. In times of crisis or change, they mended the social fabric, helping people to adjust to what they could not prevent.

It is against this background of the miraculous potency of the Mass that post-Reformation liturgical ritual is a medium of a lower, a thoroughly mundane, order of magnitude. The transubstantiational moment disappeared in theology as soon as Luther and Zwingli said so – and won the backing of their respective governments – and with it the supernatural capacity of the officiant. Inexorably, the trappings of divine presence fell away, though in the Swiss city and others under its influence far more rapidly and completely than in Wittenberg. Sooner or later, the precious equipage of the Mass – the pyxes, patens, monstrances, chalices, vestments, and elaborate altar cloths – were, depending on their nature and value, melted down for their precious metals or sold into still-Catholic territories. Few images were lost to iconoclastic rage, despite the interest of these episodes.[6] Most were discreetly purveyed by princes and magistrates to the Catholic market for religious art. Depictions that remained in Lutheran areas had to convey stories

[5] These are most of the meanings of "medium," rendered apropos of the present topic by me, listed in *Webster's New Collegiate Dictionary* (Springfield, MA, 1973), 714.

[6] Among recent works on iconoclasm, see Carlos M.N. Eire, *War Against the Idols: The Reformation of Worship from Erasmus to Calvin* (Cambridge and New York, 1986); Lee Palmer Wandel, *Voracious Idols and Violent Hands: Iconoclasm in Reformation Zurich, Strasbourg, and Basel* (Cambridge and New York, 1995); Sergiusz Michalski, *The Reformation and the Visual Arts: The Protestant Image Question in Western and Eastern Europe* (London and New York, 1993); Norbert Schnitzler, "Bilderstürmer – Aufrührer oder Blasphemiker?" in *Ordnung und Aufruhr im Mittelalter: Historische und juristische Studien zur Rebellion*, ed. Marie Theres Fögen (Frankfurt am Main, 1995), 195–215.

from or concepts based on the Bible, particularly the Gospels. Crucifixes no longer displayed the contorted, agonized image of a dying but not-yet-expired Christ; instead, as on Lucas Cranach the Elder's predella in the Wittenberg city church, the Savior's body hung limp, for His work of atonement was accomplished.[7] In Zurich music ceased, whereas in Wittenberg Luther busily composed and compiled a hymnal.[8]

In both the northern and the southern spheres, the revised medium quickly became separated from the concept of the Mass. Except on those few occasions when the Lord's Supper was celebrated, the populace was compelled, as it had not been under Catholicism, to come together at least weekly to the service of God, the *Gottesdienst*. We have often heard that the sermon was the centerpiece of this meeting. Sometimes it was and sometimes it was not. On Sundays (more often in cities, though not necessarily in each church), the pastor or the deacon did preach. Uneducated as the majority of clergymen still were, particularly in the countryside, and unlettered as most of the laity were, these messages were extremely basic. Leaders of the church now considered it urgent to impress the rudiments of the faith upon the humblest laypeople, and the only way to accomplish this was to force them to come to church and to remain there. This was one of the factors that promoted the erecting of pews in every sanctuary during the sixteenth century: Bodies needed to be held in place.

As topics on which to preach, the principal alternative to the explication of the catechism was Christian behavior. These were not of necessity separate. These two main themes intertwine incessantly in those homilies that have come down to us, though our impression of sermons is distorted by the survival chiefly of the rhetoric of prominent men in metropolitan pulpits.

## II. THE MESSAGE

### A. *Intentional aspects*

To describe the medium is already to address its messages. Let me summarize what I see the message of the revised, the Protestant, liturgy to

---

[7] On late medieval cricifixes and Christ's agony, see Valentin Groebner, "Der Blick auf den Gekreuzigten am Ende des Mittelalters und in der Reformation," in *Kulturelle Reformation: Sinnformationem im Umbruch 1400–1600*, eds. Bernhard Jussen and Craig M. Koslofsky (Göttingen, 1999); Helmar Junghans, *Wittenberg als Lutherstadt* (Berlin, 1979), the predella, fig. 68, opposite 133. On some more abstract meanings of Christ's tormented body in the late Middle Ages, see also Sarah Beckwith, *Christ's Body: Identity, Culture, and Society in Late Medieval Writings* (London and New York, 1993).

[8] Charles Garside, *Zwingli and the Arts* (New York, 1966).

have been as it was intended by the framers themselves – and most of this is as true in the Lutheran sphere as in the later Calvinist. First, as observed previously, the world was disenchanted. Just as the age of miracles was past, mere mortals could work no wonders through the manipulation of secular or religious objects. God's Providence, to be sure, did permit of interventions, but these were impenetrable by human act or reason. Ecclesiastical rites, then, could not gain advantages for humankind except in the impalpable respect that they pleased God by according with his wishes. Ritual set people apart from animals. God *desired* that his children come together in orderly ways and *worship* him.

Second, that worship had to be grounded in legitimate theological content. I will not dwell here on the conviction of each and every leading religious figure that his definition of that content was the *correct* one. God was the author of one overriding Truth, which ritual had to embody.

Third, in the act of embodying, liturgy instructed in doctrine. The words of Bible readings, prayers, words of consecration, admonitions, and hymns (where hymns were used) were all intended to inculcate a knowledge of basic precepts upon pastors' human flocks. Although, as I have pointed out, sermons were not given at numerous services, *sermon* became a near-eponym for religious gatherings.[9] During the sixteenth century, and particularly after midcentury, sermons became a newly prominent literary genre. They were not only given and aurally received in church, but thousands were now printed and disseminated in pamphlet and book form, to be reread at home by pious and educated urban dwellers. For the most part, peasants simply heard sermons, but the growing urban literate classes also read them. Preaching occurred at Sunday and at least some midweek services, and in Lutheran territories (in contrast to Calvinist) it took place at weddings and funerals, too.

Fourth, the Reformers and heads of state intended that rituals should discipline the laity. As the century wore on, the lengthening liturgy increased space for admonitions (*Vermahnungen*). The word itself conveys a sense of warning, such as before distribution of the Lord's Supper. The people should dispose themselves mentally toward humble acknowledgement of their unworthiness. Elector August of Saxony specified in his detailed ecclesiastical ordinance of 1580 that in each of his parishes, the people should be admonished verbatim before coming forward to commune:

Dear friends of Christ, because we are gathered here in the name of the Lord, in order to receive His holy testament, so I admonish you, first of all, to lift your

---

[9] Karant-Nunn, *The Reformation of Ritual*, 125–7.

hearts up to God and pray the Lord's Prayer with me. . . . So that God our Father in heaven will regard us, His wretched children on earth, with mercy and give us grace to hallow His holy name here and throughout the world; by means of the pure, honest teaching of His Word and by [implanting] a burning love [for Him] in our lives, may He graciously turn aside all false teaching and sinful living (through which His worthy name is defamed and dishonored). [We pray too] that His kingdom may come and be increased; and that all sinners, those who are deluded, [and others] trapped in the empire of the Devil be brought to recognition of the true faith in Jesus Christ.[10]

This is but a fraction of the text provided in this instance. Admonitions were a major form of liturgical embroidery within early modern Lutheranism, significantly lengthening services of worship. They were added to baptisms, weddings, and funerals. Indeed, clergymen coming to the dying chamber were required, unless death were truly imminent, to deliver an admonition or short admonitory sermon to the person who was about to expire as well as to the gathered relatives, servants, and neighbors. Increasingly, the governors of church and state provided scripts for the officiants to read, for they did not trust them to give accurate and fulsome messages otherwise. The message by the deathbed was essentially that of the Catholic *memento mori*: Christians must be perpetually aware that death may come to them at any moment; they must prepare all their lives, through piety and repentance, for that often unexpected instant when their Maker shall call them.[11]

The disciplining intention of the liturgy is even more clearly visible in the Lutheran additions that were designed to humiliate transgressors before the entire congregation and finally to readmit them to full fellowship in the life of the Church. A prominent example of this kind of shaming ritual was that used when an engaged couple had engaged in sex and the future bride had become pregnant. In Rothenburg in 1618 and after, the pastor was obliged to read out, as the pair stood before their assembled neighbors:

Inasmuch as it is said and apparent that both of you have joined yourselves dishonorably under the influence of the Evil Enemy and your own sinful, evil lusts, contrary to God's ordinance and will; that you have lived unchastely and not waited for the Christian going-to-church, after which with God['s blessing], honor, and good conscience you would have been able to live together; you have thereby angered God the most highly praised Trinity, driven away the dear holy little angels and chaste spirits, injured your own consciences, annoyed the

---

[10] Emil Sehling, ed., *Die evangelischen Kirchenordnungen des 16. Jahrhunderts*, vol. 1 (Leipzig, 1902), 368.
[11] I take up the deathbed *Vermahnung* in *The Reformation of Ritual*, 152–5.

Christian Church and the dear youth, afflicted the office of preacher, offended the government, wounded the hearts of your parents, and thus fallen into the court and judgment of God.[12]

Only after undergoing such a ritual could the bride and groom proceed to their nuptials, but without the customary wreaths or music and dance. Often the bride had to bind up her hair prematurely and wear a veil.

## B. *Subliminal messages*

It is hard to say to what extent the Reformers and their immediate successors, the crafters of revised ritual in the sixteenth century, were aware of other messages that the new rites communicated to clergy and laity alike. Certainly, some of these messages coincided seamlessly with the fabricators' outlook on the world. Whether the learned authors of ritual prescriptions were conscious of the additional values or not, these were transmitted nonverbally to the people, who may, then, have received them beneath the level of articulate awareness. In considering this question, we need to look not just at the liturgical rubrics themselves but at the settings within which the acts were to be performed. Precisely these settings reinforced ideas contained in the words and physical gestures, and/or they relayed auxiliary ideas.

One of these values is hierarchy. In the Catholic sphere, the priest was clearly the center of attention in his mediatory and sacrificial roles. But if we leave him aside and glance around, we see that at least in the large urban church, there may be much else going on visually and structurally. There were likely to be side chapels with their own clergy. In relation to the high and sacrally most potent altar, even where there were as yet few seats, the laity had their customary standing places, with those of higher station closer to the front and those of lowest rank at the back. By 1500 such high-and-mighty people as magistrates and the nobility had chairs or pews, sometimes placed perpendicular to the standing masses so that their occupants could see and be seen. Tradition aside, the rank-and-file themselves were likely to be unfettered and to be able to enter and leave the sanctuary at will or to shift their position. In depictions of late medieval and early Reformation preaching, we see men, women, and children placed randomly beneath the pulpit, some squatting on collapsible three-legged stools. We hear complaints from the Reformers of the helter-skelter way in which the people were accustomed to go

---

[12] Emil Sehling, *Die evangelischen Kirchenordnungen*, vol. 13, no. 3 KOO, 13.3 (Tübingen, 1966), 551.

forward to receive the Eucharist. There was, nevertheless, a certainly hierarchical principle visible even in its violation.

It is, however, of additional interest that the bearers of the Reformation perceived a laxity of hierarchy in the old Church. Whereas on the one hand they desired to "domesticate" the clergy and integrate them into mundane society, on the other they enhanced the earthly power of pastors to intervene in parishioners' personal lives. A new clericalism was but one aspect of assigning people rank and standing, and, in part, this was both accomplished and conveyed by means of ecclesiastical ritual. The building of pews grew apace, and a greater proportion of the populace sat than stood. This heightened discipline as well, for the people were held in place, their faces directed toward the pulpit; and they were not to get up or go out without good reason. With fixed seating, it was easier for authorities to tell who was missing, and attendance was now legally binding. Every aspect of ritual contains more than one message.

People sat within their rows in accordance with local perceptions of status. This was not a function solely of wealth but could be influenced by such factors as whether one was a burgher, whether one was married or not (married people having higher rank), one's age, and one's gender. Gender is a very important aspect of station. I need hardly state which sex was thought to be the better one. From early Christianity men had sat on the (superior) south side of the sacred space and women on the (inferior) north.[13] In the late medieval Church, girls and boys were treated differently in the baptismal rite, with the boys baptized first (in case two children were brought to the sacrament at the same time) and with gender-specific prayers and exorcisms.[14] Differences in gender roles were impressed upon infants literally from the hour – or at least within three days – of their birth. Whereas Reformation baptismal rubrics, whether Lutheran, Zwinglian, or Calvinist, eliminated these, the evidence of art and of parish visitation protocols confirms that Protestants were equally as concerned to ensure the differential

---

[13] Johann P.B. Kreuser, *Heilige Meßopfer, geschichtlich erklärt*, 2nd ed. (Paderborn, 1854), unpaginated schematic plan inserted at back of volume. For a broader context, see Joan Cadden, *Meanings of Sex Difference in the Middle Ages: Medicine, Science, and Culture* (Cambridge, 1993), passim. On the negative associations with the north side, see Jeffrey Burton Russell, *Lucifer: The Devil in the Middle Ages* (Ithaca, NY, 1984), 69, 71.

[14] Susan C. Karant-Nunn, "'Lasset die Kindlein zu mir kommen und wehret ihnen night': Die Taufe, der Leib Christi, und die Gemeinde im 16. und 17. Jahrhundert," paper presented March 1998 at Max-Planck-Institut für Geschichte, Göttingen, Germany; and in English as "'Suffer the Little Children to Come unto Me and Forbid Them Not': Baptism, the Body of Christ, and the Community," September 1998, Yale Divinity School, New Haven, Connecticut.

treatment of the sexes. In rural churches, where the altar was not big enough for men and women to come forward simultaneously to receive Holy Communion at its separate corners, men and boys went first (in that order) and women and girls second. Females played a secondary part in funeral observances, and in the case of burial rites for nobles, women often remained at home, a practice that we have recently witnessed in the Moslem world in connection with the funeral of King Hussein of Jordan.[15]

Other alterations in the decoration of the sanctuary, that paramount ritual space, conveyed other meanings. I have argued elsewhere that the Lutheran Reformation produced the near removal of female holy figures from the church and that this signaled, however subtly, the demotion of women from the sacred sphere.[16] The myriad women saints who were so prominent in late medieval religiosity all but disappeared. The one who remained, but in a newly subordinate position, was Mary, the mother of Jesus, who was now mainly depicted as one of the two people at the foot of the cross, and shown only occasionally in a surviving nativity scene. Gone were the birth of the Virgin, the Annunciation, the Visitation, the Purification of Mary, the pains of Mary, the death of Mary, her Assumption, and her coronation by Christ.

Along with women went the ideal of affective piety. Women had always been prominently associated with emotion, and it was hardly a coincidence that when feminine images were removed, the people were informed semiotically that religious fervor was being reassessed and moderated. Men, too, had shared in the model of intense religious feeling, and paintings and statues that displayed male saints in torment were now eliminated. Gone were Sebastian and Lawrence and Bartholomew. As noted previously, crucifixes underwent a metamorphosis; the agonized Christ, the Man of Sorrows, was now replaced by the slack-bodied, definitely dead Savior. Swept away along with all of these was the legitimacy of spiritual agony and spiritual ecstasy.[17] It is significant, however, that Lutheranism adhered to the physical presence of Christ's body and blood in the Eucharist, and I shall return to that

---

[15] In his profound grief over the death of his and Katharina's fourteen-year-old daughter Magdalena in 1542, Luther wrote repeatedly about the dying and the burial. It would seem from these references that Käthe did not attend her daughter's funeral.

[16] Susan C. Karant-Nunn, "Continuity and Change: Some Effects of the Reformation on the Women of Zwickau," *Sixteenth Century Journal* 13.2 (1982): 17–42, here at 28.

[17] See Susan C. Karant-Nunn, "'Gedanken, Hertz und Sinn': Die Unterdrückung der religiösen Emotionen in der Reformationszeit," in *Kulturelle Reformation: Semantische Umordnung und soziale Transformation 1400–1600*, eds. Bernhard Jussen and Craig M. Koslofsky (Göttingen, 1999), 66–90.

shortly, for it tended to contradict the calming messages of other rites. In addition, it promoted schoolboys' multipart and Latin singing during services, and this could have an arousing rather than a tranquilizing effect.

More limited still was the approved place of strong feeling in the Calvinist or Reformed sanctuary: From it *every* image, whether male or female, disappeared. The walls were uniformly whitewashed; the location of the medieval high altar, with its "superstitious" and "idolatrous" associations, was concealed and a plain table was erected along one of the long side walls of the ecclesiastical space. Table decoration sometimes took the form of a word-painting – of the Ten Commandments, for example. Candles could not be lit by day. Song was confined to the Psalms, and the organs were stilled, at least until the end of the century, when some were reintroduced. Pulpits protruded, as they now did in many Lutheran sanctuaries, too, into the midst of the people, who were held in their echelons. What could they gaze at besides the preacher? That they should be compelled to attend to him was precisely their governors' intent. They could not find distraction in his apparel, for the flowered vestments of yore had been supplanted by simple black clothing. Every space, even those of the pastor's suit, bespoke order, quiescence, the spiritual nature of God.

### III. THE MESSENGER

The success of all ecclesiastical and social goals hinged upon the pastorate. Without its conversion to the evangelical cause, the Reformers' and the rulers' efforts would have been in vain except among those individuals who felt personally attracted to the new teachings. How numerous these individuals were, however, is a matter of ongoing discussion.[18] In the late Middle Ages, the parish clergy normally derived from the community they served, or at least from the vicinity. They were part of an existing social network. Their ordination set them above their neighbors with respect to access to the divine, security of living,

---

[18] My own view remains, as it was at the time I finished writing my Ph.D. dissertation in 1970 ("Luther's Pastors: The Reformation in the Ernestine Countryside" [Philadelphia, 1979]), that a majority of ordinary people at every rank had to be convinced of the superiority of evangelism and oftentimes compelled to adopt it. Peter Blickle, however, like confessional scholars of the early twentieth century, sees the German-speaking populace as overwhelmingly drawn to the new teachings (for example, *From the Communal Reformation to the Revolution of the Common Man* [Leiden, 1998], 129: "It is very probable that the Reformation owed its global repercussions to the unparalleled support for its theology among the population at large").

training, if not education, and at least occasional association with the diocesan rank above. At the same time, they remained rooted in the community, sharing its cosmic outlook and its sense of interrelatedness. They were even glad to avail their parishioners of their supernatural powers by distributing such substances as holy water and by blessing houses, candles, loaves of bread, fields, and livestock. They and their spiritual flocks knew these objects and rites to be efficacious in healing and protecting against evil. In one sense, then, all were bound together in a sacral economy that was beneficial to all. Even before the Reformation "domesticated" the clergy, as we are wont to say,[19] the curate and his immediate helpers were integrated into the eternal community, symbolized by the concrete and earthly one. The men who practiced the cure of souls and the laity in their charge mainly understood one another.

Abuses were no figments of the Reformers' imagination, to be sure. The institutional Catholic Church was often all too indifferent to these. In addition, the people's resentment tended to focus far more on "extraneous" ecclesiastics, such as monks and friars, who may have been less open to collective concerns and more intent on promoting their own interests. No generalization can have been true of all, however.

It was the curates on whom the Reformation depended, after the suppression of monasticism; and in them it had to work its changes. In a series of as yet unpublished essays, Amy Nelson Burnett has studied this process in regard to the clergy of Basel and its hinterland.[20] Especially at first, parish visitors compelled these priests to adopt the new doctrines, including their liturgical embodiments, or depart. The humble men of the cloth, whose intellectual preparation for their profession had often been minimal, had no initial means of informing themselves other than instructions from the visitors, which were distributed. Clergymen who wished to retain their posts sometimes had to prepare a sermon on a key point of theology, and often owed their survival to the severe dearth of men eligible to replace them. As a token of their submission and in keeping with evangelical belief, they had to wed the "cooks" and "housekeepers" with whom they had been living, or set them aside and marry someone else.

---

[19] I do not know whether William S. Stafford originated this term in *Domesticating the Clergy: The Inception of the Reformation in Strasbourg, 1522–1524* (Missoula, MT, 1976).

[20] Amy Nelson Burnett, "Controlling the Clergy: The Oversight of Basel's Rural Pastors in the Sixteenth Century," *Zwingliana* 25 (1998): 129–42; "Basel's Rural Pastors as Mediators of Confessional and Social Discipline," *Central European History* 33 (2000): 67–85; "Controlling the Clergy: Synods and Visitations in Basel, 1529–1601 (unpublished)." I am most grateful to her for letting me read these.

As the century wore on, and in keeping with the Reformers' implicit understanding that clerical conformity was the crux of the Reformation's future, authorities improved methods of oversight, launching visitation committees, and establishing superintendencies, synods, and consistories. They increased pastoral compensation to a degree that a "better sort of man," that is, men from the middling levels of society, were attracted to the post. Indeed, such men came increasingly from the towns instead of the countryside and were thus no longer indigenous members of the community. By the end of the sixteenth century, their different provenance formed part of the wedge that tended to divide their sympathies from those of the rustic laity. In addition, by century's end, a course of study was in place that prospective clergymen were expected to undertake. This study all by itself placed them on a level above those whom they served and in its content shaped a view of the world that no longer coincided with the peasants'. Future pastors were trained to shun "superstition": every manifestation of folk belief in an animated and manipulable environment. Many people continued to believe in supernaturally charged, efficacious objects; the clergy were forbidden to share that conviction.

At the sociological level, pastors and their wives, sextons, schoolmasters, organists, and cantors (in Lutheran territories) were enjoined not to fraternize with parishioners. They should not drink with the men at the tavern; they should prefer increasingly to receive a monetary substitute for wedding dinners and baptismal ales. In the countryside, they sometimes saw the lower nobility on social occasions. In the towns, they were apt to interact with the magistracy, and especially the ranks of officialdom, with which they intermarried.[21] They should exhibit appropriate (affectionate, restrained, decorous) relations with members of their household: wives, children, and servants. They should provide a *model* for their flocks – but a model is something set apart from those who observe and imitate it.

These were the men who were supposed to instruct, oversee, counsel, admonish, and discipline the laity. The institutional church and the state depended on them to do so. They presided over the liturgy and formulated the sermons that signaled the new type of religion. They stood at the communicative center from which post-Reformation messages issued. The liturgical rites that they administered were no longer "lent"

---

[21] For a most detailed treatment of a regional clergy from the sixteenth into the eighteenth century, see Luise Schorn-Schütte, *Evangelische Geistlichkeit in der Frühneuzeit: Deren Anteil an der Entfaltung frühmoderner Staatlichkeit und Gesellschaft* (Gütersloh, 1996).

to the people for their extracurricular purposes but were rigorously defined and *confined* to specific occasions.

## IV. THE MISUNDERSTANDING

How were the messages that were delivered by the messengers received by the laity? In her superb guide to ritual theory, Catherine Bell explores the manifest goals of ritual from the perspective of those who prescribe and supervise it. Summarizing the work of anthropologist specialists in the power of ritual, she states, "These studies yield at least three ways in which the empowerment of those who most control ritualization is constituted: the objectification of office, the hierarchization of practices, and traditionalization." Yet, she continues, "This should not be taken as a definitive list of the strategies of this form of empowerment. Nor should the potential efficacy of such strategies obscure the real limits of the power so constituted."[22] Although she is not writing about early modern Europe, these generalizations appear to fit the Reformation setting if we admit continuities with late medieval Catholic practice. First, those who prescribed and those who presided over post-Reformation ritual hardly broke with the past in claiming objective validity for the functions they performed. The propriety of their activities seemed to them inscribed in the universe and conferred upon them by the Deity. The populace fundamentally subscribed to the same scheme, albeit with qualitative differences in its definitions of propriety.[23] Second, I have taken up the subject of hierarchization previously. Third, while at one level the Reformers disputed the authority of tradition, at least insofar as the Catholic Church employed it, at another they believed themselves to be reestablishing and reaffirming their descent from a yet earlier, worthier tradition, that of the early Christian Church.

Of greater pertinence here are the limitations on the might of those who wield official ritual. Bell finds hegemonic interpretations of ritual inadequate. She is assuredly right in asserting limitations and arguing that lay participants must be able to, and inevitably will, appropriate

---

[22] Catherine Bell, *Ritual Theory, Ritual Practice* (Oxford and New York, 1992), 212.

[23] On all aspects of late medieval and Reformation anticlericalism, see Peter A. Dykema and Heiko A. Oberman, eds., *Anticlericalism in Late Medieval and Early Modern Europe* (Leiden, 1992); also see R.W. Scribner, "Anticlericalism and the Reformation in Germany," in idem, *Popular Culture and Popular Movements in Reformation Germany* (London and Ronceverte, 1987), 243–75; Hans-Jürgen Goetz, *Pfaffenhaß und Großgeschrei: Die reformatorischen Bewegungen in Deutschland 1517–1529* (Munich, 1987); Susan C. Karant-Nunn, "Neoclericalism and Anticlericalism in Saxony, 1555–1675," *Journal of Interdisciplinary History* 24.4 (1994): 615–37.

ritual for their own purposes. She regards resistance and appropriation as essential dimensions of such observances.[24] Resistance and appropriation may well not be conscious, for observers cannot help but interpret ritual transactions within their own frame of reference.[25] What that frame of reference is, is a matter for debate. Surely those iconoclasts of the early Reform movement who destroyed images out of their own will and conviction need to be accounted for and their mentalities assessed. Lee Palmer Wandel has made an excellent start at distinguishing among motives in three southwest German/Swiss contexts.[26] Images were *ritual* artifacts, but they had other associations, which are crucial to our complete understanding of why they were objectionable.

Yet iconoclasm was rarely a major form of ritual resistance. Practically universal was a simple misunderstanding or misinterpretation of official intention. The prefix "mis-" does confer legitimacy upon the elites who officiated, just as it inherently accuses the laity of falsification. As a scholar who is influenced by anthropology, I must for the present purpose repudiate this implied meaning. At the same time, I do not mean to suggest that lay understandings were somehow superior to those of theologians, princes, pastors, and magistrates. They were what they were, and that is the point, whatever the limitations of our language may be.

The themes of resistance and misunderstanding could be taken up in connection with each major ecclesiastical rite. My evidence is drawn very heavily from visitation protocols in various parts of Lutheran Germany, but we might take similar anecdotes from consistory records, and in fact, for the Calvinist "capital" Geneva, from the minutes of the great consistory there, which are now being published.[27] I shall briefly take up baptism and the Eucharist as examples.

Within late medieval Catholicism, baptism was of such urgency that even a woman, an infidel, or a heretic could, *in extremis*, administer it. Popular and elite opinion nearly coincided in regarding it as a prerequisite of salvation, the essential mark of a Christian. Even though the Reformers preserved baptism as a sacrament, they differed among themselves on whether its absence absolutely barred a soul from paradise.

---

[24] Bell, *Ritual Theory*, esp. 215–23.

[25] For a persuasive argument on this point, see James W. Fernandez, "Symbolic Consensus in a Fang Reformative Cult," *American Anthropologist* 67 (1965): 902–29.

[26] Lee Palmer Wandel, *Voracious Idols and Violent Hands*.

[27] Thomas A. Lambert and Isabella M. Watt, comps., *Registres du Consistoire de Genève au temps de Calvin*, vol. 1 (1542–1544) (Geneva, 1996). For a preliminary overview, see Robert M. Kingdon, "The Geneva Consistory in the Time of Calvin," in *Calvinism in Europe, 1540–1620*, eds. Andrew Pettegree, Alastair Duke, and Gillian Lewis (Cambridge and New York, 1994), 21–34.

Lutheran divines accused Calvinists of invalidating the sacrament by not regarding it as obligatory for all Christians, and the Reformed reproached Lutherans for not having departed from "popish superstition" concerning the necessity of rituals.[28]

I have shown elsewhere how Reformers in the southwest, including Zwingli, Oecolampadius, and Bucer, restored the ancient metaphor of baptism as engraftment onto the body of Christ by ordaining that baptism could only take place before the congregation. This restoration developed only gradually in the rest of the German-speaking lands until, in the seventeenth century, the analogy stood revived in much of Germany.[29] The sense of commonality was surely persuasive in those regions that, Peter Blickle has told us, were particularly drawn in secular life to communal ideals. More important to the laity, however, was the concept of baptism as salvific. Bits of evidence from across Germany inform us that the people themselves continued to regard baptism as essential to salvation. They generally hastened their newborns to the rite, with the proviso that, if their infants' apparent health allowed, they wanted to delay long enough to gather in the godparents of their choosing. We may see this as resistance to ritual changes, based on theology, that were introduced by the Reformation.

For from the lay perspective, baptism not only provisionally assured salvation in the next life, but it afforded concrete advantages in this one, and these were crucial to mundane well-being. Throughout the sixteenth and seventeenth centuries, clergy and rulers on the one hand contended with the popular view on the other that the social dimensions of baptism were indispensable. Sumptuary and ecclesiastical ordinances rail in vain, becoming more intense and detailed in the age of orthodoxy and confessionalization, against excessive gifts, guests, food, and moral license during postbaptismal festivities. We may see this as resistance to strictly ecclesiastical, spiritual definitions of baptism, and as the ongoing appropriation of the liturgy for socioeconomic purposes.

Others areas of resistance include the popular conviction that baptismal water possessed apotropaic qualities that could benefit humans and beasts, and that clerical rites of exorcism were effective and thus

---

[28] For instance, Sächsisches Hauptstaatsarchiv Dresden, Loc. 10601, "Erster Theill Der im Churfurstenthumb Sachssen . . . im 1592 gehaltenen . . . Visitation," fols. 104–16, in which the visitors have drawn up a chart showing Lutheran teaching on the left and their perception of Calvinist teaching on the right; on baptism, fols. 104–6. Also see some of the fliers (poorly) reproduced in Harry Oelke, *Die Konfessionsbildung des 16. Jahrhunderts im Spiegel illustrierter Flugblätter* (Berlin, 1992), such as figs. 38, 39.
[29] Karant-Nunn, "'Lasset die Kindlein zu mir kommen'," unpublished manuscript; see note 14 in this chapter.

salubrious for infants. Parish visitors repeatedly enjoined sextons to dispose of the water immediately and in such a way that it could not be recovered, as by pouring it into a flowing stream, or at least pouring it onto the ground when and where no one was watching. When Saxon authorities decided not to revive baptismal exorcism in 1591, after the death of Elector Christian I, who had introduced Reformed theology and practice to his domains, the people were incensed.[30] In a famous episode in the Holy Cross Church in Dresden, a butcher threatened the pastor with a meat cleaver if he did not include the words of exorcism in his child's baptismal liturgy, and many people took their newborns across territorial borders to obtain exorcism.[31] In Württemberg exorcism was reintroduced in the church ordinance of 1553.[32]

The populace at large continued to regard the Eucharist as having supernatural authority. This was particularly and persistently true in Lutheran territories, where, after all, the very body and blood of Christ remained present on the Communion table and were ingested by the faithful. It would have been difficult for unlettered folk to reconcile theologians' insistence that transubstantiation was nothing but execrable hocus pocus with their just-as-firm assertion that the bread and the wine mysteriously did coexist with the Savior's very flesh. Lutheran divines failed to demystify the Mass and perceptibly left their parishioners persuaded of its supernatural power. Reinforcing the leftover Catholic attitude were the facts that elevation continued until 1542 in Wittenberg; that candles, vestments, and decorative altar cloths remained in use, being replaced as they wore out; that at least some images and many crucifixes continued to adorn the sanctuaries, albeit their nature had altered; and a measure of pomp, music, and Latin remained.

The laity may hardly have noticed a change, even though the catechism was now preached hard upon them. We detect their traditional attitude in several ways. The visitation records expose the tendency to take bits of the Host out of the church in the hand or mouth for use in "superstitious" rites elsewhere. This is an appropriation and extension

---

[30] Bodo Nischan, "The Exorcism Controversy and Baptism in the Late Reformation," *Sixteenth Century Journal* 18.1 (1987): 31–51; summarized in idem, *Prince, People, and Confession: The Second Reformation in Brandenburg* (Philadelphia, 1994), 141–3; Sächsisches Hauptstaatsarchiv Dresden, Loc. 9477, "Visitation Acta Wegen Abschaffung des Exorcismi (1592)."

[31] Ernst Koch, "Ausbau, Gefährdung und Festigung der lutherischen Landeskirche von 1553 bis 1601," in *Das Jahrhundert der Reformation in Sachsen*, ed. Helmar Junghans (Berlin, 1989), 212–15.

[32] Martin Brecht and Hermann Ehmer, *Südwestdeutsche Reformationsgeschichte* (Stuttgart, 1984), 345. The authors remark that this was done in order to come closer to Luther's *Taufbüchlein*, and this may be so, but the people did not object.

of the Mass that is consistent with medieval practice. If a pastor or a deacon dropped the Host in the process of distributing Holy Communion, the people seem to have thought it a serious infraction and reported it to the visitors when they next appeared. Pregnant women and the sick sought Communion as often as possible, suggesting their conviction that it contained healing powers. When people lay on their deathbeds, they sought out the pastor *not* to hear his sermons of admonition but to receive the sacrament one last time, as if certain that this would aid their passage into the next life. The official churches fought these views, which they regarded as papal remnants, but without success. It may well be that Calvinist churches indoctrinated their flocks more successfully, and one of the reasons surely was their sweeping away of the entire semiotic vocabulary of Catholicism. The use of common table bread in the Lord's Supper by itself informed the laity that things were radically different. Just as importantly, in the cities where Calvinism was imposed, oversight was strict and consistent to a degree that it could not be in a larger and rural setting.

Popular resistance and appropriation, taken altogether, possessed two common features. First of all, they rejected the elite assertion that the divine was no longer physically among human beings. It carried at least into the nineteenth century the cosmic view that supernatural forces, both godly and diabolical, were accessible to people by various means, among which were the condoned sacraments and prayers, to be sure, but also disapproved incantations and other ritualized behavior, substances, objects, and practitioners (cunning or wise men and women). When theologically trained and unlettered citizens met in church, their perceptions of the liturgy were likely to differ. Nevertheless, across the spectrum of degrees of education, people found something to supply their needs in church services. That is, it may be that some did not, but the discipline imposed upon them on into the eighteenth century by church and state moved any ideological nonconformists to conceal their dissent.

Second, the people never relinquished the socioeconomic dimensions of ritual. Going to church itself was a social occasion, a time of courting and the exchange of information. The laity clung tenaciously to the interactive and extra-ecclesiastical observances that accompanied each and every liturgically marked rite of passage. In many parishes after the Reformation, the clergy were urged not to participate in these celebrations and ceased to do so. Only the most extreme and consistent governmental disapproval, such as existed in Calvinist towns, could dissuade the people from holding baptismal feasts, post-churching ales, boisterous wedding breakfasts and dances, and wakes. People who lived along confessional boundaries blithely slipped back and forth to uncondoned weddings and baptisms and even received different denominations' Holy Communion without compunction. They did not even mind the Anabaptists in their midst.[33]

Every individual brought to church the person that he was. This is hardly profound. The wonder is that so many people, through the processes of (mis)understanding and (mis)appropriation, thought that they benefited from the rituals they witnessed. That they were so persuaded indicates the strength of the early modern liturgy. I am, though, curious about these processes within the Reformed churches. Did the unrelenting, intrusive probing into states of mind by the Calvinist magistracy and clergy triumph over folkish outlook? Could discipline suppress not just the outward manifestations of belief but the very belief itself? I shall look forward to the later volumes of the Genevan consistory minutes.

---

[33] See my "Confessional Ambiguity along Borders: Popular Contributions to Religious Tolerance in Sixteenth-Century Germany," Seventeenth Sivert O. and Marjorie Allen Skotheim Lecture (published as a separate pamphlet: Walla Walla, WA, 1998).

CHAPTER XI

# Self-correction and social change in the Spanish Counter-Reformation[1]

SARA T. NALLE

THE Counter-Reformation was for Spain, as it was for other European countries, a great watershed, a time when long-standing beliefs and behaviors usually characterized as traditional or medieval were discarded in favor of new ones. Official changes in religious ideas were made carefully, for early modern theologians and rulers fully understood both religion's integrative and disintegrative power. They saw the intimate connection between formal theology and social dealings, and if they embarked on the perilous course of changing religious law, they also expected concomitant change in society. Early modern people intuitively understood Clifford Geertz's conclusion that culture does not consist of a catalog of gestures per se but of the meanings that give gestures their significance, hence their willingness to fight (endlessly, it seems to us) over the religious laws and symbols, both humble and exalted, that gave meaning to their lives.

Both Reformations are distinguished by their self-conscious efforts to direct the beliefs and actions of entire populations or, to put it another way, their attempt to ensure cultural conformity through the shared understanding of symbols of faith. No transformation of cultural attitudes had been attempted on this scale in Europe since the original conversion of the Germanic tribes in the early Middle Ages, which took place under vastly different circumstances. This early modern battle for symbols and souls was waged on several fronts, through religious education, propaganda, and social discipline. Since the 1970s, historians of early modern Europe have embraced research on all of these aspects of the Reformations, but Spanish historiography has come later to a

[1] The author wishes to thank Peter Brown, Sir John Elliott, Lu Ann Homza, and Ronnie Po-Chia Hsia for their comments and encouragement.

302

reappraisal of the Counter-Reformation and brings more excess baggage to the topic – first, the Inquisition's legacy had to be exorcised. As a result, many recent studies of aspects of the Spanish Counter-Reformation tend to be descriptive, or focus on the cruder forms of religious control summed up in the inquisitorial auto-da-fé. Without a doubt, much of the Counter-Reformation's labor was meant to discipline the general population, and the Inquisition relentlessly punished those who refused to conform to the majority religious identification.[2] Yet, religion in Counter-Reformation Spain does not have to be conceived wholly as a matter of force and submission. The image of the auto-da-fé may be balanced against that of the religious play known as the *auto sacramental*, which enjoyed enormous popularity during the Counter-Reformation.[3] Even the auto-da-fé was perceived by its audience as having several functions: to reintegrate into society those who accepted their errors, to mark or exclude those who refused to conform, and finally to heal the religious body through the public affirmation of faith.[4]

If the leaders of the Reformations were not content with external conformity, how do we assess the inward changes of heart, the habits of mind that they wanted to inculcate? Certainly it is possible to show that changes did occur, as I did in my book, *God in la Mancha*, but it has been harder to explain why they did so.[5] Were behaviors altered through coercion – out of fear, even, as some historians have suggested – or did

[2] For examples of this, the reader need go no further than Allyson Poska, *Regulating the People. The Catholic Reformation in Seventeenth-Century Spain* (Leiden, 1998). Certainly the Counter-Reformation Church set limits and enforced them: Extreme cases required extreme measures. However, it would be misleading to argue from rare cases that people conformed out of fear of punishment. Willful heresy and deliberate unfaithfulness were to the seventeenth century what murder is to our own century. Correctly socialized, functioning members of society believe that such crimes lie beyond them; it is not fear of punishment that prevents such people from committing murder/heresy, but their own socialization, which prevents them from considering these things as options. Thus, when they do commit such crimes, public reaction often is that the individual must be insane, for there is no other explanation for the breakdown of internal control.

[3] The *auto sacramental* evolved out of the short mystery plays (*autos* or *farsas*) that were held inside the churches on major holidays. During the seventeenth century, Spain's leading playwrights wrote *autos sacramentales* for the commercial theaters or individual patrons, which might be a city seeking to celebrate Corpus Christi with particular style.

[4] Examples of recent studies are Jesús Vegazo Palacios, *El auto general de fe de 1680* (Malaga, 1995); Consuelo Maqueda Abreu, *El Auto de fe* (Madrid, 1992); and Maureen Flynn, "Mimesis of the Last Judgement: The Spanish *Auto de fe*," *Sixteenth Century Journal* 22 (1991): 281–97. Public acknowledgment of error at this time was the continuation of an age-old approach to dealing with sin inside the Christian community, and we can easily find examples of the rationale behind the auto-da-fé in Protestant congregations that formally exposed or expelled their nonconformist members.

[5] Sara T. Nalle, *God in La Mancha: Religious Reform and the People of Cuenca, 1500–1650* (Baltimore, 1992).

teaching and sermons have a positive impact on individuals' decision making? Historians may despair of answering such questions for lack of suitable sources. Personal testimonials of faith, besides being rare, by nature are exceptional. Perhaps there is some other way of getting at the problem. In this chapter, I propose to examine certain behaviors that we might take for the moment to be external barometers of the inward change that was hoped for. These were swearing, sexual relations, and mourning rituals. Each arose out of very different circumstances, reflecting varying degrees of self-control and attitudes about one's relationship to others (living and dead) and God.

Before beginning with these examples, it is necessary to make a few points about the nature of propaganda, catechism, and confession as they relate to this discussion. The Counter-Reformation was a massive attempt to shape the meaning of cultural symbols in order to promote a common identity. Although much of this effort took the form of the visual propaganda and spectacle for which the Counter-Reformation is famous, this chapter will contend that the most revolutionary innovation of the Counter-Reformation was its emphasis on the active articulation of belief. By teaching the words and concepts one hoped to restructure behavior and even habits of mind. As Maureen Flynn points out in her recent study of blasphemy, "scholastic philosophers of the medieval and early modern periods believed that all language, and particularly spontaneous utterances, exposed our intimate relationship to the sacred order of things, revealing the true sentiment of our souls."[6] Ordering the words, then, was of paramount importance to ordering the signs of religious conformity. At every step, the faithful were exposed to sermons, forced to memorize bits of doctrine and then to contrast what they had learned to the reality of their own behavior. The passive observation of an image or the witnessing of ritual no longer sufficed; now Catholics were expected to know dogma to an extent never before demanded of them. The inarticulate image or gesture remained important, but it was to be coupled to intellectual and emotional understanding. The *auto sacramental*, in which theological ideas are given parts and moved around the stage, is the culmination of the Counter-Reformation's determination to put words to the symbols.

The surest way to achieve a common understanding of religion was to make sure that everyone knew a basic minimum about the tenets of their faith *and* performed a minimum of actions that signified belief. Just as the crime of heresy by definition could not take place in the mind, but

---

[6] Maureen Flynn, "Blasphemy and the Play of Anger in Sixteenth-Century Spain," *Past and Present* 149 (1995): 34.

had to be expressed outwardly,[7] the practice of right religion consisted of internal belief and outward action. Ignatius Loyola meant for his *Spiritual Exercises* to be the implementation of just such a concept when he wrote, "we make acts of the understanding in reasoning and acts of the will in being moved to action." Loyola went on to insist that Catholics should verbalize their approval for the various points of doctrine that he lists and avoid talking about others.[8] On a more popular level, Juan de Avila expressed the same idea in his Second Memorial to the Council of Trent, in which he wrote that it was absurd to teach the catechism in Latin because it precluded the possibility of ordinary people forming the connection between the ideas conveyed by the catechism and the behavior it promoted.[9] What made the nominally converted Moriscos so threatening and hateful to early modern Christian Spaniards was the Moriscos' adherence to the Muslim precept of *taqiyya*, which permitted them to go through the motions of being Christian while remaining inwardly faithful to Islam, thus divorcing action from meaning.

The first step in ordering meanings, then, was to make sure that every member of the community knew the basic words with which to express their faith. This was true for Protestants as well as Catholics; in mirror image of one another Catholic and Protestant societies printed prayer booklets, established Sunday schools, sent out inspectors to evaluate progress in rural areas, and devised methods to ensure continued compliance. During the 1540s, Spanish church officials began to insist on popular catechization, attendance at Sunday mass, and annual confession. Knowledge of one's prayers (i.e., a profession of faith, a sign that one had accepted the meanings) became the prerequisite for undertaking such key social and religious obligations such as marriage, communion, and god parenthood. Every conceivable method was used to teach the prayers: group recitation in church, Lenten catechism classes, children's primers and popular songs, home instruction, specially organized confraternities, and schools. By the end of the sixteenth century, we must conclude that the campaign was successful in the privileged,

---

[7] Diego de Simancas, *De Catholicis Institutionibus. Liber ad praecavendas et extirpandas hereses admodum necessarius* (Valladolid, 1552). In *Tractatus Illustrium in utraque tum pontificii, tum caesarei iuris facultate Iurisconsultorum*, vol. 11, pt. 2, *De Iudicijs Criminalibus S. Inquisitionis* (Venice, 1584), "De Occultis," tit. xlii, fol. 173v. Simancas was not entirely happy with the ruling that the crime of heresy was committed only when expressed externally via actions or words. This stems from the principle of Roman law that a person cannot be punished for thinking of a crime, only for committing one.

[8] Ignatius de Loyola, *The Spiritual Exercises of Saint Ignatius*, trans. T. Corsbishley, S.J. (Wheathampstead, 1973), nos. 352–70, point 3, 12–13.

[9] A. Huerga, "Sobre la catequesis en España durante los siglos XV–XVI," *Analecta Sacra Tarraconensia* 41 (1968): 314–15.

central Castilian dioceses. In interrogations by the Inquisitions of Toledo and Cuenca, thousands of defendants from all walks of life, male and female, literate and illiterate, villager or town dweller, demonstrated that they had successfully memorized the basic prayers of the church – the Lord's Prayer, Hail Mary, Salve, Creed, and Ten Commandments – and more besides. Importantly, although earlier in the century the catechism was often learned in Latin, by 1600 Latin had virtually disappeared from the prayers. The Ten Commandments, the most important component of the prayers for promoting social control, from the beginning were always taught in the vernacular.[10]

Inquisition records show us that people from all walks of life discussed their religion in all sorts of settings. Occasionally, in ordinary conversations, we find them specifically applying to their lives what they had learned in the catechism. Diego Ortiz, for example, was a poorly educated farmer from El Toboso who in a conversation that took place in 1585 maintained that there would be no Last Judgment, and the world would not come to an end as long as God was God. One of those who was listening immediately challenged him, "Don't you know the articles of faith where it says that there will be Judgment?"[11] Nicolás Martínez, a shopkeeper in Santa María del Campo, certainly had absorbed the meaning of the Ten Commandments even if he was in error about who created them. He confessed in 1561 to the inquisitors that he had said, "The [first] three commandments were to honor God and the other seven had been made by men for their own good and that of their neighbor."

---

[10] For Toledo, J.-P Dedieu summarizes briefly his results in *L'Administration de la foi: L'Inquisition de Tolède (XVIe–XVIIIe siècle)* (Madrid, 1989), 51–2, where he notes steady improvement over the course of the sixteenth century. Circa 1531 only forty percent of men were able to recite correctly the Our Father, Hail Mary, Creed, and Salve, but during the first half of the seventeenth century, over eighty percent were successful. For fuller details, see his "'Christianisation' en Nouvelle Castille: catéchisme, communion, messe et confirmation dans l'archevêché de Tolède, 1540–1650," *Melanges de la Casa de Velázquez* 15 (1979): 261–94 (available in an abridged English version, "Christianization in New Castile," in *Culture and Control in Counter-Reformation Spain*, eds. A. Cruz and M.E. Perry [Minneapolis, 1991]). On Cuenca, see Nalle, *God in La Mancha*, 104–33. In the studies of Cuenca and Toledo (contiguous dioceses), both authors use samples of approximately eight hundred subjects each. Defendants were generally male, working class, and accused of minor offenses against the faith, such as blasphemy. In most respects, defendants did not have religious training beyond what was available in the community. Nationally, in all likelihood peripheral areas where the population was poor and dispersed in small communities were not as successfully catechized. See H. Kamen, *The Phoenix and the Flame: Catalonia and the Counter-Reformation* (New Haven, CT, 1993), 348–54, 381–2, 384; and Poska, *Regulating the People*.

[11] "¿No sabéis los artículos de fe donde dice que ha de haver juicio?" Archivo Diocesano de Cuenca, Inquisición [henceforth "ADC, Inq."] 297: 4246 (1585). This sort of peer correction comes up repeatedly in trial testimony.

Martínez was also filled with remorse about his relationship with God since he did not feel sufficiently grateful to him for the riches he had earned.[12]

The most direct test of the strength of the connection between interior understanding and outward action was confession. Since the publication of Thomas Tentler's *Sin and Confession* in 1977, confession and penance have been at the center of several studies about early modern religion.[13] There has been little agreement over how confession was used or what was its psychological impact on believers. In a recent book, David Myers argues that confession, as reconfigured by the Tridentine Church, was meant to become a tool for the spiritual development of the people and did not add appreciably to people's burden of guilt.[14] As yet, there has been no monograph about confession in Counter-Reformation Spain, except in the context of solicitation in the confessional.[15] In the sixteenth century, when religious authorities discussed confession, they had in mind two sorts, annual and frequent. Annual confession and communion, a requirement for all Christians since 1215, was the gross means of religious control, so generalized that it had become a communal ritual for the people. The mass confessions at Eastertide followed by group communion were meant to purify the community and set it straight with God; such confessions had little to do with personal sin and atonement. Over the course of the sixteenth century, authorities adopted more efficient measures to ensure that everyone complied with the annual precept. During Lent, lists of parishioners were drawn up, and in

12 "Los tres mandamientos eran para honrar de dios y los otros siete que los habían hecho los hombres para el provecho de los hombres y del próximo." Martínez was a case of self-denunciation. He told the inquisitors that he was guilty of wishing "that God had not given him as much wealth as he had because it made him uneasy that he did not serve God as he should nor did he give Him thanks as he ought and he did not go to Mass" ("que dios no le oviera dado tantos bienes como tenía por desasosiegos que tenía, que no servía a dios como era obligado ni le daba gracias como debía y no oía misa") ADC, Inq., 225: 2790 (1561).
    The best way to appreciate the range of what could be said or done and in what context is to read one of the Inquisition's *libros de testificaciones*, which collected all the preliminary testimony received during a visitation. As yet, this source has remained completely overlooked by historians except for John Edwards, "Religious Faith and Doubt in Late Medieval Spain: Soria *circa* 1450–1500," *Past and Present* 120 (1988): 3–25.
13 Thomas Tentler, *Sin and Confession on the Eve of the Reformation* (Princeton, 1977); a survey is Jean Delumeau, *L'aveu et le pardon: les difficultés de la confession, XIIIe–XVIIIe siècle* (Paris, 1990).
14 David Myers, *"Poor, Sinning Folk": Confession and Conscience in Counter-Reformation Germany* (Ithaca, NY, 1996).
15 In English, see Stephen Haliczer, *Sexuality in the Confessional: A Sacrament Profaned* (New York, 1996). A more thorough study on the same topic is A. Sarrión Mora, *Sexualidad y confesión: La solicitación ante el Tribunal del Santo Oficio (siglos xvi–xix)* (Madrid, 1994).

the diocese of Cuenca, those who had not confessed by the end of the season could be summoned to the capital for prosecution. Transients had to carry with them certificates of confession; even the incarcerated were being confessed in jail. In Toledo and Cuenca, again according to the testimony of Inquisition defendants, by the end of the century compliance with the precept was virtually complete.

Like the periodic recitations of prayers prior to engaging in essential social contracts (marriage, god-parenthood), annual confession was a test to be passed before the public sharing of communion with the parish at Easter. The very fact that penitents, no matter who they were, found themselves every Easter on their knees in front of the parish priest served to impress upon them the ubiquity of the system. The confession proceeded according to the elements of the previously learned catechism: the Ten Commandments, Articles of Faith, the parts of the Credo, and so on. J.-P Dedieu has described how in inquisitorial interrogations (which technically were confessions), judges sometimes used a defendant's own knowledge of the catechism to shock him into the realization that he had unwittingly broken one of the commandments. An emotional crisis often would follow upon the cognitive breakthrough. Dedieu's comment is apt: "Memorizing formulas thus functioned as the bridge between the general will of the Old Christians to be good Catholics, and, what was more difficult, the observance of the ecclesiastical institution's particular interpretations. This constituted a sign of identity, of being one of the faithful."[16]

Priests knew full well that these annual confessions, hastily made with a certain amount of reluctance and glossing over, could never match the ideal. Beyond the summary annual confessions, Spanish reformers wanted to bring their charges to realize the value of more frequent confession and communion. During the High Middle Ages, both sacraments had been used sparingly, but the trend among the religious orders had been toward practicing them on a regular basis to enhance their members' spiritual life.[17] The purely educational value of frequent confession was not lost on Spanish church officials. Two highly regarded prelates, Martín Pérez de Ayala, who participated in the Council of Trent, and San Juan de Ribera, most noted for his efforts to implement the Tridentine reforms in Valencia, thought that all people should confess frequently

---

[16] Dedieu, "Christianization in New Castile," 8.

[17] Tentler, *Sin and Confession*, 3–27, sees the late medieval emphasis on confession as placing an unbearable burden of guilt on the believer, thus paving the way to the Protestant revolt against the sacrament. Tentler's work is based on Northern and Central European confessors' manuals, many of which were commonly used in Spain.

because in that way they would be inspired not to sin.[18] One of the earlier Spanish writers on the subject, Fr. Hernando de Talavera, explained how without frequent confession, even while a person did nothing bad, sin could form in his heart in the same way that, without periodic care, moths will appear in well-packed clothes or the well-oiled knife will rust in its scabbard: "just so our soul becomes moth-eaten, rusty, corrupted by sin and weeds, if from time to time it is not aired out or weeded by holy confession."[19] Talavera's idea, although hardly original, is key to understanding the popular mentality promoted during the Counter-Reformation. Sin was not something an individual did, but was. It was, first and foremost, internal. If countermeasures were not taken, of their own accord "evil weeds" would take over in the fertile earth of the soul. Seventy years later, Teresa of Avila, describing for her nuns how to cultivate the spiritual life, returned to the image of the weeds spontaneously crowding the garden of the soul.[20]

Formal confession was the most explicit link between meaning and action, meant only for that individual; we generally find out about its impact only when something in the relationship between confessant and confessor went wrong. But the habit of confession does translate into another type of behavior that can be observed more readily. In Spain, examination of one's own sins was promoted along with the idea that individuals must denounce the sins of others, leading to what might be called a "psychology of denunciation" whereby individuals become willing enforcers of community values. In the sixteenth and seventeenth centuries, early modern Spaniards were constantly exhorted to monitor their behavior and that of others and to confess any deviations to the authorities. This psychology of denunciation for the good of oneself and others was inculcated at an early age. In their catechism classes, the Jesuits began the weekly lesson by encouraging the children to remember who had lost their temper and sworn during the week and to denounce those children in front of the others.[21] As the children grew into adults, every few years the diocesan inspector would come to the community and read the Edict of Visitation. The visitation edict was developed by Juan Bernal Díaz de Luco in 1530 and even before Trent

---

[18] E.J. Zarco Cuevas, *España y la comunión frecuente y diaria en los siglos XVI y XVII* (El Escorial, 1912), 93–4. Zarco's book collects the opinions of major Spanish religious figures on the issue, which was controversial.

[19] Zarco, *España y la comunión*, 11: "así cria polillo, orín y corrupción de pecado y malas hierbas nuestra alma, si a menudo no es meneada y escardada de la sancta confesión."

[20] Teresa of Avila, *The Life of Teresa of Avila*, trans. J.M. Cohen (Harmondsworth, 1958), Chapter 11.

[21] Monumenta Historica Societatis Jesu, *Litterae Quadrimestrales* (Madrid, 1894–1925), 3: 89.

it had become part of the diocesan inspection tours of Cuenca and Toledo.[22] The edict reduced into simple language the total of prohibited behavior for priests and parishioners. In the edict drawn up in 1602 for the diocese of Cuenca, on the pain of excommunication, parishioners were given three days to come forward with what they knew about any "public sins" committed by their priests or neighbors. Rather than list the sins by name and take the chance of not being understood, the inspectors described precisely the sinful behavior to look for: "if anyone has been excommunicated for a long time, and remaining so, has attended mass and holy services"; "if there are some married men who do not live with their wives, or, if they have married a second time while their first husbands or wives are still alive"; or "if there are any profiteers and they sell at a higher price than what the thing is worth."[23] Famous, of course, are the equally explicit inquisitorial edicts, which used the carrot-and-stick method to encourage people to discipline themselves. An Edict of Grace offered clemency to those who came forward to confess to the crimes described by the edict; the Edict of Faith held over the people the threat of formal anathema, which invoked unspeakable destruction on the rebellious, their families, animals, and crops.[24]

We can only imagine the psychological impact of these repeated appeals to people's conscience.[25] Inquisition trials show that, having been conditioned from a young age to believe that one must report transgressions of religious law, many people responded to the appeals to

---

[22] Juan Bernal Díaz de Luco, *Instruction muy prouechosa (y aun necessaria) para los visitadores: a donde se muestra como se an de regir los que van a visitar en lugar de los Perlados. Iten otro tractado de dotrina que conuiene: para los visitadores y clerigos* (Alcalá de Henares, 1530). On Toledo, see J. Tellechea Idigoras, "El formulario de visita pastoral de Bartolomé de Carranza, arzobispo de Toledo," *Anthologica Annua* 4 (1956): 385–437.

[23] Andrés Pacheco, *Constituciones synodales de Cuenca* (Madrid, 1602), bk. 3, tit. 13, const. 10: "si alguno ha estado descomulgado mucho tiempo y estándolo ha oydo misa y los diuinos oficios; si ay algunos casados que no hacen vida con sus mugeres; o que están casados dos veces siendo los primeros maridos o mujeres viuos o viuas; si ay algunos logreros y que vendan fiado por mayor precio de lo que valía la cosa a luego pagar."

[24] I.e., "we curse them and damn them in town and country, wherever they may be, and may the houses where they live and the fruits of their fields be damned, and may their animals and livestock die, may God send them hunger, pestilence and death...let them lose their wits and their eyesight...let their wives be widows and their children orphans, let them go begging from door to door and receive nothing...may all the plagues of Egypt and the evilness of Sodom and Gomorrah come over them and let them burn in the fire like they burned"; M. Jiménez Monteserín, *Introducción a la Inquisición española: documentos básicos para el estudio del Santo Oficio* (Madrid, 1980), 534–5. Inquisitors were well aware of the fact that the Edicts could furnish people with enough information to make false denunciations either of themselves or others; the more scrupulous ones attempted to distinguish between generic and specific instances of sin.

[25] For discussions see Tentler, *Sin and Confession*; and Jean Delumeau, *La péché et la peur* (Paris, 1983).

denounce themselves and one another.[26] The psychology of confession and denunciation permeated society and led to powerful lines of social control that were largely self-imposed.

The Counter-Reformation's campaign against blasphemy is an excellent example of how popular feelings of guilt and religious conviction could work hand-in-glove to promote change in behavior. For centuries, in theory, blasphemers had been subject to ferocious punishment in the Spanish law codes, but the threat of bodily mutilation did not control the crime. The mid-sixteenth century, however, was not a time for mincing words: Heresy was on the rise, and blasphemy was considered to be a sign of man's alienation from God. Since Spanish civil courts had proved unable to eradicate blasphemy, many oaths were declared heretical and placed under the Inquisition's jurisdiction. In all of the tribunals, during the Counter-Reformation, blasphemy trials accounted for a large percentage of the cases heard. We can entertain a certain amount of cynicism about these trials as revenue-enhancing schemes, but only so much. After reading many of them, we have to conclude that some blasphemers were genuinely repentant and were actively seeking forgiveness. Had individuals wished to ignore the edicts, in reality the tribunals did not have the personnel or financial resources to enforce them, since they had become blanket condemnations of all sorts of behavior and beliefs. Such a large-scale penancing of the population by the tribunals could only take place with the active cooperation of the persons involved.[27]

Blasphemy had become a sign of the wretched state of the world. As a result, working in conjunction with the Holy Office's campaign against the sin were new religious brotherhoods created to combat oath taking. Juan de Avila recommended at the 1565 Council of Toledo the founding of papal-sponsored brotherhoods of the Santísimo Nombre de Jesus, whose purpose was the suppression of blasphemy. The idea immediately took hold; within a few years of the Toledo council, brotherhoods were operating in the dioceses of Avila, Cuenca, Mallorca, Toledo, Zamora, and no doubt others. The 1583 diocesan visitation of Cuenca recorded 16 organizations in the 116 towns and villages that were inspected.[28]

These brotherhoods worked to suppress blasphemy through a combination of confession, correction, and public education. In Arévalo

---

[26] See Dedieu, *L'administration de la foi*, 121–6; 135–53; and Sara Nalle, "Inquisitors, Priests and the People during the Catholic Reformation in Spain," *Sixteenth Century Journal* 18 (1987): 567–9.

[27] Nalle, "Inquisitors, Priests, and the People."

[28] Juan de Avila, *Obras completas*, 6 vols. (Madrid, 1970–1), 6: 259–60; Nalle, *God in La Mancha*, 162.

(Ávila), with the guidance of their confessors, those who joined the confraternity became responsible for ridding themselves and their households of the habit of swearing. Brothers were encouraged to be self-vigilant; they promised to drop one *blanca*[29] into the *cofradía's* charity box for each time they swore. In addition, in the spirit of good Christian fraternal correction, members were to watch out for one another; if one heard another swear, he was obliged to correct him "with charity and humility." Members' educational and pious activities were rewarded with so many days of grace and jubilees. The brothers were charged with celebrating the Feast of the Circumcision, on which day the cult of the Name of Jesus would be honored. Several weeks before the holiday, members were to go 'round to all the priests and make sure that the holiday would be well publicized and attended. The sermon on that day always had to deal with the harm that comes from swearing, and the brothers could win more indulgences and jubilees by their attendance. The constitutions of one of the brotherhoods from Cuenca were quite similar, with an additional twist: Brothers promised to turn themselves in to the Inquisition for the worst offenses.[30]

As we can see from the example of blasphemy, the purpose of teaching prayers, Sunday sermons, and frequent confession was to make the population internalize doctrine in such a way as to become capable of self-censorship. Nothing could represent more powerfully the religion's success in ordering meanings than its ability to make people look upon their natural desires as sinful or polluting. Concupiscence weighed heavily on the minds of sixteenth-century theologians and urged them to new attacks on the flesh. For Protestants such as Luther, Zwingli, and Calvin, concupiscence was at the core of mankind's depravity, the cause of his estrangement from God, and could not be washed away by baptism. Catholics, committed to free will, preferred to see concupiscence as the spark that leads to sin in individuals not strong enough to resist the devil's wiles. In any case, reform-conscious governments, whether Protestant or Catholic, saw that their populations had to be brought to new standards of sexual conformity.[31] Compliance signaled

---

[29] A *blanca* was one half of a *maravedi*, sufficient to purchase a small wax tablet.

[30] T. Sobrino Chomón, *Documentos de antiguos Cabildos, Cofradías y Hermandades abulenses* (Avila, 1989), 345–52; Nalle, *God in La Mancha*, 159. It bears pointing out that while the majority of Inquisition cases of blasphemy involved men, the membership of the antiblasphemy *cofradías* appears to have been predominantly female!

[31] For a study of Protestant legal action against sin, see Michael F. Graham, *The Uses of Reform: "Godly Discipline" and Popular Behavior in Scotland and Beyond, 1560–1610* (Louvain, 1996).

that theology had conquered the most ungovernable corners of the soul, but defiance meant that conversion was incomplete and any form of revolt could take place. For this reason, libertinage became one of the most frightening crimes of the post-Reformation era because the libertine willfully rejected one of the basic premises of Christian theology and social order.

Given what was at stake, it is hardly surprising that the Inquisition was also enlisted in the defense of sexual order, even though morals did not originally fall within its jurisdiction.[32] It was not heretical to break any of the Ten Commandments, including the sixth (thou shalt not commit adultery) and the ninth (thou shalt not covet thy neighbor's wife). However, theologians writing for the Inquisition liked to emphasize that it was heretical to *deny* that breaking one of the Commandments was a sin.[33] The most blatant area in which laypeople's understanding of morality was at odds with church teaching was the question of simple fornication. Both men and women commonly believed that sex between single individuals, particularly when it involved prostitutes ("paying for it," as people put it), was not sinful. Such an attitude was understandable; men typically did not marry until their mid-twenties and many occupations required seasonal migration and prolonged absences from wives. One result of the delayed marriage patterns was the astonishing popular saying that it was permissible for a man to have intercourse with his mother one time if he had extreme necessity. No defendant ever admitted to performing such an act; rather, the saying expressed the sexual tension resulting from the enforced continence. The euphemistic verbs commonly used in the saying, *cabalgar* (ride) or *echarse* (go to bed with), emphasized the purely physical need of the male, the result of a marital and religious system at odds with the course of human sexual development.[34]

---

[32] This aspect of the Inquisition's activity has been studied in all the recent monographs on the Spanish Inquisition. For a broad discussion of the history of sexuality in Spain and an excellent bibliography, see Francisco Vázquez García, "Historia de la sexualidad en España: Problemas metodológicas y estado de la cuestión," *Hispania* 56 (1996): 1007–35.

[33] A. Albertinus, *De agnoscendis assertionibus catholicis et haereticis tractatus* (Palermo, 1554); reprinted in *Tractatus Illustrium*, vol. 11, pt. 2, *De Iudicijs Criminalibus*, quaes. I, nos. 5, 6.

[34] Mean age at first marriage in Cuenca in 1601–5 was 23.6 years for men and 20.7 years for women. From 1650 to 1800, the mean for men was about 25.5 years (22.3 years for women): David Reher, *Town and Country in Pre-Industrial Spain: Cuenca, 1550–1870* (Cambridge, 1990), 75. In northern Spain, the means were even higher. In Castile, although men married late, there do not seem to have been special youth groups as there were in France and Italy. The confraternities may well have provided some sort of structure for young men, but no research to date pursues that avenue.

The inquisitors were even more determined to teach the true meaning of the sixth commandment than they had been to eradicate blasphemy. In the 1570s, under the leadership of Gaspar de Quiroga, the Supreme Council launched an all-out campaign to teach Spaniards that all sexual relations outside of marriage were a mortal sin. Special edicts were posted in all the towns, and, with the usual compliance, denunciations and confessions started to pour in. From the evidence of the Tribunals of Galicia, Toledo, and Cuenca, it is clear that the inquisitors encountered a great deal more ideological resistance from the "fornicarios" than they did from the blasphemers.[35] Defendants, usually young, single males (locked within the marriage system described previously) could not accept the reality of the moral code being imposed upon them. Yes, bestiality was a mortal sin; adultery was too, but not sexual relations between consenting single adults. How could it be a sin? For these people, sin was still defined as an action that harmed another person, or God, to whom restitution should be made. In the case of blasphemy, we saw that in addition to prohibitions and punishment, there was popular resonance among laypeople, who agreed to form associations and discipline themselves because they believed that oath taking harmed God or the saints and had collective consequences, since it was thought that cursing would bring God's punishment on the community. But who was the wronged party in a case of simple fornication?[36] I have not encountered any popular association of men vowing to lay off simple fornication; instead, efforts at control were directed at what was perceived to be the inspiration of sexual sin – women.[37]

In the case of blasphemy, we saw that some laypeople took to heart the law and set out to reform themselves and others. Whether they enjoyed any success is probably impossible to determine. However, the work of historical demographers does allow us to ask whether the church's sexual teaching succeeded in changing the ways in which men and women understood and then controlled their sexual behavior.

Theologians carefully regulated the conditions under which licit sexual transactions could take place. They taught that only intercourse with

---

[35] See especially Jaime Contreras, *El santo oficio de la Inquisición de Galicia: poder, sociedad y cultura* (Madrid, 1982), 637–40.

[36] Perhaps because these particular inquisitorial cases dealt with hypotheticals rather than with real actions, and emphasized the consensual nature of the relations, there was never any discussion of honor or marriage.

[37] Here is not the place to enter into the gender wars of the Counter-Reformation. For Spain, readers can test the waters with Mary Elizabeth Perry, *Gender and Disorder in Early Modern Seville* (Princeton, 1990) and María Helena Sánchez Ortega, *La mujer y la sexualidad en el antiguo régimen: la perspectiva inquisitorial* (Madrid, 1992).

one's spouse for the purpose of procreation or to satisfy the marriage debt was completely blameless sex; all other sexual acts and relationships were transgressions to some degree. Penitents were instructed to examine even their thoughts; if they had lingered over lustful images and derived pleasure from them, they had sinned as surely as if they had in fact committed the imagined deed.[38] Knowing what was sin was one thing; not committing it, however, was another.

One common benchmark measure of the church's success in imposing its teachings on sex has been the illegitimate birth rate, although, like many statistics derived from early modern sources, such figures are difficult to interpret. Historical demographers are not always sensitive to religious questions while conducting their research. In larger towns and cities with foundling hospitals, establishing an illegitimacy rate is complicated by the problem of abandoned infants, who may have been legitimate or even may have been brought to the town from outlying villages.[39] Moreover, rates vary considerably from year to year, and from parish to parish, according to the economic conditions of the period and the neighborhood. In this situation, the more reliable indicators are figures derived from continuous data stretching over a very long period of time. Although such figures may underreport the total of illegitimate births, they do point to the general change in the population's behavior. From the sixteenth through the eighteenth century, the trend was a gradual decline in illegitimate births. For example, Talavera de la Reina's illegitimacy rate fell from 5.2 percent of births in 1550–99 to 0.9 percent in 1700–50, but was back up to 4.2 percent during the latter half of the eighteenth century. The Cantabrian village of Liebana exhibited extraordinarily low rates and slightly different timing, but the general downward trend was the same.[40]

As the authors of these studies point out, it is very difficult to sort out the factors affecting illegitimate births. A somewhat different approach to the question is to ask whether or not the Church's teaching of sexual abstinence during Lent was observed. By counting back nine months from the baptismal date (parents were required to bring the infant for baptizing within fifteen days of birth), one gains a rough idea of the date of conception. Three factors other than religious belief could

---

[38] For an extended discussion, see Tentler, *Sin and Confession*, 162–232.

[39] See Claude Larquié, "Amours légitimes et amours illégitimes à Madrid au XVIIe siècle (une approche quantitative)," in *Amours légitimes et amours illégitimes en Espagne (XVIe–XVIIe siècles)*, ed. A. Redondo (Paris, 1985), 69–91.

[40] María del Carmen González Muñoz, *La población de Talavera de la Reina (siglos XVI–XX)* (Toledo, 1974), 109, 196, 281; R. Lanza García, *Población y familia campesina en el antiguo régimen. Liebana, siglos XVI–XXI* (Santander, 1988), 149.

affect the seasonality of conceptions: the rhythm of the agricultural year, the prevalence of disease, and the timing of marriages. All over Spain, during the early modern period, conceptions were inversely correlated with adult mortality, which typically peaked in the months of August, September, or October. March, the month most affected by Lent, was a period of relative low adult mortality and agricultural inactivity (thus, in theory, ideal for conceptions). The most popular time for marriages fell between Epiphany (January 6) and Ash Wednesday (which can fall as early as February 8 or as late as March 7).

In Cáceres, A. Rodríguez Sánchez analyzed conceptions from the latter half of the sixteenth century by season, parish, and the social status of the parents. Two parishes in Cáceres were dominated by noble and ecclesiastical households; the other two were predominantly lower class. At first glance conceptions seemed little influenced by the religious injunctions of Lent; there was no shortfall of conceptions during March, although neither was there a surplus.[41] Instead, conceptions peaked in December and January, months of merrymaking and marriages, and bottomed out in the late summer, when mortality was high. However, when it came to *illegitimate* conceptions, the four parishes did alter their behavior. Commoners and nobles alike avoided illicit sexual relations during Lent; the self-control was most pronounced in the noble parishes. Few individuals seemed willing to compound their sins during Lent; at least that much of the Church's teaching was coming across.[42] When Rodríguez further examined all illegitimate conceptions, he discovered that the choice of sexual partners varied as well. In the aristocratic parishes, seventy percent of illegitimate births were to slaves and married or widowed servants, while in the working-class parishes, half of illegitimate births were to single parents. In Cáceres, then, we see acted out in the behavior of its lower-class citizens the belief that sexual relations between single persons were not sinful. Nobles, on the other hand, chose partners for whom there would be the least amount of social accounting: slaves and servants.[43]

---

[41] Angel Rodríguez Sánchez, *Cáceres: poblaciones y comportamientos demográficos en el siglo XVI* (Cáceres, 1977), 100. If sexual relations are constant, we would expect conceptions to be evenly distributed throughout the year. The expected average is then compared to the actual number, giving an index of surplus or deficit births.

[42] We may observe the same contrast in Madrid: Larquié, "Amours légitimes," 91; and in Medina del Campo: Alberto Marcos Martín, *Auge y declive de un nucleo mercantil y financiero de Castilla la Vieja. Evolución demográfica de Medina del Campo durante los siglos XVI y XVII* (Valladolid, 1978), 111–13.

[43] Rodríguez, *Cáceres*, 109–18.

Lent's impact on married couples' behavior was less pronounced, although here we encounter more ambiguity. Since Lent was preceded by the marriage season and Carnival, the asceticism of established couples could be offset by the enthusiasm of the newly married and Carnival revelers. Two demographers have tried to control for the problem. At first glance, couples in seventeenth-century Zaragoza appeared hardly affected by Lent, but when M.C. Ansón Calvo compared the behavior of established couples with that of the newlyweds, it turned out that the older couples did observe the Lenten precept.[44] In Cuenca, David Reher tracked conceptions to the precise dates of the Lenten and Easter seasons, and also controlled for first marriages. Again, among established couples, there were twenty percent fewer conceptions than had occurred in the weeks just prior to Lent.[45]

The preceding examples are not intended as conclusive proof of the influence of religious ideas on sexual behavior but rather as ways for historians to begin to evaluate in concrete ways the impact of the Counter-Reformation on Spanish society. In the cases of blasphemy and sexual relations, the Church's intent was to make people learn to control their own behavior, behavior that was virtually instinctual or at the very least impulsive. The last example for us to consider involves behavior that stems entirely from the intersection between belief and custom: the question of what should be done for the soul after the death of the body. No discussion of Spanish society during the Counter-Reformation would be complete without an examination of the baroque cult of death that gripped the country and diverted much of its resources into funeral pomp and suffrages. Peter Brown once observed, writing about Mediterranean funeral practices, that burial customs are among the most stable aspects of a culture. The durability of such customs should make us resist facile labels, such as "pagan" or "Christian," and look instead for the continuity of underlying structures of belief.[46] If basic, centuries-old patterns of care for the dead change in a relatively short amount of time, then we are confronted with a cultural shift of enormous proportions. The effect of the Counter-Reformation was to provoke such a fundamental shift in Spain.

To appreciate just how radical the changes were, we must take a macroscopic approach and begin in the late antique period. Prominent

---

[44] María del Carmen Ansón Calvo, *Demografía y sociedad urbana en la Zaragoza del siglo XVII* (Zaragoza, 1977), 85.

[45] Reher, *Town and Country*, 104–5.

[46] Peter Brown, *The Cult of the Saints. Its Rise and Function in Latin Christianity* (Chicago, 1981), 24.

features in Roman burials were graveside offerings of food and the use of torches. All of the ceremonies required the intensive involvement of the family. Roman women mourned their dead by lamenting loudly and clawing their cheeks and breasts; men poured ashes on their heads. After interment, the family observed a nine-day mourning period culminating in elaborate feasts and torches at the graveside of the deceased. An official mourning period would continue for one year after the death of the family member, with ceremonies marking the 30th, 40th, and 365th days of mourning.[47]

Christians in Roman Spain found it difficult to give up mourning their dead according to pagan tradition. At the very first Hispanic Council, Hispano-Roman Christians were told not to burn daytime torches at the graves of their dead.[48] Despite St. Augustine's complaints about Christians observing pagan funeral practices, Visigothic Christians in Spain continued the tradition of feasting at the graveside of the dead. At the Council of Braga (561), the Visigothic Church tried to undermine the private and pagan nature of grave offerings by decreeing that the goods would become the property of the priests, and a few years later, the Council of Toledo outlawed grave offerings and mourning altogether. Such orders seem to have had no effect; five hundred years later we find the Council of Coyanza (1055) still trying to outlaw graveside banquets and offerings of food to the dead.[49]

Gradually, the mourning periods and feasts were co-opted into a Christian structure. Very early on, in the seventh century, the Roman thirty days of mourning became a liturgical cycle of thirty masses known as the trental.[50] As we see from the Council of Braga, there also were attempts to transform the graveside feasting into an oblation for the priests. Eventually this became known as the *ofrenda* (typically made up

---

[47] Fred Paxton, *Christianizing Death: The Creation of a Ritual Process in Early Medieval Europe* (Ithaca, NY, 1990), 23–5.

[48] Concilio de Ilíberis (306?), in José Orlandis and Domingo Ramos-Lissón, *Historia de los concilios de la España romana y visigoda* (Pamplona, 1986), 39.

[49] Joyce E. Salisbury, *Iberian Popular Religion, 600 B.C. to 700 A.D.: Celts, Romans and Visigoths* (New York, 1985), 281; *Historia de la Iglesia en España* (Madrid, 1982), II: 2, 299. These observations emphasize the continuity of Roman customs, by which I do not mean to imply Spanish Christians were really pagans. Early Christians in Spain did exhibit a change in behavior reflecting a purely Christian belief: They wanted to be buried inside their churches near the relics of the saints. This was quite contrary to the Romans' practice of keeping their dead isolated in cemeteries, separate from the living. See particularly, Brown, *The Cult of the Saints*, Chapter 1.

[50] According to tradition, Pope Gregory I (540–604) originated the trental. The early history of the novena is not as clear. The earliest novena dates back to the tenth Council of Toledo (656) but was related to Christmas. See *The Catholic Encyclopedia* (New York, 1911), 141–3.

of the symbolic wine, bread, and wax, but sometimes including meat, cheese, and stew) and was carried to the church every day that the family held obsequies for the deceased. Only sixty-five years after the Council of Coyanza, which was still trying to prohibit banqueting, we find what seems to be the successful transformation of grave offerings into *ofrendas.* In 1120, the Fuero de Ledesma, a body of customary law, ordered that widows were now *obligated* to carry a weekly *ofrenda* to their husband's grave, although as yet this was not permitted on Sundays.[51] Late medieval testaments show that all of the important elements of the Christianized Roman burial – torches, grave offerings, and mourning cycles of 9, 30, and 365 days, public wailing by the women (*llantos*) – were still in place at the end of the Middle Ages.

Despite these mourning rituals' durability, the sixteenth and seventeenth centuries witnessed the rapid decline or disappearance of the ancient customs. In some areas, the *ofrenda* and traditional 9-, 30-, 40-, and 365-day mourning periods began to disappear or lose their intensity. In Madrid, Zamora, and Cuenca, the trental disappeared by 1580. The novena (a medieval cycle of nine masses over the course of nine days) with its accompanying *ofrenda* was well on its way out by the beginning of the seventeenth century.[52] The elaborate *cabo de año* ceremony, which usually repeated whatever services had been performed for the deceased on the day of his funeral (as it were, a second and final death), also disappeared in Cuenca in the seventeenth century. In both Cuenca and Oviedo, where there had been a tradition of carrying grave offerings for an entire year (the *añal*), the nature of offering changed from gifts of food, wine, and wax candles, to just candles, which symbolized the Resurrection.[53] Most families, however, simply stopped observing the custom, and testators ceased requiring the detailed involvement of their families in the mourning process. Some thirteen centuries after the

---

[51] Antonio Cea Gutiérrez, "Ritos de difuntos en Salamanca," *Revista de Dialectología y Tradiciones Populares* 40 (1985), 39. In sixteenth-century Alberca, the *ofrenda* was actually called "las novenas."

Ritual demonstrations of grief similarly underwent slow change. Medieval Spanish towns found it necessary to legislate excessive mourning and to restrict face scratching to the immediate female relatives of the deceased; see Heath Dillard, *Daughters of the Reconquest* (Cambridge, 1984), 96. In the early modern period, I have not encountered any references to self-mutilation, but church officials continued to exhort women not to wail in church (*llantos*) because it displayed lack of confidence in salvation.

[52] Nalle, *God in La Mancha*, 191, 194; Florián de Ocampo, *Actitudes religiosas ante la muerte en Zamora en el siglo XVI: un estudio de mentalidades* (Zamora, 1989), 48, 43; Carlos M.N. Eire, *From Madrid to Purgatory. The Art and Craft of Dying in Sixteenth-Century Spain* (New York, 1995), 223.

[53] Roberto J. López López, *Comportamientos religiosos en Asturias durante el Antiguo Régimen* (Gijón, 1989), 107–12; Nalle, *God in La Mancha*, 194.

conversion of Hispania, basic patterns of mourning finally were beginning to shift. Why?

The answer would appear to lie in the popular triumph of two powerful ideas that were successfully linked during the Counter-Reformation: purgatory and Christian individualism. Since the dogma of Purgatory was confirmed in 1274, salvation fell within the reach of virtually everyone, and anyone who had money or family could speed up the process of purging the soul's sins.[54] The ideal suffrage involved masses; funeral pomp, although important to satisfy social expectations, was secondary. During the late medieval period, Castile's elites enthusiastically embraced the doctrine of Purgatory. In the fifteenth century, the oligarchy of Valladolid, for example, began founding private chantries whose only purpose was to provide perpetual masses for the benefit of their own souls. The mendicant movement, patronized by Castile's titled families, promoted a new spirituality that encouraged one to look deeper into one's sins and to gain a greater appreciation of the judgment of the soul that was to come. Thus, among *vallisoletano* testators, half wanted to be buried in the habit of Saint Francis (as did Queen Isabel) and in the preambles to their testaments, we find a growing obsession with personal sin, death, and the need for the Virgin's intercession on behalf of the soul.[55]

Among the less affluent classes, the doctrine of Purgatory was slower to triumph.[56] In the late medieval period, funerals and mourning tended to be collective and were still tied to the traditional, Roman-inspired mourning patterns. The corporate nature of medieval society encouraged individuals to seek the solidarity of their peer groups and families for salvation; with confraternities and similar associations marching in the funeral cortege, the deceased satisfied the requirements of his earthly status and reaped the spiritual and economic benefits of such associations.[57] As yet, lower-class Spaniards did not feel the need for a large number of masses or excessive gifts of bread, wine, and wax. In fifteenth-century Murcia, the majority of testamentary bequests for masses fell

---

[54] On the creation and spread of the cult of Purgatory, see Jacques Le Goff, *The Birth of Purgatory* (Chicago, 1984).

[55] Adeline Rucquoi, *Valladolid en la Edad Media. II: El mundo abreviado (1367–1474)* (Valladolid, 1987), 310–12, 385–7.

[56] "Triumph" in the sense that concern for the soul in Purgatory dominated all funeral arrangements – I do not wish to imply that ordinary Spaniards were unaware of the concept of Purgatory as Henry Kamen claims for the sixteenth century in the *Phoenix and the Flame*.

[57] Adeline Rucquoi, *Valladolid en la Edad Media. I: Genesis de un poder* (Valladolid, 1987), 355: "In short, the *vallisoletanos* seem much more preoccupied with the completion of their last wishes on earth than with the remission of their sins."

between a total of eleven and forty (i.e., a novena or novena with trental).[58] Similar figures may be found in other cities of Castile in the first half of the sixteenth century: In the cities of Cuenca, Zamora and Madrid, about half of testators requested fewer than forty masses. As for the *ofrenda*, testators in Cuenca rarely stipulated more than a pound or two of bread, a pint of wine and a wax taper for each day of obsequies.[59]

The sixteenth century witnessed the extraordinary rise in the amount of suffrages, offerings, and number of marchers in the funeral cortege, and then their abrupt collapse, except for the suffrage of mass. Up until the last quarter of the century, testators seemed unable to discriminate between the various aspects of their funeral and suffrages: Simply, more was better, no matter what it was. In the case of the wealthy, in some parts of Spain during the sixteenth century, the *ofrenda* could involve gifts of entire cows, bushels of wheat, and vats of wine – a true frenzy of materialism. Testators had absorbed the concept that the more suffrages that were poured into the Church, the quicker they and their relatives could be redeemed from Purgatory. For example, in 1585, over half of the testators in Cuenca now wanted at least 115 masses said for their souls, several confraternities marching in the funeral cortege, and for those who wanted the *ofrenda*, increased amounts of wax, wine, and bread as well.

Right on the heels of the success of the idea of Purgatory, however, came the popularization of the new spirituality, which encouraged personal devotions and a critical attitude toward rituals. Thus, while some people equated the quasi-pagan *ofrendas*, mourning cycles, and funeral marchers with Christian faith, others began to see the practices as earthly vanity. No matter how much some priests tried to justify the gifts of bread and wine as suffrages, the fact that the *ofrenda* was specifically left on the grave of the deceased could not disguise its less than Christian origin. Even lower-class residents of the diocese of Cuenca began to see that the custom was a vanity that did nothing for the souls of the deceased. Marco López, a wool comber from Valera de Arriba, told the inquisitors in 1574: "This offering thing of bread and wine doesn't help the dead, that is an earthly custom . . . which benefits the priests . . . but does nothing for the dead." A linen weaver from Gascueña, who went to confession often, admitted to having said, "Burning candles for the dead was empty vanity." When a large amount of wax was used in a

---

[58] Amparo Bejarano Rubio, *El hombre y la muerte. Los testamentos murcianos bajomedievales* (Cartagena, 1988), 64.
[59] Nalle, *God in La Mancha*, 188, 186; Ocampo, *Actitudes religiosas*, 47; Eire, *From Madrid to Purgatory*, 178–9.

funeral in El Cañavate, Catalina Escribana, the wife of a farmer, sniffed, "[even] for King Don Felipe [II] our lord that was an awful lot of pomp." As far as she was concerned, the service of mass was worth more than any pomp that money could buy.[60]

In other words, during the latter half of the sixteenth century, we find ordinary Spaniards learning to discriminate between actions that they believed truly were for the good of their souls or those of their relatives and customs that they thought were worldly or even superstitious. The long-term trend was to order more masses, which indisputably benefited the soul, and to leave the other funeral arrangements, particularly those involving gifts of food, in the hands of the executors, or to omit the requests altogether. In all of the cities surveyed, toward the end of the sixteenth century, the mendicants began to play a larger role in funerals. They marched in the cortege, said the masses, and provided the shroud and burial ground, while the participation of lay mourners and clerics, except for orphans, fell off. The traditional mourning cycles of nine and thirty days went out of fashion; instead, all the burial and mourning rituals were collapsed into a period of three days following death, for it was during these three days that the soul was believed to be personally judged by Jesus. In late seventeenth-century Madrid, which had once led the country in extravagant funeral pomp, we see the culmination of the modern trend toward simplification. Now, a growing number of individuals wanted to be buried in secret with the total absence of ritual: They knew that whatever went on between God and the soul would not be affected by the vain efforts of humans.[61]

* * * * *

From the High Middle Ages to the Counter-Reformation, confession became progressively more frequent and private; penance, more symbolic; and the definition of sin, more abstract. These examples of blasphemy, seasonality of conceptions, and funeral customs suggest that the Spanish population embraced the policy of self-correction that was the Church's goal. For the mass of people, perhaps the great innovation in their lives was the required verbalization of doctrine and examination

---

[60] "Esto de la ofrenda de pan y vino no los sirvía a los difuntos, que aquello era uso de tierra...que para los clérigos era el provecho, que a los difuntos...no les servirá de nada"; "Quemar candelas para difuntos era una vanagloria"; "Para el rey don Felipe nuestro señor hera mucha aquella pompa." ADC, Inq., cases 257: 3494; 257: 3500; 304: 4400.

[61] Jesús Bravo Lozano, "Morir en Madrid: ¿Nueva sensibilidad a fines del siglo XVII?" *Hispania Sacra* 42 (1990): 109–209.

of conscience. For many of them, being present and participating in the required ceremonies was enough; officials were satisfied with outward conformity. For others, the weight of supervision could lead to a heightened sense of guilt as they began to internalize sin. For still others, the policies could promote a greater awareness of self as individuals learned to explore their psyches. How many? It would be impossible to tell, but certainly more than the clerical and cloistered elites. The Counter-Reformation's repeated reliance on language to forge a link between interior faith and outward action fostered the internalizing of social control and the cult of introspection, habits of mind more commonly associated with the "modern" Protestant approach to religion.[62] In other words, to characterize the Counter-Reformation as an historically "backward" movement that forced unthinking compliance through a combination of propaganda, threats, and constant surveillance simply does not do justice to the complexity of the movement or the depth of its influence. In many respects, both Reformations embraced similar programs of social control with the potential for similar changes; future research will show whether or not they left a similar impact.

---

[62] A book that explores these issues in a regional study is Oscar di Simplicio, *Peccato, penitenza, perdono, Siena 1575–1800. La formazione della coscienza nell'Italia moderna* (Milan, 1994).

# CHAPTER XII

# The disenchantment of space: Salle church and the Reformation

## EAMON DUFFY

OUR theme is religion and the early modern state, with all the polarities such a title implies. In this chapter, I want to consider the impact of the Reformation in a community in which "folk belief" and the state religion – or at any rate the religion of the local clerical and social elites – were intimately bound together, and in which the social, economic, and religious dynamics and interests of the community were represented and inscribed in a great building, one of the most harmonious perpendicular churches of fifteenth-century England. I want to explore the way in which that building even now encodes the interplay of social realities and relations within a gentry-dominated community on the eve of the Reformation. I also want to raise some questions about the extent to which the Reformation should be considered not an act of state so much as an assertion of social hegemony, a radical simplification of social as well as religious space, the elimination or overwhelming of some of the key constituent elements in the balance of a late medieval community.

### THE PARISH OF SALLE

The great church of Salle stands isolated in the north Norfolk fields near Aylsham: There is no longer anything that could be called a village.[1] The parish was once a rich and important place, weaving linen and

---

[1] Much of the surviving documentation on medieval Salle is gathered or summarized in W.L.E. Parsons, *Salle: The story of a Norfolk Parish, Its Church, Manors and People* (Norwich, 1937) [hereafter cited as *Salle*]; a brief architectural account by T.A. Heslop in *The Cambridge Guide to the Arts in Britain*: vol. 2. *The Middle Ages*, ed. Boris Ford (Cambridge, 1988), 194–9; R. Fawcett and D. King, "Salle Church," *Archaeological Journal* 137 (1980): 332–5; F. Blomefield and C. Parkin, *An Essay towards a Topographical History of the County of Norfolk* (London, 1769), IV: 421–6.

Hessian for the region as well as wool, but there were never enough people in Salle to fill the church. The population of the parish probably never exceeded four or five hundred, if so many, and it may already have been in decline in the early Tudor period. Fifty-four taxpayers are recorded in a lay subsidy of 1333, forty-two in the subsidy of 1544; the rector returned one hundred fifty communicants (i.e., adults over the age of about sixteen) in 1603.[2] So this huge building was never full and was never intended to be full; its space was intended as the setting for elaborate liturgy and processions, involving the whole parish, but also for the smaller-scale worship in screened-off side chapels, which housed the daily and occasional activities of the guilds and family chantry-chapels. In the mid-fifteenth century, this relatively small community supported up to seven priests and was the focus of a complex web of religious and social rituals and relationships that have left their marks in the material fabric of the building and in a rich deposit of documents in the diocesan, county, and national archives.

### THE GENTRY AND SALLE

The parish of Salle in the Middle Ages contained four manors and parts of several others. It was, therefore, dominated by a cluster of great and less than great gentry families, some of them with country-wide interests, like the Pastons and their various alliances, others more modest in their wealth but by the same token more solidly rooted in the parish itself, like the Brigg family, who held two manors and who built the south aisle and porch of the church. This strong gentry presence is registered on the west front of the church, where a series of heraldic shields on either side of the empty central niche (which, a will of 1528 tells us, housed "Our Lady of the West") contains the arms of the Brewes (who were patrons of the living, and whose arms therefore occur first), Ufford, Mauteby, Morley, and Kerdeston families, all major clans with landed interests in the parish.[3] The Brigg arms are similarly displayed on the south porch. Inside the church there are more gentry memorials, not least to the Boleyn family, local landlords who were to rocket to fame, fortune, and subsequently near calamity in the person of Anne Boleyn. Godfrey Boleyn, whose brass is the most dominant monument in the central aisle, was probably one of the key figures in the rebuilding of Salle church in the early fifteenth century (between ca. 1410 and 1430).

---

[2] Figures from *Salle*, 139–40.
[3] The coats of arms are detailed in *Salle*, 32–3.

Through these gentry, squires and squireens, the parish touched national politics, and not only at the Reformation. The nave roof once had the arms of the intermarried Brewes and Shardelow families blazoned on the rafters, and Sir John Brewes, patron of the living and another of the gentry whose estate probably provided much of the funding for the building of the present church, was one of four Norfolk gentlemen captured during the 1381 Peasants' Revolt and forced into an embassy to the king on behalf of the rebels. He was eventually rescued by the militaristic bishop of Norwich, Henry Dispencer. The five-paneled altarpiece of the Passion of Christ in Norwich Cathedral is sometimes said to have been commissioned by Dispencer in thanksgiving for the suppression of the Rising, though there is no contemporary evidence for this link, and the retable may predate the Rising. But whatever its date and occasion, it bears the arms of another family with landholdings in Salle: the Kerdestons, one of whose manors was partly situated in the parish, though their main base was elsewhere.[4]

The building itself, then, was paid for by a group of rich and not quite so rich families, whose fortunes were founded on the sheep who grazed the commons and fields of Salle, Cawston, and the surrounding parishes. By no means all of these families had blue blood, and the proud blazoning of their arms on the west front here at Salle as at neighboring Cawston has as much of the jumpy pride of the *arriviste* as of the confidence of those born to effortless social superiority. Most had made their money in wool, not necessarily all that long ago, like Thomas Roos (= Rose), who built the north transept chapel and who is buried there under the best brass in the church. He and his wife, Katherine, were members of the Coventry cloth guild (as were many other prosperous Salle graziers and wool-staplers: the Boleyns, Briggs, Fountaines, Gowers, Melman, Seggefords). Roos, pious patron of the Trinity guild, was fined in 1425 for grazing five hundred sheep on Cawston common when he was entitled only to graze two hundred.[5]

These wealthy men and women had an enormous impact on parish life. John Fountaine, whose brass is also in the north transept, where he and his three wives, Alice, Joan, and Agnes are buried, made in 1453 a will that shows his involvement or interest in every dimension of parish life. He left gifts to the high altar, to the light before the rood, to the guilds of the Blessed Virgin, St. Margaret, St. John, the Holy Trinity, and St. Paul; he made bequests for the building funds of eight local churches

---

[4] Jonathan Alexander and Paul Binski, eds., *The Age of Chivalry: Art in Plantagenet England, 1200–1400* (London, 1987), 516–17.
[5] Listed in *Salle*, 94–5; for Thomas Roos's misdemeanor, p. 47.

(including Cawston) and to two ploughlights and three maiden lights in Salle – perhaps those for the parts of the parish where his land was. And to emphasize both his personal and his parochial piety, he sent a priest to Rome to celebrate mass in the church of St. Paul outside the walls, the shrine where the patron saint of the parish is buried.[6] Once dead, the influence of such men was continued by the recurrence of their funeral celebrations, or "obits," every year, when candles were placed on their graves, masses and dirges were sung, and alms of food, money, and clothing were given to the poor. John Fountaine's funeral celebrations immediately after his death lasted for seven days and will have been a prominent feature of the parish's round of worship during that time, and annually thereafter on his anniversary day – as they were meant to be.

### THE GUILDS, LIGHTS, AND PRIVATE PATRONAGE

As Fountaine's will shows, Salle had a number of ploughlights and maiden lights, at Marshgate, Kirkgate, Lunton, and Steynwade, all of which maintained lamps in the church. The maiden lights are referred to in Latin documents as "puelaria" or "trepidaria" (more or less the Latin for tripping the light fantastic), and they were regularly remembered by testators, like Alice Martyn, who left 6*d* to the ploughlight and "to the daunsyng lights of the maydens to eche of them 3*d.*"[7] Identical organizations flourished in surrounding parishes, as at Cawston a mile away, where they are specially well documented. Both ploughlights and dances were organized by streets or districts, and by gender-specific youth groups, which raised money to maintain lamps in the church, and which might on occasion contribute funds toward parish projects. Maiden lights were usually funded by collections taken at dances, ploughlights by collections made by young men in January, when they harnessed themselves to a plough that they dragged round the district, raising money from householders on threat of ploughing up the ground outside their doors.[8] Parishioners often left bequests for the maintenance of their local ploughlight, like William Kechyn, a

---

[6] Norfolk Record Office [hereafter cited as NRO], Norwich Consistory Court Wills [henceforth NCC], 181/182 Aleyn.

[7] NRO, Archdeaconry of Norwich Wills [hereafter cited as ANW], 222 Gloys, Will of Alice Martyn, 1510; see NRO, ANW, 173 Cooke, Will of Margaret Greeve, 1508 (bequest of 3*d* to the ploughtlight of Kirkgate); parish organizations for women only are discussed, using evidence mainly from the southwest of England, in Katherine L. French, "Maiden Lights and Wives Stores: Women's Parish Guilds in Late Medieval England," *Sixteenth Century Journal* 29 (1998): 399–425.

[8] For ploughlights, see Ronald Hutton, *The Stations of the Sun: A History of the Ritual Year in Britain* (Oxford, 1996), 124–8.

parishioner of Sloley, in Norfolk, who left 20*d* in 1506 to "the plough light of the street there I dwell ynne," and 12*d* "to every of the odir vii plough lights in the same town."[9] Ploughlights might also be funded by ales organized by the young men of a street or settlement. The bell-ringers' gallery in the tower at Cawston has a carved beam recording that the gallery was paid for by ales organized by one such group, the ploughlight of Sygate, a settlement on the north side of the parish. We know that there were other Cawston ploughlights based on settlements at Eastgate and "the Dams," and in 1490, William Herward of Cawston left 12*d* "to the Plowlyght of Sygate," another 12*d* "to the Dawnce of Sygate," and 6*d* "to ich other plowlyght in Cawston and dawnce of the same town." The gallery inscription runs:

God spede the plow and send us ale corn enow our purpose for to make A(t) crow of cock of the plowlete of Sygate Be mery and glad Wat good ale this work mad(e).[10]

Wat Good ale here is not, of course, an individual but a joking reference to the drinking celebrations that funded the gallery.

Awareness of the existence of such groups in Salle – at Marchgate, Kirkgate, Lunton, and Steynewade – perhaps even more than the presence of the guilds, helps modify the sense the present building conveys of overwhelming gentry domination of the parish and its social and sacred space. It may well be that the sons and daughters of the gentry took part in the activities of the lights and dances, as their seniors seem to have done in the guilds, but numerically, at least, they hardly can have dominated them. The popular sociability represented by ales, dances, and plough celebrations suggests a plebian involvement in the life of the parish, invisible now but that will have been symbolically registered in the lights these bodies maintained at images and altars in the church.

There were seven guilds in Salle: of the Blessed Virgin Mary (the Assumption guild), of St. Thomas, of St. Paul (the parish dedication), of St. John the Baptist, of St. Margaret, of the Trinity, which had its altar and priest in Thomas Roos's chapel, and of St. James, which had its altar in the chapel of the south transept, built for it by Thomas Brigg (d. 1444).[11] His initials are on bosses in the roof, his name is on the outside of the chapel cornice, and the remains of his gravestone, and that of his two wives, both called Margaret, can be seen in the south end of

---

[9] NRO, NCC, 444 Ryxe.
[10] H. Harrold, ed. "Extracts from Early Norfolk Wills," *Norfolk Archaeology* 1 (1847): 119.
[11] His will is in Public Record Office [hereafter PRO], Prerogative Court of Canterbury [hereafter PCC] Wills, 44/45 Wylbey.

the transept with other Brigg burials. Thomas and his wives kneel before St. Thomas Becket in the upper registers of the reconstructed glass of the east window of this chapel. It was, therefore, very much a Brigg family chapel, partitioned from the rest of the church as Brigg's land, no doubt, was fenced off from that of his neighbors. But his chapel also was the St. James guild chapel, and along with the Brigg family name, the scallop shell of St. James can be seen carved on the outside of this transept. The Briggs dominated this southern side of the church, and not just the transept. Thomas's son, John, is buried in the south aisle under a shroud brass, paid for – somewhat belatedly – by *his* son Thomas, who left £1 6s 8d in his will in 1494, "for a marble stone for my father in Salle Church."[12] The effigy of John Brigg presents this member of one of the parish's more opulent families as the ultimate pauper, a dead man stripped and in his shroud, thrown on the mercy of his neighbors, rich and poor. The inscription runs:

> Here lyeth John Brigge under this marbil stone
> Whose sowle our Lord I.H.S. have mercy upon
> For in this worlde worthily he lived many a day
> And here is body is buried and couched under clay
> Lo friends fro whatever ye be pray for me I you pray
> As ye me se in soche degree so schall ye be another day.

The other Salle guilds had altars placed around the church. From the will of Robert Luce, chaplain to the Assumption guild,[13] we know that its altar, like that of the Trinity guild, was in the chapel of Thomas Roos in the north transept. One of the windows in the east wall of this transept has been cut away to house the reredos for an altar, and the piscina for the ritual ablutions of the mass was uncovered there in the early twentieth century. The guild of St. Margaret had its altar in the north aisle. The grave of John Ryghtwyse, who asked to be buried before the image of St. Margaret in 1475, is still visible in the aisle and pinpoints the spot.[14] The guild of St. John the Baptist had its altar at the east end of the south aisle. In 1731, there were still substantial remains of a window here depicting the life and martyrdom of St. John; it had a memorial inscription for John Holwey, rector of Salle between 1375 and 1401, so he no doubt left money for a window in the new church in honor of his patron saint. There were also two altars against the roodscreen, their presence indicated by the unprimed blank spaces on the figured panels

---

[12] NRO, NCC, 202–5 Wolman.
[13] NRO, NCC, 11–12 Brosyard.
[14] PRO, PCC Wills, 20 Wattys.

of the screen dado. The other guilds may have celebrated there, or in the chapel over the north porch.

The interior of the church was, therefore, not a single open space, but an interconnecting network of sacred zones around altars and images, some privately owned, some the property of guilds in which many parishioners were sharers, all of them in some sense part of a shared symbol system and set of resources, and manned by a clerical cadre financed by guild salaries, by the recurrent benefactions of the leading families, and by short-term benefactions like that of Robert Pull, who left eight marks in 1510 as wages for "a pryst that shalbe able to singe in the church of Saul a yere."[15] We get some sense of how these sacred spaces were viewed, at least by the chaplains, from the bequest by one of the former chaplains in 1399 of three sets of vestments "to serve the common altars," or the bequest of another chaplain in 1456 of his missal, to be used on two of the guild altars (not ones that he had himself served while alive).[16]

The guild certificates of 1389 for the guilds of St. James, St. John, and the Blessed Virgin survive in the Public Record Office.[17] Members of the guilds met at vespers on the eve of their patron saint's feast day to recite the Rosary ("the psalter of Our Lady") for the repose of the souls of dead brethren and sisters. On the feast day, itself, or the Sunday after, they had a common meal, first attending mass together and offering the priest a farthing each. Poor men and women were invited to the meal and given a farthing each in alms. The guild members attended each other's funerals and gave alms there to the poor. They paid a small pension to impoverished members, if the guild funds were able to sustain it, and they also maintained three candles to burn during services on Sundays and major feast days before their patronal image. In addition, they paid for a large torch – a flare of wax and resin around a cluster of thick wicks – to burn at the elevation of the Host at the parish mass each Sunday. These torches were very prominent objects, and therefore a noticeable addition to the splendor and reverence of parish worship. The St. John guild paid for a single torch weighing twelve pounds, the Assumption guild maintained two of six pounds each. Each torch would have been held by a guild member or a clerk assisting at the mass, and their presence gives us a hint of the scale and elaboration of worship in Salle, worship in which the largesse of the gentry and of the

---

[15] NRO, NCC, Spyltimber 291; Pull also left 6*d* to each ploughlight.
[16] *Salle*, 83 (John Lutting, chaplain, d. 1399); 98–100 (Robert Luce, chaplain, d. 1456).
[17] They are summarized in H.F. Westlake, *The Parish Gilds of Medieval England* (London, 1919), 209.

parish guilds provided a range of ritual gestures and furnishings that reminded the community of the piety – and the importance – of the donors.

Commensality – shared feasting – was clearly an important aspect of guild life, and bequests of place-settings or "a garnesse" of pewter to the guilds are common in Salle wills.[18] The lights maintained by the guilds were seen as parish amenities, not simply the possession of the guild itself, and bequests might be made directly to the lights, distinct from any gift to the guild.[19]

The sharing of chapels by gentry families and by the guilds of Salle was clearly a feature of the region. A similar pattern is evident across the fields at Cawston, which had guilds of the Holy Trinity, St. Agnes (the parish patron), St. John the Baptist, St. Mary, St. Peter, and St. Thomas. The St. John guild at Cawston had a chapel on the north side of the chancel, and the St. Mary guild met in the south transept chapel.[20] These and several other chapels in the church were screened off so that the present open arrangement of the building gives, as at Salle, a quite misleading impression of unified space. The altars in all of the chapels were regularly used for guild masses, but were also designated sites for temporary chantry arrangements, paid for by members of the parish elite. Richard Brown, a wealthy Cawston parishioner who was one of the donors of the roodscreen, left 10 marks in 1505, for example, to his brother, John Brown, who was a priest, to say mass daily for him for a year at the altar of the Lady Chapel, where Brown asked to be buried "afore the Image of oure Ladi of pitee."[21] On the east wall of this same (south transept) chapel at Cawston is further evidence of the annexation of public space by private benefactors: a wall painting of an enthroned saint, now hard to decipher – perhaps the Virgin or St. Anne teaching the Virgin to read (there is a book on the knee of the seated figure) or perhaps St. Agnes, the parish patron – with two kneeling donors, left and right.

At Salle, the association of these common spaces with two of the chief parish families, the Rooses and the Briggs, was more emphatic, more firmly encoded in the stones that those families had raised. None, however, was a perpetual foundation; none of the families concerned had the inalienable property right conveyed by royal license for a perpetual foundation in "their" part of the church, and this may account for

---

[18] *Salle*, 93.
[19] NRO, ANW, 222 Gloys (Will of Alice Martyn, 1510).
[20] Information on Cawston is from Blomefield and Parkin, *An Essay*, 3: 537–47.
[21] NRO, NCC, 22 Ryxe (fol. 131).

the curious presence in the transept chapels of guild as well as private altars.

## THE POOR

Architecturally, the poor of the medieval parish are largely invisible. They left no monuments, they annexed no portions of the churches at the back or sides of which they stood or sat. Where were the poor of Salle? Much depends, of course, on what one means by the term "poor." Salle's weaving industry will have required a pool of waged labor. There will have been relatively poor young men and women – the sons and daughters of laborers and cottagers – in the ploughlights and the dances, perhaps even in the guilds, though the guild provisions for alms to paupers makes it clear that the very poorest were likely to be "outsiders" to the guilds, the objects of compassion rather than fraternity, as they were in society generally. Paupers feature regularly, of course, at the funerals of the wealthy, holding candles and saying the rosary and receiving, in return, beef and beer and bread, or money doles. These were normally of a penny or tuppence, but Thomas Brigg in 1494 left £20 to the poor of Salle, and in 1463 Geoffrey Boleyn, son of the founder of the building who had risen to become Lord Mayor of London, left the fabulous sum of £200 to be shared by the poor householders of six Norfolk communities, including Salle.[22] In 1532, John Norman left the residue of his goods after the payment of his specified bequests to be distributed among "the poore needy creatures of the town of Sall," a vivid glimpse of an underclass who became increasingly prominent in mortuary benefactions in the course of the hungry and inflationary Tudor century.[23]

## THE RECTORS AND CHAPLAINS OF SALLE

Like the transepts, the chancel of Salle church, donated circa 1440–50 by one of the fifteenth-century rectors, John Nekton, and his patrons, the Brewes family, was itself a space emphatically in the hands of a parish subgroup – in this case, the clergy. It has a magnificent set of medieval stalls, all of them carved with misericords on their underside, against which the clergy rested their bottoms during the lengthy performance of the daily offices. These stalls alert us to the presence of a community

---

[22] NRO, NCC, 202–5 Wolman (Thomas Brigg); PRO, PCC Wills, 1 Godeyn (Geoffrey Boleyn).
[23] NRO, NCC, 46–7 Platfoote.

of priests in the parish church, serving the various altars and guilds, as well as the parish or high altar. The rectors of Salle were wealthy men, and many of them were clerical careerists, graduate high-fliers based elsewhere, employing other priests to do their work. They were often members or clients of local families, however, and they left their mark on the church. John Nekton, for example, who died in 1467, left legacies to Simon Boleyn, his deputy in the parish, to the parish clerk, and to the poor of the parish.[24]

Boleyn was officially called "parish chaplain," but the need to staff guild and chantry altars ensure the additional presence of a fluctuating body of assistant clergy. None were priests of a perpetual chantry foundation, but rather they were stipendiaries on contract to one or another of the parish guilds, or serving in the family chantries. And quite apart from the guild and family chaplains employed long term to serve the transept altars, both clerical and lay testators in Salle contributed to the clerical presence in the parish by making provision in their wills for a small stream of priests on short-term contracts to celebrate masses for one, two, or three years.[25] We have details of almost thirty such priests for the century from 1399 to 1499 and evidence of their continuance thereafter. It is clear that the absence of perpetual foundations did not prevent them from forming strong and, in many cases, life-long attachments to the parish and the parish community. The graves of several are to be seen still in the church: for example, that of Simon Boleyn (d. 1482) in the central aisle (one of several priests' graves indicated by a chalice-shaped indent in the slab), and of Robert Luce (d. 1456) in the north transept. Luce was chaplain of the guild of the Assumption. Requesting burial before the altar that he had served in Roos's chapel, he spoke proprietarily of "our" chapel, that is, the guild's.[26] Boleyn, another local man from a gentry family, as parish chaplain, was, in effect, vicar for the absentee rector.

These men formed part of a close-knit clerical subculture, with strong links out into the wider community of the parish. They left money, clothing, vestments, and books to each other (from surviving wills we can trace the passage of some of these books, including professional treatises on the work of a priest, like the *Pupilla Occuli*, through successive generations of chaplains and rectors); they entered into joint ownership

---

[24] PRO, PCC Wills, 75 Jekyn; *Salle*, 76.
[25] NRO, NCC, 11–12 Brosyard (Will of Robert Luce, chaplain, 1456); NCC, 120 Gelour (Will of Thomas Bucke, chaplain, 1475); NCC, 32 Wight (Will of William Jekkes, chaplain, 1499); NCC, 291 Spyltimber (Will of Robert Pull, 1510).
[26] NRO, NCC, 11–12 Brosyard.

of property, witnessed each other's wills, loaned or gave each other pious objects, recruited likely young men from the local families into the profession, and sometimes signaled a deeper level of friendship by requesting burial near each other.[27] The font at Salle is a monument to the embedding of these chaplains in the life of the parish community. It is one of the forty or so distinctive East Anglian octagonal fonts which portray on seven of their eight sides, with considerable theological precision, the seven sacraments of the Catholic Church. The Salle font comes from a workshop that produced similar fonts for Cley and Binham, yet it is unique in retaining not only its medieval canopy, but the mechanism for raising and lowering it. The font was a gift of the chaplain Robert Luce and his parents, William and Agnes. No doubt he donated it in memory of them; it is inscribed for them in Latin around the step:

Pray for the souls of Thomas Luce and [Agnes] his wife and Robert their son, chaplain, and for those for whom they are bound to pray, who caused this font to be made.[28]

These chaplains of Salle left money for the poor (Simon Boleyn left 2*d* each to two paupers every Friday for a year, in return for which the poor people had to say a rosary every week for his soul), and they acted as spiritual advisers – and sometimes financial consultants – to the wealthy men and women of the parish. In return, they were promoted in their careers by their gentry friends. Many prosperous Norfolk rectors started out as guild chaplains in churches like Salle. They often formed close links with the community, which survived their promotion to parishes elsewhere, like John Crome, who went on to be rector of Bale but acted as supervisor for Simon Boleyn's will, or Henry Newman, formerly chaplain of St. James's guild, who went on to be rector of Pensthorp but left substantial legacies to Salle church and to the light of St. James in his chapel. The continuous presence of a group of clergy in the parish, with a strong "esprit de corps" no doubt brought its own tensions and challenges to the community. A number of chaplains turn up in the manorial courts for poaching the local rabbit warrens, and there may have been more specifically religious frictions, too. But they were undoubtedly a tremendous resource in the parish, a source of spiritual advice and expertise, and in many cases material benefactors of the community, making gifts of books, ornaments, vestments,

---

[27] *Salle*, 73–7, 81–8, 99. Thomas Jekkes asked for burial beside Simon Boleyn.
[28] Ann E. Nichols, *Seeable Signs. The Iconography of the Seven Sacraments, 1350–1544* (Woodbridge, 1994), 345–6.

and vessels to instruct the laity, provide resources for the parish's other stipendiary clergy, and enhance the parish's worship.

## THE SCREEN

The screen at Salle was planned as part of the reconstruction of the church in the early fifteenth century. It was savagely truncated during the Reformation, the whole upper section being sawn away. The decoration on the dado, which remains, follows a common Norfolk pattern, the side panels of the screen having the twelve apostles, the doors into the chancel having the four Latin doctors, just like the screen at Cawston. But only two apostles survive on the paneling on either side of the doors: St. Thomas and St. James on the north side, St. Philip and St. Bartholomew on the south, with Gregory, Jerome, Augustine, and Ambrose on the doors between. To north and south of the apostles there are blank white panels. This is not the work of the reformers, but the original priming paint of the screen. The explanation is that the other eight apostles were painted on parclose screens, now gone, standing at right angles to the dado and forming enclosures blocking in two altars, which were pushed up against the blank sections of the screen.

The apostles have the articles of the Apostle's Creed inscribed over their heads, an unusual arrangement in Norfolk, where the texts normally occur on scrolls carried by the apostles. But in one form or another the Creed texts themselves are found on a number of screens in the county, such as Gooderstone, where there are also doors with the Latin Doctors; Weston Longville, Ringland, and elsewhere.[29] These texts underline the symbolism of doctors and apostles as expressions of the teaching of the Church. Salle, like so many other fifteenth-century parishes, prided itself on its self-consciously correct Catholicism.

The screen at Salle is notably more coherent as a conception than its equivalent, but probably somewhat later match, at Cawston. There, too, apostles and Latin doctors dominate, but without their Latin texts, and they are flanked by a rather miscellaneous group of helper saints: St. Agnes, the parish patron; St. Helena, carrying a relic of the true cross in a reliquary that looks like a representation of the reliquary at one of the region's great shrines, the shrine of the True Cross at Bromholm; and the uncanonized wonder worker, Master John Schorne. The Cawston screen, which was being built from about 1460, but which went on being painted and decorated until 1504, was certainly a commission

---

[29] The conventional texts are conveniently listed in M.R. James, *Suffolk and Norfolk* (London, 1930), 218–19.

of a common Norfolk type, involving the cooperation or, rather, the not particularly coordinated serial donations of a number of quite modest donors. The figures of the saints on the north and south screens are patently by different hands, a reflection of the mixed origins of the funding. We know from wills of many gifts ranging from one mark (13s 4d or two-thirds of a pound) to ten marks toward the building or painting of the screen. In 1505, Richard Brown left four marks to paint "a pane in the Rode lofte," and the first four "panes" or panels on the left were paid for in memory of a married couple, William and Alice Atereth in 1490; the screen has an inscription in English that runs:

Pray for the sowlis of William Atereth and Alice his wyff the wiche dede these iiij panys peynte be the executors lyff.[30]

At Salle, by contrast, there is no such evidence of piecemeal patronage. The screen's iconographic unity and the blank spaces for two symmetrically placed altars, moreover, make it look like a unitary planned commission (there is a close parallel at Ranworth in the Norfolk Broads), probably a reflection of the domination of the patronage of the church as a whole by clusters of wealthy parishioners acting in concert, and with clerical advice.[31]

### THE STAINED GLASS

Salle was once filled with cycles and sequences of stained glass.[32] The chancel windows contained the legends of the church's patrons, Saints Peter and Paul, as well as a series of bishops, popes, and kings associated with the conversion of southern England; a scheme adapted from the series in the choir clerestory of York Minster. There was also a good deal of heraldic glass, dominated by emblems of the de la Pole, Beaufort, and Brewes families. On the north side of the chancel are the remains of a series of figures of prophets with scrolls, and the Fathers of the Church; there were almost certainly the twelve apostles, also, making up a standard set symbolizing Christian teaching. In the south transept, in addition to the Briggs's window, are figures of St. Jerome, St. Margaret, St. Catherine, St. Helen, and St. Etheldreda. In the north

---

[30] NRO, NCC, 131 Ryxe (Will of Richard Brown, 1505).
[31] Eamon Duffy, "The Parish, Piety and Patronage in Late Medieval East Anglia: The Evidence of Rood-screens," in *The Parish in English Life, 1400–1600*, eds. K.L. French, G.C. Gibbs, and B. Kumin (Manchester, 1997), 133–62, esp. 145–6.
[32] The discussion of the glass in *Salle*, 61–71, largely based on notes supplied by M.R. James, has now to be supplemented by the account by David King in Fawcett and King, "Salle Church," 333–5.

aisle east window is a restored Annunciation (originally the Coronation of the Virgin in heaven) and in the north transept (Roos chapel) parts of a Visitation scene and the figures of the Virtues: Mercy, Truth, Justice, and Peace, remnants of a depiction of a scene known as the "Parliament of Heaven" in which God plans the Incarnation. Originating in the works of St. Bernard, it is replicated in such early fifteenth-century devotional classics as Nicholas Love's "Mirror of the Life of the Blessed Jhesu"; however, it is a somewhat rarified subject, which occurs only occasionally in stained glass or carving.[33] There are bits and pieces of prophets, cardinals, and patriarchs in the tracery lights of the south aisle. But the best glass in the church is in the east and south windows of the chancel, the remains of what was once a magnificent double set of the nine orders of angels.

In medieval tradition, inherited from Jewish and early church speculation, the angelic orders were divided into three groups or hierarchies. The highest division was that of Epiphany, or Revelation, and contained the orders of Seraphim, Cherubim, and Thrones. Next came Hyperepiphany, containing the orders of Dominations, Virtues, and Powers. Lastly, came the Hypophany, containing Principalities, Archangels, and Angels. All of these orders had distinctive functions and powers, encompassing both this world and the next.[34] Their representation in communities like Salle, alongside heraldic glass endorsing the rule of Henry VI and the greatness of the local aristocratic families,[35] may well have spoken to the parishioners of established order, hierarchy, and the given nature of social and religious reality. Like the screen, the evidence of the glass suggests a church whose iconography was determined by clerical and lay elites and planned programmatically as a coherent whole. Here, in contrast to the many humbler parish communities, and even in contrast to Cawston a mile across the fields, order and control rather than spontaneity seems to have been the keynote.

## SALLE AND THE REFORMATION

Any parish where the Boleyn family were major landowners was bound to feel the impact of the Reformation. James Boleyn, who was Ann Boleyn's uncle, made the most of it, acquiring yet more property here

---

[33] For an illustration of the subject and some other examples, see Francis Cheetham, *English Medieval Alabasters* (Oxford, 1984), 175.

[34] Late medieval belief about the angels is conveniently summarized in Jacobus de Voragine, *The Golden Legend or Lives of the Saints as Englished by William Caxton*, 7 vols. (London, 1900), 5: 180–99.

[35] On the heraldic glass, see *Salle*, 66–9.

and at Cawston throughout the early 1530s and 1540s, and the family held on to their status even after Ann's disgrace and execution in 1536.[36] The Henrician rector of Salle, presented to the living in 1523 by his own father who was patron, was Roger Townsend. The family had a tradition of serious piety and hard-nosed attention to the main chance. The rector's grandfather, Sir Roger, was a successful lawyer who had married into serious money: the Hoptons of Blythburgh in Suffolk. Sir Roger, was, among other things, a moneylender. His very distinctive will of 1494 established a chantry in East Raynham served by two priests, one of whom was to engage in theological studies at Cambridge, returning each year at Easter to preach God's word to the parishioners. Townsend asked for a thousand masses to be said immediately after his death, distributed through twenty towns, including Salle. He sought the prayers "of all the aungells of hevyn and patriarchs, prophets, apostles, martyrs . . . and all the hooly company of hevyn," but he also begged Christ "for the merytes of his bitter and gloriouse passion to have mercy on me and to take me to his mercy which is above all workes, unto whom it is appropused [sic] to have mercy."[37]

Sir Roger's son, Sir Roger Townsend II, was an active landowner whose marriage to Anne Brewes made him lord of the manor of Stinton and patron of both Heydon and Salle parishes. Conventionally pious, heading his notebook entries with the holy names of Jesus and Mary, and steward of four monastic houses including Walsingham Priory, he was nevertheless a ruthless opportunist, and he identified himself lock, stock, and barrel with the process of reform in Henry's reign. He was one of the commissioners for the Norfolk section of the 1535 *Valor Ecclesiasticus* and a key figure in the containment of discontent with the Reformation in north Norfolk. He profited directly from the suppressions, acquiring, among much else, the Franciscan house at Walsingham for himself. Unsurprisingly, he played a central role in uncovering and suppressing the Walsingham plot after the destruction of the shrine of the Holy House at Walsingham and in taking drastic and sometimes dubious legal action against criticism of royal religious policy in the years that followed.[38] His zeal earned him the enmity of the Norfolk

---

[36] T.H. Swales, "The Redistribution of Monastic Lands in Norfolk at the Dissolution," *Norfolk Archaeology* 34 (1966–9): 25.

[37] Colin Richmond, *John Hopton* (Cambridge, 1981), 244–5.

[38] Swales, "Redistribution," 24–5; Duffy, *The Stripping of the Altars: Traditional Religion in England, c. 1400–c. 1500* (New Haven, CT, 1992), 403; and see *Letters and Papers*, vol. 20, pt. 1, 282 no. 37 (grant in fee of the sight of the Franciscan priory at Walsingham); A.R. Martin, "The Greyfriars of Walsingham," *Norfolk Archaeology* 25 (1935): 227–71, esp. 235. A representative cross section of Townsend's activities on behalf of government

commons, especially through the late 1530s and 1540s, when the county seethed with animosity against the gentry who fattened on the spoils of the Reformation. In 1540, it was reported that John Walker of Griston had tried to raise the county against such profiteers:

"Let us kylle them, ye, evyn theyr children in the cradelles: for yt were a good thinge yf ther were so many jentylmenin Norffolk as ther be whyt bulles. . . ." They should begin, he declared, with Sir Richard Southwell, ". . . and so to Sir Roger Townsende . . . and so to spoyle them all . . . and hernesse our sylffe."[39]

This Sir Roger had appointed his own son Roger to the rectory of Salle (and to Heydon) in 1523. As might be expected from a family with these sorts of traditions, the rector was an educated man, a Cambridge-trained canon lawyer, whose library had the latest editions of Church Fathers like St. Augustine and St. John Chrysostom. He was also, again as might be expected, an archetypal Henrician careerist, pluralist rector not only of Salle, Heydon, and North Creake within the county,[40] but of St. Mary Woolnoth in London, where he is buried. In 1538, the year of his death, he also became chancellor of the diocese of Salisbury, holding the prebend of Netherby there.[41] He was, therefore, intended to be a member of the evangelical establishment Bishop Shaxton was seeking to build in Salisbury. Townsend was probably rarely resident in Salle. In addition to his various livings, he was heavily involved in the Faculty Office, the administrative body which under the royal supremacy took over the work of the Roman curia in granting dispensations and the like.[42] He was also active in the business side of the dissolution of the monasteries, though he appears not to have had much share in the loot, complaining in his will that although he had been often "in attendance . . . for the sealing and dispatching of a great number of capacities as well of houses suppressed as surrendered, never hitherto

in Norfolk is provided in Geoffrey R. Elton, *Policy and Police* (Cambridge, 1972), 17, 82, 144–5, 342. The best discussion of the Walsingham plot and on the Townsend family's role in suppressing it is C.E. Morton, "The Walsingham Conspiracy of 1537," *Historical Research 63* (1990): 29–43.

[39] C.E. Moreton, *The Townsends and their World: Gentry, Law and Land in Norfolk, c. 1451–1551* (Oxford, 1992), 29–36; Frederick W. Russell, *Kett's Rebellion in Norfolk* (London, 1859), 8–9.

[40] In 1537, "Roger Tonneshonde DCL," rector of North Creak, was described as the King's Chaplain when dispensed for plurality: D.S. Chambers, ed., *Faculty Office Registers, 1534–1549* (London, 1966), 105. I owe this and several other references to the kindness of Dr. David Crankshaw, who commented very helpfully on a draft of this essay.

[41] John Le Neve, *Fasti Ecclesiae Anglicanae 1300–1521*, 12 vols., rev. ed. (London, 1962), 3: 19; Moreton, *The Townsends*, 42–43.

[42] In 1534 Townsend signed the formal renunciation of papal supremacy, which is reproduced as plate xxiv of Denys Hay, *The Italian Renaissance in its Historical Background* (Cambridge, 1976), facing 183.

receiving one penny for the same, whereas I have always been put in hope that I should be reasonably recompensed for my pains." Townsend died in October 1538, before the Reformation entered its radical phase.

The exact extent of Townsend's evangelicalism is hard to gauge.[43] The preamble to his will is reminiscent of his grandfather's, but it also clearly confirms his sympathy with the Henrician reforms while retaining some Catholic attitudes and beliefs. The preamble commits his soul

> to God eternall the father almighty maker of hevyn and erthe; hys oonly sonne and my lord Jhesus Criste by whose passion dethe and the shedying of his precious blod upon the crosse, for all mankind and by the meryts thereof excluding all my deserving, meryts or good dedis I stedfastly truste and beleve my poure soule to be redeemed from all my synnes, deth, and hell, noon of them all never to have any power over hyt but that it shall forthwith from its departure oute of this my mortall body, have the fruycion of theternal godhed, and to be partaker of the unspeakable joys of theverlasting inheritance prepared for me and all true believers, nothing douting but the holly goost . . . dothe and will at my most need, when deth synne and hell shall most trouble me, strengthen and so staye me in this my beleve that they shall nothyn prevaile ageynst my poure soule.

Nevertheless, he added that he trusted also that

> as at all tymes so most chefly when my soule shall departe from my body, to be partaker of the charitable prayers of all saints, both quyck and deede.

He left to each of his parishes:

> a hole Bible in Englishe to be chained at my own proper cost, desireing my parisheners that they wolde so reverently here and rede the same so they increase in the fear and love of God.

This was the "Great Bible" required by all the royal injunctions of 1538, a sign of Townsend's up-to-the-moment political correctness. He left £6 to be divided among the poor of his three Norfolk parishes, and £4 to "Mr. Nicols of Raynham," asking him to preach two sermons in each of his parishes. The will contains no request for masses to be said for the repose of his soul, though it seems inconceivable that these can have been omitted at this early stage in the Reformation; such arrangements for his obsequies will have been made verbally.[44]

---

[43] The references to his evangelicalism in Susan Brigden, *London and the Reformation* (Oxford, 1989), 55, 384, appear to be based on the provisions and wording of his will, discussed later in this chapter.

[44] PRO, PCC Wills, F 21 Dyngeley, fol. 169v. The extracts transcribed in *Salle*, 130–1, are accurate in substance, but the spellings have been modernized and many omissions and paraphrases have been unacknowledged.

Townsend's will still just about envisages prayers for the dead and the intercession of saints, but like the teaching of the Henrician Ten Articles of 1536, it does not seem to believe in Purgatory – hence the reference to immediate enjoyment of the fruition of God. The rejection of Purgatory spelled the death warrant for the guilds and chantry masses, which were the main occupation of the community of priests at Salle, and with the accession of Edward VI in 1547, all guilds and chantries were dissolved, and the chaplains of Salle sang no more for the dead. The rood and the whole upper part of the screen were destroyed, the altars that filled every corner of the church were pulled down and their images and tabernacles were burned, and many of the commemorative brasses, representing the roll call of the dead benefactors of the community, were ripped up. Most of those in place today were replaced in the eighteenth and nineteenth centuries, having been rescued and kept in the church chest.

These transformations of the sacred space of Salle church – the abolition of the multiple corrals for the holy which divided the body of the church – had the effect of at once making invisible and indeed of abolishing some of the social complexity of the parish. What happened to the local loyalties of scattered parishes like Salle when the ploughlights and dances of Marchgate, Kirkgate, Lunton, and Steynewade were abolished, when the feast-day meetings as well as the altars of the seven guilds became illegal, when the opportunities – and burdens – of officeholding and stock holding within the guilds were suppressed? No guild or churchwarden's accounts survive for sixteenth-century Salle, but where such accounts do exist elsewhere we get some measure of the social transformation such changes involved. In the tiny and much poorer Exmoor village of Morebath in this period, twelve men and women, including the teenage wardens of the young men's and maiden's stores, held office in the parish and the parish's "stores" or light fraternities, a primitive form of guild. These twelve people were annually elected; they managed small flocks of sheep, handled donations, and laid out money for ceremonial and social functions, and they presented annual accounts to parish meetings. After the Reformation, the parish elected just one person a year to office, and that person was always a man.[45]

We should not idealize; there never was a merry England, and officeholding was often a serious burden that medieval parishioners wriggled to avoid. But such office holding, within guilds and light stores, was also an aspect of the complex social geography of the medieval parish community, and that geography was mapped out in the interior of the

---

[45] Eamon Duffy, "Morebath 1520–1570: A Rural Parish in the Reformation," in *Religion and Rebellion*, eds. J. Devlin and R. Fanning, *Historical Studies* 20 (Dublin, 1997): 17–39.

churches in which the guild and chantry altars were placed, and in which stood the images before which the lights burned. With the removal of altars, images, and lights, and the social and religious groups that funded them, the dynamics of local communities were permanently changed.

In terms of the social geography of the parish church, that, of course, left the wealthy in possession. The Reformation abolished altars, lights, and guilds, and with them the groups who paid for and maintained them. The Reformation also abolished family chantries, but not, of course, the families who maintained them. The rich, like the poor, are always with us. The Townsends, hard-faced men who did well out of the Reformation, remained lords of the manor and patrons of the living for another century. The chantry-chapels of Salle ceased to function; we do not know at what point they lost their parclosing, but they did not altogether lose their semiprivate function. As all the church's seating came to focus on the pulpit on the south side of the nave, they are unlikely to have been satisfactory family pews, but they certainly retained their value as semiprivate family mausolea. In 1802, Edward Hase, an early nineteenth-century parish grandee, thought nothing of bricking up one of the north transept windows to provide a suitable background for his own funeral monument. He consulted neither parson nor people.[46]

Was the Reformation in Salle a gentry coup? Without a lot more documentation than we possess, we cannot hope to answer that question satisfactorily. We have no idea, for example, how the commons of Salle at large behaved during Kett's Rebellion in the "camping time" of 1549, though one Salle man, at least, Robert Chapman, died among the rebels at Mousehold Heath, and the likelihood is that he did not march alone.[47] That rebellion, unlike the Western rising the same summer, has been widely interpreted as enthusiastically sympathetic to Protestantism,[48] and certainly the rebels ostentatiously secured prayer book worship and reformed preaching in their camp at Mousehead Heath, in which, famously, the future Archbishop Matthew Parker played a part. But Parker came within a whisker of being lynched by the rebels, and according to Nicholas Sotherton this prayer book conformity was policy rather than piety, adopted "in order to have a fayre shew and a similitude of well doinge." Sir Roger Townsend was one of those appealed to against the rebels by the mayor of Norwich, and however Townsend's tenants in Salle behaved, the men of the neighboring village of Heydon, where the

---

[46] *Salle*, 133.
[47] *Salle*, 133.
[48] D. MacCulloch, "Kett's Rebellion in Context," *Past and Present* 84 (1979): 60, and, less guardedly, A. Fletcher and D. MacCulloch, *Tudor Rebellions*, 4th ed. (London, 1997), 79.

Townsends were also patrons of the living, marched to the rebel camp carrying their church banner, a strongly traditionalist gesture reminiscent of the Pilgrimage of Grace and certainly suggesting no very strong Protestant convictions.[49]

Like the Townsend family, many of the influential people of Salle were establishment figures, men and women with a lot to lose from nonconformity. Whatever their innermost convictions, most of them will have cooperated with the processes of Reformation. We should not assume that this was ever straightforward. One might benefit from the Reformation yet not endorse all its teachings. Ann Boleyn's brother, Sir James Boleyn, who died at Blickling in 1561, was Queen Elizabeth's uncle. He remembered her in his will, leaving her a gilt basin and ewer, but also "my written book of the revelations of S. Bridget, most humbly beseeching her Highness to read well and ponder the same." We do not know whether Queen Elizabeth followed his advice and read St. Bridget's detailed descriptions of the pains of Purgatory, or her blow-by-blow accounts of the life and Passion of Christ, but it is not routine Protestant reading matter.[50]

But there may well be in any case a sense in which the Reformation barely came to mid-Tudor Salle, except for its destructive aspects. Roger Townsend was succeeded as rector in 1538 by William Worrison, who would remain in the benefice until his death, through the remainder of Henry's, Edward's, and Mary's reigns.[51] As that suggests, Worrison was a conformist who made no religious changes; the religious provisions of parish wills in the 1540s manifest no hint of Reformed convictions, and even after the disappearance of the guilds and their clergy, the parish retained enough clerical and musical resources in 1543 for a parishioner to specify with confidence that he would have "masse and dirge by note" at his burial.[52] Sir Roger Townsend, himself, hardly qualifies as a convinced Protestant and was unlikely to have been a force for radicalism in Salle. His closest allies in East Anglia came from conservative families, notably the Bedingfields, to whom he was related by his daughter's marriage, and his commitment to reform was strictly opportunist.[53] The preamble to his own will, made in May 1552, would

---

[49] Russell, *Kett's Rebellion*, 37–8; Moreton, *The Townsends*, 37–8.
[50] *Salle*, 185.
[51] His will, made on 12 July 1558, was proved in the Norwich Consistory Court on 7 February following: NRO, NCC, 322 Jerves.
[52] NRO, NCC, 10 Crawforde (Will of John Lockett, tailor, 1543).
[53] See the bitter comments about Townsend's suspicious alliances and his unscrupulous opportunism, made by Sir Nicholas le Strange to Cecil in September 1549: C. Knighton, ed., *Calendar of State Papers of Edward VI* (HMSO, 1992), no. 359.

pass superficial inspection as an evangelical document, with its emphasis on salvation by "the merite of [Christ's] most blissed passion." In
fact, however, these phrases are directly copied from the preamble to
his impeccably Catholic father's will, with the references to the Virgin
Mary, the saints and the sacraments removed, and a phrase on Scripture inserted. Indeed, it was in fact less insistent than the will of old Sir
Roger on the doctrine of predestination. Family identity is far more in
evidence here than evangelical conviction.[54]

Salle parish certainly cannot have welcomed the destructive aspects of
the Reformation. Early in Edward's reign they seem hastily to have sold
off more than £17 worth of silver and diverted the bulk of the money to
repairs in the church, to prevent the royal commissioners getting their
hands on it, a proceeding matched in many other parishes in the region. At Cawston, for example, the parish spent forty pounds of the
forty-four pounds two shillings and sixpence it raised from the sale of
the church silver on parish projects like roofing an aisle, paying for the
whitewashing and "scripturing" of the church, and repairing roads. But
at Salle much remained in the church, and in 1552 a new batch of royal
officials took away barrow-loads of ornaments and vestments: two chalices, nearly a hundredweight of candlesticks in silver and brass, eight
elaborate sets of velvet and gold high-mass sets of chasuble, tunicles
and copes, many of them black and obviously designed for use in the
elaborate requiems that had been so important a part of the worship of
Salle church, as well as another eleven sets of humbler vestments, the
handbells used in Rogationtide processions and for calling people to
prayer for the dead, and three of the five bells in the steeple.[55] One of
the leading parishioners who joined Rector William Worrison in signing
the 1552 inventory was Arthur Fountain, a member of one of the longest-
standing Salle families, whose monuments and pious benefactions were
now the target of royal religious policy. By the end of Edward's reign,
Salle had been stripped of at least six generations of pious giving.

The religious regime of Marian Salle seems to have reverted to traditional practice. Richard Locket, in May 1555, asked for "diridge and
mass," provided funds for "my neybors to have good chere," and alms
to the poor for the "profit of my soule." He also left funds to the repara-
tion of the church, and a load of squared marble for repaving the south

---

[54] NRO, NCC, 31–7 Lyncolne, and see Richmond, *Hopton*, 244–5.
[55] *Salle*, 134–6; H.B. Walters, ed., "Inventories of Norfolk Church Goods," *Norfolk Archaeology* 28 (1945): 17–18: "probably the richest inventory in quality in the county outside
Norwich." There are still two medieval bells in the tower, one inscribed in honour of
the Trinity, and the other simply with the name of its King's Lynn maker.

aisle "where most need is," which may simply indicate that his seat was there, but which may represent repair work after officially enforced Edwardian iconoclasm.[56]

From Elizabeth's reign onward, the rectors of Salle were mostly resident and were the only priests in the parish. The living lapsed to the Crown in 1558 because the patron, Roger Townsend III, was a minor. William Worrison died in July 1558, leaving a will with a Catholic preamble, bequeathing his soul to St. Mary and "all the holy companie of heaven," but otherwise containing no religious provisions of any sort. His successor, John Crane, was duly nominated by Philip and Mary. Crane was a native of Pulham, near Diss, but he was probably related to a local Salle family. One of the stipendiary chaplains in the 1490s was a Walter Crane, and one of the signatories of the 1552 inventories, signing with a mark, was a Robert Crane.[57]

John Crane was a decidedly surprising Crown appointment in 1558, for he was a theological graduate and a preacher with a notably Protestant past. As a young fellow of Christ's College in Henry VIII's reign, he had taken a prominent part in a notorious performance of Thomas Kirchmeyer's play, *Pammachius*, during Lent 1545. *Pammachius* was a scurrilous satire against the papacy and concerned a mythical pope who had sold himself, and the papacy, into subjection to Satan. Denounced by another Christ's man, Cuthbert Scot, the future Marian bishop of Chester and a dedicated defender of conservative orthodoxy, the play, which reputedly "reproved Lent fastinges [and] al ceremonies" had attracted the enraged attention of the chancellor of the university, Stephen Gardiner, bishop of Winchester. With Matthew Parker's emollient assistance, Crane had been obliged to defend himself against accusations of sacramental heresy, claiming that the objectionable aspects of the original had been bowdlerized and that "they entended not but to rebuke the popes usurped power." Crane went on to take his bachelor of divinity degree in 1549, but it is not clear whether his subsequent career before his arrival in Salle sustained the tone of this controversial beginning. His whereabouts and activities in the earlier part of Mary's reign are unknown, though by the time of his death in 1578, he had acquired the reputation of having been "an ernest Professor of Christ in the tyme of Queen Marie." His curate describes him as "a trew, a constaunt and a

---

[56] NRO, NCC, 155 Beeles. Lockett requested burial in the churchyard, so the repaving cannot have been connected with his grave; on the other hand, it is clear that many explicitly Catholic funeral inscriptions survived the Edwardian purges *in situ* at Salle: for a list made ca. 1602, see C.M. Hood, ed., *The Chorography of Norfolk* (Norwich, 1938), 145–7.

[57] *Salle*, 135–6.

devout follower of Christ unto his Death," which may or may not indicate that he was Puritanically inclined.[58] He evidently kept his head
down sufficiently to pass muster as a possible Marian incumbent, however, and, above all, he was unmarried. He can have had little impact
on Salle in any case, for he was an absentee. Crane was a pluralist, who
by 1561 was not only rector of Salle, but incumbent at Feltwell, in the
west of the county, and of Tivetshall, near Diss in South Norfolk, where
he resided.[59]

It is not clear how far Crane's successor, John Thurston, appointed in
1565 and who does not seem to have resided in the parish, qualifies as
a convinced Protestant. In 1572 he married a local girl, Dorothy Turner,
and their first son, born in 1572, was baptized Esaye (Isaiah), which
looks on the face of it like a revealing indication of the Reformed ethos
of the parsonage. But if Thurstan was a Protestant, he was not admired
by the godly. The 1586 Puritan survey of the Norfolk ministry notes that
he was a nonpreacher, "blinde, a leper, he was a shoe-maker, and then a
masse priest."[60] The next rector, Thomas Aldred, married a wife perhaps
significantly named Faith, but was not long in the parish, since he died
in 1590. His successor, Richard Wrathall, who married into one of the
parish gentry families, the Fountains, is described in a legal document
in 1615 not as rector but as "Minister of the Word of God of Saull."
Like the rector of neighboring Cawston, he was in trouble in the 1590s
for persistent failure to wear the surplice,[61] and it was for him, in 1611,
that Thomas Lord Knyvett, another Salle landlord and one with marked
Protestant credentials, turned the elegant fifteenth-century pulpit into
the dominant "three-decker" with a prayer desk and a clerk's desk below
the pulpit itself.[62] The pulpit was placed halfway down the church (not
its present position), and the pews were arranged toward it so that
everyone seated in the eastern half of the nave sat with their backs
toward the now redundant chancel.

We know something at least of the use the pulpit was put to. In 1584
Robert Sendall, a wealthy yeoman parishioner who had occupied the

---

[58] Charles Henry Cooper, *Annals of Cambridge*, 5 vols. (Cambridge, 1842), I: 423–37;
Charles Henry Cooper, *Athenae Cantabrigiensis*, 3 vols. (Cambridge, 1858), I: 461–2;
J.B. Mullinger, *History of the University of Cambridge*, 2 vols. (Cambridge, 1873), 2: 73–6;
J. Peile, ed., *Biographical Register of Christ's College, 1505–1905*, 2 vols. (Cambridge, 1910),
I: 26; Victor J.K. Brook, *A Life of Archbishop Parker* (Oxford, 1962), 28–32.

[59] Corpus Christi College, Cambridge, Parker Library, MS 97, fols. 202, 212, 225. (Norwich
diocesan certificate, compiled for Archbishop Parker ca. September 1561–January 1562.)

[60] Albert Peel, ed., *The Second Parte of a Register*, 2 vols. (Cambridge, 1915), 2: 153; *Salle*, 77.

[61] *Salle*, 77–9; J.F. Williams, "An Episcopal Visiting in 1593," *Norfolk Archaeology* 28 (1945):
82.

[62] *Salle*, 140.

lands of Nugoun's manor since 1545, made a will requesting burial "at my stooles ende" in the church, leaving 1*d* to every poor man, woman, and child who attending his funeral, 1*s* each and their food and drink to the men who carried him to the grave, and 6*d* each to the bell ringers. He also stipulated that "some learned man shall preach in Sawle Church on the day of my funeral and he to have for his paynes 5*s* of lawfull englysh money." Sendall had been one of the parishioners named in the parish inventory submitted prior to the drastic Edwardian confiscation of 1552. He was clearly proud of the church, leaving land in fee to help maintain the building in perpetuity. He also provided for an annual distribution of 20*s* "on St. John's daie in Chrystmas," "to ease and unburden the poore in Sawl." Sendall commended his soul into the hands of "Almighty God my maker and Jesus Chryste his onlye sonne my alone saviour by whose merites I hope to be saved," and he asked for a learned sermon, not a dirge and mass by note, at his funeral. Yet, in its manifest pride in the building, attachment to his own place in it, and desire for remembrance on a festal anniversary in the form of charity to the poor, his will is reminiscent of dozens of similar surviving Salle wills made over the previous century and a half. By the 1580s, Protestantism had certainly arrived in the parsonage and, at least occasionally, in the pulpit of Salle. But if the Puritan survey's contemptuous dismissal of Sendall's pastor, John Thurstan, as a blind, nonpreaching former mass-priest is anything to go by, it was a Protestantism muted and modified by continuities which had little to do with ideology. All in all, it is not clear to me whether the religion of Robert Sendall was different in kind from the religion of the pre-Reformation Briggs, Fountains, and Roos, or much the same sort of thing, working in reduced circumstances.[63]

[63] NRO, ANW, 144–8 Lawson.

*An epilogue at the parish level*

# CHAPTER XIII

# Popular religion and the Reformation in England: A view from Cornwall

NICHOLAS ORME

POPULAR religion – the religion of the generality of people, especially those of the lower orders – is a large subject. It ranges from belief, worship, private prayer, and reading to morality, charity, and the payment of church dues. These elements may vary according to people's gender, age, status, and context, presenting the historian with many aspects to study and evaluate. This chapter is concerned with three of them: worship in church, the economic support of churches, and ceremonies outside church. It begins by reviewing the systems in force in early Tudor England, continues by studying the impact of "state religion" during the Reformation of the mid-sixteenth century, and concludes by tracing the survival of some pre-Reformation beliefs and practices between about 1600 and 1750. To achieve focus, the survey centers on one English county, Cornwall, an appropriate area for this purpose because it is rich both in pre-Reformation records of popular religion and in literary descriptions of its society and customs after the Reformation. Some features of Cornish popular religion were characteristic of other parts of England and illustrate general conditions. Equally, Cornwall had attributes distinct to itself, like all English counties, and some of these were untypical of England elsewhere. Its study reveals both national verities and regional variations.

Cornwall is England's most maritime county: a long peninsula attached to the mainland by a short land border with Devon. It is also peripheral in its geographic situation, its eastern edge lying about 220 miles from London and its remotest point, Land's End, a further 86 miles westwards. As a county, its distance from London is roughly equivalent to that of north Yorkshire or County Durham. The Cornish landscape, like theirs, contains many of the features of the English highland zone. Settlement in Cornwall, in the period under review, took the form of

351

hamlets and farms more often than nucleated villages, and in many of the parishes the church building stood (and still stands) in an isolated place, serving a dispersed population. In terms of civil government, the county was a distinct unit by at least the tenth century, measuring 1,327 square miles in the period concerned.[1] For ecclesiastical purposes it formed, until 1877, an archdeaconry within the diocese of Exeter. It was unique in Tudor, Stuart, and even Hanoverian England in retaining speakers of a Celtic language, Cornish, closely related to Breton and (to a lesser extent) Welsh. By 1500, however, this language was chiefly confined to the western districts beyond Truro and declined steadily in support thereafter. English, in contrast, was used all over the county and must have been known by some who naturally spoke in Cornish.[2]

POPULAR RELIGION BEFORE THE REFORMATION

Cornwall was inhabited by "Brittonic" people, related in race, language, and culture to those of Brittany and Wales, when an organized Church first developed there in post-Roman times. Even in the early sixteenth century, many ecclesiastical sites (some religious houses, most parish churches, some parochial chapels, and possibly some holy wells) probably still stood where they had been established in that early period. Popular religion, too, reflected this long-distant past. About 140 early Brittonic saints were venerated in early-sixteenth-century Cornwall, the majority – about 112 – being unique to one church or chapel, and only 27 owning more than one site in Cornwall or, like David, Petroc, Sampson, and Winwaloe, also possessing cults in Brittany or Wales.[3] But religion in Cornwall had experienced other influences during the Middle Ages. The English had made an impact from about the ninth century onward, followed by the Normans. Some monasteries had been founded anew or reorganized, the common religious cults of western Europe introduced, and the normal English diocesan organization established. Locally, parish churches and chapels had been restored and rebuilt on a large scale, especially under the Normans and again in the fifteenth and early sixteenth centuries. The resulting synthesis can be illustrated by the saints venerated in Cornwall between about 1400 and 1550 – at least 233 of them with documented churches, chapels, altars, or images

---

[1] Excluding the parishes of North Petherwin and Werrington, which, although west of the River Tamar, were historically part of Devon until 1966.

[2] On the history of Cornish and English in Cornwall, see M.F. Wakelin, *Language and History in Cornwall* (Leicester, 1975).

[3] On the Celtic saints of parish churches, see Nicholas Orme, *English Church Dedications* (Exeter, 1996), n. 4.

in their honor.[4] This variety reflected the county's history, blending Brittonic saints with those of the New Testament, Rome, post-Roman Gaul, Anglo-Saxon England, and, most recently, the cults of recent times. The latter, including those of Anne, Roche, Syth, and King Henry VI, show that Cornwall was not isolated from the diffusion of new cults that occurred throughout Europe and England up to the Reformation.

The early-Tudor county contained a modest number of religious houses, all for men: three Augustinian priories (Bodmin, St. Germans, and Launceston), one small Benedictine house (Tywardreath), three cells dependent on monasteries in other counties (St. Anthony in Roseland, St. Carroc, and Tresco), two friaries (Bodmin and Truro), and five communities of secular clergy (St. Buryan, Crantock, Glasney, St. Michael's Mount, and Probus). The religious houses had some relevance to popular religion, since St. Germans and the secular communities (excepting the Mount) were also parish churches, and the Mount was the main focus of pilgrimage in the county. Bodmin, too, had the shrine of St. Petroc, and its clergy and those of the other houses are likely to have encouraged lay devotion to their saints. The institutions most linked to the people, however, were the parish churches, about 218 in number. Some of these, like Advent, Gwithian, and St. Ives were technically chapelries of other parish churches, but most of the 218 possessed their own clergyman, a substantial building, frequent worship, community support, and a distinct parish territory. At least eighteen of the parish churches claimed to possess the body of a Celtic saint, but the devotion to such saints was mainly confined to the home parish or its immediate neighborhood. The saint's name was sometimes bestowed on children in the parish, but rarely elsewhere.[5] Perranzabuloe, with its shrine of St. Piran, was the only parish church with a local saint who seems to have attracted wide veneration.[6]

Outside the parish churches lay the parochial chapels – a feature of parish life all over England but notable in the southwest peninsula, where they far exceeded the churches.[7] Charles Henderson counted 188

---

[4] This figure is based on a complete inventory of recorded religious cults in pre-Reformation Cornwall: Nicholas Orme, *The Saints of Cornwall* (Oxford, 2000).

[5] For example, in the parishes of Cardinham (Meubred), Constantine, St. Dominick, Gerrans (Gerent), Landulph (Dilecta), St. Keverne, Madron (Madern), St. Minver (Enodoc, Minefreda), St. Neot, Perranzabuloe (Piran), and Wendron.

[6] Charles Henderson, "Ecclesiastical History of the 109 Parishes in Western Cornwall," *Journal of the Royal Institution of Cornwall* n.s., 2–3 (1953–60): 401–2. Several Cornish wills, for example, include bequests to the saint or his church.

[7] On this subject, see Nicholas Orme, "Church and Chapel in Medieval England," *Transactions of the Royal Historical Society*, 6th ser., 6 (1996): 75–102.

in the 95 parishes of western Cornwall,[8] and the total for the whole
county has been estimated at 650 (not counting 50 foundations like
St. Ives that were virtually parish churches). This means that there
were at least twice as many chapels as churches.[9] Parochial chapels can
be roughly divided into three categories. There were private chapels
(some technically oratories) in or near the houses of the gentry at,
for example, Bodrugan in St. Goran parish, Godolphin in Breage, and
Lanherne in St. Mawgan-in-Pydar. There were chapels of ease, built to
provide supplementary centers of worship for settlements lying at a
distance from their parish churches, including such places as Boscastle,
Camelford, Grampound, and East and West Looe. Finally, there were
chapels that centered on a particular cult, like St. Day with its famous
image of the Trinity, Our Lady in the Park near Liskeard, which honored the Virgin Mary, and the chapel of the Brittonic St. Elide (now
St. Helen's) on the Isles of Scilly. These categories often overlapped, especially the two latter kinds, so that chapels of ease became cult centers
and vice versa.

Some chapels had a landscape significance. They were placed on
rocks, like those at Roche and at Rough Tor in St. Breward parish, and on
islands as at Looe and St. Clement outside Mousehole. The landscape
was also sprinkled with holy wells, which played a further role in local religion. Such wells are often thought of as distinctively Cornish,
but they occurred widely in England, too.[10] In Cornwall, their pre-
Reformation origins can sometimes be shown archaeologically by
chapels or well houses built over them, as at St. Clether or at Dupath in
Callington (formerly in St. Dominick) parish, or through their appearance as place names in early documents.[11] One, that of St. Cadoc near
Padstow, is attested by medieval writers as virtuous against intestinal
worms.[12] Their relationship to the organized Church is difficult to establish, but it seems clear that many (like St. Cadoc) were attributed

---

[8] Henderson, "Ecclesiastical History," passim.
[9] J.H. Adams, "The Mediaeval Chapels of Cornwall," *Journal of the Royal Institution of Cornwall* n.s., 3 (1957–60): 48–65.
[10] A preliminary inventory of holy wells in Devon (where there were large numbers) was made by Theo Brown, "Holy and Notable Wells of Devon," *Transactions of the Devonshire Association* 89 (1957): 205–15, with supplementary lists in later volumes.
[11] The Cornwall Archaeological Unit at Truro keeps lists of holy wells and their locations. The most complete published inventory of them, by J. Meyrick, *A Pilgrims Guide to the Holy Wells of Cornwall* (Falmouth, 1982), is useful in describing them as they are now, but unreliable about their history. For the latter, see Joanna Mattingly, "Pre-Reformation Holy Wells in Cornwall: Sites, Structure and Functions," *The Poly: The Magazine of the Royal Cornwall Polytechnic Society* (1997): 8–11.
[12] For example, William Worcester, *Itineraries*, ed. J.H. Harvey (Oxford, 1969), 72–3.

to a saint, often that of the local parish church. Some were integrated into the Church calendar, Lady Nant Well in Colan parish being especially visited on Palm Sunday and Madron well on the feast of Corpus Christi.[13] In at least one parish, Antony, offerings made at two wells were appropriated by the local church.[14] Even wells do not exhaust the religious features of the landscape. St. Breward church and St. Illick chapel in St. Endellion parish possessed holy trees associated with the local saint, St. Illick and St. Levan chapel had holy paths of a similar nature, and St. Michael's Mount boasted a rocky chair where the archangel was said to have sat.[15] Stone crosses were also to be found all over the county: marking roads, parish boundaries, and places where people rested while taking the dead to church or, perhaps, on Rogationtide processions.[16]

The social history of these institutions can be traced, here as elsewhere in England, from archaeological and documentary sources. The first category includes surviving roodscreens, benches, and glass windows. These bear witness to support for religion but do not usually make clear what was provided voluntarily and what compulsorily. Nor do they state by whom, except on the rare occasions when they contain identifiable initials, armorial coats of arms, or inscriptions to their donors like those in the early sixteenth-century windows of St. Neot church.[17] Documentary records, such as churchwardens' accounts and wills, are more helpful.[18] Accounts often indicate which resources were levied and which came willingly, while wills disclose personal preferences, albeit under the restraints of convention or advice. The most easily recoverable evidence about popular religion relates to church stores and

---

[13]  Richard Carew, *The Survey of Cornwall* (London, 1602), fols. 144r–v; Nicholas Roscarrock, *Nicholas Roscarrock's Lives of the Saints: Cornwall and Devon*, ed. Nicholas Orme, Devon and Cornwall Record Society, n.s., 25 (1992), 86, 149.

[14]  Truro, Cornwall Record Office, P 7/5/1.

[15]  Roscarrock, *Lives of the Saints*, 61, 79, 92, 168–9.

[16]  A.G. Langdon, *Old Cornish Crosses* (Truro, 1896; repr., Exeter, 1988); Andrew Langdon, *Stone Crosses in North Cornwall*, 2nd ed. (Padstow, 1996); idem, *Stone Crosses in Mid Cornwall* (Padstow, 1994); idem, *Stone Crosses in East Cornwall* (Padstow, 1996).

[17]  Frederick Bligh Bond and Bede Camm, *Roodscreens and Roodlofts*, 2 vols. (London, 1909); Joanna Mattingly, "The Dating of Bench-Ends in Cornish Churches," *Journal of the Royal Institution of Cornwall*, n.s., 2.1 (1991): 58–72; G. McN. Rushforth, "The Windows of the Church of St. Neot, Cornwall," *Exeter Diocesan Architectural and Archaeological Society Transactions*, 3d ser., 4 (1936): 150–90; Joanna Mattingly, "Stories in the Glass – Reconstructing the St. Neot Pre-Reformation Glazing Scheme," *Journal of the Royal Institution of Cornwall*, n.s., 2.3 (2000): 9–55.

[18]  The list of wardens' accounts can be extracted from Joanna Mattingly, "The Medieval Parish Guilds of Cornwall," *Journal of the Royal Institution of Cornwall*, n.s., 10 (1989): 310–29, and idem, "Cornwall," in *English Medieval Guilds: Eight Regional Studies*, ed. K. Farnhill (Hull, forthcoming). Most of the surviving pre-Reformation Cornish wills were transcribed by Charles Henderson: Truro, Royal Institution of Cornwall, Henderson Manuscripts, no. 66.

guilds. Stores were funds of money or goods dedicated to the maintenance of cults in churches or chapels, such as images or lights. They were
administered by one or more wardens but did not necessarily involve a
social organization, though their income provides a clue to the support
they enjoyed. Guilds were groups of people, often maintaining images
and lights like the stores, but placing more emphasis on fellowship. A
good example from Tudor Cornwall is the guild of Holy Trinity, Helston,
apparently founded or refounded during the Reformation period. The
founders were seven cordwainers (shoemakers), who apparently intended it for themselves, their wives, and their servants. Its spiritual
location was to be Helston parish church, where its members were to attend dirige (matins of the dead) and Mass at the Trinity altar once a year,
saying a psalter of Our Lady (i.e., the rosary). This was to be followed
by a feast. Other arrangements included the settlement of quarrels, the
assistance of members in financial distress, the support of their funerals,
and the regulation of the craft of shoemaking in Helston.[19]

Guilds and stores were numerous in pre-Reformation Cornwall, and
also further eastwards in Devon and Somerset.[20] Archaeological evidence in Golant church suggests at least seven guilds there, and churchwardens' accounts record many others elsewhere. Poughill provides
evidence of five guilds and nine stores; North Petherwin, ten guilds
and four stores; Antony, eleven guilds (one in a separate chapel) and
three stores; and Camborne, a further eleven guilds (seven in parochial
chapels) and three stores. Even a small parish is therefore likely, like
Golant, to have had at least five or six guilds or stores, and a large rural one, like North Petherwin, as many as fifteen. Bodmin, the county's
biggest community, had some thirty in the late fifteenth century, based
in the parish church or in chapels elsewhere in the town. The likely total
in Cornwall is over a thousand. Their social support probably came from
most levels of society from the gentry and clergy downward, but seems
to have especially involved laypeople of the ranks of yeomen, husband-
men, and craftsmen. Some guilds, like the Helston one, were based on
particular trades; others (such as guilds and stores in chapels) were

---

[19] Truro, Royal Institution of Cornwall, Courtney Library, BB/5/1. The document is in a
hand of the sixteenth century, with an incomplete date ending "... lix" and therefore
readable as 1449 or 1459 (if the document is a copy) or 1549 (if it is an original). The
latter date looks too late for a religious guild foundation, but the document contains one
or two features of the Reformation period, so perhaps an earlier guild was refounded
in 1549 in an attempt to accord with the religion of the period. For a discussion and
edition of the text, see Joanna Mattingly, "The Helston Shoemakers' Gild and a Possible
Connection with the 1549 Rebellion," *Cornish Studies*, 2d ser., 6 (1998): 23–45.

[20] On this topic in Cornwall, see Mattingly, "Medieval Parish Guilds," 290–329.

based on particular neighborhoods. Some included men and women but, when they did so, were likely to have been dominated by adult male householders. People outside that category formed groups of their own, and many parishes had distinct organizations of the wives, the young (i.e., unmarried) men, and the maidens (the unmarried women).

Once we leave the safety of organizations like parish churches and guilds, which generated records, it becomes difficult to establish people's religious beliefs and practices. Certainly, as we see with the guilds, the social system affected the practice of religion. The gentry and other wealthy people enjoyed religious power and status through the ownership of church advowsons and the funding of church projects. Coats of arms on surviving church furniture, like that of the Roscarrocks in St. Endellion, emphasize this fact. Gentry did not necessarily consort with lesser folk in guilds, though they may have been members. They were likely to possess prayer books and other devotional works, and sometimes mention them in their wills. They and people of the merchant class had more leisure to attend services in their own chapels or town parish churches. Gentry, merchants, and rural yeomen seem particularly to have venerated international saints, to whom they dedicated the domestic chapels and parish guilds that they founded. Lesser people, on the other hand, may have had a particular devotion to the Brittonic saints of the parish churches. The naming of children after such saints seems to have been more popular at lower social levels, as was the frequenting of saints' holy wells in later times.[21] In these respects, there were differences between elite and popular religious culture, but the differences were not absolute. Some gentry were interested in Brittonic saints. Thomas Tretherffe bequeathed a chalice and vestments to St. Enoder church in 1528 to be used in honor of its saint,[22] and Nicholas Roscarrock (fl. 1548–1633) had a special devotion to the saint of St. Endellion.[23] Support for the county's two chief shrines at St. Day and St. Michael's Mount came from the wealthy, who made them bequests in their wills, but it is likely to have included many lesser folk who went to these shrines on pilgrimage. Ordinary people probably also supported the cults of international saints in parish churches. But personal religion is hard to trace and evaluate. One suspects that it generated many activities and possessions outside the parish church: wall paintings in houses or the display of woodcuts (mass-produced by printers in the early-Tudor period) depicting the Savior or Our Lady

---

[21] See earlier, p. 353.
[22] British Library, Harley MS 597, fols. 28–9.
[23] Roscarrock, *Lives of the Saints*, 12.

of Pity. The existence of domestic images in England is mentioned by the government of Edward VI.[24] The wealthy might collect documentary indulgences (like those of the Arundell family of Lanherne, which still survive),[25] and any family might gather for prayer or reading, say grace at meals, and, of course, observe religious diets and calendar observances.

It is possible, nevertheless, to hazard some conclusions about the nature of pre-Reformation popular religion in Cornwall, based on Cornish evidence or by analogy with what is known about England generally. First, such religion was immensely diverse in the places where it took place, in the cults to which it was addressed, and in the forms in which it was practiced. It was driven by both compulsion and free will. Attendance at the parish church was expected, though how often it was practiced is hazardous to say. Confession was required once a year, the other sacraments had to be received at due times, and tithes and offerings were binding upon adults. The frequenting of other churches or chapels in addition to the parish church, however, was voluntary, as were reading, private devotions, pilgrimages, indulgences, and charity. Not only did most parishes have more than one place of worship but parish churches had more than one focus at which it was done: the high altar, secondary altars, images, font, porches, and graves. The larger churches, with more than one cleric, might offer alternative daily masses, and the religious houses made further provisions of worship. Laypeople had a large measure of choice in where and how they worshiped, and local communities probably split up into different or overlapping groups to do so. Popular religion was grounded not only in churches but also in the world outside. Church festivals developed extramural links: culinary feasts, dramas, games, and the customs of disguising and collecting that accompanied, for example, St. Nicholas's Day (December 6). Guilds like Helston's had functions both religious and economic.

Religion was also of the people in the sense that it was not as clergy-led as is often assumed. True, the Mass, celebrated only by a priest, was immensely important: the focus of Sunday worship and the accompaniment of funerals and commemorations of the dead. Only clergy provided the sacraments, including the confession of adults during Lent. They visited one's home to bless the marriage bed, anoint the sick, and administer the last rites to the dying. There were liturgical blessings for

---

[24] *Visitation Articles and Injunctions of the Period of the Reformation*, eds. W.H. Frere and W. McC. Kennedy, 3 vols., Alcuin Club Collections 14–16 (1910), ii: 126.

[25] Nicholas Orme, "Indulgences in Medieval Cornwall," *Journal of the Royal Institution of Cornwall*, n.s., 2, 1.2 (1992): 149–70.

houses and wells, presumably reflecting lay demand for such things.[26] Equally, many clergy lived under a measure of lay direction, owing their appointments to church or chantry patrons, or being hired to celebrate masses by guild members. Masses, even if said in a church every day, did not take up much of the week. The rest of it was free for individual devotions at images. In chapels, which usually lacked permanent clergy and had masses only weekly or even annually, individual lay devotion would have been the staple of worship. This was also true at holy wells and in the still mysterious world of the Christian home. When we move from liturgy to its economic and social context, lay control becomes irrefutable. Laypeople acted as churchwardens, guild wardens, and store wardens, raising money by collecting and hospitality. Many parishes in Cornwall, as elsewhere in England, possessed a second communal building by the early sixteenth century, complementing the parish church. This was the church house, usually close to the church, which formed the venue for social feasts on special days of the year. Such feasts raised money for church purposes and cemented links within the community, helping to counteract the tendency to religious diversity.[27]

## THE REFORMATION

The reshaping of popular religion during the Reformation period took place in Cornwall through the same series of measures as in England in general. It began with the dissolution of the smaller monasteries in 1536, followed by the closure of all the monastic and mendicant houses in the county by 1539.[28] In the parish sector, the first important changes were the second royal injunctions of Henry VIII (1538), forbidding the veneration of images by pilgrimage, offerings, or lights (other than lights in honor of Christ in three specified places), and requiring each church to acquire a Bible in English.[29] A proclamation of 1541 reduced the number of holy days and sought to forbid extramural celebrations like the boy bishop ceremonies of St. Nicholas's Day.[30] Under Edward VI, the

[26] *Liber Pontificalis of Edmund Lacy, Bishop of Exeter*, ed. Ralph Barnes (Exeter, 1847), 212–13, 235–6.
[27] Patrick Cowley, *The Church Houses: Their Religious and Social Significance* (London, 1970); Joanna Mattingly, "Church Houses in Cornwall," *Cornish Buildings Group Review* (1988): 1–2.
[28] For dates, see D. Knowles and R.N. Hadcock, *Medieval Religious Houses: England and Wales*, 2d ed. (London, 1971).
[29] *Visitation Articles*, ii: 35–6.
[30] For this and the changes that follow, see A.G. Dickens, *Reformation Studies* (London, 1982), 293–305.

Royal Injunctions of 1547 abolished religious processions; commanded the destruction of all images (including paintings and window glass) that commemorated "feigned miracles, pilgrimages, idolatry, and superstition"; and ordered the income of guilds and lights to be converted to the use of the poor.[31] In 1548 religious guilds, chantries, and collegiate churches were done away with, and communion in both kinds (bread and wine) was introduced. The year 1549 saw the introduction of the first Edwardian Book of Common Prayer, which recognized only a couple of dozen holy days of Christ and of the saints of the New Testament. Further landmarks were the removal of all stone altars and the institution of a communion table in each church in 1550, the second Book of Common Prayer in 1552, and the seizure of church plate in 1553. Neither the momentous "Prayer-Book Rebellion" of 1549 nor the brief restoration of Catholicism under Queen Mary I (1553–8) did much more than delay the process of change, since most of the Henrician and Edwardian reforms were reimposed in the first years of the reign of Elizabeth I.

There is nothing to show that the making of these alterations was impeded by Cornwall's relative remoteness or distinctiveness. The dissolution of religious houses, of course, was carried out by royal officials and proceeded according to their program. An apparent exception to dissolution, the prebendal church of St. Endellion, was not really one; it was suppressed in 1548 and subsequently revived, for obscure reasons, at the very end of Mary's reign or the beginning of Elizabeth's.[32] Changes that had to be carried out by local justices of the peace or by churchwardens were less easy to enforce. Yet they too seem to have taken place without inordinate delay when they involved the removal of visible objects like church furniture. When John Leland visited Cornwall, in about 1540 or a year or two later, the Royal Injunctions of 1538 against shrines and pilgrimages had already taken effect. He used the past tense to describe the chapel of Our Lady in the Park as a place "wher was wont to be gret pilgrimage" and the remote chapel of St. Elide as "wher yn tymes past . . . was gret superstition."[33] A couple of generations later, Nicholas Roscarrock believed that the shrine of the saint of St. Endellion church had been defaced in Henry's reign,[34] very likely in 1538. Dr. Robert Whiting, who investigated the impact of the Reformation

---

[31] *Visitation Articles*, ii: 124, 126–8.

[32] L.S. Snell, *Documents towards a History of the Reformation in Cornwall*: vol. 1. *The Chantry Certificates for Cornwall* (Exeter, *c.* 1953), 22–4, 56.

[33] John Leland, *The Itinerary of John Leland*, ed. Lucy Toulmin Smith, 5 vols. (London, 1907–10), i: 190, 208.

[34] Roscarrock, *Lives of the Saints*, 73.

on parish churches through churchwardens' accounts in Cornwall and
Devon, found that the government's orders to destroy Catholic furnishings and to acquire Bibles or Books of Common Prayer evoked relatively
speedy and universal compliance under Henry VIII, Edward VI, and
Elizabeth I. Moreover, an awareness of official policies deterred some
people from supporting traditional institutions and encouraged others
to attack them even before they were formally condemned.[35] Roscarrock
tells two picturesque stories about popular iconoclasm, one involving
a man who cut down the holy tree at St. Illick's well, and the other,
Mistress Borlase, who (in about 1580) took a stone from St. Nectan's
chapel in Newlyn East parish to use as a cheese press. Such actions may
have been common, despite Roscarrock's belief that the man inflicted a
fatal wound on himself and that the woman ordered the stone to be returned before her death or, according to another story, restored it herself
as a ghost![36]

It is easier to catalogue the changes to church furniture, recorded in
churchwardens' accounts, than the alterations to popular religion in
other respects: attendance and demeanor at services, involvement
in extramural rites, or personal devotions at home. We possess the directions for the performance of church services, of course, in the Prayer
Books of 1549, 1552, and 1559. Their material can be compared with the
Latin "Sarum" prayer books of the early sixteenth century to show the
changes between the two liturgies, but such sources need to be handled
cautiously. Not only do they describe what ought to take place rather
than what did, but they are primarily interested in the role of the clergyman and give us an imperfect view of the congregation and church
building. Traditionally, historians have emphasized the differences between pre- and post-Reformation worship, and these differences were
indeed felt at the time. The "Prayer-Book" rebels of 1549, men of
Cornwall and of Devon, demanded ("we wyll have") the restoration
of the old Latin services (Mass, matins, evensong, and processions), the
distribution of holy bread and water after Mass, the use of ashes and
palms on the appropriate days of the year, and all other former ceremonies. Communion should be received only at Easter and then simply
in the form of bread, baptism done on weekdays as well as on Sundays,
images set up again, the reserved sacrament replaced above the altar,
and the English Bibles taken away. These were the changes that had
struck the protesters, or more accurately were those that bothered their

---

[35] Robert Whiting, *The Blind Devotion of the People: Popular Religion and the English Reformation* (Cambridge, 1989), esp. 25–47.
[36] Roscarrock, *Lives of the Saints*, 79, 94.

leaders, and, as so often happens in Church history, changes of a visual, concrete nature seem to have made the most impact.[37]

There is no doubt that the Reformation made permanent alterations to popular religion in Cornwall. It reduced the number of places of worship and the number of people available to lead it. The dissolution of the religious houses removed about ten monasteries, friaries, and colleges. Although they were few, they were the places where the medieval liturgy had assumed its most elaborate and varied forms. The attacks on shrines, images, and pilgrimages were fatal for the far greater number of parochial chapels, nearly all of which ceased to be used. This included even the chapels of ease, with a few exceptions like St. Enodoc and Porthilly in St. Minver parish and St. Nectan in St. Winnow. The Reformers did not target chapels directly through legislation, and the Prayer Book of 1549 assumed that some would continue in being.[38] Most chapels, however, depended so much on offerings to shrines and images, the celebration of masses, and the support of guilds that the abolition or reshaping of these institutions left them lacking roles and resources. The decline in the number of clergy was another factor. Monks, friars, collegiate clergy, and chantry priests ceased to exist in their original form, and although many of them took posts as parish clergy, their numbers were not replaced and were eventually lost. The post-Reformation Church in Cornwall was normally staffed by a single clergyman in each parish and, in some of the smaller ones, by no resident man at all.

It followed that there were fewer places of worship than before and fewer services in them. This was not merely an economic consequence of the Reformation but accorded with the Reformers' aim of emphasizing the community of the people of God, rather than (as before) allowing it to divide into smaller groups centered on cults. Parish worship became largely a formal Sunday matter, confined to two services. Morning prayer consisted of matins, followed by the litany and the communion service up to the prayer for the Church militant. Evening prayer (evensong) occupied the mid afternoon. Baptism was to be carried out on Sundays or other holy days rather than, as before, on the day that the child was born.[39] The location of worship in the parish church was also simplified. Most of it now took place in the nave, west of the screen, where the clergyman in his desk or pulpit was stationed closer to the people occupying their pews or benches. The chancel was used only for the consecration and administration of the bread and wine in the

---

[37] Frances Rose-Troup, *The Western Rebellion of 1549* (London, 1913), 220–2.
[38] F.E. Brightman, *The English Rite*, 2d ed., 2 vols. (London, 1921), ii: 714.
[39] Brightman, *The English Rite*, ii: 726–7.

rare communion services, three or four times a year. Gone were the secondary altars and images, which had provided other focuses for worship before the Reformation. The bays and chapels where they once stood were either filled with seating orientated toward the nave or used for nonliturgical purposes such as burials. The font near the church porch went on being the authorized place for baptisms, but the use of the porch for the first part of the baptismal service was discontinued in 1549, and its use for marriages, in 1552.[40] There was far less scope than before for coming to church, except to the regular services or to a wedding, a churching, or a funeral. In short, there was more uniformity: of liturgy, time, place, and attendance. The chief new feature, when one came, was the emphasis on instruction, now far greater than ever before. Morning and evening prayer each had two Bible readings, communion included an epistle, gospel, and sermon or homily, while baptisms, marriages, and funerals carried exhortations about the matters with which they dealt.

State policy during the Reformation, however, was not only concerned to change tradition but to maintain and even strengthen certain aspects of it. This was most manifest in the retention of a prescribed liturgy, based on much of the material of the old Sarum prayer books and its delegation to the clergyman and parish clerk, virtually unaided by anyone else. For, while Prayer Book services aimed to make a greater impact on the minds of the congregation, little was done to change what they did with their mouths or bodies. Once, churches may have been lacking in much formal seating. When John Myrc wrote his well-known *Instructions for Parish Priests* soon after 1400, he envisaged laypeople in church as normally kneeling on the floor during Mass and reprobated those who stood (except during the gospel) or leaned on pillars or walls.[41] During the fifteenth and early sixteenth centuries, however, churchwardens' accounts bear witness to a large-scale installation of benches or pews for most of the congregation.[42] In Cornwall, for example, Bodmin church commissioned the making of a pulpit and seats for the nave and aisles in 1491.[43] Many surviving benches in the county bear traditional iconography – instruments of Christ's passion or a crowned M for Mary – and must have been in place before the mid-1540s (unless they date from Mary Tudor's reign).[44] It seems likely that a silent revolution led

[40] Brightman, *The English Rite*, ii: 726–7, 800–1.
[41] *John Mirk's Instructions for Parish Priests*, ed. Gillis Kristensson (Lund, 1974), 82.
[42] On this subject, see J.C. Cox and A. Harvey, *English Church Furniture*, 2nd ed. (London, 1908), 261–88, and J.C. Cox, *Churchwardens' Accounts* (London, 1913), 66–9, 186–94.
[43] J. Wallis, *The Bodmin Register* (n. p., 1827–38), 33–5.
[44] Mattingly, "The Dating of Bench-Ends," 58–72.

to congregations being placed in an orderly way in pews or benches, well before the Reformation, where they knelt, sat, or stood, each in a defined and stationary spot. Once congregations did this, their behavior in church was bound to be affected, even while the old Latin services went on behind the screen. Knowing what we do about the hierarchical nature of society, we can be confident that there were rights or customs about where people sat before the Reformation, as there were in later times. Seating would have reflected order – rank, residence, gender, or family – and would have made it more difficult to behave differently from other people. Benches and pews had probably caused congregations to become more static and conformist by 1500, and the official Reformers, far from changing this arrangement, encouraged it to continue.[45]

The Sarum service books had given little attention to the lay congregation at services. Such books assumed that services would be primarily a dialogue between the priest and the clerk or clergy who assisted him. Nothing was prescribed for the congregation to do, and glimpses of lay behavior in other medieval literature suggest that people had some individual freedom to read, pray, or meditate while the service went on. This was enhanced by the chancel screen separating the clergy and congregation. Such freedom must have been more restricted when, after the Reformation, the clergyman moved into the nave with the congregation, but the Books of Common Prayer still gave the latter relatively little to do and were sparing in directives about deportment.[46] The Books of 1552 and 1559 required the laity, at morning and evening prayer, to say only the general confession, the Apostle's Creed, and the Lord's Prayer. The first was to be said "after the minister," presumably repeating his phrases, while the two latter were prayers that everyone had long been expected to know in Latin, and in English since 1538.[47] In the communion service, they were to say the Lord's Prayer and a uniform response to the Ten Commandments, while the confession before communion was to be pronounced either by a single representative of the communicants or by the clergyman on their behalf. Later, the custom grew up that the congregation, or part of it, might also say or sing the psalms in metrical versions. With regard to posture, morning and evening prayer stipulated kneeling for the confession, standing for the

---

[45] I must confess a shift of view here from the emphasis on pre-Reformation congregations' freedom of action expressed in my contribution to *Unity and Variety: A History of the Church in Devon and Cornwall*, ed. Nicholas Orme (Exeter, 1991), 60, 76.

[46] On what follows, see the parallel texts of the Prayer Books of 1549 and 1552 (with other material) in Brightman, *The English Rite*, i: 130–47; ii: 640–711.

[47] *Visitation Articles*, ii: 36.

creed, and kneeling for the final versicles, responses, and collects. At communion, kneeling was prescribed for the Commandments, for the person who said the confession, and for those who received communion. Otherwise, demeanor was not mentioned, and it is quite possible that traditional postures (like standing for the gospel) went on being followed.

The great new role that Cranmer foresaw for the laity in the 1549 Prayer Book was the reception of communion more often than the traditional once-a-year practice at Easter. But this involved the laity coming out of their seats to go into the chancel, and here official wishes were rebuffed. People did not like to communicate frequently, perhaps because they regarded the action as especially solemn and unusual, or associated it (outside Easter) with times of great peril, like the deathbed. The Prayer Book rebels apparently voiced a complaint that going into the chancel with members of the opposite sex would make everyone married to one another – a supposition possibly due to the fact that people had hitherto entered the chancel only for the marriage blessing.[48] By the time of the Prayer Book of 1552, the authorities had decided that it was feasible only to demand reception three times a year, and that on ordinary Sundays the communion service should be abandoned rather than be compromised by refusal to communicate.[49] The people defeated the regime on this point, simply by staying in their seats.

## POST-REFORMATION SURVIVALS

The Reformers also failed to efface every sign of pre-Reformation religion, even in the visual forms that were easiest to identify and eliminate. Parish church buildings remained, modified in furnishings and decoration but largely unaltered architecturally. Many church furnishings stayed, notably roodscreens and benches, often with Catholic iconography. Screens and benches survived because they were not controversial in themselves and were also robust. Windows, when they featured representations of saints, were more contentious and also more frail, but equally they were expensive to replace and were often allowed to decay gradually.[50] St. Neot church retained most of its stained glass windows, despite their hagiographical imagery, and some other churches kept similar representations until well after the Reformation. Glass depicting saints is mentioned at St. Agnes, Cardinham, St. Columb Major,

[48] Joyce Youings, "The South-Western Rebellion of 1549," *Southern History* 1 (1979): 108–9.
[49] Brightman, *The English Rite*, ii: 715.
[50] William Harrison, *The Description of England*, ed. G. Edelen (Ithaca, NY, 1968), 35–6.

and Feock during the seventeenth or eighteenth centuries, and some of it survives at St. Kew and St. Winnow. Outside the churches, religious houses and chapels survived as ruins or as buildings turned to other uses. When John Norden mapped Cornwall in the late 1590s, he included the priory of St. Carroc and the chapels of St. Mary Magdalene Cosawes near Penryn, St. Saviour Fowey, and St. Saviour Padstow as topographical features – perhaps because of their importance for navigation.[51] Such remains may have encouraged remembrance of the past. Equally, of course, they might discourage traditionalists and inspire reformists by proclaiming the success of the Reformation.

The history of people's readjustment to religion in post-Reformation Cornwall remains to be written from a detailed exploration of documentary sources. The best view of the subject at the moment comes from literature about Cornwall by contemporary writers. These fall into two main groups: one active in the period around 1600 and the other during the eighteenth century. The preeminent member of the first group was Richard Carew, the gentleman-author from Antony in Cornwall, who wrote the first comprehensive description of the county, *The Survey of Cornwall*, published in 1603 (modern style). Contemporary with him was John Norden, who visited, mapped, and described Cornwall in the late 1590s, and wrote up his account for James I in about 1604. Norden utilized Carew's account for his own, much shorter work, which covers fewer general topics but provides a systematic gazetteer of place names, occasionally annotated with landscape features or historic events.[52] A third figure was Nicholas Roscarrock, born into a gentry family at St. Endellion in about the late 1540s and closely associated with the county until about 1603. He then moved northward to Naworth Castle near Carlisle, where he worked on his unpublished "Lives of the Saints" of Britain and Ireland until about the 1620s.[53] All three authors wrote under the shadow of the Reformation and were influenced by it, Carew and Norden being Protestants, while Roscarrock was a resolute Catholic who suffered imprisonment and torture in Elizabeth's reign.

Carew and Norden both concentrated on the secular aspects of the county – its physical geography, economy, society, and history – so that a detailed coverage of religion is not to be expected, but it is surprising how rarely they mention the subject at all. At times they consign it to the

---

[51] *John Norden's Manuscript Maps of Cornwall and its Nine Hundreds*, ed. W. Ravenhill (Exeter, 1972), facs. 1, 3, 4, 5, 9.

[52] Norden's text was published as *Speculi Britanniae Pars: Cornwall* (London, 1728); for his maps, see note 51 in this chapter.

[53] Roscarrock, *Lives of the Saints*, 1–14.

past. Thus Carew describes three places where customs of popular religion had formerly been observed: St. Nonn's pool at Altarnun, where the mentally sick had been "bowssened" or ducked in the water and taken to Mass in the church; Lady Nant Well, where people had made offerings to the parish priest on Palm Sundays and divined the future by throwing in their palm crosses; and Lostwithiel, where the community had chosen a king each year on Low Sunday (the Sunday after Easter), involving a service in church and a feast.[54] Carew treats the first two of these with some derision, calling the first an excess of devotion over knowledge and the second "a foolish conceit." He was more indulgent toward the third, perhaps because it was "civic" and was remembered as involving only churchgoing, not superstition; indeed he refers to the events in church as "divine service." Norden describes these ceremonies, too, with similar judgments. He also mentions pilgrimages, in the past tense, to St. Michael's Mount and the Trinity of St. Day, and the presence of ruined chapels at St. Day, Launceston Castle, Merther Uny near Wendron, and Tintagel Castle.[55]

Norden and Carew, as Protestants, could discuss what was obsolete with relative safety. When they came to the living popular religion of their day, they observed much greater caution. Norden, indeed, says scarcely anything about it, and Carew (apart from noting that some people knew the Lord's Prayer, Creed, and Ten Commandments in the Cornish language)[56] centered his attention on extramural festivities and dramas, which he classified as recreations, not religious observances. According to Carew, three kinds of festivities survived in 1602, all related to the ecclesiastical calendar.[57] Each parish still held a church-ale, organized by two young men chosen annually who collected money and financed a feast in the church house at Whitsuntide. The feast was accompanied by outdoor games, neighboring parishioners attended, and the profits were applied to church or parish expenses. Another festival, that of the patron saint, was also commonly observed, but only in private. People kept it in their own houses, giving hospitality to "foreigners" (i.e., those from other parishes) who repaid it in turn, but there was evidently no commemoration of the patron saint in church except, perhaps, where the local saint was Mary or an apostle with an authorized holy day in the Prayer Book calendar. Finally, there were "harvest dinners" provided by the wealthy for their neighbors and kindred. These

---

[54] Carew, *The Survey of Cornwall*, fols. 123r, 137v, 144r–v.
[55] Norden, *Speculi Brittaniae Pars*, 39, 44–5, 60, 77, 81, 92.
[56] Carew, *The Survey of Cornwall*, fol. 56r.
[57] Carew, *The Survey of Cornwall*, fols. 68r–69r.

were not necessarily held at harvest time, but on any date between Michaelmas (29 September) and Candlemas (2 February), when guests stayed for the night and were treated to "Christmas rule."

Carew followed these customs by describing the kind of drama popular in Cornwall: "*gwary*" in Cornish, "miracle" in English.[58] Plays of this type, he reports, were still performed in earthen amphitheatres, delivered in the Cornish language, and attended by country people from miles around. We know from pre-Reformation texts of such dramas that they had once included stories from the Bible and at least one series of plays about Sts. Meriasek and Sylvester, but by Carew's day the latter kind of drama may have disappeared, since he mentions only those compiled "out of some scripture history." A late example of such a piece, "The Creation of the World," survives in Cornish in a text of 1611.[59] Carew's account of the plays is marked by a mixture of disapproval and amusement, since he judged them as stamped "with that grossness which accompanied the Romans' *vetus comedia*" and gives half of his description to a comic story about a gentleman who joined in performing one. He falls short of condemning the plays absolutely, however, and shows some tolerance toward the parish feasts, which were also potentially controversial. "Of late times," he reports, "many ministers have, by their earnest invectives, both condemned these saints' feasts as superstitious and suppressed the church-ales as licentious," and he went on to discuss the matter at length in the form of a dialogue, which he claimed to have had with a friend. Here, he put forward points of view for and against such customs, admitting that they had faults but suggesting that they were also useful and capable of improvement, finally quoting St. Augustine in their favor.

If Carew gives the impression of willingness to tolerate old religious customs whose purpose was largely social, his attitude toward traditions more distinctively Catholic was colder. He says little about the former religious houses beyond giving a brief list of them, the subject being a sensitive one now that their properties were in lay hands. His mentions of the saints are infrequent and usually ironical. The most general reference to them speaks of the "fruitful age of canonization" when the Cornish "stepped a degree farther to holiness and helped to stuff the church calendar with divers saints, either made or born Cornish."[60]

---

[58] Carew, *The Survey of Cornwall*, fols. 71r–72r.
[59] Whitley Stokes, "Gwreans an Bys, the Creation of the World: A Cornish Mystery," *Transactions of the Philological Society* (1864), pt. 4.
[60] Carew, *The Survey of Cornwall*, fol. 58r. Compare the briefer neutral reference by Norden, *Speculi Brittaniae Pars*, 35.

Carew usually adopts a mocking tone on the other rare occasions when he talks about saints. Thus St. Nonn of Altarnun is associated with the bizarre custom of "bowssening," a verse about St. Keyne describes her as "no over-holy saint," and St. Meva and St. Issey are portrayed as unambitious in becoming patrons of such a small parish as Mevagissey.[61] Norden repeats Carew's tone, remarks about all three places, and is more hostile to St. Keyne, whose name he compares with Cain's.[62] Where wells and springs are concerned, both writers were willing to praise them in general terms as "sweet" or "wholesome for man's use,"[63] but holy wells did not prompt similar feelings. Norden mentions only one, the famous well of Madron in west Cornwall, and with a sneer. It was formerly popular

for the supposed vertue of healinge, which St. Maderne had therinto infused.... But of late St. Maderne hath denied his or hers (I know not whether) pristine ayde; and as he is coye of his Cures, so now are men coye of cominge to his conjured Well; yet soome a day resorte.[64]

Carew says nothing about Madron well, although he must have known of it, closely acquainted as he was with his county. His only example of a well in current use is St. Keyne's, where husbands and wives drank to gain mastery in marriage – something else that could be portrayed as a quaint custom rather than a superstition. The sensitivity toward wells by the Cornish governing elite in Carew's time is shown by his account of the events at Scarlet's Well near Bodmin, which took place in the 1580s. Here, inspired by news of cures at a well at Kings Newnham in Warwickshire, people flocked to the water "in huge numbers" until the local justices, "finding the abuse and looking into the consequence, forbade the resort, sequestered the spring, and suppressed the miracle."[65] Clearly, Scarlet's Well was not regarded, by the authorities at least, as a mere spa. It must have seemed, too, like a Catholic holy well with a reputation for supernatural cures.

Carew and Norden, then, are not altogether reliable witnesses to popular religion, which they report selectively. They show, however, that some of the extramural practices of the pre-Reformation laity were still in being: commemoration of saints' days, church-ales, religious places,

---

[61] Carew, *The Survey of Cornwall*, fols 123r, 130r, 140v.
[62] Norden, *Speculi Brittaniae Pars*, 86.
[63] Carew, *The Survey of Cornwall*, fol. 26r; Norden, *Speculi Brittaniae Pars*, 17.
[64] Norden, *Speculi Brittaniae Pars*, 37–8.
[65] Carew, *The Survey of Cornwall*, fols. 126v–127r. The events in Warwickshire are described by Walter Bailey, *A Briefe Discours of Certain Bathes in the Countie of Warwicke neere Newnam Regis* (London, 1587), who dates them "within these fewe yeers" and "not long since." I am grateful to Dr. Alexandra Walsham for this reference.

and recourse to holy wells. Carew implies the dissociation of such popular practices from the religion of the gentry, who had either adopted Protestantism more strongly or were obliged to play the role required of those in authority under a Protestant regime. Roscarrock differed here since he held no public office, wrote in a more religious genre – lives of the saints – and sympathized with Catholic practices. He mentions popular religious traditions in twenty-six parishes in Cornwall, in eleven of which he reports beliefs about the identity of the parish saint or saints. These must have been gathered from oral folklore rather than written saints' lives, and usually involve phrases like "the inhabitants there say. . . ." In sixteen parishes, he appears also to draw on popular tradition to supply the date of the saints' feast days, sometimes stating that it "is" so observed, sometimes "was." He mentions six holy wells including Madron, which he appears to have thought still active, since "I have heard that there hath been sundry miracles wrought and especially on the feasts of Corpus Christi."[66] Finally, he refers to four examples of religious processions, but these are all placed in the past and had evidently ceased to be held.

The problem of using Roscarrock as a source is not his suppression of evidence but his remoteness from Cornwall at the time when his work took its final form. It is difficult to be sure how many of the traditions he describes were those of his youth in the county, which went back to the 1550s, and how many flourished in the early seventeenth century. Probably he himself did not know. Evidence from later writers and documents, however, shows that many saints' feasts and holy wells continued to be remembered or frequented throughout the seventeenth century and well into the eighteenth. This was especially so at Madron, where the well recovered its fame in 1638–40 through the miraculous healing of a Cornish cripple, named John Trelille, after sixteen years of infirmity. The circumstances were investigated by the bishop of Exeter, Joseph Hall, accepted as an authentic spiritual cure, and recorded in print by both Hall and a Catholic writer.[67] According to later belief, the chapel beside Madron well was demolished in Cromwell's time to prevent superstition,[68] but as late as 1654, although the building was then roofless, it was reckoned that offerings made at the chapel furnished the parish "ordinarily with £3 per annum or more towards the reliefe of the

---

[66] Roscarrock, *Lives of the Saints*, 86.
[67] Roscarrock, *Lives of the Saints*, 148–50.
[68] William Borlase, "Parochial Memorandums, 1740" (British Library, Egerton MS 2657), fol. 38r.

poor."[69] This is an interesting example of compromise between old and new practices. The coming of people to the well for healing was tolerated, as were their offerings, but these were channeled to the acceptable Protestant cause of poor relief.

Our second group of witnesses lived in the early eighteenth century and, though later, are sometimes more informative than their predecessors. All were Protestants, but they wrote when the passions of religious controversy had cooled and when state religion was more tolerant of diverse beliefs and of popular customs. They were therefore able to take a more dispassionate view of the pre-Reformation Church and its remaining vestiges. A pioneer in this respect was the Welsh scholar Edward Lhuyd, who visited Cornwall in 1700 and was probably the author of an anonymous notebook describing a journey through Cornwall in that or a later year, with records of folklore and antiquities.[70] Another was the Buckinghamshire scholar Browne Willis, who collected material on Cornish saints and parish feast days, helped by the fact that his wife was an Eliot of the parish of St. Germans, and published it in a series of Church directories.[71] Three other writers were based in Cornwall itself. They included William Hals (d. 1737) and Thomas Tonkin (d. 1742), both Cornish gentlemen who wrote accounts of Cornwall arranged by parishes,[72] and the cleric William Borlase, who composed two unitary works about the county: *Observations on the Antiquities, Historical and Monumental, of the County of Cornwall* (1754) and *The Natural History of Cornwall* (1758).[73] All five authors recorded material bearing on the Reformation and on popular religion, valuable because it represented un-self-conscious traditions and practices, untouched by scholarly publicity or romantic revival.

---

[69] Henderson, "Ecclesiastical History," 319.

[70] Oxford, Bodleian Library, MS Rawlinson D. 997; the date 1704 is on fol. 21v.

[71] Browne Willis, *Parochiale Anglicanum* (London, 1733); the material also appeared in John Ecton, *Thesaurus Rerum Ecclesiasticarum* (London, 1742; 2nd ed., London, 1754; 3rd ed., London, 1763). Willis's manuscript collections are held in the Bodleian Library, including MS Willis 25, 41, 64, 80.

[72] Hals's "History of Cornwall" is preserved in London, British Library, Additional MS 29,762 and was partly published as William Hals, *Compleat History of Cornwall*, 2 pts. (Truro, ca. 1750), and (with Tonkin's notes) by Davies Gilbert, in *The Parochial History of Cornwall, founded on the manuscript histories of Mr. Hals and Mr. Tonkin*, 4 vols. (London, 1838), and by [J. Polsue], in *A Complete Parochial History of the County of Cornwall*, 4 vols. (Truro and London, 1867–72).

[73] William Borlase, *Observations on the Antiquities Historical, and Monumental, of the County of Cornwall* (Oxford, 1754; 2nd ed., entitled *Antiquities...*, London, 1769; repr., East Ardsley, 1973); idem, *The Natural History of Cornwall* (Oxford, 1758). On Borlase, see P.A.S. Pool, *William Borlase* (Truro, 1986).

The evidence of these five writers illustrates the survival of pre-Reformation cults in at least three respects. First, most of the patron saints of the parish churches were still remembered. This was unusual elsewhere in England, where such saints had been little honored since the Reformation and had usually been forgotten. Nearby in Devon, Browne Willis found that many people had no concept of churches having patron saints and that little about these figures could be recovered from local knowledge.[74] The better understanding of patron saints in Cornwall must have been largely due to their preservation in the place names of so many churches and parishes. Where this was not the case, the saint was not always remembered even by the Cornish. At Laneast, Lanivet, Lansallos, and Lewannick, he or she had been forgotten or an erroneous figure had been conjectured from the place name, like the fictitious St. Lanty reported to (or invented by) Willis as patron of the two churches of Lanteglos.[75] Nevertheless, a few places in Hanoverian Cornwall still held tenacious links with their saint through popular folklore, even when the name was not obvious. At Blisland he was remembered as "Pratt" (the original medieval saint was Protus), at Merther correctly as Cohan, at North Hill as Terney, and at Poughill as "Tooleda" (i.e., "St. Olaf day"), the saint being preserved through his festival.[76] Two places on the north coast still told folk tales about their patron saints. St. Agnes, in the parish so named, was said to have come from Rome to Cornwall, to have killed a local giant, and to have left various traces on the landscape of the parish.[77] At nearby Perranzabuloe, St. Piran was reported to have crossed from Ireland to Cornwall on a millstone and to have revealed to local tinners some of the secrets of their art; they still kept his day as a holiday.[78] Further west, Sancreed remembered its saint and his patronage of pigs in 1667,[79] eighteenth-century St. Levan had legends of its saint and his connection with fishing,[80] and Germoe, in the same period, preserved a saying in Cornish that its saint was a king whereas Breage, the saint of the larger neighboring parish, was only a midwife.[81]

---

[74] Orme, *English Church Dedications*, 47–9.

[75] Orme, *English Church Dedications*, 92, 95. "Lanteglos" means valley with a church, not Lanty's church.

[76] Orme, *English Church Dedications*, 69, 103–4, 108, 112.

[77] Thomas Tonkin, "The Parish of St. Agnes," *Journal of the Royal Institution of Cornwall* n.s., 7 (1973–7): 203–4.

[78] Borlase, *Natural History*, 302.

[79] Henderson, "Ecclesiastical History," 432.

[80] G.H. Doble, *S. Selevan, A Cornish Saint*, "Cornish Saints" Series, No. 19, 3d ed. (Long Compton, 1938), 8–11.

[81] [Polsue], *A Complete Parochial History*, i: 134.

The second respect related to the ecclesiastical calendar. Most English parishes in the eighteenth century held a "feast" or "revel" once a year, with feasting and social events. In England as a whole, many of these were still tied to religious festivals: Easter week, Whitsun week, St. John's Day (24 June), and Michaelmas Day (29 September) being especially popular. As these days were feasts in the Prayer Book calendar, it was lawful to hold church services and follow them with revelry, just as before the Reformation. In Cornwall, however, at least thirty-eight parishes in the eighteenth or nineteenth centuries still held their parish feast-day on that of the medieval saint, with another eight possibly doing so. The most famous example is that of the "Furry Day" in Helston, which has survived until the present day. This festivity is not recorded before 1790, but it takes place on May 8, a feast of St. Michael (the patron saint of the town's church) that ceased to be celebrated at the Reformation.[82] The best explanation for the choice of day is that it was already observed before that event. The thirty-eight cases are an unknown proportion of the whole because in many parishes we know neither the medieval feast of the saint or the date of the eighteenth-century feast, so that the number of such correspondences may have been much larger. It was not universal, however, since some parishes had come to adopt a major church festival for the purpose.

The third respect was that of the holy wells. Some of these had evidently remained in use in the late seventeenth century. We hear of a man and woman of Stratton parish being paid expenses in 1694 to go to a well in St. Columb Minor parish, probably St. Pedyr's well at Treloy, for infirmities of the legs.[83] A traveler to North Hill in about 1700 (probably Edward Lhuyd) reported that "the well by the church is call'd St. *Turne's*, much resorted (by pilgrims especially)."[84] More extended descriptions of holy wells in west Cornwall are given by Hals and Borlase. They tell us that people drank the water of Holywell in Cubert parish as a purgative; of Gulval well for unspecified medical purposes; of St. Levan well for eye problems; of Madron well for aches, pains, and stiffness of the limbs; and of Chapel Euny well in Sancreed parish for wounds and sores. Gulval and Madron were also visited for purposes of divination. Frequenting such wells, however, did not necessarily have a strong religious context by this period. The visits were not mentioned as relating to the church's calendar, as in former times, unless the popularity of Chapel Euny well on New Year's Eve is such an example, and the only

---

[82] H. Spencer Toy, *The History of Helston* (Oxford, 1936), 368–79.
[83] R.W. Goulding, *Records of the Charity known as Blanchminster's Charity* (Louth, 1898), 44.
[84] MS Rawlinson D. 997, fol. 19r.

well ceremony reported to have had religious features was at St. Levan, where "when people have wash'd they are allways advis'd to go into this chappell and sleep upon the stone which is the floor of it."[85] There had been a similar custom at Madron well in the 1630s, when Trelille was cured there, and both this custom and St. Levan's show a lingering connection between the well, a former chapel, and the medieval practice of keeping vigil at a shrine. But none of the eighteenth-century reports about wells mentions formal liturgical observances, and none describes the patients as praying.

### CONCLUSION

The reformers of the 1530s and 1540s were ambitious to impose major changes on a system of popular religion that was ancient, diverse, and deeply rooted in parishes and their subcommunities. Change was easiest to bring about in visible institutions – church buildings, furnishings, and the liturgy – and, where people were concerned, among the most amenable to discipline, the clergy. The greatest success of the reformers was iconoclastic: the destruction of images, shrines, and ceremonies. Even so, buildings, screens, seating, and windows had often to be left, at least in the short term. The reformers further aspired to make the laity more godly through Bible reading, teaching, and the discouragement of superstition, but here they were less able to command and, perhaps, wished to proceed more cautiously. True, church attendance and economic support by the laity remained obligatory and (as in pre-Reformation times) there were penalties for persistent disobedience. Churchwardens retained their responsibility for buildings and became more powerful over the community through the growth of the vestry as an organ of local government. But men or women, when they came to church to worship, were assigned few parts to play and refused to play one of them: frequent communion. The Reformation sought to change them from spectators to pupils, but left them with a role that was largely static and passive in oral and physical terms.

Even within the church doors, then, the policies of the authorities were limited by caution or resistance. Outside, such policies were even less effective. The large body of wells, so enmeshed with popular religion in Cornwall, survived largely unscathed by iconoclasm. Many of their structures remained to identify their nature to the public. They

---

[85] Egerton MS 2657, fol. 10r.

continued to be widely frequented and, as the incidents at Scarlet's Well and Madron show, resorting to them still had a religious resonance in the late sixteenth and early seventeenth centuries, though this is less clear by the eighteenth. Calendar customs – feasts, dances, disguisings, and collecting – also went on being practiced, often on the days of the medieval Church calendar with which they had once been associated.[86] The Reformation did not end them; it did, however, drive them from the church and make them (like the visiting of wells) more fully secular than they had been before. But this, like the whole effect of the Reformation on popular culture, was a long slow process, quite unlike the rapid events of the 1530s and 1540s.

[86] It is not feasible here to explore the large topic of calendar customs. See particularly, A.R. Wright, *British Calendar Customs: England*, ed. T.E. Lones, 3 vols. (1936–40), which includes Cornish evidence, and for good recent syntheses, Ronald Hutton, The *Rise and Fall of Merry England: The Ritual Year 1400–1700* (Oxford, 1994) and idem, *Stations of the Sun* (Oxford, 1996).

# Selected Annotated Bibliography of Secondary Works

The following bibliography is intended only as an introduction to the vast literature related to the study of religion in the early modern world. Brief annotations have been added to guide the reader who wishes to pursue particular topics or areas of study. In some instances, only one or two works by an author have been cited as examples of a more extensive *opera*. Readers should refer to the footnotes in each chapter for additional works and suggestions for further reading.

## PART I

Balzer, Marjorie Mandelstam, ed. *Russian Traditional Culture: Religion, Gender, and Customary Law*. Armonk, NY, and London, 1992.

This is an anthology of articles and book chapters that were originally published in Russian between 1987 and 1989 in Soviet journals and books. The editor is an anthropologist, and she has brought together essays from various disciplines, covering the period from the tenth to the twentieth century, grouped under three headings: "Religion and Ritual," "Gender and Family Life," and "Customary Law, Daily Life, Medicine, and Morality."

Carlson, E. J., ed. *Religion and the English People, 1500–1640: New Voices, New Perspectives*. Kirksville, MO, 1998.

This collection of essays tries to redefine the question of whether the Reformation succeeded or failed in early modern England, in order to deal with what people actually practiced in their religious daily lives.

Collinson, Patrick. *The Religion of Protestants: The Church in English Society, 1559–1625*. Oxford, 1982.

This book is a collection of the studies Collinson presented at Oxford in the Ford Lecture series of 1979. He develops the viewpoint that the Jacobean period was the culmination of the Protestantization of the English commonwealth, in terms both religious and political. He again argues for the importance of moderate Puritanism in the development of the mainstream church and goes on to explore the religious activities of laypeople and clergymen, emphasizing those practices that created community among them.

Frijhoff, Willem. *Wegen van Evert Willemsz. Een Hollands Weeskind op Zoek Naar Zichzelf.* Nijmegen, 1995.

This is a biography of Evert Willemsz, a seventeenth-century orphan from Woerden, who, after undergoing a mystical experience in his teens, became a preacher, changed his name to Everhardus Bogardus and took up his vocation in New Amsterdam (now New York). Additionally, the book provides a rich picture of daily life, culture, and mentality in Holland and its colonies overseas.

Haigh, Christopher. *English Reformations: Religion, Politics, and Society under the Tudors.* Oxford, 1993.

One of the main revisionist historians of the English Reformation, Haigh here produces a scholarly survey of religious continuity and change in the Tudor century. He sees the developments of the period not as abrupt and revolutionary, but rather as slow, piecemeal, and reversible. The book utilizes a wide variety of sources and emphasizes the role of politics in the possibilities for religious change.

Heller, Wolfgang. *Die Moskauer "Eiferer für die Frömmigkeit" zwischen Staat und Kirche (1642–1652).* Wiesbaden, 1988.

Heller examines political and theological developments prior to Nikon's ascension to the patriarchal throne and the schism in the Orthodox Church. Focusing on Patriarch Iosif and the Zealots of Piety (reforming clerics associated with the tsar's confessor) before 1652, Heller argues that Nikon actually continued reforms that had begun earlier.

Johnson, David, Andrew J. Nathan, and Evelyn Rawski, eds. *Popular Culture in Late Imperial China.* Berkeley, 1985.

This collection of thirteen essays sought to bring the study of popular culture into the mainstream of academic research on traditional China by attempting to reconstruct nonelite mentalities in the period from 1550 to 1920. Essays concentrate on values and the ways they were communicated, mainly through various textual possibilities: plays, journals, sacred texts, etc.

Kaplan, Benjamin. *Calvinists and Libertines. Confession and Community in Utrecht, 1578–1620.* Oxford, 1995.

Focusing on Calvinist-Libertine conflicts in the city of Utrecht, Kaplan explores how civic culture and confessional identity came to coexist in the period up to 1620. He argues that the Libertines (mainly local gentry) came to control political power, while the Calvinists (mainly skilled artisans and guildsmen) increasingly controlled the ecclesiastical life of the city. However, the political position of the Libertines allowed them to limit the wider social influences of Calvinism.

Litzenberger, Caroline. *The English Reformation and the Laity: Gloucestershire, 1540–1580.* Cambridge, 1997.

Focusing on the laity in the county of Gloucestershire, Litzenberger challenges the view that these people easily accepted the Reformation, and argues instead that Protestantism only started to gain strength in the 1580s. She suggests that most people could not be categorized as Catholics or Protestants in this period – rather, there was a diverse spectrum of lay religious practices.

Liu, Kwang-Ching, ed. *Orthodoxy in Late Imperial China*. Berkeley, 1990.
This collection of eleven essays is based on a conference on orthodoxy and heterodoxy in Ming and Qing China (1368–1911) that took place in 1981. The essays discuss social, political, and cultural aspects of Confucianism in premodern China and contribute to an understanding of how religion was practiced in society as a whole, specific kinship organizations, and by the state. Authors demonstrate that the existence of religious pluralism together with moral orthodoxy held Chinese society together.

Meyendorff, Paul. *Russia, Ritual, and Reform. The Liturgical Reforms of Nikon in the Seventeenth Century*. Crestwood, NY, 1991.
This book provides an account of the main events, people, and results of the schism in the Orthodox Church, but its centerpiece is a comprehensive study of the liturgical reforms introduced by Nikon that kindled the schism.

Pollmann, Judith. *Religious Choice in the Dutch Republic. The Reformation of Arnoldus Buchelius (1565–1641)*. Manchester and New York, 1999.
Autobiographical texts kept by Buchelius, including journals of his own activities and contemporary events, form the basis of this religious biography. Pollmann argues that Buchelius's decision to abandon Catholicism and become a member of a Calvinist church was because he wanted to help form a godly society rather than because of an abrupt personal conversion. She suggests that this pattern of evolutionary (rather than revolutionary) change in faith may be applied more widely to Dutch society in this period.

Ter Haar, B. J. *The White Lotus Teachings in Chinese Religious History*. Leiden, 1992.
In contrast to previous scholars, Ter Haar demonstrates that there was no unified, continuous, sectarian, White Lotus tradition in China. Rather, the term may be properly applied to groups in the Song, Yuan, and early Ming dynasties that were devoted to the Buddha Amitâbha. Thereafter it was used by outsiders, usually as a derogatory term to describe popular religious sects – especially those involved in uprisings of various kinds.

van Rooden, Pieter. *Religieuze Regimes. Over Godsdienst en Maatschappij in Nederland, 1570–1990*. Amsterdam, 1996.
In this collection of essays, church historian Pieter van Rooden challenges the grand narrative of secularization and attempts to bring religious issues to the fore in a broad period of Dutch history. Focusing mainly on Protestantism in a politicocultural context, van Rooden shows changes in the "localization" of religion in society: for the early modern period, from a public church in the service of public order in the sixteenth and seventeenth centuries, to the individual's inner life in the eighteenth and early nineteenth centuries.

## PART II

Baron, Samuel H., and Nancy Shields Kollmann, eds. *Religion and Culture in Early Modern Russia and Ukraine*. DeKalb, IL, 1997.
This collection of twelve essays emerged from a conference held at Stanford in 1993 designed to promote explicitly comparative and interdisciplinary

approaches to the subject. Thus the essays look at sociopolitical themes, religious experience, and art produced. The book is divided into three sections: society and cultural practice; religion and belief; images, identity, and mentality.

Benedict, Philip. *The Huguenot Population of France, 1600–1685. The Demographic Fate and Customs of a Religious Minority*. Philadelphia, 1991.

The first part of this book is a demographic study (mainly using censuses of Protestant households and Protestant church records) that seeks to determine by how much the numerical strength of French Protestantism declined up to 1685. Benedict estimates that there were about 730,000 Huguenots living in France in 1681. The second part of the book uses this fine demographic work to shed light on the social behavior of Protestants in the various regions of France.

Brook, Timothy. *Praying for Power: Buddhism and the Formation of Gentry Society in Late-Ming China*. Cambridge, MA, 1993.

Brook's study is a pioneering attempt to understand more exactly the place of Buddhism in Ming society. He surveys Ming Buddhism generally, and focuses on three counties to demonstrate that monastic patronage was almost entirely in the hands of the local gentry. Brook interprets this pattern as evidence of gentry withdrawal from the public authority of the state, coupled with increased awareness of local autonomy.

Davies, Julian. *The Caroline Captivity of the Church: Charles I and the Remoulding of Anglicanism*. Oxford, 1992.

Davies's study examines Charles I's church policies in the period 1625 to 1641, placing emphasis on the role of the king and thus terming the developments "Carolinism" rather than "Arminianism" or "Laudianism." Charles I's policies were a break from the practices of the Jacobean church, and with them he sought to reinforce his elevated notions of kingship. He advocated ritual over preaching, railed in the communion table, and allowed sports on Sundays. Davies stresses the importance of not attempting to separate politics and religion when studying this period.

Ferrell, Lori Anne. *Government by Polemic: James I, the King's Preachers, and the Rhetorics of Conformity, 1603–1625*. Stanford, CA, 1998.

Decoding the evidence to be found in court sermons, Ferrell shows that the strong divisions between Puritans and conformists that shaped the Caroline era, developed during the reign of James I. Conformist preachers painted even moderate Puritans as being on par with political and ecclesiastical extremists – refusing to kneel, for example, was rhetorically turned into refusal to acknowledge the supremacy of the king.

Gudziak, Boris A. *Crisis and Reform. The Kyivan Metropolitanate, the Patriarchate of Constantinople, and the Genesis of the Union of Brest*. Cambridge, MA, 1998.

This book recounts the background to the Union of Brest in 1596, when most of the Orthodox (Ruthenian) bishops of Poland-Lithuania submitted to the pope, thus forming the Uniate Church of present-day Ukraine and Belarus. Gudziak is particularly interested in relations between the Ruthenian Church and the Patriarchate of Constantinople, and he argues that Ruthenian bishops accepted the Union as a way to reform their own church.

Hrushevsky, Mykhailo. *History of Ukraine-Rus'*: volume 7. *The Cossack Age to 1625*. Toronto, 1999.
First published in 1909, Hrushevsky's book is now primarily interesting as a major work of nineteenth-century nationalistic myth making. In opposition to Russian historiography of the time, the book depicts the Cossacks as crucial to the formation of an essentially Ukrainian tradition and identity.

Mentzer, Raymond, ed. *Sin and the Calvinists: Morals Control and the Consistory in the Reformed Tradition*. Kirksville, MO, 1994.
A collection of six essays by eminent scholars of European Calvinism, this volume is a survey of the concerns and dealings of Reformed consistories in cities of Switzerland, Germany, The Netherlands, France, and Scotland.

Prestwich, Menna, ed. *International Calvinism, 1541–1715*. Oxford, 1985.
This collection of essays was prepared in connection with the celebration of the three-hundred-year anniversary of the revocation of the Edict of Nantes. The essays are both thematic and surveys of Calvinism in particular countries from the sixteenth to the early eighteenth centuries. Countries included are Switzerland (focused on Geneva), The Netherlands, France (four out of thirteen essays), Germany, Hungary, Scotland, England, and North America, though little attention is given to connections among them in this period.

Schilling, Heinz. *Religion, Culture and the Emergence of Early Modern Society*. Leiden, 1992.
A collection of nine essays (most previously published in German between 1979 and 1988) that integrate social, religious, intellectual, and political history and are often organized around the key role of elites. Four essays study the pattern of development of German cities in the sixteenth century; two essays are on the Second Reformation or the period of Confessionalization, as Schilling has called it; and the last three essays examine the Northern Netherlands in the seventeenth century in terms of being a "modern" nation.

Ševčenko, Ihor. *Ukraine between East and West: Essays on Cultural History to the Early Eighteenth Century*. Edmonton and Toronto, 1996.
This collection of twelve of the author's essays includes five that are newly published. The author discusses Ukraine from the Middle Ages to the eighteenth century as a cultural crossroads – focusing especially on Byzantine, Russian, and Polish influences on culture, religion, and the formation of national identity.

Thompson, Laurence G. *Chinese Religion: An Introduction*, 4th ed. Belmont, 1989.
First published in the late 1960s, this introduction to Chinese religion over the past two thousand years elucidates Confucianism, Taoism, and Buddhism (primarily), while at the same time emphasizing the particular Chinese worldview manifested here. Thompson focuses on the ways that religious expression functioned in Chinese society from family groups to the state apparatus.

Tyacke, Nicholas. *Anti-Calvinists: The Rise of English Arminianism, c. 1590–1640*. Oxford, 1987.

Tyacke charts the "Arminian revolution" in England, discussing the new theology in university and political contexts. Arminians stressed the hierarchical nature of both the church and the state, and this may have informed Charles I's decision to support the movement. Tyacke shows that the outlawing of Calvinism in the 1620s destabilized the religious status quo and gave an added bitterness to political dissensions under Charles I.

Watson, James L., and Evelyn Rawski, eds. *Death Ritual in Late Imperial and Modern China*. Berkeley, 1988.

This collection of essays by historians and anthropologists focuses on funeral and burial rituals in China between 1500 and 1911 as a window to understanding Chinese society and what held it together. The essays are grouped around two main themes: correct belief/meaning versus correct practice, and the subsidiary question of how rituals may be manipulated by different groups if they do not mean the same thing to everyone involved.

Webster, Tom. *Godly Clergy in Early Stuart England: The Caroline Puritan Movement, c. 1620–1643*. Cambridge, 1997.

A detailed study of Puritan clergy in southeast England during the reign of Charles I, Webster's book first examines matters of godly sociability. Then he looks at what happened as these men came under increasing pressure from high-church policies. They had to choose to conform, conform superficially, suffer as nonconformers, or flee – often to New England.

Yang, C. K. *Religion in Chinese Society*. Berkeley, 1961.

In this influential book, using a sociological approach, Yang seeks a relationship between religion and social order. He considers Confucianism in terms of a "socio-political doctrine having religious qualities," and thus examines the role religion played in Chinese social life and organizations, such that it provided the basis for the society's existence and development. He also looks at the structural forms that allowed this role for religion. The final chapter is entitled, "Communism as a New Faith."

## PART III

Anisimov, Evgenii V. *The Reforms of Peter the Great: Progress Through Coercion in Russia*. Armonk, NY, 1993.

A somewhat condensed and modified translation of a work first published in Russian in 1989, this study of Peter the Great follows his life chronologically, as well as discusses his goals and achievements. The author gives credit to his reforms but condemns the force constantly used to achieve them.

Bell, Catherine. *Ritual Theory, Ritual Practice*. New York, 1992.

Unlike both Karant-Nunn's and Muir's books, Bell's does not focus on a particular historical era or on a specific region. Rather, this is an analytic and theorizing treatment of the concept of ritual and of how ritual action is used in societies to negotiate power relationships. Indeed, Bell seeks to show ritual at work in all human actions and practices.

Bushkovitch, Paul. *Religion and Society in Russia: The Sixteenth and Seventeenth Centuries*. New York, 1992.
One of the first English-language monographs on a formative period in the evolution of the Russian Orthodox Church, this study simultaneously provides an introduction to and a reassessment of the age, not as one of decline but rather of development. Bushkovitch looks mainly at the upper classes and shows the way religious practices changed from public and collective observances focused on the liturgy and miracle cults, to more private and personal faithfulness stressing morality.

Duffy, Eamon. *The Stripping of the Altars: Traditional Religion in England, c. 1400– c. 1580*. New Haven, CT, 1992.
Emphasizing the corporate and vital nature of late medieval religious practices, Duffy offers a comprehensive reconstruction of beliefs and rituals in England from about 1400 to 1536 in the first part of his book. The second part describes the tragic destruction of this system under the Tudors. Nevertheless, elements of late medieval Catholicism survived these changes so that Englishmen could greet Mary Tudor's reign with relief, not as an anachronistic throwback.

Hutton, Ronald. *The Stations of the Sun: A History of the Ritual Year in Britain*. Oxford, 1996.
Hutton intended this book, on the seasonal festivals of Great Britain from the early Middle Ages to the Industrial Revolution, to be used in conjunction with his more methodologically inflected book, *The Rise and Fall of Merry England*. Using data collected by folklorists since the late eighteenth century, Hutton shows that there is little evidence for the survival of pagan practices in Christian celebrations, but certainly for Catholic rituals in post-Reformation Protestant ones. Moreover, there were wide regional variations, and celebrations were constantly evolving and being newly created.

Kamen, Henry. *The Phoenix and the Flame: Catalonia and the Counter-Reformation*. New Haven, CT, 1993.
Simultaneously detailed and wide-ranging, this book traces the progress of the Catholic/Counter-Reformation in Spain at the local, regional, and national levels, with a particular case study of Catalonia at its center. For Catalonia, Kamen argues that the Inquisition was marginal in most people's lives; that censorship was not effective, and therefore intellectual freedom remained; and that while many local practices continued, Catalans did accept Tridentine reforms of penance and marriage.

Karant-Nunn, Susan. *The Reformation of Ritual: An Interpretation of Early Modern Germany*. London and New York, 1997.
The central theme of this book is Protestant change in Catholic religious practices, focused on lifecycle rituals: betrothal, marriage, baptism, churching, penance, communion, and funerals. As a social historian influenced by anthropological theory, Karant-Nunn interprets her subject as a continuous series of negotiations between reformers and people.

Michels, George B. *At War with the Church. Religious Dissent in Seventeenth-Century Russia*. Stanford, CA, 1999.
Michels's book is a reassessment of the seventeenth-century schism between the Russian Orthodox Church and dissenters traditionally known collectively as Old Believers. Rather than being a unified dissenting movement from the 1650s onwards (when the Orthodox Church instituted various reforms and experienced widespread disobedience), Old Belief in this period, Michels shows, meant a host of different ideas and practices held by individuals and small groups, most of whom were on the margins of Muscovite society.

Moreton, C. E. *The Townshends and Their World. Gentry, Law, and Land in Norfolk, c. 1450–1551*. Oxford, 1992.
Moreton was the first to use the rich archives of the Townshend family, major nongentry Norfolk landowners who came to be involved in law in the late fifteenth century. Through focusing on the Townshends, increasing involvement in sheep raising, Moreton demonstrates that fifteenth-century factionalism gave way to ever greater co-operation with the Crown in the sixteenth century.

Muir, Edward. *Ritual in Early Modern Europe*. Cambridge, 1997.
Muir's work, suitable for use as a textbook, is concerned with religious and cultural ritual and draws upon the insights of anthropology and ritual studies. He covers the whole of Europe between 1400 and 1700. The first two sections deal with pre-Reformation Catholic Europe with an emphasis on the sensual experience of ritual. The third section discusses the Reformation as a revolution in the understanding of ritual, now focused on meaning.

Myers, David. *'Poor Sinning Folk': Confession and Conscience in Counter-Reformation Germany*. Ithaca, NY, 1996.
Focused primarily on Austria and southern Germany, this book follows changes in the practice and theology of the sacrament of penance in Catholic parishes from the Middle Ages, through the period of the Counter-Reformation and into the eighteenth century.

Nalle, Sara T. *God in La Mancha: Religious Reform and the People of Cuenca, 1500–1650*. Baltimore and London, 1992.
Nalle addresses the practical ways Tridentine reforms were implemented in the Castilian diocese of Cuenca. Her study begins with a view of medieval religious observances in the region and traces the educational and spiritual reforms of the Reformation era, emphasizing popular and elite support for many of the changes.

Nichols, Anne Eljenholm. *Seeable Signs: The Iconography of the Seven Sacraments, 1350–1544*. Woodbridge, Suffolk, 1994.
Concerned with the iconography of all seven sacraments shown together, Nichols starts with the European background, but then concentrates on England between about 1450 and 1544 – the first and last representations prior to the Reformation. These representations were concentrated in stained glass windows and baptismal fonts, mainly in the West Country and East Anglia.

Nichols argues that these images were a positive way of combating Lollardy through demonstrating the Church's teachings, rather than simply rejecting unorthodox beliefs.

Okenfuss, Max J. *The Rise and Fall of Latin Humanism in Early-Modern Russia: Pagan Authors, Ukrainians and the Resiliency of Muscovy.* Leiden, 1995.
Based on research regarding the presence of Latin Classics in Russian private libraries, as well as the printing of such works by Russian presses, Okenfuss describes the educated elite of Muscovy and the way they were educated between 1650 and 1789. His arguments center first on disproving the influence of Ukrainian clergy in establishing Western-style Latin education in Russia, and second on demonstrating that traditional Muscovite values, based on the teachings of the Orthodox Church, in fact triumphed over the secularizing claims of Westernization in the eighteenth century.

Poska, Allyson M. *Regulating the People: The Catholic Reformation in Seventeenth-Century Spain.* Leiden, 1998.
This is a study of the Catholic Reformation in the Galician diocese of Ourense, which focuses on the on going negotiative process between local beliefs and practices and official Church efforts at reform. Poska examines factors such as geography, undereducated clergy with strong local ties, and particular lifecycle rituals to demonstrate that Tridentine reforms were largely ineffective in the region.

Scribner, R. W. *Popular Culture and Popular Movements in Reformation Germany.* London, 1987.
This is a wide-ranging collection of fifteen of the author's essays (three previously unpublished) the rest published between 1975 and 1987 with the underlying theme of religious and social change. Scribner tackles political and economic factors, sociological and anthropological interpretation, the carnivalesque, folklore, ritual, early print culture, and the image/myth of Luther in the early modern period. His approach to the Reformation in Germany is predominantly social scientific, but he does not deny the importance of the sacred in everyday life.

## EPILOGUE

Hutton, Ronald. *The Rise and Fall of Merry England: The Ritual Year, 1400–1700.* Oxford, 1994.
Using mainly churchwardens' accounts for the period from 1350 to 1700, Hutton describes changes in rituals and observances that marked out the year. He argues that the "merry" rituals created in medieval England were suppressed, sterilized, or formalized by the changes introduced during the Reformation and beyond.

Orme, Nicholas. *The Saints of Cornwall.* Oxford, 2000.
This book consists of two parts: The first is an introduction to Cornish sociopolitical and church history, together with an overview of primary sources from before 900 to the eighteenth century; the second is a dictionary of saints,

listing every person venerated with a cult, as well as every site, object, ritual, and written source associated with that cult in Cornwall.

Whiting, Robert. *The Blind Devotion of the People: Popular Religion and the English Reformation*. Cambridge, 1989.

Focused on Exeter, Whiting's approach to and conclusions about the extent of the Reformation have been applied to other parts of England as well. Though people expressed some reluctance to change, for the most part they simply obeyed established authority. Changes introduced under Edward, Mary, and Elizabeth were all met with a similar degree and kind of acceptance.

# Index